Oracle Essentials
Oracle8 and Oracle8i

Oracle Essentials

Oracle8 and Oracle8i

Rick Greenwald, Robert Stackowiak,
and Jonathan Stern

O'REILLY®

Beijing · Cambridge · Farnham · Köln · Paris · Sebastopol · Taipei · Tokyo

Oracle Essentials: Oracle8 and Oracle8i
by Rick Greenwald, Robert Stackowiak, and Jonathan Stern

Published by O'Reilly & Associates, Inc. 101 Morris Street, Sebastopol, CA 95472.

Editor: Deborah Russell

Production Editor: Maureen Dempsey

Printing History:

        October 1999:   First Edition.

ISBN: 1-56592-708-7

To the two most important people in my life: my wife, LuAnn, and my daughter, Elinor Vera YuXiu. You give me everything.

—*Rick Greenwald*

For my wife, Jodie, and sons, Nick and Mike ... thanks for providing the time, support, and understanding needed for projects such as this one. My love to each of you.

—*Robert Stackowiak*

To my wife, Heather, and my children, Zachary and Sarah, for their support and understanding.

—*Jonathan Stern*

Table of Contents

Preface

The Oracle database is a product that's both rich and deep. To address the complexities and variations in this product, most Oracle books tend to be long and somewhat intimidating. Most of them either cover a broad scope of functionality in a fairly cursory way, or delve deeply into complex and rather narrow topics, sometimes missing the forest for the trees by concentrating on the multitude of details of a particular subject. The characteristics of most current books can make it difficult to find just the information you need for your own specific problem. With some Oracle books, it's a bit like a web search that returns thousands of pages: it's difficult to find the information you need efficiently.

As Oracle professionals (all of whom have worked for Oracle Corporation), we've found that a lot of Oracle users need explanations on the same topics. For some time, we've wanted a book that describes all of the underlying principles that shape the Oracle database, written concisely for an intelligent audience. We found that the explanations were scattered among many manuals and books, and were often too complex or too simplistic. After a good deal of complaining, we finally decided to write the book ourselves.

Goals of This Book

Our main goal is to give you a foundation for using the Oracle database effectively and efficiently. Therefore, we wrote with these principles in mind:

Focus

> We've tried to concentrate on the most important Oracle issues. Every topic provides a comprehensive but concise discussion of how Oracle handles an issue and the repercussions of that action.

Brevity

One of the first decisions we made was to concentrate on principles rather than syntax. There simply isn't room for myriad syntax diagrams and examples.

Uniqueness

We've tried to make this book the first Oracle book for a wide spectrum of Oracle users—but not the last! You will very likely have to refer to Oracle documentation or other, more specific books for more about details using Oracle. However, we hope that this book will act as an accelerator for you. Using the foundation you get from this book, you can take detailed information from other sources and put it to the best use.

This book is the result of over 30 years of experience with Oracle and other databases. We've tried to apply that experience as best we can here.

Audience for This Book

We wrote this book for people at all levels of Oracle expertise: *database administrators* (DBAs), who spend most of their workday interacting with Oracle; *application developers*, who build their systems on the data available in an Oracle database; and *system administrators*, who are concerned with how Oracle will affect their computing environment. Of course, some users interact more peripherally with the actual Oracle product, from IT management to end users. On the one hand, anticipating the appropriate technical level of all our potential readers presented difficulties; on the other hand, we've tried to build a solid foundation from the ground up and believe that some introductory material benefits everyone. We've also tried to ensure that every reader receives all the fundamental information necessary to truly understand the topics presented.

If you're an experienced Oracle user, you may want to skip over the material in this book that you're already familiar with. But our experience has shown us that some of the most basic Oracle principles have been overlooked, even by experts. We've also seen how the same small "gotchas" trip up even the most experienced Oracle practitioners and cause immense damage if they go unnoticed. After all, an ounce of prevention tempered by understanding is worth a pound of cure (especially when you're trying to get a system up and running). So we hope that even experienced Oracle users will find valuable information in every chapter of this book—the kind of information that will save them hours in their busy professional lives.

Our guiding principle has been to present this information compactly without making it overly tutorial. We figure that the most important ratio in a book is the amount of useful information you get balanced against the time it takes you to get it. We sincerely hope that this volume provides a terrific bang for the buck.

Structure of This Book

This book is divided into fourteen chapters and one appendix, as follows:

Chapter 1, *Introducing Oracle*, briefly describes the range of Oracle products and provides some history of Oracle and relational databases.

Chapter 2, *Oracle8 Architecture*, describes the core concepts and structures (e.g., files, processes, and so on) that are the architectural basis of Oracle8.

Chapter 3, *Installing and Running Oracle8*, briefly describes how to install Oracle and how to configure, start up, and shut down the database. It also covers a variety of networking issues.

Chapter 4, *Data Structures*, summarizes the various types of datatypes supported by Oracle and introduces the various Oracle objects (e.g., tables, views, indexes). It also provides information about query optimization.

Chapter 5, *Managing Oracle8*, provides an overview of issues involved in managing an Oracle system, including security, using the Oracle Enterprise Manager (OEM) product, and dealing with database fragmentation and reorganization issues.

Chapter 6, *Oracle8 Performance*, describes the main issues relevant to Oracle performance, especially the major performance characteristics of disk, memory, and CPU tuning, and pays special attention to parallelism in Oracle.

Chapter 7, *Multiuser Concurrency*, describes the basic principles of multiuser concurrency (e.g., transactions, locks, integrity problems) and explains how Oracle handles concurrency.

Chapter 8, *Oracle8 and Transaction Processing*, describes online transaction processing (OLTP) in Oracle.

Chapter 9, *Oracle8 and Data Warehousing*, describes basic principles of data warehouses and data marts, and how you can use Oracle to build such systems.

Chapter 10, *Oracle8 and High Availability*, discusses Oracle's facilities for doing backup and recovery, including the latest failover and data redundancy solutions.

Chapter 11, *Oracle8 and Hardware Architecture*, describes how the choice of various types of architectures (uniprocessor, SMP, MPP, NUMA) affects Oracle processing.

Chapter 12, *Distributed Databases and Distributed Data*, briefly summarizes the Oracle facilities used in distributed processing—for example, two-phase commits and Advanced Queuing.

Chapter 13, *Oracle8/8i Extensions,* discusses how Oracle8 and Oracle8*i* provide object-oriented extensions to Oracle datatypes and to the overall processing framework.

Chapter 14, *Oracle8i and the Web,* describes how Oracle is now being used as an Internet computing platform and introduces various web-related tools, such as Oracle Application Server, WebDB, and Java.

Finally, for each chapter, the Appendix lists a variety of additional resources—both online and offline—so you can do more detailed reading.

Conventions Used in This Book

The following conventions are used in this book:

Italic
> Used for file and directory names, for emphasis, and for the first occurence of terms

`Constant width`
> Used for code examples and literals

`Constant width italic`
> In code examples, indicates an element (e.g., a parameter) that you supply

UPPERCASE
> Generally indicates Oracle keywords

lowercase
> In code examples, generally indicates user-defined items such as variables

---

 The owl icon indicates a tip, suggestion, or general note. For example, we'll tell you if you need to use a particular version of Oracle or if an operation requires certain privileges.

 The turkey icon indicates a warning or caution. For example, we'll tell you if Oracle doesn't behave as you'd expect or if a particular operation negatively impacts performance.

Comments and Questions

Please address comments and questions concerning this book to the publisher:

O'Reilly & Associates, Inc.
101 Morris Street
Sebastopol, CA 95472
800-998-9938 (in the U.S. or Canada)
707-829-0515 (international or local)
707-829-0104 (fax)

To ask technical questions or comment on the book, send email to:

booktech@oreilly.com

You can also send messages electronically. For corrections and amplifications to this book, check out O'Reilly & Associates' online catalog at:

http://www.oreilly.com/catalog/oressentials

See the ads at the end of the book for information about all of O'Reilly & Associates' online services.

Acknowledgments

Each of the authors has arrived at this collaboration through a different path. But we would all like to thank the team at O'Reilly for making this book both possible and a joy to write. At the top of the list is Debby Russell, who was able to leverage her robust scalability throughout the deployment of this work (go edit *that* one!). Debby not only helped to create this book, but believed in the concept enough to take it on as a project. We are lucky to have her as an editor and a friend. The rest of the O'Reilly crew also deserve a lot of credit, especially Steve Abrams and Michael Blanding. It's incredible how they were able to strike the perfect balance—always there when we needed something, but leaving us alone when we didn't.

We're all grateful to each other. Giving birth to a book is a difficult process, but it can be harrowing when split three ways. Everyone hung in there and did their best throughout this process. We'd also like to give our sincere thanks to the technical reviewers for this book: Craig Shallahamer of OraPub, Jonathan Gennick, Jenny Gelhausen, and Dave Klein. This somewhat thankless, but crucially important, work really enhanced the value of the book you're reading.

Rick thanks the incredibly bright and gifted people who have shared their wealth of knowledge with him over the years, including Bruce Scott, Earl Stahl, Jerry Chang and Jim Milbery. In particular, he thanks the two individuals who have been his technical mentors over the course of his entire career—Ed Hickland and Dave Klein, who have repeatedly spent time explaining and discussing some of the broader and finer points of database technology. Finally, Rick would like to thank David Rogelberg and all the folks at Studio B for helping to make this project a reality.

Robert acknowledges all his friends over the years around the world at Oracle Corporation, IBM, Harris Computer Systems, and the U.S. Army Corps of Engineers. Through personal relationships and email, they have shared a lot and provided him with incredible opportunity for learning. He'd also like to thank his customers, who have always had the most practical experience using the products and tools he has worked with, and from whom he will continue to learn.

Jonathan thanks Murray Golding, an excellent friend and Oracle practitioner, for his insights and analogies; Sam Mele, a true friend, for plucking him from the "frozen North" and opening doors; and the Oracle Server Technologies members and their teams, including Juan Tellez, Ron Weiss, Juan Loaiza, Carol Colrain, and George Lumpkin for their help during his years at Oracle.

1

Introducing Oracle

Where do we start? One of the problems in comprehending a massive product such as the Oracle database is the difficulty of getting a good sense of how the product works without getting lost in the details of implementing specific solutions. This book aims to solve this problem by giving you a thorough grounding in the concepts and technologies that form the foundation of Oracle8 and Oracle8*i*.

We've tried to write a book for a wide range of Oracle users—from the novice to the experienced user. To address this range of users, we've explained the concepts and technology behind the Oracle database. Once you fully understand these facets of the product, you'll be able to handle the particulars of virtually any type of Oracle database. Without this understanding, you may feel overburdened as you try to connect the dots of Oracle's voluminous feature set and documentation.

This first chapter lays the groundwork for the rest of the discussions in this book. It covers the broadest range of topics of any chapter; most of the topics mentioned are discussed further in the book, but some of the basics—for example, the brief history of Oracle, and the contents of the different "flavors" of the Oracle database products—are unique to this chapter.

The Oracle database has grown from its humble beginnings as one of a number of relational database vendors in the 1970s to the overwhelming market leader of today. In its early days, Oracle Corporation was known as an aggressive sales and promotion organization. But over the years, the Oracle database has grown in depth and quality until its technical capabilities matched its early hype. With the last two releases, Oracle8 and Oracle8*i*, Oracle has added noticeably more power and features to its already solid base.

Oracle8, released in 1997, added a host of features, such as the ability to create and store complete objects in the database, and also dramatically improved the performance and scalability of the database. Oracle8*i*, released in 1999, has added a new twist to the Oracle database—a combination of enhancements that make the Oracle8*i* database the focal point of the new world of Internet computing.

Before we dive into the specific foundations of these new releases, we must spend a little time describing some Oracle basics—how databases evolved to arrive at the relational model, a brief history of Oracle Corporation, and an introduction to the basic features and configurations of the Oracle8 and Oracle8*i* databases.

The Evolution of the Relational Database

The concept of the relational database was first described around 1970 by Dr. Edgar F. Codd in an IBM research publication entitled "System R4 Relational." Initially, it was unclear whether any system based on these concepts could achieve commercial success. Nevertheless, Relational Software, Incorporated (RSI) was founded in 1979 and released Oracle V.2 as the world's first relational database. By 1985, Oracle could claim more than 1,000 relational database customer sites. IBM itself would not embrace relational technology in a commercial product until the Query Management Facility in 1983.

Why has relational database technology grown to become the de facto database technology since that time? A look back at previous database technology may help to explain this phenomenon.

Database management systems were first defined in the 1960s to provide a common organizational framework for what had been data stored in independent files. In 1964, Charles Bachman of General Electric proposed a network model with data records linked together, forming intersecting sets of data, as shown on the left in Figure 1-1. This work formed the basis of the Codasyl Data Base Task Group. Meanwhile, the North American Aviation's Space Division and IBM developed a second approach based on a hierarchical model in 1965. In this model, data is represented as tree structures in a hierarchy of records, as shown on the right in Figure 1-1. IBM's product based on this model was brought to market in 1969 as the Information Management System (IMS). As recently as 1980, almost all database implementations used either the network or hierarchical approach. Although several competitors utilized these technologies, only IMS remains.

Relational Basics

The relational database uses the concept of linked two-dimensional tables consisting of rows and columns, as shown in Figure 1-2. Unlike the hierarchical approach, no predetermined relationship exists between distinct tables. This means that the data needed to link together the different areas of the network or

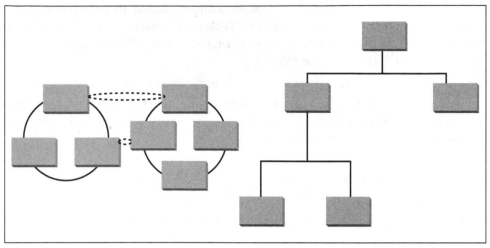

Figure 1-1. Network model and hierarchical model

hierarchical model need not be defined. And because relational users dodn't need to understand the representation of data in storage to retrieve it (many such users created ad hoc queries against the data), ease of use helped popularize the relational model.

DEPTNO	DEPTNAME	LOCATION
10	Accounting	San Francisco
20	Research	San Francisco
30	Sales	Chicago
40	Operations	Dallas

EMPNO	EMPNAME	TITLE	DEPTNO
71712	Johnson	Clerk	10
83321	Smith	Mgr	20
85332	Stern	SC Mgr	30
88888	Carter	Mgr	10

Figure 1-2. Relational model with two tables

Relational programming is nonprocedural and set-at-a-time. In a master detail relationship between tables, there can be one or many detail rows for each individual master row, yet the statements used to access, insert, or modify the data would simply describe the set of results. With early relational competitors, data access required the use of procedural languages that worked one record at a time. Because of this set orientation, programs can access relational databases more easily.

The contents of rows in Figure 1-2 are sometimes referred to as *records*. A column within a row is referred to as a *field*. Tables are stored in a database *schema*, which is a logical organizational unit within the database. Other logical structures in the schema often include the following:

Views
> Provide a single view of data derived from one or more tables or views. The view is an alternative interface to the data, which is stored in the underlying table(s) that make up the view.

Sequences
> A mechanism for providing unique numbers for column values.

Stored procedures
> Contain logical modules that can be called from programs.

Synonyms
> Provide an alternative name for database objects.

Indexes
> Provide faster access to table rows.

Database links
> Provide links between distributed databases.

The relationships between columns in different tables are typically described through the use of *keys*, which are implemented through referential integrity constraints and their supporting indexes. For example, in Figure 1-2, you can establish a link between the DEPTNO column in the second table, which is called a *foreign key*, to the DEPTNO column in the first table, which is referred to as the *primary key* of that table.

Finally, even if you define many different indexes for a table, you don't have to understand them or manage the data they contain. Oracle includes a *query optimizer* that chooses the best way to use your indexes to access the data for any particular query.

The relational approach lent itself to a Structured Query Language (SQL). SQL was initially defined over a period of years by IBM Research, but it was Oracle Corporation that first introduced it to the market in 1979. SQL was noteworthy at the time for being the only language needed to use relational databases, because you could use SQL:

- For queries (using a SELECT statement)

- As a Data Manipulation Language or DML (using INSERT, UPDATE and DELETE statements)

- As a Data Definition Language or DDL (using CREATE or DROP statements when adding or deleting tables)

- To set privileges for users or groups (using GRANT or REVOKE statements)

Today, SQL contains many extensions with ANSI/ISO standards that define its basic syntax.

How Oracle Grew

In 1983, RSI was renamed Oracle Corporation to avoid confusion with a competitor named RTI. At this time, Oracle made a critical decision to create a portable version of Oracle (Version 3) that ran not only on Digital VAX/VMS systems, but also on Unix and other platforms. By 1985, Oracle claimed the ability to run on more than 30 platforms (it runs on more than 70 today). Some of these platforms are historical curiosities today, but others remain in use. (In addition to VMS, early operating systems supported by Oracle included IBM MVS, DEC Ultrix, HP/UX, IBM AIX, and Sun's Solaris version of Unix.) Oracle was able to leverage and accelerate the growth of minicomputers and Unix servers in the 1980s. Today, Oracle leverages its portability on Microsoft Windows NT to capture a significant market share on this new platform.

In addition to multiple platform support, other core Oracle messages from the mid-1980s still ring true today, including complementary software development and decision support tools, ANSI standard SQL and portability across platforms, and connectivity over standard networks. Since the mid-1980s, the database deployment model has evolved from dedicated database application servers to client/server to Internet computing implemented with PCs and thin clients accessing database applications via browsers.

Oracle introduced many innovative technical features to the database as computing and deployment models changed (from offering the first distributed database to the first Java Virtual Machine in the core database engine). Table 1-1 presents a short list of Oracle's major feature introductions.

Table 1-1. History of Oracle Technology Introductions

Year	Feature
1979	Oracle Release 2—the first commercially available relational database to use SQL
1983	Single code base for Oracle across multiple platforms
1984	Portable toolset
1986	Client/server Oracle relational database
1987	CASE and 4GL toolset
1988	Oracle Financial Applications built on relational database
1989	Oracle6

Table 1-1. History of Oracle Technology Introductions (continued)

Year	Feature
1991	Oracle Parallel Server on massively parallel platforms
1993	Oracle7 with cost-based optimizer
1994	Oracle version 7.1 generally available: parallel operations including query, load, and create index
1996	Universal database with extended SQL via cartridges, thin client, and application server
1997	Oracle8 generally available: including object-relational and VLDB (Very Large Database) features
1999	Oracle8*i* generally available: Java Virtual Machine (JVM) in the database

The Oracle8 Family

Oracle8 describes the most recent major version of the Oracle Relational Database Management System (RDBMS) family of products that share common source code. The Oracle8 release surfaced in 1997. The family includes:

- Personal Oracle, a database for single users that's often used to develop code for implementation on other Oracle multiuser databases

- Oracle8, which was named Workgroup Server in its first iteration as part of the Oracle7 family

- Oracle8 Enterprise Edition, which includes additional functionality

In 1998, Oracle announced Oracle8*i*, which is sometimes referred to as Version 8.1 of the Oracle8 database. The "*i*" was added to denote added functionality supporting Internet deployment in the new version. Oracle8 and Oracle8*i* are used somewhat interchangeably in this book, since Oracle8*i* includes all the features of Oracle8, and the features of Oracle8 make up the bulk of the Oracle8*i* product. When we describe a new feature that was first made available for Oracle8*i* specifically, we've noted that fact.

Oracle has focused development around a single source code model since 1983. While each database implementation includes some operating system-specific source code, almost two-thirds of the code is common across the various implementations. The interfaces that users, developers, and administrators deal with for each version are consistent. Features are consistent across platforms for implementations of Oracle8*i* and Oracle8*i* Enterprise Edition. As a result, companies have been able to migrate Oracle applications easily to various hardware vendors and operating systems with minimal effort while leveraging their investments in Oracle technology. From Oracle's perspective, Oracle has been able to focus on implementing new features only once in its product set, instead of having to add functionality at different times to different implementations.

Oracle8i

When Oracle uses the names Oracle8 and Oracle8*i* to refer to a specific database offering, it refers to what was formerly known as Workgroup Server. From a functionality and pricing standpoint, this product intends to compete in the entry-level multiuser and small database category, which support a smaller numbers of users. Oracle8 and Oracle8*i* are available today on Windows NT, Netware, and Unix platforms such as Compaq (Digital), HP/UX, IBM AIX, and Sun Solaris.

Oracle8 and Oracle8i Enterprise Edition

Oracle8 Enterprise Edition and Oracle8*i* Enterprise Edition are the Oracle offerings aimed at larger-scale implementations that require additional features. Enterprise Edition is available on far more platforms than Oracle8*i* and includes advanced management, networking, programming, data warehousing features, and options.

Oracle8i Personal Edition

Oracle8*i* Personal Edition is the single-user version of Oracle8*i* most frequently used by developers because it allows development activities on a single machine. Its features essentially match those of Oracle8*i* Enterprise Edition; thus, a developer can write applications using the Personal Edition and deploy them to multiuser servers. Some companies deploy single-user applications using this product. However, Oracle8*i* Lite offers a much more lightweight means of deploying the same applications.

Oracle8i Lite

Oracle8*i* Lite is intended for single users who are typically mobile. It differs from other members of the Oracle8*i* family in that it doesn't use the same database engine. Instead, Oracle developed a lightweight engine that could fit in the limited memory and storage of handheld devices. Oracle8*i* Lite is described in more detail at the end of this chapter.

Because the SQL supported by Oracle8*i* Lite is mainly the same as the SQL for other Oracle databases, you can run applications developed for other Oracle database engines using Oracle8*i* Lite. Replication of data between Lite and other Oracle versions is a key part of most implementations.

Table 1-2 summarizes the situations in which you would typically use each database product. We've used the Oracle8*i* product names to refer to the different members of the Oracle8 and Oracle8*i* family.

Table 1-2. Oracle8i Family of Database Products

Database Name	When Appropriate
Oracle8i	Version of Oracle server for a small number of users and a smaller size database
Oracle8i Enterprise Edition	Version of Oracle for a large number of users or a large database size with advanced features for extensibility, performance, and management
Oracle8i Personal Edition	Single-user version of Oracle typically used for development of applications for deployment on Oracle8i and Oracle 8i Enterprise Edition
Oracle8i Lite	Lightweight database engine for mobile computing on notebooks and handheld devices

Summary of Oracle8/8i Features

The Oracle8 database is a broad and powerful product. The remainder of this book examines different aspects of Oracle8—for example, data structures, performance, and parallel processing. But before you can understand each of the different areas of Oracle8 in depth, you must familiarize yourself with the range of features in the Oracle8 database.

The rest of this chapter gives you a high-level overview of the basic areas of functionality in the Oracle8 product family. By the end of this chapter, you will at least have some orientation points to guide you in exploring the topics in the rest of this book.

To give some structure to the broad spectrum of the Oracle8 database, we've organized the features into the following sections:

- Database application development features
- Database connection features
- Distributed database features
- Data movement features
- Performance features
- Database management features

At the end of each of the following sections describing database features we've included a subsection called "Availability," which indicates the availability of each feature in specific Oracle products. You should be aware that as this feature list grows and Oracle implements packaging changes in new versions, the availability of these features in the version you implement may vary slightly.

In this chapter, we've included a lot of terminology and rather abbreviated descriptions of features. Oracle is a huge system. Our goal here is to quickly familiarize you with the full range of features in the system. Subsequent chapters will provide additional details. Obviously, though, whole books can be (and have been!) written about each of the features summarized here.

Database Application Development Features

Applications are built on the foundation of the Oracle8 database system. The features of the Oracle8 database and related products described in this section are used to create applications. We've divided the discussion in this section into three categories: database programming, Oracle programming and development tools, and database extensibility options.

Database Programming

All flavors of the Oracle8*i* database include different languages and interfaces for programmers to access and manipulate the data in the database. Database programming features usually interest two groups: developers building Oracle-based applications that will be sold commercially, and IT organizations within companies that custom-develop applications unique to their business. The following sections describe the languages and interfaces supported by Oracle.

SQL

The ANSI standard Structured Query Language (SQL) provides basic functions for data manipulation, transaction control, and record retrieval from the database. However, most end users interact with Oracle through applications that provide an interface hiding the underlying SQL and its complexity.

PL/SQL

Oracle's PL/SQL, a procedural language extension to SQL, is commonly used to implement program logic modules for applications. PL/SQL can be used to build stored procedures and triggers, looping controls, conditional statements, and error handling. You can compile and store PL/SQL procedures in the database. You can also execute PL/SQL blocks via SQL*Plus, an interactive tool provided with all versions of Oracle.

Java features and options

Oracle8*i* introduced the use of Java as a procedural language with a Java Virtual Machine (JVM) in the database (JServer). JServer includes support for Java stored procedures, methods, triggers, Enterprise JavaBeans (EJBs), CORBA, IIOP, and HTTP. JServer versions are available for Oracle8*i* and Oracle8*i* Enterprise Edition. A Java compiler for the Enterprise Edition of the database, JServer Accelerator, is planned after the initial release of Oracle8*i*.

The inclusion of Java within the Oracle database means that a Java developer can leverage his or her skills as an Oracle applications developer. Java applications may be deployed in the client, Oracle Application Server (OAS), or database, depending on what is most appropriate. We discuss Java development Chapter 13, *Oracle8 Extensions*, and Chapter 14, *Oracle8i and the Web*.

Large objects

Interest in the use of large objects (LOBs) is growing, particularly for the storage of nontraditional data types such as images. The Oracle database has been able to store large objects for some time. Oracle8 added the capability to store multiple LOB columns in each table.

Object-oriented programming

Support of object structures was offered as an option to Oracle8 (and is included with Oracle8*i* at no additional charge) to provide support for an object-oriented approach to programming. For example, programmers can create user-defined data types, complete with their own methods and attributes. Oracle8's object support includes a feature called Object Views through which object-oriented programs can make use of relational data already stored in the database. You can also store objects in the database as varying arrays (VARRAYs), nested tables, or index-organized tables (IOTs). We discuss the object-oriented features of Oracle8 further in Chapter 13.

Third-generation languages (3GLs)

Programmers can interact with the Oracle database from C, C++, Java, COBOL, or FORTRAN applications by embedding SQL in those applications. Prior to compiling these applications using a platform's native compilers, you must run the embedded SQL code through a precompiler. The precompiler replaces SQL statements with library calls that the native compiler can accept. Oracle provides support for this capability through optional "programmer" precompilers for languages such as C and C++ (Pro*C) and COBOL (Pro*COBOL). More recently, Oracle added SQLJ, a precompiler for Java that replaces SQL statements embedded in Java with calls to a SQLJ runtime library, also written in Java.

Database drivers

All versions of Oracle8 include database drivers that allow applications to access Oracle via ODBC, (the Open Database Connectivity standard) or JDBC, (the Java Database Connectivity open standard). You can find the most recent versions of these drivers on the Oracle web site (*http://www.oracle.com*).

The Oracle Call Interface

If you're an experienced programmer seeking optimum performance, you may choose to define SQL statements within host-language character strings and then explicitly parse the statements, bind variables for the statements, and execute the statements by using the Oracle Call Interface (OCI).

OCI is a much more detailed interface that requires more programmer time and effort to create and debug. The value in spending more time developing an application that uses OCI emerges over time in the incremental performance gains you may be able to achieve, and immediately in the functionality that may be required in your application that's unavailable in any other way.

Why Use OCI?

Why would someone want to use OCI instead of the higher-level interfaces? In certain programming scenarios, OCI improves application performance or adds functionality. For instance, in high availability implementations in which multiple systems share disks and implement Oracle Parallel Server you may want users to reattach to a second server transparently if the first fails. You can write programs using OCI to do this.

National Language Support

National Language Support (NLS) provides character sets and associated functionality, such as date and numeric formats, for a variety of languages. These are provided so Oracle can render information in the native language of the database user.

Availability

All of these database programming features and options are included in or available for both Oracle8*i* and Oracle8*i* Enterprise Edition.

Oracle Programming and Development Tools

Many Oracle tools are available to developers to help them build more sophisticated Oracle database applications. Although this book focuses on the Oracle database, this section briefly describes the main Oracle tools for application development.

Oracle Developer

Oracle Developer provides a powerful tool for building forms-based, reports-based (via Oracle Reports), and graphical applications for deployment as traditional client/server applications or as three-tier applications via the Web. Developer is a fourth-generation language (4GL). With a 4GL, you define applications by defining values for properties, rather than writing procedural code. Developer supports a wide variety of clients, including traditional client/server PCs and Java-based clients. Version 6 of Developer adds more options for creating easier-to-use applications, including support for animated controls in user dialogs and enhanced user controls. The Forms Builder in Version 6 includes a built-in Java Virtual Machine for previewing web applications.

Oracle JDeveloper

JDeveloper was introduced by Oracle in 1998 to develop basic Java applications without writing code. JDeveloper includes a Data Form wizard, a BeansExpress wizard for creating JavaBeans and BeanInfo classes, and a Deployment wizard. JDeveloper has features for database development such as various Oracle drivers, a Connection Editor to hide the JDBC API complexity, database components to bind visual controls, and a SQLJ precompiler for embedding SQL in Java code, which you can then use with Oracle8*i*. You can also deploy applications developed with JDeveloper using the Oracle Application Server (OAS), which is described later in this chapter and in greater detail in Chapter 14. Although JDeveloper uses wizards to allow programmers to create Java objects without writing code, the end result is generated Java code. This Java implementation is an advantage, because it makes the code highly flexible, but it is typically a less productive development environment than a true 4GL.

WebDB

WebDB, introduced in 1999, provides an HTML-based tool for developing web-enabled applications and content-driven web sites. WebDB application systems are developed and deployed in a simple browser environment. WebDB includes wizards for developing application components and building entire Internet sites. The application components developed with WebDB reside entirely in the database (Oracle 7.3.4 or later) in which WebDB is installed and implemented using PL/SQL.

Oracle Designer

Oracle Designer provides a graphical interface for Rapid Application Development (RAD) for the entire database development process—from building the business model to schema design, generation, and deployment. Designs and changes are stored in a multiuser repository. The tool can reverse engineer existing tables and database schemas for reuse and redesign from Oracle and non-Oracle relational databases.

Designer also includes generators for creating applications for Oracle Developer, HTML clients using Oracle Application Server, and C++. Designer not only generates applications, but can also reverse engineer existing applications or applications that have been modified by developers. This capability enables a process called *round-trip engineering,* in which a developer uses Designer to generate an application, modifies the generated application, and reverse engineers the changes back into the Designer repository.

Availability

All of these programming and development products are available as separate packages.

Database Extensibility Options

The Internet and corporate intranets have created a growing demand for storage and manipulation of nontraditional data types within the database. There is a need for extensions to the standard functionality of a database for storing and manipulating images, audio, video, spatial, and time series information. In Oracle8, Oracle provides extensibility to the database through options sometimes referred to as *cartridges.* These options are simply extensions to standard SQL, usually built by Oracle or its partners through C, PL/SQL, or Java. You may find these options very helpful if you're working extensively with the type of data they're designed to handle.

For more details regarding these optional features of Oracle8, see Chapter 13.

interMedia

Oracle8*i* *inter*Media is an option that bundles what was formerly referred to as the "Context cartridge" for text manipulation with additional image, audio, video, and locator functions.

- The text portion of *inter*Media can identify the gist of a document by searching for themes and key phrases within the document.

- The image portion of *inter*Media can store and retrieve images.

- The audio and video portions of *inter*Media can store and retrieve audio and video clips, respectively.

- The locator portion of *inter*Media can retrieve data that includes spatial coordinate information.

Some of these portions are also available with enhanced functionality as separate options for the Enterprise Edition, as described in the next three sections.

Visual Image Retrieval

The Visual Image Retrieval (VIR) option provides a means of comparing images stored within the database and retrieving images based on similarity to other images.

Spatial

The Spatial option can optimize the display and retrieval of data linked to coordinates. Several vendors of Geographic Information Systems (GIS) products now use this option as their search and retrieval engine.

Time Series

The Time Series option extends the functionality of the database in which the stored data has a timestamp associated with it. Included in this option are calendar functions (for defining business calendars) and time-based analysis functions such as the computation of moving averages.

Availability

Table 1-3 lists the availability of each of the database extensibility options for Oracle8*i*.

Table 1-3. Oracle8i Database Extensibility Options

Feature	Oracle8*i*	Oracle8*i* Enterprise Edition
*inter*Media	✓	✓
Virtual Image Retrieval		✓
Spatial		✓
Time Series		✓

Database Connection Features

The connection between the client and the database server is a key component of the overall architecture of a computing system. The database connection is responsible for supporting all communications between an application and the data that it uses, and Oracle8 includes a number of features that establish and tune your database connections.

The following features relate to the way the Oracle8 database handles the connection between the client and server machines in a database interaction. We've divided the discussion in this section into two categories: database networking and Oracle Application Server.

Database Networking

Database users connect to the database by establishing a network connection. You can also link database servers via network connections. Oracle provides a number of features to establish connections between users and the database and/or between database servers, as described in the following sections.

Net8

Oracle's network interface, Net8, was formerly known as SQL*Net when used with Oracle7 and previous versions of Oracle. You can use Net8 over a wide variety of network protocols, although TCP/IP is by far the most common protocol today.

Oracle Names

Oracle Names allows clients to connect to an Oracle server without requiring a configuration file on each client. Using Oracle Names can reduce maintenance efforts, since a change in the topology of your network will not require a corresponding change in configuration files on every client machine.

Oracle Connection Manager

Each connection to the database takes up valuable network resources, which can impact the overall performance of a database application. Oracle's Connection Manager, illustrated in Figure 1-3, reduces the number of network connections to the database through the use of *concentrators*, which provide connection multiplexing to implement multiple connections over a single network connection. Connection multiplexing provides the greatest benefit when there are a large number of active users.

You can also use the Connection Manager to provide multiprotocol connectivity when clients and servers run different network protocols. This capability replaces the multiprotocol interchange formerly offered by Oracle. However, this capability is less important today as many companies have standardized on TCP/IP as their protocol.

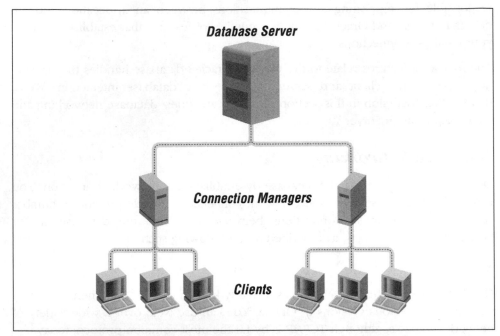

Figure 1-3. Concentrators with Connection Managers for a large number of users

Advanced Security Option

Advanced Security, now available as an option, was formerly known as the Advanced Networking Option (ANO). Key features include network encryption services using RSA Data Security's RC4 or DES algorithm, network data integrity checking, enhanced authentication integration, single sign-on, and DCE (Distributed Computing Environment) integration.

Availability

Table 1-4 lists the availibility of Oracle8*i* networking features.

Table 1-4. Oracle8i Networking Features

Feature	Oracle8*i*	Oracle8*i* Enterprise Edition
Net8	✓	✓
Oracle Names	✓	✓
Oracle Connection Manager		✓
Advanced Security Option		✓

Oracle Application Server

The popularity of the Web for Internet and intranet applications has led to a change in deployment from client/server (with fat clients running a significant piece of the application) to a three-tier architecture (with a browser supplying everything needed on a thin client). Oracle Application Server (OAS) provides a means of implementing the middle tier of a three-tier solution for web-based applications, component-based applications, and enterprise application integration.

OAS was originally called the Oracle Web Application Server. In Oracle Application Server Version 4, the architecture includes HTTP listeners, the application server itself—implemented on a CORBA 2.0 compliant Object Request Broker (ORB)—and application cartridges. The listener and application architecture can be distributed over multiple physical servers because application cartridges and system services are implemented as distributed objects. Thus, OAS is often used when a web server supports a large number of users, providing a scalable and highly available solution to handle requests.

Access to OAS may be via HTTP servers from Oracle, Netscape (Enterprise Server), or Microsoft (Internet Information Server), or directly into OAS via IIOP, the protocol used in the CORBA distributed environment. For these deployments, you don't need to distribute Net8 to clients.

OAS provides a Java Virtual Machine cartridge for running Java components accessible from HTTP clients. OAS also enables the Java Virtual Machine to run CORBA components that are accessible from CORBA/IIOP clients. The PL/SQL cartridge is linked to PL/SQL stored procedures running in the database server. Security options include directory and database-based authentication, SSL 3.0, and X.509 certificate support. Additional transaction support is provided in the Enterprise Edition.

Figure 1-4 shows many of the connection possibilities we've discussed.

Availability

Because OAS is a separate product, it can be used with either the Oracle8 server or the Oracle8*i* server in either edition. For more details about OAS, see Chapter 14.

Distributed Database Features

One of the strongest features of the Oracle8 database is its ability to scale up to handle extremely large volumes of data and users. Oracle8 scales not only by running on more and more powerful platforms, but also by running in a distributed

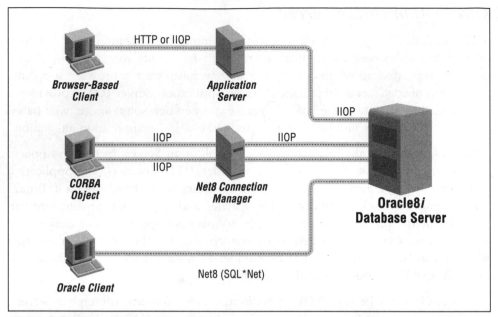

Figure 1-4. Typical Oracle8i connections

configuration. Oracle8 databases on separate platforms are combined to act as a single logical distributed database.

This section describes some of the basic ways that Oracle handles database interactions in a distributed database system.

Distributed Queries and Transactions

Data within an organization is often spread among multiple databases for reasons of both capacity and organizational responsibility. Users may want to query this distributed data or update it as if it existed within a single database.

Oracle first introduced distributed databases in response to the requirements for accessing data on multiple platforms in the early 1980s. *Distributed queries* can retrieve data from multiple databases. *Distributed transactions* can insert, update, or delete data on distributed databases. Oracle's two-phase commit mechanism, which is described in detail in Chapter 12, *Distributed Databases and Distributed Data*, guarantees that all of the database servers that are part of a transaction will either commit or roll back the transaction. Distributed transactions that may be interrupted by a system failure are monitored by a recovery background process. Once the failed system comes back online, the same process will complete the distributed transactions to maintain consistency across the databases.

You can also implement distributed transactions in Oracle8 by popular transaction monitors (TPs) that interact with Oracle8 via XA, an industry standard (X/Open) interface. In addition, Oracle8*i* adds native transaction coordination with the Microsoft Transaction Server (MTS), so that you can implement a distributed transaction initiated under the control of MTS through an Oracle database.

Heterogeneous Services

Heterogeneous Services enable the accessing of non-Oracle data and services from an Oracle8 database through tools such as Oracle Transparent Gateways. For example, Transparent Gateways allow users to submit Oracle SQL statements to a non-Oracle distributed database source and have them automatically translated into the SQL dialect of the non-Oracle source system, which remains transparent to the user. In addition to providing underlying SQL services, Heterogeneous Services provide transaction services utilizing Oracle's two-phase commit with non-Oracle databases, and procedural services that call third-generation language routines on non-Oracle systems. Users interact with the Oracle database as if all objects are stored in the Oracle database, and Heterogeneous Services handles the transparent interaction with the foreign database on the user's behalf.

Availability

All of the technology discussed in this section is included in both editions of the database. The MTS support for distributed transactions is available for Oracle8*i* only on the NT platform at press time.

Heterogeneous Services work in conjunction with Transparent Gateways, which are a separate Oracle product.

Data Movement Features

Moving data from one Oracle database to another is often a requirement when using distributed databases, or when a user wants to implement multiple copies of the same database in multiple locations to reduce network traffic or increase data availability. You can export data and data dictionaries (metadata) from one database and import them into another. Oracle also offers many other advanced features in this category, including replication, transportable tablespaces, and Advanced Queuing.

This section describes the technology used to move data from one Oracle database to another automatically.

Basic Replication

Use basic replication to move recently added and updated data from an Oracle "master" database to databases on which duplicate sets of data reside. In basic replication, only the single master is updated. You can manage replication through the Oracle Enterprise Manager (OEM).

Advanced Replication

Use advanced replication when any of the databases involved may be updated, and conflict resolution features are needed to resolve any inconsistencies in the data. Because there is more than one "master" (known as multi-masters), the same data may be updated on multiple systems at the same time. Conflict resolution is necessary to determine the true version of the data. Oracle's advanced replication includes a number of different conflict resolution scenarios, and also allows the programmer to write his own. We cover replication in more detail in Chapter 12.

Transportable Tablespaces

Transportable tablespaces were introduced in Oracle8*i*. Instead of using the export/import process, which dumps data and the structures that contain it into an intermediate file for loading, you simply move or copy these read-only tablespaces from one database to another and mount them. You must export the data dictionary (metadata) for the tablespace from the source and import at the target. This feature can save a lot of time during this maintenance process, because it simplifies the process.

Advanced Queuing

Advanced Queuing (AQ) was introduced in Oracle8 and provides the means to asynchronously send messages from one Oracle database to another. Because messages are stored in a queue in the database and sent asynchronously when the connection is made, the amount of overhead and network traffic is a lot less than it would be using traditional guaranteed delivery through the two-phase commit protocol between source and target. By storing the messages in the database, AQ provides a solution with greater recoverability than other queuing solutions that store messages in filesystems.

Oracle8*i* messaging adds the capability to develop and deploy a *content-based publish and subscribe solution* using a rules engine to determine relevant subscribing applications. As new content is published to a subscriber list, the rules on the list determine which subscribers should receive the content. This approach means that a single list can efficiently serve the needs of different subscriber communities.

Availability

Table 1-5 lists the availability of Oracle8*i* data movement features.

Table 1-5. Oracle8i Data Movement Features

Feature	Oracle8*i*	Oracle8*i* Enterprise Edition
Basic replication	✓	✓
Advanced replication		✓
Transportable tablespaces		✓
Advanced Queuing		✓

Performance Features

Oracle8 and Oracle8*i* include a number of features specifically designed to boost performance in certain situations. We've divided the discussion in this section into two categories: database parallelization and data warehousing.

Database Parallelization

Database tasks implemented in parallel speed up querying, tuning, and the maintenance of the database. By breaking up a single task into smaller tasks and assigning each subtask to an independent process, you can dramatically improve the performance of certain types of database operations.

Parallel query features became a standard part of Enterprise Edition beginning with Oracle 7.3. Examples of query features implemented in parallel include:

- Table scans
- Nested loops
- Sort merge joins
- GROUP BYs
- NOT IN subqueries (anti-joins)
- User-defined functions
- Index scans
- Select distinct UNION and UNION ALL
- Hash joins
- ORDER BY and aggregation

- Bitmap star joins

- Partition-wise joins

When you're using Oracle8*i*, the degree of parallelism for any operation is, by default, set to twice the number of CPUs. You can adjust this degree automatically for each subsequent query based on the system load. The cost-based optimizer is a key feature for optimizing performance; it utilizes statistics that you can generate in parallel.

Availability

You can perform maintenance functions such as loading (via SQL*Loader) in parallel in Oracle8*i* or Oracle8*i* Enterprise Edition. You can perform backups and index builds in parallel in Enterprise Edition. Oracle Partitioning for the Enterprise Edition enables additional parallel Data Manipulation Language (DML) (inserts, updates, deletes) as well as index scans.

Data Warehousing

The parallel features discussed in the previous section improve the overall performance of the Oracle database. Oracle has also added some performance enhancements that specifically apply to data warehousing applications. For detailed explanations of these and complementary products and features related to data warehousing, see Chapter 9, *Oracle8 and Data Warehousing*.

Bitmap indexes

Oracle added support for stored bitmap indexes to Oracle 7.3 to provide a very fast way of selecting and retrieving certain types of data. Bitmap indexes typically work best for columns that have few different values relative to the overall number of rows in a table.

Rather than store the actual value in the index, a bitmap index uses an individual bit for each potential value with the bit either "on" (set to 1) to indicate that the row contains the value or "off" (set to 0) to indicate that the row does not contain the value. This storage mechanism can also provide performance improvements for the types of joins typically used in data warehousing. The bitmap index is described in more detail in Chapter 4, *Data Structures*.

Star query optimization

Typical data warehousing queries occur against a large *fact table* with foreign keys to much smaller *dimension tables*. Oracle added an optimization for this type of *star query* to Oracle 7.3. (A figure showing a typical star schema appears in Chapter 9, *Oracle8 and Data Warehousing*.) Performance gains are realized through the use of Cartesian product joins of dimension tables with a single join back to the large fact table. Oracle8 introduced a further speed-up mechanism called a *parallel bitmap star join*, which uses bitmap indexes on the foreign keys to the dimension tables to speed star joins involving a large number of dimension tables.

Materialized views

In Oracle8*i*, materialized views provide another means of achieving a significant speed-up of query performance. Summary-level information derived from a fact table and grouped along dimension values is stored as a materialized view. Queries that can use this view are directed to the view, transparently to the user and the SQL they submit.

CUBE and ROLLUP

A growing trend in Oracle and other systems is the movement of some functions from decision-support user tools into the database. In Oracle8*i*, the ROLLUP function calculates multiple levels of subtotals while the CUBE function calculates data needed for cross tabulations.

Availability

Table 1-6 lists the availibility of these Oracle8*i* data warehousing features.

Table 1-6. Oracle8i Data Warehouse Features

Feature	Oracle8*i*	Oracle8*i* Enterprise Edition
Bitmap indexes		✓
Star query optimization	✓	✓
Materialized views		✓
CUBE and ROLLUP	✓	✓

Database Management Features

Oracle8 and Oracle8*i* include a number of features that make it easier to manage the Oracle database. We've divided the discussion in this section into four categories: Oracle Enterprise Manager, add-on packs, backup and recovery, and database availability.

Oracle Enterprise Manager

As part of every database server, Oracle provides the Oracle Enterprise Manager (OEM), a database management tool framework with a graphical interface, used to manage database users, instances, and features (such as replication). OEM also provides a framework for other useful tools, known as "Packs," that can provide additional information about the Oracle environment.

Prior to Oracle8*i*, you had to install the OEM software on Windows 95/98 or NT-based systems, and you could only access each repository of management information by a single database administrator. With the introduction of Oracle8*i*, you can use Enterprise Manager from a browser, or load it on to Microsoft Windows 95/98 or NT-based systems. Multiple database administrators can access the repository at the same time with OEM and Oracle8*i*.

Add-on Packs

Several optional add-on packs are available for Oracle, as described in the following sections and in more detail in Chapter 5, *Managing Oracle8*.

Standard Management Pack

The Standard Management Pack for Oracle8*i* is an option providing tools for the management of small Oracle databases (i.e., not Enterprise Edition). Features include support for performance monitoring of database contention, I/O, load, memory use and instance metrics, session analysis, index tuning, and change investigation and tracking.

Diagnostics Pack

You use the Diagnostics Pack to monitor, diagnose, and maintain the health of Enterprise Edition databases, operating systems, and applications. With both historical and real-time analysis, you can automatically avoid problems before they occur. The pack also provides capacity planning features that help you plan and track future system resource requirements.

Tuning Pack

With the Tuning Pack, you can optimize system performance by identifying and tuning Enterprise Edition database and application bottlenecks such as inefficient SQL, poor data design, and the improper use of system resources. The pack can proactively discover tuning opportunities and automatically generate the analysis and required changes to tune the system.

Change Management Pack

The Change Management Pack helps eliminate errors and loss of data when upgrading Enterprise Edition databases to support new applications. It can analyze the impact and complex dependencies associated with application changes and automatically perform database upgrades. Users can initiate changes with easy-to-use wizards that teach the systematic steps necessary to upgrade.

Availability

Table 1-7 lists the availability of Oracle8*i* database management features and options.

Table 1-7. Oracle8i Database Management Features and Options

Feature	Oracle8i	Oracle8*i* Enterprise Edition
Oracle Enterprise Manager	✓	✓
Standard Management Pack	✓	
Diagnostics Pack		✓
Tuning Pack		✓
Change Management Pack		✓

Backup and Recovery

As every database administrator knows, backing up a database is a rather mundane but necessary task. An improper backup makes recovery difficult, if not impossible. Unfortunately, you realize the extreme importance of this everyday task only when it is too late—usually after losing business-critical data due to a failure of a related system.

The following sections describe some products and techniques for performing database backup operations. We discuss backup and recovery strategies and options in much greater detail in Chapter 10, *Oracle8 and High Availability*.

Recovery Manager

Typical backups include complete database backups (the most common type of backup), tablespace backups, datafile backups, control file backups, and archivelog backups. Oracle8 introduced the Recovery Manager (RMAN), for the server-managed backup and recovery of the database. Previously, Oracle's Enterprise Backup Utility (EBU) provided a similar solution on some platforms. However, RMAN, with its Recovery Catalog stored in an Oracle database, provides a much more complete solution. RMAN can automatically locate, back up, restore, and recover datafiles, control files, and archived redo logs. The Oracle Enterprise Manager Backup Manager provides a GUI-based interface to RMAN.

Incremental backup and recovery

RMAN can perform incremental backups of Enterprise Edition databases. Incremental backups only back up the blocks modified since the last backup of a datafile, tablespace, or database; thus, they're smaller and faster than complete backups. RMAN can also perform point-in-time recovery, which allows the recovery of data until just prior to a undesirable event (such as the mistaken dropping of a table).

Legato Storage Manager

Various media management software vendors support RMAN. Oracle bundles Legato Storage Manager with Oracle8 to provide media management services for up to four devices, including the tracking of tape volumes. RMAN interfaces automatically with the media management software to request the mounting of tapes as needed for backup and recovery operations.

Availability

Table 1-8 lists the availability of Oracle8*i* backup and recovery features.

Table 1-8. Oracle8i Backup and Recovery Features

Feature	Oracle8*i*	Oracle8*i* Enterprise Edition
Recovery Manager	✓	✓
Incremental backup		✓
Legato Storage Manager	✓	✓

Database Availability

Database availability depends upon the reliability and management of the database, the underlying operating system, and the specific hardware components of the system. Oracle has improved availability by reducing backup and recovery times. It has done this through online and parallel backup and recovery, improving management of online data through range partitioning, and leveraging by hardware for failover through a variety of features described below.

Partitioning option

Oracle introduced partitioning as an option to Oracle8 to provide a higher degree of manageability and availability. You can take individual partitions offline for maintenance while other partitions remain available for user access. In data warehousing implementations, partitioning is frequently used to implement rolling windows based on date ranges. Hash partitioning, in which the data partitions are divided up as a result of a hashing function, is also supported with Oracle8*i* to enable an even distribution of data. You can also use composite partitioning to enable hash subpartitioning within specific range partitions.

Standby database

Oracle first introduced a standby database feature in Oracle 7.3. The standby database provides a copy of the production database to be used if the primary database is lost—for example, in the event of primary site failure. The standby database is created from a copy of the production database and updated through the application of archived redo logs generated by the production database. Oracle8*i* fully automates this process; previously, you had to manually copy and apply the logs. You can open the standby database in read-only mode and use it for querying.

Failover features and options

The failover feature provides a higher level of reliability for an Oracle8 database. Failover is implemented through a second system or node that provides access to data residing on a shared disk when the first system or node fails. Oracle Fail Safe for NT, in combination with Microsoft Cluster Services, provides a failover solution in the event of an NT-based system failure. Unix systems such as HP or Sun have long provided similar functionality for their clusters.

Oracle Parallel Server failover features

Oracle Parallel Server (OPS) option can provide failover support as well as increased scalability on Unix and NT clusters.

With OPS, you can run multiple Oracle instances on systems in a shared disk cluster configuration, or on multiple nodes of a Massively Parallel Processor (MPP) configuration. A Distributed Lock Manager (DLM) coordinates traffic among the systems or nodes, allowing the instances to function as a single database. As a result, the database can scale across hundreds of nodes. Since the DLM provides a means by which multiple instances can access the same data, the failure of a single instance will not cause extensive delays while the system recovers, because you can simply redirect users to another instance that's still operating. You can write applications with the Oracle Call Interface (OCI) to provide failover to a second instance transparently to the user.

Availability

Table 1-9 lists where Oracle8*i* database availability features are available.

Table 1-9. Oracle8i Database Availability Features

Feature	Oracle8*i*	Oracle8*i* Enterprise Edition
Partitioning option		✓
Oracle Parallel Server option		✓
Oracle Fail Safe	✓	✓
Readable and automated standby database	✓	✓
OCI client transparent failover		✓ [a]

[a] Only available with Oracle Parallel Server option

Oracle8i Lite

Oracle8*i* Lite is Oracle's suite of products for enabling mobile use of database-centric applications. Key components in the Oracle8*i* Lite suite include the Oracle8*i* Lite database, Internet Lite services for mobile web applications, EnterpriseSync Lite for sychnronization of data and applications, and Advanced Queuing Lite for messaging services.

Although the Oracle8*i* Lite database engine can operate with much less memory than other Oracle implementations (it requires less than 1 MB of memory to run on a laptop), Oracle SQL, C and C++, and Java-based applications can run against the database. Java support includes support of Java stored procedures, JDBC, and SQLJ. The database is self-tuning and self-administering. In addition to support for Windows-based laptops, Oracle8*i* Lite is also supported on handheld devices running WindowsCE and the PalmOS.

A variety of replication possibilities exist between Oracle8*i* and Oracle Lite including:

*   Connection-based replication via Net8 or SQL*Net synchronous connections
*   Wireless replication through the use of "Advanced Queuing Lite" which provides a messaging service compatible with Oracle8*i* Advanced Queuing (and replaces the Oracle Mobile Agents capability available in previous versions of Oracle Lite)
*   File-based replication via standards such as FTP and MAPI
*   Internet replication via HTTP or MIME

You can define replication of subsets of data via SQL statements. Because data distributed to multiple locations can lead to conflicts—such as which location now has the "true" version of the data—multiple conflict and resolution algorithms are provided. Alternatively, you can write your own algorithm.

In typical usage of Oracle8*i* Lite, the user will link his handheld or mobile device running Oracle8*i* Lite to an Oracle8*i* server. Data and applications will be synchronized between the two systems. The user will then remove the link and work in disconnected mode. After he has performed his tasks, he'll relink and resynchronize the data with the Oracle8*i* server.

2

Oracle8 Architecture

This chapter focuses on the concepts and structures that are at the core of Oracle8. When you understand the architecture of Oracle8, you'll have a context for analyzing the rest of the Oracle8 and Oracle8*i* features.

Instances and Databases

Many Oracle practitioners use the terms "instance" and "database" interchangeably. In fact, an instance and a database are different but related entities. This distinction is important because it provides insight into Oracle's architecture. For example, the distinction sheds light on the differences between instance recovery and media recovery.

In Oracle, the term *database* refers to the physical storage of information, and the term *instance* refers to the software executing on the server that provides access to the information in the database. The instance runs on the computer or server; the database is stored on the disks attached to the server. Figure 2-1 illustrates this relationship.

The database is *physical*: it consists of files stored on disks. The instance is *logical*: it consists of in-memory structures and processes on the server. An instance can connect to one and only one database. Instances are temporal, but databases are, with proper maintenance, forever.

Users do not directly access the information in an Oracle database. Instead, they pass requests for information to an Oracle instance.

The real world provides a useful analogy for instances and databases. An instance can be thought of as a bridge to the database, which in turn can be thought of as an island. Traffic flows on and off the island via the bridge. If the bridge is closed,

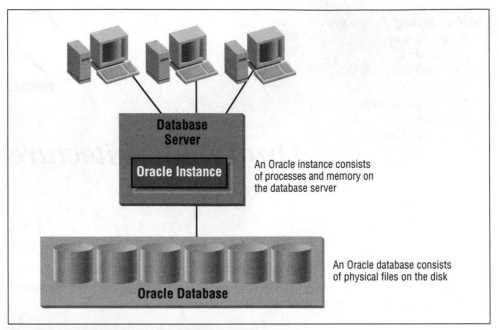

Figure 2-1. An instance and a database

the island exists but no traffic flow is possible. In Oracle terms, if the instance is up, data can flow in and out of the database. The physical state of the database is changing. If the instance is down, users cannot access the database even though it still exists physically. The instance is static: no changes can occur to it. The fact that a database without an instance is inaccessible has resulted in the misuse of terms by many Oracle users.

The Components of a Database

You assign a specific name to a database when you create it. You cannot change the database name once you create the database, although you can change the name of the instance that accesses the database.

This section covers the different types of files and other components that make up a complete database.

Tablespaces

Before you examine the physical files of the actual database, you need to understand a key logical structure within a database called a *tablespace*. All the data stored in a database must reside in a tablespace.

A tablespace is a logical structure; you cannot look at the operating system and see a tablespace. Composed of physical structures called *datafiles*, each tablespace must consist of one or more datafiles, and each datafile can belong to only one tablespace. When you create a table, you can specify which tablespace to create it in. Oracle will then find space for it in one of the datafiles that make up the tablespace.

Figure 2-2 shows the relationship of tablespaces to datafiles for a database.

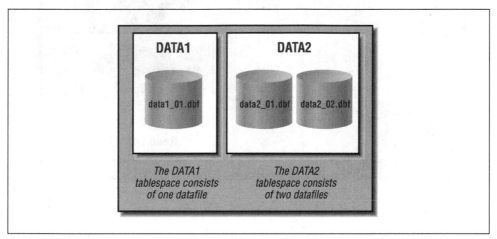

Figure 2-2. Tablespaces and datafiles

This figure shows two tablespaces within an Oracle database. When you create a new table in this Oracle database, you may place it in the DATA1 tablespace or the DATA2 tablespace. It will physically reside in one of the datafiles that make up the specified tablespace.

Physical Files in an Oracle Database

A tablespace is a logical view of the physical storage of information in an Oracle database. There are actually three fundamental types of physical files that make up an Oracle database:

- Control files
- Datafiles
- Redo log files

Other files are used within a database environment, such as password files and instance initialization files, but the three fundamental types listed represent the physical database itself. Figure 2-3 illustrates the three types of files and their interrelationships.

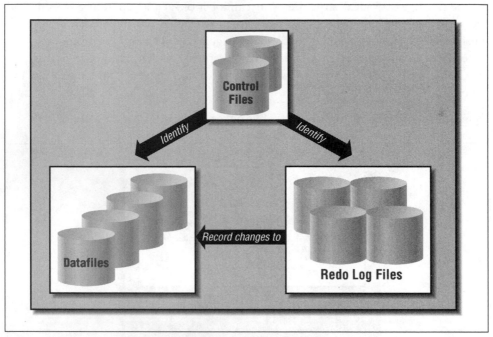

Figure 2-3. The files that make up a database

The next sections describe the role of these three types of files and their interactions.

Control Files

The control file contains a list of all the other files that make up the database, such as the datafiles and redo log files. It also contains key information about the contents and state of the database, such as:

- The name of the database

- When the database was created

- The current state of the datafiles: whether they need recovery, are in a read-only state, and so on

- If the database closed cleanly the last time it was shut down

- The time period covered by each archived redo log

- What backups have been performed for the database

Prior to Oracle8, control files were typically under a megabyte in size. With Oracle8, there is more information in the control file, such as the details of database backups. The control files in Oracle8 can easily grow to the 10 MB range or beyond. For example, the default database created when you install Oracle8 on Windows NT contains control files about 2.5 MB in size. More complex databases can contain control files as large as 7.5 MB.

Control file parameters

The size of a control file is influenced by the following initialization parameters, which are part of the initialization (*INIT.ORA*) file and are set at the time you create a database (see "The Components of an Instance" for a discussion of the *INIT.ORA* file):

MAXLOGFILES
> The maximum number of redo log file groups for the database. Redo log files are described later in this chapter in the "Redo Log Files" section.

MAXLOGMEMBERS
> The maximum number of members for each redo log file group.

MAXLOGHISTORY
> The number of redo log history the control file can contain. This history is used to simplify automatic recovery, which uses the redo logs by identifying the range of transactions held in an archived redo log.

MAXDATAFILES
> The number of datafiles the control file can track. In Oracle7, if you tried to exceed this limit you had to rebuild the control file to increase the number of datafiles that Oracle could track. In Oracle8, this parameter determines the amount of space set aside in the control file for datafiles at the time you create the database. If you add more datafiles than specified in the MAXDATA-FILES parameter, the control file will expand automatically.

MAXINSTANCES
> The amount and number of instances the control file can track. This is relevant for Oracle Parallel Server, which is discussed in Chapter 6, *Oracle8 Performance*.

For more details about these parameters, please see your Oracle documentation.

In general, it's far simpler to set these MAX values to high levels to avoid encountering any problems later on. For example, if you think that your database might eventually have five redo log file groups with two members each, why not set MAXLOGFILES to 20 (instead of the 10 required by your estimate) and MAXLOG-MEMBERS to 3 instead of 2? It's much easier to set the parameters for a control file a little high initially than to go through the time-consuming process of rebuilding control files when your database grows.

Of more significance, do not limit MAXLOGHISTORY in the interest of saving
space. If the control file does not have enough room for redo log history, recovery
will be more complex and time-consuming. When you are recovering a database,
you generally want to finish the task as quickly as possible. Trying to save a little
disk space by minimizing log history entries could result in more time recovering
from a disaster.

Multiple control files

A database should have at least two control files. Without at least one current copy
of the control file, you run the risk of losing track of some or all of your database.
Losing control files is not necessarily fatal—there are ways to rebuild them. However, rebuilding control files can be difficult and introduces risk, which is why it's
a good idea to keep multiple copies of the control file. You enable multiple copies of control files by specifying multiple locations for the control files in the
CONTROL_FILES parameter in the *INIT.ORA* file for the instance, as shown here:

```
CONTROL_FILES = (/u00/oradata/prod/prodctl1.ctl,
        /u01/oradata/prod/prodctl2.ctl, /u02/oradata/prod/prodctl3.ctl)
```

This parameter tells the instance where to find the control files. Oracle will ensure
that all copies of the control file are kept in sync so all updates to the control files
will occur at the same time.

Many Oracle systems use some type of redundant disk solution such as RAID-1 or
RAID-5 to avoid data loss when a disk fails. (RAID, which stands for "redundant
array of inexpensive disks, is covered in more detail in Chapter 6.) You might con-
clude that if storing the control file on protected disk storage eliminates the need
for maintaining multiple copies of control files, and therefore losing a disk won't
mean loss of the control file. But there are two reasons why this is not an appropriate conclusion:

1. If you lose more than one disk in a given *striped array* or *mirror-pair* (we'll
   explain these terms in Chapter 6), you will lose the data on those disks. Statis-
   tically speaking, losing two disks in a short period of time is unlikely to happen. But this type of disastrous event can occur, and it's possible that at some
   point you will suffer a failure or series of failures resulting in a damaged or
   lost control file. Because you will no doubt have your hands full recovering
   from the multiple disk failures, you should avoid the overhead of rebuilding
   control files during the recovery process. Multiplexing your control files, even
   when each copy is on redundant disk storage, provides an additional level of
   physical security for your Oracle database.

2. Redundant disk storage does nothing to protect you from the unfortunately
   perpetual threat of human error. Someone may inadvertently delete or rename
   a control file, copy another file over it, move it, and so on. A mirrored disk
   will faithfully mirror these actions, and multiplexed control files will leave you

with one or more surviving copies of the control file when one of the copies is damaged or lost.

You do not need to be concerned with the potential performance impact of writing to multiple control files versus one control file. Updates to the control files are insignificant compared to all the other disk I/O that occurs in an Oracle environment.

Datafiles

Datafiles contain the actual data stored in the database. This data includes the data dictionary, the rollback segments, and the tables and indexes created by users of the database.

A datafile is composed of Oracle database blocks that, in turn, are composed of operating system blocks on a disk. Oracle block sizes range from 2K to 32K. If you're using Oracle with Very Large Memory (VLM) support, for example on a Compaq (DEC) Alpha, you may use Big Oracle Blocks (BOBs), which can be as large as 64K in size.

Figure 2-4 illustrates the relationship of Oracle blocks to operating system blocks.

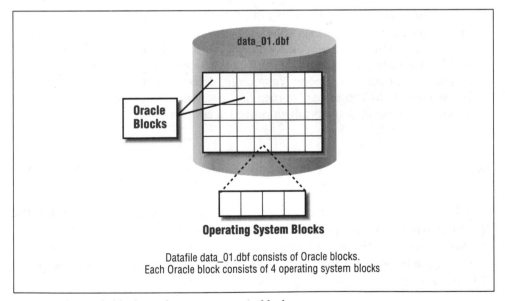

Datafile data_01.dbf consists of Oracle blocks.
Each Oracle block consists of 4 operating system blocks

Figure 2-4. Oracle blocks and operating system blocks

Datafiles belong to only one database and to only one tablespace within that database. Data is read in units of Oracle blocks from the datafiles into memory as needed, based on the work users are doing. Blocks of data are written from

Setting the Database Block Size

You set the database block size for an Oracle database at the time you create the database, and you can't change it without recreating the database. You set the block size using the DB_BLOCK_SIZE parameter in the instance initialization file (*INIT.ORA*) used when you create the database. What constitutes an appropriate block size for an Oracle database? Oracle defaults the block size to 2K, but most experienced Oracle users agree that this is too small for just about every type of application. Understanding the implications of the block size can help you to determine an appropriate setting for this parameter.

The block size influences how much data is read and written with each block transfer. In online transaction processing (OLTP) systems, a transaction typically involves a relatively small, well-defined set of rows, such as the rows used for placing an order for a set of products for a specific customer. The access to rows in these types of operations tends to be through indexes, as opposed to through a scan of the entire table. Because of this, having smaller blocks, such as 4K or 8K, might be appropriate. Oracle doesn't waste system resources by transferring larger blocks that contain additional data not required by the transaction.

Data warehouses tend to do more large-scale reading of data, often involving millions of rows and complete scans of all the data in a table. With this type of activity, having bigger database blocks means that each block read provides more valuable data to the requesting user. To support these types of operations best, data warehouses tend to use larger blocks, such as 8K or 16K. As mentioned, on systems that support Very Large Memory, Oracle can use a block size as large as 64K to create "in-memory" databases. Caching large amounts of data can result in dramatically improved access times.

memory to the datafiles stored on disk as needed to ensure that the database reliably records changes made by users.

Datafiles are the lowest level of granularity between an Oracle database and the operating system. When you lay a database out on the I/O subsystem, the smallest piece you place in any location is a datafile. Tuning the I/O subsystem to improve Oracle performance typically involves moving datafiles from one set of disks to another.

Datafile structure

The first block of each datafile is called the *datafile header*. It contains critical information used to maintain the overall integrity of the database. One of the most critical pieces of information in this header is the *checkpoint structure*. This is a logical timestamp that indicates the last point at which changes were written to the datafile. This timestamp is critical for recovery situations. The Oracle recovery process uses the timestamp in the header of a datafile to determine which redo logs to apply to bring the datafile up to the current point in time.

Extents and segments

From a logical point of view, a datafile is composed of data blocks. From a physical point of view, datafiles have two intermediate organizational levels: extents and segments. An *extent* is a set of data blocks that are contiguous within an Oracle datafile. A *segment* is an object that takes up space in an Oracle database, such as a table or an index that's comprised of one or more extents.

When Oracle8 updates data, it attempts to update the data in the same data block. If there is not enough room in the data block for the new information, Oracle8 will write the data to a new data block, which may be in a different extent.

For more information on segments and extents and how they affect performance, refer to the section on "Fragmentation and Reorganization" in Chapter 5, *Managing Oracle8*.

Redo Log Files

Redo log files store a "recording" of the changes made to the database as a result of transactions and internal Oracle activities. Oracle caches changed blocks in memory; in the event of an instance failure, some of the changed blocks may not have been written out to the datafiles. This recording of the changes in the redo logs is vital because it plays back the changes that were lost when the failure occurred.

Oracle7 supported suppressing redo generation for some operations, such as creating indexes, creating tables from a SELECT statement, and data loads. The keyword used to suppress redo was UNRECOVERABLE, while the RECOVERABLE keyword acted as the default.

Oracle8 uses the keywords LOGGING and NOLOGGING for the same functionality. Oracle8 still supports the use of the UNRECOVERABLE and RECOVERABLE keywords to preserve backward compatibility for the syntax, but you should start using the new keywords.

Oracle8 also expands support for NOLOGGING operations. In addition to the NOLOGGING keyword in certain commands, you can now mark a table or an entire tablespace with the NOLOGGING attribute. This will suppress redo information for all applicable operations on the table or for all tables in the tablespace.

Suppressing Redo Logging

By default, Oracle logs all changes made to the database. The generation of redo logs adds a certain amount of overhead. You can suppress redo generation to speed up certain operations, but suppressing redo log generation means that the operation in question won't be logged in the redo logs; thus, you cannot recover the effects of the operation in the event of a failure. You can suppress redo logging by including the UNRECOVERABLE (Oracle7) or NOLOGGING (Oracle8) keyword in the SQL statement for the operation.

Database administrators use this option to speed up large operations. If a failure occurs later, they simply repeat the operation they initially performed. For example, you can build an index on a table without generating redo information. If a failure occurs and the database is recovered, the index will not be re-created because it wasn't logged. The DBA simply re-executes the script used to create the index in the first place. The DBA gets improved performance by suppressing the redo logging and only pays the price for it if the instance fails, which is uncommon.

To simplify operations in the event of a failure, some shops make it a standard practice to back up the pieces of the database affected by these unlogged operations as soon as possible after the unlogged operations have completed. (Remember, because you didn't log the operation, you will have to repeat it if you recover from a failure that takes place after the last backup before the operation. And you must do this before the next backup that includes the new version of the database.) This procedure also avoids the problems caused if the operational staff forgets to repeat the operation. You should always take a backup after an unlogged operation if you cannot afford to lose the object created by the operation, or you cannot repeat the operation for some reason.

Of course, if taking a backup after an unlogged operation poses its own problems for you, you can simply perform the operation in question in the traditional way—with redo logging enabled.

Multiplexing redo log files

Oracle uses specific terminology to manage redo logs. Each Oracle instance uses a *thread* of redo to record the changes it makes to the database. A thread of redo is composed of redo log groups, which are composed of one or more redo log members.

Logically, you can think of a redo log group as a single redo log file. However, Oracle allows you to specify multiple copies of a redo log to protect the all-important integrity of the redo log. By creating multiple copies of each redo log file, you protect the redo log file from disk failure and other types of disasters.

Figure 2-5 illustrates a thread of redo with groups and members. The figure shows two members per group, with each redo log mirrored.

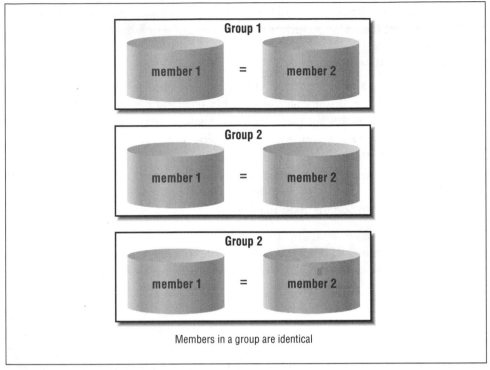

Figure 2-5. A thread of redo

When multiple members are in a redo log group, Oracle maintains multiple copies of the redo log files. The same arguments for multiplexing control files apply here. Redo logs are critical to the health and safety of your Oracle database and you should protect them. Simple redundant disk protection is not sufficient for cases in which human error results in the corruption or deletion of a redo log file.

There are ways you can rebuild the control file if you lose it, but there is no way to reproduce a lost redo log file; be sure to have multiple copies of the redo file.

Oracle writes *synchronously* to all redo log members. Oracle will wait for confirmation that all copies of the redo log have been successfully updated on disk before the redo write is considered done. If you put one copy on a fast or lightly loaded disk, and one copy on a slower or busier disk, your performance will be constrained by the slower disk. Oracle has to guarantee that all copies of the redo log file have been successfully updated to avoid losing data.

Consider what could happen if Oracle were to use *asynchronous* multiplexing, in which Oracle writes to a primary log and then updates the copies later in the background. Suppose that before Oracle finishes updating the copies, a failure occurs that brings the system down and damages the primary log. At this point you have committed transactions that are lost—the primary log that recorded the changes made by the transactions is gone, and the copies of the log are not yet up to date with those changes. To prevent this from occurring, Oracle always waits until all copies of the redo log have been updated.

How Oracle uses the redo logs

Once Oracle fills one redo log file, it automatically begins to use the next log file. Once the server cycles through all the available redo log files, it returns to the first one and reuses it. For this reason, you must create at least two redo log groups, which raises an important concept: the redo log file name versus the redo log sequence number. The redo log file name is the name of the physical file stored on disk. As the server fills each redo log file and moves on to the next one, it increments an internal counter called the *redo log sequence number*. This sequence number is recorded inside the redo log files as they are used.

Oracle's ability to reuse redo log files in a circular fashion is crucial because it allows a single transaction or unit of work to run as long as it needs to. A transaction can span multiple redo log files because there is no "end" of the redo log file structure.

To understand the concepts of redo log file names and redo log sequence numbers, consider three redo log files called *redolog1.log, redolog2.log,* and *redolog3.log*. The first time Oracle uses them the redo log sequence numbers for each will be 1, 2, and 3, respectively. When Oracle returns to the first redo log—*redolog1.log*—it will reuse it and assign it a sequence number of 4. When it moves to *redolog2.log*, it will initialize that file with a sequence number of 5.

Don't confuse these two concepts. The the operating system uses the redo log file to identify the physical file, while Oracle uses the redo log file sequence number to determine the order in which the logs were filled and cycled. Because Oracle automatically reuses redo log files, the name of the redo log file is not indicative of its place in the redo log file sequence.

Figure 2-6 illustrates the filling and cycling of redo logs.

Naming conventions for redo logs

The operating system names for the various files that make up a database are very important—at least to humans, who sometimes have to identify these files by their names. To add meaning and avoid errors, you should use naming conventions that capture the purpose and some critical details about the nature of the file. Here's one possible convention for the names of the actual redo log files shown in Figure 2-6:

```
redog1m1.log, redog1m2.log, ...
```

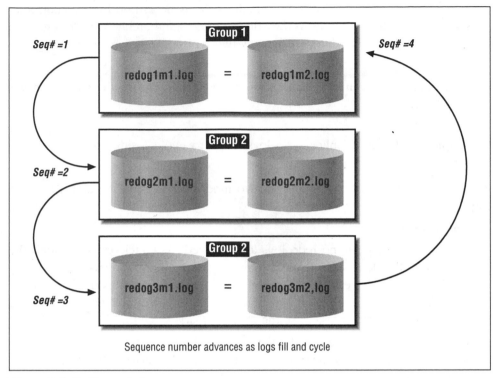

Figure 2-6. Cycling redo logs

The `redo` prefix and `.log` suffixes indicate that this is redo log information. The `g1m1` and `g1m2` character strings capture the group and member number. This convention is only an example; it's best to set conventions that are meaningful for yourself and stick to them.

Archived redo logs

You may be wondering how to avoid losing the critical information in the redo log when Oracle cycles over a previously used redo log.

There are actually two ways to address this issue. The first is quite simple: you don't avoid losing the information. You will lose the history stored in the redo file when it's overwritten. If a failure occurs that damages the datafiles, you must restore the entire database to the point in time when the last backup occurred. No redo log history exists to reproduce the changes made since the last backup occurred. Very few Oracle shops make this choice, because the inability to recover to the point of failure is unacceptable—it results in lost work.

The second and more practical way to address the issue caused by recycling redo logs is to archive the redo logs as they fill. To understand archiving redo logs, you must first understand that there are actually two types of redo logs for Oracle:

Online redo logs

   The operating system files that Oracle cycles through to log the changes made to the database.

Archived redo logs

   Copies of the filled online redo logs made to avoid losing redo data as the online redo logs are overwritten.

An Oracle database can run in one of two modes with respect to archiving redo logs:

NOARCHIVELOG

   As the name implies, no redo logs are archived. As Oracle cycles around the logs, the filled logs are reinitialized and overwritten, which erases the history of the changes made to the database. A shop that runs in this mode risks losing all the work done from the time they last took a full backup because there's no contiguous history of the changes made since the backup.

   Choosing not to archive redo logs significantly reduces your choices and options for database backups, as we'll discuss in Chapter 10, *Oracle8 and High Availability*.

ARCHIVELOG

   When Oracle rolls over to a new redo log, it archives the previous redo log. To prevent gaps in the history, a given redo log cannot be reused until it's successfully archived. The archived redo logs, plus the online redo logs, provide a complete history of all changes made to the database. Together, they allow Oracle to recover all committed transactions up to the exact time a failure occurred.

The internal sequence numbers discussed earlier act as the guide for Oracle while it is using redo logs and archived redo logs to restore a database.

ARCHIVELOG mode and automatic archiving

There are two steps to enabling automatic archiving for an Oracle database. First of all, you must turn archive logging on with the following SQL command:

```
ALTER DATABASE ARCHIVELOG
```

If the database is in ARCHIVELOG mode, Oracle marks the redo logs for archiving as it fills them. The full log files must be archived before they can be reused.

But just because the log files are marked as ready for archiving does not mean they will be automatically archived. You must also set a parameter in the *INIT.ORA* initialization file with the syntax:

```
LOG_ARCHIVE_START = TRUE
```

This will start a process that is called by Oracle to copy a full redo log to the archive log destination. This archive log destination and the format for the archived redo log names are specified using two additional parameters, LOG_ ARCHIVE_DEST and LOG_ARCHIVE_FORMAT. A setting such as the following:

```
LOG_ARCHIVE_DEST = C:\ORANT\DATABASE\ARCHIVE
```

specifies the directory to which Oracle writes the archived redo log files, and:

```
LOG_ARCHIVE_FORMAT = "ORCL%S.ARC"
```

specifies the format Oracle will use for the archived redo log file names. In this case, the file names must begin with ORCL and will end with .ARC. Oracle expands the %S automatically to the sequence number of the redo log padded with zeros on the left. The other options for the format wildcards are:

%s

Replaced by the sequence number without zero-padding on the left

%T

Replaced by the redo thread number with zero-padding

%t

Replaced by the redo thread number without zero-padding

If you want the archived redo log file names to include the thread and the sequence numbers with both numbers zero-padded, set:

```
LOG_ARCHIVE_FORMAT = "ORCL%T%S.ARC"
```

The *INIT.ORA* file is read every time an Oracle instance is started, so changes to this file do not take effect until an instance is stopped and restarted. Remember, though, that turning on automatic archiving does not put the database in ARCHIVELOG mode. Similarly, placing the database in ARCHIVELOG mode does not enable the automatic archiving process.

The LOG_ARCHIVE_START parameter defaults to FALSE. Sometimes you may see an Oracle instance endlessly waiting because of dissonance between the ARCHIVELOG mode setting and the LOG_ARCHIVE_START setting. If you have turned archive logging on, but have not started the automatic process, the Oracle instance will stop because it cannot write over an unarchived log file marked as ready for archiving. In other words, the automatic process of archiving the file has not been done.

You should also make sure that the archive log destination has enough room for the logs that Oracle will automatically write. If the archive log file destination is full, Oracle will hang since it can't archive additional redo log files.

Figure 2-7 illustrates redo log use with archiving enabled.

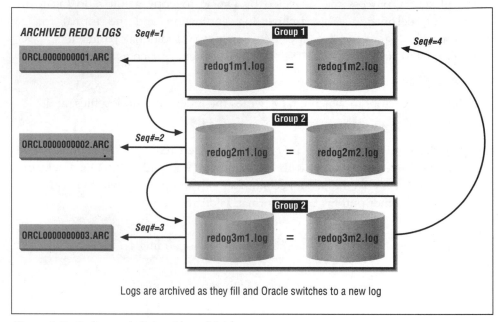

Figure 2-7. Cycling redo logs with archiving

The archived redo logs are critical for database recovery. Just as you can duplex the online redo logs, in Oracle8 you can also specify multiple archive log destinations. Oracle will copy filled redo logs to specified destinations. You can also specify whether all copies must succeed or not. The *INIT.ORA* parameters for this functionality are as follows:

LOG_ARCHIVE_DUPLEX_DEST
  Specifies an additional location for redundant redo logs

LOG_ARCHIVE_MIN_SUCCEED_DEST
  Indicates whether the redo log must be successfully written to one or all of the locations

With Oracle8*i*, you can specify up to five mandatory or optional archive log destinations, including remote systems for use in disaster recovery situations (covered in Chapter 10). Oracle8*i* also introduces automated support for multiple archiving processes to support the additional load of archiving to multiple destinations. See your Oracle documentation for the additional parameters and views that enable and control this functionality.

The Components of an Instance

An Oracle instance can be defined as an area of shared memory and a collection of background processes. A user connects to an Oracle instance and creates a user process that, in turn, provides access to the Oracle database. An instance connects to only one database. When you shut down Oracle, you shut down the instance, not the database.

The area of shared memory for an instance is called the *System Global Area,* or SGA. The SGA is not really one large undifferentiated section of memory; rather, it's made up of various components that we'll examine in the next section, "Memory Structures for an Instance." All the processes of an instance—system processes and user processes—share the SGA.

The background processes interact with the operating system and each other to manage the memory structures for the instance. These processes also manage the actual database on disk and perform general housekeeping for the instance.

There are other physical files that you can consider as part of the instance as well:

The instance initialization (INIT.ORA) file
> This critical file contains a variety of parameters that configure how the instance will operate: how much memory it will use, how many users it will allow to connect, what database the instance actually provides access to, and so on. You can alter many of these parameters dynamically at either the systemwide or session-specific level.

The instance configuration (CONFIG.ORA) file
> This is an optional parameter file, included if you want to segregate a set of initialization parameters (for example, those used for Oracle Parallel Server).

The password file
> Oracle can use an optional password file stored as an operating system file to provide additional flexibility for managing Oracle databases. This file is encrypted and contains userids and passwords that can be used to perform administrative tasks, such as starting and stopping the instance. Use of the password file is an added level of security beyond simply using operating system groups to allow users to start up and shut down Oracle. For example, on a Unix system, any user in the DBA group can start up or shut down Oracle— the operating system group gives them the authority. The password file can be used to force the entry of a password, thereby providing more security than just the operating system group. Validating a password against the value stored in the database for a user is not possible when the database is not open. The password file forces a user to authenticate herself with a password in order to start up the database.

Figure 2-8 illustrates the memory structures and the background processes, which are discussed later in the chapter.

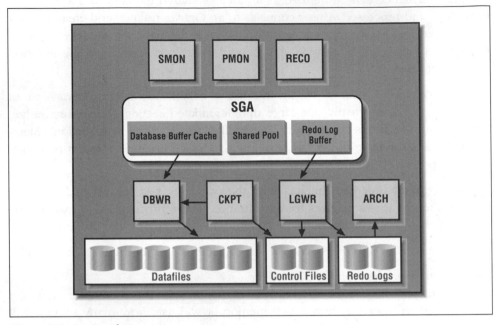

Figure 2-8. An Oracle instance

Additional background processes may exist when you use certain other features of the database: for example, the Multi-Threaded Server (MTS) or job queues and replication. For now, we'll just describe the basic pieces of an Oracle instance and leave the optional pieces for later in the book. We'll discuss the MTS processes in Chapter 3, *Installing and Running Oracle8*, and replication processes in Chapter 10.

Memory Structures for an Instance

As shown in Figure 2-8, the System Global Area (SGA) is actually composed of three main areas: the database buffer cache, the shared pool, and the redo log. There is another type of memory pool (not in shown in Figure 2-8), introduced in Oracle8—the large pool. This optional area of the SGA is used for buffering I/O for various server processes, including those used for backup and recovery. The area is also used to store session memory for the Multi-Threaded Server, and when using the XA protocol for distributed transactions, as discussed later in the book.

This alternate pool exists to reduce the demand on the shared pool for certain large memory allocations. The *INIT.ORA* parameter used to configure the large pool is LARGE_POOL_SIZE.

The following sections describe the areas of the SGA. For a more detailed discussion of performance issues for these areas, see "How Oracle Uses the System Global Area" in Chapter 6.

Database buffer cache

The database buffer cache caches blocks of data retrieved from the database. This buffer between the users' requests and the actual datafiles improves the performance of the Oracle database. If a piece of data can be found in the buffer cache, you can retrieve it from memory without the overhead of having to go to disk. Oracle manages the cache using a "least recently used" (LRU) algorithm. This means that if a user requests data that has been recently used, the data is more likely to be in the database buffer cache, and can be delivered immediately without having to execute a disk read operation.

When a user wants to read a block, if it's not in the cache, it's read and loaded into the cache. When a user makes changes to a block, those changes are made to the block in the cache. At some later time, those changes will be written to the datafile in which the block resides. This avoids making users wait while Oracle writes their changed blocks to disk.

This notion of waiting to perform I/O until absolutely necessary is common throughout Oracle. Disks are the slowest component of a computer system, so the less I/O performed, the faster the system runs. By deferring noncritical I/O operations instead of performing them immediately, an Oracle database can deliver better performance.

Oracle7 had one pool of buffers for database blocks. Oracle8 introduced multiple buffer pools. Currently, there are three pools available in Oracle8:

DEFAULT
   The standard Oracle database buffer cache. All objects use this cache unless otherwise indicated.

KEEP
   For frequently used objects you wish to cache.

RECYCLE
   For objects that you're less likely to access again.

You can mark a table or index for caching in a specific buffer pool. This helps to keep more desirable objects in the cache and avoids the "churn" of all objects fighting for space in one central cache. Of course, to use these features properly you must be aware of the access patterns for the various objects used by your application.

Shared pool

The shared pool caches various constructs that can be shared among users. For example, SQL statements issued by users are cached so that they can be reused if the same statement is submitted again. Another example is stored procedures—pieces of code stored and executed within the database. These are loaded into the shared pool for execution and then cached, again using an LRU algorithm. The shared pool is also used for caching information from the Oracle Data Dictionary, which is the metadata that describes the structure and content of the database itself.

Redo log buffer

The redo log buffer caches redo information until it's written to the physical redo log files stored on a disk. The buffer also improves performance. Oracle caches the redo until it can be written to a disk at a more optimal time, which avoids the overhead of constantly writing to the disk with the redo logs.

Background Processes for an Instance

The background processes shown in Figure 2-8 are:

Database Writer (DBWR)
> The Database Writer process writes database blocks from the database buffer cache in the SGA to the datafiles on disk. An Oracle instance can have up to 10 DBWR processes, from DBW0 to DBW9, if needed, to handle the I/O load to multiple datafiles. Most instances run one DBWR. DBWR writes blocks out of the cache for two main reasons:
>
> - To perform a checkpoint. A checkpoint is the technical term for updating the blocks of the datafiles so that they "catch up" to the redo logs. Oracle writes the redo for a transaction when it's committed, and later writes the actual blocks. Periodically, Oracle performs a checkpoint to bring the datafile contents in line with the redo that was written out for the committed transactions.
>
> - To free space in the cache. If Oracle needs to read blocks requested by users into the cache and there is no free space in the buffer cache, DBWR is called to write out some blocks to free space. The blocks written out are the least recently used blocks. Writing blocks in this order minimizes the performance impact of losing them from the buffer cache.

Log Writer (LGWR)
> The Log Writer process writes the redo information from the log buffer in the SGA to all copies of the current redo log file on disk. As transactions proceed, the associated redo information is stored in the redo log buffer in the SGA.

When a transaction is committed, Oracle makes the redo information permanent by invoking the Log Writer to write it to disk.

System Monitor (SMON)

The System Monitor process maintains overall health and safety for an Oracle instance. SMON performs crash recovery when the instance is started after a failure. SMON also coordinates and performs recovery for a failed instance when you have more than one instance accessing the same database, as with Oracle Parallel Server. SMON also cleans up adjacent pieces of free space in the datafiles by merging them into one piece and gets rid of space used for sorting rows when that space is no longer needed.

Process Monitor (PMON)

The Process Monitor process watches over the user processes that access the database. If a user process terminates abnormally, PMON is responsible for cleaning up any of the resources left behind (such as memory), and for releasing any locks held by the failed process.

Processes or Threads?

With all this talk about processes, you may be wondering whether Oracle actually uses threads or processes in the underlying operating system to implement these services.

For simplicity, throughout this book we use the term *process* generically to indicate a function that Oracle performs, such as DBWR or LGWR. Oracle on Microsoft Windows NT uses one operating system process per instance; thus each "Oracle process" is actually a thread within the one NT process. For example, DBWR and LGWR are each one thread in the one Oracle process. Oracle on Unix uses a process-based architecture. All of the "processes" are actual operating system processes, not threads. So, DBWR, LGWR, and so on are specific operating system processes.

There are some exceptions, however. For instance, the Oracle Multi-Threaded Server, introduced in Oracle7, uses real threads on NT and simulated threads on Unix.

While discussions of lightweight threads versus processes is certainly intellectually interesting, at the end of the day what matters most is how Oracle works and performs. As long as Oracle effectively leverages the operating system it's running on and provides great performance, then the relative merits of threads versus processes become less important.

Archiver (ARCH)

> The Archiver process reads the redo log files once Oracle has filled them and writes a copy of the used redo log files to the specified archive log destination(s).

> Oracle8*i* supports up to 10 archiver processes, using the notation ARCn. LGWR will start additional archivers as needed, based on the load, up to the limit specified by the *INIT.ORA* parameter LOG_ARCHIVE_MAX_PROCESSES.

Checkpoint (CKPT)

> The Checkpoint process works with DBWR to perform checkpoints. CKPT updates the control file and database file headers to update the checkpoint data when the checkpoint is complete.

Recover (RECO)

> The Recover process automatically cleans up failed or suspended distributed transactions (discussed in Chapter 10).

The Data Dictionary

Each Oracle database includes a set of what is called *metadata*, or data that describes the structure of the data contained by the database. The tables that hold this metadata are referred to as the Oracle Data Dictionary. All of the components discussed in this chapter have corresponding system tables and views in the data dictionary that fully describe the characteristics of the component. You can query these tables and views using standard SQL statements. Table 2-1 shows how you can find information about each of the components in the data dictionary.

Table 2-1. Database Components and Their Related Data Dictionary Views

Component	Data Dictionary Tables and Views
Database	V$DATABASE
Tablespaces	DBA_TABLESPACES, DBA_DATA_FILES, DBA_FREE_SPACE
Control files	V$CONTROLFILE, V$PARAMETER, V$CONTROLFILE_RECORD_SECTION
Datafiles	V$DATAFILE, V$DATAFILE_HEADER, V$FILESTAT, DBA_DATA_FILES
Segments	DBA_SEGMENTS
Extents	DBA_EXTENTS
Redo threads, groups, and numbers	V$THREAD, V$LOG, V$LOGFILE
Archiving status	V$DATABASE, V$LOG, V$ARCHIVED_LOG, V$ARCHIVE_DEST
Database instance	V$INSTANCE, V$PARAMETER, V$SYSTEM_PARAMETER
Memory structure	VSGA, VSGASTAT, VDB_OBJECT_CACHE, VSQL, V$SQLTEXT, V$SQLAREA
Background processes	V$BGPROCESS, V$SESSION

3

Installing and Running Oracle8

If you've been reading this book sequentially, you should understand the basics of the Oracle database architecture by now. This chapter begins with a description of how to install and get a database up and running. (If you've already installed your Oracle8 database software, you can skim through this first section.) We'll describe how to create an actual database and how to configure the network software needed to run Oracle8. Finally, we'll examine how to manage databases and discuss how users access databases.

Installing Oracle8i

Prior to Oracle8*i*, the Oracle installer came in both character and GUI versions for Unix. The Unix GUI ran in Motif using the X Windows system. Microsoft Windows NT came with a GUI version only. In Oracle8*i*, the installer has been completely rewritten in Java. The Oracle installer is one of the first places in which you can see the benefits of the portability of Java; the installer looks and functions the same way across all operating systems. Installing Oracle is now quite simple, requiring a few mouse clicks and answers to some questions about options and features.

The installer allows you to install Oracle software, deinstall software, or simply check which software you have installed. The launch screen for the installer is shown in Figure 3-1.

Although the installation process is now the same for all platforms, there are still particulars about the installation of Oracle8*i* that relate to specific platforms. Each release of the Oracle database server software is shipped with several pieces of documentation. Included in each release are an installation guide, release notes (which include installation information added after the installation guide was

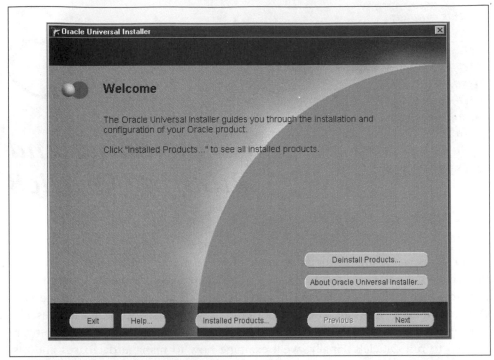

Figure 3-1. Oracle Universal Installer

published), and a "getting started" book. You should read all of these documents prior to starting the installation process, since each of them contains invaluable information about the specifics of the installation. You will need to consider details such as where to establish the Oracle home directory and where database files will reside, and these issues are covered in detail in the documentation. In addition to the hardcopy documentation, online documentation is shipped on the database server CD-ROM, which provides additional information regarding the database and related products.

You'll typically find the installation guide in the server software CD case. The installation guide includes system requirements (memory and disk), preinstallation tasks, directions for running the installation, and notes regarding migration of earlier Oracle databases to the current release. You should remember that complete installation of the software includes not only loading the software, but also configuring and starting key services.

One of the more important decisions you need to make before actually installing Oracle concerns the directory structure and naming conventions you will follow for the files that make up a database. Clear, consistent, and well-planned conventions are crucial for minimizing human errors in system and database administration. Some of the more important conventions to consider include the following:

- Disk or mount point names
- Directory structures for Oracle software and database files
- Database file names: control files, database files and redo log files

The Optimal Flexible Architecture, described in the next section, provides suggestions for naming conventions for all of these files.

Optimal Flexible Architecture (OFA)

There is one more piece of documentation that you may not know about, but will find extremely valuable in creating and managing your Oracle environment. Oracle consultants working at large Oracle sites created (out of necessity) a comprehensive set of standards for Unix directory structures and file names. This set of standards is called *An Optimal Flexible Architecture for a Growing Oracle Database* or, as it is lovingly known in the Oracle community, the OFA. The OFA provides a clear set of standards for handling multiple databases and multiple versions of Oracle on the same machine. The OFA includes recommendations for mount points, directory structures, file names, and scripting techniques. Anyone who knows the OFA can navigate an Oracle environment to quickly find the software and files used for the database and the instance. This standardization increases productivity and avoids errors.

While the OFA was created for Unix, the core standards can be and have been applied to NT and other operating systems. Through the later Oracle7 releases, the OFA standards were also embedded in the Oracle installer. All system administrators and database administrators working with Oracle will find the OFA worthwhile, even if your Oracle system is already installed. The OFA exists as part of the Oracle installation guide.

Supporting Multiple Oracle Versions on a Machine

You can install and run multiple versions of Oracle on a single-server machine. All Oracle products use a directory referred to by the environment or system variable, ORACLE_HOME, to find the base directory for the software they will use. Because of this, you can run multiple versions of Oracle software on the same server, each with a different ORACLE_HOME variable defined. Whenever a piece of software accesses a particular version of Oracle, the software simply uses the proper setting for the ORACLE_HOME environment variable.

Oracle supports multiple ORACLE_HOME variables on Unix and NT systems by using different directories. The OFA provides clear and excellent standards for this type of implementation.

Creating a Database

As you learned in Chapter 2, *Oracle8 Architecture*, an Oracle installation can have many different databases. You should take a two-step approach for any new database you seek to create. First, understand the purpose of the database, and then create the database with the appropriate parameters.

Planning the Database

As with installing the Oracle software, you should spend some time learning the purpose of an Oracle database before you create the database itself. Consider what the database will be used for and how much data it will contain. You should understand the underlying hardware that you'll use—the number and type of CPUs, the amount of memory, the number of disks, the controllers for the disks, and so on. Because the database is stored on the disks, many tuning problems can be avoided with proper capacity and I/O subsystem planning.

Planning your database and the supporting hardware requires insights into the scale or size of the workload and the type of work the system will perform. Some of the considerations that will affect your database design and hardware configuration include the following:

How many users will the database have?
> How many users will connect simultaneously and how many will concurrently perform transactions or execute queries?

Is the database supporting OLTP applications or data warehousing?
> This distinction leads to different types and volumes of activity on the database server. For example, online transaction processing (OLTP) systems usually have a larger number of users performing smaller transactions, while data warehouses usually have a smaller number of users performing larger queries.

What are the expected size and number of database objects?
> How large will these objects be initially and what growth rates do you expect?

What are the access patterns for the various database objects?
> Some objects will be more popular than others. Understanding the volume and type of activity in the database is critical to planning and tuning your database. Some people employ a so-called *CRUD matrix* that contains Create, Read, Update, and Delete estimates for each key object used by a business transaction. These estimates may be per minute, per hour, per day, or for whatever time period makes sense in the context of your system. For example, the CRUD matrix for a simple employee update transaction might be as

shown in Table 3-1, with the checkmarks indicating that each transaction performs the operation against the object shown.

Table 3-1. Access Patterns for Database Objects

Object	Create	Read	Update	Delete
EMP	✓	✓		
DEPT		✓		
SALARY		✓	✓	

How much hardware do I have now, and how much will I add as the database grows?

For example, disks tend to get cheaper and cheaper. Suppose you're planning a database of 100 GB that you expect to grow to 300 GB over the next two years. You may have all the disk space available to plan for the 300 GB target, but it's more likely that you'll buy some amount to get started, and add disks as the database grows. It's important that you plan the initial layout with the expected growth in mind.

What are the availability requirements?

What elements of redundancy, such as additional disk drives, do you need to provide the required availability?

What are my performance requirements?

What response times do your users expect, and how much of that time can you give them? How will you measure performance: average response time, maximum response time, response time at peak load, total throughput, or average load?

What are my security requirements?

Will the application, the operating system, or the Oracle database (or some combination of these) enforce security?

The Value of Estimating

Even if you are unsure of things like sizing and usage details, take your best guess as to initial values and growth rates, and document these estimates. As the database evolves, you can compare your initial estimates with emerging information to react and plan more effectively. For example, suppose you estimate that a certain table will be 5 GB in size initially and will grow at 3 GB per year. But when you are up and running, you discover that the table is actually 3 GB, and six months into production you discover that it has grown to 8 GB. You can now revise your plans to reflect the higher growth rate and thereby avoid space problems. Comparing production measures of database size, growth, and usage patterns with your initial estimates will provide valuable insights to help you avoid problems as you move forward. In this way, documented guesses at an early stage are useful later on.

The same is true for key requirements like availability and performance. If the exact requirements are not clear, make some assumptions and document them. These core requirements will heavily influence the decisions you make regarding redundancy and capacity. As the system evolves and these requirements become clearer, the history of these key decision criteria will be crucial in understanding the choices that you made and will make in the future.

Tools for Creating Databases

There are two basic ways to create an Oracle8 database:

- Use the GUI Oracle Database Configuration Assistant
- Run character-mode scripts

Oracle8 ships with a GUI utility called the Oracle Database Configuration Assistant. It is written in Java and therefore provides the same look and feel across platforms. The Assistant is a quick and easy way to create, modify, or delete a database. It allows you to create a typical preconfigured database (with minimal input required) or a custom database (which involves making some choices and answering additional questions). Both options include support for the various Oracle8 cartridges, as well as for advanced replication. The Database Configuration Assistant is shown in Figure 3-2.

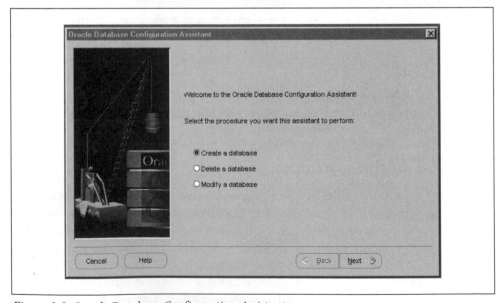

Figure 3-2. Oracle Database Configuration Assistant

If you choose to create a database, you can then select either a typical or custom database, as shown in Figure 3-3.

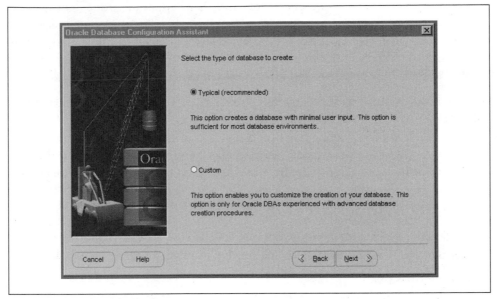

Figure 3-3. Selecting a database to create

Both the typical and custom database creation choices allow you to further specify the type of workload the database will be performing: OLTP or Decision Support (DSS).

The alternative method for creating a database is to create or edit an existing SQL script that executes the various required commands. Most Oracle DBAs have a preferred script that they Edit as needed. In Oracle7 and Oracle8, you executed the script using a character-mode utility called Server Manager. In Oracle8*i*, various core administration tasks can be performed using Server Manager or SQL*Plus, another character-mode utility. The Oracle software CD-ROM also includes a sample script called *BUILD_DB.SQL*, described in the Oracle documentation.

Configuring Net8

Net8 (or SQL*Net as it was known prior to Oracle8) is a layer of software that allows different physical machines to communicate for the purpose of accessing an Oracle database. A version of Net8 runs on the client machine and on the database server, and allows clients and servers to communicate over a network using virtually any popular network protocol. For example, it supports TCP/IP, LU6.2, DECNET, and SPX/IPX. Net8 can also perform network protocol interchanges. For example, it allows clients that are speaking SPX/IPX to interact with database servers that are speaking TCP/IP.

Net8 also provides *location transparency*—the client application does not need to know the server's physical location. The Net8 layer handles the communications, which means that you can move the database to another machine and simply update the Net8 configuration details accordingly. The client applications will still be able to reach the database, and no application changes will be required.

Net8 introduces the notion of *service names*, or *aliases* as they are sometimes called. Clients provide a service name or Net8 alias to specify which database they want to reach without having to identify the actual machine or instance for the database. Net8 looks up the actual machine and the Oracle instance using the provided service name and transparently routes the client to the appropriate database.

Resolving Net8 Service Names

The following Net8 configuration options resolve the service name that clients specify into the host and instance name needed to reach an Oracle database.

Local name resolution

For local name resolution, you install a file called *TNSNAMES.ORA* on each client machine that contains entries that provide the host and Oracle instance for each Net8 alias. You must maintain this file on the client machines if there are any changes made to the underlying database locations. Changes to your network topology are almost certain over time, so use of this option can lead to an increased maintenance load.

Oracle Names service

You can use the Oracle Names software that ships with Oracle, which will avoid the need for a *TNSNAMES.ORA* file on each client. When a client specifies a service name, Oracle Net8 automatically contacts the Oracle Names server, typically located on another machine. Oracle Names replies with the host and instance information needed by the client. You can configure multiple Oracle Names servers to provide redundancy and increased performance. Oracle Names typically minimizes the overhead of updating the local *TNSNAMES.ORA* files when there are frequent changes to the Oracle network topology. Oracle Names can also be very useful for complex networks that are widely distributed.

Host naming

Clients can simply use the name of the host that the instance runs on. This is valid for TCP/IP networks with a mechanism in place for resolving the hostname into an IP address. For example, the Domain Name Service (DNS) translates a hostname into an IP address, much as Oracle Names translates service names.

Third-party naming services

> Oracle Net8 can interface with external or third-party naming and authentication services, such as Kerberos or Radius. Use of such services may require the Oracle Advanced Security Option (known as the Advanced Networking Option prior to Oracle8*i*).

These name resolution options are not mutually exclusive. For example, you can use Oracle Names and local name resolution (*TNSNAMES.ORA* files) together. In this case, you specify the order Oracle should use in resolving names in the *SQLNET.ORA* file. (For example, check Oracle Names first, and if the service name isn't resolved, check the local *TNSNAMES.ORA* file.) This is useful for cases in which there are corporate database services specific to certain clients. You would use Oracle Names for the standard corporate database services, such as email, and then use *TNSNAMES.ORA* entries for the client-specific database services, such as a particular development database.

The Net8 Assistant

Oracle provides a GUI utility called the Net8 Assistant to create the various configuration files required for Net8. Like the Database Configuration Assistant, the Net8 Assistant is written in Java and provides the same look and feel across platforms. The Net8 configuration files have a very specific syntax with multiple levels of nested brackets. Using the Net8 Assistant can avoid the errors that are common to hand-coded files. The Net8 Assistant, which automates the configuration of various Net8 components, is shown in Figure 3-4.

Debugging Network Problems

If you're having a problem with your Net8 network, one of the first steps toward debugging the problem is to check that the Net8 files were generated, not hand-coded. If you're in doubt, back up the current configuration files and use the Net8 Assistant to regenerate them. In fact, when Oracle Worldwide Support assists customers with Net8 problems, one of the first questions they ask is whether or not the files were hand-coded.

Auto-Discovery and Agents

Beginning with Oracle 7.3, Oracle provided auto-discovery features that allowed it to find new databases automatically. Support for auto-discovery has increased and improved with each Oracle release since then. With Oracle8*i*, the Universal Installer and Net8 Assistant work together smoothly to automatically configure

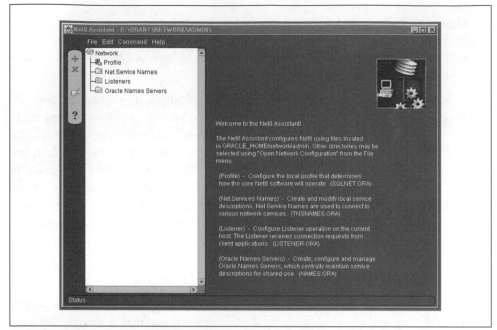

Figure 3-4. Net8 Assistant

your Net8 network. All that is required is the *INIT.ORA* entry that maps the instance to the service or application, as described in the sidebar "Generic Service Names" later in this chapter. Auto-discovery and dynamic registration take care of the rest.

A key piece of the Oracle network that enables auto-discovery is the Oracle8 Intelligent Agent. The Agent is a piece of software that runs on the machine with your Oracle database(s). It acts as an agent for various other functions that need to find and work with the database on the machine. For example, the Agent knows about the various Oracle8 instances on the machine and handles critical management functions, such as monitoring the database for certain events and executing jobs. The Agent provides a central point for auto-discovery: Net8 discovers instances and databases by interrogating the Agent. We'll examine the Agent again in Chapter 5.

Net8 Configuration Files

Net8 requires several configuration files. The default location for the files used to configure a Net8 network are as follows:

- On NT *ORACLE_HOME\net80\admin* and Oracle 8.0 and *ORACLE_HOME\network\admin* for Oracle8i

- On Unix *ORACLE_HOME/network/admin*

You can place these files in another location, in which case you must set an environment or system variable called TNS_ADMIN to the nondefault location. Oracle then uses TNS_ADMIN to locate the files. The vast majority of systems are configured using the default location.

The files that form a simple Net8 configuration are as follows:

LISTENER.ORA

Contains details for configuring the Net8 Listener, such as which instances or services the Listener is servicing. As the name implies, the Listener "listens" for incoming connection requests from clients that want to access the Oracle database over the network. For details about the mechanics of the Listener's function, please see the section later in this chapter entitled "Net8 and Establishing Network Connections."

TNSNAMES.ORA

Decodes a service name into a specific machine address and Oracle instance for the connection request. (If you're using Oracle Names, as described earlier, you don't need to use the *TNSNAMES.ORA* file as part of your configuration.) This file is key to Net8's location transparency. If you move a database from one machine to another, you can simply update the *TNSNAMES.ORA* on the various clients to reflect the new machine address for the existing service name. For example, suppose that clients reach the database using a service name of "SALES". The *TNSNAMES.ORA* file has an entry for the service name SALES that decodes to a machine named HOST1 and an Oracle instance called PROD. If the Oracle database used for the SALES application is moved to a machine called HOST2, the *TNSNAMES.ORA* entry is updated to use the machine name HOST2. Once the *TNSNAMES.ORA* files are updated, client connection requests will be routed transparently to the new machine with no application changes required.

SQLNET.ORA

Provides important defaults and miscellaneous configuration details. For example, *SQLNET.ORA* contains the default domain name for your network. If you're using Oracle Names, *SQLNET.ORA* can contain the address the client uses to find the Oracle Names server and the order Net8 should use for resolving service names.

For more details on the inner workings of Net8 and the various configuration options and files, please see your Oracle Net8 documentation.

Starting Up the Database

Starting a database is quite simple—on NT you simply start the Oracle services, and on Unix you issue the STARTUP command from Server Manager or SQL*Plus

Generic Service Names

Prior to Oracle8*i*, the Listener on a database server was configured to listen for specific instance names. Clients used a Net8 service name that decoded to the host and the specific instance name. With Oracle8*i*, you can use the SERVICE_NAMES parameter in the *INIT.ORA* file for an instance to specify a generic application name or names that the instance supports. When the instance is started on the database server, it registers the applications or services it supports with the Listener. The Net8 name resolution files use service names that decode to a host and an application, not a host and an instance. The Listener on the host then directs the client to the appropriate instance based on the applications each instance is registered to support.

For example, suppose you had SALES and HR applications using the same database with an instance name of PROD running on HOST1. Prior to Oracle8*i*, you would configure a Listener to listen for the instance called PROD. Clients for both the SALES and HR applications would use a service name that resolved to the HOST1 machine and the PROD instance. If you moved the SALES application to another instance on the same host, you would have to update the Net8 name resolution files to reflect the new instance name for the SALES application. With Oracle8*i*, the PROD instance could have an *INIT.ORA* entry for the SERVICE_NAMES parameter, specifying that it supports the SALES and HR applications. When you start the PROD instance, it registers dynamically with the Listener and is associated with SALES and HR. The entries in the Net8 name resolution files would decode to HOST1 and an application name of SALES or HR as opposed to HOST1 and the PROD instance. The Listener would direct clients that specify a service name of SALES or HR to the PROD instance.

This level of indirection avoids the need to embed instance names in the Net8 name resolution files, reducing administration and increasing the flexibility of the system. Suppose that you migrate the data for the SALES application to another database. The instance name for SALES users would now be different. Prior to Oracle8*i*, you would have to update the Net8 naming files to reflect the change to the instance name for SALES. With Oracle8*i*, you don't have to embed the instance name for SALES in the name resolution files. When the instance for the new database containing the SALES data is started, it will register with the Listener and will be associated with the SALES application. Clients requesting a connection to HOST1 for the application SALES will be directed by the Listener to the new instance automatically with no changes to the Net8 name resolution files.

(in Oracle8*i*). While starting a database appears to be a single action, it involves an instance and a database, and it occurs in several distinct phases. Starting a database automatically executes the following actions:

1. *Starting the instance*. Oracle reads the instance initialization parameters from the *INIT.ORA* file on the server. Oracle then allocates memory for the System Global Area and starts the background processes of the instance. At this point, none of the physical files of the database have been opened, and the instance is in the NOMOUNT state. There are things that can prevent an instance from starting. For example, there may be errors in the *INIT.ORA* file, or the operating system may not be able to allocate the requested amount of shared memory for the SGA.

2. *Mounting the database*. The instance opens the control files of the database. The *INIT.ORA* parameter CONTROL_FILES tells the instance where to find these control files. At this point only the control files are open. This is called the MOUNT state, and at this time, the database is only accessible to the database administrator. In this state, the DBA can perform only certain types of database administration. For example, the DBA may have moved or renamed one of the database files. The datafiles are listed in the control file but aren't open in the MOUNT state. The DBA can issue a command (ALTER DATABASE) to rename the datafile. This command will update the control file with the new datafile name.

3. *Opening the database*. The instance opens the redo log files and datafiles using the information in the control file. At this point, the database is fully open and available for user access.

Shutting Down the Database

Logically enough, the process of shutting down a database or making it inaccessible involves steps that reverse those discussed in the previous section:

1. *Closing the database*. Oracle flushes any modified database blocks that haven't been written yet to the disk from the SGA cache to the datafiles. Oracle also writes out any relevant redo information remaining in the redo log buffer. Oracle "checkpoints" the datafiles—marks the datafile headers as "current" as of the time the database was closed. Oracle then closes the datafiles and redo log files. At this point, users can no longer access the database.

2. *Dismounting the database*. The Oracle instance dismounts the database. Oracle updates the relevant entries in the control files to record a clean shutdown and then closes them. At this point, the entire database is closed; only the instance remains.

3. *Shutting down the instance*. The Oracle software stops the background processes of the instance and frees, or deallocates, the shared memory used for the SGA.

In some cases, the database may not have been closed cleanly. For example, some machine failure possibly occurred or the DBA could have aborted the instance. If this happens, Oracle doesn't have a chance to write the modified database blocks from the SGA to the datafiles. But when Oracle is started again, the instance will detect that a crash occurred and will use the redo logs to automatically perform what is called *crash recovery*. Crash recovery guarantees that the changes for all committed transactions are done, and that all uncommitted or in-flight transactions will be cleaned up. The uncommitted transactions are determined after the redo log is applied and automatically rolled back.

Accessing a Database

The previous sections described the process of starting up and shutting down a database. But the database is only part of a complete system—you also need a client process to access the database, even if that process is on the same physical machine as the database.

Server Processes and Clients

To access a database, a user connects to the instance that provides access to the desired database. A user running a program that accesses a database is really composed of two distinct pieces—a client program and a server process—which connect to the Oracle instance. For example, running the Oracle character-mode utility SQL*Plus involves two processes:

- The SQL*Plus process itself, acting as the client.

- The Oracle server process, sometimes referred to as a *shadow process*, that provides the connection to the Oracle instance.

Server process

The Oracle server process always runs on the computer on which the instance is running. The server process attaches to the shared memory used for the SGA and can read from it and write to it.

As the name implies, the server process works for the client process—it reads and passes back the requested data, it accepts and makes changes on behalf of the client, and so on. For example, when a client wants to read a row of data stored in a particular database block, the server process identifies the desired block and either retrieves it from the database buffer cache (if it's there) or reads it from the correct datafile and loads it into the database buffer cache. Then, if the user requests changes, the server process modifies the block in the cache and generates and stores the necessary redo information in the redo log buffer in the SGA. The server process, however, does not write the redo information from the log buffer to the redo log files, and it does not write the modified database block from the buffer cache to the datafile. These actions are performed by the Log Writer (LGWR) and Database Writer (DBWR) processes, respectively.

Client process

The client process, on the other hand, can be running on the same machine as the instance or, as is more commonly the case, on a separate computer. A network connects the two computers and provides a way for the two processes to talk to each other. In either case, the concept is essentially the same—two processes are involved in the interaction between a client and the database. In the case involving two computers and a network, the method by which the two processes communicate changes. When both processes are on the same machine, Oracle uses local communications via Inter Process Communication (IPC). When the client is on one machine and the database server is on another, Oracle uses Net8 over the network to communicate between the two machines.

Application Servers and Web Servers as Clients

Although the discussion in the previous section used the terms *client* and *server* extensively, please don't assume that Oracle is strictly a client-server database. Oracle pioneered client-server computing and has long been based on this notion of two tasks: a client and a server. But, when you consider multitier computing involving web and application servers, the notion of a client changes somewhat. The "client" process becomes the middle tier or application server. You can logically consider any process that connects to an Oracle instance a client in the sense that it is served by the database. Don't confuse this usage of the term "client" with the actual client in a multitier configuration. The eventual client in a multitier model is some type of program providing a user interface—for example, a browser running Java.

Figure 3-5 illustrates users connecting to an Oracle instance to access a database in both two-tier and three-tier configurations, involving local communication and network communication. The figure is based on a simplified version of the instance figure used earlier in Chapter 2 (Figure 2-8).

Figure 3-5 highlights the server process connection models as opposed to the interaction of the background processes. There is a traditional two-tier client-server connection on the left side, a three-tier connection with an application server on the right side and a local client connection in the middle of the figure. The two-tier and three-tier connections use a network to communicate with the database, while the local client uses local IPC.

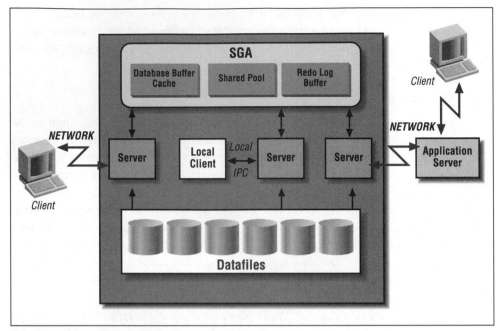

Figure 3-5. Accessing a database

Net8 and Establishing Network Connections

The server processes shown in Figure 3-5 are connected to the client processes using some kind of network. How do client processes get hooked up with Oracle server processes to begin working?

The matchmaker that arranges marriages between Oracle clients and server processes is called the Oracle Net8 Listener. The Listener "listens" for incoming connection requests for one or more instances. The Listener is not part of the Oracle instance—it directs connection requests to the instance. The Listener is started and stopped independently of the instance. If the Listener is down and the instance is up, clients accessing the database over a network cannot find the instance because there is no Listener to guide them. If the Listener is up and the instance is down, there is nowhere to send clients.

The Listener's function is relatively simple:

1. The client contacts the Listener over the network.

2. The Listener detects an incoming request and introduces the requesting client to an Oracle server process.

3. The Listener introduces the server to the client by letting each know the other's network address.

4. The Listener steps out of the way and lets the client and server communicate directly.

Once the client and the server know how to find each other, they communicate directly. The Listener is no longer required.

Figure 3-6 illustrates the previous steps for establishing a networked connection. Network traffic appears as dotted lines.

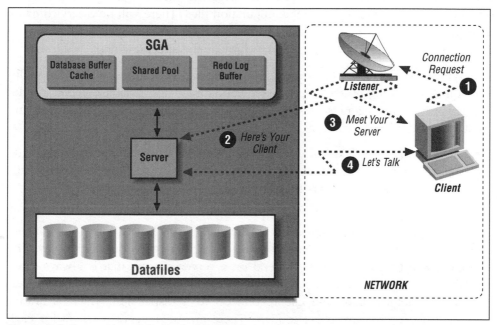

Figure 3-6. Connecting with the Net8 Listener

The Multi-Threaded Server

The server processes shown in the diagram are *dedicated*; they serve only one client process. So, if an application has 1000 clients, then the Oracle instance will have 1000 corresponding server processes. Each server process uses system resources like the memory and the CPU. Scaling to large user populations can consume a lot of system resources. To support the ever-increasing demand for scalability, Oracle introduced the Multi-Threaded Server (MTS) in Oracle7.

The MTS allows the Oracle instance to share a set of server processes across a larger group of users. Instead of each client connecting to and using a dedicated server, the clients use shared servers, which can significantly reduce the overall resource requirements for serving large numbers of users. In many systems, there are times when the clients aren't actively using their server process, such as when users are reading and absorbing data retrieved from the database. When a client is not using its server process in the *dedicated model*, that server process still has a hold on system resources but isn't doing any useful work. In the *shared server model*, when a client is inactive the shared server can do work for another client process.

You don't have to make a mutually exclusive choice between shared server processes and dedicated server processes for an Oracle instance. Oracle can mix and match dedicated and shared servers, and clients can connect to one or the other. The choice is based on your Net8 configuration files. There will be a service name that leads the client to a dedicated server, and another service name for connecting via shared servers. The Net8 manuals provide the specific syntax.

The type of server process a client is using is transparent to the client. The multi-threading or sharing of server processes happens on the database server "under the covers" from a client perspective. The same Listener handles dedicated and multithreaded connection requests.

The steps the Listener takes in establishing a shared server connection are a little different and involve some additional background processes for the instance dispatchers and the shared servers themselves.

Dispatchers

In the previous description of the Listener, you saw how it forms the connection between a client and server process and then steps out of the way. The client must now be able to depend on a server process that is always available to complete the connection. Because a shared server process may be servicing another client, the client connects to a dispatcher, which is always ready to receive any client request. There are separate dispatchers for each network protocol being used, such as dispatchers for TCP/IP and SPX/IPX. The dispatchers serve as surrogate dedicated servers for the clients, and each dispatcher can work with multiple clients. Clients directly connect to their dispatcher instead of a server. The dispatcher accepts requests from clients and places them in a request queue, which is a memory structure in the SGA. There is one request queue for the instance.

Shared servers

The shared server processes read from the request queue, process the request, and place the results in the response queue for the appropriate dispatcher. There is one response queue for each dispatcher. The dispatcher then reads the results from the response queue and sends the information back to the client process.

There is a pool of dispatchers and a pool of shared servers. Oracle starts a certain number of each based on the *INIT.ORA* parameters MTS_DISPATCHERS and MTS_SERVERS. You can start additional dispatchers up to the maximum number of dispatchers indicated by the value of the MTS_MAX_DISPATCHERS parameter. Oracle will start additional shared servers up to the value of MTS_MAX_SERVERS. If Oracle starts additional processes to handle a heavier request load and the load dies down again, Oracle gradually reduces the number of processes to the floor specified by MTS_SERVERS.

The following steps show how establishing a connection and using shared server processes differ from using a dedicated server process:

1. The client contacts the Listener over the network.

2. The Listener detects an incoming request and, based on the Net8 configuration, determines that it is for a multithreaded server. Instead of handing the client off to a dedicated server, the Listener hands the client off to a dispatcher for the network protocol the client is using.

3. The Listener introduces the client and the dispatcher by letting each know the other's network address.

4. Once the client and the dispatcher know where to find each other, they communicate directly. The Listener is no longer required. The client sends work requests directly to the dispatcher.

5. The dispatcher places the client's request in the request queue in the SGA.

6. The next available shared server process reads the request from the response queue and does the work.

7. The shared server places the results for the client's request in the response queue for the dispatcher that originally submitted the request.

8. The dispatcher reads the results from its queue.

9. The dispatcher sends the results to the client.

Figure 3-7 illustrates the steps for using the MTS. Network traffic appears as dotted lines.

Session Memory for Shared Server Processes Versus Dedicated Server Processes

There is a concept in Oracle known as *session memory* or *state*. State information is basically data that describes the current status of a session in Oracle. For example, state information contains information about the SQL statements executed by the session. When you use a dedicated server, this state is stored in the private memory used by the dedicated server. This works out well because the dedicated server only works with one client. The technical term for this private memory is the Program Global Area (PGA).

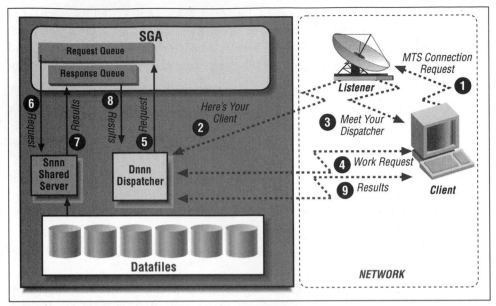

Figure 3-7. Connecting with the Net8 Listener (MTS)

If you're using the multithreaded server, however, any shared server can work on behalf of a specific client. The session state cannot be stored in the PGA of the shared server process. All shared servers must be able to access the session state because the session can migrate between different shared servers. For this reason, Oracle places this state information in the System Global Area (SGA). All shared servers can read from the SGA. Putting the state information in the SGA allows a session and its state to move from one shared server to another for processing different requests. The shared server that picks up the request from the request queue simply reads the session state from the SGA, updates the state as needed for processing, and puts it back in the SGA when processing has finished.

The request and response queues, as well as the session state, require additional memory in the SGA, so you should allocate more memory if you're using the Multi-Threaded Server. By default, the memory for the MTS session state comes from the shared pool. Alternatively, in Oracle8, you can configure something called the *large pool* as a separate area of memory for the MTS. (We introduced the large pool in Chapter 2 in the "Memory Structures for an Instance" section.) Using the large pool for MTS memory avoids the overhead of coordinating MTS memory usage with the shared SQL, dictionary caching, and other functions of the shared pool. This allows the MTS to manage its memory from the large pool and avoid competing with other subsystems for space in and access to the shared pool.

Data Dictionary Information About the Multi-Threaded Server

The data dictionary, which we introduced in Chapter 2, also contains information about the operation of the MTS in the following views:

V$MTS

Dynamic information about the MTS, such as high-water marks for connections and how many shared servers have been started and stopped in response to load variations.

V$DISPATCHER

Details of the dispatcher processes used by the MTS. This view can determine how busy the dispatchers are to help set the floor and ceiling values appropriately.

V$SHARED_SERVER

Details of the shared server processes used by the MTS. This view can determine how busy the servers are to help set the floor and ceiling values appropriately.

V$CIRCUIT

You can think of the route from a client to its dispatcher and from the dispatcher to the shared server (using the queues) as a virtual circuit. This view details these virtual circuits for user connections.

Oracle at Work

To truly understand how all of the disparate pieces of the Oracle database work together, in this section we'll walk through an example of the steps taken by the Oracle database to respond to a user request. For this example, we'll look at a user who is adding new information to the database, a user executing a transaction.

Oracle and Transactions

A *transaction*, in this case, is a work request from a client to insert, update, or delete data. The statements that change data are a subset of the SQL language called Data Manipulation Language (DML). Transactions must be handled in a way that guarantees their integrity. Although Chapter 7, *Multiuser Concurrency*, delves more deeply into the concepts of transactions, we must visit a few basic concepts relating to transactions in order to understand this example of a transaction:

Transactions are logical

In database terms, a transaction is a *logical* unit of work composed of one or more data changes. A transaction may consist of multiple INSERT, UPDATE and/or DELETE statements affecting data in multiple tables. The entire set of changes must succeed or fail as a complete unit of work. A transaction starts with the first DML statement and ends with either a commit or a rollback.

Commit or rollback

Once a user enters the data for his transaction, he can either *commit* the transaction to make the changes permanent or *roll back* the transaction to undo the changes.

System Change Number (SCN)

A key factor in preserving database integrity is an awareness of which transaction came first. For example, if Oracle is to prevent a later transaction from unwittingly overwriting an earlier transaction's changes, Oracle must know which transaction began first. The mechanism Oracle uses is the System Change Number. It is a logical timestamp used to track the order in which events occurred. Oracle also uses the SCN to implement multiversion read consistency, which is described in detail in Chapter 7.

Rollback segments

Rollback segments are structures in the Oracle database used to store "undo" information for transactions, in case of rollback. This undo information restores database blocks to their original state before the transaction in question started. When a transaction starts changing some data in a block, it first writes the old image of the data to a rollback segment. The information stored in a rollback segment is used for two main purposes: to provide the information necessary to roll back a transaction, and to support multiversion read consistency.

A rollback segment differs from a redo log. The redo log is used to log all transactions to the database and to recover the database in the event of a system failure, while the rollback segment provides rollback for transactions and read consistency.

Blocks of rollback segments are cached in the SGA just like blocks of tables and indexes. If rollback segment blocks are unused for a period of time, they may be aged out of the cache and written to the disk.

Fast commits

Because redo logs are written whenever a user commits an Oracle transaction, they can be used to speed the operation of database operations. When a user commits a transaction, Oracle can do one of two things to get the changes into the database on the disk:

- Write all the database blocks the transaction changed to their respective datafiles.

- Write only the redo information, which is typically much less I/O than writing the database blocks. This recording of the changes can be replayed to reproduce all the transaction's changes later, if needed due to a failure.

To provide maximum performance without risking transactional integrity, Oracle writes out only the redo information. When a user commits a transaction, Oracle guarantees that the redo for those changes writes to the redo logs on disk. The actual changed database blocks will be written out to the datafiles later. If a failure occurs before the changed blocks are flushed from the cache to the datafiles, the redo logs will reproduce the changes in their entirety. Because the slowest part of a computer system is the physical disk, Oracle's fast-commit approach minimizes the cost of committing a transaction and provides maximum risk-free performance.

A Transaction Step-by-Step

Let's go through a simple example to try and put it all together. We'll use the EMP table of employee data, which is part of the traditional test schema shipped with Oracle databases. In our example, an HR clerk wants to update the name for an employee. The clerk retrieves the employee's data from the database, updates the name, and commits the transaction.

For the purpose of this example, we'll assume that only one user is trying to update the information for a row in the database. Because of this assumption, we won't include the steps normally taken by Oracle to protect the transaction from changes by other users, which are detailed in Chapter 7.

Assume that the HR clerk already has the employee record on-screen and so the database block containing the row for that employee is already in the database buffer cache. The steps from this point would be the following:

1. The user modifies the employee name on-screen and the client application sends a SQL UPDATE statement over the network to the server process.

2. The server process looks for an identical statement in the shared SQL area of the shared pool. If it finds one, it reuses it. Otherwise, it checks the statement for syntax and evaluates it to determine the best way to execute it. This processing of the SQL statement is called *parsing and optimizing*. Once this processing is done, the statement is cached in the shared SQL area.

3. The server process copies the old image of the employee data about to be changed to a rollback segment. The old version of the employee data is stored in the rollback segment in case the HR clerk cancels or rolls back the transaction. Once the server process has written the old employee data to a rollback segment, the server process modifies the database block to change the employee name. The database block is stored in the database cache at this time.

4. The server process records the changes to the rollback segment and the database block in the redo log buffer in the SGA. The rollback segment changes are part of the redo. This may seem a little odd, but remember that redo is generated for *all* changes resulting from the transaction. The contents of the rollback segment have changed because the old employee data was written to the rollback segment for undo purposes. This change to the contents of the rollback segment is part of the transaction and therefore part of the redo for that transaction.

5. The HR clerk commits the transaction.

6. The Log Writer (LGWR) process writes the redo information for the entire transaction from the redo log buffer to the current redo log file on disk. When the operating system confirms that the write to the redo log file has successfully completed, the transaction is considered committed.

7. The server process sends a message to the client confirming the commit.

The user could have canceled or rolled back the transaction instead of committing it, in which case, the server process would have used the old image of the employee data in the rollback segment to undo the change to the database block.

Figure 3-8 shows the steps described here. Network traffic appears as dotted lines.

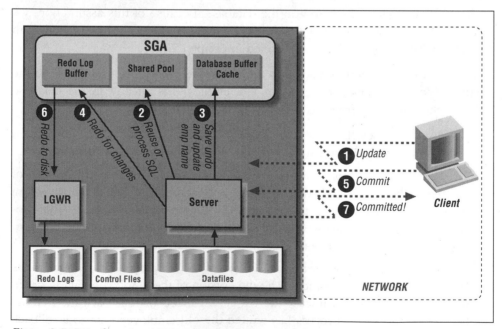

Figure 3-8. Steps for a transaction

4

Data Structures

In the previous chapters, we examined some distinctions between the different components that make up an Oracle8 database. For example, you've learned that the Oracle8 instance differs from the files that make up the physical storage of the data in tablespaces, that you cannot access the data in a tablespace except through an Oracle instance, and that the instance itself isn't very valuable without the data stored in those files.

In the same way, the actual tables and columns within the database are the entities stored within the database files and accessed through the database instance. The user who makes a request for data from an Oracle database probably doesn't know anything about instances and tablespaces, but does know about the structure of her data, as implemented with tables and columns. To fully leverage the power of Oracle8, you must understand how Oracle8 and Oracle8*i* implement and use these logical data structures.

Datatypes

The *datatype* is one of the attributes for a *column* or a variable in a stored procedure. A datatype describes and limits the type of information stored in a column, as well as some of the operations that you can perform on columns with a particular datatype.

You can divide Oracle8 datatype support into three basic varieties: character datatypes, numeric datatypes, and datatypes that represent other types of data. You use all of these datatypes when you create columns in a table, as with this SQL statement:

```
CREATE SAMPLE_TABLE(
    char_field CHAR(10),
    varchar_field VARCHAR(10),
    todays_date DATE)
```

You also use these datatypes when you define variables as part of a PL/SQL procedure.

Character Datatypes

Character datatypes can store any string value, including the string representations of numeric values. Assigning a value larger than the length specified for a character datatype results in a runtime error. You can use string functions, such as UPPER, LOWER, SUBSTR, and SOUNDEX, on standard (not large) character value types.

There are several different character datatypes:

CHAR

The CHAR datatype stores character values with a fixed length. A CHAR datatype can have between 1 and 2,000 characters. If you don't explicitly specify a length for a CHAR, it assumes the default length of 1. If you assign a value that's shorter than the length specified for the CHAR datatype, Oracle8 will automatically pad the value with blanks. Some examples of CHAR values are:

```
CHAR(10) = "Rick      ", "Jon       ", "Stackowiak"
```

VARCHAR2

The VARCHAR2 datatype stores variable-length character strings. Although you must assign a length to a VARCHAR2 datatype, the length is the maximum length for a value, rather than the required length. Values assigned to a VARCHAR2 datatype aren't padded with blanks. The VARCHAR2 datatype can have up to 4,000 characters.

A VARCHAR2 datatype can require less storage space than a CHAR datatype, because the VARCHAR2 datatype only stores the characters assigned to the column.

At this time, the VARCHAR datatype and the VARCHAR2 datatype are synonymous in Oracle8, but Oracle recommends the use of VARCHAR2, because future changes may cause VARCHAR and VARCHAR2 to diverge. The values shown for the CHAR values, if entered as VARCHAR2 values, are:

```
VARCHAR2(10) = "Rick", "Jon", "Stackowiak"
```

NCHAR2 and NVARCHAR2

The NCHAR and NVARCHAR2 datatypes store fixed-length or variable-length character data using a different character set from the one used by the rest of the database. When you create a database, you specify a character set used for encoding the various characters stored in the database. You can optionally specify a secondary character set as well. (This is known as the *National Language Set*, or NLS.) This secondary character set is used for NCHAR and NVARCHAR2 columns. For example, you may have a description field in which you want to store Japanese characters while the rest of the database uses English encoding. You would specify a secondary character set that supports Japanese characters when you create the database, and then use the NCHAR or NVARCHAR2 datatype for the columns in question.

LONG

The LONG datatype can hold up to 2 GB of character data. The LONG datatype is regarded as a legacy datatype from earlier versions of Oracle. If you want to store large amounts of character data, Oracle now recommends that you use the CLOB and NCLOB datatypes. There are many restrictions on the use of LONG datatypes in a table and within SQL statements, such as the fact that you cannot use LONGs in WHERE, GROUP BY, ORDER BY, or CONNECT BY clauses or in SQL statements with the DISTINCT qualifier. You also cannot create an index on a LONG column.

CLOB and NCLOB

The CLOB and NCLOB datatypes can store up to 4 GBs of character data. The NCLOB datatype stores the NLS data. For more information on CLOBs and NCLOBs, please refer to the discussion about large objects (LOBs) in "Other Datatypes," later in this chapter.

Numeric Datatype

Oracle8 uses a standard, variable-length internal format for storing numbers. This internal format can maintain a precision of up to 38 digits.

The main numeric datatype for Oracle8 is NUMBER. Declaring a column or variable as NUMBER will automatically provide a precision of 38 digits. The NUMBER datatype can also accept two qualifiers, as in:

```
column NUMBER( precision, scale )
```

The *precision* of the datatype is the total number of significant digits in the number. You can designate a precision for a number as any number of digits up to 38. If a value isn't declared for *precision*, Oracle will use a precision of 38. The *scale* represents the number of digits to the right of the decimal point. If no scale is specified, Oracle8 uses a scale of 0.

If you assign a negative number to the *scale*, Oracle8 will round the number up to the designated place to the *left* of the decimal point. For example, the following code snippet:

```
column_round NUMBER(10,-2)
column_round = 1,234,567
```

will give column_round a value of 1,234,600.

The NUMBER datatype is the only datatype that stores numeric values in Oracle8. The ANSI datatypes of DECIMAL, NUMBER, INTEGER, INT, SMALLINT, FLOAT, DOUBLE PRECISION, and REAL are all stored in the NUMBER datatype. The language or product you're using to access Oracle8 data may support these datatypes, but they're all stored in a NUMBER datatype column.

Date Datatype

As with the NUMERIC datatype, Oracle8 stores all dates and times in a standard internal format. The standard Oracle8 date format for input takes the form of DD-MON-YY:HH:MI:SS, where DD represents up to two digits for the day of the month, MON is a three-character abbreviation for the month, YY is a two-digit representation of the year, and HH, MI, and SS are two-digit representations of hours, minutes, and seconds, respectively. If you don't specify any time values, their default values are all zeros in the internal storage.

You can change the format you use for inserting dates for an instance by changing the NLS_DATE_FORMAT parameter for the instance. You do this for a session by using the ALTER SESSION SQL command, or for a specific value by using parameters with the TO_DATE expression in your SQL statement.

If you use the default date format, Oracle8 will assume that the dates you enter are in the 1900s and store them as such. To prevent Year 2000 (Y2K) problems, you should make sure that you use one of the format options mentioned in the sidebar to change the default date format.

Oracle8 SQL supports date arithmetic in which integers represent days, and fractions represent the fractional component represented by hours, minutes, and seconds. For example, adding .5 to a date value results in a date and time combination 12 hours later than the initial value. Some examples of date arithmetic are:

```
12-DEC-99 + 10 = 22-DEC-99
31-DEC-1999:23:59:59 + .25 = 1-JAN-2000:5:59:59
```

Other Datatypes

Aside from the basic character, number, and date datatypes, Oracle8 supports a number of specialized datatypes:

RAW and LONG RAW

> Normally, Oracle8 not only stores data, but interprets that data. When data is exported from the database or requested from the database, the Oracle8 database sometimes massages the requested data. For instance, when you dump

Y2K Issues and Oracle8

At the time of this writing, the problems that may result from the turn of the millennium are very much in the news.

But Y2K isn't a problem for the Oracle database itself because Oracle's internal date format stores all dates in a format that can accept dates from 4712 BC to 4712 AD.

However, Oracle uses a date format to specify how dates are input and output from this internal date format. You set the format with the NLS_DATE_FOR-MAT parameter in the *INIT.ORA* file for an instance or with the ALTER SESSION command for an individual session.

If the date format isn't set to recognize centuries, the Oracle database might not properly store the dates entered. For instance, the default date format for Oracle is DD-MM-YY. Using this default date format, the value "01-01-00" would be recognized as January 1, 1900 and would be stored accordingly.

Oracle has a date format that's ideal for handling Y2K issues: the RR year format. The RR format automatically assigns two-digit years from 50 to 99 to the 1900s, and two-digit years from 00 to 49 to the 2000s. The RR format gives users the option of entering dates with only two digits, while still properly assigning those digits at least until the year 2050 (when it definitely won't be our problem any more!).

Some application developers store date values in an Oracle database as character strings. These developers will have to correct their own work to prevent any potential Y2K problems, because there is no way for Oracle to know that a character string is *supposed* to be a date.

If you're reading this page in the year 2002 or beyond, you won't have to worry about this issue for at least 40 years or so—but it helps to be prepared anyway.

---

the values from a NUMBER column, the values written to the dump file are the representations of the number, not the internal storage of the number.

The RAW and LONG RAW datatypes circumvent any interpretation on the part of the Oracle8 database. When you specify one of these datatypes, Oracle8 will store the data as the exact series of bits presented to it.

The RAW datatypes typically store objects with their own internal format, such as bitmaps. A RAW datatype can hold 2,000 bytes, while a LONG RAW datatype can hold 2 GBs.

ROWID

The ROWID is a special type of column known as a *pseudocolumn*. The ROWID pseudocolumn can be accessed just like a column in a SQL SELECT statement. There is a ROWID pseudocolumn for every row in an Oracle8 database. The ROWID represents the specific address of a particular row. The ROWID pseudocolumn is defined with a ROWID datatype.

The ROWID relates to a specific location on a disk drive. Because of this, the ROWID is the fastest way to retrieve an individual row. However, the ROWID for a row can change as the result of dumping and reloading the database. For this reason, we don't recommend using the value for the ROWID pseudocolumn across transaction lines. For example, there is no reason to store a reference to the ROWID of a row once you've finished using the row in your current application.

You cannot set the value of the standard ROWID pseudocolumn with any SQL statement.

The format of the ROWID pseudocolumn has changed with Oracle8. With Oracle8, the ROWID now includes an identifier that points to the database object number, as well as the identifiers that point to the datafile, block, and row. You can parse the value returned from the ROWID pseudocolumn to understand the physical storage of rows in your Oracle database.

You can define a column or variable with a ROWID datatype, but Oracle8 doesn't guarantee that any value placed in this column or variable is a valid ROWID.

LOBs

A LOB, or large object datatype, can store up to 4 GBs of information. LOBs come in three varieties, as follows:

- CLOB, which can only store character data

- NCLOB, which stores National Language character set data

- BLOB, which stores data as binary information

You can designate that a LOB should store its data within the Oracle8 database or that it should point to an external file that contains the data.

LOBs can participate in transactions. Selecting a LOB datatype from Oracle8 will return a pointer to the LOB. You must use either the DBMS_LOB PL/SQL built-in package or the OCI interface to actually manipulate the data in a LOB.

BFILE

The BFILE datatype acts as a pointer to a file stored outside of the Oracle8 database. Because of this fact, columns or variables with BFILE datatypes don't participate in transactions, and the data stored in these columns is only available for reading. The file size limitations of the underlying operating system limit the size of data in a BFILE.

User-defined data

Oracle8 allows users to define their own complex datatypes, which are created as combinations of the basic Oracle datatypes previously discussed.

Oracle8 also allows users to create objects composed from both basic datatypes and user-defined data types. For more information about objects within Oracle8, see Chapter 13, *Oracle8/8i Extensions*.

Type Conversion

Oracle8 automatically converts some datatypes to other datatypes, depending on the SQL syntax in which the value occurs.

When you assign a character value to a numeric datatype, Oracle8 performs an implicit conversion of the ASCII value represented by the character string into a number. For instance, assigning a character value such as 10 to a NUMERIC column results in an automatic data conversion.

If you attempt to assign an alphabetic value to a numeric datatype, you will end up with an unexpected (and invalid) numeric value, so you should make sure that you're assigning values appropriately.

You can also perform explicit conversions on data, using a variety of conversion functions available with Oracle8. Explicit data conversions are better to use if a conversion is called for, since they both document the conversion and avoid the possibility of missing any unwanted implicit conversions.

Concatenation and Comparisons

The concatenation operator for Oracle8 SQL on most platforms is two vertical lines "| |". Concatenation is performed with two character values. Oracle8's automatic type conversion allows you to seemingly concatenate two numeric values. If NUM1 is a numeric column with a value of 1, NUM2 is a numeric column with a value of 2, and NUM3 is a numeric column with a value of 3, the following expressions are TRUE:

- NUM1 | | NUM2 | | NUM3 = "123"
- NUM1 | | NUM2 + NUM3 = "15" (12 + 3)
- NUM1 + NUM2 | | NUM3 = "33" (1+ 2 | | 3)

The result for each of these expressions is a character string, but that character string can be automatically converted back to a numeric column for further calculations.

Comparisons between values of the same datatype work as you would expect. For example, a date that occurs later in time is larger than an earlier date, and 0 or any positive number is larger than any negative number. You can use relational operators to compare numeric values or date values. For character values, comparisons of single characters are based on the underlying code pages for the characters. For multicharacter strings, comparisons are made until the first character that differs between the two strings appears. The result of the comparison between these two characters is the result of the overall comparisons.

If two character strings of different lengths are compared, Oracle8 uses two different types of comparison semantics: *blank-padded comparisons* or *nonpadded comparisons*. For a blank-padded comparison, the shorter string is padded with blanks and the comparison operates as previously described. For nonpadded comparisons, if both strings are identical for the length of the shorter string, the shorter string is identified as smaller. Nonpadded comparisons are used for comparisons in which one or both of the values are VARCHAR2 and NVARCHAR2 datatypes, while blank-padded comparisons are used when neither of the values are these datatypes.

For example, the comparison of the string "A " (a capital A followed by a blank) and the string "A" (a capital A by itself) is read as equal in a padded comparison, because the second value is padded with a blank. The same comparison returns the second value as smaller in a nonpadded comparison, because the second string is shorter than the first string.

NULLs

The NULL value is one of the key features of the relational database. The NULL, in fact, doesn't represent any value at all—it represents the lack of a value. When you create a column for a table that must have a value, you specify it as NOT NULL, meaning that it cannot contain a NULL value. If you try to write a row to a database table that doesn't assign a value to a NOT NULL column, Oracle8 will return an error.

You can assign NULL for a value of any datatype. The NULL value introduces what is called *three-state logic* to your SQL operators. A normal comparison has only two states: TRUE or FALSE. If you're making a comparison that involves a NULL value, there are three logical states: TRUE, FALSE, and none of the above.

This leads to the following results for a column named "A" that contains a NULL:

- A = 0 is FALSE
- A > 0 is FALSE
- A < 0 is FALSE
- A != 0 is TRUE

The existence of three-state logic can be confusing for end users, but your data may frequently require you to allow for NULL values for columns or variables.

You have to test for the presence of a NULL value with the relational operator IS NULL, since a NULL value is not equal to 0 or any other value. Even the expression:

```
NULL = NULL
```

will always evaluate to FALSE, since a NULL value doesn't equal any other value.

Should You Use NULLs?

Initially, the idea of three-state logic may seem somewhat confusing, especially when you imagine your poor end users executing ad hoc queries and trying to account for a value that's neither TRUE nor FALSE. This prospect may concern you, so you may decide not to use NULL values at all.

We feel that NULLs have an appropriate use. The NULL value covers a very specific situation—a time when a column has not had a value assigned. The alternative to using a NULL is using a value with another meaning—such as 0 for numbers—and then trying to somehow determine whether that value has been assigned or whether it exists as a replacement for NULL.

If you choose not to use NULL values, you're forcing a value to be assigned to a column for every row. You are, in effect, eliminating the possibility of having a column that doesn't require a value, as well as potentially assigning a misleading value for the column. Not only can this situation be misleading for end users, but it can also lead to inaccurate results for summary actions like AVG (average).

Avoiding NULL values simply replaces one problem—educating users or providing them with an interface that implicitly understands NULL values—with another set of problems, which can lead to a loss of data integrity.

Basic Data Structures

This section describes the three basic Oracle data structures: tables, views, and indexes.

Tables

The *table* is the basic data structure used in a relational database. A table is a collection of rows. Each *row* in a table contains one or more *columns*. If you're unfamiliar with relational databases, you can map a table to the concept of a file or database in a nonrelational database, just as you can map a row to the concept of a record in a nonrelational database.

With Oracle8 Enterprise Edition and Oracle8*i* Enterprise Edition, you can purchase an option called the Partitioning option that, as the name implies, allows you to partition tables and indexes, which are described later in this chapter. Partitioning a data structure means that you can divide the information in the structure between multiple physical storage areas. A partitioned data structure is divided based on column values in the table. You can partition tables based on the range of column values in the table, or on the result of a hash function (which returns a value based on a calculation on the values in one or more columns), or on a combination of the two. Oracle8 is smart enough to take advantage of partitions to improve performance in two ways:

- Oracle won't bother to access partitions that won't contain any data to satisfy the query.

- If all the data in a partition satisfies a part of the WHERE clause for the query, Oracle simply selects all the rows for the partition without bothering to evaluate the clause for each row.

Partitioning tables can also be very useful in a data warehouse, in which data can be partitioned based on the time period it spans.

You can perform all maintenance operations, such as backup, recovery, and loading, on a single partition. This flexibility makes it possible to handle extremely large data structures while still performing those maintenance operations in a reasonable amount of time. In addition, if you must recover one partition in a table for some reason, the other partitions in the table can remain online during the recovery operation.

If you've been working with other databases that don't offer the same type of partitioning, you may have tried to implement a similar functionality by dividing a table into several separate tables and then using a UNION SQL command to view the data in several tables at once. Partitioned tables give you all the advantages of having several identical tables joined by a UNION command without the complexity that implementation requires.

To maximize the benefits of partitioning, it sometimes makes sense to partition a table and an index identically so that both the table partition and the index partition map to the same set of rows. You can automatically implement this type of partitioning, which is called *equipartioning*, by specifying an index for a partitioned table as a LOCAL index.

For more details about the structure and limitations associated with partitioned tables, refer to your Oracle8 documentation.

Views

A *view* is an Oracle data structure constructed with a SQL statement. The results of the SQL statement make up the definition of the view. The SQL statement is stored in the database, while the data for the view is assembled when data is requested through the view. You can use a view instead of a table in a SQL query.

You can use a view for several reasons:

- To simplify access to data stored in multiple tables

- To implement specific security for the data in a table by creating a view that includes a WHERE clause that limits the data that you can access through the view

- To isolate an application from the specific structure of the underlying tables

A view is built on a collection of *base tables*, which can be either actual tables in an Oracle8 database or other views. If you modify any of the base tables for a view so that they no longer can be used for a view, then the view itself can no longer be used.

In general, you can only write to the columns of one underlying base table of a view in a single SQL statement. There are additional restrictions for INSERT, UPDATE, and DELETE operations, and there are certain SQL clauses that prevent you from updating any of the data in a view.

You can write to a non-updateable view by using an INSTEAD OF trigger, which is described later in this chapter.

Oracle8*i* introduced *materialized views*. Materialized views can hold pre-summarized data, which provides significant performance improvements in a data warehouse scenario. Materialized views are described in more detail in Chapter 9, *Oracle8 and Data Warehousing*.

Indexes

An index is a data structure that speeds up access to particular rows in a database. An index is associated with a particular table and contains the data from one or more columns in the table.

The basic SQL syntax for creating an index is shown in this example:

```
CREATE INDEX emp_idx1 ON emp (ename, job);
```

in which emp_idx1 is the name of the index, emp is the table on which the index is created, and ename and job are the column values that make up the index.

The Oracle8 database automatically modifies the values in the index when the values in the corresponding columns are modified. Because the index contains less data than the complete row in the table, and because indexes are stored in a special structure that makes them faster to read, it takes fewer I/O operations to retrieve the data in them. Selecting rows based on an index value can be faster than selecting rows based on values in the table rows. In addition, most indexes are stored in sorted order—either ascending or descending—depending on the declaration made when you create the index. Because of this storage scheme, selecting rows based on a range of values or returning rows in sorted order is much faster when the range or sort order is contained in the presorted indexes.

In addition to the data for an index, an index entry stores the ROWID for its associated row. The ROWID is the fastest way to retrieve any row in a database, so the subsequent retrieval of a database row is performed in the most optimal way.

An index can be either unique, which means that no two rows can have the same index value, or nonunique. If the column or columns on which an index is based contain NULL values, the row isn't included in an index.

An index in Oracle is the physical structure used within the database. A *key* is a term for a logical entity, typically the value stored within the index. In most places in the Oracle8 documentation, the two terms are used interchangeably, with the notable exception of the foreign key constraint, which is discussed later in this chapter.

There are four different types of index structures in Oracle8, which are described in the following sections: standard B*-tree indexes, reverse key indexes, and bitmapped indexes, and a new type of index, the function-based index, which was introduced with Oracle8*i*. Oracle8 also gives you the ability to cluster the data in the tables, which can improve performance and is described in a later section.

B*-tree indexes

The *B*-tree index* is the default index used in Oracle8. The B*-tree index gets its name from its resemblance to an inverted tree, as shown in Figure 4-1.

The B*-tree index is composed of one or more levels of branch blocks and a single level of leaf blocks. The branch blocks contain information about the range of values contained in the next level of branch blocks. The number of branch levels between the root and leaf blocks is called the *depth* of the index. The leaf blocks contain the actual index values and the ROWID for the associated row.

The B*-tree index structure doesn't contain that many blocks at the higher levels of branch blocks, so it takes relatively few I/O operations to read quite far down the B*-tree index tree structure. All leaf blocks are at the same depth in the index, so all retrievals require essentially the same amount of I/O to get to the index entry, which evens out the performance of the index.

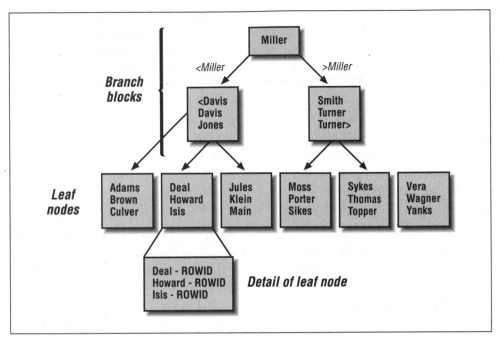

Figure 4-1. A B*-tree index

Oracle8 allows you to create *index organized tables* (IOTs), in which the leaf blocks store the entire row of data, rather than storing only the ROWID that points to the associated row. Index organized tables reduce the amount of space needed to store an index and a table by eliminating the need to store the ROWID in the leaf page. But index organized tables cannot use a UNIQUE constraint or be stored in a cluster. In addition, index organized tables don't support distribution, replication, and partitioning (covered in greater detail in other chapters).

Reverse key indexes

Reverse key indexes, as their name implies, automatically reverse the order of the bytes in the key value stored in the index. If the value in a row is "ABCD", the value for the reverse key index for that row is "DCBA".

To understand the need for a reverse key index, you have to review some basic facts about the standard B*-tree index. First and foremost, the depth of the B*-tree is determined by the number of entries in the leaf nodes. The greater the depth of the B*-tree, the more levels of branch nodes and the more I/O required to locate and access the appropriate leaf node.

The index illustrated in Figure 4-1 is a nice, well behaved alphabetic-based index. It's balanced, with an even distribution of entries across the width of the leaf pages. But some values commonly used for an index are not so well behaved.

Incremental values, such as ascending sequence numbers or increasingly later date values, are always added to the right side of the index, which is the home of higher and higher values. In addition, any deletions from the index have a tendency to be skewed towards the left side as older rows are deleted. The net effect of these practices is that over time the index turns into an unbalanced B*-tree, where the left side of the index is more sparsely populated than the leaf nodes on the right side. This unbalanced growth has the overall effect of increasing the depth of the B*-tree structure due to the number of entries on the right side of the index. The effects described here also apply to the values that are automatically decremented, except that the left side of the B*-tree will end up holding more entries.

You can solve this problem by periodically dropping and recreating the index. But you can also solve it by using the reverse value index, which reverses the order of the value of the index. This reversal has the effect of causing the index entries to be more evenly distributed over the width of the leaf nodes. For example, rather than having the values of 234, 235, and 236 be added to the maximum side of the index, they are translated to the values 432, 532, and 632 for storage, and retranslated when the values are retrieved. These values are more evenly spread throughout the leaf nodes.

The overall result of the reverse index is to correct the imbalance caused by continually adding increasing values to a standard B*-tree index. For more information about reverse key indexes and where to use them, refer to your Oracle documentation.

Bitmapped indexes

In a standard B*-tree index, the ROWIDs are stored in the leaf pages of the index. In a bitmapped index, each bit in the index represents a ROWID. If a particular row contains a particular value, the bit for that row is "turned on" in the bitmap for that value. A mapping function converts the bit into its corresponding ROWID. Unlike other index types, bitmapped indexes include entries for NULL values,

You can store a bitmapped index in much less space than a standard B*-tree index if there aren't many values in the index. Figure 4-2 shows an illustration of how a bitmapped index is stored and used in a selection condition.

The functionality provided by bitmapped indexes is especially important in data warehousing applications in which each dimension of the warehouse contains many repeating values and in which queries typically require the interaction of several different dimensions. For more about data warehousing, see Chapter 9.

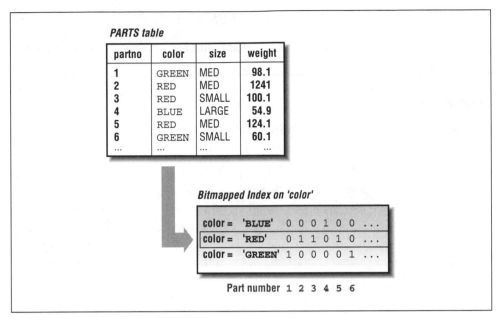

Figure 4-2. Bitmapped index

Function-based indexes

Function-based indexes are new in Oracle8*i*. A function-based index is just like a standard B*-tree or bitmapped index, except that you can base the index on the result of a SQL function, rather than just on the value of a column or columns.

Prior to Oracle8*i*, if you wanted to select on the result of a function, Oracle retrieved every row in the database, executed the function, and then accepted or rejected the row. With function-based indexes, you can simply use the index for selection, without having to execute the function on every row, every time.

For example, without a function-based index, if you wanted to perform a case-insensitive selection of data, you would have to use the UPPER function in the WHERE clause, which would have to retrieve every candidate row and execute the function. With a function-based index based on the UPPER function, you can select directly from the index. This capability becomes even more valuable when you consider that you can create your own functions in an Oracle8 database. You can create a very sophisticated function and then create an index based on the function, which can dramatically affect the performance of queries that required the function.

Additional Data Structures

There are several other data structures available in Oracle8 that are useful in some circumstances.

Sequences

One of the big problems that occur in a multiuser database is the difficulty of supplying unique numbers for use as keys or identifiers.

In such a case, Oracle8 allows you to create an object called a *sequence*. The sequence object is fairly simple. Whenever anyone requests a value from it, it returns a value and increments its internal value, avoiding the time-consuming interaction with the requesting application. Oracle can cache a range of numbers for the sequence so that access to the next number doesn't have to involve disk I/O; rather, it can be satisfied from the range in the System Global Area (SGA).

Sequence numbers are defined with a name, an incremental value, and some additional information about the sequence. Sequences exist independently of any particular table, so more than one table can use the same sequence number.

Consider what might happen if you didn't use Oracle sequences. You might store the last sequence number used in a column in a table. A user wants to get the next sequence number, so he'd read the last number, increment it by a fixed value, and write the new value back to the column. But if many users tried to get a sequence number at the same time, they might all read the "last" sequence number before the new "last" sequence number had been written back. You could lock the row in the table with the column containing the sequence number, but this would cause delays as other users waited on locks. What's the solution? Create a sequence.

Synonyms

All data structures within an Oracle8 database are stored within a specific *schema*. A schema is associated with a particular username, and all objects are referenced with the name of the schema followed by the name of the object.

For instance, if there is a table named EMP in a schema named DEMO, the table would be referenced with the complete name of DEMO.EMP. If you don't supply a specific schema name, Oracle8 assumes that the structure is in the schema for your current user name.

Schemas are a nice feature because object names only have to be unique within their own schema, but the qualified names for objects can get confusing, especially for end users. To make names simpler and more readable, you can create a *synonym* for any table, view, snapshot, or sequence, or for any PL/SQL procedure, function, or package.

Synonyms can be either *public*, which means that all users of a database can use the synonym, or *private*, which means that only the user whose schema contains the synonym can use it. For example, if the user DEMO creates a public synonym called EMP for the table EMP in his schema, then all other users can simply use EMP to refer to the EMP table in DEMO's schema. Suppose that DEMO didn't create a public synonym and a user called SCOTT wanted to use the name EMP to refer to the EMP table in DEMO's schema. The user SCOTT would create a private synonym in his schema. Of course, SCOTT must have access to DEMO's EMP table for this to work.

Synonyms simplify user access to a data structure. You can also use synonyms to hide the location of a particular data structure, making the data more transportable and increasing the security of the associated table by hiding the name of the schema owner.

Clusters

A *cluster* is a data structure that improves retrieval performance. A cluster, like an index, doesn't affect the logical view of the table.

A cluster is a way of storing related data values together on disk. Because Oracle reads data a block at a time, storing related values together reduces the number of I/O operations needed to retrieve related values, since a single data block will contain only related rows.

A cluster is comprised of one or more tables. The cluster includes a cluster index, which stores all the values for the corresponding cluster key. Each value in the cluster index points to a data block that only contains rows with the same value for the cluster key.

If a cluster contains multiple tables, the tables should be joined together, and the cluster index should contain the values that form the basis of the join.

A cluster can reduce the performance of INSERTs, so you shouldn't use a value for a cluster column that changes very often. Because the value of the cluster key controls the placement of the rows that relate to the key, changing a value in that key can cause Oracle to change the location of rows associated with that key value.

A cluster may not necessarily be appropriate for tables that regularly require a full table scan, in which a query requires the Oracle database to iterate through all the rows of a table. Because you access a cluster table through the cluster index, which then points to a data block, full table scans can actually require more I/O operations, lowering overall performance.

Hash Clusters

A *hash cluster* is like a cluster with one significant difference that can make it even faster. The values for the cluster key are stored in the cluster index. Each request for data in a clustered table involves at least two I/O operations: one for the cluster index and one for the data.

A hash cluster stores related data rows together, but groups the rows according to a *hash value* for the cluster key. The hash value is calculated with a hash function, which means that each retrieval operation starts with a calculation of the hash value, and then goes directly to the data block that contains the relevant rows. By eliminating the need to go to a cluster index, a hash clustered table can be even faster for retrieving data than a table in a cluster. You can control the number of possible hash values for a hash cluster with the HASHKEYS parameter when you create the cluster.

Because the hash cluster directly points to the location of a row in the table, you must allocate all the space required for all the possible values in a hash cluster when you create the cluster.

Hash clusters work best when there is an even distribution of rows among the various values for the hash key. You may have a situation in which there is already a unique value for the hash key, such as a unique ID. In such situations, you can assign the value for the hash key as the value for the hash function on the unique value, which eliminates the need to execute the hash function as part of the retrieval process. In addition, you can specify your own hash function as part of the definition of a hash cluster.

Data Design

Tables and columns present a logical view of the data in a relational database. The flexibility of a relational database gives you many options for grouping the atomic pieces of data, represented by the columns, into a set of tables. To use Oracle8 effectively, you must understand and follow some firmly established principles of database design.

The topic of database design is vast and deep: we won't even pretend to offer more than a cursory overview of the topic. For more information, we recommend the book *Oracle Design* by Dave Ensor and Ian Stevenson (O'Reilly & Associates).

When E.F. Codd created the concept of a relational database in the 1960s, he also began work on the concept of *normalized* data design. The theory behind normalized data design is pretty straightforward: a table should only contain the information that's directly related to the key value of the table. The process of assembling these logical units of information is called *normalization* of the database design.

Normalized Forms

In fact, there is more than one type of normalization. Each step in the normalization process ends with a specific result called a *normalized form*. There are five standard normalized forms, which are referred to as first normal form (1NF), second normal form (2FN), and so on. The normalization process that we describe briefly in this section results in third normal form (3NF), the most common type of normalization.

Explaining the complete concepts that lie behind the different normal forms is beyond the scope of this chapter and book.

The concept of normalized table design was tailored to the capabilities of the relational database. Because you could join data from different tables together in a query, there was no need to keep all the information associated with a particular object together in a single record. You could decompose the information into associated units and simply join the appropriate units together when you needed information that crossed table boundaries.

There are many different methodologies for normalizing data. Here's one example. You start by defining all the data required by your application.

1. You identify the objects your application needs to know: the *entities*. Examples of entities, as shown in Figure 4-3, include EMPLOYEE NAME, LOCATION, DEPARTMENT NAME, and JOB.

2. You identify the individual pieces of data, referred to by data modelers as *attributes*, for these entities. In Figure 4-3, EMPLOYEE NAME and SALARY are attributes. Typically, entities correspond to tables and attributes correspond to columns.

3. As a potential last step in the process, you identify *relationships* between the entities based on your business. These relationships are implemented in the database schema through the use of structures such as foreign keys. For example, the primary key of the DEPARTMENT NUMBER table would be a foreign key column in the EMPLOYEE NAME table used to identify the DEPARTMENT NUMBER in which an employee works.

Why is normalization good? Normalization avoids redundant data. Storing the department in every employee record not only would waste space, but also would lead to an unmanageable data maintenance issue. If the department name changed, you would have to update every employee record. By normalizing the department data into a table and simply pointing to the appropriate row from the employee rows, you avoid duplication of data and the associated problems.

But there is an even more important reason to go through the process of design-ing a normalized database design. You benefit from normalization because of the planning process that normalizing a data design entails. By really thinking about the way the intended applications use data, you get a much clearer picture of the needs the system is designed to answer. This understanding leads to a much more focused database and application.

Normalization also reduces the amount of data that any one row in any one table contains. The less data in a row, the less I/O is needed to retrieve a row, which helps to avoid this performance bottleneck. In addition, the smaller the data in a row, the more rows retrieved per data block, which increases the likelihood that more than one desired row will be retrieved in an I/O operation. And the smaller the row, the more rows that will be kept in Oracle8's system buffers, which also increases the likelihood that a row will be available in memory when it's needed, thereby avoiding the need for any disk I/O at all.

Finally, the process of normalization includes the creation of foreign key relation-ships and other data constraints. These relationships add a level of data integrity to your database design. We'll describe these relationships in more detail in the "Constraints" section.

Figure 4-3 shows a simple list of attributes grouped into entities and linked by a foreign key relationship.

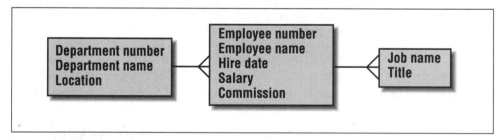

Figure 4-3. The normalization process

Creating a normalized data design isn't the only data design work you will have to do. Once you've completed an optimal logical database design, you must go back and consider what indexes you should add to improve the anticipated perfor-mance of the database, or whether you should designate any tables as part of a cluster or hash cluster.

Since adding these types of performance enhancing data structures doesn't affect the logical representation of the database, you can always make these types of modifications later when you see the way an application uses the database in test mode or in production.

Should You Normalize Your Data?

Whenever possible, we recommend that you go through the process of designing a normalized structure for your database.

Data normalization has been proven, both theoretically and in decades of practice, to provide concrete benefits. In addition, the process of creating a normalized data design is intimately intertwined with the process of understanding the data requirements for your application system. You can improve even the simplest database by the discoveries made during the process of normalization.

However, there may be times when you feel that the benefits of a fully normalized design will counteract the performance penalty that a design imposes on your production systems. For example, you may have one, two, or three contact names to be placed in their own table, with a foreign key linking back to the main row for the organization. But because you always want to see all the contact names whenever you request contact information, you might decide to save the overhead of the join and simply include the three contact names in your organization table.

Of course, this violation of the rules of normalization limits the flexibilty of your application systems—for example, if you later decide that you need four contact names, you will be in a difficult situation.

For this reason, we suggest that you always design your database fully normalized and then, if necessary, go back and denormalize certain tables as needed. With this approach, you will at least have to make a conscious decision to "break" the normalization, which involves an active consideration of the price of denormalization.

Constraints

A *constraint* enforces certain aspects of data integrity within a database. When you add a constraint to a particular column, Oracle8 automatically ensures that data violating that constraint is never accepted. If a user attempts to write data that violates a constraint, Oracle8 returns an error for the offending SQL statement.

Constraints are associated with columns when you create or add the table containing the column (via a number of keywords) or after the table has been created with the SQL command ALTER TABLE. There are five constraint types supported by Oracle8 and Oracle8*i*:

NOT NULL constraint

You can designate any column as NOT NULL. If any SQL operation leaves a NULL value in a column with a NOT NULL constraint, Oracle8 returns an error for the statement.

Uniqueness constraint

When you designate a column or set of columns as unique, a user cannot enter a value for the columns that already exist in another row in the table.

The unique constraint is implemented by the creation of an index, which requires a unique value. If you include more than one column as part of a unique key, you will create a single index that will include all the columns in the unique key. If an index already exists for this purpose, Oracle8 will automatically use that index.

If a column is unique but still allows NULL values, any number of rows can have a NULL value, because the NULL indicates an absence of a value. To require a unique value for a column in every row, the column should be both unique and NOT NULL.

Primary key constraint

Each table can have, at most, a single primary key constraint. The primary key may comprise more than one column in a table.

The primary key constraint forces each primary key to have a unique value. A primary key constraint enforces both the unique constraint and the NOT NULL constraint. A primary key constraint will create a unique index, if one doesn't already exist for the column.

Foreign key constraint

The foreign key constraint is defined for a table (known as the *child*), which has a relationship with another table in the database (known as the *parent*). The value entered in a foreign key must be present in a unique or primary key of another specific table. For example, the column for a department ID in an employee table might be a foreign key for the department ID primary key in the department table.

A foreign key can have one or more columns, but the referenced key must have an equal number of columns. You can have a foreign key relate to the primary key of its own table, such as when the employee ID of a manager is a foreign key referencing the ID column in the same table.

A foreign key can contain a NULL value if it's not forbidden through another constraint.

By requiring that the foreign key exist in another table, the foreign key enforces what is called *referential integrity* in the database. In this way, foreign keys not only provide a way to join related tables, but ensure that the relationship between the two tables will have the required data integrity.

If a row in a parent table is deleted, you can specify one of two actions with regard to the related rows in the child table. Normally, you cannot delete a row in a parent table if it causes a row in the child table to violate a foreign key constraint. However, you can specify that a foreign key constraint causes a *cascade delete*, which means that deleting a referenced row in the parent table automatically deletes all rows in the child table that reference the primary key value in the deleted row in the parent table.

Check constraint

A check constraint is a more general-purpose constraint. It's a Boolean expression that evaluates to either TRUE or FALSE. If the check constraint evaluates to FALSE, the SQL statement that caused the result returns an error. For example, a check constraint might require the minimum balance in a bank account to be over $100. If a user tried to update data for that account in a way that caused the balance to drop below this required amount, the constraint would return an error.

Constraints can cause the creation of indexes to support the constraint. For instance, the unique constraint creates an implicit index used to guarantee uniqueness. You can also specify a particular index that will enforce a constraint when you define the constraint.

All constraints can be either immediate or deferred. An *immediate constraint* is enforced as soon as a write operation affects a constrained column in the table. A *deferred constraint* is enforced when the SQL statement that caused the change in the constrained column completes. Because a single SQL statement can affect a lot of rows, the choice between using a deferred constraint or an immediate constraint can significantly affect how the integrity dictated by the constraint operates. You can specify that an individual constraint is immediate or deferred, or you can set the timing for all constraints in a single transaction.

Finally, you can temporarily suspend the enforcement of constraints for a particular table. When you re-enable the operation of the constraint, Oracle8 resumes enforcing the constraint for all subsequent changes, but doesn't check to see whether all existing rows in the table conform to the rules required by the constraint. When you're adding a constraint to an existing table, you can also specify whether you want to check all the existing rows in the table.

Triggers

You can use a constraint to automatically enforce a data integrity rule whenever a user tries to write or modify a row in a table. There are times when you want the same kind of enforcement of your own database or application-specific logic. Oracle8 includes *triggers* to give you this capability.

A trigger is a block of code fired whenever a particular type of database event occurs to a table. There are three types of events that can cause a trigger to fire:

- A database UPDATE

- A database INSERT

- A database DELETE

You can, for instance, define a trigger to write a customized audit record whenever a user changes a row.

Triggers are defined at the row level. You can specify that a trigger is to be fired for each row or SQL statement that fires the trigger event. As with the previous discussion of constraints, a single SQL statement can affect many rows, so the specification of the trigger can have a significant effect on the operation and performance of the trigger.

There are three times when a trigger can fire:

- Before the execution of the triggering event

- After the execution of the triggering event

- Instead of the triggering event

Combining the first two timing options with the row and statement versions of a trigger gives you four possible trigger implementations: before a statement, before a row, after a statement, and after a row.

INSTEAD OF triggers were introduced with Oracle8. The INSTEAD OF trigger has a specific purpose: to implement data manipulation operations on views that don't normally permit them, for example, in a view that references columns in more than one base table for updates. You should be careful when using INSTEAD OF triggers, because of the many potential problems associated with modifying the data in the underlying base tables of a view. There are many restrictions on when you can use INSTEAD OF triggers. Refer to your Oracle documentation for a detailed description of the forbidden scenarios.

All triggers can have a trigger restriction specified for the trigger. A trigger restriction is a Boolean expression that circumvents the execution of the trigger if it evaluates to FALSE.

Triggers are defined and stored separately from the tables that use them. A trigger contains logic, so a trigger must be written in a language with capabilities beyond those of SQL, which is designed to access data. Oracle8 allows you to write triggers in PL/SQL, the procedural language that has been a part of Oracle since Version 6. Oracle8*i* also supports Java as a procedural language, so you can create Java triggers with Oracle8*i*.

You can write a trigger directly in PL/SQL or Java, or a trigger can call an existing stored procedure written in either language.

 Although you can write triggers to perform the work of a constraint, Oracle8 has optimized the operation of constraints, so it's best to always use a constraint instead of a trigger if possible.

Triggers are fired as a result of a SQL statement that modifies a row in a particular table. It's possible for the actions of the trigger to modify the data in the table, or to cause changes in other tables that fire their own triggers. The end result of this may be data that ends up being changed in a way that Oracle8 thinks is logically illegal. These situations can result in Oracle8 returning runtime errors referring to *mutating tables*, which are tables modified by other triggers, or *constraining tables*, which are tables modified by other constraints. Oracle8*i* has eliminated some of the errors caused by activating constraints with triggers.

Oracle8*i* has also introduced a very useful set of system event triggers (sometimes called *database-level event triggers*), and user event triggers (sometimes called *schema-level event triggers*). You can now place a trigger on system events such as database startup and shutdown, and on user events such as logging on and logging off.

Query Optimization

All of the data structures discussed so far in this chapter are server entities. Users request data from an Oracle server through a database query. Oracle includes two different types of query optimization that determine the best way to access the data requested by a query.

One of the great virtues of a relational database is its ability to access data without predefining the access paths to the data. When a SQL query is submitted to an Oracle8 database, Oracle8 must decide how to access the data. The process of making this decision is called *query optimization*, because Oracle8 looks for the optimal way to retrieve the data. This retrieval is known as the *execution path*. The trick behind query optimization is to choose the most efficient way to get the data, since there may be many different options available.

For instance, even with a query that involves only a single table, Oracle can take either of these approaches:

- Use an index to find the ROWIDs of the requested rows, and then retrieve those rows from the table.

- Scan the table to find and retrieve the rows; this is referred to as a *full table scan.*

Although it's usually much faster to retrieve data using an index, the process of getting the values from the index involves an additional I/O step in processing the query. Query optimization may be as simple as determining whether the query involves selection conditions that can be imposed on values in the index. Rather than retrieving all the data from the table and then imposing the selection conditions, using the index values to select the desired rows would involve less I/O and therefore would perform more efficiently.

Another factor in determining the optimal query execution plan is whether there is an ORDER BY condition in the query that could be automatically implemented by the presorted index. Alternatively, if the table is small enough, the optimizer may decide to simply read all the blocks of the table and bypass the index since it estimates the cost of the index I/O plus the table I/O to be higher than just the table I/O.

The query optimizer has to make some key decisions even with a query on a single table. When a more involved query is submitted, such as one involving many tables that must be joined together efficiently, or one that has a complex selection criteria and multiple levels of sorting, the query optimizer has a much more complex task.

Oracle has had a query optimizer for a long time. In fact, in Oracle8 and Oracle8*i* you may choose between two different query optimizers: a *rule-based optimizer* and a *cost-based optimizer,* which are described in the following sections.

Rule-Based Optimization

Oracle has always had a query optimizer, but until Oracle7, the optimizer was only rule-based. The rule-based optimizer, as the name implies, uses a set of predefined rules as the main determinant of query optimization decisions.

Rule-based optimization is smarter than other random methods of optimization, despite some significant weaknesses. One weakness is the simplistic set of rules. The Oracle8 rule-based optimizer has about twenty rules and assigns a weight to each one of them. In a complex database, a query can easily involve several tables, each with several indexes and complex selection conditions and ordering. This complexity means that there will be a lot of options, and the simple set of rules used by the rule-based optimizer might not make the best choice.

The rule-based optimizer assigns an optimization score to each potential execution path, and then takes the path with the best optimization score. Another main weakness of the rule-based optimizer stems from the way that it resolves optimization choices made in the event of a "tie" score. When two paths present the same optimization score, the rule-based optimizer looks to the syntax of the SQL statement to resolve the tie. The winning execution path is based on the order in which the tables occur in the SQL statement.

You can understand the potential impact of this type of tie-breaker by looking at a simple situation in which a small table with ten rows, SMALLTAB, is joined to a large table with 10,000 rows, LARGETAB, as shown in Figure 4-4. If the optimizer chooses to read SMALLTAB first, the Oracle database will read the ten rows, and then read the LARGETAB table to find the matching rows for all ten rows. If the optimizer chooses to read the LARGETAB first, the database will read 10,000 rows from the LARGETAB table, and then read the SMALLTAB table 10,000 times to find the matching rows. Of course, the rows in SMALLTAB will probably be cached, thus reducing the impact of each probe, but the two optimizer choices still offer a dramatic difference in potential performance.

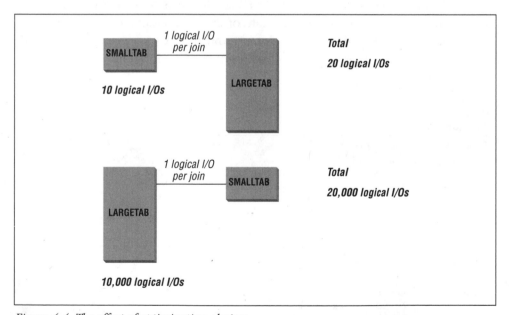

Figure 4-4. The effect of optimization choices

The dramatic differences occur as a result of the ordering of the table names in the query. In the previous situation, the rule-based optimizer returns the same results, but it uses widely varying amounts of resources to retrieve those results, based on the optimizer choice.

Cost-Based Optimization

To improve the optimization of SQL statements, Oracle introduced the *cost-based optimizer* in Oracle7. As the name implies, the cost-based optimizer does more than simply look at a set of optimization rules. It selects the execution path that requires the least number of logical I/O operations. This approach avoids the error discussed in the previous section. After all, the cost-based optimizer would know which table was bigger, and would select the right table to begin the query, regardless of the syntax of the SQL statement.

Oracle8, by default, attempts to use the cost-based optimizer to identify the optimal execution plan. To properly evaluate the cost of any particular execution plan, the cost-based optimizer uses statistics about the composition of the relevant data structures.

Statistics

Just like the rule-based optimizer, the cost-based optimizer finds the optimal execution plan by assigning an optimization score for each of the potential execution plans. However, the cost-based optimizer uses its own internal rules and logic along with *statistics*, which reflect the state of the data structures in the database. These statistics relate to the tables, columns, and indexes involved in the execution plan. The statistics for each type of data structure are listed in Table 4-1.

Table 4-1. Database Statistics

Data Structure	Type of Statistics
Table	Number of rows Number of blocks Number of unused blocks Average available free space per block Number of chained rows Average row length
Column	Number of distinct values per column Second lowest column value Second highest column value Column density factor
Index	Depth of index B*-tree structure Number of leaf blocks Number of distinct values Average number of leaf blocks per key Average number of data blocks per key Clustering factor

These statistics are stored in three tables in the data dictionary, which are described in the final section of this chapter, "Data Dictionary Tables."

You can see that these statistics can be used individually and in combination to determine the overall cost of the I/O required by an execution plan. The statistics reflect not only the size of a table, but also the amount of unused space within the blocks; this space can, in turn, affect how many I/O operations are needed to retrieve rows. The index statistics reflect not only the depth and breadth of the index tree, but also the uniqueness of the values in the tree, which can affect the ease with which values can be selected using the index.

Oracle8 uses the SQL statement ANALYZE to collect these statistics. You can analyze a table, an index, or a cluster in a single SQL statement. Collecting statistics can be a resource-intensive job; in some ways, it's like building an index. Because of its potential impact, the ANALYZE command has two options:

COMPUTE STATISTICS
> Calculates the statistics on the entire data structure

ESTIMATE STATISTICS
> Specifies a number of rows or overall percentage of the data structure for statistical analysis

The latter choice makes gathering the relative statistics for the data structure consume far fewer resources than computing the exact figures for the entire structure. If you have a very large table, for example, analyzing 5 percent or less of the table will probably come up with the same relative percentages of unused space and other relative data.

 The accuracy of the cost-based optimizer totally depends on the accuracy of the statistics it uses, so you should make updating statistics a standard part of your maintenance plan.

The use of statistics makes it possible for the cost-based optimizer to make a much better informed choice of the optimal execution plan. For instance, the optimizer could be trying to decide between two indexes to use in an execution plan that involves a selection based on a value in either index. The rule-based optimizer might very well rate both indexes equally and resort to the order in which they appear in the WHERE clause to choose an execution plan.

The cost-based optimizer, however, knows that one index contains 1,000 entries while the other contains 10,000 entries. It even knows that the index that contains 1,000 values only contains twenty unique values, while the index that contains 10,000 values has 5,000 unique values. The selectivity offered by the larger index is much greater, so that index is assigned a better optimization score and is used correctly for this query.

But even the cost-based optimizer, with all the information available to it, has flaws. Aside from the fact that the cost-based optimizer (like all software) occasionally has bugs, the optimizer uses statistics that don't provide a complete picture of the data structures. In the previous example, the only thing the statistics tell the optimizer about the indexes is the number of distinct values in the index. The statistics don't reveal anything about the distribution of those values. For instance, the larger index can contain 5,000 unique values, but these values can each represent two rows in the associated table, or one index value can represent 5,001 rows while the rest of the index values represent a single row. The selectivity of the index varies wildly, depending on the value used in the selection criteria of the SQL statement. Fortunately, Oracle 7.3 introduced support for collecting histogram statistics for indexes to address this exact problem. You create histograms using syntax within the ANALYZE INDEX command, which is described in your Oracle SQL reference documentation.

Oracle8 gives you two different ways of shaping the operation of the cost-based optimizer. These help to control the selection of the execution plan, as described in the next section.

Influencing the cost-based optimizer

There are two ways you can influence the way the cost-based optimizer selects an execution plan. The first way is by setting the optimizer mode to favor batch-type requests or interactive requests with the ALL_ROWS or FIRST_ROWS choice.

You can set the optimizer mode to weigh the options for the execution plan to either favor ALL_ROWS, meaning the overall time that it takes to complete the execution of the SQL statement, or to favor FIRST_ROWS, meaning the response time for returning the first set of rows from a SQL statement. The optimizer mode tilts the evaluation of optimization scores slightly and, in some cases, may result in a different execution plan. ALL_ROWS and FIRST_ROWS are two of four choices for the optimizer mode, which is described in more detail in the next section.

Oracle8 also gives you a way to completely override the decision of the optimizer with a technique called *hints*. A hint is nothing more than a comment inside a SQL statement with a specific format. There are a variety of hints you can use to force different decisions onto the optimizer, such as:

- Force the use of the rule-based optimizer
- Force the use of a full table scan
- Force the use of a particular index
- Force a specific number of parallel processes for the statement

Hints come with their own set of problems. A hint looks just like a comment, as shown in this extremely simple SQL statement. The hint forces the optimizer to use the EMP_IDX index for the EMP table:

```
SELECT /*+ INDEX(EMP_IDX) */ LASTNAME, FIRSTNAME, PHONE FROM EMP
```

If a hint isn't in the right place in the SQL statement, if the hint keyword is misspelled, or if you change the name of a data structure so that the hint no longer refers to an existing structure, the hint will be simply ignored, just like a comment would be. Because hints are embedded into SQL statements, repairing them can be quite frustrating and time-consuming if they aren't working properly. In addition, if you add a hint to a SQL statement to address a problem caused by a bug in the cost-based optimizer, and the cost-based optimizer is subsequently fixed, the SQL statement is still outside the veil of the optimization calculated by the optimizer.

However, hints do have a place—for example, when a developer has a user-defined datatype that suggests a particular type of access. The optimizer cannot anticipate the effect of user-defined datatypes, but a hint can properly enable the appropriate retrieval path.

For more details about why we don't recommend using hints, see the sidebar "Accepting the Verdict of the Optimizer" later in this chapter.

Choosing a Mode

In the previous section, we've mentioned two optimizer modes: ALL_ROWS and FIRST_ROWS. In fact, there are two other valid optimizer modes:

RULE
> Forces the use of the rule-based optimizer

CHOOSE
> Allows Oracle8 to choose whether to use the cost-based optimizer or the rule-based optimizer

With an optimizer mode of CHOOSE, which is the default setting, Oracle8 will use the cost-based optimizer if any of the tables in the SQL statement have statistics associated with them. The cost-based optimizer will make a statistical estimate for the tables that lack any statistics. It's important to understand that partially collected statistics can cause tremendous problems. If one of the tables in a SQL statement has statistics, Oracle will use the cost-based optimizer. If the optimizer is acting on incomplete information, the quality of optimization will suffer accordingly. If you're going to use the cost-based optimizer, make sure you gather complete statistics for your databases.

You can set the optimizer level at the instance level, the session level, or within an individual SQL statement. But the big question remains, especially for those of you who have been using Oracle since before the introduction of the cost-based optimizer: which optimizer should I choose?

Why choose the cost-based optimizer?

There are several reasons we favor using the cost-based optimizer.

First, the cost-based optimizer makes decisions with a wider range of knowledge about the data structures in the database. Although the cost-based optimizer isn't flawless in its decision-making process, it does tend to make more accurate decisions based on its wider base of information, especially because it has been around since Oracle7 and has been improved with each new release.

Second, the cost-based optimizer has been enhanced to take into account improvements in the Oracle database itself, while the rule-based optimizer has not. For instance, the cost-based optimizer understands the impact that partitioned tables have on the selection of an execution plan, while the rule-based optimizer does not. As another example, the cost-based optimizer can optimize execution plans for star schema queries, which are heavily used in data warehousing, while the rule-based optimizer has not been enhanced to deal effectively with these types of queries.

The reason for this bias is simple: Oracle Corporation has been quite frank about their intention to make the cost-based optimizer *the* optimizer for the Oracle database. Oracle isn't adding new features to the rule-based optimizer, and hasn't guaranteed support for it past the Oracle8*x* releases.

The future lies in the cost-based optimizer. But there are still situations in which you should use the rule-based optimizer.

Why choose the rule-based optimizer?

As the old saying goes, if it ain't broke, don't fix it. And you may be in an environment in which you've designed and tuned your SQL to operate optimally with the rule-based optimizer. Although you still want to look ahead to a future in which only the cost-based optimizer is supported, there may be no reason to switch over to the cost-based optimizer if you have an application that is already performing at its best.

The chances are pretty good that the cost-based optimizer will choose the same execution plan as a properly tuned application using the rule-based optimizer. But there is always a chance that the cost-based optimizer will make a different choice, which can create more work for you, because you might have to spend time tracking down the different optimizations.

Remember the bottom line for all optimizers: no optimizer can provide a performance increase for a SQL statement that's already running optimally. The cost-based optimizer is not a magic potion that remedies the problems brought on by a poor database and application design, or an inefficient implementation platform.

The good news is that Oracle8 lets you use either optimization method to shape, or even override, the way the optimizers do their job..

Saving the Optimization

There may be times when you want to prevent the optimizer from calculating a new plan whenever a SQL statement is submitted. For example, you might do this if you've finally reached a point where you feel that the SQL is already running in an optimal way, and you don't want the plan to change regardless of future changes to the optimizer or the database.

In Oracle8*i*, you can now create a *stored outline* that will store the attributes used by the optimizer to create an execution plan. Once you have a stored outline, the optimizer simply uses the stored attributes to create an execution plan.

Remember that storing an outline fixes the optimization of the outline at the time the outline was stored. Any subsequent improvements to the optimizer will not affect the stored outlines, so you should document your use of stored outlines and consider restoring them with new releases.

Understanding the Execution Plan

Oracle8's query optimizer automatically selects an execution plan for each query submitted. By and large, although both types of optimizer do a good job of selecting the execution plan, there may be times when the performance of the database suggests that it's using a less-than-optimal execution plan.

The only way you can really tell what path is being selected by the optimizer is to see the layout of the execution plan. You can use two Oracle character-mode utilities to examine the execution plan chosen by the Oracle8 optimizer. These tools allow you to see the successive steps used by Oracle8 to collect, select, and return the data to the user.

The first utility is the SQL EXPLAIN PLAN statement. When you use EXPLAIN PLAN, followed by the keyword "FOR" and the SQL statement whose execution plan you want to view, the Oracle8 cost-based optimizer returns a description of the execution plan it will use for the SQL statement and inserts this description into a database table. You can subsequently run a query on that table to get the execution plan, as shown in SQL*Plus in Figure 4-5.

Accepting the Verdict of the Optimizer

Some of you may be doubting the effectiveness of Oracle8 query optimization, especially those of you who encountered bumpy times with the early releases of the cost-based optimizer. You may have seen cases in which the query optimizer chose an incorrect execution path, one that resulted in poor performance. You may feel that you have a better understanding of the structure and use of the database than the query optimizer. For these reasons, you probably include a lot of hints to force the acceptance of the execution path you feel is correct for the cost-based optimizer.

We recommend using the query optimizer for all of your queries, as well as the CHOOSE optimizer mode for the cost-based optimizer when possible. Although the Oracle8 developers who wrote the query optimizer had no knowledge of your particular database, they did depend on a lot of customer feedback, experience, and knowledge of how Oracle8 processes queries during the creation of the query optimizer. They designed the cost-based optimizer to efficiently execute all types of queries that may be submitted to the Oracle database.

In addition, there are three advantages that the query optimizer has over your discretion in all cases:

- The optimizer sees the structure of the entire database. Many Oracle8 databases support many different applications and users, and it's quite possible that your system shares data with other systems, making the overall structure and composition of the data somewhat out of your control. In addition, you have probably designed and tested your systems in a limited environment, so your idea of the optimal execution path may not match the reality of the production environment.

- The optimizer has a dynamically changing view of the database and its data. The statistics used by the cost-based optimizer can change with each new ANALYZE operation. Although the statistics typically don't change the query optimization in more or less steady-state production databases, exceptions to this rule do occur. In addition to the changing statistical conditions, the internal workings of the optimizer are occasionally changed to fix bugs, or to accommodate changes in the way the Oracle database operates. If you force the selection of a particular query plan with a hint, you won't benefit from these changes in Oracle.

—Continued—

- A bad choice by the optimizer may be a sign that something is amiss in your database. For the most part, the query optimizer selects the optimal execution path. What may be seen as a mistake by the query optimizer can, in reality, be traced to a misconception about the database and its design, or to an improper implementation. A mistake is always an opportunity to learn, and you should always take advantage of any opportunity to increase your overall understanding of how Oracle and its optimizer work.

We recommend that you avoid using hints with your queries. The hints syntax was included in Oracle syntax as a way to handle exceptional situations, rather than to allow you to circumvent the query optimizer. If you've found a performance anomaly, and further investigation has led to the discovery that the query optimizer is choosing an incorrect execution path—then, and only then, should you assign a hint to a query.

Even in this situation, we recommend that you keep an eye on the hinted query in a production environment to make sure that the forced execution path is still working optimally.

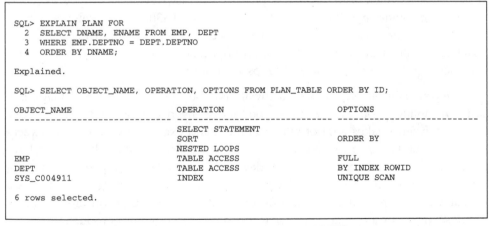

```
SQL> EXPLAIN PLAN FOR
  2   SELECT DNAME, ENAME FROM EMP, DEPT
  3   WHERE EMP.DEPTNO = DEPT.DEPTNO
  4   ORDER BY DNAME;

Explained.

SQL> SELECT OBJECT_NAME, OPERATION, OPTIONS FROM PLAN_TABLE ORDER BY ID;

OBJECT_NAME                 OPERATION                      OPTIONS
-------------------------   ----------------------------   -------------------------
                            SELECT STATEMENT
                            SORT                           ORDER BY
                            NESTED LOOPS
EMP                         TABLE ACCESS                   FULL
DEPT                        TABLE ACCESS                   BY INDEX ROWID
SYS_C004911                 INDEX                          UNIQUE SCAN

6 rows selected.
```

Figure 4-5. Results of a simple EXPLAIN PLAN statement in SQL*Plus

The plan is presented as a series of rows in the table, one for each step taken by Oracle8 in the process of executing the SQL statement. The optimizer also includes some of the information related to its decisions, such as the overall cost of each step and some of the statistics that it used to make its decisions.

The optimizer writes all of this information to a table in the database. By default, the optimizer uses a table called PLAN_TABLE, so you should make sure the table exists before you use EXPLAIN PLAN. (There is a SQL script included with your Oracle8 database that creates the default PLAN_TABLE table: *utlxplan.sql.*) You can specify that EXPLAIN PLAN uses a table other than PLAN_TABLE in the syntax of the statement. For more information about the use of EXPLAIN PLAN, please refer to your Oracle documentation.

There are times when you want to examine the execution plan for a single statement. In such cases, the EXPLAIN PLAN syntax is appropriate. There are other times when you want to look at the plans for a group of SQL statements. For these situations, you can set up a trace for the statements you want to examine and then use the second utility, TKPROF, to give you the results of the trace in a more readable format in a separate file.

You must use the EXPLAIN keyword when you start TKPROF, as this will instruct the utility to execute an EXPLAIN PLAN statement for each SQL statement in the trace file. You can also specify that the results delivered by TKPROF are sorted in a variety of ways. For instance, you can have the SQL statements sorted on the basis of the physical I/Os they used; or sort them on the elapsed time spent on parsing, executing, or fetching the rows; or sort by the total number of rows affected.

The TKPROF utility uses a trace file as its raw material. Trace files are created for individual sessions. You can start either by running the target application with a switch (if it's written with an Oracle product such as Developer) or by explicitly turning it on with an EXEC SQL call or an ALTER SESSION SQL statement in an application written with a 3GL. The trace process, as you can probably guess, can significantly affect the performance of an application, so you should only turn it on when you have some specific diagnostic work to do.

Tuning your SQL statements isn't a trivial task, but with the EXPLAIN PLAN and TKPROF utilities, you can get to the bottom of the decisions made by the cost-based analyzer. It takes a bit of work to understand exactly how to read an execution plan, but it's better to have access to this type of information than not to have any such access. In large-scale system development projects, it's quite common for developers to submit EXPLAIN PLANs for the SQL they're writing to a DBA as a formal step toward completing a form or a report. While time-consuming, this is the best way to ensure that your SQL is tuned before going into production.

Data Dictionary Tables

The main purpose of the data dictionary is to store data that describes the structure of the objects in the Oracle database. Because of this purpose, there are a lot of views in the Oracle data dictionary that provide information about the attributes and composition of the data structures within the database.

All of the views listed in this section actually have three varieties, which are identified by their prefixes:

*DBA_*
> Includes all the objects in the database. A user must have DBA privileges to use this view.

*ALL_*
> Includes all the objects in the database to which a particular user has access. If a user has been granted rights to objects in another user's schema, these objects will appear in this view.

*USER_*
> Includes only the objects in the user's own database schema.

This means that, for instance, there are three views that relate to tables: DBA_ TABLES, ALL_TABLES, and USER_TABLES.

Some of the more common views that directly relate to the data structures are described in Table 4-2.

Table 4-2. Data Dictionary Views About Data Structures

Data Dictionary View Name	Type of Information
ALL_TABLES	Information about the object and relational tables
TABLES	Information about the relational tables
TAB_COMMENTS	Comments about the table structures
TAB_HISTOGRAMS	Statistics about the use of tables
TAB_PARTITIONS	Information about the partitions in a partitioned table
TAB_PRIVS*	Different views detailing all the privileges on a table, the privileges granted by the user, and the privileges granted to the user
TAB_COLUMNS	Information about the columns in tables and views
COL_COMMENTS	Comments about individual columns
COL_PRIVS*	Different views detailing all the privileges on a column, the privileges granted by the user, and the privileges granted to the user
LOBS	Information about large object (LOB) datatype columns
VIEWS	Information about views
INDEXES	Information about the indexes on tables
IND_COLUMNS	Information about the columns in each index
IND_PARTITIONS	Information about each partition in a partitioned index
PART_*	Different views detailing the composition and usage patterns for partitioned tables and indexes
CONS_COLUMNS	Information about the columns in each constraint
CONSTRAINTS	Information about constraints on tables

Table 4-2. Data Dictionary Views About Data Structures (continued)

Data Dictionary View Name	Type of Information
SEQUENCES	Information about sequence objects
SYNONYMS	Information about synonyms
TAB_COL_ STATISTICS	The statistics used by the cost-based analyzer
TRIGGERS	Information about the triggers on tables
TRIGGER_COLS	Information about the columns in triggers

5

Managing Oracle8

Most Oracle users and developers aren't actively aware of all of the system and database management that goes on around them. But effective management is vital to providing a reliable, available, and secure platform that delivers optimal performance. This chapter focuses on how you can manage Oracle in a way that contributes to such an environment. Much of the management responsibility usually falls upon the database administrator. However, users and developers of Oracle also need to be aware of some of the techniques described here.

The DBA is typically responsible for the following management tasks:

- Installing and upgrading the database and options

- Creating tables and indexes

- Creating and managing tablespaces

- Managing control files, online redo logs, archived redo logs, job queues, and server processes

- Creating, monitoring, and tuning data loading procedures

- Adding users and groups, and implementing security procedures

- Implementing backup and recovery plans

- Monitoring database performance and exceptions

- Reorganizing and tuning the database

- Troubleshooting database problems

- Coordinating with Oracle Worldwide Customer Support Services

Particularly in smaller companies, DBAs are also often called upon to take part in database schema design and security planning. DBAs in large enterprises may also help set up replication strategies, disaster and high availability strategies, hierarchical storage management procedures, and the linking of database event monitoring into enterprise network monitors.

All of these tasks come under the heading of managing the database. This chapter explores the major products and issues involved in these tasks:

- Implementing security

- Using Oracle Enterprise Manager (OEM), which performs many database management tasks

- Managing database fragmentation, which can affect database performance

- Performing backup and recovery operations, which are the foundation of database integrity protection

- Working with Oracle Support

You will need an understanding of all of these areas if you're going to design and implement effective management strategies for your own Oracle database environment.

Implementing Security

One of the most important aspects of managing the Oracle database effectively in a multiuser environment is the creation of a security scheme to control the access to, and modification of, the database. You grant security clearance in an Oracle database to individual users or database roles, as described in the following sections.

Security management is typically performed at three different levels:

- Database level

- Operating system level

- Network security level

For example, at the operating system level, DBAs should have the ability to create and delete files related to the database, whereas typical database users should not. Oracle includes operating system-specific security information as part of its standard documentation set. In many large organizations, DBAs or database security administrators work closely with computer system administrators to coordinate security specifications and practices.

Database security specifications control who has database access, and place limits on user capabilities through the use of username/password pairs. Such specifications may limit the allocation of resources (disk and CPU) to users and may also mandate the auditing of users. Database security at the database level further enables the ability to control the access and use of specific schema objects in the database.

Usernames, Privileges, Groups, and Roles

The DBA or database security administrator creates *usernames* to provide valid user identifiers that can be used to connect to the database. Two user accounts are automatically created as part of the installation process and are assigned the DBA role: SYS and SYSTEM. (The DBA role is described later in the section "The DBA Role.")

Each database username has a password associated with it that prevents unauthorized access. Oracle can check to ensure that passwords must:

- Be at least four characters
- Differ from the user ID
- Not match any word on an internal list of simple words
- Differ from the previous password (if there is one) by at least three characters

You can tell Oracle to check for these characteristics each time a password is created or modified.

Once a user has successfully logged in to the database, that user's access is restricted based on *privileges*, which are the rights to execute certain SQL commands. Some privileges may be granted systemwide (such as the ability to delete rows anywhere in the database) or may apply only to a specific schema object in the database (such as the ability to delete rows in a specific table).

Roles are named groups of privileges and may be created, altered, or dropped. In most implementations, the DBA or security administrator creates usernames for users and assigns roles to specific users, thereby granting them a set of privileges. This is increasingly done today through the Oracle Enterprise Manager (OEM) console, which is described in the "Management Through the Oracle Enterprise Manager" section. For example, you might grant a role to provide access to a specific set of applications, such as "human resources," or you might define multiple roles so that certain roles can update hourly pay in the human resources applications, while other roles cannot.

As mentioned in the next section, every database has a pseudo role named PUBLIC that includes every user. All users can use privileges granted to PUBLIC. If database links are created using the keyword PUBLIC, they will be visible to all users who have privileges to the underlying objects for those links and synonym.

Security Privileges

There are four basic security privileges applied to the data in an Oracle database:

- SELECT for query

- INSERT to put rows into tables or views

- UPDATE to update rows in tables or views

- DELETE to remove rows from tables, table partitions, or views

In addition to these data-specific privileges, there are several other privileges that apply to the objects within a database schema:

- CREATE to create a table in a schema

- DROP to remove a table in a schema

- ALTER to alter tables or views

All of these privileges are handled with two simple SQL commands. The GRANT command gives a particular privilege to a user or role, while the REVOKE command takes away a specific privilege. You can use GRANT and REVOKE to modify the privileges for an individual or a role. You can use either of these commands with the keyword PUBLIC to issue a privilege for all database users.

Default Roles

The following default roles come predefined with your Oracle installation. Note, though, that the default roles change with each release, so see the syntax description of GRANT system_privileges_and_roles (included in all the Oracle SQL reference documentation) for a current list of all predefined roles.

CONNECT

Allows you to log into the database, create objects, and perform exports.

RESOURCE

Allows you to create procedures, triggers, and types within the user's own schema area.

DBA

Allows you virtually unlimited privileges (see the next section).

SYSOPER

Allows you to connect to the database remotely and perform a limited set of privileged actions, including starting up and shutting down.

SYSDBA

Very similar to the DBA role. Includes the SYSOPER privilege and all privileges with the ADMIN OPTION. Allows you to connect to the database and remotely perform privileged actions like starting up and shutting down the database.

EXP_FULL_DATABASE

Allows you to perform export activities on any object within the database and record the export activities to the data dictionary.

IMP_FULL_DATABASE

Allows you be become a user so that the user's objects can be imported into the appropriate schema area.

DELETE_CATALOG_ROLE

Allows you to delete rows from the SYS.AUD$ auditing table.

EXECUTE_CATALOG_ROLE

Allows you to execute any exported packages listed in the recovery catalog.

SELECT_CATALOG_ROLE

Allows you to select roles from all exported recovery catalog views and tables.

RECOVERY_CATALOG_OWNER

Allows you to create the owner of a recovery catalog.

SNMPAGENT

Used by the Oracle Enterprise Intelligent Agent.

The DBA Role

The DBA role is one of the most important default roles that comes with Oracle. The DBA role gives all system privileges to users who are members of this role. For example, the DBA role allows a user to perform the following database actions from the command line of SQL*Plus or the Oracle Server Manager (*svrmgrl*), or through the Oracle Enterprise Manager interface:

STARTUP

To start up a database instance.

SHUTDOWN

To shut down a database instance.

ALTER DATABASE OPEN

To open a mounted but closed database.

ALTER DATABASE MOUNT

To mount a database using previously started instance.

ALTER DATABASE BACKUP

To start a backup of the control file, for example. Backups are more frequently done through RMAN today, as described in the "Backup and Recovery" section later in this chapter.

ALTER DATABASE ARCHIVELOG

To specify that the contents of a redo log file group must be archived before the redo log file group can be reused.

ALTER DATABASE RECOVER

To apply logs individually or start automatic application of the redo logs.

CREATE DATABASE

To create and name a database, specify datafiles and their size, specify logfiles and their size, and set parameter limits such as MAXLOGFILES, MAX-DATAFILES, and so on.

RESTRICTED SESSION

To allow connections to databases started in Restricted mode. Restricted mode is designed to keep users out of the database for activities such as troubleshooting or some types of maintenance.

Those with the DBA role will typically assign tablespace quotas to users, set system resources limits, and establish auditing. A DBA can set system resource limits in a user's profile, such as:

- The number of concurrent sessions possible for a user

- The session and SQL call CPU processing time limits

- The amount of logical I/O (logical data block reads) from memory and disk in a session or a single SQL call

- The amount of session idle time allowed

- The amount of session connect time allowed

- Password restrictions, such as account locking after multiple unsuccessful login attempts, password expiration periods, and password-reuse and password-complexity rules

Auditing Security

If you're suspicious about the actions of a particular user and are considering reducing that user's level of privileges, you may want to make use of Oracle's audit capabilities to audit that user's actions at the statement level, privilege level, or schema object level. Auditing can also gather data about database activities for planning and tuning purposes.

You can also audit at the "user" level, which captures some basic but extremely useful statistics like the number of logical I/Os, the number of physical I/Os, and the total time logged on. The overhead for user auditing is quite minimal, since there are only write operations when a user logs on and logs off.

Audit records always contain the following information:

- User name
- Session identifier
- Terminal identifier
- Name of schema object accessed
- Operation performed or attempted
- Completion code of the operation
- Date and timestamp
- System privileges used

The records may be stored in a data dictionary table (AUD$ in the SYS schema) which is also called the database audit trail, or in an operating system audit trail.

To turn on auditing, the AUDIT_TRAIL parameter must be set in the *INIT.ORA* file. To generate audit information, you must set this parameter and specify the desired auditing options with the AUDIT command. A typical use of the AUDIT command is the auditing of a specific schema object (a table) for a certain action (UPDATE) to see who has been modifying that table.

View-Based Security

You can think of views as virtual tables defined by queries that extract or derive data from physical "base" tables. Because you can use them to create different representations of the data to different groups of users, you can use views to present only the rows or columns that a certain group of users should be able to access.

For example, in a human resources application, users from the HR department may have full access to the employee base table, which contains basic information such as employee names, work addresses, and work phone numbers, as well as more restricted information such as Social Security numbers, home addresses, and home telephone numbers. For other users in the company, you'll want to hide more personal information by providing a view that shows only the basic information.

Fine-Grained Access Control

Implementing security can be a very time-consuming process, especially if you want to base security on an attribute with a wide range of values. A good example of this type of situation in the human resources scenario previously described would be the need to limit the data an HR representative can see to only the rows relating to employees that he supports. Here you're faced with a situation in which you might have to define a view for every HR representative, which might mean *many* different views. And if you want to grant write access for a representative's own employees and read access for other employees, the situation gets even more complex. The smaller scope, or grain, of the access control you desire, the more work is involved in creating and maintaining the security privileges.

Oracle8*i* offers a new type of security that you can use to grant this type of fine-grained access control (FGAC). *Security policies* (implemented as PL/SQL functions) can be associated with tables or views. A security policy returns a condition that's dynamically associated with a particular SQL statement, which transparently limits the data that's returned. In the HR example, suppose that each representative supports employees with a last name in a particular alphabetic range, such as A through G. The security policy would return a WHERE clause, based on a particular representative's responsibilities, which limited the rows returned. You can keep the range for each representative in a separate table that would be dynamically queried as part of the security policy function.

You can associate a security policy with a particular view or table by using a PL/SQL package, which also allows you to refresh, enable, or disable a security policy.

Fine-grained security can also implement security based on the type of SQL statement issued. The security policy previously described could be used to limit UPDATE, INSERT, and DELETE operations to one set of data, but allow SELECT operations on a different group of data.

For a good description of FGAC through PL/SQL, see Steven Feuerstein's book *Oracle PL/SQL Programming: Guide to Oracle8i Features* (O'Reilly & Associates).

Security and Applications

Applications may involve data and logic in many different schemas with many different privileges. To simplify the issues raised by this complexity, roles are frequently used in applications. Application roles have all of the privileges necessary to run the applications, and users of the applications are granted the roles necessary to execute them.

Application roles may contain privileges that should be granted to users only while they're running the application. Application developers can place a SET ROLE command at the beginning of an application to enable the appropriate role and disable others only while the application is running. Similarly, you can invoke a DBMS_SESSION.SET_ROLE procedure from PL/SQL, but not from a stored procedure.

Another way application security is sometimes accomplished is by encapsulating privileges in stored procedures. Instead of granting direct access to the various tables for an application, you can create stored procedures that provide access to the tables and grant access to the stored procedures instead of the tables. For example, instead of granting INSERT privileges for the EMPLOYEE table, you might create and grant access to a stored procedure called HIRE_EMPLOYEE that accepts as parameters all the data for a new employee.

When you run a stored procedure, the procedure has the access rights that were granted to the owner of the procedure; that owner is the schema in which the procedure resides. If a particular schema has access to a particular database object, all stored procedures that reside in that schema have the same rights as the schema. When any user calls one of those stored procedures, that user has the same access rights to the underlying data objects as the procedure does.

For example, suppose there is a schema called HR_REP. This schema has write access to the EMP table. Any stored procedure in the HR_REP schema also has write access to the EMP table. Consequently, if you grant a user access to a stored procedure in the HR_REP schema, that user will also have access to the EMP table—regardless of his personal level of security privilege, but only through the stored procedures in the schema.

One small but vitally important caveat applies to access through stored procedures: the security privilege must be *directly* granted to the schema, not granted by means of a role.

In Oracle8*i*, if you attach the keyword AUTHID CURRENT_USER to a stored procedure when it's compiled, security restrictions will be enforced based on the user name of the user *invoking* the procedure, rather than the schema that owns the stored procedure (the definer of the procedure). If a user has access to a particular database object with a particular privilege, that user will have the same access through stored procedures compiled with the AUTHID CURRENT_USER.

Distributed Database and Multitier Security

All of the security features available for undistributed Oracle databases are also available for the distributed database environment, which is covered in Chapter 12, *Distributed Databases and Distributed Data*. However, the distributed database environment introduces additional security considerations. For example, user accounts needed to support server connections must exist in all of the distributed databases forming the system. As database links (which define connections between distributed database instances) are created, you will need to allow the user accounts and roles needed at each site.

For large implementations, you may want to configure global authentication across these distributed databases for users and roles. Global authentication allows you to maintain a single authentication list for multiple distributed databases. Where this type of external authentication is required, Oracle's Advanced Security Option, discussed in the next section, provides a solution.

In a typical three-tier implementation, the Oracle Application Server runs some of the application logic and serves as an interface between the clients and database servers. Security of the middle-tier applications is controlled by limiting the applications' privileges and preserving client identities through all three tiers.

In this scenario, the application server validates a client through a login and password procedure, or through the use of a Lightweight Directory Access Protocol (LDAP) directory. The application server then authenticates itself to the database server. The database server checks the application server's authentication, verifies that the username of the client is valid, and ensures that the application server has the privileges necessary to connect for this client. The application server can also enable roles for the client, obtained from a directory, on behalf of a client for whom it is connecting. The database server has the ability to audit operations performed by the application server, including those on behalf of the client.

Advanced Security Option

The Oracle Advanced Security Option (ASO), formerly known as the Advanced Networking Option (ANO), is used in distributed environments linked via Net8 in which there are concerns regarding secure access and transmission of data. This option specifically provides data encryption during transmission to protect data from unauthorized viewing; it also provides support for a variety of identity authentication methods to ensure that user identities are accurately known.

The ASO implements network data encryption, which turns data into an encrypted form during transmission to ensure data privacy. The option supports the RSA Data Security's RC4 algorithm and the Data Encryption Standard (DES) algorithm: encryption algorithms, based on various key lengths, may encrypt data either for native transmissions through Net8 or through web application server support of the Secure Sockets Layer (SSL).

Authentication methods supported by the Advanced Security Option include the following:

RADIUS (Remote Authentication Dial-In User Service) support
> Synchronous mode support of passwords, SecureID token cards, smartcards, and challenge-response asynchronous authentication

Biometric support using the Identix Biometric Authentication Adapter
> Includes a repository of stored fingerprint templates that are compared to templates transmitted from a fingerprint reader for authentication

X.509 v3 digital certificates issued by a certificate authority
> Contains a created public key and entity name, serial number, and certificate expiration date

You can use a number of additional third-party authentication services, including Kerberos, public key with SSL, and the Distributed Computing Environment (DCE). Digital certificates, Kerberos, and DCE also support single sign-on, or the ability to log in once and have access to multiple accounts and system resources. Authentication is set up via the Net8 Assistant interface or through text-based editing of the *SQLNET.ORA* file. You can deploy networks with different authentication methods for clients and servers.

Here's a typical scenario utilizing the various Oracle security features. The Oracle Enterprise Security Manager, accessible through the Oracle Enterprise Manager, configures valid users to Oracle8*i* servers (via SSL) and in Oracle's LDAP-compliant Internet Directory server. An X.509 certificate authority creates private key pairs and publishes them in Oracle wallets (through Oracle Wallet Manager) to the LDAP directory. When a user wants to log in to a database server, he will need a certificate and private key which can be retrieved from his password-protected wallet residing in the LDAP directory. When the user's key on the client device is sent to the database server, it's matched with the paired key retrieved by the server via SSL from the LDAP directory and the user is authenticated to use the database.

Management Through the Oracle Enterprise Manager

Each new set of Oracle features requires corresponding management capabilities. For instance, the addition of database partitions to Oracle not only provides more capabilities, but requires additional management functions to ride herd on these capabilities. This ever-increasing feature curve can require a fairly steep learning curve on the part of the novice. To ease this learning curve, Oracle has recently provided more intuitive management of these features through the Oracle Enterprise Manager (OEM).

The Oracle Enterprise Manager provides both a standard graphical interface across multiple platforms and a framework that can support a variety of different monitoring tools. The growth of combined Microsoft Windows NT and Unix deployment of Oracle, in particular, has resulted in many DBAs using the single OEM interface to access Oracle instances residing on multiple operating systems. Today, you can deploy the OEM standard console to a browser-based client, further adding to its flexibility.

The OEM framework provides a standard user interface and includes standard components for performing many of the basic tasks that a DBA must perform, including:

- Instance management—starting up or shutting down database instances, managing database initialization parameters, saving configurations, resolving in-doubt transactions, and managing user sessions

- Security management—creating and changing users, roles, privileges, user profiles, and passwords

- Schema management for examining tables, indexes, and views

- Storage management of tablespaces, rollback segments, redo logs, and datafiles

- Direct entry of SQL statements, PL/SQL, or server manager commands through the SQL Worksheet

- Event monitoring with notification based on administrators' predefined thresholds

- Job scheduling and execution

- Backup and recovery through wizards linked to the Recovery Manager utility provided with the database

- Replication monitoring, modification, and integration with the Oracle Replication Manager

- Monitoring of Oracle Parallel Server environments

Oracle Enterprise Manager Architecture

Oracle started distributing the Oracle Enterprise Manager as part of the database in Oracle7. The initial OEM versions required Windows 95, Windows 98, or Windows NT workstations as client machines.

OEM 2.0, which became available with Oracle8*i*, introduces a thin client version of the OEM Console that can run in any standard browser. OEM in Oracle8*i* is comprised of a number of different components:

Intelligent Agents
These agents monitor databases and services on remote nodes. An Intelligent Agent can both monitor the database and services on a remote node and communicate the results of this monitoring back to OEM.

Console(s)
For viewing the status of database components.

Management Server

> This server, located in the middle tier, provides an interface between the console clients and managed nodes.

Common services

> These include a multiuser repository, automatic services discovery, a job scheduling system, an event management system, and security. The repository stores information of interest to administrators—for example, permissions data. Also stored in the repository is information about services that have been discovered, jobs, events, and security settings.

The OEM architecture is shown in Figure 5-1.

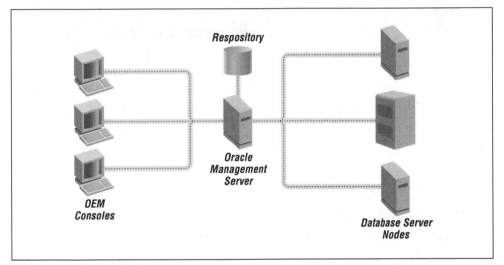

Figure 5-1. Oracle Enterprise Manager architecture

Oracle Enterprise Manager Console

Because the Oracle Enterprise Manager is one of your most important tools, we'll take a little time to explain how it works. For details, consult your Oracle OEM documentation.

The OEM console interface, shown in Figure 5-2, is divided into four panes: the Navigator pane, the Group pane, the Events pane, and the Jobs pane.

Navigator pane

> The Navigator pane, by default displayed in the upper-left corner of the OEM, displays all discovered objects on the network, such as databases, groups, listeners, and nodes, as a hierarchical tree.

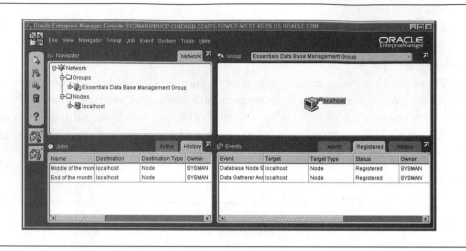

Figure 5-2. The OEM user interface for Oracle8i

Group pane

The Group pane, by default displayed in the upper-right corner of the OEM, displays discovered objects and their status determined by the event management system, on a map.

Events pane

The Events pane, by default displayed in the lower-right corner of the OEM, provides an interface to the event management system enabling the monitoring of the Oracle environment for problems such as loss of service, lack of available storage, or high CPU utilization.

Jobs pane

The Jobs pane, by default displayed in the lower-left corner of the OEM, provides a user interface to the job scheduling system. You can use this system to schedule operating system or SQL commands on remote systems in the network. Jobs can be comprised of one or more tasks. Once submitted from the console, the Management Server stores the job and places it in a queue. If the target node is up, the job is sent to the node and is accepted by its Intelligent Agent, which then executes the job whenever it's scheduled. If the node isn't up, the job remains in the queue until the node is alive and can be sent to the Intelligent Agent. Once executed, the Intelligent Agent sends any related job messages back to the Management Server for display at the appropriate console.

OEM Intelligent Agents are available for the wide variety of operating systems on which the Oracle database is available and are responsible for automatic service discovery and event monitoring, in addition to job execution on remote nodes. Intelligent Agents can also send Simple Network Management Protocol (SNMP) traps to network monitors such as CA Unicenter, IBM Tivoli, and HP OpenView.

Through the Agents, OEM can be used to manage Oracle databases running on Unix, NT, and many other operating systems.

Oracle Enterprise Manager Tools

OEM includes tools that perform the most common administrative tasks. Located on the OEM menu, the tools and tasks include the following:

Oracle Instance Manager
> For starting up and shutting down the database, viewing and editing initialization parameters, resolving in-doubt transactions, managing user sessions, and monitoring long-running operations.

Oracle Schema Manager
> For creating, altering, or dropping schema objects such as clusters, indexes, snapshots, tables, and views. Also for managing partitioned tables and indexes, advanced queues, and Java stored procedures.

Oracle Security Manager
> For managing users, roles, passwords, and profiles, which set limits on a user's database resources.

Directory-enabled Oracle Security Manager
> For managing user security using an LDAP directory server.

Oracle Storage Manager
> For administering tablespaces, datafiles, redo logs, and rollback segments.

Oracle SQL Worksheet
> For using SQL, PL/SQL, and SQL*Plus commands to administer the database.

Backup wizard
> For backing up databases, tablespaces, datafiles, and archive logs.

Recovery wizard
> For restoring and recovering a database, tablespaces, and datafiles.

Export wizard
> For extracting Oracle database data to a binary file.

Import wizard
> For importing data into an Oracle database from a binary file generated by an Oracle export from an Oracle database.

Load wizard
> For loading data from operating system files (such as text) to an Oracle database.

Oracle Replication Manager

> For setting up, configuring, and managing replication, including multimaster and snapshot replication.

Oracle Application Manager

> For managing Oracle Applications Concurrent Managers; used with the Oracle Applications vertical packages.

Oracle Parallel Server Management

> For discovering and managing Oracle Parallel Server databases. This option is available only if you're using Oracle Parallel Server.

Oracle8i interMedia Text Manager

> For managing and searching for text in an Oracle database. This option is available only if you have the *inter*Media option installed as part of your Oracle database.

Options for Oracle Enterprise Manager

The standard Oracle Enterprise Manager package provides a wealth of management options for your Oracle database. But one of the virtues of OEM is its extensibility, which allows additional services to be integrated into the OEM framework.

Oracle offers a number of additional option packs that can work through the OEM console. Many of these options may be applicable only for managing Oracle Enterprise Edition instances; we've noted any restrictions in the following sections.

Diagnostics Pack Option

The Diagnostics Pack is an option for Oracle Enterprise Manager that is used for monitoring, performing diagnostics, and planning in conjunction with Oracle Enterprise Edition. It consists of five basic components:

Performance monitor

> The performance monitor provides graphical views used in monitoring system and database resources. The views are refreshed at timed intervals that the DBA can select. Among the predefined groups of charts which can be viewed are database contention, I/O load, memory usage, database instance and operating system metrics, and parallel server performance. You can use diagnostics charts to further determine sessions or applications that are causing problems. In addition to these predefined charts, DBAs can create their own custom charts to view data gathered via SQL or the data collection framework. You can also record data viewed in charts for playback later.

Automated data collection and capacity planner

> The Diagnostics Pack includes the ability to perform automated data collection for a standard set of statistics. DBAs can also define additional perfor-

mance statistics to gather together. Collected data is stored in a historical database, which is loaded and stored in the database for periods defined by the DBA. A capacity planning feature predicts performance and resource use over time based on trends.

Advanced events monitor

The events monitor can watch more than 40 predefined events through the event management system. The event management system uses Intelligent Agents to monitor performance, space management, and resource utilization on remote systems and to react to problems occurring on those systems. DBAs typically set thresholds for issuing warnings and alerts as well as monitoring intervals. Severity levels indicated on the object severity flag in the Event pane and the object in the Group pane are the following:

- Alert cleared (green)

- Warning (yellow)

- Critical (red)

- Unknown (grey).

You can create "fixit" jobs through the OEM job management system to automatically take corrective action whenever an alert is issued.

"Top Sessions" resource utilization monitor

The "Top Sessions" chart is a handy way to rapidly determine which sessions are using the greatest amounts of resources. If you're running into a performance problem because database resources are growing short, this chart can help you quickly identify potential culprits. The top sessions are identified based on factors such as resource utilization, open cursors, and user transactions. DBAs select the criteria and polling intervals and can see database session identifications, database usernames, operating system user names, and applications. Through the interface, the DBA can terminate sessions causing excessive resource problems, or can simply drill down into the session to view more detailed statistics.

Trace facility

The trace facility provides an application programming interface (API) to build applications for collecting precise database event statistics whenever a key event occurs within the application. Oracle8 includes support for tracing logical and physical database transactions, database waits, SQL events, resource utilization, and SQL plan details for statements as they are executed. Oracle instances with trace definition files are discovered automatically from the OEM console running the Trace Manager. Because tracing can present an overwhelming amount of data, you can use the Trace Data Viewer to sort through the data so the DBA can extract and aggregate significant metrics and get to the bottom of the problem.

Tuning Pack Option

The Tuning Pack is an OEM option that helps DBAs collect, evaluate, and tune Oracle Enterprise Edition databases. It consists of the following features:

Expert utility

   Captures performance statistics during a period of time. Using Expert, you select a period of time that has the usage characteristics for which you wish to tune the instance, application, or database. Once this data is gathered, an inference engine in the tool makes suggestions aimed at improving database performance. If the DBA accepts such recommendations, scripts can be automatically generated and applied to the database.

Index tuning wizard

   Generates recommendations for optimal use of indexes.

SQL Analyze utility

   Analyzes and tunes inefficient SQL statements based on measured parameters specified by the DBA. Statements can be identified as to whether the cost-based or rule-based optimizer is used. The execution path is viewed via an execution plan. DBAs can walk through the execution of the statement step-by-step, and can test performance for various optimizer modes. (The basics of SQL optimization and execution plans were covered in Chapter 4, *Data Structures.*)

Auto Analyze utility

   Automates the collection of optimizer statistics for the database schema. The cost-based optimizer uses the statistics to determine the most efficient execution plan. Without statistics that adequately reflect the current state of the database, you can't expect the cost-based optimizer to make the appropriate decisions. With Oracle8*i*, the Auto Analyze function collects the statistics in parallel, which can significantly improve the speed of this function.

Tablespace Usage Monitor

   Provides a graphical view of tablespace details. This monitor lets you gain more efficient space usage by allowing you to reorganize tables and indexes that can, in turn, result in better database performance. Typically, the Tablespace Usage Monitor evaluates the following types of potential problems: migrated or continued rows, stagnated indexes, nonlinear extent growth, inefficient extent settings, and objects approaching maximum extent settings. For more information about fragmentation and its dangers, see the "Fragmentation and Reorganization" section later in this chapter.

Change Management Pack Option

The Change Management Pack option, as the name implies, helps manage changes to Oracle Enterprise Edition databases. Servers and objects can be difficult to manage, particularly when there are many separate instances of Oracle running in your environment. The Change Management Pack provides these tools for tracking and implementing changes:

DB Plan Manager
    An interface to all of the Change Management Pack utilities.

DB Capture
    Captures the current database schema, objects, and database definitions and sets a baseline for future comparisons.

DB Diff
    Compares two current databases or a current database to a baseline.

Quick Change
    Guides the DBA through changes to a single definition of a database object.

DB Alter
    Guides the DBA through changes to one or more objects in one or more databases.

DB Propagate
    Selects one or more object definitions and propagates those definitions to one or more target databases. You might use this tool to clone tables and data to one or more sites and reproduce database object definitions.

DB Search
    Locates objects based on characteristics of their names.

These tools are invaluable in larger installations; you can also use them in environments that contain only a few Oracle databases.

Standard Management Pack Option for Oracle8i

Companies using Oracle8*i* rather than the Enterprise Edition may need more advanced features for database management than those provided by the basic OEM framework. As we mentioned earlier, many OEM options are supported by Oracle only for use with Enterprise Edition databases. Oracle has packaged a subset of the capabilities discussed in a pack specifically for non-Enterprise Edition database installations, and now offers this option as the Standard Management Pack for Oracle8*i*.

This pack includes the ability to capture, filter, and present performance data via a GUI. The pack also includes performance monitoring tools, such as the ability to examine database contention, I/O, load, memory use, and various database instance metrics. It's also possible to drill down into more detailed data behind the charts.

The Standard Management Pack can help determine which database user sessions are having the greatest impact on database performance, based on user database resource utilization, the number of open cursors, user transactions, and block changes. You can drill down further into cache processing, redo activity, locks, and SQL (including explain plans) on a session-by-session basis. DBAs have the option of terminating sessions that are having the biggest impact on performance.

Other features of this pack include wizard-driven index tuning and database schema change investigation and tracking. The change investigation and tracking is enabled through the DB Capture and DB Diff tools (described in the previous section "Change Management Pack Option").

Management Pack Options for Oracle Applications and SAP

In 1999, Oracle planned the first release of the Management Packs for Oracle Applications and for SAP, two of the most popular enterprise resource planning (ERP) applications. These massive applications have a solid foundation in the Oracle database. The packs make OEM "aware" of these applications so OEM can monitor them.

For Oracle Applications, the OEM will automatically discover Concurrent Managers and Oracle Forms Servers. You can launch an applet that provides a subset of the Oracle Applications system administration interface. The Management Pack for Oracle Applications includes additional features that allow you to monitor applications-related events, monitor the Concurrent Managers through the Performance Manager, and automatically gather data from the Concurrent Managers for resource consumption analysis, capacity planning, and trend analysis.

For SAP R/3, the OEM console recognizes R/3 application servers, events, and jobs. The Performance Manager recognizes multiple R/3 instances, automates data gathering for resource consumption and capacity trending analysis, and handles specific SAP R/3 events such as buffer quality, response time of dialog work processes, and the sizes of rollback area, page area, and extended memory.

Fragmentation and Reorganization

Fragmentation is a problem that may negatively impact performance—and one that many DBAs struggle to manage. Fragmentation is the "free space" that appears between filled extents when data is deleted.

There are many types of fragmentation:

- Segment fragmentation (i.e., segments consisting of multiple extents)

- Tablespace free space fragmentation (i.e., chunks of free space between a segment's extents)

- Row fragmentation (i.e., a row residing in multiple blocks)

- Index leaf block fragmentation (i.e., leaf blocks with holes)

- Data block fragmentation (i.e., data block holes)

This section discusses some common misunderstandings about fragmentation and offers some tips on how to minimize the fragmentation issues DBAs typically focus on: segment fragmentation, free space fragmentation, and index fragmentation.

Segments and Multiple Extents

As mentioned in Chapter 2, *Oracle8 Architecture*, Oracle manages disk space as a collection of datafiles (grouped into tablespaces) which represent the disk space Oracle can utilize. A collection of contiguous blocks is referred to as an *extent*. A collection of extents is referred to as a *segment*. Segments can contain anything that takes up space—for example, a table, an index, or a rollback segment. Segments typically consist of multiple extents. As one extent fills up, a segment begins to use another extent. As fragmentation occurs, by database activity that leaves "holes" in the contiguous space represented by extents, segments acquire additional extents.

As of Oracle 7.3, a table (and any other object that can occupy a segment) can have an unlimited number of extents. This was not intended to result in tables with thousands of extents, but rather to avoid "hitting the ceiling" of the total number of extents, as specified by the MAXEXTENTS parameter,[*] forcing a segment rebuild. DBAs should still set a ceiling on extents for control purposes, but you can bump up that ceiling as needed, with appropriate increases in the extent allocation size. In this way, you may be able to avoid a reorganization. Despite this flexibility, many DBAs view a large number of extents as a direct cause of performance problems and don't like allowing a segment's extent count to grow, opting instead for frequent reorganizations.

In fact, one of the more popular reasons cited for a reorganization is that a table has grown into multiple extents and needs to be rebuilt into fewer extents or, in many cases, into a single extent.

---

[*] The MAXEXTENTS parameter, like all storage parameters, can be set for the complete system, for an individual tablespace, or for a specific object in the tablespace. Each higher level of specification acts as the default for the lower level, the system value for the tablespace, and the tablespace value for the individual objects.

The usual way to reorganize a table is to export the table, drop it, and import it, which makes the data unavailable while the table is in the process of being reorganized. Many DBAs claim that they see improved performance after reorganizing segments into a single extent. Over time, DBAs see a decrease in performance as the number of extents the table occupies increases. When the table is reorganized again, DBAs again see increased performance.

In fact, performance does increase from the export/import, but this improvement is *not* due to a decrease in the number of extents. When a table is dropped and recreated, several things happen that increase performance:

- Each block is loaded as full of rows as possible.

- As a consequence, the high-water mark of the table (explained later) gets set to its lowest point.

- All indexes on the table get rebuilt, which means that the index blocks are as full as possible. The depth of the index, which determines the number of I/Os it takes to get to the leaf blocks or the index, is minimized.

The high-water mark of a table is the highest block that has ever had data in it. In a busy online transaction processing (OLTP) system, there are typically blocks below the high-water mark that have empty space in them due to row deletions and updates. These "Swiss cheese" blocks contain wasted space resulting in I/O resources being wasted while reading this empty space.

The export/import process fills every block with rows, which removes the Swiss cheese pattern and helps improve I/O performance. Over time, though, the pattern creeps back in. A subsequent reorganization repeats the cycle. Because of this phenomenon, DBAs have drawn the conclusion that reorganizations into one extent help performance. In fact, the number of extents was not the performance issue; instead, the performance improvement is due to the reduction in empty space within the blocks.

If you properly set the table storage parameters PCTFREE and PCTUSED, you'll reduce the Swiss cheese effect by limiting the empty space and maximizing the rows found in blocks below the high-water mark. If the usage patterns of a table change, you can change these parameters using the ALTER TABLE command.

Free Space Fragmentation

The free space within a tablespace is managed in contiguous ranges of blocks within the tablespace's datafiles. As segments are added and dropped within a tablespace, there may be free space "trapped" in bubbles between various extents.

Segments allocate extents based on their INITIAL, NEXT, and PCTINCREASE parameters in the STORAGE clause of the CREATE TABLESPACE command.

INITIAL specifies the size of the first extent and NEXT specifies the size of the second extent. PCTINCREASE is used to increase the size of the third and subsequent extents. The third extent will be NEXT * (1 + PCTINCREASE); the fourth will be the size of the third extent inflated by PCTINCREASE, and so on.

For example, suppose that a table is created using one extent of 40 KB. As it grows, Oracle allocates nine additional extents of 40 KB for a total of 400 KB. These 40 KB extents are spread throughout the datafiles for the tablespace because the extents were not allocated at one time. In between their allocations, other segments used some space. When the table is dropped, there are ten 40 KB free space bubbles. If a table requires a 400 KB extent, it cannot use the ten 40 KB bubbles because they are not contiguous. One of the other reasons cited for reorganizations is to reclaim free space within the datafile(s) of a tablespace by "packing" all the segments into contiguous extents and freeing the free space trapped between them.

You can set the parameters for each individual segment, or you can simply allow a segment to be created without specific values, which will cause the segment to inherit the default values for the tablespace in which the segment is created. Setting the tablespace-level default storage parameters intelligently is an effective and simple way to manage extent sizing for segments and to avoid management issues for free space.

There are differing views about whether managing segment-specific storage parameters is an effective use of time. Some DBAs think that it's easier to simply set up tablespaces as small, medium, and large (based on the objects they will contain) and to set the default parameters accordingly. The specific values for small, medium, and large tablespaces will be a function of your database size and schema complexity.

Oracle8*i* introduced locally managed tablespaces. Such a tablespace manages its own extents by maintaining a bitmap in each datafile to keep track of the free or used status of blocks. Locally managed tablespaces automatically allocate uniform extents to minimize free space fragmentation.

Other DBAs would rather assign data objects to tablespaces based on other criteria, such as the need to back up a tablespace individually, so they find that managing segment-specific storage parameters is the lesser of two evils. Typically, as the number of objects grows, the greater the overhead to manage specific segment information for each object.

Research from Oracle has resulted in a set of standards that simplify space management for segments and can help prevent free space fragmentation. These standards are based on an excellent research paper by Bhaskar Himatsingka and Juan

Loaiza of Oracle Corporation entitled "How to Stop Defragmenting and Start Living: The Definitive Word on Fragmentation," which is listed in the Appendix.

Index Fragmentation

Indexes can become fragmented due to repeated changes to the underlying table. The typical solution is to reorganize the indexes by performing an index rebuild. Oracle gives you the ability to rebuild an index by itself. While the rebuild is occurring, you can use the index for queries but it cannot be updated, thus limiting the use of the underlying table for transactions.

Oracle8*i* can rebuild an index online without limits on transactional usage of the underlying table. Oracle8*i* also features the ability to perform an in-place coalescing of the index to defragment the index and reclaim free space trapped in the index blocks as a result of deletions and updates to the table.

Index organized tables (IOTs), which are tables in which the data is held in the associated index, were introduced with Oracle8. As of Oracle8*i*, you can move and reorganize IOTs online.

Backup and Recovery

This section provides only a very brief overview of standard backup and recovery options. For much more detailed information about backup and recovery options, refer to Chapter 10, *Oracle8 and High Availability*.

Even though you've taken adequate precautions, critical database records may sometimes be destroyed as a result of user error or hardware or software failure. The only way to prepare for this type of potentially disastrous situation is to perform regular backup operations.

There are two basic types of potential failures that can affect an Oracle database: *instance failure*, in which the Oracle instance terminates without going through the shutdown process, and *media failure*, in which the disks that store the information in an Oracle database are corrupted or damaged.

After an instance failure, Oracle will automatically perform crash recovery; you can use Oracle Parallel Server to automatically perform instance recovery when one of its instances crashes. However, DBAs must initiate recovery from media failure. The ability to recover successfully from this type of failure is one of the greatest challenges a DBA faces—it's also the place where the value of the DBA becomes most apparent! The recovery process includes restoring older copies of the damaged datafile(s) and rolling forward by applying archived and online redo logs.

To ensure successful recovery, the DBA should have prepared for this eventuality by performing the following actions:

- Multiplexing online redo logs by having multiple log members per group on different disks and controllers

- Running the database in ARCHIVELOG mode so that redo log files are archived before they are reused

- Archiving redo logs to multiple locations

- Maintaining multiple copies of the control file

- Backing up physical datafiles frequently—ideally, storing multiple copies in multiple locations

Running the database in ARCHIVELOG mode ensures that you can recover the database up to the time of the media failure; in this mode, the DBA can perform online datafile backups while the database is available for use. In addition, archived redo logs can be sent to a standby database (explained in Chapter 10) in which they may be applied.

Types of Backup and Recovery Options

There are two major categories of backups:

Full backups
> Includes backups of datafiles, datafile copies, tablespaces, control files (current or backup), or the entire database (including all datafiles and the current control file). Reads the entire file and copies all blocks into the backup set, skipping only datafile blocks that have never been used (with the exception of control files and redo logs where no blocks are skipped).

Incremental backups
> Includes backups of datafiles, tablespaces, or the whole database. Reads the entire file and backs up only those data blocks that have changed since a previous backup.

You can begin backups through the Recovery Manager (RMAN) or the OEM GUI interface to RMAN, which uses the database export facility, or initiate them via standard operating system backup utilities. RMAN was introduced with Oracle8 and replaces the Enterprise Backup Utility (available for some previous Oracle7 releases). In general, RMAN supports the most database backup features, including open or online backups, closed database backups, incremental backups at the Oracle block level, corrupt block detection, automatic backups, backup catalogs, and backups to sequential media. Backups of the *INIT.ORA* and password files must be made through operating system backup utilities.

Recovery options include the following:

- Complete database recovery to the point of failure

- Tablespace point-in-time recovery (recovery of a tablespace to a time different from the rest of the database)

- Time-based or point-in-time database recovery (recovery of the entire database to a time before the most current time)

- Recovery until the CANCEL command is issued

- Change-based or log sequence recovery (to a specified System Change Number, or SCN)

You can recover through the use of RMAN (utilizing the recovery catalog or control file), or via SQL or SQL*Plus.

Making Sure the Backup Works

The key to providing an adequate backup and recovery strategy is to simulate recovery from failure using the backups from your test system before going live in production. Many times, backup media that were thought to be reliable prove not to be, or backup frequencies that were thought to be adequate prove to be too infrequent to allow for timely recoveries. It's far better to discover that recovery is slow or impossible in test situations than after your business has been impacted by the failure of a production system.

Additional Backup Capabilities

A number of Oracle Backup Solutions Program (BSP) partners certify their products to perform backup and recovery to disk and tape storage devices using RMAN. Many of these third parties can reduce the overall time it takes to perform a backup by taking advantage of the parallelism of the Oracle database. One BSP partner, Legato, includes the Legato Storage Manager (LSM) tape storage management product at no charge with Oracle8 releases on popular Unix (AIX, HP/UX, Solaris) and NT platforms. The LSM's capabilities include the following:

- Media management, including tape labeling, media tracking, and retention policy management

- Ability to use up to four locally connected tape drives for concurrent read or write

- Installation integrated into the Oracle installer

- Support through Oracle Worldwide Customer Support Services

There are some limitations when using LSM. The product doesn't support networked backups; it only provides support for a limited number of tape devices; and it doesn't support robotic libraries or operating system file backups. Legato offers optional products providing additional backup capabilities.

Other Oracle BSP partners include Cheyenne ARCServe, EMC EDM, HP Omniback, IBM ADSM, Openvision Netbackup, Spectralogic Alexandria, Sun Networker OEM, and Veritas. Check with these vendors about their current certification in support of Oracle's Media Management Interface Library (MML), the interface to RMAN.

Working with Oracle Support

Regardless of the extent of your training, there are bound to be some issues that you can't resolve without help from Oracle. Part of the job of the DBA is to help resolve any issues with the Oracle database. Oracle offers several levels of support. These are currently termed "Oracle Metals," since increasing levels of support are named after increasingly valuable metals: Gold, Platinum, and so on. All of these support options cost extra, but regardless of your support level, you can get the most from Oracle by understanding how to best work with them.

Resolving problems with the assistance of Oracle Worldwide Customer Support Services can initially be frustrating to novice DBAs and others who may report problems. Oracle responds to database problems (Technical Action Requests or TARs) based on the priority or severity level at which those problems are reported. If the problem is impacting your ability to complete a project or do business, the problem should be reported as "priority level 2" in order to assure a timely response. If the problem is initially assigned a lower level and the response hasn't been adequate, you should escalate problem resolution.

If business is halted because of the problem, the priority level assigned should be "priority level 1." However, if a problem is reported at level 1, the caller must be available for a callback (even if after hours). Otherwise, Oracle will assume that the problem wasn't as severe as initially reported and may lower the priority level for resolution.

You can report problems via the phone, email, or a web interface. Contact points are listed in the Customer Support Guide shipped with your software. When calling for technical support, you will need your Customer Support Identification (CSI) number. Oracle Sales Consultants can also provide advice regarding how to report problems. Additionally, Oracle Worldwide Customer Support Services offers training for DBAs about how to effectively use the Support services.

6

Oracle8 Performance

As this book illustrates, the Oracle8 database has a wide range of features. As you gain experience with Oracle8, you'll reap more of the benefits it has to offer. One area you should focus on is performance tuning. This chapter gives you the basics you'll need to understand before you can address performance issues.

Oracle database performance tuning has been extensively documented in the Oracle community. Numerous books provide detailed and excellent information. This book is focused more on the concepts of Oracle8, so we won't delve too deeply into specific tuning recommendations. Instead, we'll touch on the importance of tuning and discuss some basic notions of how Oracle8 uses resources. Here, we're simply laying a foundation for understanding Oracle8 performance issues. This understanding will help you implement the tuning procedures most suited for your own particular implementation scenario. Where appropriate, we'll provide some basic tuning guidelines.

Performance Tuning Basics

Database performance is one of the trickiest aspects of the operation of your database. Performance is simultaneously a very simple topic—any novice user can implicitly understand it—and an extremely complex topic that can strain the ingenuity of the most proficient database administrator. But, like most complex topics, you can only address performance issues effectively if you have a firm grasp of how to analyze and identify performance problems.

There are three basic steps to understanding how to address performance issues with your Oracle database:

- Define performance problems

- Check the performance of the Oracle server software
- Check the overall performance of the server machine

Defining Performance Problems

The first step in performance tuning is to determine if there actually *is* a performance problem. This question may seem facetious, but there are many system consultants who have arrived at client sites to "tune the database" with no real indication of why or what they are tuning. A simple test can determine if a performance problem currently exists and whether or not the system is meeting the response times promised to the users. If a database wastes machine resources but users are happy with the response time, does a performance problem really exist?

If users are happy, system performance improvements may not be needed. But even in this case, it makes sense to measure resource usage to ensure that the database is performing the needed work both efficiently and effectively; an increased system workload could quickly expose underlying problems. Gaining a baseline understanding of the resources needed to deliver acceptable performance on a well-tuned system is crucial to anticipating and handling potential problems as the system's workload increases.

If users are unhappy with the system's performance (as is frequently the case), you first need to quantify their unhappiness, and second, identify which of the system's components are causing the problems. You must refine a general statement like "the system is too slow" to identify which types of operations are too slow, what constitutes "too slow," and when these operations are slowing down. For example, the problem may occur only on specific transactions and at specific times, or all transactions and reports may be performing below the user's expectations.

Once you've defined the performance expected from your system, you can begin to try and determine where your performance problem lies. One of the curious aspects of performance is that "good performance" is defined by its absence rather than by its presence. You can recognize bad performance easily, but good performance is more likely the absence of bad performance. Bottlenecks frequently cause bad performance when there is a greater demand for a particular resource beyond what's available.

Oracle Server Performance

Begin looking for bottlenecks in the Oracle database software itself. You can use the Oracle Enterprise Manager (described in more detail in Chapter 5, *Managing Oracle8*) to identify a lower than optimal use of Oracle's internal resources. Some users will run their own monitoring or auditing scripts to analyze the state of the database and determine where bottlenecks may be occurring. Simply put, bottlenecks within your database result in sessions waiting unnecessarily, and tuning is aimed at removing these bottlenecks.

Oracle's dynamic performance views (their names all begin with "V$") are one of the most powerful tools for detecting bottlenecks within your Oracle database. Two views, in particular, identify the source of these waits; these are invaluable for guiding your analysis:

V$SYSTEM_EVENT

Provides aggregated, systemwide information about the resources that sessions are waiting for

V$SESSION_WAIT

Provides detailed, session-specific information about the resources individual sessions are waiting for

Use these two views to pinpoint the resources that are causing the most waits. Focusing on the resources presenting the largest source of contention will provide the largest performance improvements.

You may find that there is a simple source of your problem, such as a lower-than-expected database buffer cache hit ratio, which indicates that the cache is not working at its optimal level. For a resource like the cache, which is controlled by the Oracle server software, you can simply increase the *INIT.ORA* file parameter DB_BLOCK_BUFFERS to increase the size of the cache, which may improve the hit ratio.

Other situations may not be quite so clear-cut. For instance, you may find that it takes a relatively long time to fetch database rows from the disk. This situation may be caused by contention on the database server's disks, which calls for more investigation into the usage of the overall resources of the machine. Also, you may not be able to locate any specific problem through the Oracle Enterprise Manager, which will lead you to the next step of performance analysis.

Later in this chapter, we'll show you how Oracle uses its own internal resources, such as disk and memory, and how understanding this will help you to manage the resources allocated to the Oracle database software.

Machine Resource Usage

You can run into problems with machine resources on the database server itself and on the machine on which the database server is running. If your Oracle database is not properly configured, adding machine resources may help reduce performance bottlenecks, but this is a fairly expensive way to solve the problem. Further, the problem will likely resurface as these additional resources are consumed. If your Oracle database is properly configured and you find that the host computer is experiencing resource shortages, then adding machine resources is in order.

The performance of your Oracle8 database is dictated by how it uses machine resources and what resources are available. These machine resources include processing power or CPU, memory, disk I/O, and network bandwidth. You can trace the bulk of database performance problems back to a bottleneck on one or more of these resources.

Network bandwidth can be a bottleneck, but since the network enables communication between the server and the client, the use of this bandwidth is more a function of the client applications communicating with the database server than a problem on the core database server itself. For this reason, this chapter focuses on how Oracle8 uses the three key machine resources: CPU, memory, and disk I/O. The slowest device in a computer is the disk drive, and, as a result, the most common source of database performance issues is disk I/O. The majority of this chapter therefore focuses on performance as it relates to physical disk I/O.

The database server machine may bottleneck on multiple resources, for example, CPU and I/O. In fact, modern computers are set up so that one resource may try to compensate for the lack of another resource, which can lead to a deficit in the compensating resource as well. For instance, if you run out of physical memory, the operating system will swap areas of memory out to the disk, which can cause I/O bottlenecks. You can identify your machine resource usage using tools provided by the machine vendor or operating system utilities. For example, on Unix systems, you can use *sar, iostat,* and *vmstat,* and on Microsoft Windows NT, you can use the Performance Monitor.

When All Else Fails

You may still have performance problems with your application system even if you've examined all the areas previously described. In this case, your performance problem may not lie in the database server, but in the design of the application or the database itself. At this point, you will face the difficult problem of having to analyze the interaction of individual modules and SQL statements in your application system and the database server. You may find that you get lucky and find a handful of SQL statements that are causing your performance problem. However, it's more likely that you will have to reconsider the design of your application system.

Needless to say, this type of analysis is far beyond the scope of this book, so the rest of this chapter will concentrate on helping you to understand Oracle machine resources.[*]

---

[*] For more details about the vast topic of Oracle performance, refer to the tuning books mentioned in the Appendix.

Oracle8 and Disk I/O Resources

From the perspective of machine resources, an input/output operation, or I/O, can be defined as the operating system of the computer reading or writing some bytes from or to the underlying disk subsystem of the database server. I/Os can be small, such as 4 KB of data, or large, such as 64 KB or 128 KB of data. The lower and upper limits on the size of an I/O operation vary according to the operating system.

An Oracle database issues I/O requests in two basic sizes:

Single database block I/Os
> For example, 8 KB at a time. This type of request reads or writes a specific block. For example, after looking up a row in an index, Oracle uses a single block I/O to retrieve the desired database block.

Multiblock I/Os
> For example, 32 database blocks, each consisting of 8 KB, for a total I/O size of 256 KB. Multiblock I/O is used for large-scale operations, such as full table scans. The number of blocks in one multiblock I/O is determined by the *INIT.ORA* file parameter DB_FILE_MULTIBLOCK_READ_COUNT.

I/O Planning Principles for an Oracle Database

When you're planning the disk layout and subsequent placement of the various files that make up your database, you need to consider the different reasons Oracle performs I/O and the potential performance impacts.

The main destinations of the I/O operations Oracle performs are as follows:

- Redo logs

- Data contained in tables

- Indexes on the tables

- Data dictionary, which goes in the SYSTEM tablespace

- Sort activity, which goes in the TEMP tablespace of the user performing the sort

- Rollback information, which is spread across the datafiles of the tablespace containing the database's rollback segments

- Archived redo logs, which go to the archived log destination, assuming the database is in ARCHIVELOG mode

The following simple principles for managing these types of I/O can optimize Oracle's use of the database server's disk subsystem:

Use disk striping technologies to spread I/O evenly across multiple spindles
These technologies are covered in detail in the next section, "Using RAID Disk Array Technology."

Use tablespaces to clearly segregate and target different types of I/O
For example, separate table I/O from index I/O by placing these structures in different tablespaces. You can then place the datafiles for these tablespaces on various disks to provide better performance for concurrent access.

Using tablespaces to segregate objects also simplifies tuning later on. Oracle tracks I/O activity at the datafile level—the physical object the operating system sees as a file. Placing specific objects in specific tablespaces allows you to measure and direct the I/O for those objects accurately by tracking and moving the underlying datafiles as needed. For example, consider a database with several large, busy tables. Placing multiple large tables in a single tablespace makes it difficult to determine which table the I/O to the underlying datafiles is for. Segregating the objects gives you the ability to directly monitor the I/O associated with each object. Your Oracle documentation details the other factors to consider in mapping objects to tablespaces.

Place redo logs and redo log mirrors on the two least busy devices
This placement maximizes throughput for transactional systems. Remember that Oracle writes to all copies of the redo log file, and this I/O is not completed until all copies have been successfully written to. So, if you have two copies of the redo log file, one on a slow device and the other on a fast device, your redo log I/O performance will be constrained by the slower device.

Distribute "system overhead" evenly over the available drives
System overhead consists of I/O to the SYSTEM tablespace for the data dictionary, the TEMP tablespace for sorting, and the tablespaces that contain rollback segments for undo information. Consider the system profile in spreading the system overhead over multiple drives. For example, if the application generates a lot of data changes versus data reads, then the I/O to the rollback segments may increase due to higher writes for changes and higher reads for consistent read functionality.

Sort activity can also affect disk I/O. If you can get the majority of sorts to occur in memory through tuning the SORT_AREA_SIZE parameter in the *INIT.ORA* file, and you can then minimize physical I/O to the TEMP tablespace. Oracle constantly queries and updates the data dictionary stored in the SYSTEM tablespace. This information is cached in the shared pool section of the SGA so sizing your shared pool properly is key to overall performance.

Use a different device for archiving and redo log files
> To avoid archiving performance issues due to I/O contention, make sure that the archive log destination uses different devices from those used for the redo logs and redo log mirrors.

Some other principles to consider from the perspective of database availability include the following:

If taking database backups to disk, store the backups on devices that don't contain any database components
> This protects the system from the potential loss of the database and the needed backups from the failure of an I/O device.

Make sure the device used for the archive log destination doesn't contain any database components or database backups
> If the failure of a single device results in the loss of both database components and archived redo logs, or backup components and archived redo logs, recovery will be endangered.

 Fault-tolerant disk arrays don't eliminate the need for a sound backup and recovery strategy. Fault-tolerant storage merely reduces the likelihood of undergoing database recovery due to the failure of a single drive. For full coverage of Oracle databases and high availability see Chapter 10, *Oracle8 and High Availability*.

Using RAID Disk Array Technology

One of the most powerful ways to reduce performance bottlenecks due to disk I/O is the use of RAID disk arrays. RAID stands for Redundant Array of Inexpensive (or Independent) Disks and is used to group disks into arrays for two reasons: redundancy and performance. The use of RAID for redundancy is detailed in Chapter 10. Our focus in this chapter is on the performance aspects of RAID technology.

RAID groups disk drives into arrays to automatically spread I/O operations across multiple spindles, reducing contention on individual drives. For example, suppose you place a datafile containing an index on a single drive. If multiple processes use the index simultaneously, they will all issue I/O requests to the one disk drive, resulting in contention.

Now suppose you placed the same datafile on a "disk" that was actually an array of five physical disks. Each physical disk in the array can perform I/O operations independently on different data blocks of the index, automatically increasing the amount of I/O Oracle can perform without causing contention.

RAID Basics

RAID disk arrays provide a hardware solution for both reliability and performance. There are different levels of RAID hardware; the following are most relevant to performance:

- RAID-0. Where availability isn't a concern, the disks may be configured as RAID-0, which is nonredundant disk *striping*.

- RAID-1. The simplest form of redundancy is full duplication of data, referred to as *mirroring*.

- RAID-0+1. Combines the one-to-one mirroring of RAID-1 with the striping of RAID-0.

- RAID-3. Provides redundancy by storing parity information on a single disk in the array. This parity information can help to recover the data on other disks should they fail. RAID-3 saves on disk storage compared to RAID-1, but isn't often used because the parity disk can be a bottleneck.

- RAID-5. Uses parity data for redundancy similar to RAID-3, but stripes the parity data across all of the disks, similar to the way in which the actual data is striped. This alleviates the bottleneck on the parity disk.

There are additional levels of RAID, including RAID-6, which adds dual parity data, and RAID-7 and RAID-8, which add performance enhancements to the characteristics of RAID-5.

Simply using disk arrays won't, by itself, give you the greatest improvement in I/O performance. As we discussed earlier, you also have to think about how to logically place the different types of Oracle8 files across the available drives, even if the drives are grouped into arrays.

Disk striping technology for RAID arrays can be implemented in various ways, which are transparent to your Oracle database, described in the following sections.

Host-based software

With host-based striping, logical volume management software runs on the database server. Examples of this type of software include Hewlett Packard's Logical Volume Manager (LVM) and Veritas Software's Volume Manager, which act as an interface between the operating system that requests I/O and the underlying physical disks. The volume management software groups disks into arrays, which are then seen by the operating system as single "disks." The actual disks are usually individual devices attached to controllers or disks contained in a prepackaged array containing multiple disks and controllers. This striping is handled by the volume management software and is completely transparent to Oracle. Figure 6-1 illustrates host-based volume management.

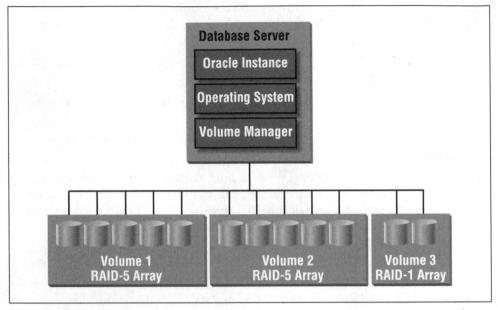

Figure 6-1. Host-based volume management

Dedicated storage subsystems

These "disk farms" contain disks, controllers, CPUs, and (usually) memory used as an I/O cache. Vendors include EMC and Storagetek. These subsystems offload the task of managing the disk arrays from the database server. The I/O subsystem is attached to the server using controllers. The disk arrays are defined and managed within the dedicated I/O subsystem, and the resulting logical "disks" are seen by the operating system as physical disks.

This type of disk volume management is completely transparent to the database server. There are many benefits: The database server does not spend CPU resources managing the disk arrays. The I/O subsystem uses memory for an I/O cache, so the performance of Oracle I/O can improve dramatically, for example, from an average I/O time of 10–12 milliseconds to 3–5 milliseconds. Write I/O is completed as soon as the data has been written to the subsystem's cache. The I/O subsystem will de-stage the data from cache to actual disk later. Read I/O can be satisfied from the cache. The subsystem can employ some type of algorithm to sense I/O patterns and preload the cache in anticipation of pending read activity.

Note that you must back up the cache with some type of battery so a power failure doesn't result in the loss of data that was written to the cache, but hasn't yet been de-staged to the physical disk. Otherwise, data that Oracle assumes made it to disk may be lost, thereby potentially corrupting the database. Figure 6-2 illustrates a database server with a dedicated I/O subsystem.

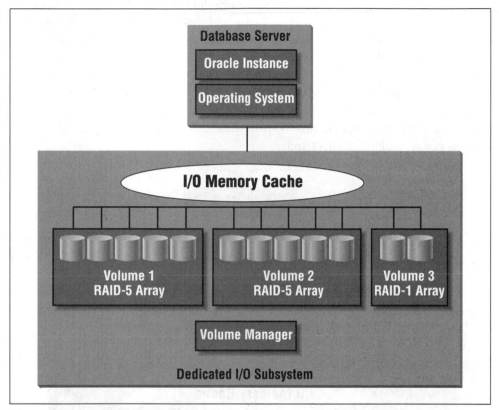

Figure 6-2. Dedicated I/O subsystems

Combined host-based and I/O subsystem volume management

In this configuration, disks are grouped into arrays within the I/O subsystem and grouped again into coarser arrays using operating system volume management. On EMC systems for example, the physical disks are grouped into either RAID-1 mirrored disk pairs or into a RAID-S striped configuration using four disks per stripe set. RAID-S is the term EMC (*http://www.emc.com*) uses for their specialized striping hardware and software that has been approved as a RAID-5 equivalent by the RAID Council.*

---

* With EMC storage subsystems, the actual disks themselves are not visible to the operating system; they are managed internally within the EMC subsystem. The horizontal slices across the disks are visible as operating system devices. Some DBAs who are accustomed to tracking I/O at the individual disk level may initially find this frustrating. EMC does have tools that can provide further insight into the internal functioning of the subsystem. However, keep in mind that tracking I/O at the individual disk level is one of the problems that led to array technology in the first place!

Using EMC technology as an example, the operating system sees horizontal sections of disk space across each RAID-1 disk or RAID-S array as single "disks." You can use the operating system volume management to group these "disks" into arrays. With RAID-1 disks, this configuration delivers the benefits of using a dedicated I/O subsystem with its own cache and processing power while leveraging striping for simplicity. With RAID-S arrays you get the benefit of the dedicated I/O subsystem and further simplify disk management by a striping multiplier effect. An array of five "disks" at the operating system level maps back to five arrays of four disks each in the I/O subsystem. This configuration maps a logical disk seen by Oracle to 20 physical disks in the underlying I/O subsystem. Figure 6-3 illustrates a logical drive on the database server mapping to horizontal sections across multiple RAID-S arrays.

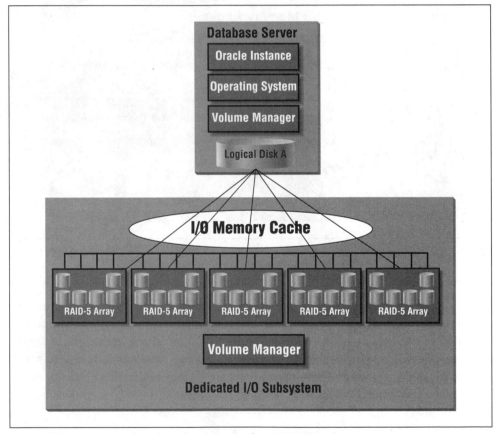

Figure 6-3. Combining host-based striping and an EMC I/O subsystem

Flexibility Versus Manageability in Disk Array Configuration

Many systems today use some type of RAID technology that groups multiple individual disk drives, also referred to as *spindles*, into arrays. Each disk array is then treated as a single logical disk for the purposes of planning I/O. Striping allows you to simply spread I/O across multiple disks, without incurring the planning and administrative overhead of dealing with many individual disk drives. Striping is transparent to Oracle, but this doesn't mean that a DBA or system administrator can ignore it. Understanding the mapping of Oracle database files to arrays, and the arrays to the underlying disks and controllers, is crucial to planning and maintaining your Oracle database.

The decision about how many disks should be in each array is often the topic of intense debate. The decision hinges on the issues of flexibility versus manageability.

At one extreme, using multiple disks without grouping any of them into arrays provides the most control and flexibility because every disk is visible and can be targeted in isolation by placing certain files on each disk. However, this approach requires more planning and certainly more ongoing administration because you must remember to deal with every individual disk drive. As databases become larger and larger, this approach becomes unmanageable.

At the other extreme, you can group all disks into one single array, seen by the operating system and Oracle as a single "disk." This makes for extremely simple planning and administration; no effort is required to analyze where you should place the various files, as there is only one "disk." However, this approach sacrifices flexibility and leads to brute force solutions to I/O bottlenecks. If I/O performance across the array is unsatisfactory, the solution is to add more controllers and disks. The entire set of disks becomes a black box that either works or doesn't work as a unit. This approach clearly isn't viable for most systems.

The most useful configuration is one that balances manageability with flexibility. For example, consider a system with 1,000 disks. A single array of 1,000 disks is not likely to be appropriate, and neither is a set of 1,000 individual disks. Perhaps fifty arrays of twenty disks each will provide the needed "I/O targetability" without any undue administrative burden. If less flexibility is needed, perhaps twenty arrays of fifty disks are more suitable. At the other extreme, grouping all the disks into one array may be the simplest way to manage a system with only five disks. There is no one answer—you must assess your needs and skills to determine the right balance.

How Oracle I/O and Striped Arrays Interact

In almost all very large databases, some type of disk striping increases disk I/O rates without adding too heavy an administrative burden for managing a large number of datafiles across many individual disks. As we've discussed, the disks may be organized into RAID arrays using a volume manager on the database server, a dedicated I/O subsystem, or a combination of both.

In setting up striped disk arrays, you can set the *chunk size* used to stripe across the disks. The chunk size is the amount of data written to one disk before moving to the next disk in the array. Understanding the interaction between different stripe chunk sizes and the two sizes of Oracle I/O is critical in maximizing your I/O performance.

Consider an Oracle database with an 8 KB data block size and DB_FILE_ MULTIBLOCK_READ_COUNT (*INIT.ORA* parameter) set to 32. There will be two sizes of I/O by Oracle: a single 8 KB data block and a 256 KB multiblock read (32 times 8 KB). Suppose you then configure a four-disk array for use by Oracle with a chunk size of 64 KB so that the 256 KB of data will be spread across the four drives, with 64 KB on each.

Each 8 KB I/O will hit one spindle, as the 8 KB will lie within one 64 KB chunk.* Striping can increase performance for small I/Os by maximizing concurrency: each disk can service a different I/O. The multiblock I/Os of 256 KB will hit all four disks. If the chunk size was 256 KB instead of 64 KB, then on average each 256 KB I/O call would hit one disk. In this case, the multiblock I/O will require fewer I/O calls with a larger chunk size on the disks. In either case, a single disk will clearly satisfy single data block I/O calls. Striping can increase I/O rates for large reads by driving multiple disks with a single I/O call, as illustrated with a 64 KB chunk size and a 256 KB multiblock I/O.

Figure 6-4 illustrates the interaction of different sized Oracle I/Os with arrays striped using different chunk sizes.

Oracle and Parallelism

The ability to parallelize operations is one of the most important features of the Very Large Database (VLDB). Database servers with multiple CPUs, which are

---

* It's difficult to say exactly what will occur due to the alignment of the stripe chunk boundaries with Oracle data blocks, but to illustrate the single versus multiple disk point, let's assume the simple case— they line up! For a more detailed discussion of striping issues, see the document "Configuring Oracle Server for VLDB" by Cary Millsap of Oracle Corporation (see the Appendix). Anyone who is tempted is welcome to perform detailed testing for all the permutations of stripe chunk size and Oracle I/O. If you happen to perform this extensive testing, please tell all the rest of us what you find!

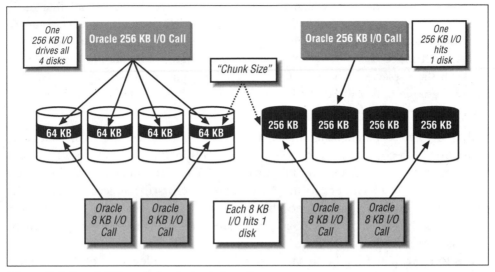

Figure 6-4. Oracle I/O and chunk size interaction

called symmetric multiprocessing (SMP) machines, are the norm today for most database servers. As performance demands increase and data volumes continue to grow you will increasingly need to use multiple processors and disks to reduce the time to complete a given task. Oracle supports parallelism within a single SMP server, as well as parallelism across multiple nodes, using Oracle Parallel Server. Executing a SQL statement in parallel will consume more of all three machine resources—CPU, memory and disk I/O—but the main potential performance gains fall in the area of disk I/O. Parallelism affects the amount of memory and CPU used to execute a given task in a fairly linear fashion. Each parallel execution process has a Program Global Area (PGA) that consumes memory and performs work, which in turn consumes the CPU resources, but disk I/O is the place in which bottlenecks can most readily appear, and which parallelism can help reduce.

There are two types of parallelism possible within an Oracle8 database:

Block-range parallelism
    Driven by ranges of database blocks

Partition-based parallelism
    Driven by the number of partitions or subpartitions involved in the operation

The following sections describe these types of parallelism.

Block-Range Parallelism

Back in 1994, Oracle 7.1 introduced the ability to dynamically parallelize table scans and a variety of scan-based functions. This parallelism was based on the notion of *block ranges*, in which the Oracle server would understand that each table contained a set of data blocks that spanned a defined range of data. Oracle7 implemented block-range parallelism by dynamically breaking a table into pieces, where each piece was a range of blocks, which then used multiple processes to work on these pieces in parallel. Oracle's implementation of block-range parallelism was unique in that it didn't require physically partitioned tables to achieve parallelism.

With block-range parallelism, the client session that issued the SQL statement transparently becomes the parallel execution coordinator, assigning block ranges to a set of parallel execution (PE) processes. The determination of the block ranges and their assignment to the PE processes occurs dynamically. Once a PE process has completed an assigned block range, it returns to the coordinator for more work. Not all I/O will occur at the same rate, so some PE processes may process more blocks than others. This notion of "stealing work" allows all processes to participate fully in the task, providing maximum leverage of the machine resources.

Block-range parallelism scales linearly based on the number of PE processes, provided you have adequate hardware resources. The key to achieving scalability with parallelism lies in hardware basics. Each PE process runs on a CPU and requests I/O to a device. If you have enough CPUs reading enough disks, parallelism will scale. If the system encounters a bottleneck on one of these resources, scalability will suffer. For example, four CPUs reading two disks will not scale much beyond the two-way scalability of the disks and may even sink below this level if the additional CPUs cause contention for the disks. Similarly, two CPUs reading twenty disks will not scale to a twenty-fold performance improvement. The system hardware must be balanced for parallelism to scale.

Most large systems have far more disks than CPUs. In these systems, parallelism results in a randomization of I/O across the I/O subsystem. This is useful for concurrent access to data as PE processes for different users read from different disks at different times, resulting in I/O that is distributed across the available disks.

A useful analogy for dynamic parallelism is eating a pie. The pie is the set of blocks to be read for the operation, and the goal is to eat the pie as quickly as possible using a certain number of people. Oracle serves the pie in helpings, and when a person finishes his first helping, he can come back for more. Not everyone eats at the same rate, so some people will consume more pie than others. While this approach in the real world is somewhat unfair, it's a good model for parallelism because if everyone is eating all the time, the pie will be consumed more quickly. The alternative is to give each person an equal serving and wait for the slower eaters to finish.

Figure 6-5 illustrates the splitting of a set of blocks into ranges.

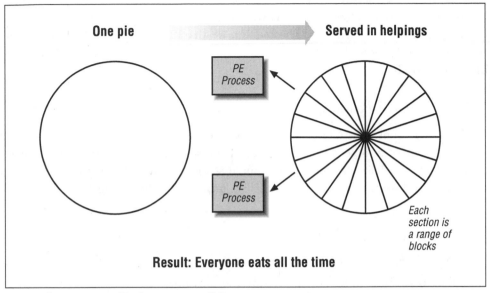

Figure 6-5. *Dynamic block-range parallelism*

Parallelism for Tables and Partitions of Tables

With *partitioned tables*, introduced in Oracle8, an operation may involve one, some, or all of the partitions of a partitioned table. There is essentially no difference in how block-range parallelism dynamically splits the set of blocks to be read for a regular table as opposed to a partitioned table. Once the optimizer has determined which partitions should be accessed for the operation, all the blocks of all partitions involved are treated as a pool to be broken into ranges.

This assumption by the optimizer leads to a key consideration for using parallelism and partitioned tables. The degree of parallelism (i.e., the number of parallel execution processes used for the table as a whole) is applied to the set of partitions that will be used for an operation. The optimizer will eliminate the use of partitions that do not contain data that an operation will use. For instance, if one of the partitions for a table contains ID numbers below 1,000, and if a query requests ID numbers between 1,100 and 5,000, the optimizer understands that this query will not access this partition.

The use of a subset of partitions has important implications for setting a degree of parallelism that provides good scalability for queries that scan some versus all of a table's partitions. A level of parallelism that may be good for the partitioned table as a whole may cause I/O contention for a query that only accesses one partition stored on fewer disks.

If you expect that your queries may use partition elimination or pruning, and you plan on using parallelism, you should stripe each partition over a sufficient number of drives to scale effectively. This will ensure scalability regardless of the number of partitions accessed. This striping can be manual through multiple datafiles on multiple disks or it can be achieved through the use of striped arrays or a combination of both.

What Can Be Parallelized?

Many people think that Oracle can only parallelize simple table scans. While the parallelization of a table scan is involved in most parallelized operations, Oracle actually can parallelize far more than simple scans. The list of operations that can be parallelized using block-range parallelism includes the following:

- Tablespace creation
- Index creation and rebuilds
- Online index reorganizations and rebuilds
- Index organized table reorganizations and movements
- Table creation, such as summary creation using CREATE TABLE AS SELECT
- Partition maintenance operations, such as moving and splitting partitions
- Data loading
- Imposing integrity constraints
- Statistics gathering
- Backup and restore
- DML operations (INSERT, UPDATE, DELETE)
- Query processing operations

The specific features of query processing that may be parallelized include the following:

- Table scans
- Nested loops
- Sort merge joins
- Hash joins
- Bitmap star joins
- Index scans
- Partition-wise joins
- Anti-joins (NOT IN)

- SELECT DISTINCT

- UNION and UNION ALL

- ORDER BY

- GROUP BY

- Aggregations

- User-defined functions

Controlling Oracle's Parallel Resource Usage

An Oracle instance has a pool of parallel execution (PE) processes that are available to the database users. These processes consume CPU, memory, and I/O resources. Controlling the maximum number of active PE processes is important; too many PE processes will overload the machine, leading to resource bottlenecks and performance degradation. The pool of PE processes is governed by the following two *INIT.ORA* file parameters:

PARALLEL_MIN_SERVERS

> A number that acts as a floor for the pool of PE processes. When the instance is started, it will spawn this number of PE processes. A typical value is twice the number of CPUs.

PARALLEL_MAX_SERVERS

> A number that acts as a ceiling for the pool of PE processes. As users request parallel operations, the instance will spawn additional PE processes up to this value. This limits the maximum parallel activity on the system and can be used to avoid overloading the machine. The effective ceiling for a given machine will vary. If the load decreases, the instance will gradually scale the pool back to PARALLEL_MIN_SERVERS.

A user session requests a number of PE processes from the pool based on the degree of parallelism for the operation the session is performing.

Setting the degree of parallelism

The degree of parallelism governs how many parallel execution processes may be used for a given operation. The degree of parallelism is determined in three mutually exclusive ways:

1. If a table has default parallelism enabled using ALTER TABLE *tablename* PARALLEL, the optimizer will set the degree of parallelism automatically. In Oracle versions 7.3 and 8.0.3, default parallelism was set to the minimum of two values: the number of CPUs in the machine or the number of distinct devices

used to store the table.* Based on customer feedback, in Oracle version 8.0.4 (and subsequent releases) default parallelism defaults to the number of CPUs to recognize the prevalent use of striped disk arrays. Large tables in which parallelism is useful are typically stored on one or more striped disk arrays such that the resulting number of actual spindles used is greater then the number of CPUs. So, CPU count represents a more realistic value for default parallelism.

2. You can set the parallelism for a table to an explicit value using ALTER TABLE *tablename* PARALLEL *N*, where *N* is the desired degree of parallelism. This is useful where you want to override the optimizer's default value because of hardware characteristics. For example, you should set the parallelism if the machine can handle a degree of twice the number of CPUs for a particular table.

3. You can override any table-level setting and explicitly set the degree using the PARALLEL optimizer hint for queries or the PARALLEL clause, which is valid for some statements, such as CREATE INDEX or CREATE TABLE AS SELECT. This is useful if you want to use more resources for a particular task like an index build, but leave the degree of parallelism for other operations unchanged.

Intra-operation parallelism

For any operation involving more than one step, such as a scan and sort, a degree of parallelism of *N* will actually use 2 * *N* PE processes, one set per sub-operation. For example, *N* scanner processes will feed *N* sorter processes. Figure 6-6 illustrates transparent parallelism within and between sets of PE processes.

At the end of the overall task, the coordinator combines the results from the separate PE processes.

Adaptive Parallelism in Oracle8i

Determining the optimal degree of parallelism in the presence of multiple users and varying workloads has proved challenging. For example, a degree of 8 for a query may provide excellent performance for one or two users, but what if twenty users query the same table? This scenario would call for 160 PE processes (eight PEs for each of the twenty users), which could overload the machine. Setting the degree to a lowest common denominator value (for example, 2) provides effec-

---

* If you use operating system or disk subsystem striping to stripe a datafile over more than one disk, this striped datafile presents itself as a single datafile on a single device to Oracle. Using a single array of five disks will not equate to five devices for default parallelism. Using five datafiles, each on a separate array, would. So, take care when using default parallelism and transparent or OS-level disk striping in these earlier Oracle versions.

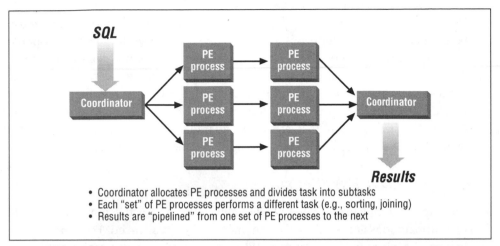

Figure 6-6. Intra-operation and inter-operation parallelism

tive parallelism for higher user counts, but does not leverage resources fully when fewer users are active.

Oracle8*i* introduces the notion of *self-tuning adaptive parallelism*. This feature automatically scales down parallelism as the system load increases, and scales it back up as the load decreases. When an operation requests a degree of parallelism, Oracle8*i* will check the system load and lower the actual degree the operation uses to avoid overloading the system. As more users request parallelism, the degree they receive will become lower and lower until operations are executing serially. If activity decreases, subsequent operations will be granted increasing degrees of parallelism. This adaptability frees the DBA from the essentially impossible task of trying to determine the optimal degree of parallelism in the face of constant changes in concurrency and workload.

Adaptive parallelism takes two factors into account in determining the degree of parallelism granted to an operation:

*   System load.

*   Parallelism resource limitations of the user's consumer group if the Database Resource Manager is active. (The Database Resource Manager is explained in Chapter 8, *Oracle8 and Transaction Processing*.) This is important, because it means that adaptive parallelism respects resource plans if they're in place.

The following two *INIT.ORA* file parameters enable adaptive parallelism:

PARALLEL_AUTOMATIC_TUNING
When set to TRUE, enables the adaptive parallelism feature.

PARALLEL_MIN_PERCENT

Determines what percentage of the requested parallelism an operation must be granted. For example, suppose this parameter were set to 50 and an operation requested a degree of 8. If Oracle grants the operation a degree of 4, then the operation will continue as it received the minimum 50 percent of the requested degree of parallelism. If Oracle grants a degree less than 4, which would be less than 50 percent of the requested degree of 8, an error will be returned to the user. If you are using adaptive parallelism, set PARALLEL_ MIN_PERCENT to 0 to allow Oracle to scale parallelism down as needed.

Partition-Based Parallelism

A small subset of Oracle's parallel functionality is based on the number of partitions or subpartitions accessed by the statement to be parallelized. For block-range parallelism, the piece of data that each PE process works on is a range of blocks. For partition-based parallelism, the pieces of data that drive parallelism are partitions or subpartitions of a table. The operations in which parallelism is based on the number of partitions or subpartitions include the following:

- Updates and deletes
- Index scans
- Index creation and rebuilds on partitioned tables

Parallelism for partitions and subpartitions of a table

Oracle8 introduced support for parallel Data Manipulation Language (DML), which is the ability to execute INSERT, UPDATE, and DELETE statements in parallel. This type of parallelism improves the performance of large bulk operations: for example, an update to all the rows of a very large table.

In Oracle8, the degree of parallelism for updates and deletes is tied to the number of partitions involved, while in Oracle8*i*, the degree of parallelism for updates and deletes is tied to the number of partitions or subpartitions involved. In Oracle8 and Oracle8*i*, a table with twelve partitions (for example, one partition for each month of the year) can have a maximum degree of 12 for a parallel update or delete. An update to only one month of data would have no parallelism because it involves only one partition. If the table were created using Oracle8*i*'s composite partitioning (for example, with four hash subpartitions by PRODUCT_ID within each month) then the maximum degree of parallelism for the entire table would be 48, or twelve partitions with four subpartitions each. An update to one month of data could have a degree of 4 because each month contains four hash subpartitions. If the table is not partitioned, Oracle cannot perform updates or deletes in parallel.

Oracle8 and Oracle8*i* can execute index creation, index rebuild, and index scans for partitioned indexes in parallel using the same semantics as parallel DML: one PE process per partition or subpartition of the index.

Fast full index scans for nonpartitioned tables

People often assume that the Oracle database can only parallelize index scans if the target index is partitioned. Oracle 7.3 introduced the ability to perform parallel index scans on nonpartitioned indexes for a certain case. If the index scan operation were "unbounded," meaning the entire index was going to be accessed to satisfy the query, then Oracle 7.3 and higher would use block-range parallelism to access the entire index in parallel. So, while Oracle can perform index scans for nonpartitioned indexes, this feature applies to a narrow set of queries. Partition-based index scans apply to a much broader range of queries.

Parallel insert for nonpartitioned and partitioned tables

Oracle can execute an INSERT statement of the form INSERT INTO *tableX* SELECT...FROM *tableY* in parallel for nonpartitioned and partitioned tables. Oracle uses a set of PE processes executing block-range parallelism for the SELECT portion of the INSERT statement. These PE processes pass the rows to a second set of PE processes, which insert the rows into the target table. The target table can be a nonpartitioned or partitioned table. So, parallelism for an insert is not exactly block-range or partition-based.

Oracle8 and Memory Resources

Accessing information in memory is much faster than accessing information on a disk. An Oracle instance uses the database server's memory resources to cache the information it uses to improve performance. Oracle uses an area of shared memory called the System Global Area (SGA), and a private memory area for each server process called the Program Global Area (PGA). Operating systems use virtual memory, which means that an Oracle instance can use more memory than is physically available on the machine.

Exhausting a database server's supply of physical memory will cause poor performance. You should gauge the size of the various memory areas Oracle uses or add more memory to the machine to prevent a memory deficit from occurring. What constitutes the right size for the various areas is a function of your application behavior, the data it uses, and your performance requirements.

How Oracle Uses the System Global Area

Oracle uses the SGA for the following operations:

- Caching of database blocks containing table and index data in the database buffer cache

- Caching of parsed and optimized SQL statements, stored procedures, and data dictionary information in the shared pool

- Buffering of redo log entries in the redo log buffer before they're written to disk

The amount of memory allocated to each of these areas within the SGA is determined at instance startup and cannot be altered without restarting the instance. The *INIT.ORA* file parameters that allocate memory are:

DB_BLOCK_BUFFERS
  Specifies the number of database blocks the database buffer cache can contain

SHARED_POOL_SIZE
  Specifies the size of the shared pool in bytes

LOG_BUFFER
  Specifies the size of the redo log buffer in bytes

Of these three memory areas, the majority of tuning efforts focus on the database buffer cache and the shared pool.

The database buffer cache

Tuning the database buffer cache is relatively simple: You assess what percentage of the database blocks requested by users are read from the cache versus read from the disk. This percentage is termed the *hit ratio*. If response times are too high and this ratio is lower than 90 percent (as a rule of thumb), increasing the value of the *INIT.ORA* file parameter DB_BLOCK_BUFFERS may increase performance.

 You can use the Oracle Enterprise Manager to get information about the cache hit ratio.

It's tempting to assume that continually increasing the size of the database buffer cache should translate into better performance. However, this is only true if the database blocks in the cache are actually being reused. Most OLTP systems have a relatively small set of core tables that are heavily used, for example, lookup tables for things such as valid codes. The rest of the I/O tends to be random, accessing a row or two in various database blocks in the course of the transaction. So having a larger buffer cache may not contribute to performance because other than the core tables, there isn't much reuse of data blocks occurring.

Furthermore, not all operations read from the database buffer cache. For example, large full table scans are limited to a small number of buffers to avoid adversely impacting other users by dominating the cache. So, if your application performs a lot of table scans, increasing the buffer cache may not help performance, as the cache will not contain the needed data blocks. Parallel table scans completely bypass the buffer cache and pass rows directly to the requesting user process. As with most performance issues, insight into how your application is actually using your data is the key that will help guide your database buffer cache tuning.

The shared pool

The shared pool is used at several points during the execution of every operation that occurs in an Oracle database. For example, the shared pool is accessed to cache the SQL sent to the database and for the data dictionary information required to execute the SQL. Because of its central role in database operations, a shared pool that's too small may have a greater impact on performance than a database buffer cache that's too small. If the requested database block isn't in the database buffer cache, Oracle will perform an I/O to retrieve it, resulting in a one-time performance hit. A shared pool that's too small will cause poor performance for a variety of reasons affecting all users. These reasons include the following:

- Not enough data dictionary information can be cached, resulting in frequent disk access to query and update the data dictionary.

- Not enough SQL can be cached, leading to memory "churn" or the flushing of useful statements to make room for incoming statements, which in turn are flushed out as more statements arrive from the application. A well-designed application issues the same statements repeatedly. If there isn't enough room to cache all the SQL the application uses, the same statements get parsed, cached, and flushed over and over, wasting valuable CPU resources and adding overhead to every transaction.

- Not enough stored procedures can be cached, leading to similar memory churn and performance issues for the program logic stored and executed in the database.

Once you've diagnosed which of these problems is occurring, the solution is fairly simple: increase the size of the shared pool. Shared pool sizes in the 150 to 250 MB range are not uncommon for large, active databases. For more information about examining shared pool activity to identify problems, see the *Oracle8x Tuning Guide*, as well as the third-party books listed in the Appendix.

The redo log buffer

While the redo log buffer consumes a very small amount of memory in the SGA relative to the database buffer cache and the shared pool, it's critical for performance. Transactions performing changes to the data in the database write their redo information to the redo log buffer in memory. The redo log buffer is flushed to the redo logs on disk when a transaction is committed or when the redo log buffer is one-third full. Oracle "fences" off the portion of the redo log buffer that's being flushed to disk to make sure that its contents aren't changed until the information is safely on disk. Transactions can continue to write redo information to the rest of the redo log buffer—the portion that isn't being written to disk and therefore isn't "fenced off" by Oracle. In a busy database, transactions may generate enough redo to fill the remaining unfenced portion of the redo log buffer before the I/O to the disks for the fenced area of the redo log buffer is complete. If this happens, the transactions will have to wait for the I/O to complete because there is no more space in the redo log buffer. This can impact performance. The ratio that detects this waiting is calculated using system statistics from the dynamic performance view V$SYSSTAT as:

redo log space requests / redo entries

As a general rule, if this ratio is greater than 1:5000, then you should increase the size of the redo log buffer. You can keep on increasing the size of the redo log buffer until the ratio does not get any lower.

Alternatively, the statistic "redo buffer allocation retries" can be used. It is also available through V$SYSSTAT and is an indication of how often a session waited for space in the redo log buffer. An example of the query you may use to obtain the statistic is:

```
SELECT name, value FROM V$SYSSTAT
    WHERE name = 'redo buffer allocation retries';
```

You should monitor these statistics over a period of time to gain insight into the trend. The values at one point in time reflect the cumulative totals since the instance was started, and aren't necessarily meaningful as a single data point. Note that this is true for all statistics used for performance tuning. Ideally, the value of "redo buffer allocation retries" should be close to 0. If you observe the value rising during the monitoring period, you should increase the size of the redo log buffer.

How Oracle Uses the Program Global Area

Each server has a Program Global Area (PGA) which is a private memory area that contains information about the work the server process is performing. There is one PGA for each server process. The total amount of memory used for all the PGAs is a function of the number of server processes active as part of the Oracle instance. The larger the number of users, the higher the number of server processes, and the larger the amount of memory used for their associated PGAs. Using the Multi-Threaded Server reduces total memory consumption for PGAs as the Multi-Threaded Server reduces the number of server processes.

The PGA consists of a working memory area for things such as temporary variables used by the server process, memory for information about the SQL the server process is executing, and memory for sorting rows as part of SQL execution. The initial size of the PGA's working memory area for variables, known as *stack space*, cannot be directly controlled because it's pre-determined based on the operating system you are using for your database server. The other areas within the PGA can be controlled as described in the following sections.

Memory for SQL statements

When a server process executes a SQL statement for a user, the server process tracks the session-specific details about the SQL statement and the progress by executing it in a piece of memory in the PGA called a *private SQL area*, also known as a *cursor*. (This should not be confused with the shared SQL area within the shared pool.) The shared SQL area contains shareable details for the SQL statement such as the optimization plan. The private SQL area contains the session-specific information about the execution of the SQL statement within the session, such as the number of rows retrieved so far. Once a SQL statement has been processed, its private SQL area can be reused by another SQL statement. If the application again issues the SQL statement whose private SQL area was reused, the private SQL area will have to be reinitialized.

Each time a new SQL statement is received, its shared SQL area must be located (or, if not located, loaded) in the shared pool. Similarly, the SQL statement's private SQL area must be located in the PGA and, if the statement's private SQL area isn't located in the PGA, the private SQL area for the statement must be reinitialized by the server process. This reinitialization is relatively expensive in terms of CPU resources.

A server process with a PGA that can contain a higher number of distinct private SQL areas will spend less time reinitializing private SQL areas for incoming SQL statements. If the server process doesn't have to reuse an existing private SQL area to accommodate a new statement, then the private SQL area for the original statement can be kept intact. Although similar to a larger shared pool, a larger PGA avoids memory churn within the private SQL areas. Reduced private SQL area reuse, in turn, reduces the associated CPU consumption, increasing performance. There is, of course, a tradeoff between allocating memory in the PGA for SQL and overall performance.

OLTP systems typically have a "working set" of SQL statements that each user submits. For example, a user who enters car rental reservations uses the same forms in the application repeatedly. Performance will be improved if the user's server process has enough memory in the PGA to cache the SQL those forms issue. Application developers should also take care to write their SQL statements so that they can be easily reused, by specifying bind variables instead of different hard-coded values in their SQL statements. This technique is discussed in more detail in Chapter 8, *Oracle8 and Transaction Processing.*

The number of private SQL areas, and therefore the amount of memory in the PGA they consume, is determined by the *INIT.ORA* parameter OPEN_CURSORS. You should set this parameter based on the SQL your application submits, the number of active users, and the available memory on the server.

Memory for sorting within the PGA

Each server process uses memory in its PGA for sorting rows before returning them to the user. If the memory allocated for sorting is insufficient to hold all the rows that need to be sorted, the server process sorts the rows in multiple passes called *runs.* The intermediate runs are written to the temporary tablespace of the user, which reduces sort performance as it involves disk I/O.

Sizing the sort area of the PGA is a critical tuning point. A sort area that's too small for the typical amount of data requiring sorting will result in temporary tablespace disk I/O and reduced performance. A sort area that's significantly larger than necessary will waste memory. The correct value for the sort area will depend on the amount of sort activity performed on behalf of your application, the size of your user population and the available memory on the database server. The sort area is determined by the following *INIT.ORA* parameters, which can be modified dynamically at the system and session level without restarting the instance:

SORT_AREA_SIZE

Specifies the maximum amount of memory a server process can use for sorting before using the temporary tablespace stored on disk.

SORT_AREA_RETAINED SIZE

Specifies the lower bound on sort memory that the server process will retain after completing sorts. Setting this parameter equal to SORT_AREA_SIZE means that each server process will eventually allocate and hold memory in the PGA equal to SORT_AREA_SIZE. Setting SORT_AREA_RETAINED_SIZE to a value lower than SORT_AREA_SIZE will reduce total memory consumption, and server processes will release memory after completing sorts, freeing memory up for use by other processes. If most sorts use the maximum amount of memory as defined by SORT_AREA_SIZE, you can set SORT_AREA_

RETAINED_SIZE to the same value. This avoids shrinking and growing the sort memory repeatedly.

 Each parallel execution process allocates its own sort area. So, if SORT_AREA_SIZE is 4 MB and you execute a query using a degree of parallelism of 8, the PE processes could allocate up to 32 MB of memory for sorting. Keep this in mind when setting the SORT_AREA_SIZE and degrees of parallelism to avoid unexpectedly high memory consumption.

Oracle8 and CPU Resources

Anything a computer does is performed through the execution of low-level instructions that initiate I/O, move data from one memory location to another, add two numbers together, compare two values, and so on. So anything and everything Oracle does requires CPU resources. Similarly, any other processes running on the server also consume CPU. If there is a shortage of CPU power, reducing Oracle or non-Oracle CPU consumption will improve the performance of all processes running on the server.

Running Oracle databases and non-Oracle applications on a single server leads to the "cannibalization" of CPU resources. Tuning Oracle frees CPU resources which are then consumed by Oracle and non-Oracle processes. Similarly, if you're running multiple Oracle databases on a single server, and if one of those databases (for example, a data warehouse) consumes a lot of CPU resources, performance across all databases will suffer. This resource cannibalization problem suggests why it's a good practice to isolate databases with demanding performance targets on to dedicated database servers.

If all the CPUs in a machine are busy, the processes line up and wait for a turn to use the CPU. This is called a *run queue* because processes are waiting to run on a CPU. The busier the CPUs get, the longer processes can spend in this queue. A process in the queue isn't doing any work, so as the run queue gets longer, response times degrade. Keep in mind that run queues (which can bottleneck) become a problem only when the demand exceeds the supply of available CPU time.

 You can use the standard monitoring tools for your particular operating system to check the CPU utilization for that machine.

The CPU consumed by your application is a direct function of the workload your application places on the database. The ever-increasing demand for larger OLTP systems and data warehouses has fueled an incredible rise in the CPU consumption seen in today's large servers.

Tuning CPU usage is essentially an exercise in tuning individual tasks: it reduces the number of commands required to accomplish the tasks, and/or reduces the overall number of tasks to be performed. You can do this tuning through workload balancing, SQL tuning, or improved application design. This type of tuning requires insight into what these tasks are and how they're being executed. Oracle databases perform a large variety of tasks when responding to user requests.

An in-depth discussion of all the various tuning points for an Oracle database is beyond the scope of this book. However, there is a set of common tasks that typically result in excess CPU consumption. Some of the usual suspects to examine if you encounter a CPU resource shortage on your database server include the following:

Bad SQL

Poorly written SQL is the number one cause of performance problems. An Oracle database attempts to optimally execute the SQL it receives from clients. If the SQL contained in the client applications and sent to the database is written so that the best plan Oracle can identify is still extremely ineffective, then Oracle will consume more resources than necessary to execute the SQL. Tuning SQL can be a complex and time-consuming process because it requires an in-depth understanding of how Oracle works and what the application is trying to do. Initial examinations will often reveal flaws in the underlying database design, leading to changes in table structures, additional indexes, and so on. Changing the SQL requires retesting and a subsequent redeployment of the application. As painful as all this sounds, the lion's share of reductions in CPU consumption will come from tuning the SQL in the application.

Excessive parsing

As we discussed in the section "Memory for SQL statements," Oracle must parse every SQL statement before it's processed. Parsing is very CPU-intensive, involving a lot of data dictionary lookups to check that all the tables and columns referenced are valid. Complex algorithms and calculations estimate the costs of the various execution plans possible for the statement to select the optimal plan. If your application isn't using bind variables (discussed in Chapter 8), then the database will have to parse every statement it receives. This excessive and unnecessary parsing is one of the leading causes of performance degradation. Another common cause is a shared pool that's too small, as discussed previously in the section "The shared pool."

Sheer database workload

If your application is well-designed and your database is operating at optimal efficiency, you may experience a shortage of CPU for the simple reason that your server doesn't have enough CPU power to perform all the work it's being asked to do. This shortage may be due to the workload for one database if the machine is a dedicated database server, or to the combined workload of multiple databases running on the server. Underestimating the amount of CPU resources required is a chronic problem in capacity planning. Unfortunately, accurate estimates of the CPU resources required for a certain level of activity demands detailed insight into the amount of CPU power each transaction will consume, and how many transactions per minute or second the system will process, both at peak and average workloads. Most organizations don't have the time or resources for the system analysis and prototyping required to answer these questions. This is perhaps why CPU shortages are so common, and why the equally common solution is to simply add more CPUs to the machine until the problem goes away—if indeed it does!

Nondatabase workload

Not all organizations have the luxury of dedicating an entire machine to an Oracle database to ensure that all CPU resources are available for that database. Use operating system utilities to identify the top CPU consumers on the machine. You may find that non-Oracle processes are consuming the bulk of the CPU resources and adversely impacting database performance.

7

Multiuser Concurrency

All information systems fulfill a single purpose: to collect, store, and retrieve information. As systems grow to handle many different users with many different needs, problems can arise as a result of the conflicting demands for concurrent access to the same data.

Concurrent user access to the same data is one of the most central and vexing issues for applications utilizing databases. Concurrency can affect two of the most important facets of any application: the underlying integrity of the data and the performance of the application system.

As Ken Jacobs, Vice President at Oracle, puts it in his paper entitled "Transaction Control and Oracle7," a multiuser database must be able to handle concurrently executing transactions in a way that "ensure(s) predictable and reproducible results." This goal is the core issue of data integrity, which, in turn, is the foundation of any database system.

As multiple users access the same data, there is always the possibility that one user's changes to a specific piece of data will be unwittingly overwritten by another user's changes. If this situation occurs, the accuracy of the information in the database is corrupted, which can render the data useless or, even worse, misleading. At the same time, the techniques used to prevent this type of loss can dramatically reduce the performance of an application system, as users wait for other users to complete their work before continuing. You can't solve this type of performance problem by increasing the resources available to an application because it's caused by the traffic visiting a piece of data, not by any lack of horsepower in the system that's handling the data.

Although concurrency issues are central to the success of applications, they are some of the most difficult problems to predict because they stem from such complex interactive situations. The difficulties posed by concurrent access continue to increase as the number of concurrent users increases. Even a robust debugging and testing environment may fail to detect problems created by concurrent access since these problems are created by large numbers of users who may not be available in a test environment. Concurrency problems can also pop up as user access patterns change throughout the life of an application.

If the problems raised by concurrent access aren't properly handled by the underlying database software, developers may find themselves suffering in a number of ways. They will have to create their own customized solutions to these problems in their software, which will consume valuable development time. They will frequently find themselves adding code during the late stages of development and testing to work around the underlying deficiencies in the database, which can alter the design of the application. Worst of all, they may find themselves changing the optimal design of their data structures to compensate for weaknesses in the capabilities of the underlying database.

There is only one way to deal successfully with the issues raised by concurrent data access. The database that provides the access must implement strategies to transparently overcome the potential problems posed by concurrent access. Fortunately, Oracle has excellent methods for handling concurrent access.

This chapter describes the basics of concurrent data access and gives you an overview of the way that Oracle handles the issues raised by concurrent access. If you've worked with large database systems in the past and are familiar with concurrent user access, you might want to skip the first section of this chapter.

Basics of Concurrent Access

To prepare you to deal with the problems posed by multiuser concurrent access to data, we should review some of the basic concepts that relate to concurrency.

Transactions

The *transaction* is the bedrock of data integrity in multiuser databases, and the foundation of all concurrency schemes. A transaction is defined as a single indivisible piece of work that affects some data. All of the modifications made to data within a transaction are uniformly applied to a database with a COMMIT statement, or the data affected by the changes is uniformly returned to its initial state with a ROLLBACK statement. Once a transaction is committed, the changes made by that transaction become permanent and are made visible to other transactions and other users.

Transactions always occur over time, although most transactions occur over a very short period of time. Since the changes made by a transaction aren't official until the transaction is committed, each individual transaction must be isolated from the effects of other transactions. The mechanism used to enforce *transaction isolation* is the lock.

Locks

A database uses a system of *locks* to prevent transactions from interfering with each other. Transactions can interfere with each other by allowing one transaction to change a piece of data that another transaction is also in the process of changing. Figure 7-1 illustrates a system without locks. Transaction A reads a piece of data; Transaction B reads the same piece of data and commits a change to the data. When Transaction A goes to commit the data, its change unwittingly overwrites the changes made by Transaction B, resulting in a loss of data integrity.

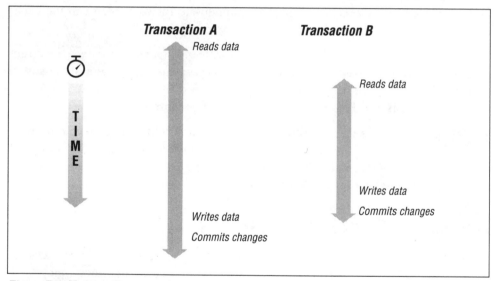

Figure 7-1. Transactions over time

There are two types of locks used to avoid this type of problem. The first is called a *write lock*, or an *exclusive lock*. An exclusive lock is taken out and held while changes are made to data in the course of a transaction and released when the transaction is ended by either a COMMIT or a ROLLBACK statement. A write lock can only be held by one user at a time, so only one user at a time can change that data.

Some databases also use *read locks*, or *shared locks*. A read lock can be held by any number of users who are merely reading the data, since the same piece of data can be shared among many readers. However, a read lock prevents a write lock from being placed on the data, as the write lock is an exclusive lock. In Figure 7-1, if a read lock were placed on the data when Transaction A began, Transaction B would not be prevented from reading the same data, but it would be prevented from acquiring a write lock on the data until Transaction A ended.

Oracle8 only uses read locks when a SQL operation specifically requests them with the FOR UPDATE clause in a SELECT statement. By default, you shouldn't use the FOR UPDATE clause because it unduly increases the probability that readers will interfere with writers, a situation that normally never occurs with Oracle8, as you will see shortly.

Concurrency and Contention

The safeguards that enforce isolation between concurrent users of data can lead to their own problems if they're improperly implemented. As you can see from the example described above, a single transaction can cause significant performance problems as the locks it places on the database prevent other transactions from completing. The interference caused by conflicting locks is called *contention*. The more contention in a database the greater the potential response times.

In most databases, increased concurrent access to data results in increased contention and decreased performance, in terms of both response time and throughput.

Integrity Problems

There are some basic integrity problems that can result if transaction isolation isn't enforced. Three of these problems are common to many databases:

Dirty reads
> A dirty read occurs when a database allows a transaction to read data that has been changed by another transaction but hasn't been committed yet. The changes made by the transaction may be rolled back, so the data read may turn out to be incorrect. Many databases allow dirty reads to avoid the contention caused by read locks.

Nonrepeatable reads
> A nonrepeatable read occurs as a result of changes made by another transaction. A transaction makes a query based on a particular condition. After the data has been returned to the first transaction, but before the first transaction is complete, another transaction *changes* the data so that some of the previously retrieved data no longer satisfies the selection condition. If the query was repeated in the same transaction, it would return a different set of results, so any changes made on the basis of the original results may no longer be

valid. Data that was read once may return different results if it's read again
later in the same transaction.

Phantom reads

A phantom read also occurs as a result of changes made by another transaction. One transaction makes a query based on a particular condition. After the
data has been returned to the first transaction, but before the first transaction
is complete, another transaction inserts new rows into the database that would
have been selected by the first transaction. If the transaction is making
changes based on the assumption that the only rows that satisfied the condition were returned, a phantom read could result in improper data. Although
all the data read by the first query is returned for the second query, additional
data also should have been returned, so any changes made on the basis of the
original results may no longer be valid.

Serialization

The goal of a complete concurrency solution is to provide the highest level of isolation between the actions of different users accessing the same data. As defined
by the SQL92 standard, this highest level is called *serializable.** As the name
implies, serializable transactions appear as though they have been executed in a
series of distinct, ordered transactions. When one transaction begins, it's isolated
from any changes that occur to its data from subsequent transactions.

To the user, a serializable transaction looks as though it has the exclusive use of
the database for the duration of the transaction. Serializable transactions are predictable and reproducible, the two cardinal virtues of data integrity.

Of course, it's not trivial to have a database server support thousands of users
while each one thinks he is the only one. But Oracle silently manages to pull off
this dramatic feat.

Oracle and Concurrent User Access

Oracle solves the problems created by concurrent access through a technology
called multiversion read consistency.

Multiversion read consistency guarantees that a user sees a consistent view of the
data he or she requests. If another user changes the underlying data during the
query execution, Oracle maintains a version of the data as it existed at the time the
query began. If there were transactions underway but uncommitted at the time the
query began, Oracle will ensure that the query neglects the changes made by

---

* The SQL92 standard is the most recent version of the SQL standard as defined by the ANSI committee.

those transactions. The data returned to the query will reflect all committed transactions at the time the query started.

This feature has two dramatic effects on the way queries impact the database. First, Oracle doesn't place any locks on data for read operations. This means that a read operation will never block a write operation. Even if a database places a single lock on a single row as part of a read operation, it can still cause contention in the database, especially since most database tables tend to concentrate update operations around a few "hot spots" of active data.

Second, a user gets a complete "snapshot" view of the data, accurate at the point in time that the query began. Other databases may reduce the amount of contention in the database by locking an individual row only while it's being read, rather than over the complete duration of the row's transaction. A row that's retrieved at the end of a result set may have been changed since the time the result set retrieval began. Because rows that will be read later in the execution of the query aren't locked, they could be changed by other users, which would result in an inconsistent view of data.

Oracle8's Isolation Levels

Oracle8, like many other databases, uses the concept of *isolation levels* to describe how a transaction will interact with other transactions and how a transaction will be isolated from other transactions. An isolation level is essentially a locking scheme implemented by the database that guarantees a certain type of transaction isolation.

An application programmer can set an isolation level at the session or transaction level with a SQL statement, such as ALTER SESSION or SET TRANSACTION, respectively. Typically, a developer weighs the potential conflicts that will result from a more restrictive isolation level with the benefits that it will deliver in terms of increased protection against data integrity problems.

There are two basic isolation levels used frequently within Oracle8: READ COMMITTED and SERIALIZABLE. Both of these isolation levels create serializable database operations. The difference between the two levels is in the duration for which they enforce serializable operations. (A third level, READ ONLY, is described later in this section.)

READ COMMITTED

Enforces serialization at the statement level. This means that every statement will get a consistent view of the data as it existed at the start of the statement. However, since a transaction can contain more than one statement, it's possible that nonrepeatable reads and phantom reads can occur within the context of the complete transaction. The READ COMMITTED isolation level is the default isolation level for Oracle8.

SERIALIZABLE

Enforces serialization at the transaction level. This means that every statement within a transaction will get the same consistent view of data as it existed at the start of the transaction.

Because of their differing spans of control, these two isolation levels also react differently when they encounter a transaction that blocks their operation with a lock on a requested row. Once the lock has been released by the blocking transaction, an operation executing with the READ COMMITTED isolation level will simply retry the operation. Since this operation is only concerned with the state of data when the statement begins, this is a perfectly logical approach.

On the other hand, if the blocking transaction commits changes to the data, an operation executing with a SERIALIZABLE isolation level will return an error indicating that it cannot serialize operations. This error makes sense, because the blocking transaction will have changed the state of the data from the beginning of the SERIALIZABLE transaction, making it impossible to perform any more write operations on the changed rows. In this situation, an application programmer will have to add logic to his or her program to return to the start of the SERIALIZABLE transaction and begin it again. There are step-by-step examples of concurrent access later this chapter (in the "Concurrent Access and Performance" section), which illustrate the different ways that Oracle responds to this type of problem.

There is one other isolation level supported by Oracle8. You can declare that a session or transaction has an isolation level of READ ONLY. As the name implies, this level explicitly doesn't allow any write operations, but the READ ONLY level provides an accurate view of all the data at the time the transaction began.

Oracle8 Concurrency Features

There are three features used by Oracle8 to implement multiversion read consistency:

Rollback segments

Rollback segments are structures in the Oracle database that store "undo" information for transactions in case of rollback. This undo information restores database rows to the state they were in before the transaction in question started. When a transaction starts changing some data in a block, it first writes the old image of the data to a rollback segment. The information stored in a rollback segment provides the information necessary to roll back a transaction and supports multiversion read consistency.

A rollback segment is different from a redo log. The redo log is used to log all transactions to the database and recovers the database in the event of a system failure, while the rollback segment provides rollback for transactions and read consistency.

Blocks of rollback segments are cached in the SGA just like blocks of tables and indexes. If rollback segment blocks are unused for a period of time, they may be aged out of the cache and written to disk.

System Change Number (SCN)

To preserve the integrity of the data in the database, it's critical to keep track of the order in which actions were performed. Oracle8 must preserve the ordering of transactions with respect to time. The mechanism Oracle uses is the System Change Number.

The SCN is a logical timestamp that tracks the order in which events occurred. Oracle8 uses the SCN information in the redo log to reproduce transactions in the original and correct order when applying redo. Oracle8 also uses the SCN to determine when to clean up information in rollback segments that's no longer needed, as you will see in the following sections.

Locks in data blocks

A database must have a way of determining if a particular row is locked. Most databases keep a list of locks in memory, which are managed by a lock manager process. Oracle8 keeps locks with an indicator in the actual block in which the row is stored. A data block is the smallest amount of data that can be read from disk for an Oracle database, so whenever the row is requested, the block is read, and the lock is available within the block. Although the lock indicators are kept within a block, each lock only affects an individual row within the block.

In addition to the above features, which directly pertain to multiversion read consistency, another implementation feature in Oracle provides a greater level of concurrency in large user populations:

Nonescalating row locks

To reduce the overhead of the lock management process, other databases will sometimes *escalate* locks to a higher level of granularity within the database. For example, if a certain percentage of rows in a table are locked, the database will escalate the lock to a table lock, which locks all the rows in a table including rows that aren't specifically used by the SQL statement in question. Although lock escalation reduces the number of locks the lock manager process has to handle, it causes unaffected rows to be locked. Because each row's lock is kept within its data block, there is no need for Oracle8 to escalate a lock so it never does.

There is a lock manager called the Distributed Lock Manager (DLM) that's used with Oracle Parallel Server to track locks across multiple instances of Oracle. This is a completely different and separate locking scheme that doesn't affect the way Oracle handles row locks. The DLM is briefly described in Chapter 8.

How Oracle8 Handles SQL Operations

If you've been reading this chapter from the beginning, you should now know enough about the concepts of concurrency and the features of Oracle8 to understand how the database handles issues related to multiuser access. However, to make it perfectly clear how these features interact, we'll walk you through three scenarios: a simple write to the database, a situation in which two users attempt to write to the same row in the same table, and a read that takes place in the midst of conflicting updates.

For the purposes of these examples, we'll use the scenario of one or two users modifying the EMP table, a part of the standard sample Oracle schema that lists data about employees via a form.

A Simple Write Operation

This example describes a simple write operation, in which one user is writing to a row in the database. In example, an HR clerk wants to update the name for an employee. Assume that the HR clerk already has the employee record on-screen. The steps from this point are as follows:

1. The client modifies the employee name on the screen. The client process sends a SQL UPDATE statement over the network to the server process.

2. The server process obtains a System Change Number (SCN) and reads the data block containing the target row.

3. The server records row lock information in the data block.

4. The server process copies the old image of the employee data about to be changed to a rollback segment and then modifies the employee data.

5. The server process records the changes to the rollback segment and the database block in the redo log buffer in the SGA. The rollback segment changes are part of the redo, since the redo log stores all changes resulting from the transaction.

6. The HR clerk commits the transaction.

7. Log Writer (LGWR) writes the redo information for the entire transaction, including the SCN that marks the time the transaction was committed, from the redo log buffer to the current redo log file on disk. When the operating system confirms that the write to the redo log file has successfully completed, the transaction is considered committed.

8. The server process sends a message to the client confirming the commit.

A Conflicting Write Operation

The write operation previously described is a little different if there are two users, client A and client B, who are trying to modify the same row of data at the same time. The steps are as follows:

1. Client A modifies the employee name on the screen. Client A sends a SQL UPDATE statement over the network to the server process.

2. The server process obtains an SCN for the statement and reads the data block containing the target row.

3. The server records row lock information to the data block.

4. The server process then copies the old image of the employee data about to be changed to a rollback segment. Once the server process has written the old employee data to a rollback segment, the server process modifies the cached database block to change the employee name.

5. The server process records the changes to the rollback segment and the database block in the redo log buffer in the SGA. The rollback segment changes are part of the redo, since the redo log stores all changes resulting from the transaction.

6. Client B modifies the employee name on the screen and sends a SQL UPDATE statement to the server.

7. The server process obtains an SCN and reads the data block containing the target row.

8. The server process sees that there is a lock on the target row from the information in the header of the data block, so it waits for the blocking transaction to complete. If Client B executed the SQL statement with the SERIALIZABLE isolation level, an error is returned to the client.

9. Client A commits the transaction, the server process takes the appropriate action, and the server sends a message to client A confirming the commit.

10. If Client B executed the SQL statement with the READ COMMITTED isolation level, the SQL statement then proceeds through its normal operation.

The previous example illustrates the default behavior of Oracle8 when it detects a problem caused by a potential lost update. Because the SERIALIZABLE isolation level has a more drastic consequence than the READ COMMITTED isolation level, many developers prefer the latter level. They can avoid some of the potential conflicts by either checking for changes prior to issuing an update or by using the SELECT FOR UPDATE syntax in their SQL to avoid the problem altogether.

A Read Operation

By looking at how a user reads data from the table, you can appreciate the beauty of Oracle8's read consistency model. In this scenario, Client A is reading a series of rows from the EMP table, while Client B modifies a row before it's read by Client A, but after Client A begins his transaction. The following steps are graphically illustrated in Figure 7-2.

1. Client A sends a SQL SELECT statement over the network to the server process.

2. The server process obtains an SCN for the statement and begins to read the requested data for the query. For each data block that it reads, it compares the SCN that timestamps the SELECT statement with the SCNs for any transactions that were active in the data block. Wherever it detects changes that were uncommitted as of the SCN of the SELECT statement, the server process uses data in the rollback segments to create a "consistent read" version of the data block, current as of the time the SELECT was issued. This is what provides the multiversion read consistency.

3. Client B sends a SQL UPDATE statement for a row in the EMP table that has not yet been read by Client A's SELECT statement. The server process gets an SCN for the statement and begins the operation.

4. Client B commits his changes. The server process completes the operation, which includes recording information in the data block that contained the modified row that allows Oracle to determine the SCN that indicated when the update transaction was committed.

5. The server process for Client A's read operation comes to the newly modified block. It sees that the data block contains changes made by a transaction that has an SCN that's later than the SCN of the SELECT statement. The server process looks in the data block header, which has a pointer to the rollback segment that contains the data as it existed when Client A's transaction started. The rollback segment uses the old version of the data to create a version of the block as it existed when the SELECT statement started. Client A's SELECT statement reads the desired rows from this consistent version of the data block.

Figure 7-2 illustrates the process of reading with multiversion read consistency.

Concurrent Access and Performance

When you read through all the steps involved in the above processes, it seems as if Oracle8 would be a very slow database. This is not at all true. Oracle8 has consistently turned in benchmarks that make it one of the fastest databases, if not the fastest, on the market today.

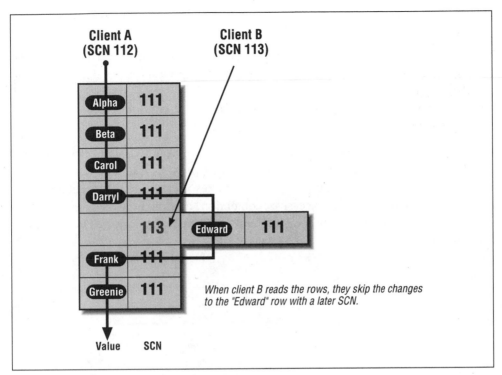

Figure 7-2. Multiversion read consistency

Oracle8 provides good performance while implementing multversion read consistency by minimizing and deferring unnecessary I/O operations. To assure the integrity of the data in a database, the database must be able to recover in the event of a system failure. This means that there must be a way to ensure that the data in the database accurately reflects the state of the committed data at the time of the crash. Oracle8 can do this by writing changed data to the database whenever a transaction commits. However, the redo log contains much less information than the entire data block for the changed data, so it's much "cheaper" to write to disk. Oracle8 writes the redo information to disk as soon as a transaction commits, and defers writing the changed data blocks to the database until several sets of changed blocks can be written together. Oracle8 can restore the database using the redo logs, and Oracle8 cuts down on time-consuming I/O operations.

But when you're considering the performance of a database, you have to think about more than simple I/O operations. It doesn't really matter how fast your database runs if your transaction is waiting for another transaction to release a lock. A faster database may complete the blocking transaction faster, but your transaction is still at a dead stop until the blocking transaction completes. Because most databases perform a mixture of reading and writing, and because Oracle8 is the only database on the market that doesn't use read locks, Oracle8 will essentially always deliver the lowest amount of database contention. Less contention equals greater throughput for a mixed application load.

There is also more than one type of performance. Performance for database operations is measured in milliseconds; performance for application developers is measured in months. Because Oracle8 provides much less contention with its read consistency model, developers have to spend less time adding workarounds to their applications to handle the results of contention.

It's not as though Oracle is the only database to give you a concurrency solution, which you can use to implement applications that provide adequate data integrity. But the multiversion read consistency model makes it easy for you to get a consistent view of data without excessive contention and without having to write workarounds in your application. If it sounds as if we're big fans of Oracle's locking scheme, well—we are.

8

Oracle8 and Transaction Processing

The insatiable corporate appetite for even larger and more sophisticated transaction processing systems has been one of the main forces driving the evolution of computing technology. As we discussed in the previous chapter, transactions form the foundation of business computing systems. In fact, transaction processing (TP) was the impetus for business computing as we know it today. The batch-oriented automation of core business processes like accounting and payroll drove the progress in mainframe computing through the 1970s and 1980s. Along the way, TP began the shift from batch to users interacting directly with systems, and online transaction processing (OLTP) was born. In the 1980s the computing infrastructure shifted from large centralized mainframes with dumb terminals to decentralized client-server computing with sophisticated GUIs running on PCs and accessing databases on other machines over a network.

The client-server revolution provided a much better user interface and reduced the cost of hardware and software, but it also introduced additional complexity in systems development, management, and deployment. After a decade of use, system administrators were being slowly overwhelmed by the task of managing thousands of client machines and dozens of servers, so the latter half of the 1990s has seen a return to centralization. Open systems server vendors like Sun, HP, Sequent (acquired by IBM in 1999), and others now provide tremendously powerful single-machine systems with mainframe-style features that deliver high availability and fault-tolerance. Browsers provide the required GUI while offering the management simplicity of terminals—just plug them in to the network!

Although many of the specific features covered in this chapter are touched upon in other chapters of this book, this chapter examines all of these features in the light of their use in large, OLTP systems—a topic of great importance to Oracle.

OLTP Basics

Before we can discuss how Oracle specifically handles OLTP, we'll start by presenting a common definition of online transaction processing.

What Is a Transaction?

The concept of a transaction and the relevant Oracle mechanics for dealing with transactions are discussed in Chapter 7, *Multiuser Concurrency*. To recap that discussion, a *transaction* is a logical unit of work that must succeed or fail in its entirety. Each transaction typically involves one or more Data Manipulation Language (DML) statements such as INSERT, UPDATE, or DELETE, and ends with either a COMMIT to make the changes permanent or a ROLLBACK to undo the changes.

The industry bible for OLTP, *Transaction Processing: Concepts and Techniques,* by Jim Gray and Andreas Reuter, introduced the notion of the *ACID* properties of a transaction. A transaction must be the following:

Atomic
>   The entire transaction succeeds or fails as a complete unit.

Consistent
>   A completed transaction leaves the affected data in a consistent or correct state.

Isolated
>   Each transaction executes in isolation and doesn't affect the state of other transactions.

Durable
>   The changes resulting from committed transactions are persistent.

If transactions execute serially—one after the other—their use of ACID properties can be relatively easily guaranteed. Each transaction starts with the consistent state of the previous transaction and, in turn, leaves a consistent state for the next transaction. Concurrency introduces the need for sophisticated locking and other coordination mechanisms to preserve the ACID properties of concurrent transactions while delivering throughput and performance.

What Does OLTP Mean?

Online transaction processing can be defined in different ways: as a type of computing with certain characteristics, or a type of computing in contrast to more traditional batch processing.

General characteristics

Most OLTP systems share some of the following general characteristics:

High transaction volumes and large user populations

The benefits of large centralized systems have driven the ever-increasing scale of today's modern OLTP systems.

Well-defined performance requirements

OLTP systems often involve Service Level Agreements that state the expected response times.

High availability

These systems are typically deemed mission-critical with significant costs resulting from downtime. The universal availability of the Web clearly increases availability requirements.

Scalability

The ability to increase transaction volumes without significant degradation in performance allows OLTP systems to handle fluctuations in business activity.

The web-enablement of OLTP systems is redefining these characteristics. The Web greatly expands the potential user population and transaction volumes and demands the highest availability and performance. Web users expect the system to be up all the time and to perform quickly—if your order entry site is down or slow, web users will go elsewhere.

Online versus batch

Online transaction processing implies direct and conversational interaction between the transaction processing system and its users. Users enter and query data using forms that interact with the back-end database. Editing and validation of data occurs at the time the transactions are submitted by users.

Batch processing occurs without user interaction. Batches of transactions are fed from source files to the operational system. Errors are typically reported in exception files or logs, and are reviewed by users or operators later on. Virtually all OLTP systems have a batch component: jobs that can execute in off-peak hours for reporting, payroll runs, posting of accounting entries, and so on.

Many large companies have batch-oriented mainframe systems that are so thoroughly embedded in the corporate infrastructure that they cannot be replaced or removed. A common practice is to "front-end" these legacy systems with online OLTP systems. Users interact with the OLTP system to enter transactions. Batch files are extracted from the OLTP system and fed into the downstream legacy applications. Once the batch processing is done, extracts are produced from the batch systems and are used to refresh the OLTP systems. This extraction process provides the users with a more sophisticated interface with online validation and editing, but it preserves the flow of data through the entrenched batch systems. While this process seems costly, it's typically more attractive than the major surgery required to remove the older systems. To compound the difficulty, in some cases the documentation of these older systems is incomplete, and the employees who understand the inner workings have retired or moved on.

The financial services industry has been a leader in information technology for transaction processing, so this notion of feeding legacy downstream applications is very common in banks and insurance companies. For example, users enter insurance claims into an online system. Once all the data has been entered and the claim has been approved, it's extracted and fed into legacy systems for further processing and payment.

OLTP Versus Decision Support

Mixed workloads—OLTP and reporting—are the source of many performance challenges and the topic of intense debate. The data warehousing industry had its genesis in the realization that OLTP systems could not realistically provide the needed transaction throughput while supporting the enormous amount of historical data and ad hoc query workload that business analysts needed for things like multiyear trend analysis.

The issue isn't simply one of adequate machine horsepower; rather, it's the way data is modeled, stored, and accessed, which is typically quite different. In OLTP, the design centers on analyzing and automating business processes to provide consistent performance for a well-known set of transactions and users. While data warehousing certainly involves analysis and requires performance, the nature of the workload isn't easy to predict. Ad hoc queries that can consume significant resources occur along with scheduled reports.

Reporting and query functions are part of an OLTP system, but the scope and frequency are typically more controlled than in a data warehouse environment. For example, a banking OLTP system will include queries for customer status and account balances, but not multiyear transaction patterns.

The OLTP system typically provides forms that allow well-targeted queries, which are executed efficiently and don't consume undue resources. However, hard and fast rules—for example, that OLTP systems don't include extensive query facilities —don't necessarily hold true. The I/O performed by most OLTP systems tends to be approximately 70 to 80 percent read and 20 to 30 percent write. Most transactions involve the querying of data, for example, product codes, customer names, account balances, inventory levels, and so on. Users submitting tuned queries for specific business functions are a key part of OLTP. Ad hoc queries across broad data sets are not.

Oracle's OLTP Heritage

Oracle has enjoyed tremendous growth as the database of choice for OLTP in the midrange computing environment. Oracle6 introduced nonescalating row-level locking and read consistency (two of the most important of Oracle's core OLTP features), but Oracle7 was really the enabler for Oracle's growth in OLTP. Oracle7 introduced many key features, including the following:

- Multi-Threaded Server (MTS)
- Shared SQL
- Stored procedures and triggers
- XA support
- Distributed transactions and two-phase commit
- Data replication
- Oracle Parallel Server (OPS)*

Oracle 8.0 enhanced existing functionality and introduced additional OLTP-related features including the following:

- Connection pooling
- Connection multiplexing
- Data partitioning
- Advanced Queuing (AQ)
- Index organized tables
- Internalization of the Distributed Lock Manager (DLM) for Oracle Parallel Server
- Internalization of the triggers for replicated tables and parallel propagation of replicated transactions

Oracle8*i* provides the following additional enhancements and technologies for OLTP:

---

* OPS was actually available for DEC VMS in 1989 and for NCR Unix with the last production release of Oracle6 (Version 6.0.36), but it became widely available, more stable, and more popular in Oracle 7.

- Support for Java internally in the database kernel

- Support for distributed component technologies: CORBA V2.0 and Enterprise JavaBeans (EJB) V1.0

- Publish/subscribe messaging based on Advanced Queuing

- Cache Fusion for Oracle Parallel Server

- Online index rebuild and reorganization

- Database Resource Manager

- Use of a standby database for queries

- Internalization of the replication packages used to apply transactions at the remote sites

The remainder of this chapter examines many of these features in more depth.

Architectures for OLTP

Although all OLTP systems are oriented towards the same goals, there are several different underlying system architectures that you can use for the deployment of OLTP, including the traditional two-tier model, a three-tier model, and a model that encompasses the use of the Web.

Traditional Two-Tier Client-Server

The late 1980s saw the rise of two-tier client-server applications. In this configuration, PCs acted as clients accessing a separate database server over a network. The client ran both the GUI and the application logic, giving rise to the term *fat clients*. The database server processed SQL statements and returned the requested results back to the clients. While database servers were relatively simple to develop using visual tools, client-server systems were difficult to deploy and maintain as they required fairly high-bandwidth networks and the installation and regular upgrading of specific client software on every user's PC. Figure 8-1 illustrates the two-tier architecture.

Stored Procedures

Oracle7 introduced stored procedures written in PL/SQL, Oracle's proprietary language for writing application logic. These procedures are stored in the database and are executed by clients issuing remote procedure calls (RPCs) as opposed to executing SQL statements. Instead of issuing multiple SQL calls, occasionally with intermediate logic to accomplish a task, the client issues one procedure call, passing in the required parameters. The database executes all the required SQL and logic using the parameters it receives.

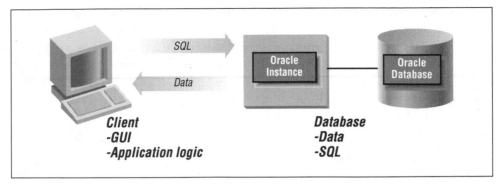

Figure 8-1. Two-tier client-server architecture

Stored procedures can also shield the client logic from internal changes to the data structures or program logic. As long as the parameters the client passed in and received back don't change, no changes are required in the client software. Stored procedures move a portion of the application logic from the client to the database server. By doing so, stored procedures can reduce the network traffic considerably. This capability increases the scalability of two-tier systems. Figure 8-2 illustrates a two-tier system with stored procedures.

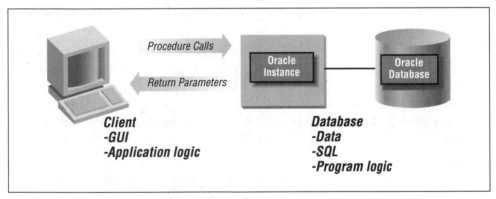

Figure 8-2. Two-tier system with stored procedures

Transaction Processing Monitors and Three-Tier Systems

The OLTP systems with the largest user populations and transaction throughput are typically deployed using a three-tier architecture. Clients access a transaction processing (TP) monitor in the middle tier that, in turn, accesses a database server on the back-end. The notion of a TP monitor dates back to the original mainframe OLTP systems. Of course, in the mainframe environment, all logic ran on one machine. In an open systems environment, TP monitors typically run on a separate machine (or machines), adding a middle tier between clients and the database server.

TP monitors provide an environment for running services that clients call. The clients don't interact directly with the database server. The calling of services provided by a TP monitor on a remote machine seems similar, in many ways, to the stored procedure architecture described in the previous section, which is why stored procedure-based systems are sometimes referred to as "TP-Lite." On the other hand, systems that make use of true TP monitors are sometimes referred to as "TP-Heavy." Examples of TP monitors include CICS from IBM on the mainframe and Tuxedo from BEA Systems on Unix and Microsoft Windows NT systems.

TP monitors provides additional valuable services such as:

Funneling

> Similar to Oracle's Multi-Threaded Server, TP monitors leverage a pool of shared services across a larger user population. Instead of each user connecting directly to the database, the client calls a service running under the TP monitor's control. The TP monitor invokes one of its services, and the service has the actual connection to the database.

Load balancing

> Client requests are balanced across the multiple-shared servers executing on one or more physical machines. The TP monitor can direct client service calls to the least loaded server, and can spawn additional shared servers as needed.

Fault tolerance

> The TP monitor acts as a transaction manager; the monitor performs the commit or rollback of the transaction.* The underlying database becomes a resource manager, but doesn't control the transaction. If the database server fails while executing some work, the TP monitor can resubmit the transaction to a surviving database server, as control of the transaction lies with the TP monitor.

Transaction routing

> The logic in the middle tier can direct transactions to specific database servers, increasing scalability.

Heterogeneous transactions

> TP monitors can manage transactions across multiple heterogeneous database servers, for example, a transaction that updates data in Oracle and DB2.

While developing three-tier OLTP systems is complex and requires specialized skills, the benefits are substantial. Systems that use TP monitors provide higher scalability, availability, and flexibility than the simpler two-tier systems.

---

* TP monitors usually control transactions using the X/Open Distributed Transaction Processing standard published by the X/Open standards body. A database that supports the XA interface can function as a resource manager under control of a TP monitor which acts as a transaction manager.

Determining which architecture is appropriate for an OLTP system requires (among other things) careful evaluation and consideration of costs, available skills, workload profiles, scalability requirements, and availability requirements.

Figure 8-3 illustrates a three-tier system using a TP monitor.

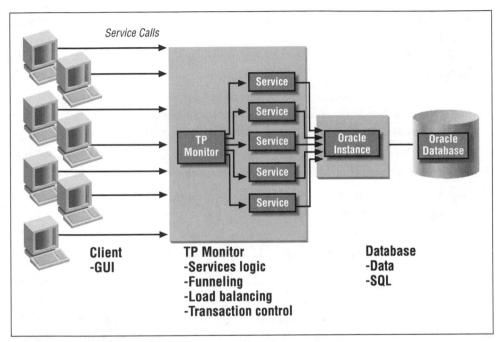

Figure 8-3. Three-tier architecture

Application Servers and Web Servers

The middle tier of web-based systems is usually an application server and/or a web server. These servers provide similar services to the TP monitor previously described, but are more web-centric, dealing with HTTP, HTML, CGI, Java, and Object Request Brokers (ORBs). While application servers are good for web technologies, they aren't as mature as proven TP monitors for handling and controlling transactions. Application servers and web servers are covered in some detail in Chapter 14, *Oracle8i and the Web*.

Oracle8 and ERP Solutions

The Oracle database is by far the most popular database foundation for the large-scale enterprise resource planning (ERP) applications that have become popular in the 1990s.

While the four best-known application suites—Oracle Applications (Oracle's own ERP solution), Peoplesoft, SAP, and BAAN—make varying use of Oracle's features, these applications have converged on a similar architecture: three-tier. All of these ERP suites involve a middle tier with some type of application server functionality:

- Oracle Applications uses the Oracle Developer Server cartridge in the middle tier. Users access the applications using a browser running a Java applet. The middle tier maintains the form runtime state for the forms in the application, generates the Java user interface, and handles database interaction.

- Peoplesoft recently rearchitected their two-tier applications to a three-tier solution that uses the Tuxedo TP monitor. Users access the Tuxedo services either through traditional Windows clients or through Java and the Web.

- SAP uses proprietary middle-tier application servers. Users connect to the application servers that, in turn, manage database interaction.

- BAAN also uses proprietary middle-tier application servers. Users connect to the application servers that, in turn, manage database interaction.

Oracle8 Features for OLTP

Oracle has many features that contribute to OLTP performance, reliability, scalability, and availability. This section presents the basic attributes of many of these features. This section is by no means exhaustive; it's only intended to be an introduction. Please see your relevant Oracle documentation and third-party books for more information.

General Concurrency and Performance

As discussed in Chapter 7, Oracle has implemented excellent support for concurrency and performance in OLTP systems. Some of the key features relevant to OLTP are as follows:

Nonescalating row-level locking
> Oracle locks only the rows a transaction works on and never escalates these locks to page-level or table-level locks. This prevents any false lock contention for cases in which users want to work on different rows but contend for locks that have escalated to higher granularity levels, such as page locks.

Multiversion read consistency
> Oracle provides statement-level and transaction-level data consistency without requiring read locks. A query is guaranteed to see only the data that was committed at the time the query started. The changes made by transactions that were in-flight but uncommitted at the time the query started won't be visible.

Transactions that began after the query started and were committed before the query finishes also won't be seen by the query. Oracle uses rollback segments to reproduce the data as it existed at the time the query started. This capability avoids the unpleasant choice between allowing queries to see uncommitted data (known as dirty reads) or having readers block writers (and vice versa). It also provides a consistent snapshot view of data at a single point in time.

Shared SQL

The parsing of a SQL statement is fairly CPU-intensive. Oracle caches parsed and optimized SQL statements in the shared SQL area within the shared pool. If another user executes a SQL statement that's cached, the parse and optimize overhead is avoided. The statements must be exactly identical to be reused; no extra spaces, line feeds or differences in capitalization are allowed. OLTP systems involve a large number of users executing the same application code. These systems provide an ideal opportunity for reusing shared SQL statements.

Stored outlines

Oracle8*i* supports execution plan stability, sometimes referred to as *bound plans*, with stored outlines. The route a SQL statement takes during execution is critical for high performance. Once application developers and DBAs have tuned a SQL statement for maximum efficiency, they can force the Oracle optimizer to use the same execution plan regardless of environmental changes. This provides critical stability and predictability in the face of software upgrades, schema changes, data volume changes, and so on.

Scalability

Both the Multi-Threaded Server and the Database Resource Manager help Oracle support larger or mixed user populations.

Multi-Threaded Server

Oracle7 introduced the Multi-Threaded Server (MTS) (described in Chapter 2, *Oracle8 Architecture*) to allow Oracle to support larger user populations. While MTS reduced the number of server processes, each client still used its own physical network connection. The resources for network connections aren't unlimited. Oracle8 provided two solutions for increasing the capabilities of the actual network socket layer at the operating system level.

Net8 connection pooling

Allows the client population to share a pool of shared physical network connections. Idle clients transparently "time out," and their network connection is returned to the pool to be used by an active client. The idle client maintains a

Bind Variables and Shared SQL

As we've mentioned, Oracle's shared SQL is a key feature for building high-performance applications. In an OLTP application, similar SQL statements may be used repeatedly, but each SQL statement submitted will typically have different selection criteria contained in the WHERE clause to identify the qualifying rows, the different values for updating and inserting rows, and so on. As we've said, Oracle can share SQL statements, but the statements must be absolutely identical.

To take advantage of this feature for statements that are identical except for specific values, such as the column values used in the WHERE clause criteria, you can use bind variables in your SQL statements. Each time the SQL statement is executed, the values substituted for the bind variables in the SQL statement may be different, but the statement itself is the same.

Consider an example application for granting raises to employees. The application submits the following SQL:

```
UPDATE emp SET salary = salary * (1 + 0.1)WHERE empno = 123;
UPDATE emp SET salary = salary * (1 + 0.15)WHERE empno = 456;
```

These statements are clearly different; they update different employees identified by different employee numbers, and the employees receive different salary increases. To realize the benefits of shared SQL, you need to write the application to use bind variables for the percentage salary increase and the employee numbers. The statements would then look like this:

```
UPDATE emp SET salary = salary * (1 + :v_incr)WHERE empno = :v_empno;
UPDATE emp SET salary = salary * (1 + :v_incr)WHERE empno = :v_empno;
```

These statements are identical and would therefore be shared. The difference in this version of the code is that the application would submit different values for the two variables :v_incr and :v_empno, a percentage increase of 0.1 for employee 123 and 0.15 for employee 456. Oracle substitutes these actual values for the variables in the SQL. The substitution occurs during the phase of processing known as the *bind phase*, which follows the *parse phase* and *optimize phase*. The end result is the same as using two different SQL statements. For more details, see the relevant Oracle8*i* guide for your development language.

virtual connection with Oracle and will get another physical connection when activity resumes. With the Oracle security model, authentication is separate from a specific connection, so a single pooled connection can represent different users at different times. Connection pooling is suitable for applications with clients that connect but aren't highly active, for example, email systems.

Net8 Connection Manager

Reduces the number of network connections used on the database server. Clients connect to a middle-tier machine running the Net8 Connection Manager. The Connection Manager multiplexes the traffic for multiple clients into one network connection per Net8 dispatcher on the database server. Unlike connection pooling, there is no notion of "time-out" for a client's virtual network connection. The Oracle network topology can include multiple machines running the Connection Manager to provide additional scalability and fault-tolerance.

In terms of scalability, you can think of connection pooling as the middleweight solution and multiplexing via Connection Manager as the heavyweight solution. Figure 8-4 illustrates these two network scaling technologies.

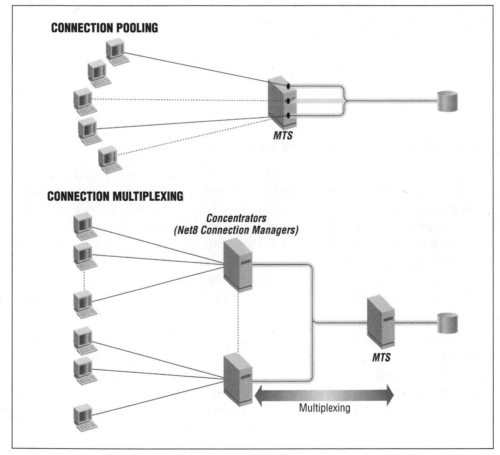

Figure 8-4. Network scaling in Net8

Database Resource Manager

Oracle8*i* introduced the Database Resource Manager (DRM) to simplify and automate the management of mixed workloads in which different users access the same database for different purposes. The DRM allocates CPU and parallelism resources to users based on resource plans. A resource plan defines limits for the amount of a particular computer resource a group of users can use. This allows the DBA to ensure that certain types of users receive sufficient machine resources to meet performance requirements.

For example, you can allocate 80 percent of the CPU resources to order entry users, with the remaining 20 percent allocated to users asking for reports. This allocation prevents reporting users from dominating the machine while order entry users are working. If the order entry users aren't using all the allocated resource, the reporting users can use more than their allotted percentage. If the order entry workload increases, the reporting users will be cut back to respect their 20 percent allocation. In other words, the order entry users will get up to 80 percent of CPU time, as needed, while the users asking for reports will get at least 20 percent of the CPU time, and more depending on how much the order entry group is using. With the DRM, you can dynamically alter the details of the plan without shutting down the instance.

Oracle Parallel Server and Partitioning

Scaling an OLTP system beyond a single physical database server requires the use of Oracle Parallel Server (OPS). With OPS, multiple machines each run an instance of Oracle and access a single shared database. Oracle's Partitioning option allows you to split a table into multiple pieces organized by ranges of business values, a hash function, or hashing within each range. The Partitioning option's ability to split a table into pieces based on a range of values, combined with the ability to route user transactions to a specific instance of OPS, provides a very powerful mechanism for controlling the traffic flow within a system to achieve maximum scalability.

You can route transactions based on the values in the transactions, such as geographically by state, in a variety of ways. The simplest way is to have users for specific values (states, for example) log onto specific machines to do their work. These specific values map users for certain states to specific instances of OPS. The activity for each instance then maps to the specific partitions for the set of states each instance's users work on. While relatively simple to implement, this manual approach only works when a natural mapping exists from users to business ranges, and when there isn't a lot of change in the mapping. For example, suppose there are many users that work across multiple states because their work is organized by line-of-business, or that different users tend to handle different states at different times. These variations disrupt the clear mapping of users to states, which in turn interferes with the mapping of users to instances for specific states. Training users as to which machine is for which state, and ensuring compliance with the mapping, would probably be difficult.

The most flexible method, and the most complex to implement, employs a middle tier to automatically route transactions to the appropriate machine based on a mapping of business values to instances of OPS. Users submit their transactions to the middle tier, which then routes the transactions to the eventual database server based on the business values in the transactions. This routing is typically done using a set of routing tables (maintained in the middle tier) that allow the routing map to be changed simply and quickly. The mapping of database servers to specific sets of data increases the scalability of the overall system by allowing each server to cache relevant data for its transactions and by avoiding undue overhead for inter-instance coordination. If multiple servers are working on the same sets of data, the servers must pass messages and data back and forth for coordination. The inter-instance coordination is based on which physical blocks each instance is accessing. Mapping the servers to distinct sets of data stored in separate table partitions minimizes this cross talk and increases scalability.

In this section we've only covered the basic concepts that lie behind the operation of OPS. The inner workings of OPS and techniques for scalability are detailed in your Oracle documentation.

Figure 8-5 illustrates a system that employs a middle tier to route transactions based on the first letter of a customer's name.

High Availability

From an operational perspective, OLTP systems represent a company's electronic central nervous system, so the databases that support these systems must be highly available. Oracle8 has a number of features that contribute to high availability.

Standby database
> Oracle provides database redundancy by maintaining a copy of the primary database on another machine, usually at another site. Redo logs from the primary server are shipped to the standby server and applied there to duplicate the production activity. Oracle8*i* introduces the automated shipping of redo logs to the standby site and the ability to open the standby database for read-only access for reporting.

Transparent Application Failover (TAF)
> TAF is a programming interface that enables you to automatically reconnect a user session to another Oracle instance should the primary instance fail.

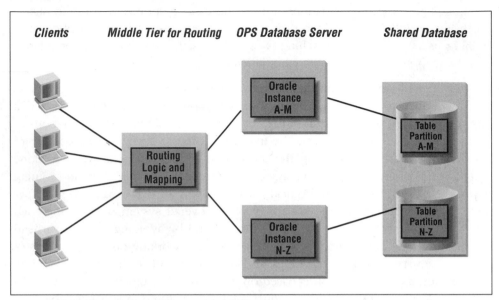

Figure 8-5. Scaling with partitioning and OPS

Advanced Queuing (AQ)

Using AQ as the basis for intersystem communication allows systems to operate more independently. Avoiding direct system dependencies can help to avoid "cascading" failures because if one system is down the others continue to function—AQ provides a method for asynchronous, or deferred, intersystem communication. Advanced Queuing is described in more detail in the following section.

Replication

You can use Oracle's built-in replication functionality to provide data redundancy. The changes made by transactions are replicated synchronously or asynchronously to other databases. If the primary database fails, the data is available from the other databases.

Oracle Parallel Server

Oracle Parallel Server increases the scalability of the Oracle database. But by supporting multiple instances with full access to one database, OPS also provides the highest levels of availability for protection from the failure of a node in a clustered or MPP environment. If one node fails, the surviving nodes provide continued access to the database

For a more detailed discussion of high availability, see Chapter 10, *Oracle8 and High Availability*.

Oracle Parallel Server and Cache Fusion

One aspect of multiuser consistency (described in Chapter 7) relates directly to the use of Oracle Parallel Server (OPS) and its performance implications. Parallel Cache Management (PCM) locks ensure cache coherency in an OPS implementation. PCM forces Oracle instances requesting data to acquire locks from holding instances before modifying or reading database blocks. Only one instance at a time can modify a block. When a block is modified, it must first be written to disk before another instance can acquire the PCM lock and modify the block. What is known as a *ping* occurs when a block must be written to the disk by an instance so that another instance can read it.

A key to obtaining optimum performance with past releases of OPS was to effectively partition the data so that locking was local to each node and pinging didn't occur. While custom-built applications can be effectively partitioned with some effort, this is not the case with many packaged applications. The three types of inter-instance contention that may be encountered are:

- Reader/reader (in decision-support applications)
- Reader/writer (in lightweight OLTP applications)
- Writer/writer (with lots of updates across instances)

Pinging may occur with reader/writer and writer/writer contention because blocks are being modified.

The Oracle8*i* Parallel Server Option features new technology for resolving reader/writer contention in an OPS environment. The technology is called Cache Fusion, and it solves the pinging problem for situations in which a reader in one instance requests a lock covering blocks currently being changed by another instance. Instead of writing the blocks in question to disk so the instance requesting the lock can read them, the instance that is changing the blocks produces consistent read blocks and ships them across the interconnect to the requesting instance, avoiding the slow disk access. If a data block requested by one instance is in the memory cache of another instance, Cache Fusion uses remote memory access to resolve the conflict. The requesting instance sends a request for a consistent-read copy of the block to the holding instance, and that image of the block is transmitted directly between the buffer caches of the two instances across an interconnect (typically of the high-speed and low-latency variety). In this way, Cache Fusion delivers a read-consistent view of data across multiple instances in an OPS environment without having to resort to disk-based pinging.

The Oracle8*i* Parallel Server continues to manage writer/writer contention using disk-based PCM, although Oracle has announced its intention to develop Cache Fusion further to provide faster writer/writer contention resolution in a future release.

Oracle8 Advanced Queuing

Messaging technology has existed for quite some time and is common in OLTP applications. Typical messaging technologies provide a reliable transport layer for shipping messages from one machine to another over a network. Oracle8 introduced Advanced Queuing (AQ) as an integrated database service.

Oracle AQ provides the benefits of simple messaging products but adds the value of database-resident queues. The information in message queues represents critical business events and should be stored in a reliable, scalable, secure, and recoverable place. Placing the queues in the database extends the core benefits of a database to the queues themselves.

The data that flows through queues represents the ebb and flow of business activity. Analyzing the types and volumes of message traffic can help to identify how different business functions are operating and interacting, which, in turn, can provide valuable insights into the operation of your business. Oracle AQ supports the notion of *message warehousing*, in which the content and details of the queues can be queried and analyzed because they're already in the database. Oracle can dequeue messages but can leave historical data in the queues for subsequent analysis.

Applications can enqueue and dequeue messages as part of a transaction or as a separate event that occurs as soon as the specific enqueue or dequeue statement is issued. Queue actions included in the scope of a transaction are committed or rolled back with that transaction. Should a failure occur, the queue activities are recovered along with the rest of the database activities.

Oracle can propagate messages from one queue to another by providing a routing engine for message traffic. Figure 8-6 illustrates the use of queuing and propagation.

Advanced Queuing for System Interfaces

Implementing OLTP systems invariably involves interfaces with other systems in the enterprise or in other companies. The effort to design, create, and manage these interfaces is substantial and can easily account for 40 percent to 60 percent of the cost of large-scale ERP implementations. Furthermore, adding other systems to the mix or changing existing systems entails reworking the interfaces, resulting in an increasing and ongoing burden. Oracle is focusing on its Advanced Queuing technology as the foundation for integrating application systems together with the Enterprise Integration Framework.

Oracle's Enterprise Integration Framework is a bundle of services and products intended to help companies solve the integration problem by implementing a

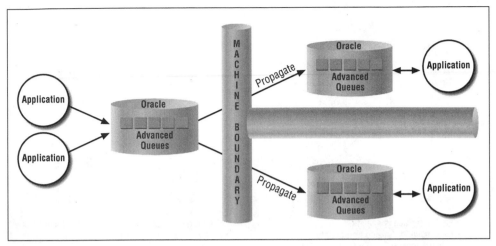

Figure 8-6. Advanced Queuing

"hub-and-spoke" architecture using a combination of messaging, routing, and transformation technologies. Traditionally, you would develop a specific interface between two systems. As you added a third system to the mix, you would have to create more specific interfaces between each of the systems. The more systems you attempt to integrate, the more custom interfaces you would be responsible for developing, and the greater the development and maintenance burden.

With the Enterprise Integration Framework, individual systems connect to a hub via the spokes, thus avoiding direct system-to-system interfaces. The spokes send and receive messages, while the hub provides routing and transformation services. This reduces the number of interfaces required to connect a set of systems. You don't need a specific interface for every specific system pair. Adding additional systems to existing systems doesn't require development of many new interfaces. You connect the new system to the hub, and leverage the routing and transformation services. Figure 8-7 contrasts the custom approach with the hub-and-spoke approach of Enterprise Integration Framework.

Oracle8i and Publish-Subscribe Technology

Oracle8*i* enhances Advanced Queuing to include publish-subscribe functionality. Applications can subscribe to a message queue by specifying the attributes of messages they're interested in receiving. When another application publishes a message by placing it in a queue, Oracle will evaluate the contents of the message to determine which of the subscribing applications is interested and can notify those applications. For example, a shipping application can subscribe to a queue used for orders and specify that only messages for orders with a status of "Ready to Ship" are of interest. As messages representing these orders flow through the

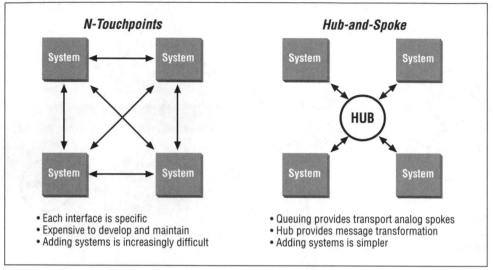

Figure 8-7. Custom interfaces versus hub-and-spoke approach

queue, the shipping application will only receive the desired messages. This pub-lish-subscribe functionality, coupled with message propagation for routing, pro-vides a very powerful messaging backbone for information flow between systems.

Object Technologies and Distributed Components

Companies spend a great deal of time and money implementing systems for spe-cific functions, for example, human resources, financial management, manufactur-ing, purchasing, and so on. While messaging technologies can assist with interfac-ing different systems, online interaction is often needed as well. For example, if the human resources system maintains information about the company's employ-ees (such as the department they work in and their role), then ideally the purchas-ing system could access the data in the HR system online at the time purchases are being made. At this point, the purchasing system could determine the spending limits of the purchaser and what department the accounting should be tied to. In practice, these online interfaces are difficult to build because they require the sys-tems to agree, and remain in agreement, about how to communicate. Each system has proprietary application programming interfaces (APIs) that allow other sys-tems to communicate with them. These specific, and often conflicting, APIs limit the reuse of the functionality within each system.

Object technologies offer a compelling solution: systems communicate by invok-ing methods on objects instead of by calling specific APIs. For example, if you want to check the department of a user, you make a standard object call to the employee object managed by the HR system.

Oracle8*i* introduces support for a number of object technologies:

CORBA

The Common Object Request Broker Architecture, a multivendor industry standard developed by the Object Management Group (OMG) for object interaction.

Java

A popular object-oriented language.

EJB

Enterprise JavaBeans, a standard architecture for computing using business components written in Java.

CORBA, EJB, and objects are covered in more detail in Chapter 13, *Oracle8/8i Extensions.*

9

Oracle8 and Data Warehousing

Although a database is a general-purpose piece of software, it handles a variety of purposes with a variety of technical requirements, such as the following:

Recording and storing data
Requires reliably storing data and protecting each user's data from the effects of other users' changes

Reading data for online viewing and reports
Requires a consistent view of the data

Analyzing data to detect business trends
Requires summarizing data and relating many different summaries to each other

Together, the last two purposes listed are known as *data warehousing*.

Data warehousing has become one of the most powerful trends in information technology. There is a very simple motivation behind this trend: data warehousing allows businesses to use their data to aid in making strategic decisions. Data warehousing unlocks the hidden value embedded in an organization's data stores.

Recognizing this trend, Oracle began adding data warehousing-related features to Oracle7 in the early 1990s. Oracle8 and Oracle8*i* contained additional features for warehousing, particularly to improve the performance and management of very large data warehouses. Oracle also developed additional tools for building a complete data warehouse infrastructure, including business analysis and data movement tools.

What is data warehousing good for? Data warehousing produces an infrastructure that can provide answers to the following business questions:

- How does this scenario relate to past results?

- What knowledge can we gain by looking at the data differently?

- What could happen in the future?

- How can we change the business to positively influence the future?

This chapter gives you an introduction to the basic concepts, technologies, and tools used in a data warehouse. Before you can really understand how Oracle addresses the issues of data warehousing, we'll have to spend a little time describing the basic terms and technologies that data warehousing encompasses.

Data Warehousing Basics

Why do you need data warehousing? Why is the data in an online transaction processing (OLTP) database difficult to use for strategic analysis? The use of data for strategic analysis has four very specific characteristics.

Strategic analysis discerns trends in data, rather than individual facts.
Because of this, data warehousing typically creates fairly simple reports based on aggregate values culled from enormous amounts of data. If OLTP databases attempted to create these aggregates on the fly, they would expend a lot of resources.

The information in a data warehouse is almost exclusively read, instead of written.
This means that the overhead of transaction control, an important part of a normal OLTP database system, isn't really needed for a data warehouse.

The data used for analysis doesn't typically have to be up-to-the-minute accurate.
Because strategic analysis is concerned with trends over time, the data used can be a day, a week, or even a month old, depending on the analysis being done. This means that data in a data warehouse can have some or all of its aggregate values created as part of a batch process offline.

The design that is required for an efficient data warehouse differs from the standard normalized design for a relational database.
Queries are typically read against a single fact table, which may contain summary information using a specific type of schema design called a *star schema*. This design lets you access facts quite flexibly along key dimensions or "lookup" values. (The star schema is described in more detail in the section "Data Warehouse Design.") For instance, a data warehouse user typically wants to compare the total amount of sales, which come from a fact table, by region, store in the region, and items, all of which can be considered key dimensions.

The Evolution of Data Warehousing

Data warehousing is not a new idea. The use of corporate data for strategic decision making, as opposed to the use of data for tracking and enabling operations, has gone on for almost as long as computing.

Quite early, companies building operational systems began to recognize the potential business benefits of analyzing the data housed in such systems. In fact, much of the early growth in personal computers was tied to the use of spreadsheets that performed analysis against data downloaded from the operational systems. Business executives began to direct IT efforts toward understanding the flow of business from the existing business data. This understanding developed business solutions and strategies, and many of these early joint initiatives led to successful data warehousing projects. Today, warehouses are used in business areas such as customer relationship management, sales and marketing campaign analysis, product management and packaging, financial analysis, and risk detection and fraud analysis.

In the 1980s, many companies began using dedicated systems for these applications, which were collectively known as *decision support systems* (DSS). Decision support queries tended to be CPU- and memory-bound and the environment was primarily read-only, while traditional OLTP was typically I/O bound with write activity. The characteristics of the queries were much less predictable (e.g., more "ad hoc") than what had been experienced in OLTP systems. This led to the development of separate data stores for decision support apart from those for OLTP.

However, it wasn't until Bill Inmon (one of the key proponents of the data warehousing movement, some of whose books are noted in the Appendix) and others popularized the term "data warehouse" in the early 1990s, that a formalized system of understanding about how these goals could be achieved came into being.

Since then, the topology of the data warehouse has evolved further, as the next section illustrates.

The Architecture of Data Warehouses

Initially conceived as a large enterprise-wide source of all information, the topology of the data warehouse has evolved into a multitier architecture, as shown in Figure 9-1.

The topology shown in Figure 9-1 is the mature result of years of experience. The evolution from a traditional client-server environment to multiple tiers occurred for a variety of reasons. Initial efforts at creating a single warehouse often resulted in "analysis paralysis." Just as efforts to define an enterprise-wide OLTP model often take years (due to cross-departmental politics and the scope of the effort), similar attempts in data warehousing also ended up taking much longer than businesses

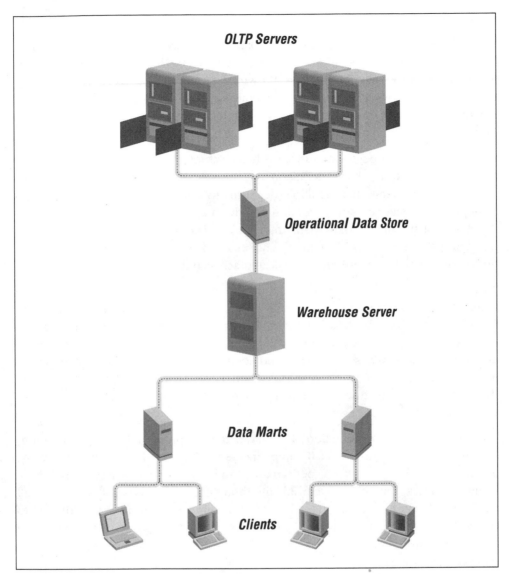

Figure 9-1. Typical data warehousing topology

were willing to accept. These efforts were further hampered by the continually changing analysis requirements necessitated by a continually changing market-place. While the data elements and requirements for operational systems can remain relatively stagnant over time, understanding business trends can be like try-ing to catch lightning in a bottle.

Consequently, attempts at building such enterprise-wide models, in an effort to satisfy everyone, often satisfied no one.

Data Marts

While some large-scale enterprise-only data warehouse efforts ended in dismal failure, business analysts at these companies became frustrated and impatient. Some analysts began building their own department-focused *data marts* by extracting data from the appropriate operational systems. Many data marts were initially quite successful because they were able to fulfill business needs relatively quickly.

However, problems began to surface. There was often no coordination between departments regarding basic definitions, such as "customer." If a senior manager asked the same question of multiple departments, the answers provided by these "independent" data marts were often different, thus calling into question the validity of any of the marts. Many departments also encountered ongoing difficulty in managing these multiple data marts and in maintaining extractions from operational sources (which were often duplicated across multiple departments).

As decision support architects took another look at their solutions, they began to realize that it was very important to have a consistent view of the detailed data at the enterprise data warehouse level. They also began to realize that data marts were a necessity for providing reasonable performance at the department level and for solving business problems and identifying return on investment in an incremental fashion. Today, most successful implementers simultaneously grow data marts one department at a time while growing the enterprise warehouse server in an incremental fashion.

The currently accepted definition of a data mart is simply a subject- or application-specific data warehouse, usually implemented within a department. Typically, these data marts are built for performance and may include a large number of summary tables. Data marts were initially thought of as being small, since not all of the detail data for a department or data from another department would need to be loaded in the mart. However, some marts get quite large as they incorporate data from outside sources (sometimes purchased), which isn't relevant in other parts of the business.

In some companies, data marts are sometimes deployed to meet specific project goals with models optimized for performance for that particular project. Such data marts are retired when the project is completed and the hardware is reused for other projects. As the analysis requirements for a business change, the topology of any particular data warehouse is subject to evolution over time, so developers must be aware of this possibility.

Operational Data Stores

The *operational data store* (ODS) is a recent concept that has grown in popularity. The ODS may best be described as a distribution center for current data. Like the OLTP servers, the schema is highly normalized and the data is recent. The ODS serves as a consolidation point for reporting and can give the business one location for viewing current data that crosses divisions or departments. The popularity of the ODS has grown in part as a result of the large number of companies in the midst of acquisitions and mergers. These organizations often face mixed application environments. The ODS acts as a staging location that can be used as the source for further transformations into a data warehouse or into data marts.

The warehouse server, or enterprise data warehouse, is a multisubject historical information store usually supporting multiple departments and often serving as the corporate database of record. When an ODS is established, the warehouse server is often fed from the ODS. When an ODS isn't present, data for the warehouse is directly extracted and transformed from operational sources. External data may also feed the warehouse server.

Data Warehouse Design

The database serves as the foundation of the data warehouse, it's the place where the data is stored. Just like a physical warehouse building used by a business to store products, a data warehouse becomes useful only when there are business users who want to gain access to the information stored within. This may seem a trivial point. Yet we've seen a number of cases of companies building data warehouses without consulting the business to determine what the company's needs actually are; thus, the database ends up with very few users and little activity.

Assuming that your warehouse is well-planned and that there is a demand for the data, your next challenge will be to figure out how to handle the demand. You will be faced with the need to design your data warehouse to deliver appropriate performance to your users: performance that may initially seem far beyond the capabilities of your system since the information requested from the data warehouse can involve summaries and comparisons of massive amounts of detailed data.

When you start designing your data warehouse, you also need to remember that a data warehouse is never complete. When the business changes, so too must the data warehouse. Thus, the ability to track changes through metadata stored in a repository often becomes critical in design phases.

Various design tools in the market provide this capability. In the Oracle world, Oracle Designer is extremely useful because, in addition to its repository, it provides the capability to reverse engineer operational tables (particularly from Oracle database sources) or other warehouse models and then forward engineer the new schema and tables. The data warehouse designer typically reverse engineers an existing schema (which consists of bringing the source database definition into the Designer repository where its design can be viewed and/or changed). The designer also removes constraints, chooses relevant items from existing tables to create new tables, and builds constraints for the new schema. The SQL to create the new tables and schema can then be automatically generated. The Oracle Designer repository product is evolving toward becoming a repository for storing all Oracle warehouse-related metadata.

As noted previously, a data warehouse has a different set of usage characteristics from those of an OLTP database. One aspect that makes it easier to meet data warehousing performance requirements is the overwhelmingly high percentage of read operations. Oracle's locking model, which is described in detail in Chapter 7, *Multiuser Concurrency*, is ideally suited to support data warehouse operations. Oracle8 doesn't place any locks onto data that's being read, thus reducing contention and resource requirements for situations in which there are a lot of database reads. Oracle8 is therefore well-suited to perform as the repository for a data warehouse.

The different set of warehousing usage characteristics, when compared to OLTP, also leads to a different type of design schema for the warehouse. In an OLTP database, the transaction data is stored in multiple tables, and data items are stored only once. If a query requests data from more than one transaction table, the tables are joined together. Typically, the database query optimizer decides which table to use as the starting point for the join, based on the assumption that the data in the tables is essentially equally important.

Data in a warehouse is usually modeled differently. The key information in a warehouse is stored in a central fact table, which may contain summarized data for data items duplicated elsewhere in the warehouse. This fact table is accessed by users specifying look-up values that reside in a number of "dimension" tables, as shown in Figure 9-2.

Ralph Kimball, author of the widely read book *The Data Warehouse Toolkit*, is largely credited with discovering that users of data warehouses typically pose their queries in such a manner that the *star schema*, shown in Figure 9-2, is an appropriate model to use. A typical query might be something like the following:

> Show me how many sales of computers (a product type) were sold by a store chain (a channel) in Wisconsin (a geography) over the past 6 months (a time).

The schema in Figure 9-2 shows a relatively large sales transactions table (called a *fact table*) surrounded by smaller tables (called *dimensions* or *look-up tables*). The query just described is often called *multidimensional*, since several dimensions are included (and time is almost always one of them). Because these queries are typical in a data warehouse, the recognition of the star schema by a cost-based optimizer can deliver enormous performance benefits.

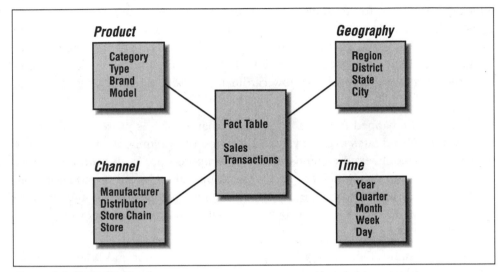

Figure 9-2. Typical star schema

Query Optimization

Oracle first provided the ability to recognize a star schema in the query optimizer in Oracle7 and has focused on making its cost-based query optimizer smarter in response to decision support queries.

How does the optimizer handle a query against a star schema? First of all, it notices that the sales transactions fact table (shown in Figure 9-2) has a lot more entries than the surrounding dimension tables. This is the clue that a star schema exists. As Oracle7 evolved, the optimizer began to produce much smarter plans. The optimizer for a standard relational database typically would have tried to join each of the dimension tables to the fact table, one at a time. Because the fact table is usually very large, involving the fact table in multiple joins takes a lot of time.

Cartesian product joins were added to Oracle7 to first join the dimension tables with a subsequent single join back to the fact table in the final step. The technique works relatively well when there aren't too many dimension tables (typically six or fewer, as a rule of thumb, since the Cartesian product can get quite large), and when data is relatively well populated.

In some situations, there are a fairly large number of dimension tables or the data in the fact table is sparse. These data warehouse schemas can be handled better by using Oracle's bitmapped indexes, which were initially described in Chapter 4, *Data Structures.*

Bitmapped indexes were first introduced in Oracle7 to speed up the type of data retrieval and joins in data warehousing queries. Bitmapped indexes in Oracle are typically considered for columns in which the data has low cardinality. *Cardinality* is the number of variations in values divided by the number of rows. There are various opinions about what low cardinality actually is, and some people consider cardinality as high as 10 percent to be low; but remember that if a table has a million rows, some might consider a low cardinality to be 100,000 different values in a column!

Essentially, a bitmapped index of "1" indicates that a value is present in a particular row and "0" indicates that the value is not present. A bitmap is built for each of the values in the indexed columns. Because computers are built on a concept of "1s" and "0s," this technique can greatly speed up data retrieval. In addition, join operations such as AND become a simple addition operation across multiple bitmapped indexed columns. A side benefit is that bitmapped indexes can provide considerable storage savings.

Figure 9-3 illustrates the use of a bitmapped index in a compound WHERE clause. Bitmapped indexes can be used together for even faster performance. The bitmapped indexes are essentially stacked together, as a set of punch cards would be. Oracle8 simply looks for those parts of the stack with all the bits turned on (which indicate the presence of the value) in the same way that you could try to stick a knitting needle through the portions of the card stack that were punched out on all of the cards.

In Oracle8, the best practice for improving star query performance is to build bitmapped indexes on the foreign keys columns of the fact table, which are the columns that link to the surrounding dimension tables. The join operation can then be a parallel bitmapped star join, that is, the bitmaps retrieve only the necessary rows from the fact table, and the rows are joined to the dimension tables. If you perform a join operation, then sparseness is recognized inherently in the bitmaps, and the number of dimension tables isn't a problem. This algorithm can also efficiently handle a *snowflake schema,* which is an extension of a standard star schema in which there are multiple tables for each dimension.

Parallelizing the queries is another obvious means of improving performance. Joins and sorts are frequent results of decision support queries. The way parallelism works is described in Chapter 6, *Oracle8 Performance.* That chapter lists all of the applications that Oracle can paralyze (see "What Can Be Parallelized?").

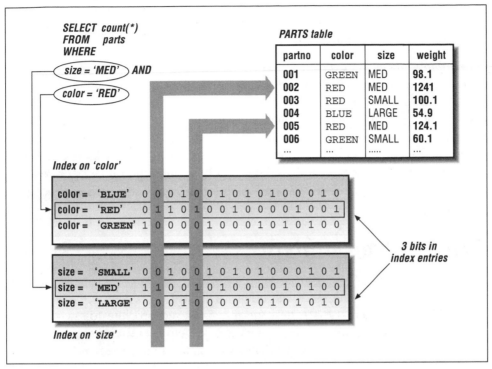

Figure 9-3. Bitmapped index operation in a compound WHERE clause

Oracle Parallel Server further expands parallelism by providing a way that queries can transparently scale across nodes in a MPP or cluster architecture.

 Remember that these Oracle features use the cost-based optimizer and that you should run statistics periodically (using the ANALYZE command) on the tables to ensure good performance. Statistics gathering can be done in parallel.

Summary Tables and Materialized Views

Data within the dimensions is usually hierarchical in nature (e.g., in the time dimension, day rolls up to week, which rolls up to month, which rolls up to quarter, which rolls up to year). If the query is simply looking for data at the month level, why should it have to sort through all of the daily and weekly information? Instead, it can simply view data at or above that level of the hierarchy. In fact, data warehousing performance consultants have been designing such summary tables—including multiple levels of precalculated summarization—for many years. For example, all of the time periods listed in Figure 9-2 can be calculated on the fly using different groupings of days. However, to speed queries based on a different time series, a data warehouse can have values precalculated for weeks and months and stored in summary tables to which queries can be redirected.

Oracle8*i* introduces the concept of *materialized views* for the creation of summary tables. A materialized view provides precomputed summary data; most importantly, a materialized view is automatically substituted for a fact table when appropriate. The cost-based query optimizer can perform query rewrites to these summary tables (once they're registered) transparently to the user, often resulting in dramatic increases in performance. For instance, if a query asks for summary data for a particular detail table based on sales by month, the query optimizer will automatically substitute the materialized view for the detail table when processing the query.

OLAP in the Database

In certain applications, it may make sense to analyze the data at its source in addition to retrieving that data. Although online analytical processing (OLAP) is often done within client tools (as we describe in a later section), the following CUBE and ROLLUP operators were added to Oracle8*i* to help client reporting and analysis tools and developers perform OLAP-style aggregation more easily and efficiently in the database:

ROLLUP operator
> Used in conjunction with a GROUP BY clause and causes the data to be grouped by multiple levels of detail. ROLLUP can deliver data from two dimensions with an increasing level of detail in one dimension.

CUBE operator
> Also used in conjunction with the GROUP BY clause. Creates a multidimensional data cube, such as one used in a crosstabulation report.

Of course, you can also use Oracle's Express Server product to store cubes and provide the fastest OLAP capabilities as we describe later in the OLAP section of "Other Data Warehouse Software."

Oracle Database Options and the Data Warehouse

A growing trend in data warehousing is the storage of multiple data types within the database. Although we discuss database options in Chapter 13, *Oracle8/8i Extensions*, we'll quickly touch on how these options might be useful in a data warehousing environment.

Time Series option

Probably the most useful option for data warehousing is the Time Series option. The Time Series option is relevant for situations in which the data includes time-stamps. This option expands the SQL functionality in two important ways:

- You can incorporate the concept of business calendars with valid business days
- You can perform additional mathematical functions (such as computations of moving averages) in the server

With this functionality, you can produce standard reports generated using sophisticated functions that might normally only be available via OLAP tools (discussed earlier in the section on "Data Warehousing Basics").

Spatial option

The Spatial option is also relevant in a data warehouse in which data is retrieved based on proximity to certain locations. Spatial data includes some type of geographic coordinates. Typically, companies use add-on products in conjunction with Oracle's Spatial option. An example of this option's use for data warehousing is a marketing analysis application that determines the viability of retail outlets at various locations.

interMedia option

The *inter*Media option opens up the possibilities of including documents, audio, video, and some locator functions in the warehouse. Of these, text retrieval is most commonly used in warehouses today. However, the number of companies storing other types of data in warehouses is growing. Often, storage of such data is first considered during the development of a web deployment strategy in which companies seek to give remote users access to all types of data.

Managing the Data Warehouse

Once you've built your data warehouse topology, you're likely to deploy multiple Oracle databases to implement the data warehouse and its data marts. Enterprise-wide warehouses are becoming more common on Unix servers, and smaller data marts are common on Microsoft Windows NT machines.

The Oracle Enterprise Manager provides a common GUI for managing these multiple instances regardless of the underlying operating system. A new feature in the Oracle8*i* release is the ability to use the Oracle Enterprise Manager from a Web browser and a multiuser repository for tracking and managing the Oracle instances. (The Oracle Enterprise Manager is discussed in much more detail in

Chapter 5, *Managing Oracle8.*) In warehousing, in addition to basic management, ongoing tuning for performance is crucial. The Diagnostics and Tuning packs are often used in tandem to help identify where performance improvements can be made.

Within the largest warehouses and data marts, you may want to manage or maintain availability to some of the data even as other parts of the database are moved offline. Oracle's Partitioning option enables data partitions based on business value ranges (such as date) for administrative flexibility, while adding enhanced query performance through the cost-based optimizer's practice of eliminating partition access for nonrelevant partitions. For an example of administrative flexibility, consider the common data warehousing requirement for "rolling window" operations, which add new data and remove old data based on time. A new partition can be added, loaded, and indexed in parallel, and optionally removed, all without impacting access to existing data.

In addition to range partitioning, hash partitioning is also supported in Oracle8*i* and allows you to spread data evenly based on a hash algorithm for performance. Hashing may be used within range partitions (composite partitioning) to increase the performance of queries while still maintaining the manageability offered by range partitioning.

Data Warehouses and Backups

Early data warehousing practitioners often overlooked the need to perform backups. Their belief was that since data for the warehouse was extracted from operational systems, the warehouses could easily be repopulated from those same systems if needed. However, as warehouses grew and the transformations needed to create and refresh them evolved, it became evident that backups of data warehouses were necessary because the transformation process had grown extremely complicated and time-consuming. Today, planning for warehouse availability includes not only an understanding of how long loading will take, but also backup and recovery operations.

Other Data Warehouse Software

A data warehouse isn't built with a single software product, nor is it simply a database. Although Oracle Corporation markets certain product bundles, such as the Oracle Data Mart Suites as "data warehouse software," a look under the covers reveals that these are simply multiple products bundled together to enable the base functionality required in a data warehouse or data mart. In addition to the database capabilities we've described, if you're going to build an effective data warehouse topology like the one we've outlined, the software must be able to do the following:

Extract data from operational data sources

The extraction process is fairly straightforward, but can be significantly optimized, since it typically involves moving large amounts of data.

Transform and/or cleanse data

Because the data in a data warehouse can come from many different sources, the data must frequently be converted into a common format. Because of inherent problems in legacy systems, the original data may also have to be cleaned up by eliminating or modifying invalid values.

Transport data from OLTP systems to the data warehouse/marts

As with the extraction process, the transportation process can be optimized for performance.

Provide basic reporting

Basic reporting can give you the same reporting capabilities as a normal database.

Provide OLAP for multidimensional analysis

OLAP tools give you the specialized type of analysis you need to spot business changes and trends. These tools typically provide a way to translate multiple dimensions into the two-dimensional world of a screen and give you the ability to easily rotate those dimensions.

Provide data mining

Data mining is a process in which the data in a data warehouse is analyzed for variations and anomalies, which can point to new business opportunities.

Provide a way to store and retrieve metadata

Metadata is frequently stored in a repository, which not only stores the data but can also provide extended management services such as versioning and impact analysis.

The following sections provide details on how each of these requirements can be met.

Extraction, Transformation, and Transportation

The first three requirements described in the previous list are often handled by what are called ETT tools (for extraction, transformation, and transportation). Those who are new to data warehousing might want to assume that the data in the operational sources is clean and that transformations can be ignored. Unfortunately, this is rarely the case because the process of understanding the data sources, designing the transformations, testing the loading process, and debugging is often the most time-consuming part of initially deploying a data warehouse. Transformations generally remove bogus data (including erroneous entries and duplicate entries), convert data items to an agreed upon format, and filter data not considered necessary for the warehouse.

The frequency with which the extraction occurs is largely determined by the required timeliness of the data in the warehouse. Most extraction and loading takes place on more of a "batch" basis with a known time delay (typically daily or even weekly or monthly). Many early warehousing efforts periodically performed a complete refresh during the loading process. As data volumes grew, this became impractical due to the limited timeframe available for loading. Today, updates to tables are more common. When a need for real-time warehousing exists, some of the more advanced warehouses are loaded nearly continuously using a *trickle feed*.

Is Cleanliness Best?

Once the data in the warehouse is "clean," is this version of the true nature of the data propagated back to the originating OLTP systems? This is an important issue for data warehouse implementation. In some cases, a "closed loop" process is implemented whereby updates are provided back to the originating systems. In addition to minimizing some of the cleansing which takes place during future extractions, operational reports thus become more accurate.

Another viable option is to avoid cleansing by improving the quality of the data at the time it's input into the operational system. This can sometimes be accomplished by not allowing a "default" condition as allowable input into a data field. Presenting the data entry person with an array of valid options, one of which *must* be selected, is often a way to ensure the most consistent and valid responses. Many companies also provide education to the data entry people at this time, showing them how the data they're keying in will be used and what the significance of it is.

Simple extraction and transportation of data is possible using one of several Oracle tools:

Transparent gateways
> Provide a means to retrieve data from non-Oracle sources using SQL against an Oracle database, although gateways are typically intended for providing access to smaller sets of data, not large bulk transfers.

Symmetric replication

> Comes bundled with Oracle server products. The asynchronous store and forward capability provides a means of moving data common to warehousing.

Transportable tablespaces

> Oracle8*i* offers yet another option for moving data. Metadata (the data dictionary) is exported from the source and imported to the target from which the transferred tablespace can then be mounted.

But none of these tools provide a way to transform data.

Transformation capabilities are offered in Oracle ETT tools targeted at extracting data from many popular applications. The Oracle Applications Data Warehouse (OADW) provides a metadata-driven interface for building extractions from Oracle Applications, scheduling them, and creating and loading a data warehouse model. Transformations are built using the Oracle SQL syntax. Add-on collection packs are available for specific application modules providing metadata-driven code generators. The metadata is stored in a repository, and after the warehouse design and the collection process definitions are complete and the metadata has been validated, you can automatically generate the objects and code necessary to build the warehouse. Similar tools exist for building extractions from SAP (the SAP toolkit) and PeopleSoft (the PeopleSoft toolkit). All of these tools are now being integrated into a common framework with a Java front-end known as the Oracle Warehouse Builder (OWB). The metadata definitions in the Warehouse Builder will be based on Oracle's Common Warehouse Metadata.

For large enterprise environments requiring ETT from mainframe data sources, warehouse implementers often look to the Oracle Warehouse Technology Initiative (WTI) partners such as ETI (*http://www.eti.com*) and Ardent (which includes the former Prism Solutions at *http://www.vmark.com/transition/index.html*). These are metadata-driven tools from vendors with extensive legacy data extraction experience. While many first-generation warehouses were built without such tools (using languages such C and COBOL to build extractions and transformations), experience has indicated that having metadata is critical, especially to determine the history of the ETT process and for ongoing maintenance.

To actually load the data warehouse database, implementers typically use Oracle's SQL*Loader. SQL*Loader's "direct path loading" option allows rapid loading by bypassing the buffer cache and rollback mechanism and writing directly to the datafile. You can run SQL*Loader sessions in parallel to further speed the table loading process (as many warehouses need to be loaded in a limited "window" of time). Many of the extraction tools can feed SQL*Loader directly.

Reporting and Ad Hoc Query Tools (Oracle Discoverer)

Data warehouses users, such as marketing and financial analysts, are rarely interested in the storage and schemas that hold their information. Their interest level rises when the discussion turns to the tools they'll be using. These tools are often evaluated and purchased within individual business areas, sometimes without close IT coordination.

Of the tools users need, the least glamorous, but most often used, are reporting tools. Reports are often frowned upon by sophisticated analysts because they require requesting help from the IT staff, which can make the process of producing a report more time-consuming and less flexible than manipulating the data directly. However, reports often appeal to executives within a company because they require no special skills (other than the ability to read them). The distribution of such reports has been greatly improved as web-based report generation becomes commonplace because the user needs only familiarity with a browser.

Oracle's tool for generating reports, Oracle Reports, has a wizard-based front-end for building reports that can then be deployed to the Web for access as Adobe Acrobat, plain text, or HTML files. With this tool, you can cache reports on a middle-tier server for better performance. The tool also provides some limited drill-down search capabilities, in which a user can ask for more detail about a particular portion of a report.

More sophisticated users need to pose frequent "what-if" questions, such as "what would happen if I looked at a section of the data limited by time?" These users need ad hocad hoc query tools. Initially developed as client-server tools, many tools are now Web-based and provide similar functionality to the earlier reporting tools. A common theme has been to make these tools much more graphically intuitive. Queries are typically posed by selecting icons that represent tables and items. End users only need be knowledgeable on where their data is stored, and what it represents. The SQL is generated behind the scenes. The challenge to IT is that this SQL can generate time- and resource-consuming queries to the detriment of other users trying to use the same system.

Oracle Discoverer, Oracle's ad hoc query tool, provides an easy-to-use front-end for picking and choosing data items to build queries around, and is typically used by the business users. Users can generate their own reports and deploy them to the Web as HTML files. Discoverer has a query governor that can predict the amount of time a query will take based on comparisons in records kept in the database server to previous similar comparisons. There is also a separate administrative layer that IT can use to place limits on the time required to perform end user queries, since an analyst can (either intentionally or accidentally) request an enormous amount of data for a particular report. This type of request can not only slow the delivery of the report, but impact the overall performance of the database.

Oracle Discoverer is most often used for querying an Oracle relational database, but ODBC (Open Database Connectivity) support does allow this tool to be used with other databases.

OLAP and Oracle Express

As end users become more sophisticated, their questions evolve from "what happened" to "what trends are present and what might happen in the future?" A class of tools known as *OLAP tools* provide the ability to handle time series and mathematical analysis for understanding past trends and forecasting the future.

OLAP initially grew around the early inability of relational databases to effectively handle multidimensional queries (described above in the section "Data Warehouse Design Considerations"). The first OLAP tools were used against data "cubes," which were essentially multidimensional joins created from the data downloaded from relational sources and stored within separate dedicated servers.

These separate database engines are called *MOLAP engines*, which stands for Multidimensional Online Analytical Processing. Examples include Oracle's Express Server and Hyperion's (formerly Arbor) Essbase, as well as the Microsoft offering that is part of SQL Server 7.0. These MOLAP engines are extremely fast for handling queries, and work best when the data isn't updated frequently (because the cube generation process takes time).

Today, OLAP tools are used more often against relational databases since a star query is supported to various degrees in many databases, and also because there is an increasing need for more frequently updated information. When used in this fashion, the interaction is called *ROLAP*, which stands for Relational Online Analytical Processing. Tools that can work against either relational databases or MOLAP engines are sometimes referred to as *hybrid tools*.

You can use Oracle Express Analyzer for forecasting and trend analysis and to build extensive report books for distribution to users. Typically used by more sophisticated business analysts, the Express Analyzer is fully web-based and can be used directly against the Oracle's MOLAP engine, Express Server. It can also be used as a ROLAP tool through the use of the Relational Access Manager (RAM) and the Relational Access Administrator (RAA). The tool can drill directly into an Oracle or another relational database.

Express Analyzer is used most often with data stored as cubes in the MOLAP engine, Express Server, in which the speed of analysis is crucial. Analyzer is also used as a ROLAP tool in cases where data changes in the warehouse relational database with such frequency that it doesn't make sense to re-create the cube.

Add-ons available for the Express Analyzer include the Oracle Sales Analyzer with marketing and campaign analysis, which can be used against the MOLAP Express Server or as a ROLAP tool, and Financial Analyzer, which you can use with data loaded in to Express Server from Oracle's Financial Applications.

Business Intelligence

Business intelligence solutions are a class of tools loosely defined today as classical decision support tools (ad hoc query and ROLAP) and also a set of new tools to provide extended reporting and "dashboard-like" interfaces to display business trends in OLTP applications.

These business intelligence tools focus on a specific area of business expertise, such as sales analysis. This focus allows these tools to include predefined queries, reports, and charts that deliver the type of information typically required for a particular type of business analysis while sparing the end user the complexity of creating these objects from scratch.

Oracle's Business Intelligence Solutions (OBIS) product is initially intended to supplement Oracle Applications; in its first release, the OBIS provides extended reporting through Discoverer. Activity-based accounting (ACTIVA) and a "Balanced Scorecard" for measuring and displaying progress toward meeting business objectives are provided in the Strategic Enterprise Management (SEM) applications used in conjunction with Oracle Applications.

The OBIS is evolving toward a classic data warehousing solution. Oracle Applications Data Warehouse and Oracle Warehouse Builder, packaged with OBIS in the winter 1999–2000 release, provide extraction and transformation from Oracle Applications and populates a number of predefined data warehousing tables in predefined schema included in the OBIS package.

The promise of more tightly integrated solutions like OBIS is that they will provide easier to deploy solutions that provide more out-of-the-box functionality.

Data Mining

Data mining, an often overused and misunderstood term in data warehousing, is the use of mathematical algorithms to discover relationships in the data that wouldn't be apparent by using any of the other tools. Most companies shouldn't approach data mining unless the following criteria are met:

- They understand the quality and meaning of the data in the warehouse.

- Analysts have successfully gained business insight using other tools and the warehouse.

- They believe there could be other undiscovered relationships that could influence the business, and all current hypotheses have been exhausted.

In other words, data mining tools are not a replacement for the analytical skills of data warehouse users.

The data mining tools themselves rely on a number of techniques to produce the relationships, such as:

- Extended statistical algorithms provided by the statistical tools vendors that can highlight unexpected statistical variations in the data.

- Clustering techniques that show how business outcomes can fall into certain groups, such as insurance claims versus time for various age brackets. In this example, once a low risk group is found or classified, further research into influencing factors or "associations" might take place.

- Logic models (if A occurs, then B or C are possible outcomes) are sometimes used and validated against small sample sets, and then applied to larger data models for prediction.

- Neural networks might be "trained" against small sets, with known results to be applied later against a much larger set.

- Visualization techniques are sometimes used to graphically plot variables and understand which variables are key to a particular outcome.

Table 9-1 shows some of the typical data mining tools available today and the algorithms they use.

Table 9-1. Typical Data Mining Tools

Vendor	Algorithms
Angoss	Decision trees, neural networking, clusters
RightPoint (formerly DataMind)	Bayesian belief (tree-like) network for clustering
DataSage	Framework for mining algorithm plug-ins
Information Discovery	Rule induction
SAS	Advanced statistics, clustering, decision trees, neural networks, visualization
SPSS	Advanced statistics, decision trees, neural networks
SRA	Decision trees, clustering, association, sequences
Oracle Darwin (formerly Thinking Machines)	Decision trees, neural networks, clustering, memory-based learning

Areas in which data mining has been most successfully used include fraud detection and micro-opportunity marketing. For example, credit card companies sometimes use data mining to track unusual credit card usage—such as the unexpected charging to a credit card of expensive jewelry in a foreign city. Discovering clusters of unusual buying patterns within certain small groups might also drive so-called micro-opportunity marketing campaigns aimed at small audiences with a high probability of purchasing products or services.

A more recent trend among relational database providers is tighter integration of data mining algorithms into the relational database. Oracle's data mining strategy so far has been to partner with a number of the data mining software providers. Oracle recently obtained the Darwin product from Thinking Machines, and is working on further integration with the Oracle database.

Today, the tools we've described usually require some consulting help to fully utilize them, but they're becoming easier to use. For example, Darwin has a wizards-driven GUI. Most often, data mining takes place against a subset of data extracted from the warehouse and is only done by the most sophisticated analysts within a company.

The Metadata Challenge

On the one hand, metadata—or data that describes data—is incredibly important. Virtually all types of interactions with a database require the use of metadata—from knowing the datatypes of the data to understanding the business meaning and history of data fields.

On the other hand, metadata is only useful if the tools and clients who wish to use it can leverage it. One of the great challenges is to create a set of common metadata definitions that allows tools and databases from different vendors to interact.

There have been a number of attempts to reach an agreement on common definitions. At the moment, it's unlikely that these efforts will result in a comprehensive widely accepted solution for a few years. Many people feel that a better approach is to find ways of translating the various metadata implementations. In the meantime, Oracle is working toward the integration and sharing of metadata among its own tools, most notably OADW, Express, and Discoverer. This effort is leading toward Oracle's own definition of Common Warehouse Metadata. Oracle has also begun to position the Designer repository as the storage location for such metadata.

Because the translation of metadata appears to be a viable approach in which multiple vendors' tools exist, many now believe that collaboration by Oracle, IBM, Unisys, and others will lead to the Object Management Group's (OMG) XML

Metadata Interchange (XMI) specification becoming the standard means of defining, validating, and sharing varying metadata formats. The Metadata Coalition and OMG further announced plans to collaborate on these specifications in 1999. We hope this means that a single standard will emerge for metadata interchange.

Best Practices

Some recent magazine articles have focused on data warehousing failures and what caused them. Those experienced in data warehousing generally agree that the following are typical reasons why data warehouse projects fail:

Failure to involve business users, IT representatives, sponsoring executives, and anyone else with a vested interest throughout the data warehousing process
> Not only do all of these groups provide valuable input for creating a data warehouse, but any one of these groups can cause a data warehouse to fail through their lack of support.

Overlooking the key reasons for the data warehouse existence
> During the sometimes long planning stages, data warehouse designers can lose sight of the forces driving the creation of the warehouse.

Overlooked details and incorrect assumptions
> A less rigorous examination of the environment for a data warehouse will doom a data warehouse project to failure.

Unrealistic timeframes and scope
> As with all projects, starting the creation of a data warehouse with too short a timeframe or too aggressive a scope will force the data warehouse team to cut corners, resulting in the mistakes previously mentioned.

Failure to manage expectations
> Data warehouses, like all technologies, are not a panacea. You must make sure that all members of the team, as well as the eventual users of the data warehouse, have an appropriate set of expectations.

Tactical decision-making at the expense of long-term strategy
> Although it may seem overly time-consuming at the start, you must keep in mind the long-term goals of your project, and your organization, throughout the design and implementation process. Failing to do so has two results—it delays the onset of problems, but it also increases the likelihood of those problems.

Failure to leverage the experience of others
> There's nothing like learning from those who have succeeded on similar projects. It's almost as good to gain from the experience of others who have

failed at similar tasks; at least you can avoid the mistakes that led to their failures.

Successful warehouse projects require the continuous involvement of business analysts and users, sponsoring executives, and IT. Ignoring this often repeated piece of advice is probably is the single biggest cause of many of the most spectacular failures. Establishing a warehouse has to produce a clear business benefit. Executives are key throughout the process because data warehouse and data mart coordination often crosses department boundaries, and funding likely comes from very high levels.

Your warehouse should provide answers to business problems that are linked to key business initiatives. Ruthlessly eliminate any developments that take warehouse projects in another direction. Your motivation behind the technology implementation schedule should be the desire to answer critical business questions. Positive return on investment (ROI) from the warehouse should be demonstrated during the building process, if possible.

Common Misconceptions

Having too simplistic a view during any part of the data warehouse building process (a view that overlooks details) can lead to many problems. Here are just a few of the typical (and usually incorrect) assumptions people make in the process of implementing a data warehouse:

- Sources of data are clean and consistent.

- Someone in the organization understands what is in the source databases, the quality of the data, and where to find items of business interest.

- Extractions from operational sources can be built and discarded as needed, with no records left behind.

- Summary data is going to be adequate, and detailed data can be left out.

- IT has all of the skills available to manage and develop all of the extraction routines necessary, tune the database(s), maintain the systems and the network, and perform backups and recoveries in a reasonable timeframe.

- Development can be done without continuous feedback and periodic prototyping involving analysts and possibly sponsoring executives.

- The warehouse won't change over time, so "versioning" won't be an issue.

- Analysts will have all of the skills needed to make full use of the warehouse or the warehouse tools.

- IT can control what tools the analysts select and use.

- The number of users is known and predictable.

- The kinds of queries are known and predictable.

- Computer hardware is infinitely scalable, regardless of warehouse design.

- If a business area builds a data mart independently, IT won't be asked to support it later.

- Consultants will be readily available in a pinch to solve last-minute problems.

- Metadata is not important, and planning for it can be delayed.

Most software and implementation projects have difficulty meeting schedules. Because of the complexity and details that emerge, most warehouse projects frequently take much longer than the initial schedule, which is exactly what an executive who needs the information to make vital strategic decisions doesn't want to hear! If you implement working prototypes along the way, however, the warehouse can begin showing positive ROI, and changes in the subsequent schedule can be linked back to real business requirements, not just to technical issues (which an executive doesn't understand anyway).

You have to avoid scope creep and expectations throughout the project. When you receive recommended changes or additions from the business side, you have to confirm that these changes provide an adequate return on investment, or else you will find yourself working long and hard on facets of the warehouse without any real payoff. The business reasoning must be part of the prioritization process; you must understand why tradeoffs are made. If you run into departmental "turf wars" over the ownership of data, you have to involve key executives for mediation and guidance.

The pressure of limited time and skills and immediate business needs sometimes leads to making tactical decisions in establishing a data warehouse at the expense of a long-term strategy. In spite of the pressures, you have to create a long-term strategy at the beginning of the project and stick to it, or at least be very aware of the consequences of modifying it. There should be just enough detail to prevent wasted efforts along the way and the strategy should be flexible enough to take into account business acquisitions, mergers, and so on.

Your long-term strategy must embrace emerging trends in warehousing such as web deployment and the need for high availability solutions. The rate of change and volume of products being introduced sometimes makes it difficult to sort through what is real and what is hype. Most companies struggle with keeping up with the knowledge curve. Traditional sources of information include vendors, consultants, and data processing industry consultants, each of which usually has a vested interest in selling something. The vendors want to sell products; the consultants want to sell skills they have "on the bench;" and the data processing industry consultants frequently resell their favorable reviews of vendors and consultants to the vendors and consultants. Any single source can lead to wrong conclusions, but by talking to multiple sources, some consensus should emerge and provide answers to questions.

The best place to gain insight is by discussing warehousing with other similar companies—at least at the working prototype stage—at conferences. Finding workable solutions and establishing a set of contacts to network with in the future can make attendance at these conferences well worth the price (and may even be more valuable than the topics presented there).

10

Oracle8 and High Availability

The data stored in the databases of your organization's computer systems is extremely valuable. In many cases, this data represents your most valuable asset. Protecting this asset is crucial for any Oracle site.

As a DBA, system administrator, or system architect, you'll probably have to use a variety of options and techniques to ensure that your data is adequately protected from a catastrophe. Of course, implementing proper backup operations is the foundation of any disaster-prevention strategy, but there are other ways to avoid a variety of disasters, from simple disk failures to a complete failure of your primary site.

Computer hardware is, by and large, extremely reliable, which may make it easy for you to postpone thinking about disaster recovery. Most software is also very reliable, and the Oracle database protects the integrity of its data even in the event of a software failure. However, components and software will, at times, fail, and the more components involved, the greater the likelihood of a disaster.

The difference between an inconvenience and a disaster is the presence or absence of adequate disaster recovery plans, so it's best to understand all of the options available with Oracle8 so you can choose the best approach for your particular site.

With Oracle8, you can guarantee that your precious data is highly available. Some of the facets of a high availability solution are part of the Oracle8 software, such as Oracle's automatic crash recovery and Parallel Server options. Some other facets are available from third-party vendors, such as hardware failover solutions and some backup managers. Finally, some of the most important facets of a high availability solution are dependent on implementing appropriate procedures to safeguard your data. This chapter will cover all three categories of solutions.

What Is High Availability?

Before we can begin a discussion of how to ensure a high level of availability for your data, you need to understand the exact meaning of the term *availability.*

Availability can mean different things for different organizations. For this discussion, we'll consider a system to be available when that system is both *up* (which means that the database can be accessed by users) and *working* (which means that the database is delivering the expected functionality to users with the expected performance).

Businesses have always depended on their data being available. With the increased use of the World Wide Web as a way to share data with the outside world, database failures can have an even more dramatic impact on business. The failure of web-based systems, with links outside a company's employees are, unfortunately, immediately visible to the outside world and can seriously affect the company's financial health as well as its image and the loyalty of its customers. Consider the Internet service offered by UPS and FedEx to share package status and tracking with their customers. As customers come to depend heavily on a service offered over the Web, interruptions in that service can cause these same customers to move to competitors. Repeated failures of systems like these would have a serious and immediate impact on customer satisfaction.

To implement a system that delivers high availability, you'll have to include techniques to avoid downtime, such as redundant hardware, as well as techniques to allow recovery from disasters, such as implementing the appropriate backup routines.

Measuring and Planning Availability

Most organizations automatically assume that they need "24 by 7" availability, meaning that the system must be available 24 hours a day, 7 days a week. Quite often, this requirement is stated with little examination of the business functions the system will support. With the perceived cost of technology components on the decline, and their reliability on the increase, most users and a fair number of IT personnel feel that achieving very high levels of availability should be simple and cheap. For example, we leave our PCs running all the time and most people have rarely experienced the joy of losing their hard drive or having their power supply fail.

Unfortunately, while some components are certainly becoming cheaper and more reliable, component availability doesn't equate to system availability. The complex layering of hardware and software in today's two- and three-tier systems introduces multiple interdependencies and points of failure. Achieving very high levels of availability for a system with varied and interdependent components is typically neither simple nor inexpensive.

To provide some perspective, consider Table 10-1, which translates the percentage of system availability into days, minutes, and hours of annual downtime based on a 365-day year:

Table 10-1. System Availability

% Availability	System Downtime Per Year		
	Days	Hours	Minutes
95.000	18	6	0
96.000	14	14	24
97.000	10	23	48
98.000	7	7	12
99.000	3	16	36
99.500	1	20	48
99.900	0	9	46
99.990	0	1	53
99.999	0	0	5

Large-scale systems that achieve a percentage of availability over 99 percent typically cost well into the millions of dollars to design and implement, with high ongoing operational costs as well. Marginal increases in availability require large incremental investments in all system components. Moving from 95 percent to 99 percent availability is likely to be very costly, while moving from 99 percent to 99.99 percent will probably cost even more. Are the required investments justified for less than a 1 percent increase in availability?

Another key aspect of measuring availability is the definition of *when* the system must be available. A required availability 99 percent of the time during normal working hours from 8 a.m. to 5 p.m. is very different from 99 percent availability based on a 24-hour day. In the same way that you must carefully define your required level of availability, you must also consider the hours during which availability is measured. For example, a lot of companies still typically take orders during business hours. The cost of a down order entry system is very high during the business day. However, the cost of downtime drops after 5 p.m. This factor points to opportunities for scheduled downtime after hours that will, in turn, help reduce unplanned failures during business hours. At the other end of the spectrum, consider web-based and multinational companies, whose global reach implies that the business day never ends.

The often casually stated default requirement that a system be available "24 by 7" must be put in the context of the high costs required. Even an initial examination of the complexity and cost of very high availability will often lead to more realistic goals and associated budgets for system availability.

The costs of achieving high availability are certainly justified in some cases. It may cost a brokerage house millions of dollars an hour for each hour that their key systems are down, while a less demanding business, such as catalog sales, may lose only tens of thousands of dollars an hour, based on a less efficient manual system that acts as a stopgap measure.

Causes of Unplanned Downtime

There are many different causes of unplanned downtime. You can prevent some very easily, while others require significant investments in site infrastructure, telecommunications, hardware, software, and skilled employees. Figure 10-1 summarizes some of the more common causes of system failures.

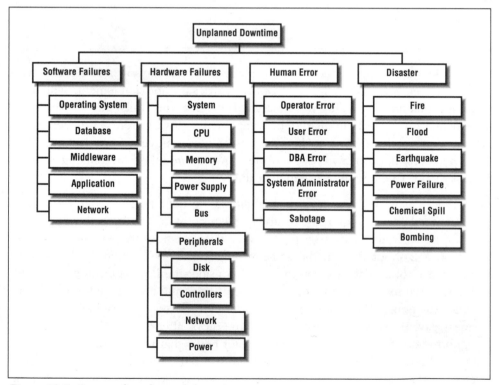

Figure 10-1. Causes of unplanned downtime

When you're creating a plan to guarantee the availability of your application, you should make a point of considering all of the items shown in the chart, as well as other potential causes of system interruption that are specific to your own circumstances. As with all planning, it's much better to consider all options, even if you quickly dismiss them, than to be caught off guard when that unexpected occurrence happens.

System Availability Versus Component Availability

A complete system is composed of various hardware, software, and networking components operating as a technology *stack*. Ensuring the availability of individual components doesn't necessarily guarantee system availability. Different strategies and solutions exist for achieving high availability for each of the system components. Figure 10-2 illustrates the technology stack used to deliver a potential system.

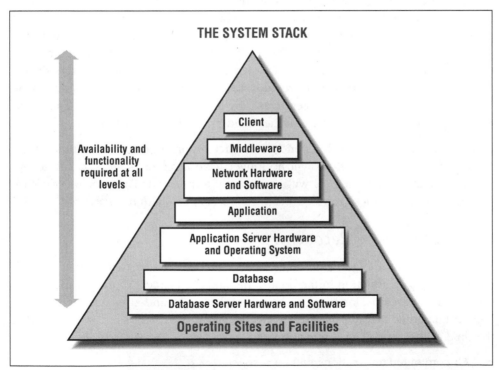

Figure 10-2. Components of a system

As the figure shows, there are a variety of physical and logical layers cooperating to deliver an application. Some systems may involve fewer components; for example, a two-tier client-server system would not have the additional application server components.

Failures in the components above the database can effectively prevent access to the database even though the database itself may be available. The database server and the database itself serve as the foundation for the stack. When a database fails, it immediately affects the higher levels of the stack. If the failure results in lost or corrupted data, the overall integrity of the application may be affected.

The potential threats to availability span all the components involved in an application system, but in this chapter we'll only examine availability issues relating specifically to the database.

System Crashes

The abrupt failure of the server machine running the database is the most common cause of unplanned downtime. The server may crash because of hardware problems, such as the failure of a power supply, or because of software problems, such as a process that begins to consume all the machine's CPU resources. Perhaps the underlying server platform may be fine, but the Oracle instance itself may have failed. Whatever the cause of the crash, the effect on Oracle is the same—the instance ceases to exist. Note that it's the instance that crashes, not the database. As you will recall from Chapter 2, *Oracle8 Architecture*, the Oracle instance runs on the server and provides access to the database that is stored on disk. This means that even a system crash, by itself, will not imperil any data that's already safely stored within the disk files used by the Oracle8 database.

The impact of the crash will depend on the activity in progress at the time of the crash. Any connected sessions will no longer have a server process to talk to. All active queries and transactions will be abruptly terminated. The process of cleaning up the resulting mess is called *instance recovery* or *crash recovery*.

What Is Instance Recovery?

When you restart an Oracle instance after a failure, Oracle detects that a crash occurred using information in the control file and the headers of the database files. Oracle then performs instance recovery automatically and uses the online redo logs to guarantee that the database is restored to a consistent state as it existed at the time of the crash. This requires two actions:

- All committed transactions will be recovered.

- In-flight transactions will be rolled back or undone.

Note that an in-flight transaction might be one that a user didn't commit or one that was committed by the user but not confirmed by Oracle before the system failure. A transaction isn't considered committed until Oracle has written the relevant details of the transaction to the current online redo log and has sent back a message to the client application confirming the committed transaction.

Tell-Tale Error Messages

The following two error messages are often good indicators that an Oracle instance is down:

```
ORA-03113:  End-of-file on communication channel
```

This message is usually received by clients that try to resubmit an operation that failed due to an instance failure. The message is somewhat cryptic but becomes clear if you interpret it very literally. Oracle works using a pipe to communicate between the client application and its associated server process in the Oracle instance. When the instance fails, the client's server process ceases to exist, so there is no one listening on the other end of the pipe. The communication channel between the client and the server is no longer valid.

```
ORA-01034:  Oracle not available
```

This terse message means that when the client requested a connection to the Oracle instance, the instance was not there. Clients that try to connect to a failed instance will typically get this message. The client can connect to the Listener but when the Listener attempts to hand the client off to the requested Oracle instance, the ORA-01034 condition results.

Phases of Instance Recovery

Instance recovery has two phases: rollforward and rollback.

Recovering an instance requires the use of the redo logs (described in Chapter 2). The redo logs contain a recording of all the physical changes made to the database as a result of transactional activity, both committed and uncommitted.

The checkpoint concept (also introduced in Chapter 2) is critical to understanding crash recovery. When a transaction is committed, Oracle writes all associated database block changes to the current online redo log. The actual database blocks may have already been flushed to disk, or may be flushed at some later point. This means that the online redo log can contain changes not yet reflected in the actual database blocks stored in the datafiles. Oracle periodically ensures that the data blocks in the datafiles on disk are synchronized with the redo log to reflect all the committed changes up to a point in time. Oracle does this by writing all the database blocks changed by those committed transactions to the datafiles on disk. This operation is called a *checkpoint*. Completed checkpoints are recorded in the control file, datafile headers, and redo log.

Rollforward

At any point in time, the online redo logs will be ahead of the datafiles by a certain amount of time or number of committed transactions. Instance recovery closes this gap and ensures that the datafiles reflect all committed transactions up to the time the instance crashed. Oracle performs instance recovery by rolling forward through the online redo log and replaying all the changes from the last completed checkpoint to the time of instance failure. This operation is called the *rollforward* phase of instance recovery.

While implementing rollforward recovery, Oracle reads the necessary database blocks into the System Global Area and reproduces the changes that were originally applied to the blocks. This process includes reproducing the undo or rollback information, in addition to the data changes. Remember that rollback segments are composed of extents and data blocks just like tables, and all changes to rollback segment blocks are part of the redo for a given transaction. For example, suppose that a user changed an employee name from "John" to "Jonathan". As Oracle applies the redo log, it will read the block containing the employee row into the cache and redo the name change. As part of recovering the transaction, Oracle will also write the old name "John" to a rollback segment as it was done for the original transaction.

When the rollforward phase is finished, all the changes for committed and uncommitted transactions have been reproduced. The uncommitted transactions are in-flight once again, just as they were at the time the crash occurred. This leads to the next logical phase of instance recovery—rollback. But before we discuss rollbacks themselves, we need to look at how Oracle uses checkpoints and how the timing of checkpoints can affect recovery time.

Fast-start checkpoints and bounded recovery time

Checkpoints cause an increase in I/O as the database writer flushes all the database blocks to disk to bring the datafiles up to the time of the checkpoint. Prior to Oracle8, DBAs controlled the checkpoint frequency using *INIT.ORA* file parameters and the size of the redo log files. The relevant *INIT.ORA* file parameters are as follows:

LOG_CHECKPOINT_INTERVAL

> The number of redo log blocks (operating system blocks) written between checkpoints.

LOG_CHECKPOINT_TIMEOUT

> The number of seconds between checkpoints. A 0 value disables time-based checkpoints.

Oracle performs a checkpoint whenever a log switch occurs, regardless of the values used for these parameters.

The most information ever recovered is the amount of information contained between checkpoints. Reducing the checkpoint interval or timeout can result in smaller amounts of data between checkpoints. This reduced data can lead to faster recovery times, but can also introduce the overhead of more frequent checkpoints and their associated disk activity. For additional details about the subtleties of these parameters, see the section "Managing the Online Redo Log" in the *Oracle8 Backup and Recovery Guide.*

A common strategy to minimize the number of checkpoints is to set these *INIT.ORA* file parameters so that checkpoints only occur with log switches. For example, a DBA might set LOG_CHECKPOINT_TIMEOUT to 0 and LOG_CHECKPOINT_INTERVAL to a value higher than the size of a redo log files. These settings result in applying a minimum of one redo log file's worth of redo in the event of a crash, which can result in unacceptably long recovery times.

Oracle8*i* introduced an *INIT.ORA* file parameter that provides a simpler and more accurate way to control recovery times: FAST_START_IO_TARGET. The bulk of recovery activity involves performing I/O for reading database blocks into the cache so that redo can be applied to them. This Oracle8*i* parameter sets a target ceiling on how many database blocks Oracle will have to read in applying redo information. Oracle will dynamically vary the checkpoint frequency in an attempt to limit the number of blocks that will need to be read for recovery to the value of this parameter. This variance will, in turn, more effectively limit the associated recovery time without setting checkpoint rates to a fixed value that isn't valid for different workloads.

Rollback

As we discussed, the rollforward phase re-creates uncommitted transactions and their associated rollback information. These in-flight transactions must be rolled back to return to a consistent state.

In Oracle releases prior to Version 7.3, the database wasn't available until all uncommitted transactions had been rolled back. Although a DBA can control the checkpoint frequency and therefore control the time required for the rollforward phase of instance recovery, the number of uncommitted transactions at the time of the crash may vary tremendously and cannot really be controlled or predicted with real accuracy. In a busy OLTP system, there are typically a fair number of in-flight transactions requiring rollback after a crash. This situation led to variable and unpredictable times for crash recovery. The solution to this was introduced in Oracle 7.3: *deferred rollback.*

Deferred rollback

In Oracle Version 7.3 and later, Oracle opens the database after the rollforward phase of recovery and performs the rollback of uncommitted transactions in the background. This process reduces database downtime and helps to reduce the variability of recovery times by deferring the rollback phase.

But what if a user's transaction begins working in a database block that contains some changes left behind by an uncommitted transaction? If this happens, the user's transaction will trigger a foreground rollback to undo the changes and will then proceed when rollback is complete. This action is transparent to the user—he doesn't receive error messages or have to resubmit the transaction.

Fast-start rollback

Oracle8*i* further optimizes the deferred rollback process by limiting the rollback triggered by a user transaction to the block the transaction is interested in. For example, suppose there is a large uncommitted transaction that affected 500 database blocks. Prior to Oracle8*i*, the first user transaction that touches one of the 500 blocks will trigger a foreground rollback and will absorb the overhead of rolling back the entire transaction. In Oracle8*i*, the user's transaction will only roll back the changes to the block it's interested in. New transactions don't have to wait for the complete rollback of large uncommitted transactions.

Protecting Against System Crashes

There are a variety of approaches you can take to help protect your system against the ill effects of system crashes, including the following:

- Providing component redundancy
- Using Oracle Parallel Server
- Using Transparent Application Failover software services

Component Redundancy

As basic protection, the various hardware components that make up the database server itself must be fault-tolerant. *Fault tolerance*, as the name implies, allows the overall hardware system to continue to operate even if one of its components fails. This feature, in turn, implies redundant components and the ability to detect component failure and seamlessly integrate the failed component's replacement. The major system components that should be fault-tolerant include the following:

- Disk drives
- Disk controllers

- CPUs

- Power supplies

- Cooling fans

- Network card

- System bus

Disk failure is the largest area of exposure for hardware failure, since disks have the shortest times between failure of any of the components in a computer system. Disks also present the greatest variety of redundant solutions, so discussing that type of failure in detail should provide the best example of how high availability can be implemented with hardware.

Disk redundancy

Disk failure is generally the most common cause of system failure. Although the mean time to failure of an individual disk drive is very high, the ever-increasing number of disks used for today's very large databases results in more frequent disk failures. Protection from disk failure is usually accomplished using RAID technology. The term RAID (Redundant Array of Inexpensive Disks) originated in a paper published in 1987 by Patterson, Gibson, and Katz at the University of California.[*] The use of redundant storage has become common for systems of all sizes and types for two primary reasons: the real threat of disk failure, and the proliferation of packaged, relatively affordable RAID solutions.

RAID technology uses one of two concepts to achieve redundancy:

Mirroring
    The actual data is duplicated on another disk in the system

Striping with parity
    Data is striped on multiple disks but instead of duplicating the data itself for redundancy, a mathematical calculation, termed *parity*, is performed on the data and the result is stored on another disk. You can think of parity as the sum of the striped data. If one of the disks is lost, you can reconstruct the data on that disk using the surviving disks and the parity data. The lost data represents the only unknown variable in the equation and can be derived. You can conceptualize this as a simple formula:

    A + B + C + D = E, in which A to D is data striped across four disks and E is the parity data on a fifth disk.

---

[*] Today, RAID also means "Redundant Array of Independent Disks."

If you lose any of the disks, you can solve the equation to identify the missing component. For example, if you lose the B drive, you can solve the formula as B = E - A - C - D.

There are a number of different disk configurations or types of RAID technology, which are formally termed *levels*. The basics of RAID technology were introduced in Chapter 6, *Oracle8 Performance*, but Table 10-2 summarizes the most relevant levels of RAID in a bit more detail, in terms of their cost, high availability, and the way Oracle uses each RAID level.

Table 10-2. RAID Levels Relevant to High Availability

Level	Disk Configuration	Costs Relative to Unprotected Storage	Comments	Oracle Usage
0	Simple striping, no redundancy	Same cost	Also referred to as JBOD—Just a Bunch of Disks. Striping increases read and write throughput. This is not really RAID, as there is no actual redundancy, but the term RAID-0 is used to describe striping.	Striping simplifies administration for Oracle datafiles. Suitable for all types of data for which redundancy isn't required.
1	Mirroring	Twice the cost	Same write performance as a single disk. Read performance may improve through servicing reads from both copies.	Lack of striping adds complexity of managing larger number of devices for Oracle. Often used for redo logs, since the I/O for redo is typically relatively small sequential writes. Striped arrays are more suited to large I/Os or to multiple smaller, random I/Os.
0 + 1	Striping and mirroring	Twice the cost	"Best of both worlds;" striping increases read and write performance and mirroring for redundancy avoids "read-modify-write" overhead of RAID-5.	Same usage as RAID-0, but provides protection from disk failure.

Table 10-2. RAID Levels Relevant to High Availability (continued)

Level	Disk Configuration	Costs Relative to Unprotected Storage	Comments	Oracle Usage
5	Striping with rotating or distributed parity	Storage capacity reduced by $1/N$ where N is number of disks in the array. For example, the storage is reduced by 20 percent or 1/5 of the total disk storage for a 5-disk array	Parity data is spread across all disks, avoiding the potential bottleneck found in some other types of RAID arrays. Striping increases read performance. Maintaining parity data adds additional I/O, decreasing write performance. For each write, the associated parity data must be read, modified, and written back to disk. This is referred to as the "read-modify-write" penalty.	Cost-effective solution for all Oracle data except redo logs. Degraded write performance must be taken into account. Popular for data warehouses as they involve mostly read activity. However, write penalties may slow loads and index builds. Often avoided for high-volume OLTP due to write penalties. Some storage vendors, for example EMC, have proprietary solutions (RAID-S) to minimize parity overhead on writes.

Which RAID Levels Should You Use with Oracle8?

Some people say that you should never use RAID-5 for an Oracle database because of the degraded write performance of this level of RAID. RAID-1 and RAID-0+1 offer better performance, but double the cost of disk storage. RAID-5 offers a cheaper and reasonable solution, provided that you can meet performance requirements despite the extra write overhead for maintaining parity data. Use these generic guidelines to help determine the appropriate uses of different RAID levels:

- Use RAID-1 for redo log files

- Use RAID-5 for database files, provided that the write overhead is acceptable

- Use RAID-1 or RAID-0+1 for database files if RAID-5 write overhead is unacceptable

Figure 10-3 illustrates the disk configurations for various RAID levels.

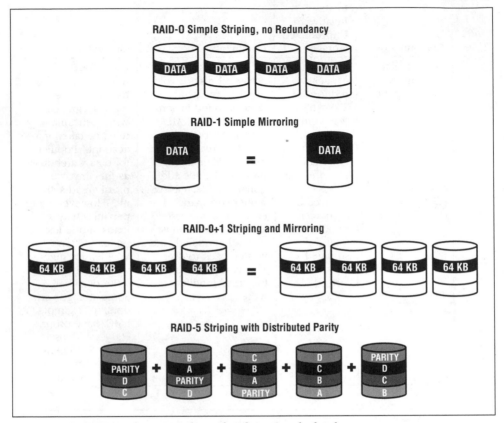

Figure 10-3. RAID Levels commonly used with an Oracle database

Simple Hardware Failover

As we've discussed, Oracle8 recovers automatically from a system crash. This automatic recovery protects the integrity of the data, which is the most essential feature of any relational database, but it also results in downtime as the database recovers from a crash. While redundant components do help prevent system crashes, at some point it's virtually inevitable that a crash will occur. Quickly detecting a system crash and initiating recovery is crucial to minimizing the associated downtime.

When an individual server fails, the instance running on that node fails as well. Depending on the cause, the failed node may not return to service quickly, or the failure may not be detected immediately by a human operator. Either way, companies that wish to protect their systems from the failure of a node typically employ a cluster of machines to achieve simple hardware *failover*. Failover is the ability of a surviving node in a cluster to assume the responsibilities of a failed node. Although failover doesn't directly address the issue of the reliability of the underlying hardware, automated failover can reduce the downtime from hardware failure.

The concept is very simple: a combination of software and hardware "watches" over the cluster. Typically, this monitoring is done by regularly checking a "heartbeat," which is a message sent between machines in the cluster. If Machine A fails, Machine B will detect the failure through the loss of the heartbeat and will execute scripts to take over control of the disks, assume Machine A's network address, and restart the processes that failed with Machine A. From an Oracle8 database perspective, the entire set of events is identical to an instance crash followed by an instance recovery. The instance uses the control files, redo log files, and database files to perform crash recovery. The fact that the instance is now running on another machine is irrelevant—the various Oracle files on disk are the key.

Most Unix failover solutions include software that runs on the machine to monitor specific processes, for example, the background processes of the Oracle instance. If the primary node itself has not failed but some process has, the monitoring software will detect the failure of the process and take some action based on scripts set up by the system administrator. For example, if the Oracle instance fails, the monitoring software may attempt to restart the Oracle instance three times. If all three attempts are unsuccessful, the software may initiate physical hardware failover, transferring control to the alternate node in the cluster.

Figures 10-4 and 10-5 illustrate the process of implementing a simple failover.

Outage duration for hardware failover

The time for failover to take effect, and therefore the length of the associated database downtime, depends on the following intervals:

Time for the alternate node to detect the failure of the primary node
> The alternate node monitors the primary node using a heartbeat mechanism. The frequency of this check is usually configurable—for example, every 30 seconds—providing control over the maximum time that a primary node failure will go undetected.

Time for the alternate node to execute various startup actions
> The time needed for such actions (e.g., assuming control of the disks used to store the Oracle database) may vary by system, and should be determined through testing. One important consideration is the time required for a filesystem check. The larger the database, the larger the number of filesystems that may have been used. When the alternate node assumes control of the disks, it must check the state of the various filesystems on the disks. This time can be reduced by using a journaled filesystem, such as the one provided by Veritas

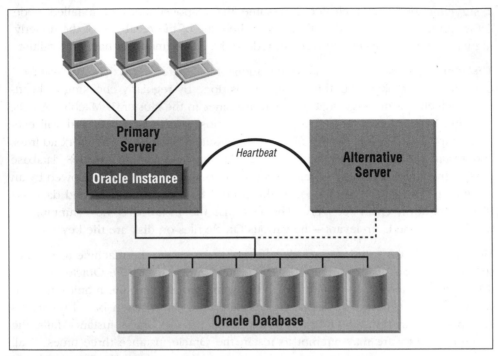

Figure 10-4. Before failover

Software (*http://www.veritas.com*). This software essentially uses a logging scheme similar to Oracle's to protect the integrity of the filesystem, thus eliminating the need for a complete filesystem check. Even with journaled filesystems, disk takeover can easily take several minutes, particularly on a busy system with high levels of disk activity.

Time for Oracle crash recovery

As we mentioned, you can effectively control this time period using checkpoints. Oracle8*i* provides a simple way to control recovery times using the *INIT.ORA* file parameter FAST_START_IO_TARGET.

When the instance fails, users will typically receive some type of error message and will attempt to log in again. Users won't be able to connect to the instance until Oracle crash recovery is complete and the database is completely open. Application developers can deal with this sequence of failover events with generic or specific error handling in their applications, or they can use the Transparent Application Failover functionality described later in this chapter.

Failover and operating system platform

Failover capability has long been available in the Unix world; more recently, it has been introduced to Microsoft Windows NT with the availability of Microsoft Cluster

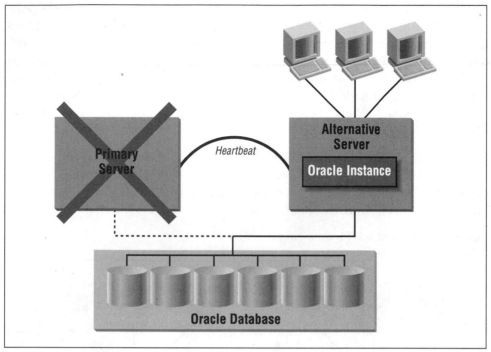

Figure 10-5. After failover

Server clustering technology. The Unix vendors typically offer a failover solution consisting of two machines, an interconnect between the machines, and the required software. There is no additional software required from Oracle. In the NT arena, Oracle8 includes FailSafe, software that provides a GUI interface for configuring the Oracle database for hardware failover. The mechanics of the failover are the same—the GUI is simply an administrative convenience.

Oracle offered a failover solution for NT with Oracle7 even before Microsoft had delivered its clustering solution. Early versions of FailSafe were available on NT hardware from vendors with clustering and failover experience, for example, Digital Equipment Corporation (now Compaq) and Data General. When Microsoft delivered its Cluster Server, Oracle simply implemented FailSafe using the Cluster Server interfaces instead of the hardware vendor interfaces previously used.

Oracle Parallel Server

Oracle first introduced Oracle Parallel Server (OPS) in 1989 on Digital Equipment Corporation's VAX clusters running the VMS operating system. OPS became available in the Unix environment in 1993. Oracle now offers Parallel Server on virtually every commercially available cluster or Massively Parallel Processing (MPP) hardware configuration.

At first glance, Oracle Parallel Server may look similar to the clustered solutions described earlier in the "Simple Hardware Failover" section. Both failover and OPS involve clustered hardware with access to disks from multiple nodes. The key difference is that OPS involves multiple Oracle instances with concurrent access to the same database. With hardware failover, only one node has an active instance, but with OPS, each node has an Oracle instance up and running simultaneously. Clients can connect to any of the instances and can access the same data but there is only one database.

With OPS, each Oracle instance runs on its own node. If a node fails, the instance on that node also fails, but the overall Oracle8 database is still available from the surviving instances still running on the other nodes. The instances continue to run uninterrupted on the other working nodes.

Figure 10-6 illustrates OPS on a cluster.

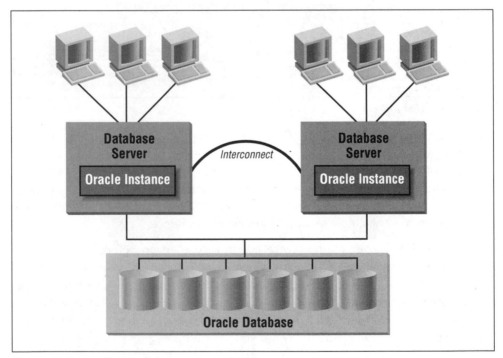

Figure 10-6. Oracle Parallel Server on a cluster

OPS and hardware failover

Which technology achieves better availability, OPS or the hardware failover capability? OPS can typically provide higher levels of availability than hardware failover, as we explain in the remainder of this section. OPS can also provide additional flexibility for scaling the application across multiple machines. OPS is an additional option on Oracle8 database licenses and does require more sophisticated system and database administration skills. Simply put, if the higher availability and flexibility of OPS doesn't justify the additional expense and complexity, then the use of a hardware failover solution is likely a more appropriate choice.

While OPS is an add-on option to your Oracle8 database licenses, it's not a separate database product. OPS runs across multiple nodes, but it's based on and requires the core Oracle database product. Oracle has only one database code base. Installing OPS adds code to the Oracle executable but doesn't replace the core database program.

OPS can increase availability by avoiding a complete database blackout. With hardware failover, the database is completely unavailable until you've completed node failover, instance startup, and crash recovery. With OPS, clients can connect to a surviving instance any time. Clients may be able to continue working with no interruption, depending on whether the data they need to work on was being used by the failed instance. You can think of the failure of an OPS instance as a potential database "brownout" as opposed to the guaranteed blackout caused by hardware failover.

Some other key differences between hardware failover and OPS include the following:

- OPS avoids the various activities involved in disk takeover: mounting volumes, validating filesystem integrity, opening Oracle database files, and so on. Not performing these activities can significantly reduce the time required to achieve full system availability.

- OPS doesn't require the creation and maintenance of the complex scripts typically used to control the activities for hardware failover. For example, there is no need to script which disk volumes will be taken over by a surviving node. The automatic nature of OPS avoids the complex initial system administration to set up the failover environment, as well as avoiding the ongoing administration needed as additional disk volumes are used. In fact, adding disk volumes to your database but forgetting to add the volumes to the various failover scripts can cause a hardware failover solution to fail itself!

In a simple two-way cluster used for hardware failover, both machines should have equal processing power and should be sized so that each can handle the entire workload. This equivalence is clearly required since only one node of the cluster is used at any point for the entire workload. If one node fails, the other should be capable of running the same workload with equal performance.

With OPS, you can use both nodes of the cluster concurrently to spread the workload, reducing the load on one machine. You still want to make sure that each machine will be powerful enough to handle the entire workload, for the same reasons as for the simple hardware cluster, that if one node fails, the other will have to process the entire workload.

Of course, using OPS to spread the workload over several machines will result in a lower percentage of each machine's resources being used in normal operating conditions, which is typically more expensive than using fully utilized machines. You will have to weigh the benefits of carrying on without any performance degradation in the event of a node failure versus the cost of buying more powerful machines. The economics of your situation may dictate that a decrease in performance in the event of a node failure is more palatable than a larger initial outlay for larger systems.

Using OPS for scalability is typically more complex than it is for high availability. Interested readers can find more details about OPS scalability in the Oracle8 documentation and third-party books mentioned in the Appendix.

Node failure and OPS

OPS instances provide protection for each other—if an instance fails, one of the surviving instances will detect the failure and automatically initiate OPS recovery. This type of recovery is different from the hardware failover discussed previously. No actual "failover" occurs—there is no disk takeover required, since all nodes already have access to the disks used for the database. There is no need to start an Oracle instance on the surviving node or nodes, since Oracle is already running on all nodes. The Oracle software performs the necessary actions without using scripts—the required steps are an integral part of OPS software.

The phases of OPS recovery are the following:

Cluster reorganization
> When an instance failure occurs, OPS must first determine which nodes of the cluster remain in service. OPS interfaces with the cluster management software provided by the platform or operating system vendor to determine the remaining nodes that make up the cluster. The time required for this operation is typically very brief.

Distributed Lock Manager (DLM) lock database rebuild
> The DLM database, which contains the information used to coordinate OPS traffic, is distributed across the multiple active instances. Therefore, a portion of that information is lost when a node fails. The remaining nodes have sufficient redundant data to reconstruct the lost information. Once the cluster membership has been determined, the surviving instances reconstruct the DLM database. The time for this phase depends on how many locks must be recovered, as well as whether the rebuild process involves a single surviving node or multiple surviving nodes. With a two-node cluster, node failure leaves a single surviving node. The single node acts as a dictator and processes the lock operations very quickly.

Instance recovery

Once the DLM database has been rebuilt, the redo logs from the failed instance perform crash recovery. This is similar to single-instance crash recovery—a rollforward phase followed by a nonblocking, deferred rollback phase. The key difference is that the recovery isn't performed by restarting a failed instance. Rather, it's performed by the instance that detected the failure.

While OPS recovery is in progress, clients connected to surviving instances remain connected and can continue working. In some cases, users may experience a delay in response times, but their sessions aren't terminated. Clients connected to the failed instance can reconnect to a surviving instance and can resume working. Uncommitted transactions will be rolled back and will have to be resubmitted. Queries that were active will also have been terminated and will require resubmission. A very powerful feature introduced in Oracle8, Transparent Application Failover, described in the next section, can be used to automatically continue query processing on a surviving node without requiring the user to resubmit the query. You can also use TAF to resubmit transactions without user intervention.

Oracle8 Transparent Application Failover

Oracle introduced the Transparent Application Failover (TAF) capability in the first release of Oracle8. As the name implies, TAF provides a seamless migration of users' sessions from one Oracle instance to another. You can use TAF to mask the failure of an instance for transparent high availability or to migrate users from an active instance to a less active one. Figure 10-7 illustrates TAF with OPS.

As shown in the figure, TAF can automatically reconnect clients to another instance of OPS, which provides access to the same database as the original instance. The high availability benefits of TAF include the following:

Transparent reconnection

Clients don't have to manually reconnect to a surviving instance. You can optimally reconfigure TAF to preconnect clients to an alternate instance in addition to their primary instance when they log on. Preconnecting clients to an alternate instance removes the overhead of establishing a new connection when automatic failover takes place. For systems with a large number of connected clients, this preconnection avoids the overhead and delays caused by flooding the alternate instance with a large number of simultaneous connection requests.

Automatic resubmission of queries

TAF can automatically resubmit queries that were active at the time the first instance failed and can resume sending results back to the client. Oracle will re-execute the query as of the time the original query started. Oracle's read

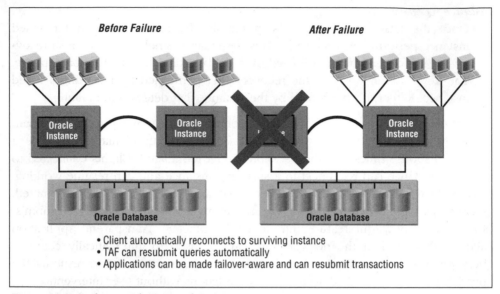

Figure 10-7. Failover with TAF and OPS

consistency will therefore provide the correct answer regardless of any activity since the query began.

Callback functions

Oracle8*i* further enhances TAF by allowing the application developer to register a "callback function" with TAF. Once TAF has successfully reconnected the client to the alternate instance, the registered function will be called automatically. The application developer can use the callback function to re-initialize various aspects of session state as desired

Failover-aware applications

Application developers can leverage TAF by writing "failover-aware" applications that resubmit transactions that were lost when the client's primary instance failed, further reducing the impact of failure. Note that unlike query resubmission, TAF itself doesn't automatically resubmit the transactions that were in-flight. Rather, it provides a framework for a seamless failover that can be leveraged by application developers.

How TAF works

TAF is implemented in the Oracle Call Interface (OCI) layer, a low-level API for establishing and managing Oracle database connections. When the instance a client is connected to fails, the client's server process ceases to exist. The OCI layer in the client can detect the absence of a server process on the other end of the channel and can automatically establish a new connection to another instance. The alternate instance to which TAF reconnects users is specified in the Net8 configuration files, which are described in Oracle's Net8 documentation.

Since OCI is a low-level API, writing programs with OCI requires more effort and sophistication on the part of the developer. Fortunately, Oracle uses OCI to write client tools and various drivers, so that applications using these tools can leverage TAF. Table 10-3 summarizes the TAF support for various tools and drivers.

Table 10-3. TAF Support by Oracle Interfaces

Oracle Development Tool/Driver	TAF Support
Oracle Call Interface (OCI)	Release 8
ODBC driver	Release 8.0.5
JDBC driver	Release 8 (thick driver only)
Pro*C pre-compiler	Release 8.0.6 for transparent reconnect Oracle8*i* for full transparent functionality
SQL*Plus	Release 8.0.4
Oracle Developer	Planned for later release
Oracle Objects for OLE	Planned for later release

Support for TAF in ODBC and JDBC drivers is especially useful; it means that TAF can be leveraged by any client application that uses these drivers to connect to Oracle. For example, TAF can provide automatic reconnection for a third-party query tool that uses ODBC. To implement TAF with ODBC, you set up an ODBC data source that uses an Oracle Net8 service name that has been configured to use TAF in the Net8 configuration files. ODBC uses Net8 and can therefore leverage the TAF feature.

TAF and various Oracle configurations

Although the TAF-OPS combination is the most obvious combination for high availability, TAF can be used with a single Oracle instance or with multiple databases, each accessible from a single instance. Some possible configurations are as follows:

- TAF can automatically reconnect clients back to their original instance for cases in which the instance failed but the node did not. An automated monitoring system, such as the Oracle Enterprise Manager, can detect instance failure quickly and restart the instance. The fast-start recovery features in Oracle8*i* enable very low crash recovery times. Users that aren't performing heads-down data entry work can be automatically reconnected by TAF and might never be aware that their instance failed and was restarted.

- TAF and simple clusters. TAF can reconnect users to the instance started by simple hardware failover on the surviving node of a cluster. The reconnection cannot occur until the alternate node has started Oracle and has performed crash recovery.

- TAF and two distinct databases, each with a single instance. TAF can reconnect clients to an instance that provides access to a different database running in another data center. This clearly requires replication of the relevant data between the two databases. Oracle fortunately provides automated support for data replication, which is covered in the later section entitled "Complete Site Failure."

Recovering from Disasters

Despite the prevalence of redundant or protected disk storage, media failures can and do occur. In cases in which one or more Oracle datafiles are lost due to disk failure, you must use database backups to recover the lost data.

There are times when simple human or machine error can also lead to the loss of data, just as a media failure can. For example, an administrator may accidentally delete a datafile, or an I/O subsystem may malfunction, corrupting data on the disks. The key to being prepared to handle these types of disasters is implementing a good backup and recovery strategy.

Developing a Backup and Recovery Strategy

Proper development, documentation, and testing of your backup and recovery strategy is one of the most important activities in implementing an Oracle database. You must test every phase of the backup and recovery process to ensure that the entire process works, because once a disaster hits, the complete recovery process *must* work flawlessly.

Some companies test the backup procedure but fail to actually test recovery using the backups taken. Only when a failure requires the use of the backups do companies discover that the backups in place were unusable for some reason. It's critical to test the entire cycle from backup through restore and recovery.

Taking Oracle Backups

There are two basic types of backups available with Oracle—*hot backups* and *cold backups.*

Hot backup
    The datafiles for one or more tablespaces are backed up while the database is active.

Cold backup
    The database is shut down and all the datafiles, redo log files, and control files are backed up.

With a hot backup, not all of the datafiles must be backed up at once. For instance, you may want to back up a different group of datafiles each night. You must be sure to keep backups of the archived redo logs that date back to your oldest backed-up datafile, since you'll need them if you have to implement rollforward recovery from the time of that oldest datafile backup.

Some DBAs with very large databases back up the various datafiles over several runs. Some DBAs back up the datafiles that contain data subject to frequent changes more frequently (for example, daily), and back up datafiles containing more static data less often (for example, weekly). There are commands to back up the control file as well, which should be done after all the datafiles have been backed up.

If the database isn't archiving redo logs, (this is known as running in NOARCHIVELOG mode and is described in Chapter 2), you can only take complete cold backups. If the database is archiving redo logs, the database can be backed up while running.

Regardless of backup type, you should also back up the *INIT.ORA* file and password files—these are key files for the operation of your Oracle database. While not required, you should also back up the various scripts used to create and further develop the database. These scripts represent an important part of the documentation of the structure and evolution of the database.

For more information about the different types of backups and variations on these types, please refer to your Oracle documentation as well as the third-party books listed in the appendix.

Using Backups to Recover

There are two basic types of recovery possible with Oracle, based on whether you are archiving the redo logs or not:

Complete database recovery
> If the database did not archive redo logs, then only a complete cold backup is possible. Correspondingly, only a complete database recovery can be performed. You restore the database files, redo logs, and control files from the backup. The database is essentially restored as of the time of the backup. As no archived redo logs are available, all work done since the time of the backup is lost. If no archived redo logs are available, this complete recovery must be performed even if only one of the datafiles is damaged. The potential for lost work, coupled with the need to restore the entire database to correct partial failure, are reasons most shops avoid this situation by running their databases in ARCHIVELOG mode. Figure 10-8 illustrates backup and recovery for a database without archived redo logs.

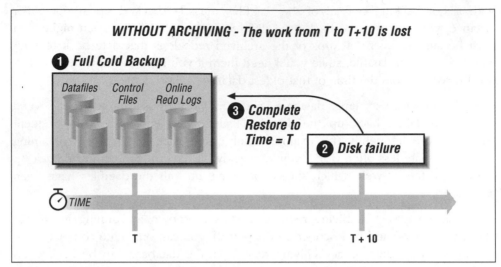

Figure 10-8. Database backup and recovery without archived redo logs

Partial or targeted restore and rollforward recovery

When you're running the Oracle database in ARCHIVELOG mode, you can restore only the damaged datafile(s) and can apply redo log information from the time the backup was taken to the point of failure. The archived and online redo logs reproduce all the changes to the restored datafiles to bring them up to the same point in time as the rest of the database. This procedure minimizes the time for the restore and recovery operations. Partial recovery like this can be done with the database down. Alternatively, the affected tablespace(s) can be placed offline and recovery can be performed with the rest of the database available.

Figure 10-9 illustrates backup and recovery with archived redo logs.

Read-only Tablespaces

Oracle 7.3 introduced read-only tablespaces. Using the ALTER TABLESPACE command in SQL, you can mark a tablespace as read-only. No changes are possible to the objects stored in a read-only tablespace. A tablespace can be toggled between read-write and read-only states as you wish.

Once a tablespace is in read-only mode, it can be backed up once and doesn't have to be backed up again, since its contents cannot change unless it's placed in read-write mode. Marking a tablespace as read-only allows entire sections of a database to be marked read-only, backed up once, and excluded from regular backups thereafter.

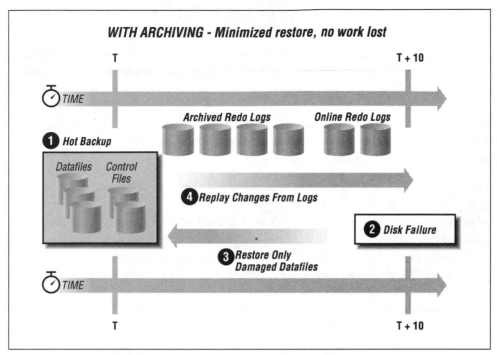

Figure 10-9. Database backup and recovery with archived redo logs

If a datafile of a read-only tablespace is damaged, you can restore it directly from the backup without any recovery required. Because there were no changes made to the datafiles of the read-only tablespace, no redo log information needs to be applied. For databases with significant static or historical data, this option can significantly simplify and streamline backup and restore operations.

Read-only tablespaces, combined with Oracle8's ability to partition a table on a range of column values (for example, a date) provide powerful support for the rolling windows common to data warehouses (described in Chapter 9, *Oracle8 and Data Warehousing*). Once a new month's data is loaded, indexed, and so on, the relevant tablespaces can be marked read-only and backed up once, removing the tablespaces datafile(s) from the cycle of ongoing backup and significantly reducing the time required for those backup operations.

Point-in-Time Recovery

Oracle 7.3 introduced point-in-time recovery (PITR) for the entire database. Point-in-time recovery allows a DBA to restore the datafiles for the database and apply redo information up to a specific time or System Change Number (SCN). This limited type of recovery is useful for cases in which an error occurred—for example, if a table was dropped accidentally or a large number of rows were deleted incorrectly. The DBA can restore the database to the point in time just prior to the event to undo the results of the mistake.

The difficulty with database-level point-in-time recovery is that the entire database has to be restored. In response to this limitation, Oracle8 introduced point-in-time recovery at the tablespace level within the database. Point-in-time recovery based on a tablespace allows a DBA to restore and recover only a tablespace or set of tablespaces to a particular point in time. Only the tablespace(s) containing the desired objects need to be recovered. This is a very useful improvement given the ever-increasing size of today's databases.

You should use this tablespace feature carefully, since objects in one tablespace may have dependencies, such as referential integrity constraints, on objects in other tablespaces. For example, suppose Tablespace1 contains the EMP table and Tablespace2 contains the DEPT table, and there is a foreign key constraint that links these two tables together for referential integrity. If you were to recover Tablespace2 to an earlier point than Tablespace1, you might find that you had rows in the EMP table that contained an invalid foreign key value, since the matching primary key entry in the DEPT table had not been rolled forward to the place where the primary key value the EMP table refers to had been added.

Recovery Manager

Recovery Manager (RMAN) debuted with Oracle8 and provides server-managed backup and recovery. RMAN includes the ability to perform and track backup and recovery operations. RMAN does the following:

- Backs up one or more datafiles to disk or tape
- Backs up archived redo logs to disk or tape
- Restores datafiles from disk or tape
- Restores and applies archived redo logs to perform recovery
- Automatically parallelizes both the reading and writing of the various Oracle files being backed up

RMAN performs the backup operations and updates a catalog, which is stored in an Oracle database with the details of what backups were taken and where they were stored. You can query this catalog for critical information, such as datafiles that have not been backed up or datafiles whose backups have been invalidated through NOLOGGING operations performed on objects contained in those datafiles.

RMAN also uses the catalog to perform incremental backups. RMAN will only back up database blocks that have changed since the last backup. When RMAN only backs up the individual changed blocks in the database, the overall backup and recovery time can be significantly reduced for databases in which a small percentage of the data in large tables changes.

Another major advantage RMAN offers is to make it simpler to perform hot or online backups. RMAN also reduces the overhead required to make online backups.

In Oracle7, you took hot backups by issuing ALTER TABLESPACE BEGIN BACKUP commands for the tablespace whose datafiles were to be backed up: you backed up the datafiles using operating system commands and issuing ALTER TABLESPACE END BACKUP commands. Oracle continued to write blocks to the datafiles while they were being backed up, and there was no restriction on user activity. This meant that the datafile backups could contain blocks from different points in time, since the backup process itself occurred over time and blocks were being written to the datafiles during this time.

Consider the following example. The operating system process reading the datafile reads the first operating system block within an Oracle block composed of two operating system blocks and writes it to tape at Time T. At T+1, Oracle updates the database block in the datafile. Both operating system blocks in the datafile on disk are now consistent as of Time T+1. The operating system process for the backup then reads and backs up the second operating system block as of T+1. The datafile backup now contains a "fuzzy" database block. The two operating system blocks that make up the Oracle block in the backup are from different points in time—the first operating system block is as of Time T, and the second is as of Time T+1.

To address this potential inconsistency, Oracle7 automatically includes extra redo information to correct this situation for any tablespace for which an ALTER TABLESPACE BEGIN BACKUP has been issued.

With Oracle8, RMAN is an Oracle process, so it reads and writes Oracle blocks, not operating system blocks. While RMAN is backing up a datafile, Oracle blocks may be written to it but RMAN will read and write in consistent Oracle blocks, not operating system blocks within an Oracle block. This removes the possibility of fuzzy Oracle blocks in the datafile backups and therefore removes the need for the ALTER TABLESPACE commands and the additional redo.

Complete Site Failure

Protection from the complete failure of your primary Oracle site poses significant challenges. Your company must carefully evaluate the risks to its primary site. These risks include physical and environmental problems as well as hardware risks. For example, is the data center in your area prone to floods, tornadoes, or earthquakes? Is the data center located in a facility with manufacturing activity involving hazardous or flammable chemicals? Are power failures a frequent occurrence? Even some extremely remote possibilities, such as a terrorist attack or an airplane crash into the data center, must at least be given cursory attention, since the complete destruction of corporate data that would occur in such a situation would have such a disastrous effect.

Protection from primary site failure involves monitoring of and redundancy controls for the following:

*   Data center power supply

*   Data center climate control facilities

*   Database server redundancy

*   Database redundancy

*   Data redundancy

The first three items on the list are aimed at preventing the failure of the data center. Data server redundancy, through simple hardware failover or Oracle Parallel Server, provides protection from node failure within a data center but not from complete data center loss.

Should the data center fail completely, the last two items—database redundancy and data redundancy—provide for disaster recovery.

Emerging Technologies: Clusters Across a Distance

Some vendors are now offering clustering solutions that allow the nodes of the cluster to be separated by enough distance to allow one node to survive the failure of the data center that contains the other node. The clustering of nodes separated by a few kilometers is becoming possible using sophisticated interconnect technologies that can function over greater distances. The disks are mirrored with a copy at each site to allow each site to function in the event of a complete failure of the other site.

These solutions are very intriguing because they can provide data server redundancy and data center redundancy in a single solution. If one node fails or the data center containing one node fails, the other node in a separate data center provides failover. Using OPS across these widely separated nodes may also be possible, providing even more latitude, but you must ensure that the increased distance messages must travel for OPS coordination doesn't result in unacceptable performance.

Standby Database for Redundancy

Oracle's standby database functionality, introduced in Oracle 7.3, provides database redundancy. The concept is simple—keep a copy of the database files at a second location, ship the redo logs to the second site as they are filled, and apply them to the copy of the database. This process keeps the standby database "a few steps" behind the primary database. If the primary site fails, the standby database is opened and becomes the production database. The potential data loss is limited to the transactions in any redo logs that have not been shipped to the standby site. Figure 10-10 illustrates the standby database feature.

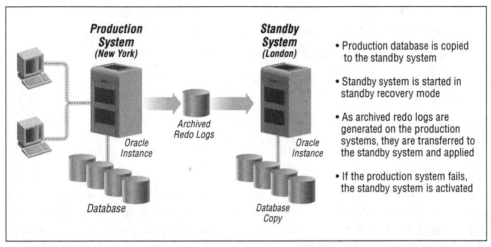

Figure 10-10. Standby database

Oracle8*i* allows you to open the standby database for read-only access. You can use read-only access to offload reporting, such as end-of-day reports, from the primary server to the standby server. The ability to offload reporting requests provides flexibility for reporting and queries and can help performance on the primary server while making use of the standby server.

While the standby database is used for reporting, the archived redo information from the primary site isn't applied. Recovery can continue when the standby database is closed again. This factor has important implications for the time it will take to recover from an outage with the standby database. If the primary site fails while the standby database is open for reporting, the archived redo information from the primary site that accumulated while the standby database was querying must be applied before the standby is brought online. This application of archived redo information increases the duration of the outage. You'll need to weigh the benefits of using the standby database for reporting against the recovery time and the duration of the outage should a failure occur while archived redo information is not being applied at the standby.

Once a standby database is opened for read-write access, as opposed to read-only access, it can no longer be used as a standby database, and you cannot resume applying archived redo information later. The standby database must be "re-cloned" from the primary site if the standby database is opened accidentally in read-write mode.

Possible Causes of Lost Data with a Standby Database

There is a possibility that you will lose data, even if you use a standby database. There are three possible causes of lost data in the event of primary site failure:

- Archived redo logs have not been shipped to the standby site

- Filled online redo logs have not been archived yet

- The current online redo log is not a candidate for archiving until a log switch occurs

These three potential problems are addressed in different ways, as described in the following sections.

Copying archived redo logs to a standby site

Oracle 7.3 and Oracle 8.0 don't automate the copying of archived redo logs from the primary to the standby site. With these versions, customers were free to use any method to copy the files across the network. For example, you could schedule a batch job that copies archived logs to the standby site every *N* minutes. If the primary site fails, these copies would limit the lost redo information (and therefore the lost data) to a maximum of *N* minutes of work.

Oracle8*i* provides support for the archiving of redo logs to a destination on the primary server as well as on multiple remote servers. This feature automates the copying and application of the archived redo logs to one or more standby sites. The lost data is then limited to the contents of any filled redo logs that have not been completely archived, as well as the current online redo log. Oracle8*i* also automatically applies the archived redo logs to the standby database as they arrive.

Unarchived redo information and the role of geo-mirroring

While certainly useful, Oracle8*i*'s automated remote archiving doesn't provide higher availability for any filled but unarchived logs or the current online redo log. If you require primary site failure not to result in the loss of *any* committed transactions, the solution is to mirror all redo log and control file activity from the primary site to the standby site.

You provide this level of reliability by using a remote mirroring technology sometimes known as *geo-mirroring*. Essentially, all writes to the online redo log files and the control files at the primary site must be mirrored synchronously to the standby site. For simplicity, you can also geo-mirror the archived log destination, which will duplicate the archived logs at the remote site—in effect, copying the archived redo logs from the primary to the standby site. This approach can simplify operations; you use one solution for all the mirroring requirements, as opposed to having Oracle copy the archived logs and having geo-mirroring handle the other critical files.

Geo-mirroring of the online redo logs results in every committed transaction being written to both the online redo log at the primary site and the copy of the online redo log at the standby site. This process adds some time to each transaction for the mirrored write to reach the standby site. Depending on the distance between the sites and the network used, geo-mirroring can hamper performance, so you should test its impact on the normal operation of your database.

An example of geo-mirroring technology is EMC Corporation's Symmetrix Remote Data Facility (SRDF) and associated software called Timefinder. Setting up geo-mirroring and understanding the exact steps to take in the event of primary site failure is not trivial. Oracle and EMC have certified this technology with the standby database and produced a detailed joint paper entitled "No Data Loss Standby Database." If you believe that your situation requires this level of redundancy, we strongly encourage you to read this paper first.

Geo-mirroring provides the most complete protection against primary site failure and, accordingly, it's a relatively expensive solution. You will need to weigh the cost of the sophisticated disk subsystems and high-speed telecommunication lines needed for nonintrusive geo-mirroring against the cost of losing the data in any unarchived redo logs and the current online redo log; see the Appendix for more information.

Data Redundancy Solutions

Redundant data is another option for dealing with primary site failure. Implementing a redundant data approach differs from using a standby database, which duplicates the entire primary database. Data redundancy is achieved by having a copy of your critical data in an entirely separate Oracle database with a different structure. The data, not the database itself, is redundant. If the primary site fails, users can continue working using the redundant data in the secondary database.

Oracle provides automated synchronous and asynchronous data replication features to support data redundancy. For simplicity, in the following sections we'll examine replication using a simple two-site example—a primary and a secondary.

Oracle can, however, perform *N*-way or multimaster replication involving more than two sites with all sites replicating to all others.

Data Replication—Synchronous and Asynchronous

Whenever you have a data replication scenario, you always have a primary site, from which the replication originates, and a secondary site, which is the recipient of the data replication. (In a multimaster scenario, you can have more than one master site, and a single machine may be a master for one replication plan and a secondary site for another.) When you design your replication plan, you must consider the degree to which data at the secondary site may differ for a period of time from the data at the primary site. This difference is referred to as *data divergence*. When you implement replication, Oracle generates triggers on all specified tables. These triggers are fired as part of the primary site transactions. The triggers either update the secondary site's data as part of the same transaction (*synchronous replication*) or place an entry in a deferred transaction queue that will be used later to update the secondary site (*asynchronous replication*).

Key considerations in setting up a replication environment include the following:

Tolerance for data divergence
> The smaller the data divergence, the more individual replication actions will have to be performed. You will reduce the resources needed to implement the replication by increasing the data divergence.

Performance requirements
> Since replication requires resources, it can have an impact on performance.

Network bandwidth
> Since replication uses network bandwidth, you have to consider the availability of this resource.

Distance between sites
> The further the distance between sites, the longer the physical transfer of data will take, and the longer each application will take.

Site and network stability
> If a site or a network goes down, all replications that use that network or are destined for that site will not be received. When either of these resources come back online, the stored replication traffic can have an impact on the amount of time it takes to recover the site.

The experience level of your database administrators
> Even the most effective replication plan can be undone by DBAs who aren't familiar with replication.

Figure 10-11 illustrates these two types of replication.

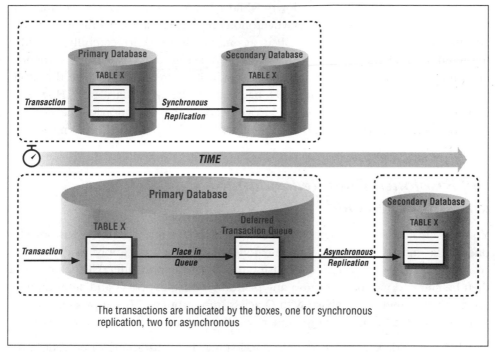

Figure 10-11. Oracle replication for redundant data

Synchronous, or real-time, replication can be used when there is no tolerance for data divergence or lost data. The data at the secondary site *must* match the primary site at all times and reflect all committed transactions. Each transaction at the primary site will fire triggers that call procedures at the secondary site to reproduce the transaction. Synchronous replication uses distributed transactions that will add overhead to every transaction at the primary site. Whether or not this additional overhead is acceptable will clearly depend on your specific requirements. Synchronous replication introduces system interdependencies—the secondary site and the network connecting the sites must be up or the primary site will not be able to perform transactions.

You can also use asynchronous, or deferred, replication to provide redundant data. Transactions are performed at the primary site, and these changes are replicated some time later to the secondary site. Until the deferred transaction queue is "pushed" to the secondary site, replicating the changes, the data at the secondary site will differ from the primary site data. If the primary database is irrevocably lost, any unpushed transactions in the deferred queue will also be lost.

The extent of the data divergence and potential data loss resulting from the divergence is a very important consideration in configuring asynchronous replication. In addition, asynchronous replication allows the primary site to function when the network or the secondary site is down, while synchronous replication *requires* that the secondary site be available. Asynchronous replication adds overhead to transactions at the primary site, so once again, you'll need to carefully consider throughput requirements and perform appropriate testing. Typically, asynchronous replication adds less overhead than synchronous replication, since the replication of changes can be efficiently batched to the secondary site. However, asynchronous replication will still add overhead to the operation of the primary site, so you should consider and test the effect of both types of replication on your database environment.

Old-Fashioned Data Redundancy—Export/Import and Unload/Reload

You can also achieve redundant data using Oracle's standard utilities. Historically, one of the most common backup methods for Oracle was simply to export the contents of the database into a file using the Oracle Export utility. This file could then be shipped in binary form to any platform Oracle supports and subsequently imported into another database with Oracle's Import utility. This approach can still provide a simple form of data redundancy if the amount of data is manageable.

Oracle 7.3 introduced a *direct-path export* feature that runs about 70 percent faster than a traditional export. The direct-path export avoids some of the overhead of a normal export by directly accessing the data in the Oracle datafiles.

You can also improve the performance of an import with some planning. An import is essentially a series of INSERT statements, so you can optimize the insert process by inserting the data into a table without indexes and then adding the indexes after the table is built. The time and resources needed to perform large exports and imports may make this an appropriate option.

Another export solution is to unload data from the desired tables into simple flat files by spooling the output of a SELECT statement to an operating system file. You can then ship the flat file to the secondary site and use Oracle's SQL*Loader utility to load the data into duplicate tables in the secondary database. For cases in which a significant amount of data is input to the primary system using loads, such as in a data warehouse, a viable disaster recovery plan is simply to back up the load files to a secondary site on which they will wait, ready for reloading to either the primary or secondary sites should a disaster occur.

While relatively crude, these import/export and loading methods can provide simple data redundancy for targeted sets of data.

11

Oracle8 and Hardware Architecture

In Chapter 2, *Oracle8 Architecture*, we discussed the architecture of the Oracle8 database, and in Chapter 6, *Oracle8 Performance*, we described how Oracle8 uses hardware resources. Although Oracle8 operates in the same way on many different hardware platforms, different hardware architectures can ultimately determine the specific scalability, performance tuning, management, and reliability options available to you.

This chapter explains each of these hardware systems:

- Uniprocessors
- Symmetrical Multiprocessing (SMP) systems
- Clusters
- Massively Parallel Processing (MPP) systems
- NUMA systems

The chapter explains how Oracle8 takes advantages of the features inherent in each of the platforms. We'll also discuss the use of different disk technologies and how to choose the hardware system that's right for your purposes.

System Basics

Any discussion of hardware systems begins with a review of the components that make up a hardware platform and the impact these components have on the overall system. You'll find the same essential components under the covers of any computer system:

- CPU, which executes the basic instructions that make up computer programs
- Memory, which stores recently accessed instructions and data

- Input/output (I/O) system, which typically consists of disk, diskette, and tape controllers for pulling data and programs off physical media and network controllers for connecting the system to other systems on the network.

The number of each of these components and the capabilities of the individual components themselves determine the ultimate cost and scalability of a system. A machine with four processors is typically more expensive and capable of doing more work than a single-processor machine; new versions of components, such as CPU chips, are typically faster and more expensive than older versions. In decision support or data warehousing systems, CPU and memory are often the performance limiting components. In online transaction processing (OLTP) systems, I/O is often the most critical component.

Each component has a latency cost and capacity associated with it. The *latency cost* of a component is the amount of latency the use of that component introduces into the system, in other words, how much slower each successive level of a component is than its previous level (e.g., Level 2 versus Level 1; see Table 11-1).

The CPU and the Level 1 memory cache on the CPU have the lowest latency, as shown in Table 11-1, but also the least capacity. Disk has the most capacity but the highest latency.

 There are several different types of memory: a Level 1 cache, which is on the CPU chip; a Level 2 cache, which is on the same board as the CPU; and main memory, which is the remaining memory on the machine.

Table 11-1. Typical Sizes and Latencies of System Components

Element	Typical Storage Capability	Typical Latency
CPU	None	10 nanoseconds
Level 1 cache (on the CPU)	10s to 100s of KB	10 nanoseconds
Level 2 cache (on same board)	100s of KB to MBs	40–60 nanoseconds
Main memory	MBs to 10 GBs	200–400 nanoseconds
Disk	GBs to TBs	10–15 million nanoseconds (10–15 milliseconds)

An important part of tuning any system involves reducing the need to read data from the slow disk as much as possible and, when a disk must be accessed, to ensure there are as few bottlenecks as possible in the I/O subsystem. As a program (or the Oracle database a program uses) accesses a greater percentage of its data from memory rather than disk, the overall latency of the system is correspondingly decreased. For more information about some of these tuning issues, see Chapter 6.

Uniprocessor Systems

Uniprocessor systems, shown in Figure 11-1, are the simplest systems in terms of architecture. These systems (typically a standard personal computer), contain a single CPU and a single I/O channel and are made entirely with industry-standard components. They are most often used as single-user standalone machines, perhaps used for database development or as client machines in a network. Some uniprocessor machines are also used as small servers for databases. Versions of this architecture made with more exotic RISC-based CPUs are typically used as engineering, scientific, or graphics workstations today.

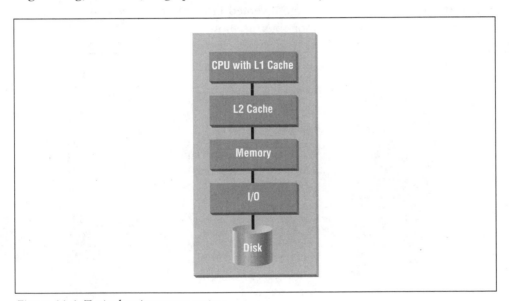

Figure 11-1. Typical uniprocessor system

Until the 1990s, uniprocessor systems were frequently used as servers because of their low price and the limited ability of relational databases to fully utilize other types of systems. However, Oracle evolved to take advantage of systems containing multiple CPUs through improved parallelism and more sophisticated optimization. At the same time, the price points of symmetric multiprocessing (SMP) systems (described in the next section) have plummeted dramatically, making SMP systems the database hardware servers of choice.

Although there is only a single processor in a uniprocessor system, the server operating systems used by these systems now support multiple threads. Each thread can be used to support a concurrent process, which can execute in parallel. By default, the PARALLEL_THREADS_PER_CPU parameter in the *INIT.ORA* file is now set at 2 for most platforms on which Oracle runs. Oracle8*i* further determines the degree of parallelism based on parameters set in the *INIT.ORA* file and the new adaptive multiuser feature. This adaptive multiuser feature (which assigns the degree of parallelism based on user load) makes use of algorithms that take into account the number of threads. Additional tuning parameters can also affect parallelism. For more information about the parallel thread capability of Oracle8, see Chapter 6.

Symmetric Multiprocessing Systems

One of the limiting factors for a uniprocessor system is the ultimate speed of its single processor—all applications have to share this one resource. Symmetrical Multiprocessing (SMP) systems were invented in an effort to overcome this limitation by adding CPUs to the memory bus, as shown in Figure 11-2.

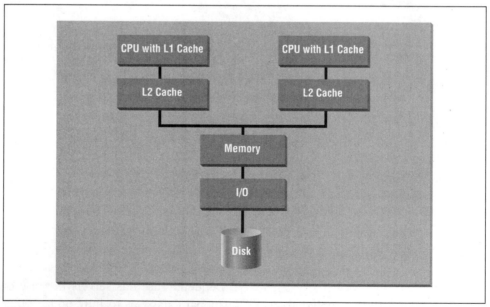

Figure 11-2. Typical Symmetric Multiprocessing (SMP) system

Each CPU has its own memory cache, but there might be data in a cache associated with one CPU that's being requested by another CPU. Because of this potential sharing of data, the CPUs for such machines must be able to "snoop" the memory bus to determine where copies of data reside and whether the data is being updated. This snooping is managed transparently by the operating system that controls the SMP system, so standard Oracle releases of Oracle8 Server and Oracle8 Enterprise Edition can be used on such platforms.

SMP platforms have been available since the 1980s as midrange platforms, primarily as Unix-based machines. Today, there is a relatively new category of SMP PC servers based on Intel (or Intel instruction set compatible) CPUs. The most popular operating system in this category is Microsoft Windows NT, although there are various Unix operating systems variations including SCO Unix and Linux.

Larger and more expensive SMP servers feature variations on this basic design. For example, SMP systems might include Reduced Instruction Set Chips (RISC), which are usually significantly faster CPUs; larger Level 2 cache; and multiple I/O channels. Each of these enhancements is intended to remove potential bottlenecks that can limit performance. Unix is the most common operating system used in Oracle implementations on high-end SMP servers.

Historically, the number of CPUs possible on a single SMP machine was limited by the system (memory) bus. As more CPUs were added to the bus, the bus itself became saturated with traffic between CPUs attached to the bus.

One of the key enabling technologies for these very large SMP servers is the high-speed system bus that supports communication traffic among a far higher number of CPUs. Oracle offers a 64-bit version for a variety of such platforms, including Compaq (formerly Digital Equipment Company), Unix, HP/UX, IBM AIX, and Sun Solaris. The most scalable versions of SMP servers today feature 64-bit CPUs, which can handle large amounts of data more efficiently than standard 32-bit CPUs can; they support as many as 64 CPUs; and extended memory into the tens of gigabytes.

Of course, the database must be parallelized to take full advantage of the SMP architecture. Oracle operations, such as query execution, and other DML activity and data loading, can run as parallel processes within the Oracle server, allowing Oracle8 to take advantage of the benefits of multiprocessor systems. Oracle8, like all other software systems, will benefit from parallel operations, as shown by "Amdahl's Law:"

> Total execution time = (parallel part / number of processors) + serial part

Amdahl's Law, formulated by mainframe pioneer Gene Amdahl in 1967 to describe performance in mixed parallel and serial workloads, clearly shows that moving an operation from the serial portion of execution to a parallel portion provides the performance increases expected with the use of multiple processors. In the same way, the more serial operations that make up an application, the longer the execution time because the sum of the execution time of all serial operations is directly added to any performance gains realized from the use of multiple processors. In other words, you cannot speed up a serial operation or a sequence of serial operations by adding more processors.

Each subsequent release of Oracle has added more parallelized features to speed up the execution of queries, as well as the tuning and maintenance of the database. For a list of Oracle operations that can be parallelized, see the section "What Can Be Parallelized?" in Chapter 6.

Oracle's parallel operations work by taking advantage of available CPU resources. If you're working with a system on which the CPU resources are already being completely consumed, this parallelism will not help improve performance; in fact, it could even hurt performance by adding the additional demands for CPU power required to manage the parallel processes. However, with the Multi-Threaded Server and Net8 concentrators (discussed in Chapter 2), parallelization may make more sense because there will be more CPU power available per Oracle connection.

Clusters

Clustered systems have provided a high availability and scalability solution since the 1980s, initially via DEC's VAXcluster. Clusters can combine all the components of separate machines, including CPUs, memory, and I/O subsystems, into a single hardware entity. However, clusters are typically built by using shared disks linked to multiple "nodes" (computer systems) as well as an interconnect between systems as a means of exchanging data and instructions without writing to disk (see Figure 11-3). Each system runs its own operating system copy and Oracle instance.

Oracle's support for clusters dates back to the VAXcluster. Oracle provided a sophisticated locking model so that the multiple nodes could access the shared data on the disks. Clusters required such a locking model, because each machine in the cluster had to be aware of the data locks held by other, physically separate machines in the cluster.

Today, that Oracle solution has evolved into Oracle Parallel Server (OPS) and is most frequently used for NT and Unix-based systems. Oracle provides an integrated Distributed Lock Manager (DLM) used to manage concurrent access to the shared disk. Simply stated, the DLM works like a traffic cop and provides control over ownership of data that may be accessed by more than one user from more than one system. Thus, if two users try to update the same data at the same time, the first user will have taken out a lock on it; this lock ensures that the first user's update can't be erased by the second user. Chapter 7, *Multiuser Concurrency*, provides a more complete discussion of the issues raised by multiple users accessing the same data.

You can configure clusters to deliver higher throughput for the system or greater availability for the system. In the high availability scenario, if a single node fails, a secondary node attached to the shared disk can get access to the same data. Users can have their queries run to completion without further intervention, since Oracle8 introduced failover client support.

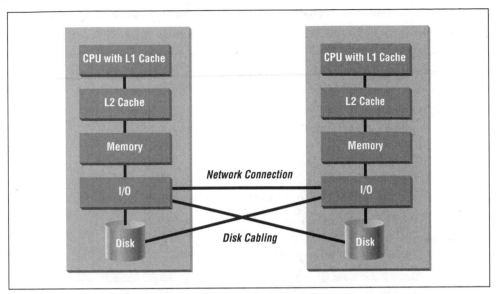

Figure 11-3. Typical cluster (two systems shown)

Clusters and OPS are increasingly being used today in NT environments, where a single NT platform cannot scale adequately to meet a company's needs and where the organization doesn't possess (or have the desire to possess) the skills needed to run Unix-type solutions. In addition, Oracle offers FailSafe on NT for simple failover. Data is not shared among the two systems and a second system provides "standby" access to this data. However, because concurrent access isn't provided, the failover solution doesn't offer the scalability that OPS can provide. The use of clusters for high availability (both with and without Oracle Parallel Server) is discussed in Chapter 10, *Oracle8 and High Availability*.

Massively Parallel Processing Systems

Clusters historically have been limited in the throughput they can deliver by the number of physical shared disk connections possible, since the disks have to be linked physically to each system. Recent advances in serial and fiber channel disk technology (discussed in the section "Disk Technology") have raised disk performance and capacity. But this increased capability has also raised issues of management complexity because each node introduces another discrete copy of the operating system and another Oracle instance to maintain.

Massively Parallel Processing (MPP) systems appeared in the early 1990s to address these limitations. Unlike clusters, the disks in an MPP environment are not shared across multiple nodes, except for high availability configurations, so the architecture is sometimes called a "shared nothing architecture" (shown in Figure 11-4). A special console provides additional operating system management tools to make management of the many operating system copies appear to be more transparent.

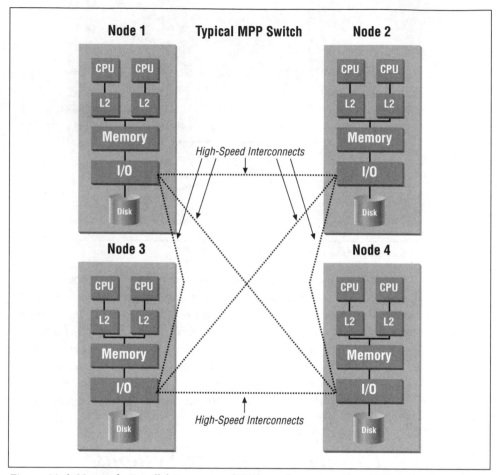

Figure 11-4. Massively Parallel Processing (MPP) configuration (four SMP nodes shown)

In a typical MPP configuration, multiple nodes reside in a single cabinet, but MPP configurations may grow to a series of cabinets with hundreds of nodes. The nodes are linked together via a high-speed switch and may be linked to other cabinets of nodes via cables that physically link the switch to the other cabinets. The switch provides each of the nodes with multiple interconnects to adjacent nodes. As additional nodes are added, additional paths are enabled between the nodes, and the total throughput possible by the switch continues to scale with the connections. Individual nodes can be single processors or symmetrical multiprocessors. Oracle Parallel Server can use either configuration, though SMP nodes can be utilized for additional parallelism against data residing on a local node and are becoming the default configuration.

The overall performance is a function of the power of individual nodes, the total number of nodes, the throughput offered by the switch, and the distribution of data. As an example, in a data warehousing query, a 64-way SMP platform could outperform a MPP platform with 16 nodes, each a 4-way SMP, since these types of queries are usually CPU-bound, and because MPP interconnects are slower than an SMP memory bus. The tradeoff is that you can use a much larger MPP configuration than a single SMP platform, although the cost of the MPP solution can be much more expensive than an SMP system.

The most common implementation of Oracle in the MPP world is on the IBM RS/6000 SP. In this type of environment, Oracle Parallel Server is implemented on a version of IBM AIX for the SP that includes Virtual Shared Disk (VSD). This software enables the disk on the SP to appear as a shared disk, even though the disk is directly connected to an individual node. As we mentioned earlier, Oracle provides an integrated Distributed Lock Manager. The DLM works in conjunction with the VSD in much the same way as if the disks were physically connected to each node, as we discussed previously in "Clusters." Recovery with twin-tailed SCSI (described later in the "Disk Controllers" section) or other disk controller options is enabled through the use of IBM's Recoverable Virtual Shared Disk (RVSD) and Oracle's Recoverable Lock Manager.

NUMA Systems

Nonuniform Memory Access (NUMA) computers, introduced in the mid-1990s, provide even greater throughput than SMP by linking multiple SMP components via linked distributed memory, as shown in Figure 11-5. Like MPP systems, these systems provide scaling of memory and I/O subsystems in addition to the advantages of using multiple CPUs. However, a single operating system copy manages the platform and a directory-based cache coherency scheme to keep data synchronized. Memory access between nodes is in the hundreds of microseconds, which is much faster than going to disk in MPP or cluster configurations, but slower than local memory access in a single SMP system.

There are also some major advantages of NUMA over MPP and cluster solutions:

* Parallel versions of applications don't need to be developed to run on these machines (though there may be additional performance gains realized when such applications can be tuned for NUMA)

* Management is much simpler on NUMA systems than on clusters because there is only one copy of the operating system to manage

Oracle works with various NUMA vendors to provide highly tunable Oracle versions that can take advantage of the benefits offered by these platforms, such as

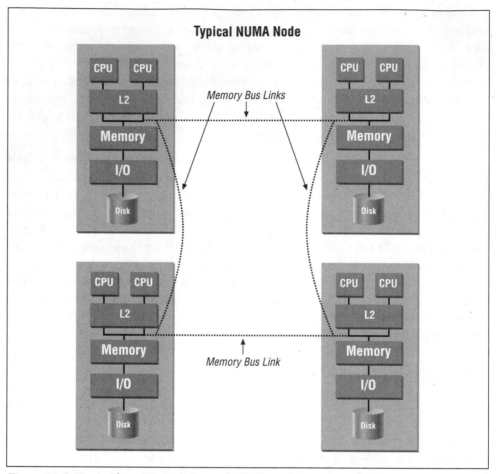

Figure 11-5. Nonuniform Memory Access (NUMA) configuration

having data available on local nodes when a query is submitted, which can deliver better performance. Today, Data General, Hewlett Packard, and Sequent (acquired by IBM in 1999) produce systems using a NUMA architecture. The vendors of such systems typically provide a very high-speed local memory bus for a limited number of local processors. As a result, the average latency when using linked memory is only slightly slower than a large SMP local memory bus.

Disk Technology

The discussion of hardware architectures in this chapter so far has centered around ways of increasing performance by increasing system resources such as CPUs, memory, and I/O subsystems, and the resulting parallelism that can take advantage of these resources.

Another way to increase performance by adjusting hardware is to tune for I/O, which includes tuning for disk layout. Since disk access has the greatest latency, the major focus of I/O tuning should initially be on keeping what has been retrieved from disk in memory. The actual performance of retrieving that data from disks can also be improved by spreading the data evenly across multiple disks, and by making sure there are enough disk controllers to transfer the data from disk onto the I/O bus and into memory.

Usually, disk performance issues can be identified on systems with sluggish performance but relatively low CPU utilization. You can use tools such as the Oracle Enterprise Manager Tuning Pack to identify where the bottlenecks are.

Disk Controllers

The slowest but most common disk controller used today is the Small Computer Systems Interface (SCSI). The origin of the name comes from the fact that these controllers were initially intended for PCs. Over the years and through several generations of SCSI controllers, performance has improved and the controllers now appear in the largest MPP and SMP systems with faster variations such as "fast and wide SCSI" and "Ultra SCSI." The benefit of using SCSI disk devices is that they are reasonably priced and widely available. Twin-tailed SCSI disk devices provide a means of attaching a SCSI disk to two controllers for high availability configurations.

A number of other disk technologies have appeared. Fiber Channel Loop controllers and IBM's SSA disk controllers provide much greater sustained data throughput per adapter, allowing many more disks to be attached to a single adapter. Sequential read performance can be as much as two to three times that delivered by SCSI controllers.

RAID Disk Arrays

Disks may be configured in a variety of ways for redundancy, eliminating the possibility of single points of disk failure resulting in loss of access to data. The configurations are set up through the hardware platform, operating system, storage management software, and disk devices, all transparently to Oracle.

The industry standard for disk arrays is RAID (Redundant Array of Inexpensive/ Independent Disks). You can use RAID drives as a part of any of the hardware configurations we've discussed to provide higher performance and reliability. RAID disk arrays were introduced in Chapter 6 and discussed in the context of their use in high availability scenarios in Chapter 10. Please refer to those chapters for more information about RAID disk arrays.

Which Hardware Solution?

In a world where there was no limit to the amount of money you could spend on hardware, you could make a simple decision about the most appropriate hardware: simply choose the level of throughput and reliability you need, and go buy it! Unfortunately, we have yet to discover the locale of this kind of world, so your choice of a hardware solution will often be a compromise.

The most commonly implemented hardware architecture for an Oracle8 server is the SMP system, which strikes a nice balance between power and price. SMP systems are popular for the following reasons:

- SMP systems offer more and simpler scalability options for the future than uniprocessor systems.

- The introduction of 64-bit processors and operating systems with extended memory support allow SMP systems to handle the needs of very large databases, even multi-terabyte databases.

- SMP systems have a single operating system and a single Oracle instance to manage and maintain, unlike cluster and MPP configurations.

- Far more applications are available that can leverage SMP systems than cluster or MPP configurations.

- SMP systems are less expensive than NUMA, clusters, or MPP configurations in similar CPU configurations because memory and I/O subsystems are not duplicated to the same degree.

This is not to say that clusters or MPP systems are not a valid approach. Certainly, if scalability demands exceed the capabilities of SMP machines, clusters or MPP systems may provide the only viable solution.* With careful planning and an enterprise computing management style, such configurations can provide powerful and highly available solutions.

NUMA offers an interesting alternative approach. At this point, there are fewer vendors offering NUMA solutions—Data General, Hewlett Packard, and Sequent (IBM) are such vendors—but we expect this architecture to continue to grow in popularity.

---

* At press time, there is no known example of a database on a single SMP system scaling to support tens of terabytes of data in a production implementation.

Table 11-2 provides a comparison of the relative strengths of the different basic hardware architectures for price, availability, manageability, and scalability.

Table 11-2. Relative Strengths of Hardware Architectures

Ranking	Scalability	Manageability	Availability	Price
Best	MPP	Uniprocessor	Cluster	Uniprocessor
	Cluster	SMP	MPP	SMP
	NUMA	NUMA	NUMA	Cluster
	SMP	MPP	SMP	NUMA
Worst	Uniprocessor	Cluster	Uniprocessor	MPP

You should select a storage technology based on your performance and recovery requirements and budget. In general, more expensive solutions offer better performance and more flexible availability options. Remember that SSA or Fiber Channel architectures may require more expensive disks.

Approaches to Choosing Hardware Architectures

When selecting a particular hardware architecture, most organizations choose systems that will meet anticipated performance and scalability needs for the near future, taking into account management and availability requirements. However, there are two additional approaches to be considered.

First is the truism we're all familiar with—the longer you wait, the cheaper computer hardware (and related components) get. According to Moore's Law, credited by Intel to Gordon Moore in 1965 (and proven many times over since then), each chip will double in capacity every 18–24 months, each time providing huge leaps in performance.

This continual reduction in price and increase in performance characteristics is an ongoing fact of life in the computer hardware industry. But how can you use this fact in planning deployment strategies for your organizational system architecture?

Buy what you need, when you need it, and plan for the obsolescence of hardware by recycling it into the organization when it no longer meets the needs of an individual application. For instance, today's departmental server may turn into tomorrow's web listener.

Second, look toward planned hardware upgrades, particularly the CPUs. Remember that SMP systems require that all CPUs be identical, so if you upgrade one you will have to upgrade all of them. At some point, the vendor will recommend a new system anyway, because other features will have been improved, partly to match the increased capabilities of the new CPUs.

It's also tempting to consider clusters and MPP systems with the idea of streaming in new machine types as they become available. When parallel workloads occur, remember that this will lead to more complicated tuning considerations, such as putting the data to be queried on the fastest nodes, and logging datafiles on slower nodes. In general, the more system variation, the greater the tuning variation and difficulty. There is a human cost associated with more complicated configurations, and while hardware pricing continues to decline relative to performance, the human costs do not.

12

Distributed Databases and Distributed Data

Data in large and midsized companies frequently resides in multiple servers. The data may be distributed across various sized servers running a mix of operating systems for a number of reasons: scalability, performance, access, or management. As a result, the data needed to answer business questions may not reside on a single local server. The user may need to access data on several servers simultaneously, or the data required for an answer may need to be moved to a local server. Inserts, updates, or deletions of data on these distributed servers may also be necessary.

There are two basic ways to deal with data in distributed databases: as part of a single distributed entity, in which the distributed nature of the architecture is transparent, or by using a variety of replication techniques to create copies of the data in more than one location. This chapter will examine each of these options, along with the technologies associated with each solution.

Accessing Multiple Databases as a Single Entity

Users may need to query or manipulate data that resides in multiple Oracle databases or in a mixture of Oracle and non-Oracle databases. This section describes a number of techniques and architectures that you can use to enable these capabilities in a distributed environment.

Distributed Data Access Across Multiple Oracle Databases

For many years, Oracle has offered access to distributed data residing in multiple Oracle database servers on multiple systems or *nodes*. Users don't need to know the location of the data in distributed databases. Data is accessed by a table name, the physical location, network protocol, and the operating system, all in a manner transparent to users. A distributed database residing on multiple database servers can appear to users to be a single logical database.

Developers can create connections between individual databases by creating database links in SQL. These connections form a distributed database. For example, the statement:

```
CREATE PUBLIC DATABASE LINK employees.northpole.bigtoyco.com
```

creates a path to a remote database of that name containing Bigtoyco's North Pole employees. Any application or user attached to a local employees database can access the remote North Pole database by using the global access name (`employees.northpole.bigtoyco.com`) in SQL queries, inserts, updates, deletions, and other statements. SQL*Net or Net8 handles the interaction with any network protocols used to communicate with the remote database.

Let's look briefly at how queries and updates issued for distributed Oracle databases differ from those issued for a single Oracle database. When using distributed data in a query, your primary concern is to properly optimize the retrieval of data for a query. Queries in a single Oracle database are optimized for performance, most frequently using the cost-based optimizer, as discussed in Chapter 4, *Data Structures*. Oracle7 added global cost-based optimization for the improvement of query performance across distributed databases as well. For example, the cost-based optimizer considers indexes on remote databases when choosing a plan whereas the rule-based optimizer does not. The cost-based optimizer also considers statistics on remote databases. Improvements to the Oracle8*i* optimizer include both optimizing for join and set operations to be performed on the nodes offering the best performance, and minimizing for data sent between systems. For these reasons, the cost-based optimizer is more frequently recommended and used for distributed databases today.

When a user wants to write data back to distributed databases, the issue becomes a bit more complicated. As we've mentioned before, a transaction is an atomic logical unit of work that typically contains one or more SQL statements. These statements write data to a database and must either be committed or rolled back as a unit. Distributed transactions can take place across multiple database servers. When distributed transactions are committed via the SQL COMMIT statement, Oracle uses a two-phase commit protocol to ensure transaction integrity and consistency across multiple systems. This protocol is further described in the "Two-Phase Commits" section of this chapter.

Access to and from Non-Oracle Databases

Oracle's Transparent Gateways (illustrated in Figure 12-1) are Oracle software products that provide users with access to non-Oracle databases via Oracle SQL. Oracle SQL is automatically translated into the SQL of the target database allowing the use of applications developed for Oracle to be used against non-Oracle databases. Native SQL of the target database can also be transmitted directly if you wish. Oracle datatypes such as NUMBER, CHAR, and DATE are converted into the datatypes of the target. Oracle data dictionary views are provided for target data store objects. As with Oracle databases, heterogeneous databases can be linked to Oracle through database links to create a distributed database.

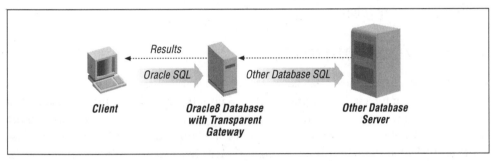

Figure 12-1. Typical configuration and use of Transparent Gateways

There are three basic types of gateways: standard Transparent Gateways, Procedural Gateways, and Access Managers.

Transparent Gateways

Transparent Gateways exist for dozens of non-Oracle data stores, including DB2/400, DB2 for OS/390, ODBC, Informix, Sybase, Microsoft SQL Server, IBM Distributed Relational Database Architecture (DRDA), and many others. Transparent Gateway performance was improved with the Oracle8 release by moving the Heterogeneous Services from the Transparent Gateway software, in which they were layered on top of the database, into the database kernel. Heterogeneous Services determine optimal SQL strategies for the remote site. Performance was further improved in the Oracle8*i* release with the introduction of multithreading for these services.

Procedural Gateways

Procedural Gateways implement remote procedure calls (RPCs) to applications built on non-Oracle data stores. The Gateway for APPC, the standard IBM protocol for RPCs, is used when Oracle applications need procedural access to applications built on CICS, DB2, IMS, VSAM, and other data stores on the mainframe and that use SNA LU6.2 to communicate to the mainframe. The Oracle Procedural Gateway for IBM MQSeries allows Oracle-based applications to exchange messages with applications that communicate via MQSeries message queues.

Access Managers

Access Managers provide access from non-Oracle based applications into Oracle. The Oracle Access Manager for AS/400 resides on the AS/400 and provides AS/400 applications written in RPG, C, or COBOL access to Oracle running on any platform. You can access Oracle from these applications through ANSI-standard SQL or through Oracle DML or DDL. Because PL/SQL is also supported, AS/400 applications can call Oracle-stored procedures. TCP/IP and LU6.2 are supported for connectivity (via Net8). Additional Access Managers for CICS and IMS/TM have been available as part of the Oracle for MVS (OS/390) client solution.

Two-Phase Commits

One of the biggest issues associated with the use of distributed databases is the difficulty of guaranteeing the same level of data integrity for updates to distributed databases. Because a transaction that writes data to multiple databases must depend on a network for the transmission of information, it's inherently more susceptible to lost information than a single Oracle instance on a single machine is. And since a transaction must guarantee that all writes occur, this increased instability can adversely affect data integrity.

The standard solution for this problem is to use two message-passing phases as part of a transaction commit; hence, the protocol used is referred to as *two-phase commit*. The main database first polls each of the participants to determine if they are ready; if they are, the transactional updates are then tentatively sent to them. In the second phase, if all of the participants are in agreement that the messages have properly been received, the changes are committed. If any of the nodes involved in the transaction cannot verify the appropriate receipt of the changes, the transactions are rolled back to their original state.

For example, if a transaction is to span databases on machines A, B, and C, in the first phase of the commit operation, each of the databases is sent the appropriate transactional update. If each of these machines acknowledges that it has received the update, the second phase of the update actually executes the COMMIT command.

You can compare this approach with a single-phase update in which the transactional update information is sent along with the COMMIT command. There is no way of knowing whether the update ever reached all of the machines, so any sort of interruption in the delivery of the update to any of the machines would cause the data to be in an inconsistent state. When a transaction involves more than one machine, the possibility of the loss of an update to one of the machines increases greatly, which, in turn, mandates the use of the two-phase commit protocol. Of course, since the two-phase commit protocol requires more messaging to be passed between machines, a two-phase commit can take longer than a standard commit, but the corresponding gain in all-important data integrity more than makes up for the decrease in performance.

Transaction Processing Monitors

In 1991, X/Open defined an open systems standard interface through which transaction processing (TP) monitors could communicate with XA-compliant resource managers (the role of the Oracle RDBMS and other XA-compliant databases in the X/Open model). Popular TP monitors supporting XA and used with Oracle include BEA Tuxedo and IBM's CICS and Encina (which are primarily used on IBM AIX or Windows NT and bundled today in IBM TXSeries).

Oracle also added the Oracle Manager for Microsoft Transaction Server (MTS) to Oracle8*i* for NT. MTS works as an application server for COM-based distributed applications, and the Oracle Manager provides MTS integration to Oracle8*i*.

We have mentioned transaction processing monitors in previous chapters in connection with their role in online transaction processing. Among their other duties, transaction processing monitors assure that transactions between multiple applications and resources complete properly. As noted previously, Oracle provides its own two-phase commit for distributed transactions, one of the early primary uses of a TP monitor. Transaction processing monitors are typically used today in very high-transaction-volume computing environments in which the monitors introduce a middle-tier application server to offload processes from the database server (see Figure 12-2). Examples of why TP monitors are used with Oracle databases include:

- Migration of legacy applications (usually originally written using CICS and COBOL for a mainframe) to CICS on Unix or NT

- Two-phase commit between Oracle and other databases that are XA-compliant

- Management of the flow of transactions, balancing workload across processors and/or dynamically managing the number of services available

- Three-tier implementations for ActiveX/DCOM applications deployed on Windows 95/98 and NT (using Microsoft MTS)

BEA Tuxedo and IBM TXSeries also provide integration with the Open Group's Distributed Computing Environment (DCE) services, which include security, directory, and time services. (Note, though, that DCE is not widely used today.)

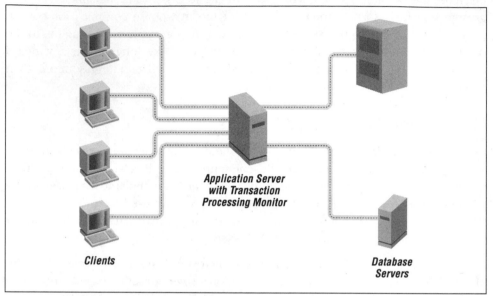

Figure 12-2. Application server with transaction monitor

Moving Data Between Distributed Systems

The previous section discussed the use of multiple database servers acting together as part of a single logical database for users. The following situations call for the contents of a database to be duplicated and moved between systems:

- When data available locally eliminates network bandwidth issues or contention for system resources

- When mobile database users can take their databases with them and operate disconnected from the network

- When redundant databases can help to deliver higher levels of reliability, as each database can be used as a backup for other databases

The biggest issue facing users of multiple identical or similar databases is how to keep the data on all of the servers in sync with each other as the data is changed over time. As a user inserts, updates, or deletes data on one database, you will need to find some way to get this new data to the other databases. In addition, you will have to deal with the possible data integrity issues that can crop up if the changes introduced by distributed users contend with each other.

Oracle8 offers a number of strategies to address this situation. The following sections discuss techniques for data and table movement among distributed systems.

Advanced Replication

The copying and maintaining of database tables among multiple databases on distributed systems is known as *replication*. Changes that are applied at any local site are propagated automatically to all of the remote sites. These changes can include updates to data or changes to the database schema. Replication is frequently implemented to provide faster access for local users at remote sites or to provide a disaster recovery site in the event of loss of a primary site. Oracle's Advanced Replication features support both asynchronous replication and synchronous replication.

Replication was improved with Oracle8*i* so that the replication can be triggered by changes to selected rows or columns of a table. The execution of replication triggers was moved into the database kernel in Oracle8, as well as automatic parallelization of data replication routines. Both of these improvements speed up the replication process.

Asynchronous replication is the storage of changes locally for later forwarding to a remote site. Some of the different types of asynchronous replication include read-only snapshots replicated from a single updateable master table and updateable snapshots that, though disconnected, can also be updated.

In the standard edition of Oracle8, you can only have a single master site, which replicates changes to other child sites. When you're using Enterprise Edition, multiple master sites can exist, and updates can take place at any of these masters. The updates to these sites must be *synchronized*, meaning that an update is not completed until all of the target sites have been updated; otherwise conflicts can remain unresolved. Conflicts can occur when more than one site updates the same data element during the same replication interval. Changes are propagated using deferred Remote Procedure Calls (RPCs) based on events or at points in time when connectivity is available or communications costs are minimal.

There are some conflict resolution routines provided with Enterprise Edition that can be automatically used to resolve replication conflicts. An administrator can simply choose which conflict resolution strategy he wishes to use for a particular replication. For updates that may affect a column or groups of columns, standard resolution choices include the following:

Overwrite and discard value
> Used when there is a single master (originating) site for new values to update current values at destination sites.

Minimum and maximum value

Minimum compares the new value at the originating site and the current value at the destination and applies the new value only if it's less than the current value.

Maximum compares the new value at the originating site and the current value at the destination and applies the new value only if it's greater than the current value.

Earliest and latest timestamp value (with designation of a column of type DATE)

Earliest dictates that when there are multiple new values, the value used for updates will be in a row with the earliest timestamp.

Latest dictates that when there are multiple new values, the value used for updates will be in a row with the latest timestamp.

Additive and average value for column groups with single numeric columns

Additive takes the difference of new and old values at the originating site and adds them to the current value at the destination site.

Average takes the current value at the destination and the new value at the originating site and divides by 2.

Priority groups and site priority

When priority levels are assigned to columns and multiple new values occur, columns with a lower priority will be updated by columns with a higher priority.

You can also use built-in uniqueness conflict resolution routines, which will resolve conflicts that result from the distributed use of primary key and unique constraints. The built-in routines include the following:

Append site name to duplicate value

Appends the global database name of the originating site to the replicated column

Append sequence to duplicate value

Appends a generated sequence number to the column value

Discard duplicate value

Discards the row at the originating site that causes errors

You can also write your own custom conflict resolution routines and assign them based on business requirements not addressed by the standard routines.

Managing advanced replication

You can manage replication through Oracle's Replication Manager, which is launched from the Oracle Enterprise Manager. Administrators can configure database objects that need to be replicated, schedule replication, troubleshoot error conditions, and view the deferred transaction queue at each location through this central interface. A deferred transaction queue is a queue holding transactions that will be replicated (and applied) to child sites.

For example, to set up a typical multimaster replication, you must first define master groups and tables and objects to be replicated in each of the databases.

The Replication Manager wizard, which is a part of the Oracle Enterprise Manager, then defines and sets up how replication will occur. You define a connection to the master definition site, then create one or more master groups for replicating tables and objects to the multiple master sites. You then assign conflict resolution routines for replicated tables in each master group. Finally, you grant appropriate access privileges to users of applications that access the data at the multiple sites.

Transportable Tablespaces

Transportable tablespaces are a way to speed up the distribution of complete tablespaces between multiple databases. Transportable tablespaces were introduced with Oracle8*i* Enterprise Edition to rapidly copy and distribute tablespaces among database instances. Previously, tablespaces needed to be exported from the source database and imported at the target (or unloaded and loaded). Transportable tablespaces enable copies to be moved simply through the use of file transfer commands such as *ftp*. Before you copy and move a copy of the tablespace, you should make the tablespace read-only to avoid changing it. Data dictionary information does need to be exported from the source prior to transfer, then imported at the target.

Some of the most popular reasons to use transportable tablespaces include:

- Rapid copying of tablespaces from enterprise data warehouses to data marts
- Copying of tablespaces from operational systems to operational data stores for use in consolidated reporting
- Publishing of tablespaces for distribution on CD-ROM
- Use of backup copies for rapid point-in-time tablespace recovery

To use transportable tablespaces, all the instances that will use the tablespaces must have the same Oracle version on the same operating system version with the same block size and character set.

Advanced Queuing

In the 1980s, *message-oriented middleware* (MOM) became more commonly used. Message-oriented middleware used the concept of *messages* to transmit information between different systems. MOM doesn't require the overhead of two-phase commit because the MOM itself guarantees the delivery of all messages. Products such as IBM's MQSeries store control information (message destination, expiration, priority, and recipients) and the message contents in a file-based queue. Delivery is guaranteed in that the message will remain in the queue until the destination is available and the message is forwarded.

Oracle's Advanced Queuing facility, introduced with Oracle8 Enterprise Edition, provides a complete queuing environment by storing the queue in the Oracle relational database. Advanced queues are Oracle database tables that support queuing operations—in particular, *enqueue* to create messages and *dequeue* to consume them. These messages, which can either be unstructured (raw) or structured (as Oracle objects, which are described in Chapter 13, *Oracle8 Extensions*), correspond to rows in a table. Messages are stored in normal queues for normal message handling or in *exception queues* if they cannot be retrieved for some reason.

Queue Creation and Management

Queues are created through PL/SQL commands or the Java API. The queue is created by an administrator through the following steps:

1. Create a queue table.

2. Create and name the queue.

3. Specify the queue as a normal queue or an exception queue.

4. Specify how long messages remain in the queue: indefinitely, for a fixed length of time, until a particular time elapses between retries, or based on the number of retries.

Queues can be started and stopped by the administrator, and the administrator also grants users the privileges necessary for using the queue and revokes those privileges when necessary.

Producers of messages specify a queue name, enqueue options, message properties, and the payload to be put into the queue, which is then handled by a producer agent. Consumer agents listen for messages in one or more queues that are then dequeued so users can use the contents. Notification of the existence of messages in the queue can occur via OCI callback registration or through a listen call that can be used by applications to monitor for messages in multiple queues.

Because messages are stored in queues in the database, a number of message management features are available. End-to-end tracking is enabled since each message carries its history with it, including location and state of the message, nodes visited, and previous recipients. Messages that don't reach subscribers within a defined lifetime are moved to the exception queue from which they may be traced. Messages that successfully reach subscribers may be retained after consumption for additional analysis including enqueue and dequeue times. As messages may be related (for example, one message may be caused by the successful execution of two other messages), retaining the messages can be used to track sequences.

Oracle Advanced Queuing is also supported by many third-party messaging vendors who are partners of Oracle, including Level8, TIBCO, TSIsoft, and Vitria.

Publish-and-Subscribe Capabilities

Oracle8*i* Enterprise Edition introduced publish-and-subscribe capabilities to Advanced Queuing. As illustrated in Figure 12-3, a *publisher* puts a message onto a queue, while a *subscriber* receives messages from a queue. The publisher and subscriber interact separately with the queue, and neither party needs to know of the existence of the other. Publishers decide when, how, and what to publish, while subscribers express an interest. Messages can be published and subscribed to based on the name of a subject or on its content (through filtering rules). Asynchronous notification is enabled when subscribers register callback functions.

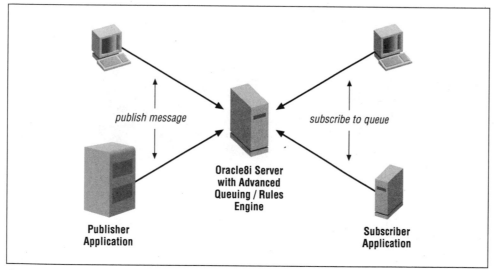

Figure 12-3. Advanced Queuing configuration for publish-subscribe applications

Queue management through Oracle Enterprise Manager includes the following:

- Creating, dropping, starting, and stopping queues
- Adding and removing subscribers
- Scheduling message propagation from local to remote queues

- Displaying queue statistics, including the average queue length, the number of messages in the wait state, the number of messages in the ready state, and the number of expired messages

You can use Advanced Queuing and its publish-and-subscribe features for additional notification of database events that, in turn, improve the management of the database or business applications. Database events such as DML (inserts, updates, deletions) and system events (startup, shutdown, and so on) can be published and subscribed to. As an example, an application may be built to automatically inform a subscriber when a shipment occurs to certain highly valued customers; the subscriber would then know that he should begin to track the shipment's progress and alert the customer that it's in transit.

In this chapter:
- *Object-Oriented Development*
- *Extensibility Options*
- *Using the Extensibility Framework in Oracle8i*

13

Oracle8/8i Extensions

You can use traditional data types, such as those described in Chapter 4, *Data Structures*, to represent only a small portion of the information that your organization needs to store and manage. Oracle8 provides several different additional data types that are specifically designed to provide optimal storage, performance, and flexibility for specific types of data.

Real-world information used in business, such as purchase orders, claims forms, shipping forms, and so on, may sometimes be best represented as object types, which are more complex than the simple atomic datatypes discussed in Chapter 4. Data that includes a timestamp may be better manipulated as a time series. Location-oriented data may best be represented using spatial coordinates. Documents, images, video clips, and audio clips have their own special requirements for storage and retrieval.

Oracle has now extended the functionality of its basic relational database engine to support the storage and manipulation of nontraditional data types through the introduction of additional features and options. Oracle8 extends the types of data and the SQL that manipulates it. And Oracle8i has extended the basic Oracle service framework so that you can modify and extend its capabilities even further.

Object-Oriented Development

An object-oriented approach to software development shifts the focus from building computing procedures that operate on sets of data to modeling business processes. By building software components that model business processes with documented interfaces, programming can become more efficient, and applications can offer more flexible deployment strategies and be easier to modify when business conditions change. In addition, since the modeling reflects real business use, application performance may improve as objects are built that don't require excessive manipulation to conform to the real-world behavior of the business process they represent.

Oracle has chosen to take an evolutionary approach to object technology by adding data abstraction, which is the creation of such user-defined data types as objects and collections as extensions to the Oracle relational database. Initially offered as the Objects option to Oracle8 and now included with Oracle8i in the Objects and Extensibility features, these features position Oracle as an object-relational database.

The introduction of the Java language as one of the languages for Oracle8i is complementary to this approach. Available for Oracle8i, the JServer feature is a Java Virtual Machine integrated with the database. It supports the building and running of Java components, as well as Java stored procedures and triggers, in the server.

The Promise of Object Orientation

Although a number of object-oriented approaches and technologies have been introduced since the 1980s, many of the improvements promised in software development efficiency haven't been realized. One of the reasons that these productivity improvements have failed is the difficulty many developers have had in making the adjustment to building reusable components. In addition, the need to learn new languages (such as C++) and technologies (object-oriented databases, CORBA, DCOM) slowed the widespread adoption of object-oriented development. Developers are becoming more familiar with these techniques and skills as Java moves into the mainstream of development.

One of the other factors limiting the growth of object-oriented development has been the work needed to adapt existing data to meet the new requirements of the object-oriented world. Oracle's evolutionary approach has made this particular transition easier to deal with.

Object-Relational Features

This section describes the major object-relational features available in Oracle8 and Oracle8i.

Objects in Oracle8

Objects created in Oracle8 are reusable components representing real-world business processes. The objects created using the database Objects and Extensibility features occupy the same role as the table in a standard relational model: the object is a template for the creation of individual "instances" of the object, which take the same role as a row within a table. An object is "instantiated" using Oracle8-supplied "constructors" in SQL or PL/SQL.

An *object* consists of a name, one or more attributes, and methods. *Attributes* model the structure and state of the real-world entity, while *methods* model the operations of the entity. Methods are functions or procedures, usually written in PL/SQL or externally in a language such as C. Methods make up the interface between an object and the outside programming environment. Each method is identified by the name of the object that contains the method and a method name, and each method can have one or more parameters, which are the vehicles for passing data to the method from the calling application.

For example, a purchase order can be represented as an object. Attributes can include a purchase order number, a vendor, a vendor address, a ship-to address, an item number, a quantity, and a price. You can use a method to add an item to the purchase order, delete an item from the purchase order, or return the total amount of the purchase order.

You can store objects as rows in tables or as values in columns. Each row object has a unique object identifier (OID) created by Oracle. Row objects can be referred to from other objects or relational tables. The REF datatype represents such references. For column objects, Oracle adds hidden columns for the object's attributes.

Object views provide a means of creating virtual object tables from data stored in the columns of relational tables in the database. Object views can also include attributes from other objects. They are created by defining an object type, writing a query that defines the mapping between data and the tables that contain attributes for that type, and specifying a unique object identifier. When the data is stored in relational tables, the unique identifier is usually the primary key. This implementation means that you can use object programming techniques without converting existing relational tables to object-relational tables. The tradeoff when using this approach is that performance may be less than optimal, since the data representing attributes for an object may reside in several different tables. Hence, it may make sense to convert the relational tables to object tables in the future.

Objects that share the same methods are said to be in the same datatype or *class*. For example, internal and external purchase orders can be in the same class as purchase orders. *Collection types* model a number of objects of the same datatype as varying arrays (VARRAYs) if the collection is bounded and ordered, or as nested tables for an unbounded and unordered collection of objects. If a collection has fewer than 4,000 bytes, it's stored as part of the database table; if it's larger, it is stored as a Binary Large Object or BLOB. Nested table rows are stored in a separate table identified through a hidden NESTED_TABLE_ID by Oracle. Typi-cally, VARRAYs are used when an entire collection is being retrieved, and nested tables are used when a collection is being queried, particularly if the collection is large and only a subset is needed.

An application can call object methods through SQL, PL/SQL, Pro*C/C++, Java, OCI, and the Oracle Type Translator (OTT). The OTT provides client-side map-pings to object types by generating header files containing C structure declara-tions and indicators. Developers can tune applications by using a client-side object cache to improve performance.

Inheritance is one of the most powerful features of object orientation. Inheritance is the way that you can use one class of objects as the basis for another, more spe-cific class. The child class inherits all the methods and attributes of the parent class and also adds its own methods and attributes to supplement the capabilities of the parent class. The great power of inheritance is that a change in a parent class auto-matically ripples down to the child classes. Object orientation supports inherit-ance over many levels of parent, child, and grandchild classes.

Polymorphism describes the ability of a child class to supersede the operation of a parent method by redefining the method on its own. Once a method has been replaced in a child class, subsequent changes to the method in the parent class don't ripple down to the child class or its descendants. In the purchase order example, as shown in Figure 13-1, purchase orders from contracted and noncon-tracted suppliers inherit the methods and attributes of external purchase orders. However, the procedure for placing the order can exhibit polymorphism because additional approvals may be required for ordering from noncontracted suppliers.

Although inheritance and polymorphism aren't supported in Oracle8 objects, the Oracle8 database can act as persistent storage for objects, and an application inter-face in an object-oriented language such as C++ or Java can add these features to the client-side implementation of objects.

Other features in Oracle8i

Several other extensibility features were added in the Oracle8*i* Objects and Exten-sibility features. These include:

- The ability to create new index types by defining the structure of the index
- The ability to store the index data inside or outside the Oracle database
- The ability to create user-defined operators for use in standard SQL statements
- An interface to the cost-based optimizer to extend support for user-defined object types and indexes

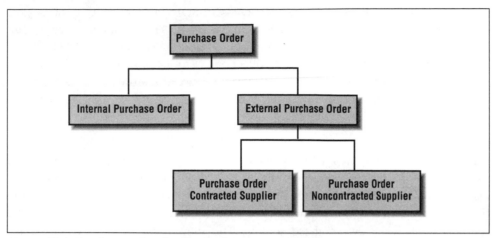

Figure 13-1. Purchase order class hierarchy

The use of object-relational features is most common today among software developers who are building database extensions. Oracle itself has made use of these features in the creation of many of the database options, including the Time Series, Spatial, and *inter*Media options.

Java's Role

Java has gained wide acceptance as an application language, particularly for building Web-based applications, due to its portability and availability on a wide variety of platforms. For Java developers wanting to use the Oracle database as a "back-end" to their applications, Oracle offers support for the two common approaches to accessing the database from a Java program: JDBC and SQLJ. Both of these approaches are based on industry-standard application program interfaces (APIs).

SQLJ
> An industry standard typically used when static SQL statements have been embedded into a Java program. SQLJ is similar to other Oracle precompilers in that Java source files are created with calls to the SQLJ runtime (as well as to additional profile files). The Java source code is then compiled, and the application is run with the SQLJ runtime library.

JDBC
> Used when the SQL is dynamic.

SQLJ and JDBC can be mixed in the same program when some SQL is static, and other SQL is dynamic.

The Oracle8*i* JDBC driver includes the ORACLE.SQL package that contains Java classes representing all of the Oracle8*i* SQL datatypes. These datatypes include all of the numeric types, CHAR, VARCHAR, VARCHAR2, DATE, RAW, ROWID, CLOB, BLOB, BFILE, REF, object types, and collections (VARRAYs or nested tables). This interface allows the use of the Oracle8 object-relational features (see the "Objects in Oracle8" section) within Java code. Java applets can communicate with the database via the Net8 protocol (which is separately deployed to the client machines) or in a "thin version" that uses TCP/IP directly.

The thick driver requires the installation of the Net8 software on the client machines, while the thin driver doesn't. The Java applet receives additional Java classes that mimic the Net8 protocol. Typically, you would install Net8 and use the thick driver on middle-tier application servers to communicate with Oracle, since there are relatively few of these servers. The thin driver is more common for browser-based applications, because installing software on the machines with the browsers negates the "thin client" advantages.

Oracle8*i* JServer introduces additional component and object-based development options. In addition to JServer providing a Java Virtual Machine (JVM) tightly integrated in the database, along with support for Java stored procedures in the database, component-based development can take place through the use of Enterprise JavaBeans (EJBs) and Common Object Request Broker Architecture (CORBA) objects.

For more about the role of Java, see Chapter 14, *Oracle8i and the Web*.

Enterprise JavaBeans

Server-side Java components are referred to as *Enterprise JavaBeans* or EJBs, in contrast to client-side reusable interface components, which are referred to as simply JavaBeans. You can deploy EJBs in the database server or with the Oracle Application Server (OAS). The tight integration of the Java Virtual Machine in the database makes use of database System Global Area (SGA) memory management capabilities to provide EJB server scalability beyond what would be expected in most JVM implementations. For example, each client within the JVM requires only about 50 KB to 150 KB of memory for session state.

CORBA programmers can develop business logic as CORBA objects, and then deploy them in Oracle8*i*. However, most organizations are far more likely to have developers with a Java programming background who will program using EJBs. EJBs are programmed at a higher level of abstraction than CORBA objects so the CORBA level is hidden from the programmer. Furthermore, EJBs are portable across a range of JVMs. Calls into and out of the database occur over the CORBA Internet Inter-ORB Protocol (IIOP).

In its initial release, Oracle8*i* supports the *session bean*, which is an EJB created by a specific call from the client that usually exists only during a single client-server session. Session beans may be *stateless* so that the EJB server reuses instances of the bean to service clients, or *stateful* in that that beans are bound to clients directly. Database cache information maintained by the stateful session beans is synchronized with the database when transactions occur by using JDBC or SQLJ. *Entity beans*, also known as *persistent beans* in that they remain in existence through multiple sessions, were not supported in the initial release of the Oracle8*i* JServer.

Extensibility Options

Oracle's extensibility options extend SQL to perform tasks that can't otherwise be easily programmed in a relational database. These include manipulation of time series data, spatial data, multimedia data, and image comparison. These options are typically used by application developers, but are sometimes bundled with applications sold by Oracle partners.

Time Series Option

A time series is a set of data in which each entry contains a timestamp. Such data is typically used in financial and trading applications and is often obtained from data collection devices. In general, tables with time series data don't contain a lot of columns, but do contain many rows of data (perhaps representing a long history). A common example of a time series is the daily reporting of a stock's highs and lows, opens and closes, and volumes, as shown in Table 13-1. The Time Series option, first introduced for Oracle8, provides functions for analyzing this data through the inclusion of calendar and time series functions.

Table 13-1. Typical Historical Time Series of Stock Trading Data

Symbol	Timestamp	Open	Close	High	Low	Volume
BIGCO	03-01-1999	30.125	29.75	30.50	29.50	285,000
BIGCO	03-02-1999	30.00	29.50	30.00	28.50	290,000
BIGCO	03-03-1999	29.25	30.125	30.50	29.00	275,000
BIGCO	03-04-1999	30.00	30.50	31.125	30.00	285,000
BIGCO	03-05-1999	30.25	31.125	32.00	30.00	310,000
BIGCO	03-08-1999	31.00	30.25	31.50	29.75	295,000
BIGCO	03-09-1999	30.50	31.00	30.50	32.125	300,000

You can store time series data in Oracle in nested index organized tables (IOTs), flat IOTs, or flat tables. IOTs are tables in which the data is held in its associated index. Flat IOTs and tables need less disk space, but require object views since the Time Series option was written using object-relational extensions, and some performance penalties occur as a result. For this reason, nested IOTs are recommended for performance.

The data in an IOT consists of time series detail data; calendars that define the frequency, pattern, and exceptions when data is collected; and time series metadata for describing attributes. When flat IOTs or flat tables are used, this data is stored in three separate tables with the time series detail data being stored as multiple rows in its table. When stored in a nested IOT, the time series data is stored as an object.

Calendar functions range in granularity; they may be as fine as seconds or as coarse as years. Calendar granularity possibilities are limited to the frequencies supported by the DATE datatype in Oracle8: year, week, 10 day, semi-monthly, quarter, month day, hour, minute, and second. Available calendar functions include equivalent testing, intersection, union, and validation of calendars. You can modify calendar definitions and create new calendars.

Time series query functions include the following:

Extraction functions
>   Return one or more time series rows.

Retrieval and trim functions
>   Return a time series.

Shift functions
>   Lead or lag a time series by a specified number of units.

SQL formatting functions
>   Allow time series values from an object to be displayed.

Aggregate functions
>   Compute the average, count, maximum, minimum, median, standard deviation, product, sum, and variance.

Arithmetic functions
>   Add, subtract, multiply, and divide.

Cumulative functions
>   Compute the cumulative average, maximum, minimum, product, and sum.

Moving average and moving sum functions
>   Compute an average or sum for successive timestamps over a specified time interval.

Conversion functions
>   Fill in missing timestamps from a time series.

Time series scaling functions include the following:

Scaleup functions
   Produce summary information (or rollups) from finer granularity data.

Scaledown functions
   Produce finer granularity data from coarser (or summary level) data.

Spatial Option

Spatial data is data that contains location information. The Oracle8*i* Spatial option provides the functions and procedures that allow spatial data to be stored in an Oracle8*i* database and then accessed and analyzed according to location comparisons. An example of using the spatial query options to combine spatial and standard relational conditions would be to "find all homes within two square miles of the intersection of Main Street and First Avenue in which the residents' income is greater than $100,000, and show their location." This query might either return a list of home addresses, or, when used with a Geographic Information System (GIS), plot the home locations on a map, as shown in Figure 13-2. Geocoding matches references such as addresses, phone numbers (including area codes and phone numbers), and postal codes (with longitude and latitude), which are then stored in the database.

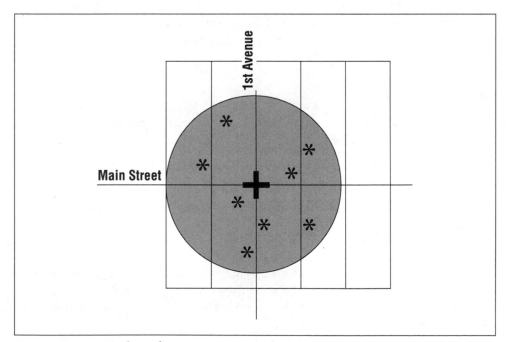

Figure 13-2. Geographic Information System display of a spatial query

Multiple geometric forms are supported by the Oracle8 Spatial option to represent many different types of spatial data, including points and point clusters, lines and line strings, polygons and complex polygons with holes, arc strings, line strings, compound polygons, and circles. You can determine the interaction of these features through the use of operators such as touch, overlap, inside, and disjoint.

Data that shares the same object space and coordinates, but represents different characteristics (such as physical and economic) is often modeled in layers. Each layer is divided into tiles representing smaller subareas within the larger area. A representation of this tile is stored with a spatial index that provides for quick lookups of multiple characteristics in the same tile. The Spatial option uses these representations to rapidly retrieve data based on spatial characteristics. For example, you can perform a query against a physical area to examine where pollutants, minerals, and water are present. Each of these characteristics is likely to be stored in a separate layer, but can be quickly mapped to their common tiles. The designers of these spatial-based databases can increase the resolution of the maps by increasing the number of tiles representing the geography.

The Spatial option now fully leverages Oracle's object features through the use of a *spatial object type* that represents single or multielement geometries. Spatial coordinates are stored in VARRAYs.

In the real world, most spatial implementations in business aren't custom built from SQL, but instead utilize purchased GIS solutions that are built on top of databases. Many of these GIS providers are now beginning to include Oracle's Spatial option as part of their product bundle.

interMedia Option

The *inter*Media option is new to Oracle8*i*, but some of the features in it have been available as options in previous versions of Oracle:

- The text management feature was formerly known as the ConText option.

- The Locator feature evolved from the Spatial option and supports the location queries and the geocoding described in the "Spatial Option" section.

- Image storage and manipulation features were formerly bundled in the Image option.

*inter*Media now lets you store and manipulate audio and video clips. Oracle positions *inter*Media as being a useful product for web-deployed applications that typically include multiple media types, since *inter*Media integrates all of these key datatypes and their associated functions.

The *inter*Media option utilizes a number of the underlying database storage options, which are described in Table 13-2.

Table 13-2. Storage Options for interMedia

*inter*Media Type	Storage Options
Text/images	VARCHAR2 BLOB CLOB VARCHAR CHAR LONG LONG RAW Object attribute Master-detail stores (in which the master table identifies the text or image and the detail table contains the content) BFILEs URLs that point to content
Audio and video clips	BLOB BFILE URLs that point to content
Locator ordinates	VARRAYs

*inter*Media also supports a number of popular document formats:

- Documents can be indexed while stored in formats such as ASCII, Microsoft Word, Excel, PowerPoint, WordPerfect, HTML, and Adobe Acrobat (PDF).

- Image and compression formats supported include TIFF, GIF, CCITT, and JPEG.

- Audio formats supported include AUFF, AIFF, AIFF-C, and WAVE.

- Video formats supported include AVI, QuickTime, and MPEG.

With text management capabilities in *inter*Media you can identify the strongest theme (or gist) of a document and generate document summaries based on the theme. Searching capabilities include full-text searches for word and phrase matching, theme searches, and mixed searches for both text and non-text data. Typical users of the *inter*Media option are news services that publish news items to interested users via the Web.

Image support includes conversion among image and compression formats, access to raw pixel data, and support for basic image manipulation functions such as scaling and cropping.

Clients can access audio and video files through Java Media Framework (JMF) players. Streaming servers can also deliver audio and video content including the RealAudio Server (for audio content), the RealVideo Server (for video content), and Oracle Video Server (for audio and video). The product also supports Live Picture FlashPix image format servers.

You can access images stored in Oracle8*i* and *inter*Media through Java or C++. You can implement audio, video, and image features as part of a web site using a variety of web authoring tools, including Oracle WebDB, Symantec Visual Page, and Microsoft Front Page.

Visual Information Retrieval Option

The Visual Information Retrieval (VIR) option is used for content-based retrieval of images stored in or accessed via the database. Images are retrieved based on feature matching, including global color (the amount of each color in an image), local color (distribution of color), texture (patterns), and structure (shapes). You can place a weight on each attribute and rank images based on similarity or can assign threshold values, below which images are determined to be different. You can also index images to improve retrieval performance. An example of an image search and possible results returned is shown in Figure 13-3

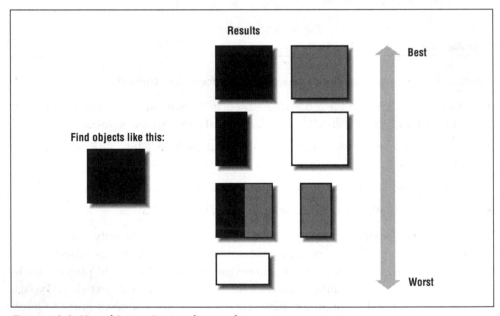

Figure 13-3. Visual Image Retrieval example

Images can be in a number of file formats including BMP, CALS Raster, GIF, JFIF, PCX, PICT, Sun Raster, Targa, and TIFF. Conversion between most formats is provided on demand. Raw Pixel Format, a new format added in the Oracle8*i* VIR option, allows you to directly access pixel data in an image. You can store images in the database as binary large objects (BLOBs) or outside the database through the use of BFILEs or URLs. Often, images are stored with associated text and keyword information, and complex queries (text and image) can use this combination of information to locate the desired image.

The format of the content can be Big or Little Endian (depending on the hardware platform used), and a number of monochrome, grayscale, truecolor, and RGB formats. Because images can be quite large, the VIR provides a number of compression algorithms to reduce storage requirements. The VIR includes support for CCITT G3, CCITT G4, JPEG, LZW, and RLE.

Using the Extensibility Framework in Oracle8i

With Oracle8*i* you can extend the basic functionality of the Oracle database. New interfaces allow an individual or software vendor to replace portions of the software with their own extensions.

Essentially, Oracle8*i* contains an extensibility framework that provides entry points in which developers can add their own features to the existing feature set. By using this framework you can do the following:

Add new relational or set operators for use in SQL statements
These new operators can be very useful when working with extended data types, such as multimedia or spatial data. You can create relational operators that relate specifically to a particular data type, such as the relational operator CLOSER TO, which you can use in SQL statements that access spatial data.

Create cooperative indexing
Cooperative indexing is a scheme in which an external application is responsible for building and using an index structure that you can also use with extended data types.

Extend the optimizer
If you use extended indexes, user-defined data types, or other features, you can extend the statistics collection process or the selectivity and cost calculations for these extended features to be used by the cost-based optimizer.

Cartridge services
The services used by what used to be called data cartridges (the ConText cartridge, for example) have now been made available to third parties so they can extend the operation of the Oracle database.

All in all, the new extensibility framework serves the same purpose as the Oracle8 extensibility options discussed earlier in this chapter. They allow you or a third-party software developer to integrate additional functionality into the main Oracle8*i* database, while still using the core features of the database, such as security management, backup and recovery, and the SQL interface.

14

In this chapter:
- *The Internet Computing Platform*
- *Oracle8i as an Internet Server*
- *Oracle in the Middle Tier*
- *Oracle Tools and the Internet Client*

Oracle8i and the Web

In this final chapter, we'll take a look at the Oracle database solution from the standpoint of the Web. Although we've already introduced some of the features, products, and capabilities mentioned in this chapter, here we'll look at Oracle technology strictly as it relates to the Web. In particular, we'll see how different Oracle products and technologies operate in the different tiers of an Internet computing system: the server, the client, and the middle tier. Because so many of the topics covered in this chapter specifically relate to the Oracle8*i* release, the Oracle8*i* database will be the standard for this chapter.

The Internet Computing Platform

In 1998, Oracle Corporation began talking about a "new" type of computing, which they termed "Internet computing." We don't believe that intrinsically there's much that's new about Internet computing. But actually, that is much to Oracle's benefit.

Regardless of the hype surrounding it, Internet computing is just another computing platform. The difference between Internet computing and other types of computing is not an earth-shaking change from the way that client-server computing operates. In fact, Internet computing is really a "best of both worlds" scenario that combines the lower cost of ownership of centralized server maintenance with a user-driven, standardized GUI.

Client-server computing was a far bigger advance, because, for the first time, it made computers respond to the actions of users, rather than the other way around. The GUI that made this method of interaction possible seemed much easier to use, and the standardization of the interface reduced training costs.

Unfortunately, client-server computing also tried to take advantage of the computing power on the client-side machine, which led to enormous headaches as MIS departments had to maintain thousands of computers, rather than the dozens of mainframes or servers they were accustomed to handling.

Enter Internet computing, in which the client requires a bare minimum of resources and the computing power is centralized, lowering the cost of maintenance. Tie this in with a massive expansion of available information and a universal accessibility scheme, coupled with the enormous buzz that's associated with any and all things related to the Internet, and enter Oracle, whose core competencies have long included both support of large enterprise servers and multiple client platforms. The Internet computing platform is just one of many platforms that Oracle supports, and this fact allows Oracle to use most of the technology that was already a part of their standard architecture.

The overall effect of the new platform is good news for Oracle users. Internet computing allows Oracle users to continue to use the power of their existing data in their Oracle database, and makes it easy to reuse the logic contained in stored procedures. And Oracle8*i*'s Internet computing solution is additive—you don't have to replace any of your existing systems to start using some of the new capabilities.

The Internet computing platform, like the client-server computing platform, consists of three main parts: the client, the network connection, and the server. And, like all new platforms, Internet computing comes with a new set of standards that implement its architecture. The following section describes this platform and its standards.

The Topology of the Internet Computing Platform

The Internet computing platform, as shown in Figure 14-1, has a topology similar to that of client-server computing. The platform includes:

- A server, which can run a variety of operating systems, including Unix, Linux, or Microsoft Windows NT

- A web server, which receives the network requests and routes them to the server, among other tasks.

- A network, which runs the HTTP protocol on top of a TCP/IP

- A client

The big difference between the Internet platform and the client-server platform is in the client and, to some extent, in the way that requests are passed between the network and the server.

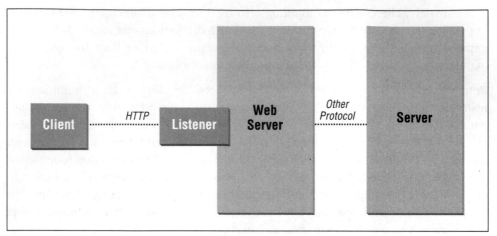

Figure 14-1. The Internet computing platform

The Internet computing platform features a *thin client*. The basic feature of a thin client is that all of the functionality that's needed can be supported with a minimum of client-side resources. All that a thin client really needs is a browser, which includes the ability to parse and display HTML pages, and usually, a Java Virtual Machine (JVM). Aside from the browser, a thin client only needs the ability to talk to a network connection to dispatch its HTTP calls.

The key to a thin client is its limited resource requirements, which give the thin client several significant advantages. The first advantage is that a thin client is truly portable—the browsers and communication software it requires are available on virtually every existing client hardware platform, from Unix workstations to Windows computers to handheld machines. The second advantage is that by only requiring a limited set of software, thin clients don't require the extensive maintenance and upgrades that are typical of Windows PCs. The complexity of the fat clients used for client-server computing has threatened to overrun the support resources of most large organizations.

Thin clients are also a window to the future. As the scope of client devices expands toward even more compact devices, such as handheld devices and setup boxes to control televisions, the thinness of the Internet computing client makes it a natural to integrate with the existing structure of the Internet.

In addition to the thin client, the Internet computing platform also includes a piece of software referred to as a *web server*. A web server can perform a variety of tasks. All Web servers include a piece of software called a *Listener*. As the name implies, the Listener is a program that listens on the ports of a server machine for HTTP calls and is also responsible for returning HTML pages to the client. Some

Web servers also include more advanced features, such as the ability to interpret scripting logic or to implement load balancing for incoming requests.

Internet Standards

The enormous popularity of the Internet has a lot to do with its universality. With a connection to the Web and a simple browser, a user gains access to an incredible wealth of information from around the world. Oracle8*i* has embraced most of the Internet standards used to implement the Internet computing platform:

HTTP

HyperText Transmission Protocol (HTTP) is the standard communication protocol between Internet clients and servers. An HTTP request is received by either an Oracle Web listener or by a standard Web listener, which can make CGI calls to Oracle procedures.

CGI

Common Gateway Interface (CGI) is used as a callout to languages and environments from most Web servers. Oracle8*i* can receive CGI calls.

URLs

Through the use of Data Access Descriptors (DADs) and PL/SQL Agents, Oracle8*i* gives developers the ability to call any stored procedure through the use of a standard Uniform Resource Locator (URL). A browser user can access stored procedures in the same way they can access a static HTML page or any other resource called through a CGI interface.

HTML

HyperText Markup Language (HTML) is a set of document structures and formatting tags that is the common formatting language for Web browsers. Oracle8*i* includes a set of PL/SQL procedures and the PL/SQL Toolkit, which helps developers format data from an Oracle database into HTML. Oracle8*i* also includes WebDB, a development and deployment environment for creating HTML clients that interact with Oracle8*i*.

Java

Java is a relatively new object-oriented language that has received wide attention due to its association with the Internet. You can easily download Java applications from a server to a Web client, which typically includes a *virtual machine* that acts as a runtime environment. The Java Virtual Machine (JVM) can run on a variety of platforms, even on thin clients with limited resources.

Oracle8*i* embraces Java in a big way by allowing Java stored procedures and triggers that run in a virtual machine in the Oracle8*i* database (JServer). In addition, Oracle8*i* supports several Java-based client-side interfaces to Oracle data, including SQLJ and JDBC.

XML

XML is the emerging open standard for describing a wide variety of data. The Internet File System (*i*FS) coming in a subsequent release of Oracle8*i*, will use XML as a way to define the structure of all types of data. Oracle has also released a set of XML interpreters for C and other languages, which are available for free on the Oracle Technet web site (*http://technet.us.oracle.com*).

LDAP

The Lightweight Directory Access Protocol (LDAP) is a directory service associated with the Web. LDAP calls allow clients to get information that's normally stored in the directory of an Oracle server, such as usernames and passwords. Oracle and many other vendors, with the notable exception of Microsoft, have teamed together to create an extended LDAP standard.

SSL

The Secure Sockets Layer (SSL) is a standard form of security encryption that's supported as a part of the Oracle8*i* Advanced Security Option.

Oracle's support of most of these major features is described in greater detail in the remainder of this chapter.

Oracle8i as an Internet Server

Oracle8 is the most popular enterprise database server in the world. By adding a few new features to their existing product, Oracle has been able to position the Oracle8*i* server as the core of the Internet computing environment.

Listener

To respond to requests from the Web, the Oracle8*i* server has to have a way to receive requests that come to it over the standard web protocol of HTTP. Oracle8*i* includes the WebDB product, which is described in detail later in this chapter, and WebDB includes a lightweight web listener. The Listener doesn't really do very much—it simply listens on a particular port number for requests for stored procedures that are intended for the Oracle server.

When a user calls an Oracle8*i* procedure, the Listener uses two types of configuration information—a Data Access Descriptor (DAD) that defines the Oracle database and username/password combination that will be used to access the database, and some form of passthrough, which routes the call to a PL/SQL procedure. In the Oracle Application Server (OAS), this passthrough mechanism is called a *PL/SQL agent*, while in WebDB, the passthrough is handled transparently.

The connection to the database is established with the DAD. The DAD identifies the target database and either uses a specific username and password combination or prompts the user for a username and password. Each PL/SQL agent is associated with a DAD, while more than one PL/SQL agent can be associated with the same DAD.

The Listener is configured to listen on a particular port, and the requests come in the form of a URL which consists of the name of the server, the port number of the server, the name of the PL/SQL agent that will service the request, and the name of a stored procedure that is to be executed. For instance, suppose that the server name is homeserver, the PL/SQL agent that is to service the request is netu, and that is listening on port 4000. a request for a stored procedure called return_ time would look like the following:

```
http://homeserver:4000/netu/return_time
```

If this stored procedure accepts parameters, those parameters can be included in the standard URL syntax following the name of the procedure. Of course, this stored procedure would be designed to return HTML code in response to this call. A developer can use the PL/SQL Toolkit or WebDB to create an appropriate PL/SQL procedure.

You can also use the Oracle Application Server, which includes a Listener as part of its architecture. The Oracle Application Server, described later in this chapter, can also execute PL/SQL and other types of code.

Java in the Server

Oracle8*i* includes its own Java Virtual Machine called JServer. Java programs can be developed with any standard Java tool and either loaded into the Oracle database at runtime or stored in the database. Once a Java program is loaded into the database, Oracle8*i* converts the program from bytecode into a compiled binary.

JServer runs in the same process space as the standard Oracle8*i* database and can directly access the information in the database buffers, which can help to improve the performance of data access through Java. The JServer virtual machine also uses shared connections to the Oracle database, which can improve performance for database access. Because it's a part of the Oracle8*i* server, the JServer Virtual Machine uses the same security and authentication methods as its host database.

The JServer Accelerator included with Oracle8*i* is a native code compiler that can deliver performance for Java binaries that's close to the performance of compiled C code. It operates by converting Java binaries into specialized C programs, which are then compiled into native libraries. Oracle claims that the garbage collection process (an integral part of a Java Virtual Machine) they've implemented in JServer also provides better performance than most other Java Virtual Machines.

Enterprise JavaBeans (EJBs) are a type of Java program that can be run on a server machine within the context of an EJB transaction server. The EJB transaction server provides system wide services for all EJBs, such as transaction and state management and communication with other EJB servers. The EJB server implemented by Oracle8*i* can use some of the internal management capabilities of the Oracle database server, such as those in the Multi-Threaded Server. Oracle8*i* includes automated tools to load and publish EJBs, which makes them easier to use with Oracle8*i*.

Oracle8*i*'s JServer also supports the ability to implement CORBA* servers through an embedded version of the Visigenic's Object Request Broker (ORB). You can call out from the Oracle8*i* server through the standard IIOP† protocol used by CORBA, and EJBs running with JServer can receive IIOP calls. This capability allows the Oracle8*i* server to become part of a CORBA-distributed system.

PL/SQL and Java

PL/SQL procedures can be called from any JServer application through the SQLJ interface embedded in the server. However, you will have to "publish" the top-level Java methods, which, in effect, creates a PL/SQL interface for the methods, in order to make them available to PL/SQL procedures. Once the wrapper is created, you can use the Java application just as you would any other PL/SQL procedure— even as part of a standard SQL statement.

The JPublisher tool, which comes as a part of Oracle8*i*, creates the interface between user-defined data types and Java wrapper classes. This capability allows you to extend the object-relational data types you may have already created with Oracle8 to the Java environment, or to create user-defined data types that can act as persistent storage for the Java objects you use in your Java applications.

Extended Media Types

As the Web grows and flourishes, Web designers are continually adding new types of data into their Internet applications. The extensions provided by the Oracle *inter*Media cartridge (described in Chapter 13, *Oracle8 Extensions*) can be used to help deliver these multimedia forms of data to Internet clients.

You can use the Java Media Framework, which is designed to integrate multimedia data into Java applications, to directly interact with the types of information stored with *inter*Media. With what's possibly the longest product name in recorded history, the Oracle8*i* *inter*Media Audio, Image, and Video Java Client is a client-side component designed to ease integration with these extended media types.

---

* Common Object Request Broker Architecture, a standard for distributed computing.

† IIOP, or Internet Inter-ORB Protocol, is the standard communication protocol for CORBA.

PL/SQL and Java

With this discussion of Java as a server language, some of you experienced Oracle users may be wondering about the position of PL/SQL in Oracle's future. After all, the description of Java in the server sounds similar to a description of the role of PL/SQL in the server. Is PL/SQL going away?

Although it's never good policy to speculate in print about the future of any particular technology, it's a pretty safe bet that PL/SQL will continue to be a part of the Oracle technology offerings for a long time. There is an enormous base of applications that use PL/SQL to implement logic, including Oracle's own vertical application package. If Oracle were to diminish the position of PL/SQL, they would be obliged to help their hundreds of thousands of customers migrate to its replacement. And since PL/SQL procedures are callable from Java methods, and vice versa, there is really no need for anything other than mutual coexistence.

Oracle has taken pains to position these two different languages as fulfilling two different purposes. Java is an object-oriented application language that can be used to create logic that is transportable between the client, a middle tier, and the server. PL/SQL is oriented around the SQL language and has a natural integration with the type of data manipulation offered by SQL.

Future Directions

Almost all of the features described in this chapter are available as part of the Oracle8*i* release, which is still fairly new at the time this book is being written. But there are some significant features of Oracle8*i* that are not available in the first release of the product. Although this book focuses on existing technology, we'll quickly mention two additional features—*i*FS and the Oracle Internet Directory— that directly relate to the use of Oracle on the Internet. Oracle has said that these features will be available in subsequent incremental releases of Oracle8*i*.

We can't guarantee a timeframe for delivery or the exact shape of these features, but from our investigations, we believe that the eventual release of these new components will include the following features.

*i*FS

The Internet File System (*i*FS), does exactly what its name implies—it extends the functionality of a file server to operate over the Internet. Oracle expects *i*FS to be available in late 1999 or shortly thereafter. *i*FS is both simple and radical. With *i*FS, you can create a virtual disk drive whose contents can be accessed from a wide variety of clients, from the thin client of the Internet to the standard fat client of a

Windows PC. The contents of the drive are stored within an Oracle8*i* database, which means that these contents are stored with the same reliability as standard data and can be backed up with the standard Oracle utilities.

In addition, *i*FS uses the standard features of the *inter*Media data cartridge to add full text search capabilities for the data in the virtual drive. *i*FS also implements version control for every type of data it stores.

*i*FS uses XML to describe the data within its environment. XML allows the common description of relational, nonrelational, and unstructured data, and allows you to combine multiple sources of data into complex documents.

At the time we're writing, Oracle is moving to widely embrace XML, (eXtensible Markup Language) to act as a standard way to describe and exchange data. Oracle's support of XML as it relates to data warehousing is described in Chapter 9.

Oracle Internet Directory

The Oracle Internet Directory is also due in a later release of Oracle8*i*. The Oracle Internet Directory essentially makes the security and configuration information stored in the Oracle system tables available through the LDAP protocol. For instance, the Oracle Internet Directory will allow you to use the security already defined in your Oracle database with other application systems that aren't involved with the Oracle database.

Oracle in the Middle Tier

The Internet computing environment naturally lends itself to a three-tier architecture for two reasons:

- The Internet itself is a public environment, so many companies want to have a middle tier to act as a security barrier to protect their proprietary data. The Internet Computing Architecture, when it's implemented over a three-tier architecture, uses the Oracle Application Server (described in this section).

- The basic protocol used for Internet communications, HTTP, is different from the Net8 protocol normally used to access Oracle8 data. The Oracle Application Server can act as an intermediary between incoming HTTP communications and the Net8 interface required for Oracle8.

Oracle Application Server

The Oracle Application Server (OAS) is a product designed to host business logic and applications in the middle tier. As you might expect, OAS is based on the standard Oracle database server architecture, with a few differences and additions. OAS comes in a Standard Edition and an Enterprise Edition.

Cartridges

The most important feature of OAS is the *cartridge*. A cartridge is simply a process that's designed to handle a certain type of application logic, such as PL/SQL procedures or Java programs. OAS comes with a variety of cartridges included as part of the product:

PL/SQL cartridge
> Can run PL/SQL procedures and packages

JWeb Java cartridge
> Can run Java applets

LiveHTML cartridge
> Oracle's version of a scripting language used to create dynamic HTML pages

Perl
> Can run Perl applications, the most popular logic language for the Web

C language
> Can run applications written in C

VRML
> Can run applications in Virtual Reality Modeling Language (VRML), a language that implements sophisticated graphic displays

JCORBA
> Enables OAS to host CORBA components

ODBC
> Available only with the Enterprise Edition of OAS, ODBC is a standard interface to a variety of data sources

OAS also includes a cartridge interface definition that allows you to create your own cartridges. The interface definition is very simple, with only a few calls to initialize, shut down, and accept commands through OAS.

Each cartridge can have one or more instances running in OAS. Each instance of a cartridge can handle incoming requests.

OAS Architecture

The basic OAS architecture is shown in Figure 14-2. This architecture includes three basic components: a Listener, a request broker, and one or more instances of cartridges.

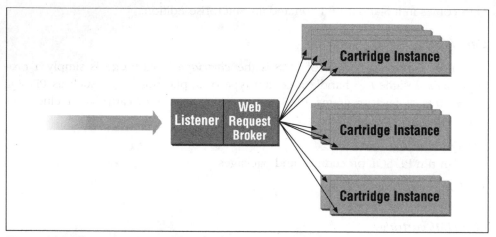

Figure 14-2. The architecture of the Oracle Application Server

The Oracle Application Server comes with a Listener, which receives HTTP and IIOP requests. You can use OAS with a number of other listeners, such as the Microsoft Internet Information Server, Netscape's Enterprise Server, or the Apache server.

Once a request is received for a service other than a standard HTML page or CGI call, it is passed on to the Web Request Broker. The Broker is responsible for both doling out requests to different cartridge instances and managing the number of instances.

Each cartridge can specify a minimum and maximum number of cartridge instances. When OAS starts, the Web Request Broker starts the minimum number of cartridge instances. If the Broker receives a request and finds that all cartridge instances are busy, it will start a new cartridge instance as long as the maximum number of instances for the cartridge has not been reached. If the maximum number of instances of a cartridge is already running, the request is put into a queue. When a cartridge completes a request, it takes the next request off its queue. If a cartridge is idle for a certain period of time, the Broker shuts down the cartridge. The length of this idle period is configurable for each cartridge.

Each separate cartridge occupies its own process space. This separation means that if any one cartridge fails, it will not affect the other cartridges or OAS itself. In OAS 3.0, each cartridge instance was in its own process space. With OAS 4.0, you can use a cartridge server, which allows multiple instances of a cartridge to exist in a single process space.

OAS can be implemented as a distributed system. The broker can route requests to cartridge instances on more than one machine, as long as you have configured the OAS instance to recognize the existence of other nodes.

OAS features

Oracle Application Server provides the following services for all cartridges.

Load balancing

Load balancing is the ability to direct incoming requests for a cartridge service to the appropriate cartridge instance automatically. The base version of OAS supports round-robin load balancing, which simply routes requests to cartridge instances sequentially. No one instance will receive a second request until all other instances have received one. The Enterprise Edition of OAS gives you more sophisticated load balancing algorithms, such as the ability to route requests based on a weighting principle you assign for each node, or on an algorithm based on system loads.

Failure recovery

OAS can detect if an instance of a cartridge has expired and will start another cartridge instance to compensate for its loss.

Transaction support

Any cartridge can use the built-in transaction support provided by OAS. OAS maintains a context for a web client through the use of *cookies*, which identify the session and client IDs. A transaction can span multiple HTTP requests using these cookies.

Intercartridge communication

OAS provides an API for cartridges to communicate with each other, which allows a developer to use OAS to combine the functions implemented in a range of different languages and dialects.

In addition, the JCORBA cartridge allows OAS to host CORBA objects. OAS includes an embedded version of the Visigenics Object Request Broker to host CORBA objects. OAS accepts IIOP requests to its JCORBA cartridge.

The PL/SQL Toolkit

As part of the development of the Oracle Application Server, Oracle created a number of PL/SQL packages that deliver the ability to create HTML pages dynamically. Some of the packages are preceded by the letters "OWA", which stand for Oracle Web Application—the first three words in the original name of the Oracle Application Server, which was once called the "Oracle Web Application Server." These packages, which are also used by WebDB (described later in this chapter) are collectively known as the PL/SQL Toolkit.

These packages provide stored procedures and functions that other stored procedures can use to create an HTML page. The client browser calls a stored procedure, which executes directly in the database and produces an HTML page that is returned to the browser. There are eight different packages in the Toolkit:

HTP

> This package contains the basic PL/SQL procedures for generating most common HTML elements. A typical HTP procedure will take the text of an element as a parameter and be named after the element—for example:
>
> ```
> HTP.TITLE('This is the title of the HTML page')
> ```
>
> This procedure would take the text supplied as a parameter, bracket it with the appropriate HTML tags, and put it into the HTML page being built in memory.
>
> The HTP package also includes a PRINT procedure, which allows you to add any ASCII text to the in-memory HTML page. This procedure gives you the flexibility to add any text to an HTML page, regardless of whether or not there is a specific HTP procedure designed for a particular element.

HTF

> This package contains functions that return HTML strings, rather than place them into the in-memory HTML page. All of the procedures that are part of the HTP package have analogs in the HTF package.

OWA_TEXT

> This package manipulates large strings of text. OWA_TEXT overcomes the limitation of PL/SQL, which only allows text strings of 32 KB characters.

OWA_PATTERN

> One of the most popular languages for developing Internet applications is Perl, and one of the most popular features of Perl is its ability to manipulate strings. The OWA_PATTERN package includes search-and-replace procedures that deliver much of the Perl functionality.

OWA_OPT_LOCK

> As readers of this book should understand by now, multiuser access to data requires the use of locks to protect each user from changes implemented by another user. However, HTTP, the standard protocol for web applications, is a *stateless* protocol, which means that each user interaction is a separate transaction. This, in turn, means that standard locking strategies can't be used for web applications. If a user reads data in one HTTP request and then goes to update the data in another request, it's difficult to view the two separate requests as part of a single transaction, especially since this type of transaction can span many seconds or even minutes.

The OWA_OPT_LOCK package gives developers two ways to detect changes in data since the data was initially read: you can store the initial values in hidden fields in the HTML page, or compute a checksum on the original values for the data.

OWA_SEC

This package includes a variety of security-related procedures and functions that help you to authenticate users.

OWA_COOKIE

A cookie is a piece of information stored outside of a particular HTML page. Cookies are usually associated with individual browser sessions, and can be stored on a user's machine. Because of this persistence, most browsers give users the ability to accept or reject cookies. You can set and receive cookies with the procedures in the OWA_COOKIE package.

OWA_UTIL

As the name implies, the OWA_UTIL package is a catch-all package that contains a variety of procedures. Some of these procedures are extremely powerful, such as the CALENDARPRINT function, which will create an HTML structure that looks like a calendar, with hyperlinks from calendar entries to other HTML pages.

You can use the PL/SQL Toolkit to create your own HTML-based clients that will interact with data in your Oracle database; however, if this is your goal, you might also want to take a look at the WebDB product that's is described later in this chapter. WebDB uses the same packages, but includes a set of wizards that will automatically generate the underlying PL/SQL code for the user interface components.

Oracle Tools and the Internet Client

Oracle is regarded primarily as a database company, because a large part of its revenue comes from database sales. However, Oracle has been offering development tools as part of its overall solution for over a decade. Oracle's embrace of the Internet computing platform also includes enhancements to its current development offerings, as well as two entirely new products, Java and WebDB, devoted to the thin client of the Internet.

Java

One of the strengths of the Java language is its portability to a wide variety of platforms. Oracle terms its support of Java as "300 percent Java," by which they mean that Java can run in three places: on the server, on a middle tier, and as a client—therefore, 100 percent Java on three tiers. Oracle's client-side Java offerings include a complete Java development environment, the integration of Java with Oracle's longstanding Developer product, and support of two Java-based APIs for accessing Oracle data, as described in the following sections.

JDeveloper

JDeveloper is a complete Java development environment offered by Oracle. The foundation of JDeveloper was the JBuilder product, which was licensed from the company currently known as Inprise (and formerly known as Borland). Oracle took this basic product and extended it with additional functionality for interacting with databases.

Developer

Oracle's Developer product has been around for over a decade in various guises. Developer is moving towards the Internet platform with two key enhancements.

The first key enhancement came in 1998, when Developer offered a Java runtime client for its applications. The Java runtime made it possible to run virtually any existing Developer application on a thin client, as long as the client supported the appropriate version of Java. This solution is not without its limitations: if you used extended components, such as ActiveX controls, in your user interface, you will have to replace them with something that can run on a Java Virtual Machine. Also, you need a particular version of the JVM to support Developer, and the initial download of the runtime environment could take a while. However, the ability to move the rich user interface of a Developer application to a Java thin client is a major advance in the product.

The 6.0 release of Developer also includes the ability to include Java components within the user interface of a Developer application. We expect to see further advances in the integration of Developer and the Internet computing platform in subsequent releases.

Java 3GL interfaces

Oracle8i includes two lower-level interfaces to data from the Java environment: JDBC and SQLJ. JDBC is a fairly low-level interface that gives a Java developer complete control over the interaction between a Java application and data in the Oracle8i database. JDBC is the functional equivalent of existing APIs like ODBC. Like ODBC, JDBC is a vendor-independent API.

The JDBC interface is standard, but Oracle offers it in three flavors:

- A thin client, 100 percent Java version, which is compact (150 KB compressed) and ideal for clients that only use Java

- A slightly fatter client version that is based on the Oracle Call Interface (OCI), which therefore requires some form of Oracle networking software that supports OCI

- A server-to-server version

The OCI version of the JDBC interface is a little faster than the pure Java version, so it's most appropriate for use in places like a middle-tier component. The server-side JDBC driver is used for Java stored procedures that run inside the Oracle8*i* server.

Oracle8*i* also includes the SQLJ interface. SQLJ is a Java library that allows developers to use embedded SQL statements in their Java applications. The SQLJ interface works like the Pro* interfaces that already exist for other 3GL languages, such as Pro*C and Pro*COBOL, but, unlike these interfaces, SQLJ is an industry standard interface. You can simply insert SQL statements into your Java code, and the SQLJ translator will translate those calls into their underlying JDBC equivalents.

There are a couple of significant differences between JDBC and SQLJ. Because JDBC simply submits SQL statements as strings, any problems with your SQL syntax won't be found until they are detected by the Oracle database at runtime. With SQLJ, the translator parses the SQL statements and returns errors. On the other hand, SQLJ can only be used for static SQL statements, while JDBC can submit dynamically constructed SQL statements. Much of the flexibility built with dynamic SQL statements can be implemented using bind variables, but there may be times when you'll need to use the JDBC interface. You can easily mix and match SQLJ and JDBC in your Java application, but the presence of any SQLJ code will require the use of the SQLJ translator.

WebDB

WebDB is a relatively new Oracle development and deployment environment. In one sense, WebDB is involved in some way with all three portions of the Internet computing platform, because it accesses data from an Oracle server from a browser client and can be hosted on an Oracle Application Server machine. WebDB uses the PL/SQL Toolkit originally developed for the middle tier and it produces HTML pages for the client. But since WebDB is primarily a development tool, we'll discuss it mainly in this context.

What is WebDB?

Simply put, WebDB is a tool for building and deploying HTML-based applications that dynamically interact with Oracle data. Since the WebDB development and deployment environment is made up entirely of standard HTML, you can run WebDB components in almost any browser, as well as use the WebDB development environment from a browser. WebDB and the components you create with it have been tested against Microsoft's Internet Explorer 4.x and Netscape's Navigator 4.x versions for compatibility.

WebDB began life as Webview, which was a group of PL/SQL packages based on the PL/SQL Toolkit that could be used to create other PL/SQL procedures. These, in turn, would generate dynamic HTML pages for return to a browser.

WebDB itself is written completely in PL/SQL and can be used against any Oracle database from version 7.3 onward.

WebDB architecture

To understand the use of WebDB, it helps to understand the basic architecture of WebDB, as shown in Figure 14-3.

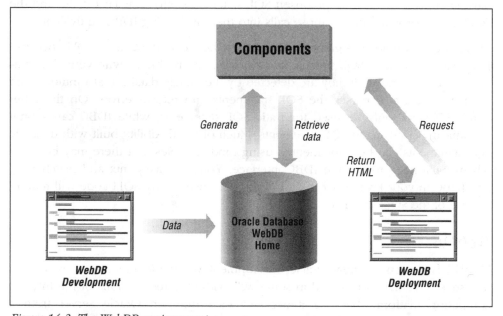

Figure 14-3. The WebDB environment

When you call the WebDB development environment from a browser, you're presented with a series of HTML pages. You interact with these pages to create WebDB components and perform other functions.

When you're in the process of creating a WebDB component, you're actually entering values for a series of parameters that are inserted into tables in the Oracle database that acts as the home of WebDB. Once you've entered values for the parameters, WebDB generates a PL/SQL package that's shaped by the parameter values.

When a WebDB component is run, the user calls the PL/SQL package, which typically interacts with the data in the Oracle database to generate HTML pages that are returned to the user's browser.

WebDB features

WebDB gives you five basic development options:

Create user interface components

With WebDB you create eight different types of user interface (UI) components, including the following:

Forms

Retrieve data through a query-by-example (QBE) interface, insert new data, and update existing data. Forms can use JavaScript procedures on the client for implementing specific client-side logic.

Reports

Can include user-entered parameters to limit selection.

Charts

Give you a basic graphical method of displaying summary data.

Menus

Create a navigational structure for a WebDB application system.

Hierarchies

Present multilevel displays of recursive data relationships.

Calendars

Display date-ordered data in the graphical form of a calendar.

Dynamic HTML pages

Dynamic data from an Oracle database is intermixed with virtually any type of developer-created HTML page.

Frame drivers

Allow a developer to create a specific type of user interface that uses HTML frames.

Most of these components use more than one type of user interface. For instance, the creation of a report includes the automatic creation of a parameter form, as well as the creation of the actual report that's delivered to the user. You can use the parameter form to allow a user to enter selection criteria, change the ordering of the report, limit the number of rows per page, or even specify the format of the returned data.

Create shared components

As the name implies, shared components are shared between multiple WebDB components. There are many types of shared components, but the two most important ones are templates and links.

A *template* is a graphical style that you can apply to any of the user interface components. A template can include navigational buttons, a color scheme, a background image, or any other type of common components or logic. Templates make it very easy to give a standard look and feel to an entire WebDB application.

A *link* acts as a connection from a WebDB component to another WebDB component or HTML page. A link can include parameters that are passed to the child component to shape the content of the resulting page. Because a link can be used by more than one parent, it's considered a shared component.

Interact with the database

WebDB includes the ability to browse database structures, as well as simple forms for inserting, updating, and deleting rows from the database. You can even create database structures from the WebDB environment and perform basic maintenance functions. Although these capabilities of WebDB are somewhat limited in their scope, the fact that you can use them from any web browser with a connection to an Internet or intranet makes them very handy.

Perform administrative functions

You can manage the components you create in WebDB from the WebDB environment. Whenever you modify a component in WebDB, the new version of the component is saved under a different version number, so you can easily return to a previous version. With WebDB you can export, import, and copy components. WebDB also includes a handy Component Finder that allows you to search the components available in your WebDB database. You also have the ability to monitor the way that the WebDB components, and their users, are using the host Oracle database.

Create complete Web sites

As we mentioned, WebDB began life as Webview, which was used to create components. The WebDB product added a whole new area of functionality to the original Webview with SiteBuilder, a tool designed to help you create entire web sites. A SiteBuilder Web site can be a home for the components you create with WebDB, as well as a collection of other resources, such as news items or other HTML-based information.

SiteBuilder sites also can include the ability for users to submit their own information for inclusion in the site. Also, SiteBuilder sites allow you to specify *categories*, which classify the type of information, and *perspectives*, which are preselected views of items. Both of these help you to organize the site.

Using WebDB to create application systems

When you build a WebDB component, you initially create it through a series of HTML pages called *builder wizards*. As shown in Figure 14-4, these pages prompt you for information that describes a variety of the component's attributes, such as the data that is to be used in the component, the appearance of the component, and the specifics of the operation of the component

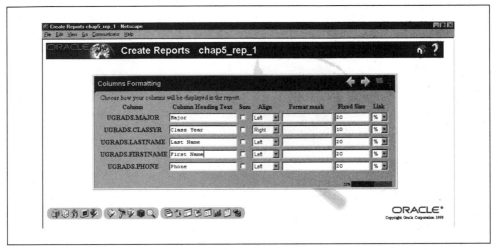

Figure 14-4. A page from the WebDB Report Builder Wizard

Once you've completed the initial building process, WebDB will generate the PL/SQL package for the component. You can always return to a component and edit the parameters for that component in a series of pages that look just like the pages of the builder wizards.

After you have built the user interface components that will make up a WebDB system, you typically implement a menu structure and join related components together through a series of links. You can also organize your components by adding them to the framework of a site created with SiteBuilder.

Integration with the Oracle environment

Although WebDB gives you the ability to create its own type of components, you can reach beyond the bounds of the WebDB development environment when building a component or an application. For instance, the WebDB Report Builder and Chart Builder wizards contain a query wizard that allows novice developers to graphically design queries without knowing any SQL syntax. However, you can also base a report on a SQL statement that you specifically write, which means you can use virtually any standard Oracle SQL statement as the basis for a report.

You can create forms based on PL/SQL procedures, with some limitations. WebDB gives you the ability to call any PL/SQL procedure at the following four (or more) specific points when an HTML page is dynamically built: before the page is built, after the header is built, before the footer is built, and after the page is built. In addition, you can specify a PL/SQL procedure that can be called whenever a user successfully inserts or updates any data.

You can also use most WebDB components to link to objects through a URL. Because WebDB places data into standard HTML format, you can store a URL as a piece of data in a data table and format it with the appropriate tags surrounding it in your standard SQL statement.

As mentioned, you can also easily add information referenced by a URL to the sites that are built with SiteBuilder. You can allow users to submit URLs for inclusion in the site and can specify that these submissions can either go directly to the site or be submitted to an administrator for approval.

Security and WebDB

WebDB is designed to work with any Oracle database from 7.3 onward. Until Oracle8*i*, which introduced the concept of *invoker rights* on PL/SQL procedures, a stored procedure used the security privileges of the schema that owned the procedure when it accessed data in an Oracle database. Unlike invoker rights, the standard security scheme for stored procedures is for the procedure to have the same security rights that have been *explicitly granted* to the owning schema. Rights that have come to the schema through a role do not apply.

This particular condition has a significant impact on WebDB applications, since all WebDB components are nothing more than PL/SQL packages that produce HTML pages. If you configure the default Data Access Description (DAD) for the WebDB environment without a username and password, a user will be prompted for a username and password the first time he calls a WebDB component. WebDB will use the Oracle database to authenticate the user, but the WebDB component will still use the privileges of the owner of the component package when accessing the Oracle database.

The net effect of this situation is that you typically will create a separate schema for each WebDB application and give this schema the access privileges needed by the application. If you want to grant differential access to data, such as allowing some users to write to the database and other users to only read from the database, you can create separate WebDB components, integrate them in a SiteBuilder site, and assign SiteBuilder security to them.

In the next release of WebDB, the concept of invoker rights may be introduced as an option, which will allow you to use the added flexibility of this security implementation in your WebDB components.

When to use WebDB

Like most contemporary tools for creating HTML front-ends, WebDB is primarily intended for read-intensive applications. If your main goal is to make data in your Oracle database available to users, the wizard-driven nature of WebDB will make it easy to accomplish. The SiteBuilder component of WebDB also helps you to create dynamic web sites, and the capability of storing the entire web site in your Oracle database adds a level of security and integrity to the wild and wacky world of the Web.

Although WebDB does allow you to create forms that you can use to insert data into an Oracle database, these forms neither impose any locks nor check for lost updates. If you think that there may be concurrency issues with the writes implemented with your system, you would probably be better off creating these forms directly using the PL/SQL Toolkit, which allows you to implement your own optimistic locking schemes with the OWA_OPT_LOCKING package.

Remember that the stateless nature of HTTP does impose limitations on the interactions you can implement over the protocol. This doesn't mean you can't use the Internet computing platform for application systems that write data; it just means that you will have to design these systems to account for this difference or use a Java user interface, such as the one available as part of Developer, to implement them.

Appendix:
Additional Resources

In this concise volume, we've attempted to give you a firm grounding in all of the basic concepts you need to understand and use Oracle8 effectively. We hope we've accomplished this goal.

At the same time, we realize that there is more to using a complex product such as Oracle8 than simply understanding how and why it works the way it does. Although you can't use Oracle8 without a firm grasp of the foundations of the product, you will still need details if you're actually going to implement a successful system.

This appendix lists two types of additional sources of information for the topics covered in the book—relevant web sites, which act as a constantly changing resource for a variety of information, and a chapter-by-chapter list of relevant books, articles, and Oracle documentation.

For the chapter-by-chapter list, the sources fall into two basic categories: Oracle documentation and third-party sources. Typically, the Oracle documentation provides the type of hands-on information you will need regarding syntax and keywords, and the third-party sources cover the topics in a more general and problem-solving way. We've listed the third-party sources first and ended each listing with the relevant Oracle documentation. You will find several of the listed papers available at the O'Reilly web site.

Web Sites

Oracle Corportation—*http://www.oracle.com*

> The home of the company. Latest information and marketing, as well as some good technical and packaging information.

Oracle Technology Network—*http://technet.oracle.com*

> The focal point of Oracle Corporation's attempt to reach a wider audience of devleopers. You can find tons of stuff at TechNet, including low-cost developer versions or free downloads of most Oracle softoware and lots of information and discussion forums.

OraPub Inc.—*http://www.orapub.com*

> Craig Shallahamer's site devoted to all things Oracle. Craig was a long-time Oracle employee in the performance analysis group and acted as one of the tech reviewers for this book.

RevealNet—*http://www.revealnet.com*

> The source for all things PL/SQL-oriented, as well as information on Java database programming and other topics.

O'Reilly & Associates—*http://www.oreilly.com*

> The O'Reilly web site which contains web pages for each book and a variety of other helpful information. See *www.oreilly.com/catalog/oracless/* for errata and other information for this book.

Quest Software—*http://209.37.83.55/index.htm*

> Home of the Tool for Oracle Application Developers (TOAD), a nifty utility for all Oracle users. Freeware and commercial versions available.

DigitialThink—*http://www.digitalthink.com*

> Online Oracle training.

Rama K. Nalam's Oracle links site—*http://members.spree.com/rnalam/html/oracle/oralinks.html*

> I don't know who this gentleman is, but he has a great set of links!

Oraclezone—*http://www.oraclezone.com*

> A new site that promises to provide a wealth of Oracle material.

Books and Oracle Documentation

The following books and Oracle documentation provide additional information for each chapter in this book.

Chapter 1, *Introducing Oracle*

Ellison, Lawrence. *Oracle Overview and Introduction to SQL*. Belmont, CA: Oracle Corporation, 1985.

Kreines, David, and Brian Laskey. *Oracle Database Administration: The Essential Reference*. Sebastapol, CA: O'Reilly & Associates, 1999.

Loney, Kevin. *Oracle DBA Handbook*. Berkeley, CA: Oracle Press / Osborne McGraw-Hill, 1994.

Anthony Ralston, ed. *Encyclopedia of Computer Science and Engineering*. New York: Nostrand Reinhold Company, 1983.

—*Getting to Know Oracle8i*. Belmont, CA: Oracle Corporation, 1999.

—*Oracle8i Server Concepts*. Belmont, CA: Oracle Corporation, 1999.

—*Oracle8i Concepts*. Belmont, CA: Oracle Corporation, 1999.

Chapter 2, *Oracle8 Architecture*

Kreines, David, and Brian Laskey. *Oracle Database Administration: The Essential Reference*. Sebastopol, CA: O'Reilly & Associates, 1999.

Oracle8i Concepts (Chapters 5-9). Belmont, CA: Oracle, 1999.

Chapter 3, *Installing and Running Oracle8*

Kreines, David, and Brian Laskey. *Oracle Database Administration: The Essential Reference*. Sebastopol, CA: O'Reilly & Associates, 1999.

Oracle8i Concepts (Chapter 5). Belmont, CA: Oracle, 1999.

Oracle8i Enterprise Edition Getting Started. Belmont, CA: Oracle, 1999.

Oracle8i Enterprise Edition Installation (CD booklet). Belmont, CA: Oracle, 1999.

Oracle Enterprise Manager Configuration Guide. Belmont, CA: Oracle, 1999.

Oracle Enterprise Manager Installation (CD booklet). Belmont, CA: Oracle, 1999.

Oracle8 Networking Manuals. Belmont, CA: Oracle Corporation (the exact names change slightly with releases)

Chapter 4, *Data Structures*

Ensor, Dave, and Ian Stevenson. *Oracle Design*. O'Reilly & Associates, Sebastopol, CA: O'Reilly & Associates, 1997.

Harrington, Jan L. *Relational Database Design Clearly Explained*. **City**: AP Professional, 1998.

Oracle8i Concepts (Chapters 5-9). Belmont, CA: Oracle, 1999.

Chapter 5, *Managing Oracle8*

Himatsingka, Bhaskar, and Juan Loaiza. *How to Stop Defragmenting and Start Living: The Definitive Word on Fragmentation.* Belmont, CA: Oracle Corporation paper no. 711.

Kreines, David, and Brian Laskey. *Oracle Database Administration: The Essential Reference.* Sebastopol, CA: O'Reilly & Associates, 1999.

Lomasky, Brian, and David C. Kreines. *Oracle Scripts.* Sebastopol, CA: O'Reilly & Associates, 1998.

Theriault, Marie, and William Heney. *Oracle Security.* Sebastopol, CA: O'Reilly & Associates, 1998.

Legato Storage Manager Administrator's Guide. Belmont, CA: Oracle Corporation, February 1999.

Oracle Intelligent Agent User's Guide. Belmont, CA: Oracle Corporation, 1999.

Oracle8i Administrator's Guide. Belmont, CA: Oracle Corporation, 1999.

Oracle Backup and Recovery, An Oracle Technical White Paper. Belmont, CA: Oracle Corporation, 1999.

Oracle8i Backup and Recovery Guide. Belmont, CA: Oracle Corporation, 1999.

Oracle8i Concepts (Chapters 29-32). Belmont, CA: Oracle Corporation, 1999.

Oracle Enterprise Manager Concepts Guide, Release 2.0. Belmont, CA: Oracle Corporation, 1999.

Oracle Enterprise Manager Configuration Guide, Release 2.0. Belmont, CA: Oracle Corporation, 1999.

Chapter 6, *Oracle8 Performance*

Gurry, Mark, and Peter Corrigan. *Oracle Performance Tuning, 2d ed.* Sebastopol, CA: O'Reilly & Associates, 1996.

Millsap, Cary V. *Configuring Oracle Server for VLDB.* Belmont, CA: Oracle Corporation, 1996.

Rich Niemiec, Bradley Brown, and Joe Trezzo. *Oracle Performance Tuning Tips & Techniques.* Belmont, CA: Oracle Press, 1999.

Oracle8i Concepts (Chapters 22-24, 26). Belmont, CA: Oracle Corporation, 1999.

Oracle8i Parallel Server Concepts and Administration. Belmont, CA: Oracle Corporation, 1999.

Oracle8i Tuning. Belmont, CA: Oracle Corporation, 1999.

Chapter 7, *Multiuser Concurrency*

Oracle8i Concepts (Chapter 27). Belmont, CA: Oracle, 1999.

Chapter 8, *Oracle8 and Transaction Processing*

Gray, Jim and Andreas Reuter. *Transaction Processing: Concepts and Techniques.* Morgan Kaufman Publishers; 1992.

Edwards, Jeri, with Deborah DeVoe. *3-Tier Client/Server at Work.* New York: John Wiley and Sons, Inc., 1997

Oracle8i Concepts Guide. Belmont, CA: Oracle Corporation, 1999.

Oracle8i Parallel Server Concepts and Administration. Belmont, CA: Oracle Corporation, 1999.

Oracle8i Call Interface Programmer's Guide. Belmont, CA: Oracle Corporation, 1999.

Oracle8i Application Developer's Guide - Fundamentals. Belmont, CA: Oracle Corporation, 1999.

Oracle8i Application Developer's Guide - Advanced Queuing. Belmont, CA: Oracle Corporation, 1999.

Oracle8i Enterprise JavaBeans and CORBA Developer's Guide. Belmont, CA: Oracle Corporation, 1999.

Oracle8i Java Stored Procedures Developer's Guide. Belmont, CA: Oracle Corporation, 1999.

Oracle8*i* Networking Manuals. Belmont, CA: Oracle Corporation, 1999.

Chapter 9, *Oracle8 and Data Warehousing*

Berry, Michael J.A., and Gordon Linoff. *Data Mining Techniques.* New York: John Wiley and Sons, New York, 1997.

Dodge, Gary, and Tim Gorman. *Oracle8 Data Warehousing.* New York: John Wiley and Sons, 1998.

Inmon, W. H. *Building the Data Warehouse.* New York: John Wiley and Sons, 1996.

Kelly, Sean. *Data Warehousing, The Route to Mass Customisation.* Chichester, England: John Wiley and Sons, 1996.

Kimball, Ralph. *The Data Warehouse Tookit.* New York: John Wiley and Sons, 1996.

Peppers, Don, and Martha Rogers. *Enterprise One to One*. New York: Currency Doubleday, 1997.

Don Peppers, Martha Rogers, and Bob Dorf; *One to One Fieldbook*. New York: Currency Doubleday, 1999.

Stackowiak, Robert. *Why Bad Data Warehouses Happen to Good People*. The Data Warehousing Institute Journal, April 1997.

Getting to Know Oracle8i. Belmont, CA: Oracle Corporation, 1999.

Oracle8i Concepts (Chapter 24). Belmont, CA: Oracle Corporation, 1999.

Chapter 10, *Oracle8 and High Availability*

Lee Chen, Kate Gibson, and Patterson Gibson. *Raid: High Performance, Reliable Secondary Storage*. ACM Computing Surveys, vol. 26 no. 2, June 1994.

Kreines, David, and Brian Laskey. *Oracle Database Administration: The Essential Reference*. Sebastopol, CA: O'Reilly & Associates, 1999.

Velpuri, Rama. *Oracle8i Backup and Recovery Handbook*. Belmont, CA: Oracle Press, 1998.

Oracle8i Concepts Guide, Oracle Corporation, 1999.

Oracle8i Networking Manuals, Oracle Corporation, 1999.

Oracle8i Backup and Recovery Guide, Oracle Corporation, 1999.

Oracle8i Replication, Oracle Corporation, 1999.

Oracle8i High Availability Enhancements. Ron Weiss et al. Belmont, CA: Oracle Corporation. 1998.

Gupta, Deepak, and Erik Peterson. *Designing Very Large Databases for High Availability: Making it Easy*. Belmont, CA: Oracle Corporation, 1996.

Peterson, Erik. *No Data Loss Standby Database*. Belmont, CA: Oracle Corporation and Paul Manning, EMC Corporation, 1998.

Millsap, Cary V. *Configuring Oracle Server for VLDB*. Belmont, CA: Oracle Corporation, 1996.

Chapter 11, *Oracle8 and Hardware Architecture*

Morse, H. Stephen. *Practical Parallel Computing*. Cambridge, MA: AP Professional, 1994.

Pfister, Gregory. *In Search of Clusters*. New Jersey: Prentice-Hall PTR, 1995.

Chapter 12, *Distributed Databases and Distributed Data*

Cerutti, Daniel, and Donna Pierson. *Distributed Computing Environments*. New York: McGraw-Hill, 1993.

Dye, Charles. *Oracle Distributed Systems*, Sebastopol, CA: O'Reilly & Associates, 1999.

Oracle8i Application Developer's Guide - Advanced Queuing. Belmont, CA: Oracle Corporation, 1999.

Oracle8i Concepts (Chapters 33-34). Belmont, CA: Oracle Corporation, 1999.

Oracle8i Distributed Database Systems. Belmont, CA: Oracle Corporation, 1999.

Oracle8i Replication. Belmont, CA: Oracle Corporation, 1999.

Ortalie, Robert, Dan Harkey, and Jeri Edwards. *The Essential Distributed Objects Survival Guide*. New York: John Wiley & Sons, 1996.

Chapter 13, *Oracle8 Extensions*

Siegal, Jon. *CORBA Fundamentals and Programming*. New York: John Wiley and Sons, 1996.

Taylor, David A.. *Object-Oriented Technology: A Manager's Guide*. Alameda, CA: Servio Corporation, 1990.

Oracle8i Concepts (Chapters 13-15). Belmont, CA: Oracle Corporation, February 1999.

Oracle8i Enterprise JavaBeans and CORBA Developer's Guide. Belmont, CA: Oracle, February 1999.

Oracle8i interMedia Audio, Image, and Video User's Guide and Reference. Belmont, CA: Oracle, February 1999.

Oracle8i interMedia Locator User's Guide and Reference. Belmont, CA: Oracle, February 1999.

Oracle8i interMedia Text Reference. Belmont, CA: Oracle, February 1999.

Oracle8i Java Stored Procedures Developer's Guide. Belmont, CA: Oracle, February 1999.

Oracle8i JDBC Developer's Guide and Reference. Belmont, CA: Oracle, February 1999.

Oracle8i Spatial User's Guide and Reference. Belmont, CA: Oracle, February 1999.

Oracle8i SQLJ Developer's Guide and Reference. Belmont, CA: Oracle, February 1999.

Oracle8i Time Series User's Guide. Belmont, CA: Oracle, February 1999.

Oracle8i Visual Information Retrieval User's Guide and Reference. Belmont, CA: Oracle, February 1999.

Chapter 14, *Oracle8i and the Web*

Greenwald, Rick, and James Milbery. *The Oracle WebDB Bible.* San Francisco, CA: IDG, 1999.

Odewahn, Andrew. *Oracle Web Applications: PL/SQL Developer's Introduction.* Sebastopol, CA: O'Reilly and Associates, 1999.

Getting to Know Oracle8i. Belmont, CA: Oracle Corporation, February 1999.

Oracle WebDB Getting Started - Installation and Tutorial. Belmont, CA: Oracle, January 1999.

Oracle8i Java Stored Procedures Developer's Guide. Belmont, CA: Oracle, February 1999.

Oracle8i JDBC Developer's Guide and Reference. Belmont, CA: Oracle, February 1999.

Oracle8i SQLJ Developer's Guide and Reference. Belmont, CA: Oracle, February 1999.

Index

About the Authors

Rick Greenwald has been active in the world of computer software for over 15 years, including stints with Data General, Cognos, and Gupta. He is currently an analyst with Oracle Corporation. He has published five books and countless articles on a variety of technical topics, and has spoken at conferences and training sessions across six continents. Rick's books include *Oracle Power Objects Developer's Guide* (principal author with Kasu Sista and Richard Finklestein, Oracle Press, 1995); *Mastering Oracle Power Objects* (principal author with Robert Hoskins, O'Reilly & Associates, 1996); *Using Oracle Web Server*, Second Edition (principal author with many others, Que Publishing, 1997); *The Oracle WebDB Bible* (principal author with Jim Milbery, IDG Books Worldwide, 1999); and *Administering Exchange Server* (principal author with Walter Glenn, Microsoft Press, 1999).

Robert Stackowiak is a data warehousing specialist at Oracle Corporation in Chicago. He works with Oracle's largest customers in the central area of the U.S., providing insight into the company's products and data warehousing strategy. In addition, he frequently assists Oracle Corporate in developing product strategy and training. Prior to joining Oracle in 1996, Robert was the Decision Support Segment Manager in IBM's RISC System/6000 Division. There, he met with IBM's largest customers throughout North America who were implementing RS/6000s and the IBM RS/6000 SP. He also previously worked as a Senior Field Analyst at Harris Computer Systems and as Chief of Programming at the St. Paul District of the U.S. Army Corps of Engineers. Articles written by Bob have appeared in publications including *The Data Warehousing Institute Journal, Informix Tech Notes,* and *AIXcellence Magazine.*

Jonathan Stern has more than 11 years of IT experience, including senior positions in consulting, systems architecture, and technical sales. He has in-depth experience with the Oracle RDBMS across all major open systems hardware and operating systems, covering tuning, scaling and parallelism, Parallel Server, high availability, data warehousing, OLTP, object-relational databases, N-tier architectures, and emerging trends such as Java and CORBA. He has authored papers and presented at internal and external conferences on topics such as scaling with Oracle's dynamic parallelism and the role of reorganizing segments in an Oracle database. Jonathan is the Central USA Technical Team Leader at Ariba, Inc., the leading vendor of electronic commerce solutions for strategic procurement. Previously, he led a team of highly experienced database specialists at Oracle Corporation, providing technical depth and strategic assistance to Oracle's largest customers in the North Central USA.

Colophon

Our look is the result of reader comments, our own experimentation, and feedback from distribution channels. Distinctive covers complement our distinctive approach to technical topics, breathing personality and life into potentially dry subjects.

The animal on the cover of *Oracle Essentials: Oracle8 and Oracle8i* is a cicada. There are about 1,500 species of cicadas. In general, cicadas are large insects with long, thin wings that are perched above an inch-long abdomen. Their heads are also large and contain three eyes and a piercing and sucking mechanism with which to extrude sap from trees. Cicadas are known for their characteristic shrill buzz that is actually the male's mating song, one of the loudest known insect noises.

Cicadas emerge from the ground in the spring or summer, molt and shed their skin in the form of a shell. They stay near trees and plants, where they live for four to six weeks with the sole purpose of mating. The adult insects then die, and their young hatch and burrow into the ground where they attach to tree roots and feed off the sap for 4–17 years, after which time they emerge and continue the mating cycle. Cicadas have one of the longest life spans of any insect; the most common species is the periodical cicada, which lives underground fro 13–17 years.

Maureen Dempsey was the production editor and proofreader for *Oracle Essentials: Oracle8 & Oracle8i*. Mark Nigara copyedited the book. Nancy Kotary and Jane Ellin provided quality control. Jeff Holcomb and Colleen Gorman provided production support. Mike Sierra provided technical support. Elizabeth Belton wrote the index.

Edie Freedman designed the cover of this book, using an illustration created by Lorrie LeJeune. The cover layout was produced by Kathleen Wilson with QuarkXPress 3.32 using the ITC Garamond font. Whenever possible, our books use RepKover™, a durable and flexible lay-flat binding. If the page count exceeds RepKover's limit, perfect binding is used.

The inside layout was designed by Alicia Cech, based on a series design by Nancy Priest, and was implemented in FrameMaker 5.5 by Mike Sierra. The text and heading fonts are ITC Garamond Light and Garamond Book. The illustrations that appear in the book were produced by Rhon Porter and Robert Romano using Macromedia FreeHand 8 and Adobe Photoshop 5. This colophon was written by Nicole Arigo.

How to stay in touch with O'Reilly

1. Visit Our Award-Winning Web Site

http://www.oreilly.com/

★ "Top 100 Sites on the Web" —*PC Magazine*
★ "Top 5% Web sites" —*Point Communications*
★ "3-Star site" —*The McKinley Group*

Our web site contains a library of comprehensive product information (including book excerpts and tables of contents), downloadable software, background articles, interviews with technology leaders, links to relevant sites, book cover art, and more. File us in your Bookmarks or Hotlist!

2. Join Our Email Mailing Lists

New Product Releases

To receive automatic email with brief descriptions of all new O'Reilly products as they are released, send email to:
listproc@online.oreilly.com
Put the following information in the first line of your message (*not* in the Subject field):
subscribe oreilly-news

O'Reilly Events

If you'd also like us to send information about trade show events, special promotions, and other O'Reilly events, send email to:
listproc@online.oreilly.com
Put the following information in the first line of your message (*not* in the Subject field):
subscribe oreilly-events

3. Get Examples from Our Books via FTP

There are two ways to access an archive of example files from our books:

Regular FTP

- ftp to:
  ftp.oreilly.com
  (login: anonymous
  password: your email address)
- Point your web browser to:
  ftp://ftp.oreilly.com/

FTPMAIL

- Send an email message to:
  ftpmail@online.oreilly.com
  (Write "help" in the message body)

4. Contact Us via Email

order@oreilly.com
To place a book or software order online. Good for North American and international customers.

subscriptions@oreilly.com
To place an order for any of our newsletters or periodicals.

books@oreilly.com
General questions about any of our books.

software@oreilly.com
For general questions and product information about our software. Check out O'Reilly Software Online at **http://software.oreilly.com/** for software and technical support information. Registered O'Reilly software users send your questions to: **website-support@oreilly.com**

cs@oreilly.com
For answers to problems regarding your order or our products.

booktech@oreilly.com
For book content technical questions or corrections.

proposals@oreilly.com
To submit new book or software proposals to our editors and product managers.

international@oreilly.com
For information about our international distributors or translation queries. For a list of our distributors outside of North America check out:
http://www.oreilly.com/www/order/country.html

O'Reilly & Associates, Inc.
101 Morris Street, Sebastopol, CA 95472 USA
TEL   707-829-0515 or 800-998-9938
           (6am to 5pm PST)
FAX   707-829-0104

International Distributors

UK, EUROPE, MIDDLE EAST AND AFRICA (EXCEPT FRANCE, GERMANY, AUSTRIA, SWITZERLAND, LUXEMBOURG, LIECHTENSTEIN, AND EASTERN EUROPE)

INQUIRIES

O'Reilly UK Limited
4 Castle Street
Farnham
Surrey, GU9 7HS
United Kingdom
Telephone: 44-1252-711776
Fax: 44-1252-734211
Email: josette@oreilly.com

ORDERS

Wiley Distribution Services Ltd.
1 Oldlands Way
Bognor Regis
West Sussex PO22 9SA
United Kingdom
Telephone: 44-1243-779777
Fax: 44-1243-820250
Email: cs-books@wiley.co.uk

FRANCE

ORDERS

GEODIF
61, Bd Saint-Germain
75240 Paris Cedex 05, France
Tel: 33-1-44-41-46-16 (French books)
Tel: 33-1-44-41-11-87 (English books)
Fax: 33-1-44-41-11-44
Email: distribution@eyrolles.com

INQUIRIES

Éditions O'Reilly
18 rue Séguier
75006 Paris, France
Tel: 33-1-40-51-52-30
Fax: 33-1-40-51-52-31
Email: france@editions-oreilly.fr

GERMANY, SWITZERLAND, AUSTRIA, EASTERN EUROPE, LUXEMBOURG, AND LIECHTENSTEIN

INQUIRIES & ORDERS

O'Reilly Verlag
Balthasarstr. 81
D-50670 Köln
Germany
Telephone: 49-221-973160-91
Fax: 49-221-973160-8
Email: anfragen@oreilly.de (inquiries)
Email: order@oreilly.de (orders)

CANADA (FRENCH LANGUAGE BOOKS)

Les Éditions Flammarion ltée
375, Avenue Laurier Ouest
Montréal (Québec) H2V 2K3
Tel: 00-1-514-277-8807
Fax: 00-1-514-278-2085
Email: info@flammarion.qc.ca

HONG KONG

City Discount Subscription Service, Ltd.
Unit D, 3rd Floor, Yan's Tower
27 Wong Chuk Hang Road
Aberdeen, Hong Kong
Tel: 852-2580-3539
Fax: 852-2580-6463
Email: citydis@ppn.com.hk

KOREA

Hanbit Media, Inc.
Sonyoung Bldg. 202
Yeksam-dong 736-36
Kangnam-ku
Seoul, Korea
Tel: 822-554-9610
Fax: 822-556-0363
Email: hant93@chollian.dacom.co.kr

PHILIPPINES

Mutual Books, Inc.
429-D Shaw Boulevard
Mandaluyong City, Metro
Manila, Philippines
Tel: 632-725-7538
Fax: 632-721-3056
Email: mbikikog@mnl.sequel.net

TAIWAN

O'Reilly Taiwan
No. 3, Lane 131
Hang-Chow South Road
Section 1, Taipei, Taiwan
Tel: 886-2-23968990
Fax: 886-2-23968916
Email: taiwan@oreilly.com

CHINA

O'Reilly Beijing
Room 2410
160, FuXingMenNeiDaJie
XiCheng District
Beijing, China PR 100031
Tel: 86-10-86631006
Fax: 86-10-86631007
Email: beijing@oreilly.com

INDIA

Computer Bookshop (India) Pvt. Ltd.
190 Dr. D.N. Road, Fort
Bombay 400 001 India
Tel: 91-22-207-0989
Fax: 91-22-262-3551
Email: cbsbom@giasbm01.vsnl.net.in

JAPAN

O'Reilly Japan, Inc.
Kiyoshige Building 2F
12-Bancho, Sanei-cho
Shinjuku-ku
Tokyo 160-0008 Japan
Tel: 81-3-3356-5227
Fax: 81-3-3356-5261
Email: japan@oreilly.com

ALL OTHER ASIAN COUNTRIES

O'Reilly & Associates, Inc.
101 Morris Street
Sebastopol, CA 95472 USA
Tel: 707-829-0515
Fax: 707-829-0104
Email: order@oreilly.com

AUSTRALIA

WoodsLane Pty., Ltd.
7/5 Vuko Place
Warriewood NSW 2102
Australia
Tel: 61-2-9970-5111
Fax: 61-2-9970-5002
Email: info@woodslane.com.au

NEW ZEALAND

Woodslane New Zealand, Ltd.
21 Cooks Street (P.O. Box 575)
Waganui, New Zealand
Tel: 64-6-347-6543
Fax: 64-6-345-4840
Email: info@woodslane.com.au

LATIN AMERICA

McGraw-Hill Interamericana
Editores, S.A. de C.V.
Cedro No. 512
Col. Atlampa
06450, Mexico, D.F.
Tel: 52-5-547-6777
Fax: 52-5-547-3336
Email: mcgraw-hill@infosel.net.mx

O'REILLY®

O'REILLY™

O'Reilly & Associates, Inc.
101 Morris Street
Sebastopol, CA 95472-9902
1-800-998-9938

Visit us online at:
http://www.ora.com/
orders@ora.com

O'REILLY WOULD LIKE TO HEAR FROM YOU

Which book did this card come from?

_____

Where did you buy this book?
- ❏ Bookstore
- ❏ Direct from O'Reilly
- ❏ Bundled with hardware/software
- ❏ Computer Store
- ❏ Class/seminar
- ❏ Other _____

What operating system do you use?
- ❏ UNIX
- ❏ Windows NT
- ❏ Macintosh
- ❏ PC(Windows/DOS)
- ❏ Other _____

What is your job description?
- ❏ System Administrator
- ❏ Network Administrator
- ❏ Web Developer
- ❏ Programmer
- ❏ Educator/Teacher
- ❏ Other _____

❏ Please send me O'Reilly's catalog, containing a complete listing of O'Reilly books and software.

Name _____ Company/Organization _____

Address _____

City _____ State _____ Zip/Postal Code _____ Country _____

Telephone _____ Internet or other email address (specify network) _____

Nineteenth century wood engraving
of a bear from the O'Reilly &
Associates Nutshell Handbook®
Using & Managing UUCP.

POST CARD

BUSINESS REPLY MAIL

FIRST CLASS MAIL   PERMIT NO. 80   SEBASTOPOL, CA

Postage will be paid by addressee

O'Reilly & Associates, Inc.
101 Morris Street
Sebastopol, CA 95472-9902

Sage 50® Accounts

for dümmies®
A Wiley Brand

4th edition

by Jane E. Kelly, ACMA
Chartered Management Accountant and Sage trainer

dümmies®
A Wiley Brand

Sage 50® Accounts For Dummies®, 4th Edition

Published by: **John Wiley & Sons, Ltd., The Atrium, Southern Gate, Chichester,** www.wiley.com

This edition first published 2016

© 2016 by John Wiley & Sons, Ltd., Chichester, West Sussex

Registered Office

John Wiley & Sons, Ltd., The Atrium, Southern Gate, Chichester, West Sussex, PO19 8SQ, United Kingdom

For details of our global editorial offices, for customer services and for information about how to apply for permission to reuse the copyright material in this book, please see our website at www.wiley.com.

For general information on our other products and services, please contact our Customer Care Department within the U.S. at 877-762-2974, outside the U.S. at 317-572-3993, or fax 317-572-4002. For technical support, please visit https://hub.wiley.com/community/support/dummies.

Wiley publishes in a variety of print and electronic formats and by print-on-demand. Some material included with standard print versions of this book may not be included in e-books or in print-on-demand. If this book refers to media such as a CD or DVD that is not included in the version you purchased, you may download this material at http://booksupport.wiley.com. For more information about Wiley products, visit www.wiley.com.

A catalogue record for this book is available from the British Library.

ISBN 978-1-119-21415-1 (pbk); ISBN 978-1-119-21416-8 (ebk); ISBN 978-1-119-21417-5 (ebk)

10 9 8 7 6 5 4 3 2 1

Contents at a Glance

Table of Contents

Introduction

S age is a well-known accounting system used in more than three-quarters of a million small- and medium-sized businesses in the U.K. The range of business software continually evolves, and Sage's developers pride themselves on listening to their customers for feedback on how to improve the software. This results in regular revisions and updates that add new features to Sage each time.

This book offers you a chance to understand how Sage 50 Accounts can help you run your business effectively. Thoroughly revised to cover all the latest Sage updates, I hope you get a lot out of this fourth edition, which covers Sage 50 Accounts version 22.

About This Book

The aim of this book is for you to get the most from Sage. I use lots of screenshots to help you navigate your way around the system and offer tips to help you customise the programs and reports contained in Sage in language you can understand, even if you're not an accountant.

Wherever possible, I show you the quickest way to do something, because you can often do the same thing in more than one way. I understand that you want a quick start, so I show you the easiest methods of doing things. You can always add details later, when time permits.

This book presents information in a modular fashion so that you get all the information to accomplish a task in one place. I don't ask you to remember things from different parts of the book; if another chapter has information relevant to the discussion at hand, I tell you where to find it, so you don't have to read the chapters in order. You can read the chapters or sections that interest you when it suits you.

This book includes a lot of instructions on how to proceed with various tasks in Sage. Wherever possible, I use numbered lists to indicate the order in which to do things. Names of windows, screens and menu choices are capitalised. This little arrow → indicates the path you click through in a series of menu options.

Because examples can help you see how a concept works in real life, I created Jingles, a fictitious party-planning company, and I use its owner Jeanette to demonstrate some of Sage's reports and functions.

Within this book, you may note that some web addresses break across two lines of text. If you're reading this book in print and want to visit one of these web pages, simply key in the web address exactly as it's noted in the text, pretending as though the line break doesn't exist. If you're reading this as an e-book, you've got it easy – just click the web address to be taken directly to the web page.

Foolish Assumptions

While writing *Sage 50 Accounts For Dummies*, 4th Edition, for version 22 of Sage 50 Accounts, I made some key assumptions about who you are and why you picked up this book. I assume that you fall into one of the following categories:

>> You're a member of staff in a small business who has been asked to take over the bookkeeping function and will be using Sage.

>> You're an existing bookkeeper who has never used Sage before or who needs to refresh your knowledge.

>> You're a small-business owner who wants to understand how Sage can help in your business.

Icons Used in This Book

Every *For Dummies* book uses icons to highlight especially important, interesting or useful information. The following icons are used in this book:

TIP

Look at this icon for practical information that you can use straightaway to help you use Sage in the most effective way.

REMEMBER

This icon indicates any items you need to remember after reading the book – and sometimes throughout it.

TECHNICAL STUFF

The paragraphs next to this icon contain information that is, er, slightly technical in nature. You don't *need* to know the information here to get by, but it helps.

WARNING

This bombshell alerts you to potential problems you may create for yourself without realising it. Don't ignore this icon!

Beyond the Book

In addition to the material in the print or e-book you're reading right now, this product also comes with some access-anywhere extras on the web.

Head to www.dummies.com and search for "Sage 50 Accounts For Dummies Cheat Sheet" for a useful cheat sheet, which includes a handy keyboard shortcut checklist, a list of at-a-glance U.K. tax codes and information on how to contact Sage. You can also find a table comparing the features in the Sage 50 Accounts product range to ensure you're using the best version for you.

Where to Go from Here

You're now ready to enter the world of Sage. If you're a complete beginner, starting at the beginning and gradually working through is probably best. If you're an existing user but a little rusty in certain areas, you can pick the chapters that are most relevant to you, probably in Parts 4 and 5. This book is designed for you to dip in and out of. I hope that you find it a useful tool for developing and managing your business.

1

Getting Started with Sage 50 Accounts

Chapter 1

Introducing Sage 50 Accounts

In this chapter, I introduce you to the Sage 50 Accounts software range. I show you how easily you can install the software and give you a guided tour, so that you can get up and running quickly – essential for busy people.

Sage works on the principle that the less time you spend inputting your accounts, the more time you spend on your business, so it makes each process as simple as possible.

Looking at the Varieties of Sage

Sage's developers understand that every business is different, and each business has different needs. As a result, they've developed a range of accounting software designed to grow with your business, whatever it is. The three levels of Sage 50 Accounts software start with basic features and finish with a product that contains all the bells and whistles you can possibly want. These versions of Sage are as follows:

>> **Sage 50 Accounts:** This is the entry-level program. Sage 50 Accounts provides all the features you need to successfully manage your accounts. You can professionally handle your customers and suppliers, manage your bank

reconciliations and value-added tax (VAT) returns, and provide simple reports, including monthly and year-end requirements. This basic version is suitable for small businesses with a simple structure and businesses that need basic stock systems but don't need systems for project costing, foreign currency, or sales/purchase order processing. If you do need foreign currency, you can pay an additional fee to add this module.

>> **Sage 50 Accounts Plus:** This contains all the features of the entry-level model but also lets you manage project costs versus budgets and control costs of manufactured and assembled products, and has an improved stock control system to produce bills of materials and allocate stock. You also still have the ability to add the foreign currency module (at an additional cost).

DECIDING ON SAGE COVER

You can purchase Sage Cover at the same time you buy Sage. Sage Cover gives you technical support in case you have any problems using Sage. It may seem an additional cost burden to begin with, but I think Sage Cover is well worth the money in case you have any software problems.

Most people who use accounting packages know something about accounting but don't necessarily know much about computer software. When your screen pops up with an error message that you simply don't understand, a quick phone call to your Sage Cover support line can soon solve the problem.

For Sage 50 Accounts, you can choose between two different types of cover:

- **Sage Cover Online Support:** The key features are the opportunity to use the web chat facility, where you can communicate with Sage advisors in real time by sending instant messages online. Email support is available for more detailed questions. You also get Ask Sage, which gives you online access to thousands of frequently asked questions. In addition you get access to software updates.

- **Sage Cover Extra Support:** You get all the options for Online Support, as well as telephone support, which includes call-backs, and email and online question-and-answer support. There is also an option for remote support, which means that with your permission, Sage technicians can remotely access your PC to help solve queries. In addition you can access customized reports support and webcasts.

Sometimes the Help button just doesn't answer your question. Having someone on the end of the phone to talk you through a problem is a real bonus. The technical support team can help you solve the most awkward problems that would otherwise have you throwing your laptop out of the window in pure frustration.

>> **Sage 50 Accounts Professional:** This includes all the features of Accounts Plus but adds sales and purchase order processing, foreign trading, bank account revaluation, and Intrastat support. Accounts Professional can handle up to 20 users and manage multiple companies. This product is suited to both small- and medium-sized businesses and offers customers a product flexible enough to suit a multitude of different businesses, including those that trade in both the U.K. and abroad.

Installing the Software

There is more than one way to install your Sage 50 software. Currently, Sage offers the software as a digital download, but if your Internet speeds are not what they should be, then you may prefer the traditional method of buying the product off-the-shelf and loading the CD. Whichever you choose, Sage guides you seamlessly through the process to ensure you load the software as efficiently as possible.

REMEMBER

Check the technical specifications required to run your software: Ensure your laptop or PC is sufficiently powerful to run it. Sage is quite a big program, and you need a relatively powerful computer to run it.

Getting what you need before you get started

Whichever method of purchase you use, you should receive a serial number and activation key. Without these two pieces of information, you can't successfully load the software. But don't worry: If you purchase a genuine copy of Sage software, you have the necessary activation information.

You also need some details about your company:

>> **When your company's financial year begins:** If you're not sure of this date, ask your accountant.

>> **Whether you use a VAT scheme:** Your accountant can tell you whether you operate the VAT cash accounting scheme or the standard VAT scheme. If you have a VAT registration number, keep it handy.

Moving to the installation

Follow the download instructions or insert your CD into the disk drive and follow the instructions on-screen. The Installshield wizard runs and proceeds to install Sage on your computer.

Sage lets you know when the program has installed successfully. Then you can really get cracking.

Setting Up with the Active Setup Wizard

Of course, you're champing at the bit and want to get going with Sage, so double-click the new Sage icon on your desktop to get started. The Activate Sage Software window opens, as in Figure 1-1. Sage asks you to enter your activation key and serial number. If you don't have this information, click the MySage button and follow the online instructions.

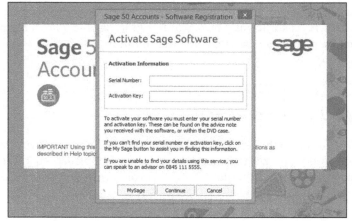

FIGURE 1-1:
Activating your
Sage software.

After you enter your activation key and serial number, click Continue and the Active Setup wizard opens. The wizard guides you through several different screens where you enter information as requested.

The first screen, shown in Figure 1-2, gives you four options:

>> **Set up a new company:** If you're new to Sage, choose this first option. Sage guides you through the automatic steps of the Active Setup wizard.

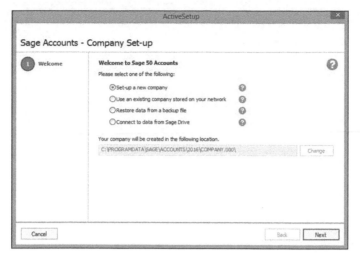

FIGURE 1-2:
Putting the
Active Setup
wizard to work.

Source: Jane Kelly

>> **Use an existing company stored on your network:** If you already use Sage and are upgrading, choose this option, which lets you copy accounts data from your previous Sage installation.

>> **Restore data from a backup file:** Choose this option if you're restoring data from an earlier version. If your backup was taken from an earlier version than version 14 (2008), contact Sage for further support.

>> **Connect to data from Sage Drive:** You'll need your Sage ID, username and password to connect to Sage Drive to see the data that you have been granted access to.

Choose whichever option is best for you and click Next.

The following steps take you through the process of setting up Sage for the first time.

1. **Click Set Up a New Company and then click Next.**

   The Company Setup screen opens and Sage prompts you to enter your company's information such as name, address, and contact details, as in Figure 1-3.

TIP

   Make the setup speedier by putting in just the company name. You can complete the other information later by clicking Settings on the main toolbar and then selecting Company Preferences.

2. **Click Next to access the Select Business Type screen.**

   A screen appears that prompts you to Select Business Type, as shown in Figure 1-4.

FIGURE 1-3:
Asking for your
company's info.

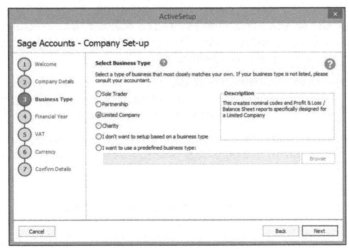

FIGURE 1-4:
What type of
business are you?

3. **Click the appropriate business type.**

   For example, I chose Limited Company for my fictional greeting card company, Jingles. If you don't know your business type, ask your accountant. Whichever business structure you choose, Sage applies the appropriate nominal codes and profit-and-loss and balance-sheet reports for your accounts.

4. **Click Next and select your financial year.**

   Jingles ends its financial year on 31 March 2017, so the financial start date is April 2016, as in Figure 1-5.

FIGURE 1-5:
Beginning the
financial year.

Source: Jane Kelly

5. **Click Next and fill in your VAT details.**

If you're not VAT registered, click No and go to Step 6.

If you're VAT registered, enter your registration number and use the drop-down arrow to select the appropriate VAT rate, as shown in Figure 1-6. You must enter the current standard VAT rate if that's the rate you've selected. Our example, Jingles Ltd, is VAT registered.

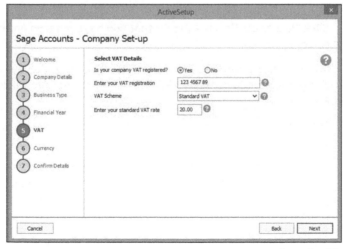

FIGURE 1-6:
Registering your
VAT status.

Source: Jane Kelly

WARNING

Don't enter any transactions until you're certain of the VAT scheme under which you operate. Failure to use the correct scheme means Sage calculates your VAT incorrectly. Applying the wrong VAT scheme can be extremely messy.

6. **Click Next and choose the type of currency you use, as shown in Figure 1-7.**

   Click Next again. Note the currency option is available only if you use Sage 50 Accounts Professional, unless you have chosen to add this as a module.

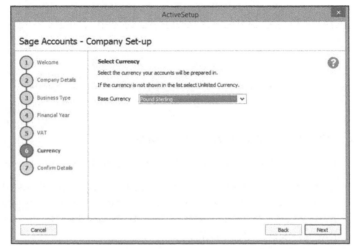

Source: Jane Kelly

FIGURE 1-7:
Telling Sage what currency to use to prepare your accounts.

7. **Click Next to confirm the details that you have entered on the previous screens.**

   If you are happy with those details, then click Create. If you need to make any changes to your data, you can click Back and revise the information. See Figure 1-8.

   The system now configures, and the next screen asks if you want to customise your company. See Figure 1-9.

   Click the Customise company button, and a wizard-style menu appears, where you can choose to set up the defaults for your customers, suppliers, bank, products, financials and administration. Sage offers some helpful videos to assist you in setting up the individual modules. Fill the tick-boxes as you complete each section.

   If you click Setup Now on the main wizard-style menu, Sage automatically takes you to the default screen for whichever module you want to set up. Figure 1-10 shows an example of the Customer Defaults window in the Customers & Sales module.

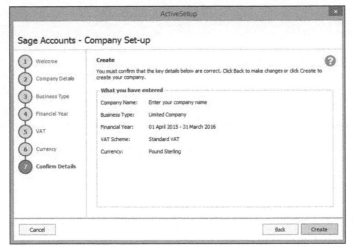

FIGURE 1-8:
Checking your
details.

Source: Jane Kelly

FIGURE 1-9:
Customising your
company.

Source: Jane Kelly

If you prefer to use a step-by-step process, Setup Now is probably the way for you. However, in this chapter I work through setting up the modules manually so you can see where all the options are within Sage. To set up manually, click Close on the Customisation screen (refer to Figure 1-9) and return to the Getting Started page.

Note: If you don't have time to continue with customising your company, then you can click Close and choose to do this later. In order to restart the customisation process, simply click Help from the main toolbar and choose the Customise your company option from the drop-down menu that appears.

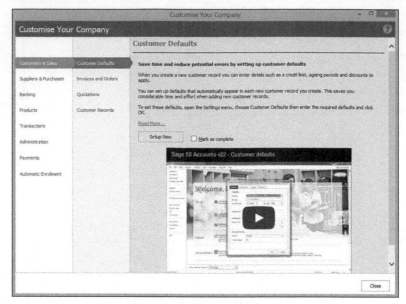

Source: Jane Kelly

Registering Your Software

After you install Sage, when you next open Sage it may prompt you to register it. You have the option to register now or later, as shown in Figure 1-11. Registering straightaway is quick and easy. Click Register Now and the next screen prompts you to complete your personal details.

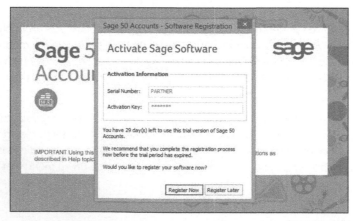

Source: Jane Kelly

After you complete your details, click Register Now. Sage checks your details. If registration is successful, a new activation key appears on the screen and in your email inbox. The email confirms you've registered your product and shows you your Serial Number and Activation Key. Keep this information in a safe place, because you may need it if you ever need to speak to Sage customer services.

Finding Out How Easy Sage Is to Use

Sage is a user-friendly system, using words and phrases that people easily understand rather than accounting jargon. Sage also has a lot of graphics to make the pages look more appealing and easy to navigate. For example, the icons that appear on the Bank module screen look like the entrance to a grand building – like the Bank of England, perhaps.

Sage uses terms that users understand and combines a mix of accounting terms with words such as 'customers' and 'suppliers' instead of 'debtors' and 'creditors'. Accounting terminology isn't done away with altogether, however – for example, Sage refers to nominal codes, and you still have to print aged debtors and creditors reports.

Navigating around Sage

When you open Sage, the first screen you come across is the Welcome screen, as shown in Figure 1-12. This screen provides useful links and various Help pages, including a page that shows you what's new in Sage 50 Accounts.

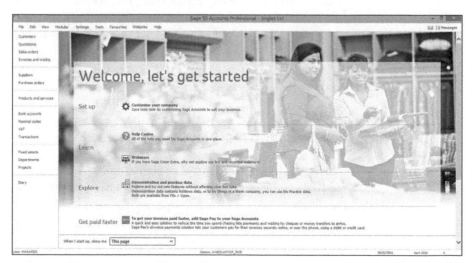

FIGURE 1-12: Getting started with Sage.

Source: Jane Kelly

TIP

You can elect to not show this screen by using the drop-down menu options and selecting the page that you would prefer to see on start-up. For example, you may want to open with your current list of customers; the choice is yours. I choose to open Sage with my customers list – which to begin with is blank until I set up some customers. You can also select not to show the welcome screen upon start-up by clicking Tools, then Options and then View, and then selecting 'Don't display the Welcome Page' in the Global Settings section.

At the top of the Welcome screen is the name of your version of Sage – Sage 50 Accounts Professional, for example – followed by the company name you entered when you set up Sage. (Refer to the earlier 'Setting Up with the Active Setup Wizard' section, which walks you through getting Sage up and running.)

The Sage 50 desktop is divided into four key areas:

>> **Menu bar:** This bar runs horizontally across the top of the screen and is one method of navigating around Sage 50. (I give more info on this area in the section 'Exploring the Menu bar'.)

>> **Navigation bar:** This bar runs vertically down the left side of the screen, listing the key modules within your chosen Sage product.

>> **Icon ribbon:** Depending on which module you choose from the Navigation bar, the list of icons changes across the top of the screen. These icons show you all the functionality contained within each module. For example, the customer module includes icons such as Batch Invoice/Credit, Customer Receipts and Statements, to list just a few.

>> **Work area:** This is the main central space of your screen. You can configure your viewing preferences by choosing Tools and then Options from the Menu bar. You can change your screen view to List format, Process Maps (similar to a flowchart) or Dashboard (a graphical display). The screen automatically defaults to the List format, which is the screen that I use throughout this book.

Exploring the Menu bar

The Menu bar runs horizontally across the top of your screen and provides many navigational tools to help you find your way around Sage.

By clicking the different Menu bar options, you gain access to submenus and different parts of the system. I talk about each option on the Menu bar in the following sections.

File

Clicking File gives you options to create, access, save and share data. The submenu options are as follows:

>> **New Report:** This takes you into Sage Report Designer, where you can use the Report wizard to design new reports.

>> **New Batch Report:** This lets you bundle a set of individual reports together and view, export, print, or email them at the same time. Click F1 for Sage Help and type 'batch reporting' for more details.

>> **Open:** This lets you access the demonstration data and practice data from here, open a report and open previously archived data, including the VAT archive.

>> **Close:** This closes the drop-down menu.

TIP

>> **Backup:** This lets you back up your data. You can also back up your data when you exit the program. I recommend you back up your data each time you use Sage, or at least at the end of each day. Backing up more often during the day is a good idea if you process significant amounts of data. For the lowdown on backing up your data, check out Chapter 9.

>> **Schedule Backup:** This opens the Sage Accounts Backup Manager and enables you to schedule backups for a specific time each day. Use the Settings tab to determine the details of the backup that you require. I cover this in more detail in Chapter 9.

>> **Maintenance:** This lets you check and correct data, compress, recover, re-index and even rebuild data. I talk about maintenance in more detail in Chapter 9.

>> **Restore:** This helps you retrieve data from a previous backup. You may need this function if your data has been corrupted and you want to return to a known point in time when the data was free of problems.

>> **Import:** This opens the Data Import wizard where you can import records, such as customer, supplier, stock, assets, nominal accounts and project records, from other sources, such as Microsoft Excel, as long as they're in a predetermined comma-separated values (CSV) format. This option is very useful when you set up Sage and want to import information. You can speed up the data-entry process if you import information instead of keying in each individual record. I cover importing and CSV formatting in more detail in Chapter 19.

>> **Sage Drive setup:** This walkthrough guide shows you how to set up Sage Drive, which gives you real-time access to your data wherever and whenever you need it. Sage Drive uses a Sage Identity (ID), which ensures secure access

to your data. You'll be asked to login using your Sage ID or create one if you don't have one already.

>> **Microsoft Integration:** Using this option, you can export data to Microsoft Excel, Word or Outlook.

>> **Send:** This lets you send a message by using your default email program.

>> **Log off:** Clicking this option logs you out of Sage.

>> **Exit:** Clicking this exits you from Sage. You can also exit Sage by clicking the black cross in the top right corner of the screen.

Edit

You can use Edit to cut, copy, paste, insert or delete rows, duplicate cells, or memorise or recall data.

View

The *status bar* is the narrow strip across the bottom of your screen, showing the name of your Sage product, today's date, the start of the financial year and the current transaction number. You can switch this bar on and off. You can also view the user list, which shows who is currently logged in to Sage.

Modules

The *modules* are essentially the different components that form the whole of the Sage accounting system. The modules include the usual accounting ledgers, such as customers, suppliers, bank, nominal ledger and reporting functions, but they also include (depending on which version of Sage you purchased) additional components, such as projects, sales order processing and purchase order processing. You can also access invoicing, quotations, fixed assets, departments, VAT, and transactions functions, wizards and a diary.

Settings

The settings include the Configuration Editor and Company Preferences, which hold some of the basic information about your company and the way you installed Sage. Settings also include many of the default screens for the ledgers, which save you time when setting up records at a later date. If you use the Customisation wizard when you install Sage, you may have already seen these default screens. If you need to change the system date or check the financial year, you can do it within settings. Settings also give you access to your Sage security settings and passwords to protect your accounts data. The settings include the following:

>> **Configuration Editor:** This holds the basic information you enter when you complete the Active Setup wizard. Some of the things you can do here include editing your customer and supplier trading terms, amending your VAT codes, and managing your project cost types and cost codes. Since version 22 it is also now possible to create new customer, supplier and project analysis fields. I discuss this further in Chapter 3.

>> **Company Preferences:** This lets you enter extra information if you didn't add everything when you used the Active Setup wizard. You may want to update your address information or check your VAT details, for example.

>> **Customer/Supplier/Bank/Product/Invoice and Order/Email Defaults:** These settings let you amend parts of the default data you set up on installation.

>> **Financial Year:** This identifies the start of the company's financial year. This date is fixed when you start to enter data.

>> **Change Program Date:** This lets you change dates when you run a month-end or year-end report. The date is normally set to the current day's date, but there may be times, such as period ends, when you want to change the date temporarily.

>> **Lock Date:** Here you can enter a *lock date* into the system, which means you can prevent postings before a specific date. This is useful when you process year ends. Only users with access rights to lock dates can post.

>> **Currencies:** This lets you edit your currency requirements if you use multiple currencies.

>> **Countries:** This lists all the countries in the world and their country codes, and identifies countries that are currently members of the EU. The Sage 50 Accounts Professional package uses this information to comply with Intrastat reporting requirements. (I talk more about Intrastat in Chapter 17.) You can amend the Countries table as and when countries enter or leave the EU.

>> **Control Accounts:** This gives you an at-a-glance list of all the control accounts within Sage. A *control account* is a summary of all entries within a specific ledger. For example, the sales ledger control account includes all transactions for all sales ledger accounts – the balance on the control account tallies with the sum of the sales ledger accounts. Control accounts are used as a check on the numerical accuracy of the ledger accounts and form part of the double-entry system that Sage performs when you enter transactions.

WARNING

If you want to change the control accounts, do so before you enter any transactions – otherwise, leave them alone!

You can reconcile a control account. Just click Help and follow the instructions for reconciling debtors or creditors.

>> **Access Rights:** Here you can set up or change access rights for particular individuals to allow them access to only certain parts or even all parts of the system.

>> **Change Password:** This lets you change your password periodically as part of your data protection and security routine.

>> **Internet Resources:** This gives you an Internet Resources list that you can use to set your courier and credit bureau information. You can launch your website browser from within Sage and go to your credit bureau to check the status of a customer or go to a courier's website to track the progress of a parcel.

Tools

The Tools option is a hotchpotch of items. You can run the Global Changes wizard, carry out contra entries, run period ends, open up Report Designer and convert reports, to name but a few. I outline the options here:

>> **Global Changes:** Here you can globally change customer or supplier credit limits, turnover values, nominal budgets, product sales or purchase prices, reorder details and discount table values.

>> **Activation:** This lets you upgrade your program and enable third-party integration with the Construction Industry Scheme (CIS) and foreign traders (if you have Sage 50 Accounts Professional). Third-party integration lets you use add-on software tailored to your specific industry. Sage has a separate module for CIS and the recording of payments to subcontractors. You can activate this scheme by clicking Tools and then Activation for businesses that fall under the scheme.

TIP

You can use the Upgrade Program option to register after your initial 30-day Sage trial period runs out.

>> **Opening Balances:** This gives you a series of actions that you need to complete to enter your opening balances. In Chapter 4 I guide you through the Opening Balances wizard.

>> **Period End:** Here you can clear your audit trail, clear and delete stock as well as run your month end, allowing you to post accruals, prepayments and depreciation. This option also clears the current-month turnover figures. You can run your year end, which sets your profit and loss nominal accounts to zero for the new financial year.

>> **Transaction Email:** This lets you exchange invoices and orders with your customers and suppliers via Microsoft Outlook. You can import any orders or invoices that you receive via email directly into your Sage accounts.

>> **Report Designer:** Here you can edit and create new reports customised for your business.

>> **Convert Reports:** If you have reports within Sage that are from version 12 or earlier, you may need to convert the report types (as the file extensions have changed). You can do this here.

>> **Event Log:** This shows a history of system events. If you contact the Sage helpline with a system problem, your event log may come in handy.

>> **Options:** This gives you options to change the settings and appearance of Sage. For example, you can change the default view of the Customers and Suppliers screens from the process map to customer or supplier lists, using the View tab. Sage has recently enabled users to change the colours of the screen. You can choose from white, light colours or dark colours. You need to play around with each option to see which one you prefer. The changes are implemented only when you reboot Sage.

>> **Batch Reporting:** You can generate several reports from any area of the Sage software at the same time. For example, you could create a 'Period End' batch report and get Sage to print off the Trial Balance, Profit & Loss and Balance Sheet, all at the same time! Type 'batch reports' into the Search field in Sage to find more information.

>> **Data Service Manager:** The Sage Accounts Data Service runs on the computer or server where your Sage Accounts data is held. The service acts as a gateway and controls the reading and writing of data. Using this service increases the robustness of the system, improves data security and helps optimise performance. You shouldn't need to change or amend this in any way.

>> **Internet Options:** Here you can vary the Sage update criteria, enter Sage Cover login details, and enable Sage Mobile by clicking the Mobile tab.

Favourites

You can store your favourite reports here. To find out how to set up favourite reports, use the Help menu supplied with Report Designer, which you access via Tools on the Browser toolbar. In Chapter 18 I go into more detail about the Report Designer.

Weblinks

Weblinks gives you a number of links to useful websites, such as Sage shop and HM Revenue & Customs (HMRC).

Help

Help is the last entry on the Menu bar but probably one of the most useful. If you want to understand more about the system and want to know how to do something, click the Help option. You have several help options to choose from, all of which take you to a Webhelp page where you can enter your keyword and click Search to find answers to your problems. In addition you can find the Customise Your Company wizard here, which you may have discovered when you first installed Sage. You can access these screens and amend your module defaults and other administrative functions at any time.

The About page now contains a raft of information about your computer, including system details, licence information and contact details for Sage. Sage support staff often find this page very useful if you ask them for help with software problems.

Using Wizards

A number of wizards wield their technological magic through Sage. Their job is to help you through a wide variety of setups and tasks. You can access these helpful creatures from the Menu bar by clicking Modules and then Wizards.

REMEMBER

A wizard's job is to make your work easy. All you have to do is follow the prompts and enter the information the wizard requests. Magic!

Wizards can help you in setting up Sage and day-to-day processing. They can help you set up new records for customers, suppliers, nominal accounts, bank accounts, products and projects. You can also use wizards to do the tricky double-entry bookkeeping for items such as opening and closing stock, fuel scale charges and VAT transfers. Sage even provides a wizard to help you set up the foreign trader features. In Chapter 23 I offer lots more info about Sage's wizards.

Chapter 2

Creating Your Chart of Accounts and Assigning Nominal Codes

I n this chapter, I get down to the nitty-gritty of the accounting system – the chart of accounts (COA), which is made up of nominal codes. Think of the COA as the engine of the accounting system. From the information in your COA, you produce your profit and loss report, your balance sheet, your budget report and prior-year reports. Set up your COA properly and the chart grows with your business – but set it up wrongly and you'll have problems forever.

Luckily, Sage gives you a lot of help and does the hard work for you, but you still need to understand why Sage is structured in the way that it is and how you can customise it to suit your business.

Understanding as Much as You Need to about Accounting

To use Sage, it helps if you have an appreciation of accounts and understand what you want to achieve. But you certainly don't need to understand all the rules of double-entry bookkeeping. In this section I give you the basics of accounting principles so you can use Sage more comfortably.

Dabbling in double-entry bookkeeping

Accounting systems and accounting programs such as Sage use the principle of *double-entry bookkeeping*, so called because each transaction is recorded twice. For every debit entry, you record a corresponding credit entry. Doing the two entries helps balance the books.

For example, if you make a cash sale for £100, your sales account receives a £100 credit and your cash account gets a £100 debit.

Some knowledge of double-entry rules helps when you use Sage. That way, you can interpret information a little more easily. The following is a short summary of the rules of double-entry bookkeeping:

>> **Asset and expense accounts:** Debit the account for an increase and credit the account for a decrease in value.

>> **Liability and income and sales accounts:** Debit the account for a decrease and credit the account for an increase in value.

Fortunately, you don't need to book yourself into a bookkeeping evening class, as Sage does the double-entry for you . . . phew! If you're intrigued by the double-entry system, though, pick up a copy of *Bookkeeping For Dummies* by Jane Kelly, Paul Barrow and Lita Epstein (Wiley), which explains double-entry and more.

Having said that, understanding the double-entry method does help with Sage, particularly if you intend to do your own nominal journals. This knowledge also comes in handy if you intend to produce monthly management accounts. Sometimes, you need to post nominal journals to correct mistakes, and understanding the principles of double-entry bookkeeping lets you confidently process journals. Don't panic, though – Sage has many wizards that can post things like depreciation, accruals and prepayments for you – so if you struggle with journals, leave them to your accountant or at least seek advice if you aren't sure.

Naming your nominals

In accounting and in Sage, you bump into the term *nominal* quite a bit. And for good reason, as several key concepts use the word:

>> **Nominal account:** Every item of income, expense, asset and liability is posted to a nominal ledger account. The nominal ledger accounts categorise all your transactions. The individual nominal accounts are grouped into ranges and can be viewed in your COA.

>> **Nominal code:** A four-digit number is given to each account that appears in the nominal ledger. For example, 7502 is the nominal code for office stationery, which is an account in the nominal ledger. Sage categorises each nominal code into nine different ranges, and these categories form the basis of your COA.

>> **Nominal ledger:** The nominal ledger is an accumulation of all the nominal accounts – it's the main body of the accounting system. Each nominal account shows all the transactions posted to that specific code, so it follows that the nominal ledger represents all the transactions of the business in one place. Deep joy, I hear you say!

To find the nominal ledger, click on Nominal Codes on the Navigation bar, down the left side of the screen.

>> **Nominal record:** Each nominal code has an individual nominal record. To create a new nominal code, open up a new nominal record and give it the new nominal code as its reference. See Chapter 3 for more details about nominal records.

REMEMBER

Sage categorises nominal codes in a specific way, so don't change them without careful consideration. Using common sense and planning at the early stages of implementing Sage can pay huge dividends in the future. You need to correctly categorise your nominal codes in order to create meaningful reports.

Preparing reports

One of the reasons you're investing in Sage is probably so you can run reports to see how your business is doing. And your money is well spent, for Sage has many reports you can run at the click of a button. The important thing to remember is that reports are only as good as the information contained within them. The old saying 'Rubbish in, rubbish out' is never truer.

The two key financial reports every business and every accounting system uses are as follows:

>> **Balance sheet:** This report shows a snapshot of the business. It identifies assets and liabilities and shows how the business is funded via the capital accounts.

>> **Profit and loss report:** This report shows the revenue and costs associated with the business for a given period and identifies whether the business is making a profit or incurring a loss.

REMEMBER

The profit and loss and balance sheet reports are created from the information in the COA, so it's important to get the COA right.

I discuss the profit and loss report and balance sheet more fully in Chapter 18, where I also cover producing monthly accounts and the types of report you may need.

Looking at the Structure of Your COA

The COA is a list of nominal codes, divided into the following ten categories:

>> Fixed Assets

>> Current Assets

>> Current Liabilities

>> Long-term Liabilities

>> Capital and Reserves

>> Sales

>> Purchases

>> Direct Expenses

>> Overhead

>> Taxation

The first five categories form the balance sheet; the remaining categories create your profit and loss report. So the COA is a pretty important part of the system.

A look at the nominal list on the Nominal Ledger screen shows that the list runs in numerical order, with the balance sheet codes first. If you click the Chart of Accounts icon within the nominal ledger and look at the default layout of accounts, you notice a tab for Profit and Loss and another for Balance Sheet. You can click on either of these two tabs and a preview of the report appears on the right side of the screen.

Checking out the default COA

Being a caring, sharing software developer, Sage provides a default COA for you to use, with a ready-made list of nominal codes. (You select the type of COA you want using the Active Setup wizard, which I go through in Chapter 1.) Your COA is determined by the type of business you operate. When you install Sage, it asks you what business type to use. I use the Limited Company business type to demonstrate Sage in this book.

Although Sage can spot if a new nominal code is outside the range of the usual COA, it can't really help with the structure of the coding system that you choose to use, so plan ahead to avoid costly mistakes.

You can also customise the default COA to suit your business. I tell you how in the 'Editing Your COA' section later in this chapter.

The COA is in the Nominal codes module. To display it, click Modules on the Menu bar and then select Nominal codes, or simply click Nominal codes from the Navigation bar down the left side of the screen.

The Navigation bar is in full view all the time you use Sage.

The opening screen for the Nominal codes module is shown in Figure 2-1. You can access the COA by clicking on the icon shown in the Nominal codes module.

The Nominal codes screen shows a series of icons, one of which is the Chart of Accounts icon. You can also create and amend nominal codes from this screen; create journals, accruals and prepayments; and run your Trial Balance, Profit and Loss and Balance Sheet as well as several other nominal ledger reports.

For a better look at the Chart of Accounts screen, follow these steps:

1. **Click the Chart of Accounts icon on the Nominal codes toolbar.**

The Chart of Accounts window opens, which gives you a list of all the COAs you have created. At first, only the Default Layout of Accounts shows, but any subsequent COAs you create also show here.

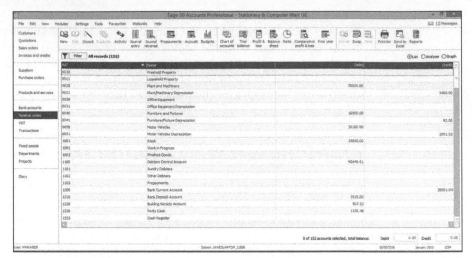

FIGURE 2-1:
Looking at a list
of nominal codes.

Source: Jane Kelly

2. **Highlight the COA you want to view and click the Edit button at the bottom of the next screen.**

Initially, the COA you want is the Default Layout of Accounts.

The Edit Chart of Accounts window for the Default Layout of Accounts screen opens, as shown in Figure 2-2. This screen shows the category types and a description in the top left of the screen, and the Category Accounts list showing the nominal codes associated with those categories outlined below. To the right of the screen, you see a preview of the profit and loss report layout.

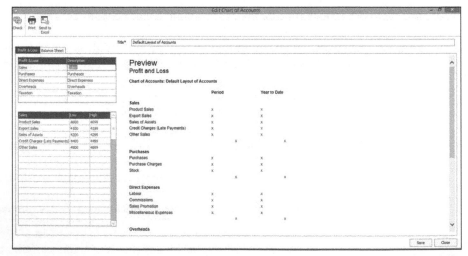

FIGURE 2-2:
Looking at the
Edit Chart of
Accounts window.

Source: Jane Kelly

As you click each category type in the first box, you see that the nominal codes shown in the Category Account List below change to match the category type.

The first category is Sales, as in Figure 2-2. Because Sales is highlighted in the first box, you notice that the Category Account List below shows the high and low ranges of nominal codes within each sales category. I explain the nominal code ranges in the next two sections.

If you're not sure which nominal codes fall into the range described, you can print a complete list of nominal codes. Alternatively, you can click the number in the Low or High column and use the drop-down arrow next to the field to see which account the nominal code refers to. You can then scroll down the list of accounts that appears and view the range of codes.

To print a hard copy of the nominal list, use the following steps. The list usually consists of two or three pages, but the length depends on the number of codes you create. The more codes, the longer the list.

1. **From the Navigation bar, click Nominal codes.**

2. **Click the Print List button at the top right (third from the end) of the screen.**

   A command is sent to your printer to run off a hard copy of the existing codes.

The list of nominal codes may look rather daunting at first, but I talk you through the basics in the next sections.

Identifying balance sheet codes

The *balance sheet* is a snapshot of your business at a fixed point in time. The balance sheet identifies your company's assets and liabilities and shows how your business has been funded via the capital accounts. To achieve this snapshot, the balance sheet looks at your business's assets and liabilities, so it draws on the numbers in a range of nominal codes. *Note:* I use the default nominal codes when demonstrating the following categories of codes.

>> **Fixed assets (0010–0051):** A *fixed asset* is an item likely to be held in the business for a long period of time – more than 12 months. The range of fixed-asset codes is used for transactions relating to freehold and leasehold property and other items the company plans to hold for a while. You can add other capital items, such as computer equipment, to this list.

- » **Current assets (1001–1250):** A *current asset* is an item that has a lifespan of 12 months or less. You should be able to *liquidate* (turn into cash) current assets reasonably quickly. Common current assets include stock, debts owed to the business, and bank and cash items. Current assets are normally ordered in the least liquid order first, meaning items that take the longest to convert into cash appear at the top of the list. Therefore you expect to see cash, which is so liquid it runs through some people's hands like water, at the bottom of the current assets list.

- » **Current liabilities (2100–2230):** *Current liabilities* are amounts the business owes, normally outstanding for less than 12 months. At the top of the list is the Creditors control account, which is basically the total owed to all suppliers. The list also includes amounts owed to HM Revenue & Customs (HMRC), such as value-added tax (VAT) and Pay As You Earn (PAYE), if applicable.

- » **Long-term liabilities (2300–2330):** *Long-term liabilities* are amounts owed by the business for a period of more than 12 months. They include long-term loans, hire-purchase agreements and mortgages.

- » **Capital (3000–3200):** Capital accounts show how the business is funded. These codes include share issues, reserves, and the current profit and loss balance.

  Reserves is another word for earnings retained within the business – they're officially called *retained earnings*. Annual profits swell this account, and any distributions of dividends to owners of the business reduce the balance.

REMEMBER

  In order for the balance sheet to balance, the capital account includes the current-year profit, as shown in the profit and loss report.

Table 2-1 shows the range of nominal codes that form the balance sheet.

TABLE 2-1

Balance Sheet Nominal Codes

Category	Low	High
Fixed Assets		
Property	0010	0019
Plant & Machinery	0020	0029
Office Equipment	0030	0039
Furniture & Fixtures	0040	0049
Motor Vehicles	0050	0059

Category	Low	High
Current Assets		
Stock	1000	1099
Debtors	1100	1199
Bank Account	1200	1209
Deposits & Cash	1210	1239
Credit Card (Debtors)	1250	1250
VAT Liability	2200	2209
Current Liabilities		
Creditors: Short Term	2100	2199
Taxation	2210	2219
Wages	2220	2299
Credit Card (Creditors)	1240	1240
Bank Account	1200	1209
VAT Liability	2200	2209
Long-term Liabilities		
Creditors: Long Term	2300	2399
Capital & Reserves		
Share Capital	3000	3099
Reserves	3100	3299

Looking at profit and loss codes

In the default set of nominal codes, all codes from 4000 onward are profit and loss codes, which, appropriately enough, include the numbers that show how much money the business brings in and spends. The profit and loss codes include the following:

>> **Sales (4000–4999):** Sales codes apply to goods or services that your business offers; they indicate how you earn your money. The 4000–4999 range also includes income other than sales, for example, royalty commissions.

TIP

The default descriptions against the sales codes are nonsense. The names Sales type A, B, C, D and so on are not meaningful to anyone. You need to change the sales types to make them applicable to your business. If you own a card shop, for example, Sales type A may become nominal code 4000 for birthday cards, sales type B may become nominal code 4005 for get-well cards and so on. I look at editing nominal codes in Chapter 3.

» **Purchases (5000–5299):** These codes identify material purchases and purchasing costs such as carriage, packaging and transport insurance. *Material purchases* is a very general term for the purchase of the raw materials used to make the products the business sells. For example, flour is a material purchase for a bakery.

» **Direct expenses (6000–6999):** A *direct expense* is a cost directly associated with the product being manufactured or created by the business. Labour costs, including subcontractors, come under these codes. The codes also include expenses such as sales commissions, samples and public relations costs that can be associated directly with the products.

» **Overheads (7000–8999):** By far the largest range of codes is *overheads*, which covers all other expenses not directly associated with making and providing the products or service. You can see the overheads subsections in Table 2-2.

» **Taxation (9000–9001):** This code sits almost at the bottom of the nominal code list. It is not classed as an overhead but is an expense of the business.

In addition, the default nominal codes also includes 9998 as a suspense account, which is used as a temporary posting account when you don't know which nominal code to use initially, and 9999 as a misposting account.

Table 2-2 lists the nominal codes that form the profit and loss report.

TABLE 2-2

Profit and Loss Nominal Codes

Category	Low	High
Sales		
Product Sales	4000	4099
Export Sales	4100	4199
Sales of Assets	4200	4299
Credit Charges	4400	4499
Other Sales	4900	4999

Category	Low	High
Purchases		
Purchases	5000	5099
Purchase Charges	5100	5199
Stock	5200	5299
Direct Expenses		
Labour	6000	6099
Commissions	6100	6199
Sales Promotion	6200	6299
Miscellaneous Expenses	6900	6999
Overheads		
Gross Wages	7000	7099
Rent & Rates	7100	7199
Heat, Light & Power	7200	7299
Motor Expenses	7300	7399
Travelling & Entertainment	7400	7499
Printing & Stationery	7500	7549
Telephone & Computer Charges	7550	7599
Professional Fees	7600	7699
Equipment Hire & Rental	7700	7799
Maintenance	7800	7899
Bank Charges & Interest	7900	7999
Depreciation	8000	8099
Bad Debts	8100	8199
General Expenses	8200	8299
Taxation	9000	9001
Suspense & Mispostings	9998	9999

TIP

You use the suspense and mispostings nominal accounts when you can't find another suitable nominal code. Suspense and mispostings nominal accounts serve as holding pens – somewhere to post an item while you try to find a better code to post it to. At the end of each month, review the suspense and mispostings accounts and put the items in their correct locations. Unfortunately, the suspense account can become a dumping ground – try to use this account only when absolutely necessary.

Leaving gaps and mirroring codes

The ranges of codes leave plenty of gaps between the categories. For example, Sales codes start at 4000 but Purchase codes don't begin until 5000. You can fill the large gap between 4000 and 4999 with Sales codes, which provides a great deal of flexibility for a growing business.

TIP

I suggest leaving gaps of ten between each code to allow for growth, but it's entirely up to you to decide the best fit for your business.

You may consider mirroring corresponding sales and purchase codes, so the last two digits are the same for the sale and purchase of each item, as shown in Table 2-3, which shows the nominal codes for Jingles, a fictional card shop and party-planning company I created to serve as an example throughout this book.

TABLE 2-3 **Mirroring Nominal Codes**

Nominal Code	Description	Nominal Code	Description
4000	Sale of greetings cards	5000	Purchase of greeting cards
4020	Sale of party balloons	5020	Purchase of party balloons
4030	Sale of party gifts	5030	Purchase of party gifts

Accommodating floating nominals

A *floating nominal* is a code that can be placed as a current asset or current liability, depending on whether the balance is a debit or a credit. For example, if your bank account is in the black, it's a current asset – but if your account is overdrawn, it shows as a current liability. Another example is the VAT liability account, as you can sometimes get a refund from HMRC.

Sage automatically places floating nominals to the correct side of the balance sheet, but only if you identify the specific codes that can be treated as an asset or a liability in the Floating Nominal Accounts section on the Edit Chart of Accounts screen. Sage normally designates accounts as floating nominal codes, so you don't have to do anything.

Editing Your COA

One of the first things to consider when setting up Sage is how well the COA suits your business. Have a look at the categories and nominal codes to make sure they contain suitable descriptions for your products or services. For example, the Product Sales category doesn't suit a business that primarily provides a service. You may want to change a few categories, or you may decide to make wholesale changes, in which case it may be simpler to create an entirely new COA. The next sections tell you how to change and create COAs.

WARNING

If you place a nominal code in the wrong category, you may find inaccuracies in the reports you produce. Miscodings are every accountant's nightmare. When you create new codes, be sure you know whether the code should be a balance sheet or a profit and loss item. You can usually rely on your common sense, but if you're unsure, give your accountant a quick call. Accountants don't mind answering a quick question like this, but they do mind if you mix up balance sheet and profit and loss codes and they then have the task of unpicking your mistakes.

Amending your COA

You can edit the default COA to suit your business.

In Figure 2-2 (in the earlier 'Checking out the default COA' section), the category types showed profit and loss items on the first tab and balance sheet items on the second tab. If you move your cursor down the list of categories in the first box, you notice the details in the Category Account list below change to reflect the heading names and nominal codes contained within the highlighted category types. To view the nominal code ranges in more detail, click the nominal code and then use the drop-down arrow to identify the name of the nominal code.

REMEMBER

You can change the description of each category in the first box on the COA screen. You can also change the description of the ranges of nominal codes shown in the Category Account list. One of the first things to change is the Product Sales headings. These headings are very general descriptions and won't suit all businesses. For example, if you're a baker, you may want to change the sales types to bread sales, cake sales and so on.

TIP

The headings in the COA show up in your profit and loss report and balance sheet (which you can preview on the right side of the COA screen), so you need to give careful consideration to which headings you want to see on your financial reports. If you don't want an extensive list of different types of sales categories on your profit and loss account, consider grouping together several nominal codes under more general headings.

After you decide on the level of detail you want to show on your reports, you're ready to amend your COA by following these steps:

1. **From the Navigation bar, click Nominal codes and then click Chart of Accounts.**

2. **Highlight Default Layout of Accounts and then click Edit.**

3. **Make any changes to headings within the category account.**

   Changes available are:

   - **Rename a heading:** Simply click the title and overtype with the new name. Jeanette, the owner of Jingles, changes Product Sales to Shop Sales.

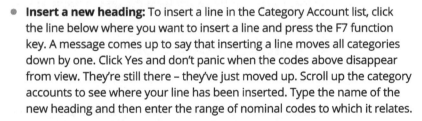

TIP

   When you rename a heading, make sure all the nominal codes included within the renamed heading relate to the new heading. (Check out Chapter 3 for more help with this.)

   - **Insert a new heading:** To insert a line in the Category Account list, click the line below where you want to insert a line and press the F7 function key. A message comes up to say that inserting a line moves all categories down by one. Click Yes and don't panic when the codes above disappear from view. They're still there – they've just moved up. Scroll up the category accounts to see where your line has been inserted. Type the name of the new heading and then enter the range of nominal codes to which it relates.

   Figure 2-3 shows the newly created Party Fees heading for Jingles. At the moment, the new heading has only one relevant nominal code (4035 Party Fees), so this code is both the low and high range. If Jeanette wants to add more nominal codes at a later date, she can include them in the high range. If the new code was 4055, the range of nominal codes for Party Fees would be 4035–4055.

   - **Delete a heading:** You can use F8 to delete a heading line, but make sure you won't want to use those nominal codes in future.

4. **Click Save when you're happy with the changes you've made.**

   You need to go through your COA for errors, so take a look at the 'Checking Your COA' section later in this chapter.

FIGURE 2-3:
Inserting a
new heading
in the COA.

Source: Jane Kelly

Creating a new COA

If the existing COA doesn't suit your business at all, you may find that creating your own COA is less work than adapting the COA Sage provides. You may decide to use your existing nominal codes from your old accounting system, in which case you can customise the COA with your existing codes.

Alternatively, you may find your business has particular geographical locations or segments that you want to report on. You can create a new COA for each segment or location, but make it specific for your business. For example, you may have an office in London and one in Edinburgh. With the creation of suitable nominal codes, you can produce a profit and loss report to the gross profit line for each office. So you group together all the sales codes associated with the London office and deduct from them all London office purchases and direct costs. This results in a London office gross profit. You can do the same exercise for the Edinburgh office with a separate COA, and then you can compare the two, to see which office was the most profitable.

The ability to analyse any further than gross profit requires an extremely complex set of nominal codes. Speak to your friendly accountant, who can assist with complicated nominal code structures.

WARNING

When you add a new COA with the purpose of producing a profit and loss report to gross profit level, be aware that you can only select the nominal codes specific to that geographical location or segment of the business. As a result, the word *partial* appears after the COA name because you haven't selected all the nominal codes. In addition to the gross profit reports, you must always have a fully complete COA for the whole business, which you must check for errors before you run reports, as I explain in the section 'Checking Your COA' later in this chapter. Don't try to check a COA that has 'partial' in the title, as Sage always brings up a list of codes that are missing.

To add a COA, follow these steps:

1. **From the Navigation bar, select the Nominal codes module and click Chart of Accounts.**

2. **Click Add from the Chart of Accounts window.**

   The New Chart of Accounts window appears.

3. **Enter the name of your new COA and click Add.**

   A new Edit Chart of Accounts window opens, with the title of your new COA in the top right corner.

4. **Select each category type by clicking the Description field in the first box and then enter a description in the Category Account List box below.**

   Enter new headings and assign a range of codes for each heading for the Profit and Loss tab and the Balance Sheet tab.

5. **When you have finished editing, click Save.**

   An 'incomplete chart of accounts' message appears. This is fine; it simply means that you haven't selected all the nominal codes. This is why you see the word 'partial' after your new Chart of Accounts.

Figure 2-4 shows a new COA called Jingles Card Shop. The Jingles business consists of two parts: One part is the card shop, which sells cards, balloons and so on, and the other part is party-planning. To see the gross profit made on each part of the business, I created a separate COA for each segment. I selected only the nominal codes specific to the card shop and ignored any party-planning codes. Because I didn't include all the nominal codes in this COA, Sage includes the word 'partial' in the title.

To get accurate reports for the whole of the business, I need to use the default COA, because this COA includes all nominal codes.

After you add a new COA, you can run your profit and loss report to see what information pulls through. Pay attention to the descriptions that you use in your COA, because they transfer through to your profit and loss and balance sheet reports. At this point, you can see the gross profit for each part of the business and determine what is making money or what isn't, as the case may be.

DELETING A COA

You may find that when you play around designing new COAs, you create too many variations and want to delete some of them. Follow these steps to delete a COA:

1. **Click Nominal codes and then Chart of Accounts.**

   The Chart of Accounts window opens.

2. **Highlight the COA that you want to delete and click Delete.**

3. **Click Yes to confirm that you want to delete the COA.**

   If you decide that you don't want to delete, click No and return to the main Chart of Accounts window.

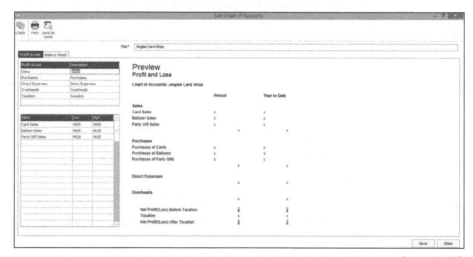

FIGURE 2-4:
A new COA created for the Jingles Card Shop.

Source: Jane Kelly

TIP

When you edit your COA, you can use the F7 function key to insert a line and the F8 key to delete a line.

REMEMBER

If you want just one code within the range, then the code is the same in both the High and Low columns.

Checking Your COA

After you make changes to your COA, you need to ensure your COA doesn't contain any errors. If an error is present, the profit and loss or balance sheet reports may be incorrect, and a warning message flashes up every time you run these reports.

To check your COA, follow these steps:

1. **Go to the Nominal codes module and click Chart of Accounts.**

2. **Click Edit.**

3. **Click Check.**

If no problems are present, Sage tells you no errors were found in the COA and you can breathe a sigh of relief. However, if a little window entitled Chart of Accounts Errors appears, be prepared to take corrective action.

Previewing errors

The Chart of Accounts Errors window gives you four output options for displaying the error report:

>> **Printer:** This sends the report directly to your printer.

>> **Preview:** This lets you look at the errors on the screen before you decide to print or exit.

>> **File:** This saves the report to a new location.

>> **Email:** This lets you email the document to another person.

Usually, the best method is to preview the report first, to make sure it provides the information you expected, and then print a hard copy if you like what you see.

Make sure the option you want has a filled-in circle next to it and then click the Run button at the bottom of the pop-up screen. Figure 2-5 is a sample error report, showing that a nominal code is not represented in the chart. The missing code must be included within the nominal code ranges to stop the error report coming up.

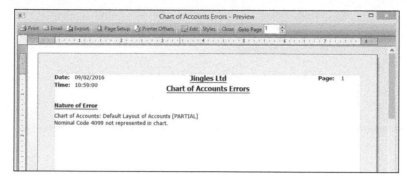

Looking at some common errors

Whenever you add new nominal codes, it is possible that the codes may not fit neatly within the nominal code structure currently in place. Common errors that can be made within the COA are listed in this section.

TIP

Check the steps in the 'Amending your COA' section earlier in this chapter for advice on how to fix the errors I list here.

Common errors include the following:

>> **Overlapping ranges:** The same nominal code occurs in two different ranges and is therefore counted twice.

For example, Jeanette, the owner of Jingles Card Shop, assigned the Sale of Cards category nominal codes from 4000 to 4199, and then assigned the Sale of Balloons category nominal codes from 4100 to 4299. The error report points out that the categories overlap between 4100 and 4199. Jeanette needs to amend the ranges so they don't overlap.

>> **Enclosing one range within another range:** Assigning a range of codes within another range is a big no-no.

For example, Jeanette assigned the Sale of Balloons category a range from 4100 to 4299, and then assigned the Sale of Party Gifts category codes from 4200 to 4250, which is within the Sale of Balloons range. She needs to fix this so she knows whether she's selling mostly balloons or mostly party gifts.

>> **Using a floating code in one category but not in its complementary category:** You may require a floating code so that an item such as the bank account can be both a current asset and a current liability, depending on whether the account is in the black or overdrawn. If you set up a floating code in Current Assets but not in Current Liabilities or vice versa, you get an error message.

IN THIS CHAPTER

Choosing a quick start or step-by-step process

Setting up records for customers and suppliers

Creating nominal records

Registering your bank accounts

Accounting for your products

Depreciating your fixed assets

Chapter 3

Setting Up Records

After you install your Sage software, you quickly realise that the hard work is only just beginning. You now have to create the records necessary to operate your accounting system, including records for your customers, suppliers and existing bank accounts. Depending on your business, you may also need to set up stock and project records. In this chapter I tell you how to do these things.

Choosing How to Create Your Records

Setting up records may seem a daunting task, but Sage provides at least two ways of doing things. You can use the quick way, which uses the New icon within the relevant module, or you can use the step-by-step way, which uses the Wizard icon. If you like the belt and braces approach, click the Wizard icon, as the wizard helps you complete each section of the record thoroughly. If you're a bit of a speed freak and want to get on with things as quickly as possible, and you don't mind leaving a few less important data fields blank (you can always update them later), choose the quick start option. I always use the quick start method, as my time is invariably of the essence.

Getting a quick start using the New icon

If you want a quick start, find the module you want to create a new record for and click the New icon. This opens up a new blank record, where you can start typing in the details straightaway.

Following the wizards brick by brick

Like Dorothy and friends finding their way to the Emerald City, going brick by brick or step by step can take some time, but it does get you where you need to be. Using the wizards is slower than using the New icon, as the wizards guide you through the completion of every box in each record. For example, if you're keen on keeping customers within their credit limit and offer discounts for early settlement, you may want to use the Customer wizard to guide you through setting up the intricacies of your credit control.

To awaken a wizard, click the module you want to create a new record within and then click the Wizard icon. The program takes you through a step-by-step wizard, which prompts you to dot every i and cross every t. Wizards are thorough, but using them can be time-consuming. (For more information about wizards, check out Chapter 23.)

Creating Customer and Supplier Records

Setting up customer and supplier records is essentially the same process, so I cover both in this section. Wizards can walk you through creating both types of record – just click the Wizard icon in the relevant module.

If you prefer to use the quick start method, click the New icon within Customers and a blank customer record appears, as in Figure 3-1. When you open a blank record, you see five icons across the top left of your screen and then more options available in a mini navigation bar down the left side of your blank record. The screen automatically defaults to the 'Details' option for your record.

I look at the options available in the navigation bar first:

>> **Details:** Type the usual contact details in these fields.

WARNING

The A/C* (short for Account) field is first, so you need to decide how you want to set up the account name before you begin your data entry. Think carefully about this first data-entry field and the eight-digit short name you give each account. Sage recommends you use an *alphanumeric* reference – containing both letters and numbers – in case you have clients with the same name. For example, you may have the references Smith01, Smith02 and so on. Alternatively, you can use customers' initials, so the reference for Julian Smith is SmithJ, Sarah Smith becomes SmithS and so on.

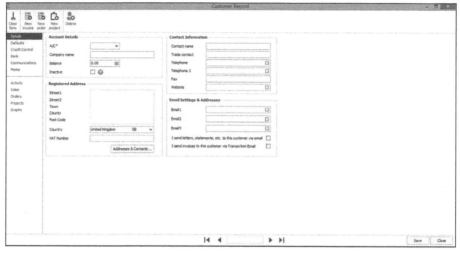

FIGURE 3-1:
An example of a blank customer record.

Source: Jane Kelly

After you type in the account reference, tab through the other fields and enter the relevant information.

TIP

If you transfer from a different computer package, you may be able to import the customer records from your old system to Sage. See Chapter 19 for info on how to do this.

» **Defaults:** The basic defaults are shown in each record. You can override the details for each individual record and tailor the defaults for your customers.

For example, the default nominal code is currently set at 4000, but if you have a customer for whom this code never applies, you can change the code to something more suitable. For example, Jingles may sell only balloons to one customer, so it makes sense to set the default nominal code for that customer as Sale of Balloons.

The analysis fields are a new feature on the default tab. To start they are shown as Analysis 1, 2 and 3. However, you can change the name of each analysis field to make it more meaningful to your business. For example, I show Sales Type, Sales Rep and Region in Figure 3-2. The user has a chance to enter additional information, such as which sales rep or which region, to provide further analysis for the business. To set up these fields, go to Settings, Configurations and then the Customer fields tab.

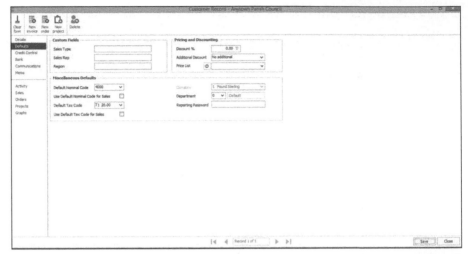

FIGURE 3-2:
Creating customer analysis fields.

Source: Jane Kelly

>> **Credit Control:** You can enter your credit control details here for both customers and suppliers. For example, you can set credit limits so if a customer exceeds those limits, Sage warns you and you can take steps to get the customer's account back under control. You can note details such as credit reviews and settlement discounts to assist you in your credit control.

TIP

I suggest you tick the Terms Agreed box in the bottom left corner of the Credit Control screen. If you don't, every time you open that record, you get an audio and visual prompt saying you haven't agreed to the terms with this account.

>> **Bank:** You can enter bank details on each record. This option is useful if you do a lot of online banking, particularly payment of suppliers.

>> **Communications:** When you open the communications tab, you will notice that a lot more icons appear at the top of your customer/supplier record. For example, you can add, edit or delete entries that you have made in your record. You can also print or send to Excel any notes that you have made on this record. It is also possible to record details of telephone conversations with both customers and suppliers. For example, if you're making a credit control call, you can make notes of promised payments and follow-up dates for callbacks, which creates an event in your Sage Diary. This information also appears in the Task Manager.

TIP

If your business charges on a time basis, you can directly invoice a customer from the Communications tab for time spent on a phone call. See Chapter 6 for more details on this.

» **Memo:** You can attach electronic documents and files for all your customer and supplier records using the Document Manager function. For more details on this function, see Chapter 19. You can also make notes about your customers and suppliers, including details of phone calls.

» **Activity:** I use this screen a lot. It shows a list of every transaction ever made on the selected account. You can see all the invoices and credit notes, payments and receipts. The screen also shows the balance, amounts paid and received, and turnover for the account.

Each line on the Activity list represents a single invoice, credit note, receipt, payment, or payment on account. You can drill down into additional detail by clicking the plus sign (+) shown in the bottom section of the record. You can also view the aged detail of your customer or supplier accounts, shown at the bottom of the Activity tab. Future, Current, 1 Month, 2 Months, 3 Months, and Older buttons show values according to the age of the outstanding amounts.

» **Sales (customer record):** You can view a history of all invoices, credit notes, balances, receipts and payments against this account, helping you identify trends in the customer's monthly transactions.

» **Purchases (supplier record):** You can view a history of all invoices, credit notes, balances, payments and receipts applied to this supplier's account, so you can see trends developing in your transactions with the supplier.

» **Orders:** This screen is available in Sage 50 Professional only. You can see the history of all sales orders applied to this account. Double-click any of the orders to enter the details of the sales order record. You can also create a new sales invoice or a new order from this screen.

» **Projects:** You can view a list of all the projects associated with this customer. You can also create a new project record for the customer by clicking New Project Record (I explain this in more detail in Chapter 13). *Note:* This module is available only in Sage 50 Plus and Sage 50 Professional.

» **Graphs:** Prepare to be wowed with a graphical representation of the history of your month-by-month transactions.

Setting customer and supplier defaults

Whenever you create a customer or supplier record, you enter details such as the credit limit, discounts and terms of payment. If all the same terms apply to *all* your customers or suppliers, you can set up this information only once so it then applies to all customer or supplier records that you create. This option can save you time, particularly at the start when you create lots of records. If terms are different for a few individual customers or suppliers, or if the terms change for some reason, you can override the defaults in individual customer or supplier records at any time.

If all your customers and suppliers are different, don't set up defaults.

If you set up Sage using the Customise your company option (which I explain in Chapter 1), you can ignore this section.

The following steps apply to setting up customer defaults, but you can use the same process for supplier defaults:

1. **Click Settings from the Menu bar, and then click Customer Defaults (or Supplier Defaults).**

   The Customer Defaults (or Supplier Defaults) screen opens, displaying the Record tab. Here you can enter the currency if Foreign Trader is enabled (otherwise, it's greyed out) and edit the value-added tax (VAT) code, nominal code and any discounts applicable.

2. **Click the Statements tab if you want to change the way some of the wording shows on customer statements.**

   For example, when invoices are shown on statements, and the default wording is 'Goods/Services', you can change this to whatever you like – 'Fees charged', for example.

3. **Click the Ageing tab if you want to switch from Period Ageing to Calendar Monthly Ageing.**

   Period ageing sets periods of less than 30 days, 60 days, 90 days, and 120 days or more. For example, if an invoice is dated 15 January 2016, the invoice falls into the current period between 15 January and 13 February (within 30 days) and the 30-days plus period between 14 February and 14 March.

   Calendar monthly ageing means all the month's transactions are classed as outstanding on the first day of the month. For example, if the invoice is dated 15 January 2016, the invoice falls into the current period if an aged report is run between 1 January and 31 January. If the aged report is run between 1 February and 29 February, the invoice falls into Period 1, and so on.

4. **Click the Discount tab if you apply different discount percentages, depending on the value of the invoices.**

   This option applies to customer defaults only, not supplier defaults.

Deleting customer and supplier records

You may want to delete a record if you set up a duplicate account in error.

WARNING

You can delete a record only if there are no transactions on the account and the account balance is zero. If neither condition is met and you try to delete an account, Sage lets you know in no uncertain terms that you can't do it.

If there are no transactions on the duplicate account, you can delete it. If you have unwittingly added transactions to the duplicate account, you can change them using the File Maintenance option, which I describe in Chapter 9. You then need to rename the duplicate account with the words 'Do Not Use!' in the title.

To delete a record, follow these steps:

1. **Open the appropriate customer or supplier ledger and select the account you want to delete.**

2. **Click Delete.**

   When the confirmation message appears, click Yes.

Having a change of view

When you create a customer or supplier record, you can choose a couple of other alternative ways to view your customers or suppliers module, either a process map or a dashboard layout. The default settings within Sage have these options switched off – to look at and activate these screens, you need to do the following:

1. **From the Menu bar, click Tools.**

2. **Select Options.**

3. **Click Yes to the confirmation screen if you have other windows open.**

4. **In the Options menu, select the View tab.**

   When the Options window opens, as in Figure 3-3, uncheck the boxes in the Global settings module. Select the options you'd like to see each time you open a new record.

5. **Click OK.**

The process map option shows a chronological display of all the processes involved with either the customer or supplier module. When you uncheck the Global changes boxes on both customer and supplier defaults, this automatically adds the alternative viewing options to your Navigation bar on the customer and supplier modules.

The dashboard option shows a graphical representation of some key data for both customers and suppliers. For example, it shows the Customer Cash Overview in a pie chart format, as well as your company's Aged Debt in a graphical format.

Creating Your Nominal Records

Nominal records are the main body of an accounting system. They're categorised into a chart of accounts structure, which I explain in Chapter 2.

In this section, I look at how you can amend and customise the nominal codes for your own business. This may involve amending existing nominal codes, creating new ones or even deleting codes that aren't needed. I also discuss how you can search for nominal codes and, when you find what you're looking for, how to explore the details shown within each nominal record.

Exploring your nominal records

To explore your nominal records, click Nominal codes from the Navigation bar to open up the Nominal codes screen. Alternatively, click on Modules from the Menu bar and then click Nominal codes. You can change the way the information is presented on this screen by clicking on the List, Analyser or Graph button at the top right of the screen. Sage automatically defaults to the Nominal list layout, but I have chosen to show the analyser layout in Figure 3-4 as a comparison.

FIGURE 3-4:
Looking at the nominal ledger through the Analyser layout.

Source: Jane Kelly

When using the Analyser layout, the main body of the screen shows the categories of the nominal codes. To see which codes lie within the categories, click the plus sign (+) next to each category. This drills down to the next level and shows the subcategories. You can click the plus sign next to a subcategory to see the actual codes that form part of that subcategory.

Alternatively, you can keep the default settings and use the List layout, which shows all the nominal codes at a glance. Follow these steps to switch back to the List view:

1. **Click the List button at the top right corner of the screen.**

   The screen changes to show a list of all your nominal codes along with a description or name. After you enter your transactions, you also see Debit and Credit columns containing figures next to each nominal code.

2. **Scroll up and down the page to see the numerous codes.**

   The codes start at 0010 and finish at 9999. You may think this is an awful lot of numbers, but the numbering system has gaps.

TIP

The Graph layout shows a pie chart of the nine categories of accounts within the nominal ledger – this option is colourful but not particularly useful. My preferred option is the List layout, which shows the nominal codes in their clearest format.

Renaming existing nominal records

You may want to rename some of your nominal records. For example, Sage helpfully gives you several sales type codes from A to E – but these descriptions are meaningless, so you need to change them to suit your business. For example, Jeanette, the owner of Jingles, wants to change nominal code 4000, currently designated as Sales Type A, to Sale of Greeting Cards.

Follow these steps to rename the nominal records:

1. **Click Nominal codes.**

   The list of nominal codes appears.

2. **Click one of the nominal codes and then click the Edit icon.**

3. **Type the number of the nominal code you want to change in the N/C (nominal code) box and press Enter.**

   In the Jingles example, Jeanette types in 4000.

4. **Place your cursor in the Name box and delete the current name.**

   Replace the name with the name of your new sales type. For Jingles, Jeanette replaces Sales Type A with the name Sale of Greeting Cards.

5. **Click Save and then click Close.**

Adding a new nominal record

When you add a new nominal record, make sure the nominal code you use fits into the correct part of the chart of accounts. Refer to Chapter 2 to see the different ranges of nominal codes that make up the chart of accounts.

If you want to add new codes into your range, you need to decide where you can slot the codes into your existing structure. For example, if you want to add a nominal record with a new nominal code for mobile phones, look at the profit and loss account, because mobile phones are an expense item. Mobile phones aren't a direct product cost, so place them in the Overhead section, close to the telephone costs for the business, around the 7500 range of nominal codes.

In the Jingles example, Jeanette wants to add a new sales nominal record, Sale of Birthday Cakes, with the new nominal code 4040.

Follow these steps to add a new nominal record:

1. **On the Navigation bar, click Nominal codes.**

2. **On the Nominal codes toolbar, click the New icon.**

3. **In the N/C box, type the new nominal code number and then tab to the Name field.**

   For Jingles, Jeanette enters the new nominal code 4040. The words 'new account' pop up next to the nominal code because Sage doesn't recognise the nominal code.

4. **In the Name field, type the name of your new record.**

   For Jingles, Jeanette enters Sale of Birthday Cakes, as in Figure 3-5.

5. **Click Save and close the box.**

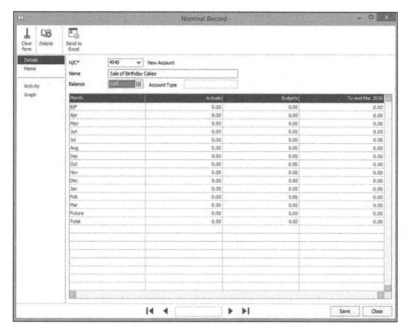

FIGURE 3-5: Adding Sale of Birthday Cakes to Jingles's nominal ledger.

Source: Jane Kelly

After you add a new nominal record, check to verify that your chart of accounts is free of errors. Refer to Chapter 2 for more on how to do this.

Looking for a nominal record

Each nominal record has its own nominal code, but not every nominal code is easy to find. Sage doesn't try to make things difficult, but it does need to slot an awful lot of codes into categories – and some codes fit into categories better than others.

I have memorised a lot of the nominal codes, but as a Sage beginner you may need some tricks to find those elusive codes.

Searching for a record alphabetically

If you know the name but not the number of a record, follow these steps to find the record:

1. **Click Nominal codes.**

The list of nominal codes opens. The codes appear in numerical order.

2. **Click the dark grey Name bar.**

Sage re-sorts the codes in alphabetical order.

3. **Type the first letter of the record you want to find.**

For example, if you want to find the nominal record Telephone, pressing 'T' on the keyboard takes you to the first record beginning with the letter T, which just so happens to be Taxation. The next record is Telephone and Fax with the nominal code of 7550.

To see where a record sits in the overall range, sort the nominal records back into number order by clicking the dark grey N/C (nominal code) heading and scrolling down to the appropriate codes.

TIP

After you sort the records back into number order, if you want to get to a specific number range again, click on one of the nominal codes and then type the first digit of the nominal code you require. Sage takes you to the first code starting with that number.

Finding a record numerically

If you know the approximate nominal code range but not the specific code to use, click on Nominal codes and then click one of the nominal codes on the list. Enter the first numerical digit in Sage. Sage scrolls down the list to the number you specified.

In the Jingles example, Jeanette is looking for a code for mobile phones. She thinks it will be close to the telephone codes, which are usually around the 7500 mark. She types **7** and then scrolls down the list until she finds Telephone and Fax at 7550. A bit further down the list she spots code 7553, called Mobile Charges.

Looking around a nominal record

Sage offers a number of different ways to view the information contained within a nominal record. It also provides some demonstration data. I sometimes find it helpful to explore parts of the system with dummy data already entered.

To view the demonstration data, use the following steps:

1. **From the Menu bar, choose File → Open → Open Demo Data.**

Click Yes to the confirmation window that appears.

2. **Type 'manager' into the Logon field.**

No password exists, so click OK. The 'Stationary and Computer Mart' company opens, which has a lot of dummy data that you can play around with to explore the system.

3. **Click Nominal codes and then click on one of the records (for example, 4000 – Sales North).**

Click the Edit icon.

4. **The nominal record for the nominal code that you have highlighted opens.**

I show the nominal record 4000 – Sales North in Figure 3-6.

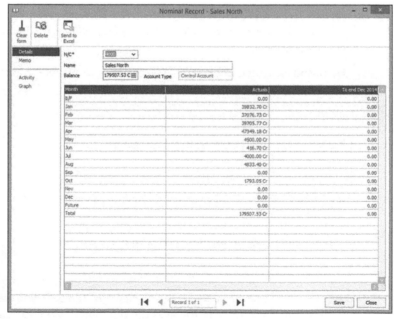

FIGURE 3-6:
Looking at a nominal record with Sage's demonstration data.

Notice that there are three icons across the top of the record, where you can either clear the nominal record that is currently open, delete the nominal record (subject to various conditions, as you find out later in this chapter) or send the nominal record details to Microsoft Excel. There are an additional four options in a navigation bar down the left side of the nominal record. Sage automatically defaults to the Details screen. I discuss the four options as follows:

>> **Details:** This screen shows actual amounts posted to the account on a month-by-month basis and prior-year figures if they're available. You can see a column for budget figures. In the Budget field you can enter figures directly into each month for each nominal record as part of your budget-setting process. These figures then appear on the Budget report (which I tell you about in Chapter 18).

TIP

If you can't see the column for budget figures, change your budgeting method from Advanced to Standard on the Budgeting tab in Company Preferences. You can access this by clicking on Settings from the Menu toolbar and then clicking Company Preferences. For more details on advanced budgets, look at the Sage Help menu by pressing F1.

>> **Memo:** You can make notes that relate to this account. You can also attach electronic documents with the Document Manager (which I talk about in Chapter 19).

>> **Activity:** In this screen you can scroll up and down to see exactly what transactions have been posted using this nominal code. Any credit notes or journals also show here.

Because 4000 is a sales code, you can see exactly which sales invoices have been posted.

>> **Graph:** Using this tab, you can view a graphic format of the account information in lots of pretty colours.

Deleting a nominal code

You can delete nominal codes that you never use to tidy up the list. For example, if you sell only one product, you may want to delete the codes associated with Sales Types B, C, D and E.

To delete a nominal code, follow these steps:

1. **Click Nominal codes from the Navigation bar.**

2. **Click on the Nominal list screen to highlight the code you want to delete and then click the Delete icon at the top right of your screen.**

3. **A confirmation message appears asking whether you want to delete this record. Click Yes; the record will be automatically deleted.**

   Note: You may get an audible bleep, and an information box may appear. This happens when Sage will not allow you to delete a nominal code. For example, Sage will not allow you to delete a nominal code if there are transactions associated with that code.

WARNING

You can delete a nominal record only if no transactions are associated with that code.

TIP

If you are still in the demonstration data, to get back to your own data, simply click File and then Open Company data. You will be asked to put in your login details; once you've done this, you will be back working on your own dataset. To check, make sure your own company details are displayed at the top of the screen, and not Stationery and Computer Mart.

Recording Your Bank Accounts

Sage automatically gives you seven bank accounts, as shown in Figure 3-7. The accounts include an ordinary bank current account and a credit card receipt account. I suggest you review the list of bank accounts and rename them, add new ones and delete those that don't apply to your business. I tell you how to do these tasks in the following sections.

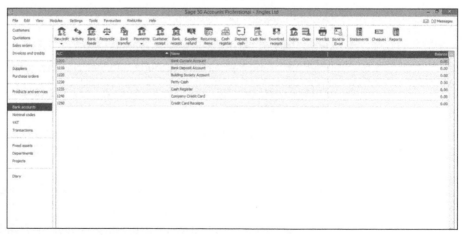

FIGURE 3-7:
The default list of bank accounts that Sage provides.

Source: Jane Kelly

Renaming an existing account

You probably need to rename the bank accounts that Sage gives you to suit your business. For example, you may want to specify the name of the bank or the type of account.

TIP

Don't create a new account if you can simply rename an existing account. Then you don't need to amend your chart of accounts for new nominal codes.

To rename an account, follow these steps:

1. **Click Bank accounts and then highlight the bank account you want to edit in the list of accounts displayed.**

   Click the New/Edit icon and then click Edit.

2. **Your chosen bank record opens.**

   In the Nominal Name field, overtype the new name for your bank account.

3. **Click Save.**

Creating a new account

If you have a lot of bank accounts, you may need to create additional bank account records to accommodate your business needs. The simplest way to create a new bank account is as follows:

1. **From the Bank accounts module, click the New/Edit icon and select New.**

   A blank bank account record opens.

2. **Click the drop-down arrow in the Account Reference box.**

   Sage lists all the existing bank accounts and their nominal codes.

3. **Enter a new nominal code reference for your bank account in the Account Reference field.**

TIP

   Try to keep all the current accounts and deposit accounts between 1200 and 1229 and the credit card accounts between 1240 and 1249. This makes the chart of accounts more presentable.

   I used nominal code 1205 to create a new bank account for Jingles, as shown in Figure 3-8.

4. **Tab down to the Nominal Name field and give your new bank account a name.**

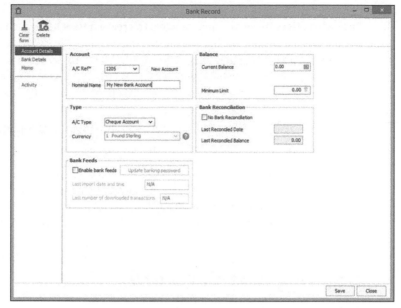

FIGURE 3-8:
Creating a new
bank record
for Jingles.

Source: Jane Kelly

5. **From the Account Type box, use the drop-down arrow to select cash, cheque or credit card account.**

The default setting is cheque account.

6. **Ignore the Balance box.**

Have a look at Chapter 4 for information on opening balances.

7. **If you operate foreign currency accounts, select a currency.**

8. **Tick No bank reconciliation if you don't want to reconcile the bank account.**

REMEMBER

You'll probably choose this option only for the petty cash account. You need to reconcile all accounts, including credit card accounts, to a bank or credit card statement to get a good picture of how your business is doing.

9. **Click the Enable bank feeds option only if you want to automatically download your bank transactions ready to reconcile.**

I strongly recommend that you do, as it is a massive time-saving device. Follow the on-screen bank feed setup instructions and enter your bank details as requested.

10. **Click Save and then close the record.**

Your new bank account appears on the list of bank accounts in the main window.

Sage also offers these alternative ways to create a new bank account:

>> **Set up a new account using the wizard:** Click Bank accounts on the Navigation bar, click the New/Edit icon, and then choose Wizard from the menu options displayed. After the wizard opens, click through each screen and enter the details Sage requests.

>> **Access the Bank accounts window from the Menu bar:** Click Modules and click Bank accounts, and then select the New/Edit icon.

>> **Duplicate an existing account:** From the Bank accounts module, highlight the account you want to duplicate and click the New/Edit icon. Select Duplicate from the list of options given. A duplicate bank record appears. Give the account an appropriate nominal code and name, click Save and off you go.

Deleting a bank record

To keep your bank account list tidy, you can delete any bank records you don't want to use. You can delete a bank account record only if the following conditions apply:

>> The bank account has no transactions associated with it.

>> The balance is zero.

>> The bank account is not a control account.

To delete an account that meets these conditions, highlight the bank account concerned and click Delete. Sage shows an affirmation message. Click Yes to continue or No to return to your original record.

Getting Your Product Records in Order

Planning your nominal codes is important, but planning your product records is just as crucial. The product records that you create eventually become your *product list* – a list of all your stock items. As your business grows, the number of stock items also grows, so you need to design a stock-coding system that's easy to use. You need to be able to identify a product type quickly and easily from a stock list or stock report.

Creating a product record

Sage offers three methods for creating a product record. The simplest method follows these steps:

1. From the Navigation bar, click Products and services.

Click the New icon. A blank product record opens, as shown in Figure 3-9. Notice that there are a couple of icons across the top, which allow you to either clear the product record details showing or delete the product record (assuming certain conditions are met, as you find out later in this chapter). In addition, there is a navigation bar on the left side of the record, which automatically defaults to the Details page of the record. I look at each of the options in the remaining steps.

2. Enter your chosen product code on the Details screen.

Use 30 digits or fewer.

3. Type in a description of the product and fill in as many of the product details as you can.

In the Description field you can enter up to 60 characters.

In the defaults section, you may need to change the default sales nominal code and purchase nominal code. For example, a stock record for birthday cards requires a nominal code for birthday cards.

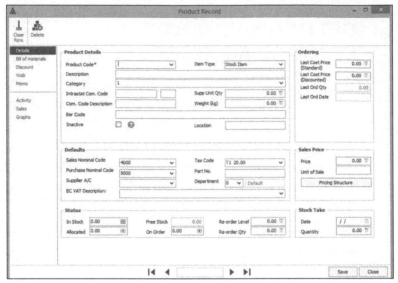

FIGURE 3-9:
Viewing a blank
product record.

Source: Jane Kelly

When you enter your product details, you can choose the following item types:

- **Stock Item:** A regular item of stock with a product code and description. You can give a stock item a project code and issue it to a project.

- **Non-Stock Item:** An item that isn't a usual item of stock, perhaps purchased for use within the business instead of to sell. You can't post non-stock items to a project because they aren't stock and can't be issued.

- **Service Item:** Usually a charge – for example, a labour charge – that can be set up as a product code. You can't post service items to a project because they aren't physical products in stock and can't be issued.

4. **Other than the Details page there are also the following additional pages for you to complete (if required):**

- **Bill of Materials (BOM):** Here, you can create a product from an amalgamation of other products that you have in stock. BOM is a list of products and components required to make up the main product. (See Chapter 12 for more details on this.) This feature is available only in Sage 50 Accounts Plus and Professional.

- **Discount:** This tab lets you give up to five different quantity discounts per product.

- **Web:** Using this tab, you can enter information about your web shop, including images of your product.

- **Memo:** You can attach electronic documents to the product record or enter additional notes about the product.

- **Activity:** Clicking this tab shows the individual transactions created for each product – for example, goods in, goods out, goods transferred or stock adjustments. You can also view the quantity of the item in stock, on order, allocated and available.

- **Sales:** This tab shows the sales value and quantity sold month by month for that product. The Actuals column is driven from actual invoices raised. You can enter budget values and prior-year information for each month. This information lets you produce useful comparison reports for the product.

- **Graphs:** Clicking this tab shows a graphical representation of products sold against budget and the prior year at a glance.

5. **When you've finished entering your product details, click Save.**

   Your first record is saved and the screen goes blank, waiting for your next record.

Sage also offers the following methods to create a product record:

» **Use the wizard:** Click Products and services from the Navigation bar, and then click the Wizard icon. This opens up the Product wizard, where you have several screens of information to complete. Fill in as much detail as you need. Click Next on each screen until you get to the end. Using this wizard can be quite time consuming, which is why I recommend instead using the method that I outline in the preceding steps.

» **Duplicate an existing record:** Highlight a product and then click the Duplicate icon. A duplicate record opens, where you can change the necessary fields. Click Save to save the product record.

Editing a product record

You can edit a product record at any time by double-clicking the product to bring up the Product Record screen. You can then make the necessary changes, click Save and close the screen.

Alternatively, highlight the product record from the list of products and services, and then click the Edit icon. The product record appears for you to edit.

Deleting a product record

You can delete a product record if the record meets the following criteria:

- >> The product record has no transactions on the product activity. You need to remove any history using the Clear Stock option – see Chapter 16 for info on how to do this.
- >> The In Stock, On Order and Allocated balances are all zero.
- >> The product is not a component of a bill of materials.
- >> The product has no outstanding transactions, such as outstanding orders.

To delete a product record, follow these steps:

1. **In the Products and services module, highlight the product you want to delete.**

2. **Click Delete.**

An affirmation message appears. Click Yes.

Entering a project record

Creating a project record gives you a place to hold all the relevant information describing your project. Sage offers a few different ways to create a project record. The simplest way is to follow these steps:

1. **In the Navigation bar, click Projects.**

The project main window opens, showing a list of the existing projects. If this new project is the first project, the screen is blank.

2. **Click the New icon.**

The project record opens. Work through the following options:

- **Details:** Enter your project details, including start dates, completion dates, and contact names and addresses. You must give the project a unique project reference before you save the project. You can link the project directly to a customer by clicking on the A/C Ref field in the Customer Details section and selecting the customer using the drop-down arrow; if the project is internal, leave this section blank.

- **Analysis:** Enter the price quoted for a project on this screen. All the other information falls into the look-but-don't-touch category (with the exception of the Analysis fields) – you can see it, but you can't change it. As you create and post invoices to raise bills to your customer for the project, the billing total is updated. This tab also shows an analysis of the total budget and costs associated with the project.

The Analysis fields can be customised to suit your business and used to analyse your projects. For example, you can call the Analysis 1 field "Project Leader" and the Analysis 2 field "Region" – you could then analyse all the projects run within a certain region or by a particular project leader. To rename the Analysis fields, you need to click on Settings from the main toolbar, followed by Configuration Editor and then the Project costing tab. You can then change the names of the fields and save this information.

- **Budgets:** The Budgets tab records monies allocated to the project.

- **Structure:** The Structure tab is used to maintain a project with several phases. You may have several smaller projects that make up a larger one. You can manage the costs associated with each phase of the project as well as look at the overall costs associated with the whole project.

- **Memo:** Using the Attachments pane, you can add electronic documents or filing references to the project. You can edit the memo pad as you require. See Chapter 19 for more information on Document Manager.

- **Activity:** You can view the transactions posted against the project, such as invoices, costs and product movements.

3. **After you enter the project details, click Save.**

   Your new project appears in the Projects screen.

TIP

When you create a sales order with the product code S3, you have the option to create a project for that order.

Sage also offers the following methods to create a project record:

>> **Summon the Project Record wizard:** Click Projects on the Navigation bar and then click the Wizard icon. The wizard takes you through a step-by-step process to complete the details of your project through a number of different screens – just follow the directions to set up your project record.

>> **Duplicate an existing project:** Highlight a project that you want to duplicate and click the Duplicate icon. A duplicate project record appears on-screen – you can amend the relevant details and save your new project record.

Setting Up Fixed Asset Records

Fixed assets are items usually held in the business for at least 12 months or more. When your business purchases a fixed asset, such as a building, a vehicle or machinery, instead of deducting the whole expense at the time of purchase, you *depreciate* the asset over the extent of its useful life. The charge to your profit and loss account is apportioned over a longer period of time – for example, you may apportion the cost of a car over a four-year period instead of charging the whole cost in the first year.

To keep track of your depreciated items, you need to set up a fixed asset record so Sage knows what items are fixed assets, over what period and at what rate they depreciate.

TIP

Fixed assets are available only if you have purchased either Sage 50 Accounts Plus or Accounts Professional.

To set up a fixed asset record, follow these steps:

1. **Click Fixed Assets from the Navigation bar, or click Modules from the Menu bar, followed by Fixed Assets.**

The main screen is blank. As you start to record your assets, the screen fills up with detail, one line per asset.

2. **Click the New icon.**

A blank asset record appears. Use the Details tab to describe the asset and give it a reference. Enter information as necessary on the Posting tab, as shown in Figure 3-10:

- Select a department, if required.

- Use the Balance Sheet Depreciation N/C drop-down arrow to select the appropriate code. This record requires a balance sheet code, so it starts with 00. For example, Plant and Machinery Depreciation is 0021.

- Use the Profit and Loss Depreciation N/C drop-down arrow to select your code. Then select a profit and loss code. For example, Plant and Machinery Depreciation is 8001.

REMEMBER

  You may feel confused by the two codes for depreciation – one in the balance sheet and one in the profit and loss account – but Sage operates a double-entry bookkeeping system and needs two codes to post your transactions to. Be careful to select the correct codes.

FIGURE 3-10:
Entering
information into
a fixed asset
record.

Source: Jane Kelly

- Select the Depreciation Method, usually straight line or reducing balance. If you're not sure, check with your accountant. After you select the method, you can't change back, except to write off the asset.

- Set the Depreciation Rate. The depreciation rate is the percentage rate that reduces the value of the asset. For example, if you want to depreciate a machine over four years and apply the straight line method, you apportion the value of the asset equally over four years and apply a 25 per cent depreciation charge per year.

- Enter the cost price, net of VAT of the asset.

3. **Enter the current book value of the item you want to depreciate.**

   If the item is brand new, the book value is the same as the cost price. If the item has already been depreciated, the book value is cost price less depreciation. If you decide to use the reducing balance method, the book value is the value used to calculate the depreciation amount. Sage automatically updates the remaining boxes.

4. **Click Save when you're happy with the information you've entered.**

Sage posts depreciation when you run the month-end option. (For more details on running the month-end, go to Chapter 16.)

If you want to delete an asset because you sold it or it was stolen or damaged, follow these steps:

1. **Click Fixed Assets.**

   Highlight the asset you want to delete.

2. **Click Delete.**

   Click Yes to agree to the confirmation message, or click No to return to the previous menu.

Chapter 4

Recording Your Opening Balances

I n this chapter I explain how to transfer the individual account balances from your previous accounting system, whether it's manual or computerised, into Sage 50 Accounts. Effectively, you take the values that make up what your business is worth on the day you swap from your old system and start using Sage. You need to set up your nominal records before you record balances, so check out Chapter 3 if you haven't done that yet.

Opening balances give you a true picture of your business's assets and liabilities to use as a starting point. If you don't enter your opening balances, you don't have accurate information about who owes you money, how much money you owe, or how much money you have in the bank. You won't even be able to reconcile your bank balance. In short, without opening balances, the information in your Sage program isn't worth the paper it's printed on.

WARNING

Entering your opening balances can be a bit tricky, so make sure you're not going to be disturbed too much. After you do this, you can print an opening balance sheet to check you've entered your balances correctly.

Timing Your Switch to Sage

The best time to start with a new system is at the beginning of a financial year. You roll the closing balances from the previous year end forward so they become your opening balances for your new year. Take advice from your accountant if you have one, as everyone's circumstances are different.

TIP

If you can't wait until the new financial year to switch to Sage and you're registered for value-added tax (VAT), at least wait until the start of a new VAT quarter. This way, you avoid having a mixture of transactions in your old and new systems that makes reconciling your data extremely difficult.

Enter your opening balances before you start entering transactions. You can then check your accuracy by proving your opening trial balance matches your closing trial balance from your previous system. Without the clutter of day-to-day transactions, you can check much more easily.

Obtaining Your Opening Balances

Whether you transfer to Sage from a manual or computerised bookkeeping system, the process is still the same. Essentially, you transfer into Sage the balance sheet information that shows the net worth of your business.

An opening *trial balance* is a list of all account balances carried forward from the previous year end. Your previous accounting system is your source for your trial balance. As you zero down your profit and loss items at the end of the financial year, any retained profit and loss items from the previous year now sit in your balance sheet, so an opening trial balance contains only balance sheet codes. An opening trial balance report looks quite short and shows debit and credit entries for all your balance sheet items, with grand totals at the bottom of your Debit and Credit columns.

If you start to use Sage at the beginning of a new financial year, ask your accountant to provide your opening balances.

TIP

If you transfer from a manual bookkeeping system, make sure you balance off all your individual accounts for the previous period. You may find it easier to print off a list of your newly created nominal accounts in Sage and create two columns, one for debit balances and one for credit balances. (To print a nominal list, click Nominal codes from the Navigation bar, which takes you to the Nominal codes screen, and then click the Print List icon at the top right of the screen.) You can then total each column to create an opening trial balance.

The figures contained within a trial balance are simply the accumulated value of items. For example, the Debtors control account is the combined value of all monies owed by customers at that point in time. To establish your opening balances, you need to know the specifics of which customers owe you money and what invoices are outstanding. The same applies to your suppliers: You need to see a full breakdown of who you owe money to. You obtain this information from a variety of sources. Table 4-1 shows the types of report you need from a computerised or manual system.

TABLE 4-1   ## Information Sources for Entering Opening Balances

Category	Computerised System	Manual System
Customers		
For a standard VAT system, record the transaction including VAT. For a VAT cash accounting scheme, record both the net and VAT amounts. If this figure isn't the same as your opening debtors balance, you need to investigate why.	An aged debtors report, showing a breakdown of who owed you money at the start of the year/period.	A list of customers who haven't paid at the year end, including the amount outstanding.
Suppliers		
For a standard VAT scheme, record the transaction including VAT. For a VAT cash accounting scheme, show both the net and VAT amounts. If this figure isn't the same as your opening creditors balance, you need to investigate why.	An aged creditors report, showing a breakdown of who you owed money to at the start of the year/period.	A list of suppliers who you haven't paid at the year end, along with the monies owed.
Bank		
When you start reconciling the first month's bank account, you may see cheques from the prior year clearing through the bank account. You don't need to worry about unpresented cheques and lodgements, because they've already been taken into account in the previous year and are included in the opening balance for your bank account. Simply mark the items on your bank statement as being prior-year entries. Don't post the items again.	A copy of the bank statements showing the balance at the year end and a copy of the bank reconciliation showing a list of any unpresented cheques or outstanding deposits. (Your accountant can help with this.)	A copy of the bank statements showing the balance at the year end and a copy of the bank reconciliation showing a list of any unpresented cheques or outstanding deposits. (Your accountant can help with this.)

(continued)

TABLE 4-1 *(continued)*

Category	Computerised System	Manual System
Products		
	A stocktake list showing the number of items in stock at the start of the year/period.	A stocktake list showing the number of items in stock at the start of the year/period.

Entering Opening Balances Using the Wizard

Sage has developed a wizard to help you magically enter your opening balances with ease. To access the wizard, click Tools and then Opening Balances from the Menu bar. The Opening Balances window opens, as shown in Figure 4-1.

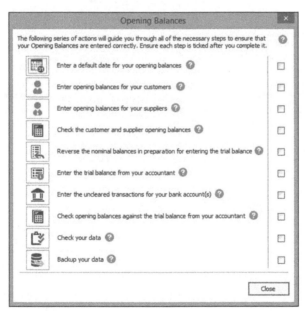

FIGURE 4-1: Entering your opening balances using the wizard.

The opening balances represent the financial position of your business on the day you start entering transactions into Sage. Even a new business has opening balances as the funds used to start up the business need to be accounted for – the owner's money or grant funding, for example.

In this section, I take you through the steps necessary to enter your opening balances using the wizard as your mystical guide. Click the first button on the list of icons shown in Figure 4-1 and you can begin to enter your default date.

After you perform each task, Sage puts a tick in the box next to that task. Go through the list in the given order to ensure maximum accuracy.

Entering your default date

The default date is usually the last day of the previous month, normally the day before the start of your financial year. So, if your financial year starts on 1 April 2016, your default date is 31 March 2016.

When you click the first button, a new window opens, as shown in Figure 4-2, and Sage asks you to enter your default date. If you're not sure of the default date, check with your accountant. Click Save once you're happy that the date is correct.

WARNING

When you enter your date, you use the last date of the prior period/year. For example, I used 31 March 2016. The system flags up a warning message saying the date is outside the financial period. Click Yes to continue.

FIGURE 4-2:
Entering your
default date.

Entering customer and supplier balances

Despite the fact that customers owe you money and you owe money to suppliers, the process for entering opening balances for both is pretty much the same, so I talk about them together in this section.

Using your aged debtors report or debtor list for customers and your aged creditors report or creditor/supplier list for suppliers, access each individual account and enter each opening balance, recording each invoice individually.

TIP

Enter your opening balances as separate invoices, as this helps with ageing the debts and affects any future reports that you run. You definitely need to enter transactions separately if you choose to use VAT cash accounting or the U.K. flat VAT rate (cash-based).

Whether you click the customer icon or the supplier icon, Sage presents very similar screens. Figure 4-3 shows the entry screen for entering customer opening balances.

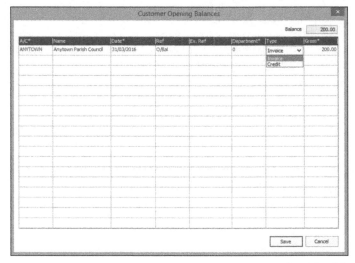

FIGURE 4-3:
Entering customer opening balances.

Source: Jane Kelly

Use the drop-down arrow to select the customer for whom you have an opening balance to record and click OK. The screen displays the full account name, and Sage automatically enters the default date. The reference O/Bal is used to identify the transaction, but you may want to edit this reference field and type in the actual invoice number – that way, it appears on any future statements that you send out, rather than the word O/Bal. You have space to enter an additional reference in the Ex. Ref column, perhaps an order number. You can also enter a department reference.

Notice that the word 'Invoice' already appears in the Type column. If you have credit notes to enter, use the drop-down arrow at the side of the Type column and select Credit instead.

Then you need to enter the gross value of the invoice. When you're happy with the details on the screen, click Save. You now see a tick against the Customer and Supplier Opening Balances line.

Note: If you're using VAT cash accounting, the Customer Opening Balances screen looks slightly different, in so much as you will be asked to enter the net invoice figure, followed by the tax code and then the VAT amount.

REMEMBER

You need to record customer balances only if you keep customer records. If you run a shop that collects all receipts at the till and doesn't send out invoices, you don't need to keep customer records. If you send invoices to your customers, keep records for each customer and record how much each customer owes you at the start of your new accounting period with Sage.

If you used wizards to create your customer and supplier records, you've already entered your opening balances because the wizards ask for them.

Checking the customer and supplier opening balances

When you click this option, Sage opens up a Criteria Value window. If you click OK, you see a preview of your aged debtor, aged creditor and trial balance reports. Check the system-generated reports with the information that you're using to enter your opening balances. They should be the same; if not, recheck and amend all your entries until they are correct.

Reversing the nominal balances in preparation for entering the trial balance

Wow, what a mouthful! If you struggle to understand what this means, don't worry – it's an automatic process, and Sage does all the hard work for you. In a nutshell, after you enter the balances for your customers and suppliers, Sage enters values into the nominal account for both debtors and creditors. When you start entering the information from the opening trial balance in the next step, you duplicate entries for debtors and creditors, but thankfully Sage intercepts at this point and reverses out the duplicated entries.

All you need to do is click the icon next to Reverse the Opening Balances. Sage asks if you want to make a backup before proceeding. (I say yes, because it's always a good idea to make a backup.) Then a new screen opens called Opening Balances Reversals, as shown in Figure 4-4.

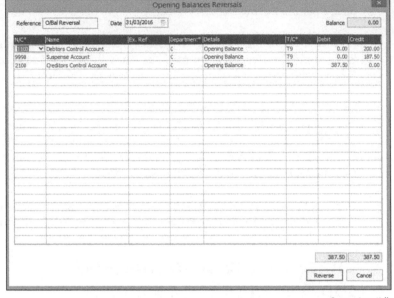

Source: Jane Kelly

FIGURE 4-4:
Reversing the nominal balances in preparation for the opening trial balance.

Sage has already completed the journals for you, but you can check them before clicking Reverse in the bottom right corner. If you're not happy, you can click Cancel, and Sage returns to the opening balances wizard.

When you click Reverse, Sage brings up a warning message saying that the date is prior year. Click Yes because you're entering a prior-year date. The screen then returns to the Wizard list.

It may look as if Sage hasn't actually done anything, but in reality it has. You can check on the Financials page to see evidence that Sage has posted reversing journals.

Entering the trial balance from your accountant

You may already have an opening trial balance from your accountant; if not, I recommend you ask for one. You need an opening trial balance if you traded in the previous year and you're moving your accounts from your old system to Sage.

If you're a business start-up and have no previous accounts records, you may simply want to enter the odd invoice or transaction as an opening balance. You can do this manually, as I explain in the 'Manually recording opening balances' section later in this chapter.

Click the icon next to Enter the trial balance from your accountant and the Trial Balance Entry window opens, as shown in Figure 4-5.

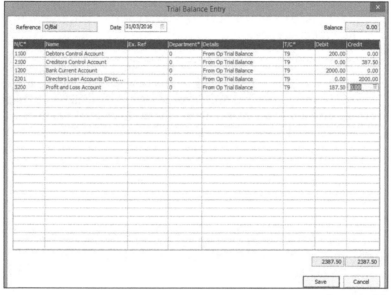

N/C*	Name	Ex. Ref	Department*	Details	T/C*	Debit	Credit
1100	Debtors Control Account		0	From Op Trial Balance	T9	200.00	0.00
2100	Creditors Control Account		0	From Op Trial Balance	T9	0.00	387.50
1200	Bank Current Account		0	From Op Trial Balance	T9	2000.00	0.00
2301	Directors Loan Accounts (Direc...		0	From Op Trial Balance	T9	0.00	2000.00
3200	Profit and Loss Account		0	From Op Trial Balance	T9	187.50	0.00

Source: Jane Kelly

FIGURE 4-5: Entering your opening trial balance from your accountant.

Using your opening trial balance, enter each item systematically into the Trial Balance Entry window.

TIP

If you use the Sage default set of nominal codes, use common sense and match the items from your opening trial balance to those of Sage. For example, Accruals in Sage has the nominal code 2109. Take the balance for Accruals from your opening trial balance and use nominal code 2109.

If you use your own existing nominal codes, enter them here. If you use your own codes, you need to choose to use a customised chart of accounts when you set up Sage – refer to Chapter 1 for company setup information.

After you enter your opening trial balance, check that the Debits and Credits columns on both your Sage trial balance and your opening trial balance match. Check each individual entry and ensure each account is correctly entered. When you're satisfied, click Save.

You return to the Opening Balance Wizard list. A tick should now show in each completed step.

Entering the uncleared transactions for your bank account

This is where you enter items that haven't cleared your bank account. This includes cheques that you wrote before the previous year end but haven't cleared the bank account yet, and bank receipts that you paid into the bank but that haven't cleared yet.

Sage lets you enter individual transactions that haven't cleared the bank account. When you run your first bank reconciliation, each of these individual payments or receipts is listed and available for selection. This allows you to perform a full bank reconciliation when you receive your next bank statement. Uncleared items entered in this way are marked as unreconciled and don't affect the opening bank balance. It is assumed that they were already included in the trial balance.

Click the icon next to Enter the uncleared transactions for your bank account(s) and the screen shown in Figure 4-6 opens.

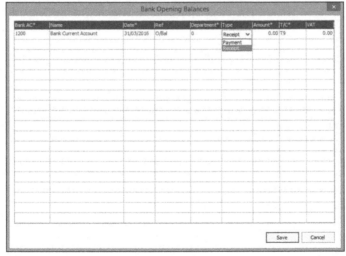

Source: Jane Kelly

FIGURE 4-6: Entering uncleared bank transactions.

Using the drop-down arrow, select the appropriate bank account. Sage prefills some of the columns, but you must select the type of transaction, such as Receipt or Payment. You then enter the amount and the appropriate VAT code. The amount is the Net amount if you select VAT code T1.

When you're happy with the details, click Save.

TIP

As an additional prompt, I enter the cheque number or paying-in slip reference in the reference field (next to where it says O/Bal) – this extra detail makes reconciling the bank account a lot easier.

Checking opening balances against the trial balance from your accountant

When you click on the icon next to the line Check opening balances against the trial balance from your accountant, Sage opens up the Criteria for Period Trial Balance window. Using the drop-down arrows, select the brought forward date for your trial balance report, as shown in Figure 4-7.

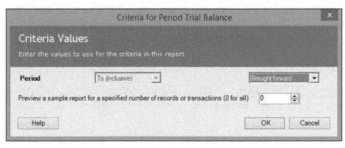

FIGURE 4-7:
Selecting the opening trial balance report.

Click OK, and your opening trial balance appears on the screen. You can print Sage's opening trial balance and double-check it against your accountant's opening trial balance.

Checking your data

Sage gives you an option to check your data to ensure everything is okay. I do this just for peace of mind.

Click the icon next to Check your data. Sage automatically runs the File Maintenance process and informs you of any errors or warnings associated with your data.

Backing up your data

Sage asks you to back up your data. When you click on the icon, Sage asks if you want to check your data. If you click No, Sage takes you straight to the backup window. Choose an appropriate filename, perhaps something referring to the backup after posting opening balances, and click OK.

That's it! You've now completed all the steps necessary to enter your opening balances. You should now have a tick in all the boxes on the screen, and you can now close the Opening Balances window.

Manually Entering Information

As with most things in life, there's always more than one way to do things. I'm not a great fan of using wizards to enter records and data, as I find them rather cumbersome and slow to use, but many people find wizards incredibly useful. The Opening Balances wizard is much more useful than most wizards, however, and I believe it guides you correctly and smoothly through the whole process, letting you check details as you go along. The Opening Balances wizard also gives you a visual aid of your progress, as you can see at a glance which items you have already ticked off the list.

If you still don't want to use a wizard, you can enter information manually, as I explain in the following sections.

Manually recording opening balances

If you want to manually enter the opening balances in the old-fashioned way, here's how to do so. Depending on whether you want to enter balances for customers or suppliers, you start from different places:

>> **Customers:** From the Navigation bar, click Customers, highlight the correct customer account, and click the Edit icon.

>> **Suppliers:** From the Navigation bar, click Suppliers, highlight the correct supplier record, and click the Edit icon.

Then follow this process:

1. **Check you've selected the correct account and then click the OB (Opening Balance) button to the right of the Balance box.**

   The Opening Balance Setup window appears, as shown in Figure 4-8.

2. **Click the Reference field and type 'opening balance'.**

   It may be useful to enter the invoice number here as well, as that information will be shown on any future statements sent to customers.

FIGURE 4-8:
The Opening
Balance Setup
window.

Source: Jane Kelly

3. **Tab to the Date field and enter the original date of the invoice or credit note.**

   Entering the original invoice date ensures the invoices are allocated to the correct period when printing aged debtors or creditors reports.

4. **Tab to the Type field and select Invoice or Credit.**

5. **Enter the invoice or credit amount in the Gross field.**

   Record the gross amount including VAT if you use standard VAT accounting. Record the net amount and VAT separately if you use the VAT cash accounting scheme.

6. **Press Enter to move to the next line if you have more transactions to enter for that customer or supplier, and then repeat Steps 2–6.**

   The system warns you that the date you've used is outside the financial year. Click Yes to continue.

7. **Click Save to accept the details you entered; click Cancel if you aren't happy with the accuracy of your entries and want to return to the main customer record without saving.**

8. **Check your customer balance agrees with your aged debtors or customer list for customers and with your aged creditors or supplier list for suppliers.**

Manually recording opening bank balances

You need to record the opening balance for each bank account associated with your business. Use the following steps to enter opening balances for each bank account:

1. **From the Navigation bar, click Bank accounts, highlight the bank account you want to enter an opening balance for, and click the New/Edit icon.**

   Select the Edit option from the drop-down list that appears.

2. **The bank record opens; click the OB button next to the Current Balance box.**

The Opening Balance Setup window opens. The reference automatically defaults to O/Bal (Opening Balance), which is fine – leave it as it is.

3. **Enter the date.**

Enter the prior year's end date. For example, if you start with Sage on 1 April 2016, the date should be 31 March 2016 to ensure Sage posts this as an opening balance. The closing balance as at 31 March 2016 is the same as the opening balance as at 1 April 2016.

4. **Enter the account balance.**

If the account is in the black, enter the account balance in the Receipt box. If the account is overdrawn, put the amount in the Payment box.

5. **Click Save when you're happy that the opening balance figure is correct.**

TIP

You may have uncleared payments or receipts already included in your bank balance shown on the opening trial balance. The best way to deal with uncleared payments is to obtain a copy of your bank reconciliation statement at the year end and identify the items shown as unpresented cheques or outstanding paid-in items. After your bank statement arrives, mark these items on your statement as being pre–year end transactions. When you come to reconcile your bank account in Sage, you can ignore these items as they're already included in your opening balances.

Manually recording nominal opening balances

If you're manually entering your opening balances, you've probably already entered the debtors control account, the creditors control account and the opening bank balances, so you don't want to enter them again.

WARNING

When you enter the individual opening balances on to each customer record, Sage does some double-entry bookkeeping in the background, crediting the sales account and debiting the debtors control account. When you come to enter the remaining nominal account balances from your trial balance, don't post the debtors control account total; otherwise, you're double-counting. If you do post the debtors control account balance in error, you need to reverse the posting by using a nominal journal. Turn to Chapter 16 for information on journals.

REMEMBER

If you use the Opening Balance wizard, Sage does the reversing journals automatically for you, so you don't need to worry about double-counting anything.

Working in a methodical manner, using your opening trial balance, enter all the remaining balances, such as fixed assets, stock, loans and so on, using the following steps:

1. **From the Navigation bar, click Nominal codes and then click the New icon.**

2. **A blank nominal record appears; enter the nominal code.**

   If you use the Sage default set of nominal codes, use common sense and match the items from your opening trial balance to those of Sage. For example, Accruals in Sage has the nominal code 2109. Take the balance for Accruals from your opening trial balance and use nominal code 2109.

   If you use your own existing nominal codes, enter them here. If you use your own codes, you need to use a customised chart of accounts when you set up Sage – refer to Chapter 1 for company setup information.

3. **Click the OB button next to the Balance box.**

   The Opening Balance Setup window appears.

4. **Keep the reference as O/Bal (opening balance), tab along to the Date field and then enter the closing date of the prior period.**

5. **Tab to the Debit or Credit column and enter a debit or credit figure from the opening trial balance.**

6. **Click Save.**

WARNING

You must use the prior year-end date as your opening balance date so the trial balance you bring forward is correct. If you inadvertently enter 1 April as your date, the figure you enter drops into the current year and not into the brought-forward category. To rectify this, enter a nominal journal to reverse the previous journal that Sage automatically posted for you. (See Chapter 16 for help with journals.) If you want to view the automatic journal that Sage has posted, click Transactions from the Navigation bar.

Putting in opening balances for products

You need to add opening balances for products if you want to track stock items. Make sure you create product records for all the items of stock that you want to put an opening balance to before you try to enter opening product balances. (Refer to Chapter 3 for information on creating records.)

I use Jingles, a fictional greeting card company, in the following steps. Jeanette, the owner, created a record with the product code Card–HB for birthday cards. Her stocktake at the year end showed 1,000 cards in stock.

1. **From the Navigation bar, click Products and services; highlight the product you want to enter an opening balance for, and then click the Edit icon.**

   For Jingles, Jeanette highlights Card-HB. The product record opens.

2. **Click the OB button next to the In Stock button (at the bottom left corner of the record).**

   The Opening Product Setup window opens.

3. **Keep the reference as O/Bal and enter the date as the prior year end.**

4. **Enter a quantity and cost price for the item.**

   In the Jingles example, Jeanette enters 1,000 as the quantity and 50p as a cost price, as shown in Figure 4-9.

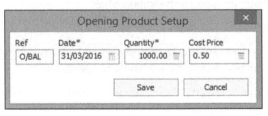

FIGURE 4-9: Entering product opening balances.

Source: Jane Kelly

5. **If you're happy with the details, click Save.**

   If you're not happy, click Cancel to return to the product record and start again from Step 2.

   After you click Save, Sage posts an Adjustment In (AI) transaction to the product record, which you can see in the Activity tab. To view activity on an item, from the main screen, click the stock item you want to view and double-click the product to take you into the record. From the Navigation bar on the left of the record, click Activity to see the adjustment posting. Alternatively, you can highlight the product item and click the Activity icon to access the same information.

REMEMBER

The product opening figures don't automatically update a stock value into your nominal ledger. Opening stock is one of the figures you enter as part of your nominal ledger opening balances, as I explain in the section 'Manually recording nominal opening balances', earlier in this chapter.

Checking Your Opening Balances

If you enter your opening balances manually, you need to make sure the figures are correct and agree with the opening trial balance you used to enter those figures. The best way to do this is to print your own opening trial balance from Sage and compare it with the document you've been working with. If you find discrepancies, go back and fix them.

Printing an opening trial balance

Follow these instructions to run an opening trial balance:

1. **From the Navigation bar, click Nominal codes and then click the Trial Balance icon.**

2. **Select Preview and then Run in the Print Output box.**

3. **Change the date in the Criteria Values box to Brought Forward, using the drop-down arrow.**

4. **Click OK.**

   This previews the opening trial balance.

5. **Click the Print icon to print the trial balance and check your report.**

Look for the following information on the report:

» You should check to see whether there is a balance in the *suspense account* (the temporary account where you put problematic transactions until you determine where they properly belong). If the balance is zero, then it won't appear on the trial balance. If a balance does appear in the suspense account, then you must investigate further.

» Verify that the totals on your new trial balance are the same as the totals on the trial balance from your previous system.

If you have problems with either of these balances, see the next section.

Dealing with errors

If the suspense account doesn't have a zero balance, check you haven't entered the debtors or creditors control account twice. If you've entered something twice, turn to Chapter 16, where I tell you how to reverse the duplicated item using a nominal journal.

If your total balance doesn't match the total of your opening trial balance, make sure you entered an opening balance for each nominal code and you haven't missed anything by mistake.

After you enter all of your opening balances and your opening trial balance matches that of your previous system, you're ready to begin entering your transactions.

2
Looking into Day-to-Day Functions

Chapter 5

Processing Your Customer Paperwork

I n this chapter I show you how to process the sales invoices for your company. If you want to process invoices created manually or from another system, such as Microsoft Word, this is the chapter for you. Alternatively, if you prefer to produce your sales invoices directly from Sage, check out Chapter 6.

Posting Batch Entry Invoices

Don't you just groan when you see a huge pile of invoices that you need to enter? Sage can help you speed your way through those invoices by letting you post batches of invoices. In other words, you can enter several invoices on the same screen and post them all at the same time as a batch on to the system – *post* simply means enter information into an account.

You can use this method to record sales invoices raised from a system other than Sage. For example, you can issue invoices with Microsoft Word and then enter the invoices on to Sage by using batch entry.

TIP

You can enter any number of invoices in one sitting. For example, if you have 20 invoices to process for the day, you can enter them all on to one screen and then check the total of the batch to ensure accuracy. Larger companies often process large quantities of invoices in a number of smaller batches, making processing a much more manageable task.

You can enter one invoice per line on your Batch Entry screen, but if you have an invoice where the value needs to be split into two different nominal codes, you need to use two lines for that one invoice.

When you have a whole batch of invoices in front of you, follow these steps:

1. **Click Customer and then click the Batch Invoice icon.**

   The Batch Customer Invoices screen appears.

2. **Click the A/C (Account) field and use the drop-down arrow to select the correct customer account for the invoice.**

   You can also start typing the known account name, and Sage presents you with a list of alternatives where you can select the correct account.

3. **Enter the invoice date.**

WARNING

   Sage automatically enters the system date, which is usually the current day's date. Make sure you change this date to the one on the invoice.

4. **Enter the invoice number in the Ref (Reference) field.**

   Every invoice needs a unique number derived from a sequential system.

5. **Add any additional references in the Ex.Ref field.**

   You can choose to leave this field blank or enter order numbers or other references.

6. **Change the nominal code, if necessary, in the N/C (Nominal Code) field.**

   This field automatically defaults to 4000, unless you changed the nominal default code on the Default tab of your customer record.

7. **Click the department for your invoice.**

   You can leave this field blank if you don't have any departments set up. If, on the other hand, you want to be able to analyse information from different offices or divisions within the company, setting up departments is the way to go. To set up departments, from the Navigation bar click Departments. Click the department number and then click the Edit icon. This opens up the Department Record window, where you enter the department details. Click Save.

8. **If you use projects, click the drop-down Project Ref arrow (on the Batch Customer Invoices screen) to select the appropriate project.**

You can leave this field blank if you don't use projects. *Note:* Projects are available only if you have Sage 50 Accounts Plus or Professional.

9. **Describe what the invoice is for in the Details field.**

10. **Enter the amount net of VAT in the Net field.**

11. **Choose the tax code applicable for this invoice in the T/C (Tax Code) field.**

Some common VAT codes include the following:

- T0: Zero-rated transactions

- T1: Standard rate (currently set at 20 per cent)

- T2: Exempt transactions

- T4: Sale of goods to VAT-registered customers within the European Community (EC)

- T5: Lower VAT rate (currently set at 5 per cent)

- T7: Zero-rated purchases of goods from suppliers in the EC

- T8: Standard-rated purchases from suppliers in the EC

- T9: Transactions not involving VAT, for example journal entries

- T20: Sales and purchases of reverse charges

- T22: Sales of services to VAT-registered customers in the EC

- T23: Zero-rated purchases of services from suppliers in the EC

- T24: Standard-rated purchases of services from suppliers in the EC

- T25: Flat rate accounting scheme, purchase and sale of individual capital items greater than £2000

The system updates the VAT field according to the tax code you choose.

WARNING

Make sure the VAT Sage calculates is the same as the amount on the invoice. Sometimes Sage rounds up the VAT, and you may find you have a penny differ-ence. If this happens, overwrite the VAT amount in Sage so the amounts match.

12. **Perform a quick check of the total value of the invoices you're about to post.**

To check the value:

- Add up the gross value of the pile of invoices you entered.

- Check this total against the total on your Batch Entry screen in the top right corner of your Sage screen.

- If the totals are different, check each line on your Batch Entry screen against the invoices.

13. **Click Save when the totals in Step 12 are the same.**

TIP

To speed up the entry of invoices, you can use the function keys. To see how the F6, F7 and F8 keys can help you, have a quick look at Chapter 22. However, in the latest edition of Sage 50, Sage has helpfully included new icons at the top of the Batch Customer Invoices screen to allow you to insert or delete rows, as well as additional icons for copying rows. This eliminates the need to use the function keys, but they are still there if you prefer that method. See Figure 5-1.

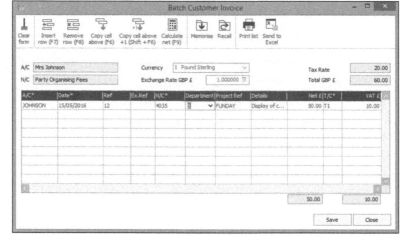

FIGURE 5-1:
The Batch
Customer Invoice
screen, showing
the new icons for
adding and
deleting rows.

Source: Jane Kelly

Creating Credit Notes

A *credit note* is the opposite of an invoice. Instead of charging the customer, as you do with an invoice, you refund money to a customer through a credit note. Posting a credit note reverses or cancels an invoice you entered previously.

You use credit notes for a number of different reasons. For example, you may need to cancel an invoice because you sent the wrong product or the customer returned the goods.

TIP

To ensure you raise the credit note correctly, you must identify which invoice you want to correct. You need to know the invoice number, the date the invoice was raised, and the nominal code the invoice was posted to. It's important to use the same nominal code on your credit note as on your invoice. This way, the double-entry bookkeeping posts the entries in the correct nominal codes, and you don't find odd balances in your accounts.

You can produce credit notes from the Invoicing module that I describe in Chapter 6. If you're not invoicing directly from Sage, you must use the batch-entry method for processing them, which is what I describe here.

To enter a credit note, follow these steps:

1. **Click Customer and then the Batch Credit icon.**

   Note the font colour changes from black to red. This feature is useful, as the Credit Note screen looks identical to the Invoice screen. You won't be the first person to merrily continue entering credit notes rather than invoices.

2. **Select the account you want to enter the credit note against.**

3. **Change the date in the Date field if necessary.**

   Unless today's date is acceptable, remember to use your desired date for raising the credit note.

4. **Put the credit number in the Credit No field.**

   Use a unique sequential numbering system for your credit notes. Some people prefer to have a separate numbering system for credit notes, but others just use the next available invoice number. The method you choose doesn't matter, as long as you're consistent.

5. **Enter any additional references in the Ex.Ref field.**

   This step isn't necessary if you don't have any further references.

6. **Make sure the nominal code (N/C) is the same as the invoice you're trying to reverse.**

7. **Select the department the original invoice was posted to.**

8. **Select the project the original invoice was posted to in the Project Ref field.**

   This step isn't necessary if you're not using projects.

9. **Use the Details field to record the specifics of the credit note.**

   Type something like 'Credit note against Invoice No. 123'. If possible, add a description to explain why the credit is necessary – the goods were faulty, for example.

10. **Enter the Net, Tax Code and VAT.**

    If you're completely refunding the invoice, these three values are the same as on the original invoice. Otherwise, you need to apportion the net amount and allow the VAT to recalculate.

11. Click Save when you're happy with the information you've entered.

Sage posts the credit note: It debits the sales account and credits the debtor's control account.

You can check to see whether the credit has been posted properly by viewing the Activity screen for the nominal code you used – see Figure 5-2 for an example. You can see the original invoice being posted to the sales nominal code as a credit and then the credit note showing the debit in the nominal code at a later date. If you've written a description in the Details field linking the credit note to the invoice, it comes in useful here.

FIGURE 5-2:
A credit note and invoice on the Activity screen for nominal code 4020.

Source: Jane Kelly

Registering Payments from Your Customers

Ideally, when a customer sends you a cheque, you also receive a *remittance advice slip*. This slip identifies which invoices the customer is paying with the cheque sent in. You then pay the cheque into the bank, using a *paying-in slip*, which is kept for your accounting records.

To match the cheque to the correct invoice, follow this procedure:

1. From the Navigation bar, click Customers and then click the Customer receipt icon.

2. **Select the account you want to post the receipt against by using the drop-down arrow.**

As soon as you open an account, Sage displays all outstanding items for that customer on the main body of the screen. The first column shows the transaction number and the second column displays the transaction type: *SI* indicates a sales invoice, and *SC* indicates a sales credit.

The top part of the Customer Receipt screen is split into three sections. The first column identifies the bank account, the second column shows the customer details and the third column shows the receipt details.

Figure 5-3 shows a list of two outstanding invoices and a credit note on the Balloon Madness account – a Jingles Card Shop customer.

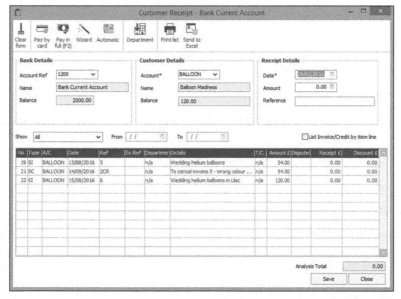

Source: Jane Kelly

FIGURE 5-3:
Outstanding items on a customer's account.

3. **Enter the date the money was received in the Receipt Details column.**

If you're recording a cheque paid into the bank, type the date from the paying-in slip.

4. **Tab past the Amount field without entering an amount.**

5. **Type BACS (Bankers' Automated Clearing Services) in the Reference field if the customer pays the invoice automatically, or type the paying-in slip reference if the customer pays by cheque.**

6. **To allocate a receipt against a specific invoice, click the receipt column on the line of the invoice that you want to allocate the receipt against.**

7. **Click the Pay in Full icon at the top left of the screen.**

   The top right box (the Amount field you ignored in Step 4) now shows the amount of the invoice paid. In the Jingles example in Figure 5-4, the amount shows £120, which is the total of invoice 6.

   Note: If the customer is paying by card, then you can click the Pay by Card icon, but you need to have set up your Sage Pay credentials in Company Preferences in order to be able to use this functionality.

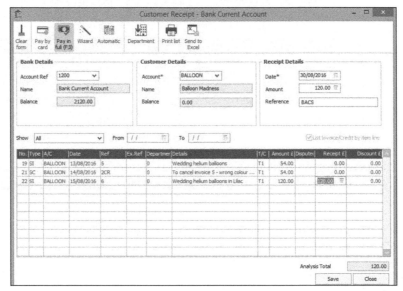

FIGURE 5-4: A customer receipt after clicking the Pay in Full button.

8. **Click Save at the lower right of the screen if you're happy that the receipt amount is correct.**

   If things aren't right, click Close, or click the Clear form icon. A confirmation button appears. Click Yes to clear your data, ready to start again.

   After you click Save, the screen returns to the original Customer Receipt screen ready for your next customer receipt.

9. **Click Close to finish after you enter all your receipts.**

You need to enter and save each receipt individually.

REMEMBER

If you want to see what's happened in your Customer account, click the Activity tab. Figure 5-5 shows the Activity tab for Jingles's customer Balloon Madness. The sales receipt shows on the account. However, two unallocated items still remain on this account – these are the items with asterisks against them. In the next section, I show you how to allocate credit notes to invoices rather than payments to invoices.

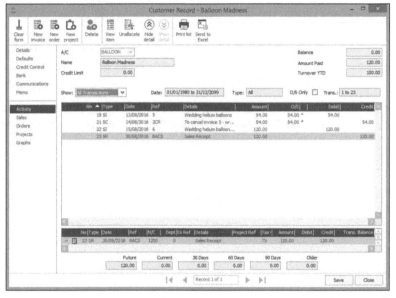

Source: Jane Kelly

FIGURE 5-5:
The Activity tab
for Balloon
Madness.

Giving credit where due – allocating credit notes

Allocating means matching a specific invoice to a specific payment or credit note. As well as knowing how to allocate a payment specifically to an invoice, you also need to know how to allocate a credit note against an invoice. Because a credit note is usually raised to cancel the whole or part of an invoice, it stands to reason that the two are matched off against one another.

In Figure 5-5, two of the entries have an asterisk against them. The asterisk means the item is unallocated or unmatched. The two unallocated items are sales invoice 5 and credit note 2CR. You can tell they should be allocated against each other because the description on the credit note refers to invoice 5.

The steps you follow to allocate a credit note are almost identical to allocating a customer receipt:

1. **From the Navigation bar, click Customers and then click the Customer Receipt icon.**

2. **Select the customer account you need to allocate the credit note to.**

3. **Put the date of the credit note in the Date field.**

   In the example, the date is 14 August 2016.

4. **Tab past the Amount field and the Reference field, down to the Credit Note line. With the cursor sitting in the Receipt column on the Credit Note line, click Pay in Full.**

   Figure 5-6 shows the Balloon Madness account with a –£54 balance in the Analysis Total field in the bottom right corner. This indicates the credit note value is ready to allocate against the invoice.

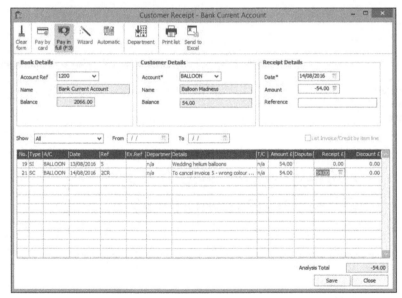

Source: Jane Kelly

FIGURE 5-6: Allocating a credit note.

5. **Click the Receipt column on the line that has the invoice you want to allocate against. Then either click Pay in Full or, if the credit note is less than the value of the invoice, manually enter the value of the credit note you're allocating.**

   The Analysis Total now reduces to zero.

6. Click Save if you're happy that you've allocated the correct amount against the invoice.

The Customer Activity tab for Balloon Madness now shows a zero balance outstanding, as all invoices have either been allocated against a credit note or been paid. A small letter *p* against a balance on an account means that the account is part paid or part allocated.

Recording payments on account

You may receive payment from a customer that you can't match to a specific invoice. For example, a customer may inadvertently pay an invoice twice or forget to include the remittance advice slip so you're not sure which invoice to allocate the payment to.

You can still enter the receipt on to your customer account, but you may not be able to allocate it against a specific invoice.

To enter the receipt, follow these steps:

1. From the Navigation bar, select Customers and then click the Customer Receipt icon.

Select the customer account.

2. Enter the date of the receipt in the Date field.

3. Enter the amount received in the Amount field.

4. Note in the Reference field why the payment isn't allocated against an invoice.

For example, if you think the customer has duplicated a payment, type 'duplication'.

5. Click Save.

6. Click Yes after you see the message saying there's an unallocated balance and asking if you want to post this payment on account.

The Customer Activity screen shows a payment on account as transaction type SA. In the event of a customer overpaying, you may find the account now has a negative balance. To rectify this, you can send the customer a cheque or leave the balance on account and wait until you start raising more invoices to net this off against.

Deleting Invoices and Credit Notes

The traditional accounting method for reversing an invoice is to create a credit note for the same amount. However, Sage has made it even easier to sort out such problems: You simply delete the invoice. That way, you don't have to raise the credit note or allocate it to the invoice. You maintain an audit trail, as any deleted items still show and are highlighted in red, so your accountant can always see what you've been up to.

Clicking on Transactions from the Navigation bar lets you look at the details of any transaction and edit or delete the transaction. See Chapter 9 for details on deleting transactions.

Chapter 6

Invoicing Your Customers

You can generate invoices directly from your Sage accounting software, which means you can streamline your paperwork process by printing invoices quickly – and even directly from sales orders if you use Sage Accounts Professional. You end up with more time to make more money for your business – or more time to take a break from making money for your business.

REMEMBER

Sage is an integrated system, so when you produce a sales invoice, the system automatically updates the nominal ledger and the customer account, along with products and projects if you use those options.

Deciding on an Invoice Type

Depending on the type of business you run, you probably issue mainly one of two types of invoice:

>> **Product invoices:** Used for businesses that sell physical items – cards, widgets, and so on. A manufacturing company issues product invoices, using product codes.

>> **Service invoices:** Used for businesses that don't sell tangible products but provide a service to their clients.

A business that sells physical products may need to generate a service invoice occasionally. For example, Manufacturers of Widgets might service some of the products they manufacture, and the engineer's time is charged using a service invoice. However, a business that provides services rarely needs to send a product invoice. For example, a consultant charges for the time spent providing a service but usually doesn't need to issue product invoices.

TIP

It is possible to set up a product record and categorise it as a nonstock item. Technically that product could be a service. For example, Jeanette of Jingles has set up a nonstock item for the services of a magician for her children's parties. When she sends out the invoices for the children's parties, she can create a product invoice to include all the party items such as party poppers and party plates, which are true stock items, but she can also select the nonstock item for a magician and include this within her product invoice.

Creating Invoices

You create product and service invoices in much the same way, so I combine the two methods in this section and simply highlight the differences between the two as I go along.

WARNING

Before you start your product invoices, make sure you set up your product records, which I explain in Chapter 3.

To create your invoice, from the Navigation bar, click Invoices and credits. Click the New Invoice icon and the Product Invoice screen comes up, as shown in Figure 6-1. The next sections cover the four options available to you on the Product Invoice screen.

FIGURE 6-1:
Creating a blank product invoice.

Source: Jane Kelly

Putting in the details

The Invoice screen automatically defaults to the Details page, where the default invoice type is for a product invoice, as indicated in the top right corner of the screen. Starting in that corner, you can set the following options for your invoice:

>> **Type:** Use the drop-down arrow if you want to change from an invoice to a proforma invoice. This is available only if you use the Professional version of Sage; refer to the nearby sidebar 'Issuing a proforma invoice'.

- » **Format:** You can choose a product or service invoice. In the Professional version, you can produce invoices that include both elements. The nearby sidebar 'Mixing product and service invoices' tells you how to do this.

- » **Date:** The date automatically defaults to today's date, so change the date if necessary.

- » **Account:** Select your customer account using the drop-down arrow.

- » **Invoice Number:** The <AutoNumber> notation here indicates that Sage automatically numbers your invoices. It starts with number 1 and automatically increases by one for each subsequent invoice. If you want to start with a different number, click Settings from the Menu bar and then Invoice/Order Defaults and select the Options tab.

- » **Order Number:** You can enter your own order number or leave it blank. However, if you use Sage Professional and generate the invoice using Sales Order Processing, an order number automatically appears within this box.

- » **Item Number:** This shows the item line of the invoice that the cursor is currently sitting on.

- » **Rate:** This field appears in Professional versions of Sage when you enable the Foreign Trader facility, which I explain in Chapter 14.

MIXING PRODUCT AND SERVICE INVOICES

If you use the Professional version of Sage, you can produce invoices that include both products and services. Start by raising a product invoice and then when you want to raise a service charge, select the S3 special product code. The Edit Item line for a service invoice opens. Follow the steps in the later section 'Selecting service invoices' for details on how to complete this transaction.

You can process all other info, including order, footer (see the 'Getting down to the footer details' section later in this chapter for more on footers) and payment details, in the normal manner.

You can save the invoice and print it whenever you decide. If you're not happy with the invoice contents, click the Clear Form icon to clear your entries and start again. Alternatively, you can click Close and then No to saving any changes.

Even though you've saved the invoice, you can still make changes and resave it.

Getting to the main attraction

The main body of the invoice has the most differences between product invoices and service invoices. As you would expect from a product invoice, you must select the product code, which in turn comes up with the product description and a quantity field. A service invoice doesn't require these items and instead has a details field.

Producing product invoices

Enter the following fields to create a product invoice:

» **Product Code:** Normally you set up product codes within product records. You can type in the relevant product code directly or use the drop-down arrow.

You may encounter instances where a regular everyday product code isn't suitable and you need a special product code, such as the following:

- **M Message Line:** Use this to add extra lines of description or to make comments about the products.

- **S1 Special Product Item Tax Chargeable:** Use this for product items that are standard VAT rated (VAT stands for value-added tax) and don't have their own product code.

- **S2 Special Product Item Zero Rated:** Use this code for zero-rated items that don't have their own product code.

- **S3 Special Service Items Tax Chargeable:** Use this code when you want to add service items to product invoices and sales orders. It uses the standard VAT code. (Available only in Sage 50 Accounts Professional)

TIP

If your S1–S3 codes don't appear in your drop-down list, click Settings in the main toolbar and select Invoice/Order Defaults. Tick the Show Special Product Codes invoicing box.

» **Description:** The product description displays automatically from the product record, but you can overwrite it if necessary. You can also click F3 to edit the item line and add any one-off product details or comments.

» **Quantity:** Enter the number of items you're invoicing. Sage automatically shows *1* if a quantity is in stock or *0* if no items are in stock. If you don't have enough stock for the quantity you enter, Sage issues a warning – it's difficult (not to mention illegal) to charge people without delivering the product, so pay attention to the warning.

» **Price:** The unit price for the product record appears here, but you can change this if you need to.

Selecting service invoices

A service invoice has fewer columns in the main body than a product invoice.

After you enter the header details for your invoice (customer details, date and so on), you need to add the details of the service provided:

» **Details:** You can expand the information entered in the Details field by using the F3 key. This function lets you add additional information to the invoice detail. You can use F3 only after you enter some information into the Details field.

» **Amount:** You can enter the amount using the Edit Item Line window that appeared if you used the F3 key in the Details field. Alternatively, if you didn't need to use the F3 key for additional details, add only one line of detail on the main screen and then tab across to the Amount column and enter the amount there.

Figure 6-2 shows what happens after Jeanette from Jingles inserted the detail Hire of Clown for Party into the Details field. As soon as you type in the description, press F3 and the edit box appears. Sage duplicates the words typed into both the Description and the Details fields.

FIGURE 6-2:
Using the F3 function key to expand the details of the service invoice.

Source: Jane Kelly

You can now apply the number of hours worked and enter the unit price. You can also check that the nominal code is one that you want to use or adjust it where necessary. In the Jingles case, Jeanette chooses to change the nominal code from 4000 for Sale of Cards (the default nominal code) to a more suitable code, such as Party Organising. Because Party Organising isn't an existing code, she needs to create a new nominal code. It's possible to click New from the drop-down list and enter a new nominal code directly from the F3 edit screen, but you need to ensure that you're creating the nominal code in the correct place. If in doubt, refer to Chapter 3 to see how to create new nominal codes.

After you enter the details on the main body of the invoice, you can work through the following, which are the same for both product and service invoices:

REMEMBER

» **Net:** This is an automatic calculation, which applies any discount attached to the customer account. You can change the discount by using the F3 key.

An additional Discount and Discount Percentage column shows if you selected this option within Invoice/Order defaults. Click the Discount tab and tick the Show Discount on Main Invoice/Order box.

» **VAT:** Sage automatically calculates this column. You can edit this column only if you selected the Item VAT Amendable box on the VAT tab of Company Preferences on the main toolbar.

» **Total:** Sage totals the invoice, showing net, VAT and any carriage charges applied.

» **Deposit:** This feature has a smart link – a little grey arrow that takes you to the Payment tab of the invoice so you can record any deposits received against the invoice.

» **Deduction:** This lets you provide a net value discount on the Details tab of your invoice (see the next bullet). You can use the deduction feature to offer seasonal discount promotions and one-off offers.

» **Net Value Discount:** Clicking the drop-down arrow in the Description box reveals an Edit Item line, where you can enter information referring to the discount and a discount value. If you press Tab, Sage automatically calculates the percentage discount. If you enter a discount percentage, the value is calculated for you.

Filling in the order details

If you click on Order, you will be able to fill in details of where the goods are delivered and who took the order. You can also add up to 60 characters of text in the Notes box for additional information. For example, if the customer tells you the order can be left outside by the chicken shed, this is the place to share that information.

When you press F3 from the Description line of an invoice, an edit box appears where you can amend some of the details of your invoice. The nominal code, tax code and department all appear in the posting details in this edit box. The details shown are defaults. You can amend the tax and nominal codes for each item line on the invoice by using the drop-down list. Alternatively, if you want to use the same nominal code and tax code for all lines of the invoice, you can click the Footer tab of the invoice and enter the appropriate codes in the Global section. The new codes overwrite any codes used on an individual line of the invoice.

In addition, from version 22 onwards, Sage has introduced some Custom fields that allow you to include additional analysis fields to your invoices (this also applies to Credit notes, Quotations and Sales Orders). In Figure 6-3, you see that Jeanette has renamed the Analysis 1, 2 & 3 fields to Sales Type, Sales Rep and Region. She now has the opportunity to enter additional data into these fields, such as whether the sale was made online, in the shop or at an event. She can also see which region the invoice relates to and also which salesperson generated the sale. This is all useful information that can be collated and viewed for all the sales invoices that are raised. By clicking on the Reports icon and selecting the Sales by analysis code option, Jeanette can review all sales invoices by each analysis code.

Getting down to the footer details

You can enter carriage terms, settlement terms and global details if you click on Footer:

» **Carriage Terms:** You may want to assign postal or courier costs to the invoice. You can set up specific nominal codes to charge carriage costs. If you set up departments, use the drop-down list to select the appropriate department. You can also add the consignment number and courier details and track your parcel by accessing the courier's website.

» **Settlement Terms:** You may already see some information in these boxes if you entered the details on the customer record. For example, you can enter how long an early settlement discount applies, and what discount percentage is applied. It also shows you the total value of the invoice. *Note:* Please be aware that VAT rules have changed from 1 April 2015 regarding the VAT treatment of early settlement discount (sometimes known as Prompt payment discount). Please refer to the HM Revenue & Customs (HMRC) Brief 49 (2014) Prompt Payment Discounts, which provides further details.

Source: Jane Kelly

FIGURE 6-3:
Jeanette adds
some custom
fields to the
sales invoice.

>> **Global:** This section lets you apply global terms to the whole of the invoice or credit note. If you choose to do this, only one line is added to the audit trail, although carriage is always shown as a separate line.

You can apply one nominal code to the whole invoice. If you do this, you can also enter details (using no more than 60 characters) to accompany the posting to the nominal ledger.

The same global effect can be applied to your tax code and your departments.

>> **Tax Analysis:** The tax analysis for each product item appears at the bottom of the Footer tab. The list shows a breakdown of all the VAT into the separate VAT codes (assuming you haven't used the Global Tax option).

Going over payment details

In Accounts Plus and Accounts Professional, you can record a payment directly to your sales invoice by clicking on the Payment tab. This opens the Payment Details screen, where you can enter details of deposits already received, make a payment on account if you don't want to allocate the payment to a specific invoice, or allocate the money to a specific invoice.

If you enter a deposit, Sage updates the details of the deposit on the Details tab of your invoice. If you click Payment Already Received, Sage displays the deposit but doesn't post a receipt transaction. You don't want to double-count the deposit receipt if it's already been posted.

After you're happy with the detail on your invoice, click Save to keep a copy of it on the Invoice list. If you're not happy with your invoice, click the Clear Form icon, or click Close and then say No to saving the invoice details.

Checking your profit on a product invoice

You can check the profit you've made on each product invoice. This is a nifty little device, but treat this feature with a little caution, as it only compares the sales price of your product with the unit cost price – at least it gives you an idea of whether you're making any money.

You can either check the profit whilst you are preparing the product invoice or later when you have saved the invoice. If you want to check the profit whilst preparing the invoice, then once you have entered the product line details (and assuming that you have set up both selling prices and cost prices in the product record), all you do is simply click the Profit Analysis icon at the top of the invoice screen. A Sales Profit Analysis window will open, which shows you the profit you will make on this invoice.

WARNING

A word of caution – this is only the gross profit on the invoice and doesn't take into account any other selling costs that you may have.

If you want to check the profit after you have saved the invoice, follow these steps:

1. **From the Navigation bar, click Invoices and credits to view a list of invoices.**

2. **Double-click the invoice you want to check. At the top of the screen, click the Profit Analysis icon. The Sales Profit Analysis window opens, as described earlier.**

   Sage calculates the profit using the information you entered in your product record. It simply displays the difference between the sales price and the cost price. If either of these fields isn't completed in the product record, the calculation doesn't work.

   Sage gives you a profit value in pounds sterling and the profit percentage.

3. **Click Close to return to your invoice.**

   Alternatively, you can print the information.

PREPARING CREDIT NOTES

You prepare credit notes in a very similar way to product and service invoices. The screens look exactly the same, but after you type in the details of the credit note, the font becomes red. From the Navigation bar, click on Invoices and credits and then choose the New Credit icon. Update your credit notes in the same way you do invoices. If you don't, the credit notes aren't updated to the nominal ledger.

Remembering that Communication Is Key

Communication and credit control are keys to the success of any business. With this in mind, Sage lets you record details of telephone calls, emails, letters and meetings and then record follow-up actions via the Communications page of each customer record. This function is particularly useful if you're a credit controller, as it can record follow-up phone calls to customers. Sage makes diary entries to remind you of your future tasks.

From the Navigation bar, click on Diary, which lets you access and view any appointments or follow-up calls made via the Communications screen.

TIP

INVOICING FROM A PHONE CALL

This option lets you charge your clients when you talk to them on the phone. For service businesses that bill by their time, this service is essential. For example, if you're a solicitor, you may need to charge clients for the time you spend on the phone with them. So, before you pick up the phone, follow these steps:

1. **From the Navigation bar, choose Customers, highlight the customer of your choice and click the Edit icon.**

   This opens up the customer's record.

2. **From the Navigation bar on the left side of the record, click Communications. Then click the Add Entry icon.**

   The Customer Communications History window appears.

(continued)

(continued)

3. **Keeping the Telephone option highlighted, enter some details in the Subject field and then dial the phone number. When the call is answered, click Start on the Telephone Timer in the top right-hand corner of the screen.**

   The system automatically starts recording the duration of the call. You can type notes in the Communication Results part of the screen. When you've finished the call, click Stop on the Telephone Timer.

4. **Click the Invoice icon to raise an invoice for the time spent on the phone call.**

   A Communication Invoice Details box appears, which lets you enter the hourly rates, nominal codes, departments and VAT details. Any notes from the Communication Results field pull through to the Details To Invoice field, where you can edit them as necessary. The time of the phone call is recorded in the Invoice Details box.

   If you simply want to record details of the phone call without billing for it, skip this step.

5. **Click Save when you're happy with the details. A confirmation message appears. Click Yes to raise the invoice and then click Save again to return to the customer record.**

   The invoice now appears on the Invoice List. Click Customers and credits from the Navigation bar to view it.

Managing Your Invoice List

After you save an invoice, it appears on your Invoice List, and you can then do all sorts of businesslike things with it.

Printing invoices

As soon as you save your invoice, you can print it. If you still have the invoice open in front of you, simply click Print. The Layouts window opens, which initially opens on the Favourites tab. Select Layouts and the right side of the window displays the different report options, as shown in Figure 6-4. When you scroll down the screen and highlight your chosen report, some floating icons appear, giving you the options of previewing, printing, exporting, exporting to Excel and emailing the document.

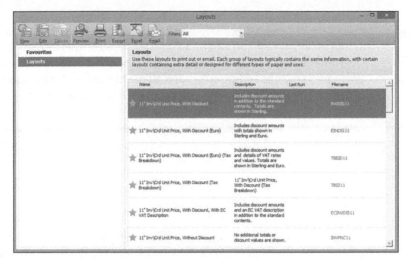

FIGURE 6-4:
Choosing the
layout before you
print your invoice.

Source: Jane Kelly

If you haven't got the invoice open in front of you, click Invoices and credits from the Navigation bar to display a list of all the invoices and credit notes that have been raised (in chronological order). Highlight the invoice you want to print from the list, click the Print icon to open the Layout window, select Layouts as before, choose the appropriate report required and click the floating print icon.

The layout choices are pretty self-explanatory: You choose a layout based on paper size and whether the customer is offered a discount. Some of the layouts are designed to be printed on plain paper rather than preprinted headed paper, and the plain paper options are self-evident as you scroll down the list of layouts.

You can preview the invoice before you print to make sure the details are correct. Click the floating preview icon to load the invoice on to the screen. If you're happy with what you see, you can print the invoice directly from this screen or choose to email it directly to the customer.

TIP

You can print the invoice without previewing it, but I always check to ensure I'm happy with the details. You can edit or change an invoice at any point before you send it to the customer and update the ledger.

You can print off a number of invoices at the same time by highlighting all the invoices you want to print and clicking Print. Then select your desired invoice layout.

TIP

You can choose an invoice layout as a favourite by clicking the grey star at the side of the report when you select an invoice layout. This copies the invoice to the Favourite screen, which is the first screen to open when you click the Print icon. This saves you time scrolling through all the layouts each time you print. The colour of the star changes to orange once you have selected that report as a favourite.

After you print an invoice, the Printed column on the Invoice List has the word Yes in it. You can reprint at any time, but you can easily identify which invoices have already been printed.

Using Quick Print

Sage has a feature called Quick Print that lets you select a default print layout and print items with a single click. The Quick Print icon sits alongside the Print icon when you view the list of invoices.

This is a quick way of printing invoices, particularly if you want to select more than one invoice. Be aware, though, that you won't see a preview of the invoice before it prints, so you need to make sure you select the correct layout.

If you try to use the Quick Print icon without having set up the default layout, a warning message appears and Sage asks if you want to set up the default now. If you know which report layout you want to use, click Yes. Sage then directs you to the Layout window, where you can click the appropriate layout. Highlight the invoice layout that you require and click OK. The report now prints. Be aware that you don't get the opportunity to preview this invoice.

Another way of setting up your default Quick Print invoice layout is to click Settings, followed by Invoice/Order defaults, and then click the Quick Print tab. Here, you can select the default print layouts for Invoices, Quotations for invoices, Sales Orders, Purchase Orders, and Quotations for Sales Orders.

Updating ledgers

When you're 100 per cent happy with your invoices, you're ready to *update ledgers*, a process that posts the invoice to both the nominal ledger and the customer ledger.

Before you update your invoices, you should be aware of a new feature that Sage has introduced in version 22. You now have the ability to determine what information is automatically shown in the Reference (Ref) and Ex Reference (Ex Ref) fields for your invoice. Click on Settings from the main toolbar, followed by Invoice/Order defaults from the drop-down list, and then click the Update ledgers tab. See Figure 6-5.

FIGURE 6-5:
Choosing your Ref and Ex Ref field options.

The default settings show that Sage uses the invoice number for the Ref field and your order number for the Ex Ref field. However, using the drop-down arrows, you can choose additional options for the Ref field, such as your order number or the customer order number. You can also change the Ex Ref field to show the invoice number, the customer order number or nothing at all. You should play around with these settings and choose the options that work for your business. Click OK to accept the changes or simply click Cancel to close the screen.

You can update invoices individually or in batches. First, check to see which invoices have been updated and printed already. To find out the status of each invoice, work through these steps:

1. **From the Navigation bar, click on Invoices and credits to view the Invoice List.**

2. **Look at the last two columns – the Posted and Printed columns.**

   The word Yes indicates whether an invoice has already been printed or posted.

To update the invoices:

1. **Highlight the invoices you want to update.**

2. **Click the Update Ledgers icon.**

   The Update Ledger box opens and you have the opportunity to print, preview or send to file. You may want to leave Preview highlighted, so after you click OK you can view all the invoices you've updated. You can print this report if you want to, but it isn't really necessary. Close this preview screen by clicking on the cross in the top right corner, or click Close at the top of the preview screen. You are now able to view the main screen where you can see that there is a Yes against that invoice in the Posted column.

Deleting invoices

Deleting invoices and credit notes is easy, but be aware that if you've already posted the invoice to the nominal ledger, deleting the invoice or credit note doesn't reverse the posting in the ledger.

To delete an invoice or credit note:

1. **From the Navigation bar, select Invoices and credits to open up the Invoice List.**

   Select the required invoice or credit note from the Invoice list.

2. **Click the Delete icon.**

   An affirmation message appears. Click Yes to continue or No to exit.

Saving Time While You Ask for Money

When you create invoices, it's useful to know about some of the time-saving features that you can use. I explain some of these features in this section.

Duplicating existing invoices

If you need to send the same invoice details to a number of different clients, this function is very useful. From the Invoice List, highlight an existing invoice and click the Duplicate icon at the top of the screen. The system produces an exact replica of the original, but you can edit the details, such as changing it from today's date to the actual date you require and changing the customer's name. Check all the details of the invoice and amend where necessary before saving.

When you duplicate an invoice, Sage replicates the details but gives the invoice a new sequential number, so you have an accurate audit trail.

Repeating recurring transactions

This feature is useful if you invoice for the same product or service on a recurring basis. After you set up your recurring transaction, you can continue to process the invoice in the same way.

To set up a recurring sales invoice, follow these steps:

1. **From the Navigation bar, click Invoices and credits and then click New Invoice.**

2. **Enter your invoice details as shown in the earlier section 'Creating Invoices'.**

3. **Click Memorise.**

The Memorise box appears and Sage asks you to provide the following:

- Reference and description for your recurring item.

- Frequency – is it every day, week or month, and when does it start and finish?

- Last processed – for ongoing recurring transactions, the date shown is the date the invoice was last processed.

4. **To save your recurring transaction and return to the invoice, click Save. To exit without saving, click Cancel.**

When you click Save, a copy of the new invoice shows on your invoice list.

TIP

Every time you open Sage, it asks if you want to post your recurring entries. Choose Yes if you want to post the transaction or choose No if you don't want to post the transaction. You can turn this reminder off by clicking Settings from the main toolbar, selecting Company Preferences from the drop-down list, and then clicking on the Parameters tab. Select the No Recurring Entries at Startup checkbox.

To process the transactions, follow these steps:

1. **From the Invoice list, select the Recurring Items icon.**

The Memorised and Recurring Entries box appears.

2. **Click the item you want to process and click Process.**

The Process Recurring Entries box appears and asks you what date you want to process transactions up to. After you put your date in, Sage lists all the items included. Make sure all the transactions you want to process have a green tick in the box next to them. If you don't want to include a transaction, make sure the box doesn't have a tick in it.

If you clear a tick from the Process Recurring Entries box and then click Process, the system asks, Do you wish to update the last posted date for excluded transactions? Select No if you want to post transactions at a later date. If you want to exclude a transaction because you don't want to put it through this month, click Yes.

3. **Click Process.**

   Sage processes the recurring items and says Processing Complete.

4. **Click Cancel to return to the Invoice List screen.**

Using defaults

You may have invoices and credit notes with similar items or characteristics, and you can enter defaults for them. For example, you may want to assign carriage costs to all your customers.

To access the defaults, from the main toolbar, click Settings, followed by Invoice/Order Defaults. To adjust carriage defaults, click Footer Defaults.

For help with other invoice defaults, select Help from the main toolbar, click Contents and Index, and select Invoices followed by Defaults.

Getting paid faster

From version 22 onwards, Sage has introduced a new Pay Now button that can be added to your e-invoices (in other words, invoices that you email your customers). This option is available only with Sage Cover Extra Support and subscription contracts. It allows customers to be able to quickly pay an invoice by clicking on the Pay Now button, which is directly on the face of the emailed invoice. By doing this, the customer is taken to a secure payment gateway (courtesy of Sage Pay) and can elect to pay the invoice by credit card or PayPal. The payments and stock levels are automatically updated with your Sage accounts software, thus speeding up processing.

This service comes at an additional charge, and more details can be obtained by accessing the Sage Pay website: www.sagepay.co.uk/getpaidfaster.

Chapter 7

Dealing with Paperwork from Your Suppliers

You probably receive lots of invoices from your suppliers, so you need to put systems in place to help you easily locate those invoices if required. Sometimes Sage contains enough detail to answer a query about an invoice, but on some occasions you may need to pull the actual invoice out of the file.

As you process each invoice, Sage allocates it a sequential number. Use this sequential number as a reference, so you can always track down an invoice quickly and easily.

Receiving and Posting Invoices

You need a good system for capturing all the purchase invoices that come into your business, so you pay your bills on time and you can continue doing business. Two steps are involved in making sure this gets done: Receiving the invoices properly and posting the invoices.

Setting up your receiving system

TIP

Send all invoices to one person or department (depending on the size of the business). You don't want lots of different people receiving your invoices, as more people means more chance of invoices getting misplaced or entered incorrectly.

Enter invoices on to the accounting system as soon as possible after you receive them so the liability is recorded in the business accounts. Depending on the size of the business, you may want to make a copy of the invoice: Keep one copy within the accounts department and send the other copy to the person who requested the goods so he can check the details for accuracy and authorise the invoice for payment.

Posting invoices

The term *posting* doesn't mean putting the invoice into a letterbox. In accounting terms, *posting* means processing an invoice to the nominal ledger. I talk about the nominal ledger in Chapter 2.

You can post a number of invoices in one sitting. If you have large quantities of invoices to process, separate them into smaller batches and total the values of each batch so you can check those same values against Sage to ensure you haven't made any mistakes.

TIP

If you use Sage Accounts Professional, you have two different ways of posting invoices:

>> If you receive an invoice as a result of raising a purchase order, you can update your order details and Sage automatically posts the invoice. See Chapter 11 for more information about processing purchase orders.

>> If you don't have an order for your invoice, you need to use the Batch Entry screen to process your invoice, which I describe in this section.

TIP

Sort the invoices into date order before separating them into batches. This ensures you enter the invoices in chronological order, which helps when you view them on-screen.

To enter a batch, follow these steps:

1. **From the Navigation bar, click Suppliers and then click on the Batch Invoice icon.**

This brings up the Batch Suppliers Invoice box.

2. **Select the correct supplier account for the invoice.**

TIP

When you have several items on an invoice, enter each item from the invoice separately on the Batch screen, as you may need to give each item a different nominal code. You can use the same supplier account, date, and reference so that Sage can group those items together.

3. **Put the invoice date in the Date field.**

Sage automatically defaults to today's date, so you may need to overtype the invoice date. If you don't, Sage won't age the invoice correctly, and you'll have a distorted view of the transaction on your aged creditor reports.

4. **Enter your sequential number in the Ref (Reference) field.**

Your *invoice reference number* is the number order in which you file your invoices. I usually give each invoice a sequential number and mark this in pen at the top right corner of the invoice. I then use the Ref field to enter this number into Sage.

5. **Add details in the Ex.Ref field.**

Note: If you are using purchase order processing, you have the option to automatically select which reference you would like to use for both the Ref field and the Ex.Ref field when you update the ledgers. I discuss this in more detail in Chapter 11.

TIP

You can add more references here or leave this field blank. I always enter the supplier's own invoice number here, as it acts as a secondary means of identification. This is important when you need to retrieve an invoice from your filing system. Having an additional reference particularly helps if you have invoices from a supplier with the same value.

6. **Select the nominal code in the N/C field using the drop-down arrow; otherwise, Sage uses the default code 5000.**

7. **Click the department applicable for your invoice in the Department field.**

You can leave this field blank if you don't have any departments set up.

8. **Click the drop-down Project Ref arrow to select the appropriate project.**

9. **Enter the Cost Code if you're using project costing.**

See Chapter 13 for further details on project costing.

10. Enter information describing what the invoice is for in the Details field.

Put as much detail as you can here. In addition to entering the supplier's invoice number in the Ex.Ref field, I also enter the supplier's invoice number and the description in the Details column. You can then identify the invoice quickly using the supplier's number. If you need to contact the supplier about an invoice, it helps to use the supplier's reference numbers.

TIP

I use both the Ex.Ref field and the Details columns for the supplier's invoice number, because different reports sometimes include one but not the other. This is a bit belt and braces, but experience has taught me this system works.

11. Enter the amount net of VAT in the Net field.

12. Choose the tax code applicable for this invoice in the T/C (Tax Code) field.

Depending on the tax code, Sage updates the VAT field. (VAT is value-added tax.)

WARNING

Make sure the VAT that Sage calculates is the same as the amount on the invoice. Sometimes Sage rounds up the VAT, and you need to overwrite the amount in Sage to match the VAT on the invoice.

13. Repeat Steps 2–12 for each invoice in your batch.

14. Check the total of your batch of invoices matches the total in the right corner of the Batch Entry screen, as in Figure 7-1.

If the totals match, click Save. Doing this check confirms you've entered accurate data. When you click Save, Sage posts the invoices to the nominal ledger, posting a debit to the Cost account and a credit to the Creditors control account.

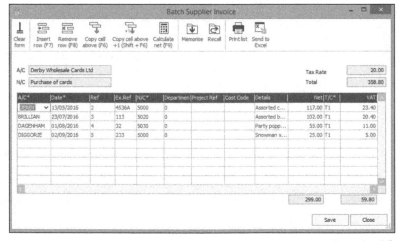

FIGURE 7-1:
A batch of purchase invoices entered on to Sage before posting.

Source: Jane Kelly

MEMORISING AND RECALLING BATCH INVOICES AND CREDIT NOTES

You can use the Memorise and Recall functions in Sage Accounts Plus and Professional versions to save you entering the same information again and again. For example, if you regularly buy the same product from the same supplier, you can use the Memorise function to save time when ordering the product.

Another great function is memorising a batch of invoices that you're in the middle of sorting out so you can come back and amend them later. You can save the batch, go away and check some details, and then come back, recall the batch, make the amendments, and post.

To memorise a batch of invoices from within the Batch Entry screen, click Memorise, add a filename for the batch, and click Save. To recall a batch of invoices, click Recall from within the Batch Entry screen, select the appropriate file, and click Open.

TIP

Check out Chapter 22 to see how using the function keys speeds up the batch-entry process.

After you post your purchase invoices (shown as PI in Sage), you can view them on the Supplier Activity screen, which is split into two parts. The top part has one line entry for each transaction (in other words, all the individual lines of each invoice are grouped together), and the bottom part has the details of each transaction. Clicking an invoice highlights it in blue, and the bottom part of the screen shows each line entry of that invoice.

Getting Credit

Credit notes are raised for a variety of reasons. You may have received faulty goods, or the goods may be the wrong colour, for example. The supplier assumes you've already posted the original invoice supplied with these goods and sends a credit note to reduce the amount you owe. The credit note may completely reverse the value of the original invoice or partially credit the invoice.

Processing a credit note is much the same as processing an invoice, so follow the steps in the earlier section 'Posting invoices', paying special attention to the following points:

>> **From the Navigation bar, click Suppliers, click the Batch Credit icon, and select the account to enter the credit note against.** The screen looks very similar to that of the Invoice screen, but the font colour is red rather than black to alert you to the fact that you're processing a credit note.

>> **Remember to change the date, unless today's date is acceptable.**

>> **Enter a credit number instead of a reference number.** Use a unique sequential numbering system for your credit notes. Some people have a separate numbering system for credit notes, but others just use the next available invoice number.

>> **Enter the supplier's credit note number in the Ex.Ref field.** This gives you an additional way of identifying the credit note.

>> **Make sure the nominal code (N/C) is the same as the invoice you're reversing.** This ensures the correct cost code is reduced in value.

>> **Put some notation in the Details field.** I suggest you type something like 'Credit note against Invoice No. 123' plus a description of why it's necessary.

>> **If the credit note is reversing just part of an invoice, apportion the Net and VAT amounts.**

When you click Save, Sage posts the credit note, crediting the Purchase account and debiting the Creditors control account. The credit note shows the reference PC in Sage, which stands for Purchase Credit.

You can check to see if everything is posted by viewing the Activity screen for the nominal code you used. The Jingles example in Figure 7-2 shows the Activity screen for nominal code 5000. You can see transaction number 26, the purchase of assorted cards (debiting code 5000), and transaction 31, the credit note (crediting the nominal record). The Activity screen shows the original invoice posted to the purchase nominal code as a debit and then the credit note showing at a later date, crediting the nominal code. Here's where having a description in the Details field linking the credit note to the invoice comes in handy.

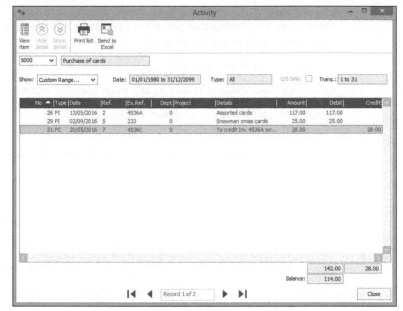

Allocating a Credit Note

You allocate credit notes in the same way as you make payments. You need to allocate a credit note specifically against an invoice.

TIP

You can tell if something hasn't been allocated if a transaction in the Supplier Activity screen has an asterisk against it.

To allocate a credit note, follow these steps:

1. **From the Navigation bar, click Suppliers and then click Supplier Payment.**

2. **Select the account you require.**

All outstanding transactions are shown.

3. **Enter the date, usually the date of the credit note.**

4. **In the Payment column, click Pay in Full Against the Credit Note.**

Doing so puts a negative value in the Analysis total at the bottom right side of the screen.

5. Move up to the invoice that you want to allocate the credit note to, and type in the value of the credit note.

The Analysis total becomes zero.

6. Click Save. Click Close to return to the main supplier window.

Saving posts the allocation, as shown in Figure 7-3.

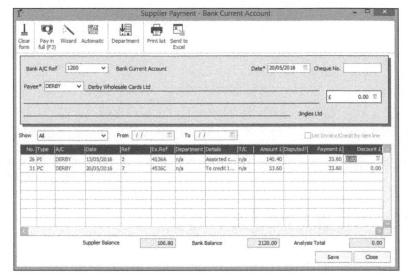

Source: Jane Kelly

FIGURE 7-3:
Allocating
a credit note to a
supplier invoice.

Paying Your Suppliers

When you process the payments for your supplier, you can still use the Supplier module. In previous versions of Sage, you had to use the Bank module – you can still do this, but you now have the option to make your payment using the Supplier module:

1. From the Navigation bar, select Suppliers and then click the Supplier Payment icon.

A screen that looks a bit like a chequebook opens up.

2. Check that the Bank A/C Ref field shows the correct account.

This field automatically defaults to account 1200, which is usually the bank current account. If this isn't the account you want to use, select the appropriate account.

3. **Enter the supplier name or use the drop-down arrow to select the payee.**

   As soon as you select an account, Sage brings up a list of outstanding transactions for that account.

4. **Enter the payment date in the Date field.**

   Usually you use the date on your cheque stub or the date of the direct debit or other form of payment.

5. **Record the cheque number or method of payment in the Cheque No. field.**

   Type DD for direct debit, BP for bank payment, or any other short description to help identify the transaction when you reconcile your bank account.

6. **Click the Payment column.**

   You have several options here:

   - **Paying in full:** Click the Pay in Full icon at the top left of the screen. The amount appears in the £ box at the top of the screen, as shown in Figure 7-4.

     If you have a discount for early payment, enter the discount amount in the Discount column. Sage calculates the amount you owe and shows this value in the £ box and in the Payment column.

   - **Paying part of an invoice:** Enter the amount you want to pay against the invoice. The amount shows up in the £ box at the top of the screen.

   - **Making a payment on account:** Enter the amount you want to pay in the £ box.

     You may find you need to make a payment against a supplier account but can't specify an invoice to allocate the payment to. You can make a payment to the supplier account without matching it to a specific invoice.

7. **Click Save. Click Close to return to the main supplier window.**

   If you make full or partial payments to an invoice, the payment posts to that invoice in the supplier account.

   If you make a payment on account, Sage gives you a confirmation message, asking, 'There is an unallocated cheque balance of £x. Do you want to post this as a payment on account?' Click Yes to accept or No to cancel.

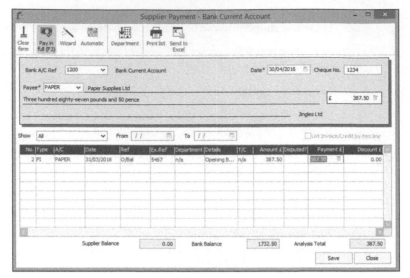

Source: Jane Kelly

FIGURE 7-4:
A happy
supplier, paid
in full.

Printing a Remittance Advice Note

You may want to print a remittance advice note to accompany your cheque. A *remittance advice note* tells your supplier which invoices you're paying. Alternatively, you can just make a note of the invoice numbers on a compliments slip.

If you select Always Create a Remittance in your Bank defaults, the system automatically stores a remittance for you. When I loaded my version of Sage, this default was already set, but you can change it by clicking Settings from the Menu bar and then Bank Defaults. If you uncheck the Always Create a Remittance box, Sage creates a new Create Remittance button on your Payment screen. You can then selectively create remittances.

To print a remittance from the Bank accounts module, click the Payments icon and then select Remittances from the drop-down menu. The Remittance window opens, allowing you to select the remittances that you want to print. Sage lists all the remittances generated, whether manually or automatically (depending on how you set your defaults). Highlight the remittances you want to print, or select the date range if you have several, and click Print Remittances. You can preview the remittances or send them straight to your printer. *Note:* After the remittance is printed, it is hidden from view. If you need to reprint a remittance, then simply tick the Show Printed Items box and the remittances reappear.

If you prefer to email the remittance rather than print it, click the Print Remittances box, select the appropriate layout and click Email for your output option. Then click Run. Click Close to exit the Remittance window. For successful emailing, you need to ensure that you have your email defaults set up correctly within Sage. Click Settings from the main toolbar followed by Email Defaults and complete the appropriate boxes.

In addition, you need to ensure that you have amended the Email Settings & Addresses box found in the details page of the Supplier record. You also need to tick the box that says, 'I send letters, remittances, etc to this supplier via email'. After you have done all these things, your emails should work!

Chapter 8

Recording Your Bank Entries

I f you're the sort of person who likes checking your bank accounts and keeping track of spending on the company credit card, this chapter is for you. In this chapter I show you how to process bank payments and receipts that aren't related to sales invoices or purchase invoices. I look at processing credit card transactions and dealing with petty cash – one of the bookkeeping jobs that can be a real pain in the backside if you don't do it properly.

I also show you how you to transfer money between bank accounts – perhaps to take advantage of earning some extra interest (every little bit helps!). As many businesses often have a lot of banking transactions, I show you ways to speed up the processing by using recurring entries.

Understanding the Different Types of Bank Account

Clicking Bank accounts from the Navigation bar shows you the default bank accounts that Sage provides, including the following:

>> **Bank accounts:** These include current, deposit and building society accounts.

>> **Cash accounts:** These include a petty cash account.

>> **Credit card accounts:** These include a credit card receipts account in case you receive customer payments via credit card.

You can add new bank accounts, rename existing accounts and delete accounts you don't need – refer to Chapter 3 to find out how.

In the following sections, I show the account number or range of numbers Sage assigns to each account. These account numbers are the same as the nominal code for that bank account.

Keeping up with current (1200) and deposit (1210) accounts

The Bank Current account is the default bank account in Sage that automatically pops up when you enter a bank transaction. You can choose another account if the Bank Current account isn't the right one for your transaction.

Most people use a current account for the majority of their transactions, although you may have additional bank accounts for different areas of your business. If you have surplus cash that you want to earn a bit of interest on, you may have a deposit account and then transfer surplus cash between the current account and the deposit account to take advantage of higher rates of interest. I talk about transferring money between accounts in the 'Transferring Funds between Accounts' section later in this chapter.

Many companies regularly transfer funds to a separate deposit account from their current account to accumulate enough money to pay their value-added tax (VAT) bills or PAYE.

TIP

Change the name of the Bank Current account to that of your own business current account. If you have more than one business current account, include the account number within the bank account name – for example, Barclays Current Account 24672376. To add or amend bank accounts, check out Chapter 3.

Sage's deposit account functions in the same way as the current account. You can make transfers between the deposit and current accounts in Sage.

Sage also includes a building society account, although not many businesses actually have one of those.

Counting the petty cash (1230) account

You use the petty cash account for cash stored somewhere other than a bank or building society – a strong box or safe in the office, perhaps.

You can operate the petty cash account in the same way as a normal bank account, although most people don't choose to reconcile it as you don't have bank statements to reconcile to.

You can transfer funds into the petty cash account from any of the other Sage bank accounts and make payments accordingly. I give further details in the later section 'Dealing with Petty Cash'.

Handling your cash register (1235)

Sage offers a separate bank account to handle your cash register transactions. You may want to use this function to record receipts of cash and card payments.

The default cash register bank account is automatically set at 1235. Check your Cash Register settings in your Bank Default menu. From the Menu bar, click Settings and then Bank Defaults. Here, you can select the sales nominal code for your Cash Register takings, which automatically defaults to 4000 (you can change this). When using a cash register account, you may find discrepancies exist between the account and actual takings. If so, use the Discrepancy account to balance the books – the default code is 8206 (which you can change). The account has a tick-box to confirm whether your cash takings include VAT.

To process takings that are recorded in your till at the end of the day, you simply click the Cash Register icon when in the Bank accounts module and then complete the details of the cash takings in the window that appears.

You are able to specify whether the takings have been received by way of cash, cheque, card or bank transfer. You can also specify any discrepancies between what the cash till reports say you have taken and the actual takings.

TIP

For further help in using the Cash Register function within Sage, click Help on the main toolbar and select Ask Sage; then follow the screen directions to guide you to the Help Centre, where you can enter your query. I typed 'Recording Cash Till Takings' and got a very useful report telling me how to do this.

Managing the company credit card (1240) and credit card receipts (1250)

You can set up a bank account for each individual credit card and manage these accounts as normal bank accounts – reconciling them, for example, with your credit card statements. See the 'Paying the Credit Card Bill' section later in this chapter for further details about the mechanics of processing credit card transactions.

If you accept payment by credit card, keep a separate bank account for these transactions. You deposit batches of credit card vouchers into your account in the same way that you deposit cheques. Use the Customer option if you receive money against a customer invoice. The credit card company then deposits the real cash into your nominated bank account, and you can make a transfer between that and the Credit Card Receipts account. You receive a statement detailing all the transactions, including a service charge, which can be reconciled.

TIP

For Sage Pay users, it is recommended that you use a separate bank account for your Sage Pay transactions. This is because Sage Pay transactions are often paid into your regular bank account as amalgamated totals, which may be difficult to easily match up with your transactions in your accounts software. If you send all Sage Pay transactions to a designated bank account, you can then transfer totals across to your current account with actual dates and amounts that match up with your Sage accounts transactions.

Tracking Bank Deposits and Payments

Sage helps you keep track of how much money you put in the bank with the Bank accounts module. Sage also keeps tabs on any bank payments you make, such as wages, interest charges, loan payments and dividend payments.

For both types of transaction, start from the Navigation bar and click Bank accounts. This opens up the Bank accounts module:

>> For receipts, click the Bank Receipt icon.

>> For payments, click the Payments icon. This gives you a drop-down menu that provides you with a number of different payment options. Please select Bank payment. *Note:* You can also choose Supplier payments here, but this chapter is discussing other types of bank payments that you might make (other than to a supplier). See Chapter 7 for payments to suppliers.

In both cases, a new window appears. Although the receipt and payment screens are different, they ask you for the same basic information. Use the Tab key to move across the screen and enter the details Sage asks for:

>> **Bank:** Select the correct bank account using the drop-down arrows. Sage automatically defaults to account 1200, which is normally the Bank Current account.

>> **Date:** Sage defaults to today's date, so make sure you change this detail to match the date of the transaction.

>> **Reference (Ref):** If you have a cheque number, payslip reference, or BACS reference, enter it here as it proves very useful when you come to reconcile your bank account.

When you make a payment, be aware that the reference you enter appears on the audit trail in the Reference (Ref) column for that transaction. Use notations you can understand, such as DD for direct debit or SO for standing order. If you paid by cheque, enter the cheque number.

>> **Ex.Ref:** A new field has been added for additional references. For example, if you were entering a direct debit as a bank payment, you could use DD (direct debit) in the first reference field, and perhaps use a more specific reference for that direct debit in the extra reference field. This may be useful if you pay several direct debits to the same supplier/service provider, particularly if the amount is the same.

>> **Nominal Code (N/C):** Using the drop-down arrow, select the appropriate nominal code. You can create a new nominal code here if you need to.

>> **Dept:** Enter the department using the drop-down arrow. Ignore this field if you don't use departments.

>> **Project Ref:** This is available only for Sage 50 Accounts Plus or Professional users. Enter your project reference here. When the transaction is saved, Sage updates the project activity and analysis information. If you make a payment, enter the relevant cost code.

>> **Cost code:** You see this only if you select a bank payment. It is available only if you have Sage 50 Accounts Plus or Professional. It is part of the project analysis feature.

>> **Details:** Record any details that may help you with reconciling your account or identifying the transaction.

>> **Net:** Enter the net amount of the transaction before VAT. If you are not VAT registered, put the gross amount here and use the non-vatable tax code T9.

TIP

If you have only the gross amount of your receipts or a payment, you can enter this number and then click Calc Net at the top of the Bank Payments/Receipts box (or press F9). Provided the tax code is set correctly, Sage calculates the net and VAT amounts for you.

>> **Tax Code (T/C):** Use the drop-down arrow to select the appropriate tax code.

>> **Tax:** Sage calculates the amount of VAT for the transaction based on the net amount and the tax code selected. You must ensure that the VAT agrees to the paperwork that you have; if necessary you can overtype the correct amount of VAT. Sometimes Sage might round up the VAT by a penny, and you must correct this to ensure that the bank payment or receipt agrees to your banking paperwork.

In addition to the preceding fields, there are also a number of icons that appear on both the Bank Payment and the Bank Receipt windows. Most of the icons are the same, and very obvious, but the two described here require further explanation:

>> **Pay by Card:** This can be found on the Bank Receipts screen. You can select this option if you have configured Sage Pay. You must enter your Sage Pay credentials in Company Preferences in order to benefit from this feature. *Note:* Sage Pay is an additional chargeable service that your business can use if you trade online. It fully integrates your online transactions with Sage Accounts, which in turn automates and streamlines your sales and stock control. You can therefore be sure that the information supplied online is the same as the data that is integrated within Sage Accounts. This reduces the scope for data entry error and also speeds up the accounts process.

>> **Print Cheque:** This icon is available only in Sage Accounts Plus and Professional. It can be found on the Bank Payments window. Once you have entered a bank payment, click the Print Cheque icon. The cheque window opens, and unless you want to select a supplier, move across to the next field and enter details of who you are paying. The amount and date should already be prefilled, so simply press Save. You can then close the Bank Payments window and click on the Cheque icon (top right corner of the screen). When the Cheque window opens, you are presented with a list of cheques that have been created, and you can select the appropriate one to print. This is useful when you have the correct stationery and ability to print cheques from your software. For many small businesses, this may not be relevant. I'm simply mentioning this as it is a new feature that Sage has implemented.

You can continue to enter receipts or payments in a batch. Figure 8-1 shows a Payment Batch Entry screen. As you enter new transactions, the total in the bottom right corner of the screen increases. Check the batch total you calculated against the total Sage reached in the Total box in the top right of the screen.

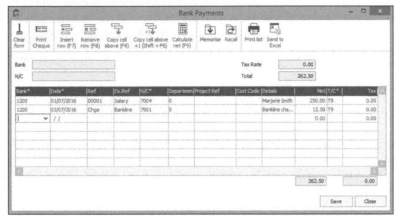

Source: Jane Kelly

FIGURE 8-1:
A Payment Batch
Entry screen.

USING A TEMPLATE TO AVOID TEDIUM

If you regularly record the same types of receipt and payment, such as regular receipts of bank interest or regular payments of interest charges, you can set up a template and load it whenever you need to. You can change the date and any values or additional information as necessary without having to enter tedious details such as the nominal code and tax information. A template not only saves you time but also reduces the possibility of errors.

To use the Memorise option for a batch of bank receipts or payments, enter the transactions as normal and then click the Memorise icon at the top of the screen. Select the directory where you want to save your template and enter a filename. (If you're making payments, Sage defaults to an invoices directory, but you can browse to find a more suitable alternative.) Click Save to preserve the template (otherwise, click Cancel) and then click Close.

To recall the template, click Recall from the Bank Receipts or Bank Payments window and choose the directory where you saved the template. Click Open to load the appropriate template. Make any changes necessary and then click Save.

Note: This feature is available only in Sage 50 Accounts Plus and Professional.

The boxes at the top of the screen show which bank account the receipt is going to, the nominal code, and the tax rate. You can also see a Total box that subtotals all the lines of information in the batch.

When you're happy that the details on the screen are correct, click Save at the lower right of the screen to post payments to the appropriate nominal accounts and bank accounts. If you aren't happy with the information on your Batch Entry screen, click Close and don't save the information entered.

Transferring Funds between Accounts

Just as big banks move money around, you may occasionally want to move money from one account to another. For example, when you pay off your company credit card each month, you make a payment from your current account to your credit card account. You can create a bank transfer between the two accounts to process this transaction easily.

To process a bank transfer, follow these steps:

1. **From the Navigation bar, click Bank accounts and then click the Bank Transfer icon.**

   The Bank Transfer window opens.

2. **Select the bank account you want to transfer the money from, using the drop-down arrow.**

3. **Select the account you want to transfer the money to, using the drop-down arrow.**

4. **Complete the information on-screen:**

   - **Date:** Enter the date of the transaction. You need to overtype this, as the system uses today's date.

   - **Reference (Ref):** Enter a reference relating to the transaction.

   - **Ex.Ref:** This is an additional reference field.

   - **Details:** You have up to 60 characters to describe the transaction.

   - **Dept:** Select a department, if applicable.

   - **Payment Amount:** Enter the amount of the transaction.

   - **Exchange Rate:** Use this only if you have Sage Accounts Professional and set up a foreign exchange rate as I explain in Chapter 14.

5. **Click Save if you're happy with the information you entered.**

   Sage updates both bank accounts. If you aren't happy, click Close and don't save the transaction.

6. **Click Close to exit the Bank Transfer screen.**

Note: In the event that you make a mistake with a bank transfer, it is now possible to correct it at a later event. Sage 50 Accounts actually posts your bank transfer as a journal debit and a journal credit, and in previous versions of Sage you were unable to edit a journal entry. However, with the advent of Sage 50 Accounts version 22, it is now possible to edit a journal entry, and if you've made a complete hash of it, you can even delete it! I discuss this further in Chapter 9.

TIP

With the new version 22 of the Sage 50 software, the method of processing bank transfers has changed. In the past you used a wizard-style screen to process a bank transfer between two different accounts. With the latest version, it is now possible to do transfers between more than two accounts, because the bank transfer window now allows you to complete multiple lines of entries. This could prove to be a time-saving device – only time will tell.

Repeating Recurring Entries

Designating recurring entries is extremely useful. Doing so speeds up the processing of data and saves time because you enter the information only once, at the setup stage, and then process all future transactions with the click of a button. You don't have to re-enter the full details of those transactions again.

You can treat many different transactions as recurring items, although they're typically direct debits and standing orders. In the next sections, I explain the different types of recurring transaction you can set up.

Going for consistency with your bank entries

You probably make regular payments into and out of your current and credit card accounts and transfer money between accounts on a monthly basis. To set up any of these transaction types as recurring, follow these steps:

1. **From the Navigation bar, click Bank accounts and then click the Recurring items icon.**

   The Recurring items window opens.

2. **Click Add to open the Add/Edit Recurring Entry box.**

Fill in the Recurring Entry From/To section. The information Sage asks for includes:

- **Bank A/C:** Select the bank account the transaction is coming from or going to.

- **Nominal Code:** Enter the nominal code for the transaction.

3. **Enter details of the recurring entry.**

These details include:

- **Transaction Type:** Choose from Bank/Cash/Credit Card Payment, Bank/Cash/Credit Card Receipts, Bank/Cash/Credit Card Transfer, Customer Payment on Account, Journal Debit, Journal Credit and Supplier Payment on Account.

- **Transaction Ref:** Enter a reference here. Note that Sage already uses DD/SO (direct debit/standing order), which may be sufficient for you, but you can change it as necessary.

- **Transaction Details:** Enter details of the transaction. In the example in Figure 8-2, I set up a recurring building insurance payment.

- **Dept:** Enter a department, if applicable.

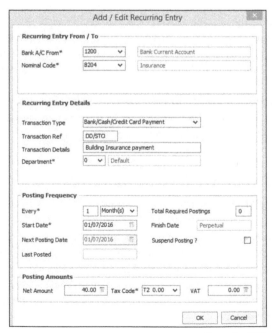

FIGURE 8-2:
Creating a
recurring bank
payment.

Source: Jane Kelly

4. **Determine posting frequency.**

Make selections about frequency:

- **Every:** Enter the posting frequency here – for example, daily, monthly, weekly or yearly.

- **Total required postings:** If you know the exact number of postings you need to make, enter the number here. The finish date automatically updates. If you leave this field as zero, Sage assumes that the payment will be ongoing in perpetuity.

- **Start date:** This is the date you want the recurring entry to start. The system automatically defaults to today's date, but you can overtype it with the correct date.

- **Finish date:** If you haven't updated the total number of postings, leave this date blank. This means the recurring entry continues until you choose to suspend posting or delete the recurring entry.

- **Next posting date:** The system shows you when the next posting is due. This date cannot be changed.

- **Last posted:** This shows the date of the last posting made. You can't change this date.

- **Suspend posting?** Tick this box if you don't want to continue posting the recurring entry. You can untick the box after you decide to resume posting.

5. **Type in the posting amount.**

Break down the amount as follows:

- **Net Amount:** Enter the net amount of the transaction.

- **Tax Code:** Select the appropriate tax code, using the drop-down arrow.

- **VAT:** This displays the VAT amount, determined by the net amount and tax code selected.

6. **To save the recurring entry, click OK. To exit without saving, click Cancel.**

The Recurring item now appears in your Recurring items window. Click Close to return to the main Bank accounts screen.

TIP

To view existing recurring entries, from the Bank module on the Navigation bar, click the Recurring items icon. The Recurring items window appears, showing a list of recurring bank transactions that you have created.

Repeating customer and supplier payments

If a customer pays you or you pay your suppliers regularly, you can set up recurring payments, particularly if the amount's the same each time (although it doesn't have to be):

1. **From the Navigation bar, click Bank accounts and then click the Recurring items icon.**

2. **In the Recurring items window, click Add.**

   Fill in the following information:

   - **Transaction Type:** Select Customer Payment On Account for a customer payment or Supplier Payment On Account for a supplier payment. Notice the Recurring Entry To/From box changes to accept the Bank A/C and Customer or Supplier A/C details.

   - **Bank Account:** Select the account you want to deposit the payment into or the account that you want to pay a supplier payment from.

   - **Customer/Supplier Account:** Choose the relevant account using the drop-down arrow.

   - **Transaction Ref:** Enter a reference for your recurring transaction here.

   - **Department:** Select a department, if required.

3. **Select the posting frequencies as in Step 5 in the section 'Going for consistency with your bank entries'.**

4. **Enter the posting amount.**

5. **If you're happy with the information supplied on the screen, click OK to save the recurring entry.**

   If you click Cancel, Sage asks if you want to save the changes. Click No to return to the main screen.

REMEMBER

If you use this method to post payments on account to both suppliers and customers, allocate the receipts or payments to the specific invoices as a separate exercise. I don't tend to use this type of recurring option very often because it's quicker to process directly to the invoice in one step: It takes two steps to process a payment on account and then allocate that payment. But every business has different needs and different sets of circumstances, so this recurring option may appeal to you.

Making regular journal entries – if you dare

This option is useful if you have to make an adjustment to the accounts where only a journal is possible. For example, if you make regular payments on a loan, you can set up the payment as a journal and record both the payment and the interest (the specific journal depends on how the loan has been set up).

WARNING

Use a journal only if you're confident with double-entry bookkeeping. If you aren't competent with your bookkeeping, this is dangerous territory.

To make a regular journal entry, follow these steps:

1. **From the Navigation bar, click on Bank accounts and choose the Recurring items icon.**

   In the Recurring items window, click Add. The Add/Edit Recurring Entry box appears.

REMEMBER

   Although you enter your debit and credit transactions separately, you need to ensure your journal entries balance; otherwise, you get an error message. For every debit entry, you need to make a credit entry of the same amount.

2. **Enter the transaction information in the boxes.**

   You need to enter the following details:

   - **Transaction Type:** Select either Journal Debit or Journal Credit.
   - **Nominal Code:** Using the drop-down arrow, select the nominal account to use. The name of the nominal account appears in the box next to the code selected.

3. **Complete the transaction details, posting frequency and amounts fields, as in Steps 4–6 in the section 'Going for consistency with your bank entries'.**

4. **Click OK if you're happy with the journal details, or click Cancel if you don't like the changes.**

Your newly created recurring entry now appears on the Recurring list.

Processing and posting recurring entries

After you set up recurring entries, every time you start up Sage, it asks if you want to process your recurring entries. Generally, you need to answer No at this stage, as processing your recurring entries in a controlled manner is better.

TIP

You can turn off this reminder by selecting the No Recurring Entries At Start Up checkbox in the Parameters tab of Company Preferences (click Settings and then Company Preferences).

You normally process your recurring entries just before you reconcile your bank account so they're ready and waiting to be reconciled. To process your recurring transactions, you need to do the following:

1. **From the Navigation bar, click Bank accounts and then click the Recurring items icon.**

   The Recurring items window opens.

2. **Select the entry you want to post and click the Process icon.**

   The Process Recurring Entries box displays the message 'Show due entries up to:'.

3. **Enter the date you want to process recurring entries up to.**

   Normally, use the month-end date. For example, to reconcile the bank account to 30 April 2016, type that date.

   After you enter the date, Sage shows you the recurring entries due to be posted up to the chosen date.

4. **Click Post.**

REMEMBER

Sage doesn't post recurring entries with a zero value. Cancel the Posting screen and go back and edit the recurring entry so that a value is entered, or choose to suspend the item. Also, Sage won't process recurring entries if there are no balancing debits and credits, so ensure you post your recurring journal entries correctly.

SAGE PAYMENTS

While I briefly mention Sage Pay earlier in this chapter (linking Sage Accounts with your online activity), it would be remiss of me if I didn't briefly refer to Sage Payments. This is an additional chargeable service that Sage provides that integrates with your accounting package and allows you to manage and make payments straight from your Sage software. This includes payments of all kinds, including those to suppliers as well as payroll payments. This service claims to save time and reduce errors by automating the payment process. Effectively, you don't have to log out of Sage, log in to your banking service and then retype the payment transactions that you want to process. It is also possible to view payments information from your mobile or tablet device.

If you operate the Foreign currency module, you are able to make international payments and the Sage Payments service adjusts the foreign currency calculations if there is a change in the currency rates between transactions being posted and subsequently paid on the accounting system.

Dealing with Petty Cash

Petty cash, funds kept in the office for incidental expenses, is often an absolute pain to administer. Normally a company has a petty cash tin containing a small amount of cash and stuffed full of receipts. As members of staff are given money from the petty cash fund, they exchange the money with a receipt. If you count up the amount of cash and receipts, the total of both should equal the value of the petty cash float. Unfortunately, some people request £20 from petty cash to buy some stationery and pop the receipt in the tin, but forget to return the change. In the following sections I help you keep the petty cash tin in order.

Funding petty cash

Normally, you write out a cheque for petty cash or take the cash out of the bank and put the cash in the petty cash tin. To account for this arrangement within Sage, you can easily show this transaction as a bank transfer.

To do a bank transfer, follow the instructions in the 'Transferring Funds between Accounts' section earlier in this chapter. Make sure the Bank Current account is selected as the *account from* and the Petty Cash account is selected as the *account to*. If you write a cheque for petty cash, you can use the cheque number as a reference.

Making payments from the tin

TIP

Make one person solely responsible for the petty cash tin. That person can then ensure that if someone returns and doesn't have the correct change and receipts, at the very least an IOU goes in the tin for the money owed. That individual must get the money returned to the tin as soon as possible.

When a payment is made from the petty cash tin, make sure a receipt replaces the money or use a petty cash voucher to record where the money has been spent. This ensures all payments are recorded correctly and should also ensure that the petty cash tin balances to the agreed float amount.

To record a payment made from petty cash in Sage, follow the instructions for bank payments in the section 'Tracking Bank Deposits and Payments' but select the Petty Cash account instead of the Bank Current account.

Reconciling the petty cash tin

Periodically, you need to reconcile the petty cash tin. The best time to do this is when you decide to top it up. To reconcile the petty cash tin, follow these steps:

1. **Extract all the petty cash receipts, batch them up and total them.**

2. **Give this batch a unique reference number, such as PC01.**

   You can then use PC02 for the next batch, PC03 for the next, and so on. You can use this reference in the Reference field for recording the petty cash bank payments.

3. **Count the remaining petty cash.**

   The sum of the actual cash added to the total from Step 1 should equal the petty cash float.

   TIP

   If the petty cash float doesn't balance, check to see if anyone is holding back any petty cash receipts or if anyone has been given cash to do something and hasn't returned all the change or the receipt.

4. **Write a cheque for cash for the value of the receipts and use this to top up the petty cash float.**

   TECHNICAL STUFF

   This method is known as the *Imprest system* – you replenish only what you've spent.

Paying the Credit Card Bill

Many businesses use credit cards as a convenient way to purchase goods and ser-vices. Just like other financial accounts, you need to include credit card payments in the monthly processing of transactions.

Making credit card payments

After you receive a credit card statement, you need to match up the invoices and till receipts with the statement:

>> **Invoices:** If you paid a supplier using your credit card, you probably received an invoice, which you entered and filed away. To process this payment, select the Credit Card bank account and then click the Payments icon and select Supplier Payment from the drop-down menu. Make sure you insert a reference to the method of payment somewhere. For example, in the Cheque No. field use the reference *CC* for credit card. Alternatively, use a unique

reference number for each credit card statement, particularly if several employees have their own credit cards. In this case, give the statement sheet for each individual its own unique reference number, such as *CC001*. This makes it easier to find the supporting papers for a transaction.

>> **Till receipts:** If you have a till receipt rather than a proper invoice for something purchased using the company credit card, attach the receipt to the credit card statement and record the transaction as a bank payment. Make sure you select the Credit Card account as the account from which the payment is to be made. Also, make sure you're careful with the VAT element of the payment, as the amount of VAT attributable to a transaction isn't always obvious.

Reconciling the credit card statement

After you enter all the transactions from the credit card statement on to Sage, you're in a position to reconcile the Credit Card account in the same way as a normal bank statement. (In Chapter 15 I talk about reconciling your bank account.)

When you enter the credit card statement balance, it should be a negative figure because it's money that you owe the credit card company.

The statement is usually paid via a direct debit from your bank account on a monthly basis. You can treat this as a bank transfer between the Bank Current account and the Credit Card account, which I describe in the section 'Transferring Funds between Accounts' earlier in this chapter. You can reconcile the statement in the same way as any other bank account. Provided you enter all the transactions and set the statement balance to a negative figure, you can't go too far wrong.

Chapter 9

Maintaining and Correcting Entries

E veryone makes mistakes. Sage understands this and makes it very easy for you to correct your errors. You can completely delete an item, change elements of a transaction such as the date or tax code, or find an item to double-check something.

In this chapter, I show you how to make changes to your data and correct any mistakes you find.

Finding Ways to Find Transactions

To amend or delete a transaction, you need to know the transaction number and then locate the transaction.

To find a transaction, you use the Transactions module:

1. **Using the Navigation bar, click Transactions.**

2. **Click the Find button at the top of the screen.**

   This brings up the Find box, as shown in Figure 9-1, which you use to find the transaction.

3. **Enter details into the boxes.**

   Tell Sage what to find and where to look:

   - **Find:** The information you enter here depends on what the Search In field shows. For example, in Figure 9-1, the Search In field reads Transaction Number, so the entry in this field should be a transaction number.

   - **Search In:** A drop-down box gives you different variables to search with. The default variable is Transaction Number, but you can also choose Account Reference, Reference, Details, Date, Net Amount, Bank Account Reference, Nominal Account Reference, Ex Reference, Tax Amount, Amount Paid, Date Reconciled and Late Entry Date.

   - **Match:** You don't have to search using the exact data. You can also select how close a match you can make.

     Selecting Any finds all transactions that contain the details you entered anywhere in the field you're searching on. For example, if you're searching for an account reference and you enter RED, Sage finds references such as RED, REDMOND and CALLRED.

     Selecting Whole finds the transaction that contains the exact details you enter in the Find field. In our example, when you search for account references, it brings up the RED account transactions.

     Selecting Start finds all transactions beginning with the details you enter. In the example, Sage finds transactions beginning with RED, such as RED and REDMOND, but it doesn't find CALLRED.

   - **Case sensitive:** Tick this box if you want Sage to find transactions that contain exactly the same upper- and lower-case letters as those in the Find What field.

4. **Click Find First.**

   If Sage finds a transaction, it highlights it in blue. If this isn't the transaction you want, click Find Next. You may need to cancel the Find box to see the transaction properly.

   If Sage finds no transactions, it tells you. Click OK to return to the Find window so you can enter new search details.

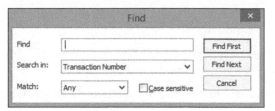

FIGURE 9-1:
The Find box.

Source: Jane Kelly

Searching for Records

You can search for records using the Filter button in the Customers, Suppliers, Nominal Codes, Invoices and Credits, Products and Services, Projects, Sales and Purchase Orders, Departments and Transactions modules. The Search button is simply another method of tracing transactions.

TIP

I tend to search from the Transactions module, as Sage performs a search on all the transactions from this module. If you search from the other modules, Sage limits the search solely to the information in that one module – which may be precisely what you want to do, in which case, choose that specific option.

To perform a search from Transactions, follow these steps:

1. **From the Navigation bar, click Transactions and then click the Filter button.**

   The Filter box opens, as shown in Figure 9-2.

2. **Choose the variables to perform the search.**

   Your choices are:

   - **Join:** From the Join drop-down list, choose the Where option, which is the only option available. (Sage doesn't explain the connection between Join and Where, and I can't either. It's just one of Sage's mysteries.)

   - **Field:** Click the Field column and select the variable you want to search by. In Figure 9-2, Total Amount Paid is selected.

   - **Condition:** Click the Condition column and choose a condition, such as 'is equal to' or 'is greater than'.

   - **Value:** Enter the value you want to search for.

TIP

     You can enter *wildcards*, which are special characters to represent a line of text or an individual character. For more help with wildcards, in the Search box click F1, the Help function key.

   Figure 9-2 shows a search for a transaction for the amount £250.

3. **Click Apply.**

   Sage identifies all transactions that meet the conditions you selected. If Sage can't find a transaction, nothing comes up.

4. **Close the Filter box to view the transactions that Sage finds.**

You can click the Edit icon to view the transaction in more detail.

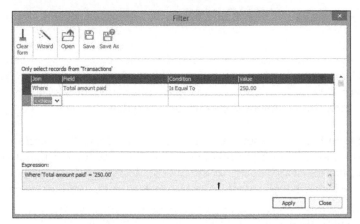

Source: Jane Kelly

TIP

You can save a search so you can find records with the same criteria later. Just follow the first two steps in the preceding list and then click the Save icon instead of Apply. Enter a suitable filename and then click Save again. To access this saved file, open the Search box, click Open and select the chosen file.

After you use the Find facility, you can return back to viewing all transactions by clicking the icon next to the filter button (it has a red circle with a cross through it).

Making Corrections

Sage makes corrections to the individual transactions themselves, so identifying the precise transaction that you want to correct is important. To make a correction to a transaction, you can delete the whole transaction or correct a part of the transaction. Just follow these steps:

1. **From the Navigation bar, click on Transactions.**

   The screen shows you a list of all your transactions, listed in transaction number order.

FIGURE 9-2:
Searching
for – and
finding – £250.

2. **Find the transaction you want to correct.**

You can click Find or use the up and down arrows to scroll through the data.

3. **Choose how to make the correction.**

You have three options:

- **Edit:** This option opens a new window showing the details of the transaction. In Figure 9-3 I've chosen a bank payment. The windows differ slightly, depending on the transaction type. On the first screen, any item in black type can be changed. Click the Edit button to change greyed-out items. You then have the option of changing most other parts of the data. Make your changes and click Save. Sage asks, 'Do you wish to post these changes?' Click Yes to save or No to return to the original screen. Click Close and then Yes to return to the Corrections screen. Click Close again to return to the Transactions screen.

- **Unallocate:** This option is greyed out, unless you select either a PP (Purchase payment transaction), an SR (Sales Receipt transaction), a PC (Purchase Credit) or an SC (Sales Credit). If you click the Unallocate icon when one of the preceding transactions is highlighted, a confirmation message will appear asking if you want to Unallocate that transaction; click Yes to continue or No to discard this action. If you say Yes, the status of the transaction will change from either PP to PA (Payment on Account) or from SR to SA (Sale on Account). The status doesn't change for a PC or an SC, but you can check the individual sales or purchase account to find that the credit note concerned has been unallocated. You will also notice that the sales or purchase invoice that was previously allocated to the credit note now has an N (No) against the paid column, where previously it had been Y (Yes).

- **Delete:** If you know you want to delete an item, highlight it and click the Delete Item icon. The individual transaction window appears. You can click the View button to see more of the transaction. If you definitely want to delete it, click Delete. A confirmation message appears, asking if you want to delete the transaction. Click Yes to continue the deletion or No to take you back to the individual transaction window. You can then click Close to return to the main Transactions screen.

WARNING

All actions you take are recorded in the audit trail, so your accountant can see how many corrections you've made. From an audit point of view, transactions need to be traceable even if you've made mistakes. Unfortunately, any deletions or changes to data are highlighted in red on the audit trail, so if you make wholesale changes to your data, they stick out like a sore thumb.

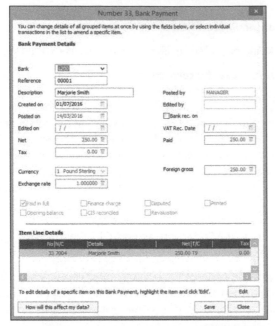

Source: Jane Kelly

FIGURE 9-3:
Editing a bank
payment.

Editing a Journal Entry

It is now possible from version 22 of the Sage 50 software to edit a journal entry made in Sage 50 Accounts. (This is a major step forward, as it was always very frustrating that you couldn't do this in the past). Here's how to do it:

1. **From the Transactions window, highlight one of the journal entries that you want to change.**

   Then click the Edit icon.

2. **The Edit Journal Entry window opens.**

   You can change pretty much all the details of the journal, from the initial reference to even the date of the journal. You can change the nominal codes using a drop-down arrow, you can edit the details in the reference field and you can also change the amount of the journal. It is also possible to add and delete lines of the journal using the icons at the top of the window.

3. **Once you are happy with your journal changes, you simply click Save.**

   You are then returned to the main Transactions window. Depending on the level of changes made, you will either see the revised text or reference, but if you have changed the amount (for example) you will find that the original journal has been deleted and changed to red font, and some new transactions have been created, showing the details of the new journal.

TIP

A bank transfer is shown as a journal entry on Sage, so these can also be amended in the same way as described earlier.

Deleting a Journal Entry

In the same way that you can edit a journal entry (see the preceding section), it is now possible to delete one. Simply do the following:

1. **From the Transactions window, highlight the journal entry that you want to delete and click the delete icon.**

2. **The Delete Journal Entry window opens, showing you the details of the whole journal.**

   Click the Delete button at the bottom right of the screen.

3. **A confirmation message appears, asking if you are sure you want to delete the journal.**

   Click Yes to delete the journal or No to return to the main transactions screen.

TIP

The deleted journal is visible on the transaction screen and can be identified by its red font and the words Deleted JD (Journal Debit) or Deleted JC (Journal Credit) in the details column of the list of transactions.

Perhaps you're wondering whether these corrections are noted. If you look at the list of transactions (click on Transactions on the navigation bar), you can easily identify transactions that have been deleted by looking for items with a red font. However, to investigate further, scroll across the transactions page to the far right. You will see that Sage has added two new columns, called Edited By and Edited on. Here you can see which user made those corrections and when she did it. You can also view these changes in report format as follows:

1. **From the Transactions module, click the Report icon at the top right of the screen.**

2. **The Transaction Reports window opens.**

   Click on Audit Trail, to the left of the window, and a series of reports will open up on the right-hand side of the screen.

3. **Choose Audit Trail (Amended Transactions by User).**

Double-click on this option to generate the Criteria box, where you can choose from a number of different options such as date, transaction number and so on. I just clicked OK and left the boxes blank so that it brought forward all changes that have been made. If you preview the report first, you can determine how large the report is going to be and select your criteria accordingly before printing your final document.

Checking and Maintaining Your Files

In this section I help you explore the file maintenance options. From the Menu bar, click File and then Maintenance. A Sage warning message opens saying that you must close all windows before proceeding. Click Yes. The File Maintenance box appears, as shown in Figure 9-4.

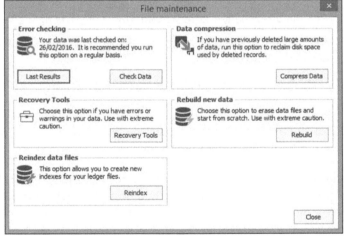

FIGURE 9-4:
File maintenance options let you check and correct your data.

Source: Jane Kelly

The File Maintenance screen may look a little daunting, but you probably need to use only the Error Checking option regularly. I go through each function in the following sections.

Checking errors

The Error Checking facility lets you check your data to make sure it's not corrupt. If your computer switches off in the middle of using Sage, I recommend you use this facility. If Sage closes without being shut down properly, your data may be corrupted.

To verify that no errors are present, perform an Error Checking routine, following these steps:

1. **From the Menu bar, click File and then Maintenance.**

2. **Click Check Data in the Error Checking section of the File Maintenance window.**

   The system checks each file. If no problems are evident, Sage gives you a message confirming there are no problems to report.

3. **Click OK to return to the File Maintenance screen.**

4. **Click Close to exit the File Maintenance Problems Report window and then Close again to exit the File Maintenance screen.**

If Sage finds any problems with your data, it shows a box with several tabs that you can click for more information:

» **Comments:** These messages tell you your data may have inconsistencies. The Comments tab shows you which accounts you need to look at. Comments are usually insignificant and don't require data correction.

» **Warnings:** These messages alert you to problems that may require further investigation.

WARNING

» **Errors:** An Error message indicates a problem with the data. You can fix errors in Sage, but I recommend you make a backup before you do so. If you find errors in your data, I recommend you restore your data back to a point where you know it was fine. I help you do this in the section 'Restoring Data' later in this chapter. Clicking 'How to fix errors and warnings in your Sage data' takes you to a Sage website that guides you through resolving any errors or warnings in your data.

Using Recovery Tools

WARNING

Recovery Tools is the second option on the File maintenance window, as shown in Figure 9-4. This is to be used with extreme caution and only really with the super-vision of a Sage technician/support person.

Once you have clicked on the Recovery Tools button, Sage will automatically prompt you to back up your data. You must make sure you do this, as you don't know what will happen next, and you need to have an accurate backup to start with.

Once the backup has been completed, you are presented with the Recovery Tools window, which shows eight different options, all of which look equally scary. I outline them briefly here:

>> **Reindex and Compress All:** This option reindexes and compresses all the data files.

- **Reindex:** This is where each data file has a matching index file, which tells the software what order the data should be in. If these files don't match up, the order of your data may appear incorrectly. When you use the Reindexing option, Sage creates a new index file based on the indexes that you have selected to re-create.

- **Compress:** When you delete data within Sage, the program doesn't delete the space that is left behind in your data files. This can lead to data appearing to be the incorrect size. Compressing the data resolves this issue.

>> **Recalculate Transaction History:** This option rebuilds the balance of any customer, supplier or nominal records with transactions.

>> **Recalculate Period Values:** This rebuilds the values within customer records, supplier records and nominal records.

>> **Reset Transaction Status:** This checks for any unallocated transactions that should be allocated and changes the transaction type. For example, a Sales Receipt (SR) will be changed to SA (Sale on Account). You then have the ability to correctly allocate the transactions.

>> **Recalculate Order Allocations:** The order levels are corrected on the stock records to match the sales orders, purchase orders and project allocation values. Sage requests that you do this only as a last resort and would prefer that you restore a backup prior to errors being found.

>> **Recalculate Stock:** This option re-links the stock transactions and resets the assembly level and link level within the product record BOM (Bill of Materials) tab and recalculates the stock quantities.

>> **Recalculate Project History:** This option rebuilds the project transactions and the values within the project record.

>> **Recreate CIS History:** This option removes any unsubmitted CIS (Construction Industry Scheme) Returns from within the CIS data files.

Reindexing data

WARNING

Sage recommends using the Reindexing option only under the guidance of Sage Customer Support. When Sage recommends this course of action, it's usually pretty serious! I've never had to use this option myself, so I can only emphasise what Sage says: Contact Sage Customer Support if you need to reindex your data.

Compressing data

WARNING

Compressing data files is pretty serious stuff and outside the scope of this book. Briefly, this function constructs a new set of data files and removes deleted records, thereby reducing the file sizes. The files are compressed to create more disk space. As the compression procedure is irreversible, you need to back up your data first, just in case any problems occur.

Rebuilding data

WARNING

Use this tool with extreme caution. You need to tread carefully when using this part of the system because you can end up wiping all the data off your machine. I suggest you make a backup before you rebuild your data, so you can restore everything fairly easily if necessary.

You can choose to create new data files for all or part of the Sage Accounts system.

Click the Rebuild button to open the Rebuild Data Files window, with all the boxes ticked. A tick indicates that you don't want to create new data files for that part of the system. Removing the ticks tells Sage which parts of your software you want to create new data files for.

If you type 'rebuild data files' into the Sage Help menu, Sage guides you through the process. However, I suggest you have Sage Customer Support on standby just in case anything goes wrong, so they can talk you through the steps.

Backing Up Data the Manual Way

REMEMBER

Performing regular backup routines is extremely important. If your data becomes corrupt or you need to reinstall Sage for whatever reason, you then have a backup that you can restore onto your computer, letting you continue to work with the least amount of disruption.

To back up your data, follow these steps:

1. **From the Menu bar, click File and then Backup.**

   A message asks if you want to check your data. Sage recommends you check your data, which normally takes a matter of seconds, depending on how many records you have. Click Yes to check or No to continue with the backup.

2. **Make adjustments on the Backup window that comes up.**

   The navigation bar on the left of the Backup window contains three options:

   - **Backup Company:** This displays the filename SageAccts, followed by your company name, today's date, time and the .001 file extension, as shown in Figure 9-5.

     You can change the filename to one that has meaning for your business. For example, the filename 'Jingles accounts end of day 2016-03-18.001' indicates a backup of Jingles's data at close of business on 18 March 2016. I often add the last transaction number (found at the bottom right of the screen) for extra detail.

     Choose a location that you can find easily if you need to restore the data. Use the Browse button to change the location if you're not happy with the location Sage chooses.

   - **Advanced Options:** This lets you choose how much you back up. For example, you can include only data, or data plus reports, templates and so on. At the very least, I suggest you back up your data files. This is the default option.

     You can tick a box to Select all file types to include in backup, but note that this will make the file extremely large; it will take up more space and potentially take longer to run the backup.

   - **Previous Backups:** This lets you see a list of previous backups.

3. **Click OK.**

   Sage starts the backup. When the process is complete, you receive a confirmation message saying the backup was successful.

REMEMBER

Give each backup a different name. Sage makes this easy by adding the date to the filename, but if you perform more than one backup in a day, you have to change the name slightly or a backup with the same name overwrites the first set of data. This is where adding the last transaction number can become quite useful.

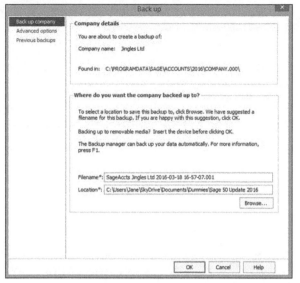

FIGURE 9-5:
The Sage Backup
screen.

Scheduling Backups

Sage lets you schedule your data backups at a time to suit you, using the new Sage Accounts Backup Manager.

Follow these steps to schedule your backups:

1. From the Menu bar, click File and then Schedule backup.

The Sage Accounts Backup Manager window opens on the Overview screen. Here you can see who is logged on, when the last backup was done and whether there are any problems to report on the data, as shown in Figure 9-6.

2. Click the Settings option to amend the backup details.

Here you can change the backup times, the file types that you want to back up and the backup location, as shown in Figure 9-7. You can also choose to adjust the amount of free space left on your server's hard drive. Sage will not create new backup files once the server has run out of space. By default, 20 gigabytes of space will be left free on the server's hard disk drive. You can adjust this figure up or down to suit your business.

3. On the Settings tab, click Save when you're happy with the backup details.

Close the Overview screen using the cross in the right-hand corner of the box.

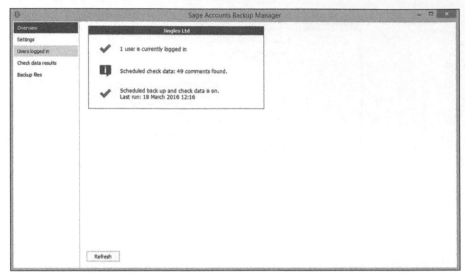

FIGURE 9-6:
Backing up data.

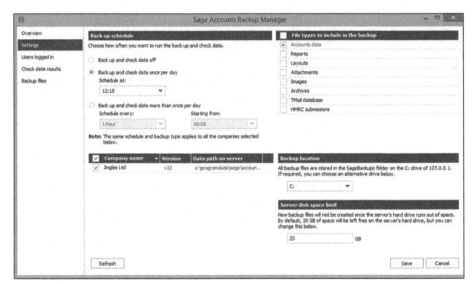

FIGURE 9-7:
Checking what
data to back up.

Restoring Data

When you restore data, you erase the current data on the computer and replace it with data from your backup files. Ideally, you'll never need to do this – but in case you do, follow these steps:

1. **From the Menu bar, click File and then Restore.**

   Sage tells you that it can't run this function without closing windows. Click Yes to show the Restore window.

2. **Click Browse and select the file that you want to restore.**

3. **Click OK.**

   A message appears saying you're about to restore, and the process overwrites any data currently on the computer. Click Yes to continue or No to exit.

TIP

After you successfully restore your data, use the Error Checking facility in the File Maintenance screen to check for errors, as I explain in the earlier section 'Checking errors'.

3

Functions for Plus and Professional Users

Chapter 10

Processing Sales Orders

S ales orders occur when a customer requests some of your goods or services. In this chapter, I walk you through the steps for processing a sales order, from the moment a quote is confirmed to allocating and despatching the stock and then issuing an invoice to the customer.

Note: Sales order processing is available only if you have Sage Accounts Professional. If you don't have this version of Sage, feel free to skip most of this chapter – though the bit on quotations also applies to Sage Accounts Plus, so you may want to read that section.

Giving a Quote

I don't mean recording your words for the enlightenment of the masses. In the business sense, a *quotation* is what you prepare when a potential customer asks for a price for a product or service that you offer. You can create a quotation within Sage that you can ultimately convert into an order if the customer accepts your price.

Amending your invoice and order defaults

If you use Accounts Plus, you don't have Sales Order Processing as an option, but you can still double-check the invoice and order defaults to ensure the quotations you raise can convert to sales invoices. Follow the instructions outlined here, but make sure that in Step 2 you set the Convert Quotes To field to Invoice.

If you use Accounts Professional, you also need to amend the invoice and order defaults. For example, you can tell Sage what number you want invoices and orders to start from – especially useful if you're continuing on from a previous system. Click the Options tab of the Invoice/Order defaults to make these changes in Sage.

To amend your invoice and order defaults, follow these steps:

1. **From the Menu bar, click Settings and then Invoice/Order Defaults.**

2. **On the General tab, set the Convert Quotes To field to Sales Orders.**

3. **Click OK to accept your changes.**

From version 22 onwards, a new tab has been added called Update ledgers. It enables you to select specific pieces of information to be automatically entered into the Reference and Extra Reference fields when the sales order is converted to an invoice, and then that invoice is subsequently updated to the ledger. I cover this in more detail in Chapter 6.

Creating a quotation

After you check your defaults, you can create a quotation by following these steps:

1. **From the Navigation bar, click Quotations.**

   The Quotation window opens.

2. **Click the New icon.**

   The Product Quote SOP window opens, which looks very similar to the Product Invoicing screen.

3. **Enter the account for which you want to create a quotation by using the drop-down arrows.**

   You can add an expiry date if you want.

4. **Enter the rest of the quotation details, including the product code and quantity.**

   In Figure 10-1, I show a sample quotation created by Jingles for the Village Shop.

5. When you're happy with your quotation details, click Save.

The quotation is saved to the Quotations list.

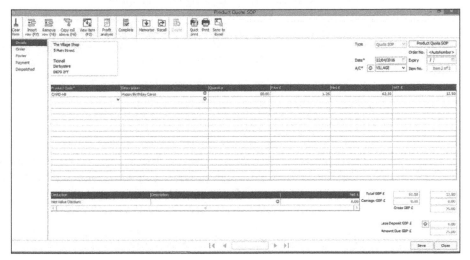

FIGURE 10-1:
A quotation
Jingles created for
the Village Shop.

Source: Jane Kelly

REMEMBER

You can access the Quotations list by clicking Quotations on the Navigation bar. If you want to edit the details of any quote, highlight the quote you want to edit, click the Edit icon, make the necessary amendments, and click Save.

Sage can list quotations using the following status categories. Generally speaking, the status of the quote is assigned automatically, unless another company gets the business, in which case you have to amend the status yourself.

» **All quotes:** Sage displays all quotations of any category.

» **Quotes won:** Sage displays all quotations that you've won. Sage automatically shows a quotation as won when you convert the quote to an order or invoice. Alternatively, you can manually highlight the quote you want to convert to won and click the Mark as Won icon.

» **Quotes lost:** Sage displays all quotations that you've lost. You can amend a quote by clicking the Mark as Lost icon.

» **Open quotes:** Sage displays all quotations that haven't passed their expiry dates.

» **Expired quotes:** Sage displays all quotations that have expired. A quotation expires after it has been open for a period longer than your specified expiry date. You can reopen an expired quotation by changing the expiry date.

You can change the status of a quote by highlighting and right-clicking a quote from the Quotations list or simply by highlighting the quote and then using the appropriate icon at the top of the screen to amend the status to either open, won or lost. That said, the following criteria apply:

>> Only open or expired quotes can be marked as lost.

>> Only lost quotes can be marked as open.

>> Expired quotes can be marked as lost.

>> Only open quotes can be converted to won.

Whilst this looks quite complicated, sometimes, depending on the situation, it may be worth amending the expiry date of a quotation, and thus changing it from expired to open. This then provides you with more options for changing the status. You can now mark the quotation as won or lost.

Allocating and amending stock for a quote

You can allocate stock to an open quotation. To allocate stock, simply select the quotation and click Allocate Stock, and then click Yes to confirm. If you want to amend the allocation of stock, select the quotation and click Amend Allocations. You can now amend the amount of stock allocated.

Converting a quotation to an invoice or order

Depending on your invoice and order default settings, you can convert your quotation to an invoice or an order. I use the example of an order in the sample steps throughout the rest of this chapter.

If you want to convert a quotation to an invoice instead of an order, set your Invoice/Order defaults to Convert quotes to an invoice and then follow the same steps as described in this chapter. You can look at the new invoice on your Invoice list by clicking on the Invoices and credits link on the Navigation bar.

From the Quotations list, select the quote you want to convert and click Mark as Won. Sage asks if you're sure you want to convert the selected quote, so click Yes.

The status of the quote changes to won, and the quotation type becomes an order. Sage also creates a sales order in the Sales Order list.

Creating a Sales Order

You can create a sales order by converting a quotation, as I describe in the previous section. You can then access the new sales order by clicking Sales orders on the Navigation bar, highlighting the order, and clicking the Edit icon.

Alternatively, you can create a new sales order by clicking Sales orders from the Navigation bar and then clicking the New icon. The Product Sales Order window opens on the Details screen, but there are five more screens that can be viewed as outlined here:

>> **Details (default screen):** This screen lets you enter the main sales order details, including customer, dates, items ordered and prices.

>> **Order:** In this screen you can amend the delivery details and add any notes about the order. You also find (from version 22 onward) some new analysis fields in the Custom Fields section at the bottom of the order page. You can rename these fields using meaningful terms for your business. As long as you are consistent with the data that you enter in these new fields, you can produce additional meaningful information that can be analysed within your business. To amend the analysis fields, click Settings from the main toolbar and then click Configuration Editor followed by Custom Fields.

It is also possible to enter a due date for the Sales order in the Sales Order Status box, found on the Order tab. This same date is then replicated in the Despatch tab for the sales order.

>> **Footer:** You can use this tab to enter information about carriage and courier charges, settlement terms and discounts.

>> **Payment:** You can record a payment on this tab, including details of deposits already received and payments on account. It is also possible to pay a deposit by card, using the button with the same name, but you have to use Sage Pay to operate this feature.

>> **Despatched:** This tab shows the order status and details of any goods despatched notes. It updates only after you record a delivery of goods.

A *goods despatched note* (GDN) is essentially the paperwork assigned to stock as it's despatched to your customers. The GDN shows the date the goods were despatched; the customer the goods were sent to; and details of the products, quantity ordered and quantity despatched. I talk about GDNs in more detail in the section 'Using goods despatched notes'.

The main body of the Despatched tab shows the GDN number, the customer's GDN and the date the goods were despatched. It shows *Y* for yes if you've printed the GDN and is blank if you haven't printed. The Despatched tab also contains the following information:

- **Order Status:** The status of the order appears here automatically. It may be full, part or cancelled – or it may be blank, which means the order is complete or has no stock allocated to it.

- **Despatch:** This box shows the despatch status of the order and can be part or complete. If no items have been despatched for the order, the box is blank.

- **Invoice Status:** This box contains *Y* for yes if you've raised an invoice for the order, or *N* for no if you haven't raised an invoice.

- **Complete:** This box shows *Y* for yes if the order is complete, or *N* for no if the order isn't complete.

- **Due Date:** This date cannot be amended in this field, but you can amend the due date of the order from the Order tab, and this is the date that is shown here.

- **Intrastat:** This box appears only if Intrastat reporting is enabled in the Invoice/Order defaults. The box displays the Intrastat declarations status of the order. *Intrastat* is a system for collecting statistics on the movement of goods between member states of the European Union. (I address Intrastat more fully in Chapter 17.)

» **Invoices:** This tab shows which invoices are raised against an order. If you want to see the full details of an invoice, double-click the invoice from the list.

Entering the sales order details

You can create a sales order from a quotation, but if you want to create a sales order without creating a quotation first, follow these steps:

1. **From the Navigation bar, click Sales orders.**

   The Sales order screen opens. Click the New icon to open the Details tab for a product sales order.

2. **Enter the header details.**

   Sage asks you to select or provide information:

   - **Type:** Use the drop-down arrow to select Sales Order or Proforma Sales Order.

   - **Order Number:** Sage automatically assigns each order a sequential number after the order has been saved. The first order is number 1, the next number 2, and so on. If you want to start from a different number, change the number on the Options tab on Invoice/Order defaults.

- **Date:** Enter the date of the order. The system defaults to the current day's date, unless you change it.

- **Invoice Reference:** When you update your sales order to match an existing invoice, the last invoice number relating to the sales order appears.

- **Account:** Enter the customer account reference here.

- **Item Number:** This is the number of the item currently highlighted on the order. For example, if there are five item lines, and the cursor is currently on the second line, the box says Item 2 of 5.

3. **Complete the main body of the order by entering the product items you've sold.**

Enter the basic information about the products:

- **Product Code:** Use the drop-down arrow to select the product code required. If you don't have a specific product code to use, you can use a special product code. (See Chapter 6 for more details on special product codes.)

- **Description:** This field automatically updates when you select a product code. You can edit the description by pressing F3. (Refer to Chapter 6 to find out more about using the F3 button.)

- **Quantity:** Enter the quantity of stock the customer has ordered.

- **Price:** The unit price from the product record appears here.

- **Discount:** The customer's discount for the item displays here. A discount appears only if it has been selected within the Invoice/Order defaults. Choose the Discounts tab and then tick the box 'Show discount on main invoice/order'.

- **Discount percentage:** This shows the percentage discount that the customer receives.

- **Net:** The net amount is calculated automatically. You can't change this value.

- **VAT:** The VAT amount calculates automatically. You can't change the value.

- **Total:** The order is totalled at the bottom, showing the net value, carriage charges if they're applicable, the amount of VAT and the gross amount.

- **Deposit:** This new feature has a smart link to the Payment tab of the order, allowing you to record any deposits received against the order or for customers to make a payment by card – if Sage Pay is activated.

- **Deduction:** Here, Net Value Discount offers a drill-down arrow in the Description box, which, when clicked, reveals an Edit Item line. You can enter information referring to the discount and a discount value, and then press Tab – Sage then automatically calculates the percentage discount. If you enter a discount percentage, Sage calculates the value instead.

4. **Click Order from the Navigation bar on the left side of the screen to add a delivery address or any notes to the order.**

   Additionally, you can add any details in the Custom fields at the bottom of this screen if you are using them.

   Sage pulls some information from the customer record, such as telephone number and contact. A Sales Order Status section shows whether stock has been allocated to the order and the delivery status of the goods. You can enter an estimated despatch date for the sales order if required.

5. **Click Footer from the Navigation bar on the left side of the screen to add carriage details.**

   The information requested includes assignment numbers and courier details:

   - **Carriage:** You may want to assign carriage costs to the order if it involves postal or courier costs. You can set up specific nominal codes for charging the carriage costs. If you've set up departments, use the drop-down list to select the appropriate department. You can also add the consignment number and courier details and track your parcel by accessing the courier's website.

   - **Settlement Terms:** Some information may already be present in these boxes, depending on what details you entered on your customer record. You can enter the number of days during which an early settlement discount applies and see the discount percentage applied. Settlement Terms also shows you the total value of the invoice.

   - **Global:** This section lets you apply global terms to the whole order. If you use this option, only one line is added to the audit trail. Carriage is always shown as a separate line.

     You can apply a global nominal code to the whole order. This global code is posted to the nominal ledger when you update the invoice that Sage eventually generates from the order. You can enter global details to accompany the posting to the nominal ledger. This information appears on all reports that show the Details field. Up to 60 characters are available for you to use.

     You can also apply the same global option to your tax code and your departments.

   - **Tax Analysis:** The tax analysis for each product item is shown at the bottom of the Footer tab. The list shows a breakdown of all the VAT into the separate VAT codes (assuming you haven't used the Global Tax option).

6. **Click Save when you're happy with the details you've entered.**

   Sage asks whether you want to allocate stock now or later. Click Allocate later, as I discuss later in this chapter.

   The Sales Order screen reverts to a blank order. Sage has saved your order, which now shows on the Sales Order list. You can find the Sales Order list when you click on Sales orders on the Navigation bar.

Dealing with cash sales

Some orders are completed at point of sale, particularly if you have over-the-counter sales. The customer pays for the goods and takes them away immediately. You can receive payment for cash sales online by using the Sage Pay wizard. (Type 'Sage Pay' into the Sage Help facility to find out more.)

Instead of manually completing each element of the sales order life cycle from stock allocation through ledger updates, you can automate the whole process by choosing the cash sales option when you create the sales order.

To activate the cash sales option, enter the sales order details as explained in Steps 1–5 in the section 'Entering the sales order details'. Then click the Cash Sales icon at the top of the order on the Details screen. A confirmation message asks if you wish to complete this order as a cash sale. Click Yes to continue or No to return to the order. If you click Yes, the Layout window opens, expecting you to select your chosen despatch note layout. When you highlight the layout you require, the floating icons appear and you can choose to preview, print, export, export to Excel or email the despatch note. The system completes all stock allocations, creates an invoice and creates a bank transaction for the receipt of cash.

REMEMBER

You must have sufficient stock levels to satisfy the whole order unless you set Sage to allow negative stock values, in which case the order goes through regardless of stock levels.

You can limit the order paperwork produced for a cash sale to only those documents that you actually need. To select the documents that you need for a cash sale, follow these steps:

1. **From the Menu bar, click Settings, select Invoice/Order defaults, and click the Cash Sales tab.**

2. **Select the documents you want to generate for a cash sale.**

   You can choose sales order, goods despatched note or sales invoice.

3. **Add a message to the invoice if you like.**

   The default message is currently Cash Sale – paid in full, as shown in Figure 10-2. If you prefer, you can untick the box so the message doesn't print.

4. **Use the drop-down arrow to select the default cash sales bank account you want the value of the cash sale applied to.**

5. **To save your changes, click OK; to exit without saving, click Cancel.**

To complete the order, Sage generates the order and allocates a sales receipt to it.

Source: Jane Kelly

Editing your order

If you want to change something after you create an order, you can easily amend the details as follows:

1. **From the Navigation bar, click Sales orders.**

   The Sales order list opens.

2. **Select the sales order you want to amend and click the Edit icon at the top of the screen.**

FIGURE 10-2:
The Cash
Sales screen.

3. **Make your changes.**

When you're happy with the order, click Save.

Putting sales orders on hold

You may find you need to put an order on hold while you check out the credit status of a new customer or see if you have enough stock. To temporarily halt an order, follow these steps:

1. **From the Navigation bar, click Sales orders.**

2. **Select the sales order you want to put on hold and click the Amend allocations icon.**

3. **From the Amend Allocations screen, click the Off Order icon.**

The Order Status window appears.

4. **Click Held and then OK.**

5. **Close the Amend Allocations screen.**

You return to the Sales Order Processing screen, where you can see that the status of the order is now held.

If you want to take the order off hold, highlight the order, click the Amend Allocations icon and then click the Order icon. Close the Amend Allocations screen.

Duplicating a sales order

TIP

You can copy the details from an existing order into a new order. I use this time-saving device a lot when processing data. To duplicate a sales order, follow these steps:

1. **From the Navigation bar, click Sales orders.**

2. **Select the sales order you want to copy from the Sales Order Processing screen.**

3. **Click the Duplicate icon.**

A new sales order opens that's an exact copy of the previous order. Notice it has a heading showing that it's a duplicate order. After you save the duplicated order, it acquires an order number of its own. You may also need to change the order date, as it appears as today's date.

4. **Check that the details of the order are correct and amend any parts where necessary.**

5. **To save the new order, click Save.**

   Sage asks if you want to allocate stock now or later. If you choose Allocate Now, Sage automatically allocates the stock and then returns you to a blank sales order screen. Click Close to go to the Sales order list, where you can see your new order with the word Full in the Allocated column.

Printing the order

The print facility lets you print as many copies of the order as you want. Follow these steps to print an order:

1. **From the Navigation bar, click Sales orders.**

2. **Select the sales order you want to print by highlighting the order on the list.**

   Click the Print icon.

3. **The Layout window opens.**

   If you've already selected a favourite report layout, the layout appears in the first screen – otherwise, click Layout and choose the layout you want. Use the floating icons to choose the output method – preview, print, export, export to Excel, or email. Preview the report first to ensure the details are correct and you're happy with the layout.

   To make a layout a favourite, click the star icon next to the report layout you like. This copies the layout to your favourites page.

TIP

4. **Click Print to print the report.**

   The Print window opens. Click OK if you're happy to continue printing the order.

Allocating Stock to an Order

After you save your sales order, Sage asks if you want to allocate stock now or later. If the order has already been despatched and you've completed the order, Sage automatically allocates the goods for you. In the next sections I describe how to apportion stock automatically and manually.

Going on automatic

Sage automatically allocates as much stock as possible to your orders, so the amount of *free stock* (stock available to fulfil orders) decreases and the amount of *allocated stock* (items earmarked for specific orders) increases.

To allocate stock automatically, follow these steps:

1. **From the Navigation bar, click Sales orders.**

   Highlight the order you want to allocate stock to, and then click the Allocate Stock icon.

2. **Click Yes when Sage asks if you want to allocate all stock to the order.**

   If you don't have enough stock to allocate to the order, Sage lets you know.

   The Sales Order Processing window reappears, and the order shows the word Full in the Allocated column. If there isn't enough stock to allocate to the order, the column reads Part.

Assigning stock yourself

Allocating stock manually gives you greater control over your stock. For example, if you have two orders, each for ten boxes of cards, but you have only ten boxes in total, you can manually allocate five boxes of cards to each order and tell each customer that the balance of the order is to follow.

To manually allocate stock, follow these steps:

1. **From the Navigation bar, click Sales orders.**

2. **Highlight the order and click the Amend Allocations icon at the top of the Sales Order Processing screen.**

3. **On the Amend Allocations screen, manually add the number of units to allocate to the order.**

4. **To save your changes, click Close.**

   The word Part shows in the Allocated column against the order.

Sage reduces the amount of free stock and increases the amount of allocated stock in the same way that it does if you automatically allocate stock. Figure 10-3 shows a partially allocated order.

Amending the allocation of stock

If you've allocated stock to an order but haven't actually despatched the order, you can still amend the order and reallocate stock. To do this, select the sales order from the Sales Order list and click Amend Allocations. You can then change the amount of stock you've allocated to that order.

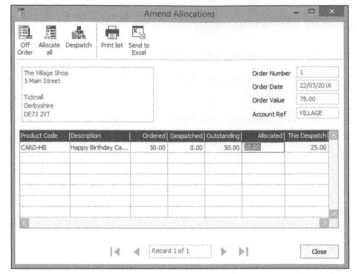

FIGURE 10-3:
The results of
allocating stock
for part of
an order.

Source: Jane Kelly

Using the shortfall generator

Sage lets you know if you don't have enough stock to fulfil all the orders raised. To check your stocks, select the orders from the Sales Order list and click the Shortfall icon on the Sales Order Processing toolbar. The Shortfall Generator window shows a list of any products that have a stock level less than the quantity required for the order, as shown in Figure 10-4. If you highlight the product that is showing as a shortfall and then click the Create Order icon, you can generate a purchase order for the specific products you're running short of.

FIGURE 10-4:
Predicting
a shortfall in
stock is a handy
Sage tool.

Source: Jane Kelly

Despatching Orders

After you allocate the stock to the order, you can despatch the goods using one of the four methods Sage offers. I explain each of these methods in the next sections.

Completing an order

You complete your order once the goods are ready to be sent to the customer. Sage allocates stock to the order and marks the order as being despatched. To complete an order, follow these steps:

1. **Highlight the order from the Sales Order list, click the Edit icon to view the order, and then click the Complete icon at the top of the Details screen.**

2. **A confirmation window asks whether you want to complete the order in full.**

   Click Yes to continue. Sage tells you if an order can't be completed – for example, because you have insufficient stock – and then lets you amend the order accordingly.

3. **Another confirmation message asks if you want to create an invoice, update your stock and record a despatch note for the selected order.**

   If you only want to print a despatch note at this stage, click No; otherwise, click Yes.

4. **A third confirmation window asks if you want to print out the goods delivery note (GDN).**

   Choose whether to print now or later.

5. **A final confirmation message asks if you want to print out your sales order.**

   Select Yes or No. Sage then marks your order as complete or part complete.

Using goods despatched notes

Using a GDN automatically records the goods you despatch and provides maximum traceability because you can view all the GDNs on the Despatch tab for each order.

Before you use GDNs, you need to set up your GDN options in the Options tab of Invoice/Order defaults. You have the following choices:

>> **Generate for all despatches:** This is the default option. Sage gives you the choice of printing a GDN now or later.

>> **Prompt at each despatch:** Sage prompts you each time you record a despatch as to whether you want to generate a GDN now or later. If you don't generate the GDN, Sage doesn't store the GDN in the Despatched tab of the Sales Order, so you can't view or print the note later.

>> **Do not generate:** If you select this option, Sage updates your sales order and your stock level but doesn't produce a GDN.

You also have the option to tick a box to determine whether the GDN prompt appears or not.

Sage issues a GDN depending on the default options you select. You can raise a GDN by clicking the Despatch button, or you can click the GDN button – I outline both methods in the next sections.

Using the despatch facility

You can use the Despatch facility to record complete deliveries of orders to your customers. Follow these steps:

1. **From the Navigation bar, click Sales orders.**

2. **Select the orders from the Sales Order Processing screen and click Despatch Orders.**

   Then follow Steps 3–5 from the earlier section 'Completing an order'.

   Sage generates a GDN if this option is selected in your defaults, creates a product invoice and updates the stock level for each product on the order.

Recording a despatch manually

If you don't despatch the whole order, you can manually record the delivery of the stock you do send. Follow these steps to use the Amend Allocations facility to record complete or part despatches:

1. **From the Sales Order Processing window, click the Amend Allocations icon.**

2. **Edit the quantity shown in the This Despatch column in the Amend Allocations window.**

3. **Click the Despatch icon to update the product records.**

A prompt asks if you want to create invoice details, update stock and record the despatch for the previous order, as shown in Figure 10-5. Choose one of the following answers:

- **Yes:** This lets you continue with the despatch of the goods. For more details, see Step 3 in the earlier section 'Completing an order'.

- **No:** This prints a delivery note only (according to the options chosen).

- **Cancel:** This returns you to the Allocations screen, which you can close if you want.

After you complete the despatch process, you return to the Sales Order List, where you can see that Sage has amended the status to part despatched.

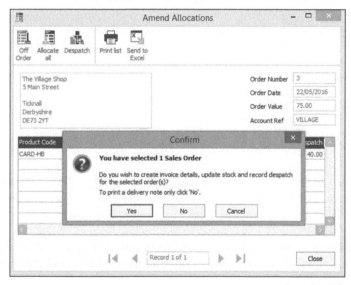

FIGURE 10-5: Recording a part despatch of an order.

Source: Jane Kelly

Invoicing Your Customers

After you allocate and despatch all stock relating to your order, you need to print the invoices created from your order and update the ledgers to complete your sales order cycle.

When you despatch an order, Sage automatically generates a product invoice for each order or partial order. Sage also updates your stock levels at the same time.

You can check that Sage has raised an invoice by looking at the Invoice tab for your order to see the invoice number. You can view and print the invoice from the Invoice tab. If you've already selected a default print layout, you can use the Quick Print option. Alternatively, you can print the invoice by using the following method:

1. **From the Navigation bar, click Invoices and credits.**

   The Invoice list appears.

2. **Choose the invoice you want to print.**

3. **Click Print and select the layout you prefer.**

   When the invoice layout window opens, it may show your favourite layout. If not, choose a layout and click Print from the floating icons. Alternatively, select the Quick Print option if you've already selected a default print layout.

When you're ready to update your invoices, from Customers, click the Invoice list. Select the invoices you want to post and then click the Update Ledgers icon, following the instructions on-screen. Sage posts the invoices to the sales and nominal ledgers.

Deleting and Cancelling Sales Orders

You can delete cancelled or completed orders, and you can also cancel orders before fulfilling them. To free up disk space on your computer, you can remove fulfilled or cancelled orders by compressing your data.

WARNING

Before you delete any orders, I suggest you back up your data in case you change your mind and need to restore the data later. I cover backing up in Chapter 9.

Deleting an order

To delete an order, follow these steps:

1. **From the Navigation bar, click Sales orders.**

   The Sales Order List appears.

2. **Select the order you want to delete and click the Delete icon.**

   A confirmation message asks you to confirm that you want to delete.

When you delete an order, Sage deletes any GDNs associated with the order. Make sure you don't need the GDN information before you delete the order.

3. **To continue deleting the order, click Yes.**

Cancelling an order

You can cancel an unfulfilled sales order. After you cancel an order, it remains on the Sales Order list, but its status changes to cancelled. Any stock that was allocated to that order reverts to free stock again. To cancel a sales order, follow these steps:

1. **From the Navigation bar, click Sales Orders.**

   The Sales order list appears.

2. **Select the order you want to cancel and then click the Amend Allocations icon.**

3. **Click the Off Order icon when the Amend Allocations window appears.**

   The Order Status window appears.

4. **To cancel your order, click Cancel Order.**

   Click OK to confirm the cancellation or click Cancel if you decide you don't want to cancel the order.

When you cancel a sales order, the Off Order button changes to Order. If you want to put a cancelled order back on order, click the Order button from the Amend Allocations window.

When you cancel an order, Sage cancels all the items in the order. If you want to cancel only a specific item on an order, choose the Edit icon from the Sales Order Processing window. Delete the unwanted item from the order, or press the F8 key to delete specific lines on the order.

Chapter 11

Processing Purchase Orders

I f you have Accounts Professional, Sage helps you process your purchase orders. If you don't have this version of Sage, you can skip this chapter.

You raise purchase orders for goods that you place on order with your suppliers. The purchase order processing (POP) system is directly linked to other parts of Sage: The system updates stock records and project records if you use these functions of Sage.

In this chapter, I cover the various stages that a purchase order goes through.

Creating, Changing and Copying a Purchase Order

When you order supplies, materials, widgets or similar items, you need to create a paper trail – or at least an electronic trail – that you can send to your supplier to tell them what you need, how much you need, when you need it and for what price. This paper trail is called a *purchase order*, or PO. Sage Accounts Professional has the perfect process for conveying this information.

Creating a purchase order

Creating a purchase order in Sage consists of completing the information Sage requests on four different screens:

1. **From the Navigation bar, click Purchase orders.**

   A window appears listing all the purchase orders. Click the New icon to open a blank purchase order.

2. **The Product Purchase Order window opens on the details page.**

   Sage asks you for the following basic information:

   TIP

   - **Order Number:** Sage automatically issues each order a sequential number, although you don't see the number until you save the order.

     Sage gives the first order number 1, the next number 2, and so on. If you want to start from a different number, change the number on the Options tab on Invoice/Order defaults, which you can find by clicking Settings on the Menu bar.

   - **Date:** Enter the date of the order. Keep in mind that Sage defaults to the current day's date, unless you change it.

   - **Account:** Enter the supplier account reference here.

   - **Project Reference:** You see this reference only if you switch on Project Costing. Use the drop-down arrow to link the order with a specific project if you want to do so.

   - **Cost Code:** This code appears only if you switch on Project Costing. You can use the drop-down arrow to select an appropriate cost code.

   - **Reference:** You can enter an additional reference here.

- **Item Number:** This field shows the number of the item currently highlighted on the order. For example, if you have five item lines and the cursor is currently on the second line, the box says Item 2 of 5.

- **Rate:** The rate appears only if you enabled the Foreign Currency option.

3. **Complete the main body of the order.**

   List the details of the product items that you want to purchase:

   - **Product Code:** Using the drop-down arrow, select the product code you require. If you don't have a specific product code to use, you can use a special product code. See Chapter 6 for more details on special product codes.

   - **Description:** The description updates automatically when you select a product code. However, you can edit the description by pressing the F3 key.

   - **Quantity:** Enter the quantity of stock that you want to order.

   - **Price:** The unit price from the product record appears here.

   - **Net:** This amount calculates automatically – you can't change this value.

   - **VAT:** This amount calculates automatically – you can't change the value. (VAT is value-added tax.)

   - **Total:** The order total appears at the bottom, showing net, VAT and any carriage charges applied.

4. **Click Order on the Navigation bar on the left to add a delivery address or any notes to the order.**

   Sage pulls certain information from the supplier record, such as the supplier's telephone number and contact information. From version 22 onward, Sage has added some new custom fields at the bottom of the order page. This provides opportunities for individual businesses to customize these fields to suit their business. For example, you may want to create a custom field called Region to identify where your suppliers are based.

5. **Click Footer on the Navigation bar on the left to add carriage details.**

   You can include assignment numbers and courier details here:

   - **Carriage Terms:** You may want to assign postal or courier costs to the order. You can set up specific nominal codes for the carriage costs to be charged to. If you set up departments, use the drop-down list to select the appropriate department. You can also add the consignment number and courier details and track your parcel by accessing the courier's website.

- **Settlement Terms:** Some information may already be present in these boxes, depending on what details you entered on your supplier record. You can enter the number of days during which an early settlement discount applies, see what discount percentage is applied and see the total value of the invoice.

- **Tax Analysis:** The tax analysis for each product item appears at the bottom of the Footer Details tab. The list shows a breakdown of all the VAT into separate VAT codes.

6. **Click Deliveries on the Navigation bar on the left to see details of the GRN (goods received notes) generated from purchase orders.**

   When you record delivery of goods using the GRN option, the system automatically updates the Deliveries screen.

   In addition to the GRN information, you can also see the order status, delivery status, delivery due date, invoice status and Intrastat declarations status.

7. **Click Save to preserve the order.**

   Sage asks, 'Do you want to place this order On Order now?' Click either Order Now or Order Later.

   If you click Order Now, Sage asks if you want to print the order. If you click Yes, the Layout window opens so you can choose a report layout. You can create a favourite report layout by clicking on the star, which turns orange, at the side of the chosen report. This copies the layout and places it on the Favourites tab.

   If you don't select a favourite layout, click on the Layout tab and select one of the series of report layouts listed on the right-hand side of the screen. As you scroll down the list, a floating set of icons offers you options to preview, print, export, export to Excel or email the report directly to your supplier. If you choose to print, your report prints out. Then click the cross in the right corner of the Layout window to close it. The Purchase Order screen then shows a blank order, but Sage has saved your order and is ready for the next one.

   If you click Order Later, the Purchase Order screen goes blank, waiting for you to enter a new order. The order shows on the Purchase Order list, which you can view from the Links pane.

After you close the Purchase Order screen, you can view a copy of your order on the Purchase Order list.

Editing your order

If you want to change something after you create your order, you can easily amend the details as follows:

1. **From the Navigation bar, click Purchase orders.**

   This opens a window showing a list of all your purchase orders.

2. **Select the purchase order that you want to amend and click the Edit icon at the top of the screen.**

   You can then amend any part of the order.

3. **Click Save when you finish editing the purchase order.**

WARNING

I recommend you amend details only if you haven't already placed the order On Order; otherwise, you may experience stock problems when products arrive and don't match what you need. Sage gives you a warning message telling you the order is already On Order, and it may affect the status of the order if you change anything.

Duplicating a purchase order

You can copy an existing order with the same details as those you want to enter for a new order. I use this feature a lot when processing orders, as it speeds up the entry time. To use the duplication feature, follow these steps:

1. **From the Navigation bar, click Purchase orders.**

   A window appears listing all your purchase orders.

2. **Select the purchase order you want to copy and click the Duplicate icon.**

   An exact copy of the previous order opens, as shown in Figure 11-1. Notice the heading proclaims it's a duplicate of the original purchase order. **Note:** You may need to change the date from the system-generated date, which is the current day's date, to the date that you require. You can easily do this by overriding the data in the date field.

3. **Check to be sure the details of the order are correct and change anything that needs to be different.**

4. **To save the new purchase order, click Save.**

   You will be asked if you want to Order Now or Order Later. If you say later, Sage will create an order for you, which you will see on the list of purchase orders on the Purchase Order window. You can then decide later how you want to proceed with this order.

5. **To close the order and return to the main purchase orders screen, click Close.**

   The Purchase Order list appears, showing the new order.

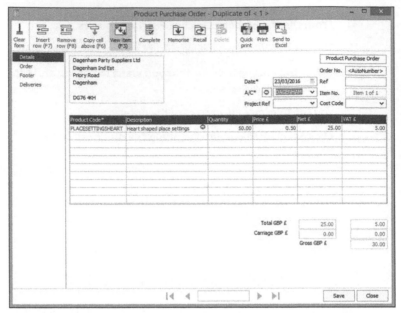

FIGURE 11-1:
Cloning a
purchase order
is easy and
helpful.

Placing the Goods on Order

After you create a purchase order and are ready to send it to your supplier, you need to put it on order with Sage.

In the following sections, I assume you clicked Order Later rather than Order Now when you saved your purchase order. You can check to see the status of your order by checking the Purchase Order list. If the On Order column is blank, you need to place the order on Sage.

Ordering via the conventional method

In the following steps, you change the status of the order to on order and update your on-order stock levels for the appropriate product codes:

1. **From the Navigation bar, click Purchase orders.**

2. **Select the purchase order you want to place on order by clicking the Place Orders icon in the POP screen.**

    A confirmation message appears, asking if you want to print the order. Click Yes if you want to print it or No if you want to continue without printing.

3. **To place the goods on order, click Yes when Sage asks if you want to place all selected items on order.**

   The POP window reappears, showing the status of the order as on order.

When the goods come in, you can now receive them properly.

The On Order status column on the Purchase Order list is now updated to reflect the status of the new order that you placed.

Manually placing goods on order

An alternative method of placing your goods on order lets you view the order again before you place it on order. If you want to double-check the items on the order, follow these steps:

1. **Select the order from the Purchase Order list.**

2. **Click the Amend Deliveries icon.**

   You see all the product records contained within your order, one line per product. The This Delivery column will be zero until you click Order.

3. **To put your purchase order on order, click Order.**

   The full order quantity appears in the This Delivery column; see Figure 11-2.

4. **Click Close to return to the POP window.**

   The purchase order now shows on order.

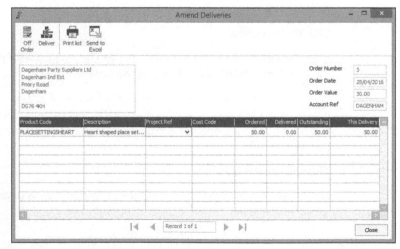

FIGURE 11-2: Manually placing goods on order lets you check the order beforehand.

Source: Jane Kelly

Completing Your Purchase Order

REMEMBER

Completing your order is necessary only if you've already received your goods. The process of completing your order means that Sage saves the order, completes the order and records the delivery of stock immediately.

If the order is linked to a project, Sage automatically allocates the goods to the project and then applies the costs. Sage applies actual costs at different stages, depending on the type of item ordered:

>> **Stock item:** Sage applies actual costs when the stock item is issued to the project.

>> **Nonstock or service item:** Sage applies actual costs when the invoice is recorded for the purchase order.

To complete your order, follow these steps:

1. **From the Navigation bar, click Purchase orders.**

   The list of purchase orders appears.

2. **From the Purchase orders window, select the order you want to complete and click the Edit icon.**

   An information window opens, confirming the current order status. Click OK to take you to the Details screen of the order.

3. **Click the Complete icon at the top of the screen and then click Yes when you get the confirmation message saying you've selected to complete the order in full.**

   Click Yes to continue.

4. **Click Yes again when another confirmation message asks if you want to update stock and record delivery of the order.**

   Sage generates a goods received note (GRN) and asks if you want to print it now or later. Make your choice and then at the next window, decide whether to print the purchase order as well by clicking Yes or No to the print confirmation window.

5. **Close the Purchase Order screen.**

   The screen returns to the Purchase Order list and the status of your order shows as complete.

If you look on the Deliveries tab of your order, you see that Sage has generated a GRN. You can view or print the GRN from this screen.

Printing Your Purchase Order

You can print or spool a copy of one or more purchase orders so you can send them out to suppliers or keep a hard copy for your records.

Print spooling is the process of transferring data to a temporary holding place known as a *buffer*, usually an area on a disk. The printer can pull the data off the buffer when required, leaving you free to carry out other computer tasks while the printing goes on in the background.

TIP

Printing purchase orders in batches makes sense, if only because you can put a wodge of the correct stationery in the printer.

To print a batch of purchase orders, follow these steps:

1. **From the Navigation bar, click Purchase orders.**

A list of purchase orders opens.

2. **Select the purchase orders that you want to print and click the Print icon.**

You can choose Quick Print if you've chosen a default print layout.

3. **From the Layout list box, select the layout you require for your purchase orders.**

Sage presents you with a multitude of layouts. Alternatively, you can choose to email the purchase order.

4. **Select the output you require from the floating list of icons.**

You can choose to print, preview, export or email.

- **Print:** Choosing this option opens the Print window. Select the pages you want to print and change your printer settings if required. You can print orders as many times as you like.

- **Print Preview:** The Print Preview window shows the first purchase order in the batch. If you're happy with the preview, you can send the order directly to the printer by choosing the Print option from the File menu.

- **Export:** You can either Export to Excel or Export. If you click Export, the Save As window appears. Select a directory to store the file in and enter a filename. If you choose Export to Excel, a new Excel file is created with the details of the purchase order.

- **Email:** This opens your email system, where you can send the purchase order as an attachment. Just follow the prompts on the screen.

Getting the Goods In

After you send a purchase order, you typically receive the goods. (If you don't, you need to pursue the issue with the supplier!) When the goods arrive, you need to book them into Sage.

If you placed the order for a project and completed the purchase order as I describe in the earlier sections in this chapter, Sage automatically records the stock as delivered and allocates it to the proper project.

In the following sections, I cover three alternative ways of recording the delivery of goods.

Using goods received notes

Goods received notes (GRNs) are a quick and easy way to record the delivery of stock. GRNs let you record deliveries against more than one order at the same time. Sage keeps a record of all GRNs raised against each order. You can view and print these GRNs by going to the Deliveries tab of each order.

Setting GRN defaults

To adjust the settings for GRNs, follow these steps:

1. **From Settings on the Menu bar, click Invoice/Order defaults and then click the Options tab.**

2. **Amend the default setting for GRNs using the drop-down arrow.**

   Your options are as follows:

   - **Generate for all received:** This is the default option. Sage generates a GRN for each delivery but gives you the option to print now or later.

   - **Prompt at each received:** Each time you record a delivery Sage asks whether to generate a GRN. If you choose not to generate the GRN, Sage doesn't store a copy of it, so you can't view or print the GRN later.

   - **Do not generate:** Sage updates the purchase order and stock levels but doesn't produce a GRN. The GRN option doesn't appear on the Purchase Order Processing toolbar.

3. **Click OK.**

Generating the GRNs

If you selected the Do Not Generate GRNs option, ignore this section, as the GRN icon doesn't appear on your toolbar. If you want to process your GRNs, then read on:

1. **From the Navigation bar, click Purchase orders.**

Select the order you want to raise a GRN for.

2. **Click the Received Note icon.**

The Received Notes window opens. You can use the GRN option only if the status of the goods is on order.

3. **Enter the date and supplier information in the boxes provided.**

As soon as Sage identifies the supplier, all the outstanding items from the selected purchase order appear, as shown in Figure 11-3. You may want to enter the supplier's GRN, if you have it.

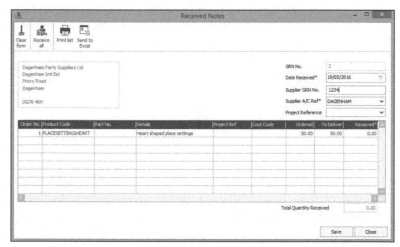

Source: Jane Kelly

4. **Check the details.**

If the delivery is all there, click the Receive All icon. If not all of your order was delivered, enter the actual quantities received in the Received column. The Received column changes from zero to the value of the items received.

5. **To save the goods received information, click Save.**

A message appears saying 'A Goods Received Note has been generated for this order and stored under the Deliveries tab of the order'. You can print the GRN now or later. You can tick the Do Not Show This Message Again box so you don't see this message every time.

6. **To return to the Purchase Order Processing window, click Close.**

   The status of the order on the Purchase Order list changes either to Complete or to Part if you received less than your full order.

Accepting delivery of everything

If everything on your purchase order comes in, you can use the Deliver function to record that, as long as you've already placed the purchase order on order, as I explain in the earlier section 'Placing the Goods on Order'.

To accept delivery, follow these steps:

1. **From the Navigation bar, click Purchase orders.**

2. **From the Purchase orders window, select the order you want to process and click the Receive Deliveries icon.**

   Sage asks if you want to update stock and record delivery of the items. Click Yes to continue. Depending on which GRN options you selected (see 'Setting GRN defaults' earlier in this chapter), Sage may ask whether you want to print a GRN. Print as required. The Purchase Order window then reappears, showing the status of the order as complete.

Taking in part of an order

You can use the Amend Deliveries facility to manually record delivery of a complete or partial order. Here you can check the order line by line against what you have received instead of automatically updating and recording stock. Also, you can choose to process part or complete deliveries instead of being forced to record complete deliveries only.

REMEMBER Before you can amend your order, you must place it on order.

To use the Amend tool, work through the following steps:

1. **From the Navigation bar, click Purchase orders.**

2. **Highlight the order you want to change and then click the Amend Deliveries icon.**

   The Amend Deliveries window appears, showing the full order quantity in the This Delivery column.

3. **To record a partial delivery, amend the actual quantity received in the This Delivery column.**

   If you want to record a complete delivery, move to Step 4 without amending the This Delivery column.

4. **Click the Deliver icon to update the product records with the new delivery information.**

   A confirmation message appears asking if you want to update the stock and record delivery of the items. Click Yes to continue or No to return to the Amend Deliveries screen.

   Depending on the GRN options you chose, Sage may ask you to print your GRN.

5. **Click Close to return to the Purchase Order list.**

   If you received a partial order, the Purchase Order window shows the new status of the order as Part.

Creating an Invoice from an Order

As part of the life cycle of the purchase order process, ultimately you want to match the invoice received from the supplier to the order that you raised in Sage. Sage lets you do this by converting the purchase order to an invoice by using the Update Ledgers icon. This icon lets you mirror the information from the invoice received from the supplier. You save time by doing this, as you don't have to type in all the supplier invoice details, because you entered most of them at the order stage.

The purchase order has a Posted column. If the Posted column is blank, the order hasn't been posted to the purchase ledger. If the order has been updated, you see a Y in the column. When the order is updated, it posts to the purchase ledger and the nominal ledger.

REMEMBER

You can update part-delivered orders. Each part creates its own invoice, so you may have more than one invoice relating to the same order.

To create a purchase invoice for a partially or fully delivered order, follow these steps:

1. **From the Navigation bar, click Purchase orders.**

2. **Highlight the order(s) against which you want to raise an invoice and click the Update Ledgers icon.**

If you've enabled transaction email and linked the selected orders to a supplier record that's marked 'I send orders to this supplier electronically', a prompt appears asking you whether you want to send the orders now.

The Purchase Order Update window opens.

3. **Edit any of the details shown in the Purchase Order Update window by highlighting the lines you want to change and clicking the Edit icon.**

You may want to change the date to reflect the invoice date, although you get the opportunity to do this later, on the batch invoice screen.

Note: If you have changed your Invoice/Order default settings to show different details in your Reference and Extra Reference box, then these will show here. For example, the Ref field automatically defaults to your Order No (Order Number), but this can be changed by using the drop-down menu and selecting a different variable. I recommend leaving this one as the order number. The Extra Ref field can be changed to the Suppliers order number, order number, order reference or nothing. I chose the Suppliers order number. While the Ref field automatically pulls through the next order number, the Extra Ref field pulls the data from a manually entered field on the order page of your Purchase order, so it's up to you to complete this field.

Make any changes you require.

4. **Click Save.**

5. **Select the components of the order that you want to update and click the Update icon.**

The Batch Supplier window appears, showing the details of your purchase invoice.

6. **Match the actual invoice received from your supplier with the details on the Batch Supplier window.**

Although your Extra Ref field currently shows your Suppliers order number (assuming that is what you have selected in the Invoice/Order defaults), you also need to add the supplier's invoice number, either in the Extra Ref field or the Details field. You also need to enter your sequential number for your purchase invoice in the Ref field. You can overtype the order number that automatically pulls through in the Ref field. If you are not using a sequential numbering system for your purchase invoices and are filing them alphabetically by supplier, then you can put the supplier's invoice number in the Ref field.

TIP

When you file your purchase invoices, you can attach a copy of the printed order to the back of the invoice.

7. **To update the purchase ledger and create an invoice from the details, click Save.**

   An information message appears about Project references – answer yes or no as appropriate. If you click Yes to continue, Sage processes the information and returns you to the Purchase Order list. The Purchase Order list now shows a Y in the Posted column for the invoice you just updated.

Deleting, Cancelling and Reinstating Orders

Sage knows the realities of the business world and accommodates them and human foibles too – sometimes you need to delete or cancel an order, and sometimes you think you need to cancel a purchase order only to find out that you need it after all.

Deleting orders

You can delete purchase orders from the Purchase Order list. If you try to delete an order that isn't complete or cancelled, Sage issues a warning message asking if you really want to delete it.

WARNING

When Sage deletes a purchase order, it also deletes any associated GRNs – so if you need to keep copies of GRNs, take copies before you delete the order.

TECHNICAL STUFF

After you delete the purchase orders, you can use the Compress Files facility in File Maintenance to remove deleted orders from the data files and make the unused disk space available.

To delete purchase orders, follow these steps:

1. **Take a backup of your data in case things go pear-shaped and you need to restore a clean set of data.**

   I cover backups in detail in Chapter 9.

2. **From the Navigation bar, click Purchase orders and select the order you want to delete.**

3. **Click the Delete icon at the top of the screen.**

   A confirmation box appears asking you to confirm that you want to delete the items highlighted. Click Yes to continue or No to halt the process.

Cancelling orders

With Sage, you have the ability to cancel orders. Just follow these steps:

1. **From the Purchase Order list, select the order you want to cancel and click the Amend Deliveries icon.**

The Amend Deliveries window appears, showing the details of the order, with one line per product.

2. **Click the Off Order icon.**

REMEMBER

If you want to cancel one line from an order, first you must cancel the order by highlighting the appropriate order from the Purchase Order list and then click the Amend Deliveries icon, followed by the Off Order icon. Then close the Amend Deliveries screen. Don't worry; it doesn't completely disappear! The word 'Cancel' appears in the On Order column on the main purchase order screen. You can now edit the order by clicking the Edit icon and delete the required row from the order by using the F8 key.

The status of the PO needs to be on order before you can cancel it. Otherwise, when you click Amend Deliveries, the Off Order button isn't available.

3. **To return to the Purchase Order list, click Close.**

The status of the order shows as cancelled.

Putting a cancelled order back on order

If you change your mind and decide that you want to reinstate a previously cancelled order, follow these steps:

1. **From the Purchase Order list, select the order you want to place back on order.**

Click the Amend Deliveries icon.

2. **Click the Order icon in the Amend Deliveries window.**

The button changes to Off Order.

3. **Exit the Amend Deliveries window by clicking Close.**

The status of the order now shows as on order.

Chapter 12

Keeping Track of Your Products

A lot of business money is often tied up in stock. Having proper control over your stock procedures makes good business sense.

In this chapter, I give you the tools to manage your stock. I cover recording a stocktake, which you can do with any version of Sage. I also explore the added features available only in the Sage 50 Accounts Plus and Professional versions.

Taking Stock

Every business should undertake a stocktake periodically – once a year at the very least – so the year-end accounts show an accurate stock position. However, actually carrying out a stocktake can prove a logistical nightmare, particularly if you have a vast array of products.

Usually, recording a stocktake is best undertaken when the factory or office is closed for normal business. Many a time I've rolled out of bed on a Saturday to help do a stocktake. Sage doesn't allow you the luxury of a weekend lie-in, but it does help you organise your company's stock methodically.

Before you run the Stock Take option in Sage, run one of the Sage stocktake reports to assist you with the physical stock count. I show an example of one of the reports, Stock Take Report (by Stock Category), in Figure 12-1. You can see that Sage helpfully provides the quantity of stock as recorded in Sage, followed by a blank box, where you can record the actual stock quantity.

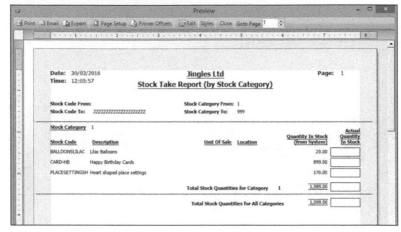

FIGURE 12-1: Running a stocktake report.

Source: Jane Kelly

WARNING

You can't run a stocktake for service or nonstock items.

After you complete your physical stocktake, you can adjust the data in Sage if there are any stock differences by following these steps:

1. **On the Navigation bar, click Products and services.**

The screen opens with a list of existing products.

2. **Select the products you want to amend the stock for and click the Stock Take icon.**

Using the drop-down arrow in the Stock management window, select each product where you need to make a stock adjustment and amend the quantities in the Actual column. This calculates an adjustment figure in the Adjustment column, as shown in Figure 12-2.

If you want to select all products for the stocktake, click Swap from the Products list page and then click the Stock Take icon. All the products then appear.

3. **When you're happy with your stock adjustments, click Post Stock Take.**

Close the Stock management window. Sage displays the new stock quantities on the product main screen. You can see the adjustments by selecting a product and clicking the Activity icon. Any adjustments contain the default

Stock Take reference. The adjustments shown have an AI (Adjustments In) or AO (Adjustments Out) transaction.

If you have Sage 50 Accounts Plus or Sage 50 Accounts Professional, you can keep a copy of the changes before posting by clicking Memorise and entering a filename where you want to save the information before clicking Save. To open the file later, click Recall and select the appropriate file.

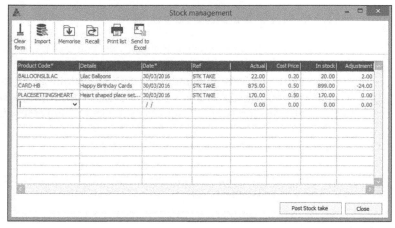

FIGURE 12-2:
Showing stocktake adjustments for Jingles Ltd.

Source: Jane Kelly

Importing your stocktake

If you have lots of stock records and you have the information saved in Excel or CSV (Comma Separated Values) format, you can import your stock information.

Some stocktake reports help you prepare your stock information in these formats, so take a look to see whether one of the standard Sage reports meets your requirements.

To import the stock, do the following:

1. **From the Navigation bar, click Products and services and then click the Stock Take icon.**

2. **Select the appropriate product records and click the Import icon.**

3. **Select the file type you want, browse and select the actual file you want to import, and click Next.**

4. **If the data you want to import doesn't include a headings row, clear the First Row Contains Headings checkbox and then click Next.**

5. **Use the field mappings page to link your imported file fields to the correct Sage fields.**

6. **Complete the imported field column and choose the relevant field from the drop-down lists provided.**

7. **When all the required fields have been mapped, click Next.**

   Click Import and then Close.

8. **Click Post Stock Take and then Close.**

Adjusting stock levels

Sage helps you adjust stock levels. For example, you may need to return some goods to stock without generating a credit note – a *stock in* movement – or record the fact that you sent some stock as samples to potential customers – a *stock out* movement. As you don't process credit notes or sales orders with these movements, you need to change the stock numbers manually to reflect the movement in stock.

To make a stock adjustment, follow these steps:

1. **From the Products and services window, select the product you want to make an adjustment to.**

   Click the Adjustments In icon to put stock back into your stores, or click the Adjustments Out icon to remove items.

   The Stock Adjustment In or Stock Adjustment Out window appears, depending on which adjustment you chose.

2. **Enter the adjustment details, using one line per product.**

TIP

   Entering a reason for the adjustment in the Details column is a good idea. You have 60 spaces to enter a description. The cost price and sale price automatically appear from the stock record.

3. **To save the details entered, click Save and then Close.**

   The stock is automatically adjusted.

If you want to check on stock, highlight the product and click the Activity icon. You can see a history of all stock movements for that product item.

Checking stock activity

You can look at a product's activity and view stock movements. The Activity screen records all movement of stock in and out and written off. (I talk about writing off stock in the section 'Processing Stock Returns' later in this chapter.) You can also look at allocated stock, stock on order, the quantity in stock and the quantity available.

You can also use the Activity screen to view the precise sales orders and purchase orders responsible for the goods in and out. Click the little grey and white arrow next to the Goods In/Out description, and Sage shows you the order and its current status.

To check product activity, follow these steps:

1. **From Products and services, select the product you want to view.**

2. **Click the Activity icon.**

   The Activity screen opens, showing all movements of stock.

3. **You can print a list of activities, send to Excel or click Close to exit this screen.**

   You return to the Products list.

Using the stock shortfall facility

If you have Sage 50 Accounts Plus or Sage 50 Accounts Professional, you can use the shortfall facility to see if your stock levels have fallen below the reorder levels you set in your product records. If you use Accounts Professional, you can automatically create a purchase order for those items.

In Figure 12-3 I show a shortfall report for Jingles, generated because the reorder level for Heart Place settings is set at 250 units and the place settings in stock/on order have fallen below that level. Clicking the Create Order icon at the top left of the screen produces a purchase order for the supplier of those cards. If the Create Order icon is greyed out, then simply click the product line shown in the Shortfall window and you will then be able to proceed.

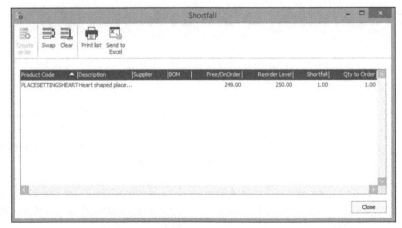

FIGURE 12-3:
In Accounts Professional you can generate a purchase order from a shortfall report.

Source: Jane Kelly

TIP

If you have a number of products on your shortfall list, sort the list into supplier order by clicking the top of the Supplier column. Print the list so you can place orders methodically with each supplier.

If you always buy the same products from the same suppliers, you can enter the supplier reference in the appropriate field within the product record, making it easier to place orders. You then select all the products with the same supplier reference and place a bulk order. The Create Order button in Accounts Professional lets you do this automatically.

To create a product shortfall list, follow these steps:

1. **From Products and services, click the Swap icon.**

   All your product records are highlighted.

2. **Click the Shortfall icon.**

   The Product Shortfall Generator window opens, showing a list of all items that have fallen below the reorder level.

   If you use Accounts Professional, you can automatically create a purchase order from this screen by highlighting the products showing a shortfall and then clicking Create Order.

3. **Click Print List and use the output as a basis for creating your orders.**

4. **Click Close to exit this report.**

You can tell if a product has fallen below its reorder level as the product details display in red rather than black on the main Product and services window.

Understanding a Bill of Materials

Note: Bills of materials are available only if you are using Sage 50 Accounts Plus or Sage 50 Accounts Professional.

A *bill of materials* (BOM) is a list of products (components) used to make up another product – the component parts of the main product. You set up each component as a separate product record and link them all together with a BOM. The various levels of component have different names.

As an example, I use a Magic Party product that our fictional card shop Jingles offers. The *product assembly*, or the list of items that make up the Jingles Magic Party product, includes the following components:

» A magician

» A box of tricks

» A wizard-themed party dishes pack

Each of these three items is a *component* of the product assembly – it may be an individual element (such as the magician) or a group of elements (subcomponents) that together form a product (component), for example the box of tricks.

The box of tricks contains the following *subcomponents*:

» A pack of cards

» Six feather dusters

» Six silk scarves

» A box of party poppers

» A bag of balloons

Creating a BOM

Creating a BOM is a relatively simple process – a bit like making a shopping list. You essentially create a new product, the BOM, from other products that you hold in stock. You create a product record for the new product and then use the BOM tab on the product record to build the list of products required to make it.

To set up a BOM, follow these steps:

1. **From the Navigation bar, click Products and services.**

   Highlight the product record you want to create a BOM for and click the Edit icon to open the Product Record screen.

2. **Click Bill of materials on the left side of the screen.**

   A blank BOM information table appears.

3. **Enter the product code and quantity required of each item needed for the BOM:**

   - **Product Code:** Select the product items required for your main product.

   - **Assembly Level:** This field shows how many levels of subcomponents are below this component. Sage automatically generates this number.

   - **Link Level:** This is the number of assemblies to which this component belongs. Each product can be a component of more than one assembly. Sage automatically creates a link count for each component on the BOM.

- **Available to Makeup:** Situated in the bottom right corner of the screen, this field shows the number of units that can be made with the current stock levels.

Figure 12-4 shows the BOM for the Jingles Magic Party's components, which include a box of tricks, a magician and a party dishes pack.

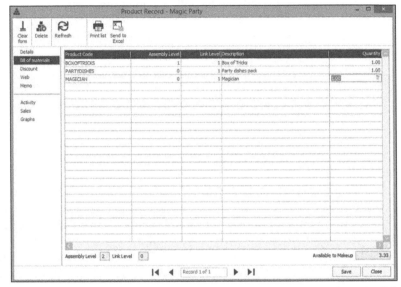

FIGURE 12-4: Jeanette has created a BOM for a Jingles Magic Party.

Before Jeanette sets up a BOM for the Jingles Magic Party, she needs to determine the components. She decides upon a magician, a box of tricks and a party dishes pack. She has to set up a product record for each of these components before she can set up her Magic Party BOM. As she sets up the Box of Tricks product record, she can click the BOM tab and select the list of products (subcomponents) required to make a box of tricks. She does the same exercise for the party dishes product record and lists the parts on the BOM tab.

After the product records are set up, Jeanette clicks the BOM tab for the Magic Party and selects the relevant component. As soon as she enters Box of Tricks, the assembly level becomes 1 rather than 0. The number 1 indicates that Box of Tricks is a component of the main assembly. The magician remains as assembly level 0 because it has no further subcomponents.

Checking stock availability for a BOM

You can use the Check bill of materials icon to see if you have enough stock available to assemble the main product. Follow these steps to check your stock availability:

1. **From Products and services, highlight the product you want to check and then click the Check bill of materials icon.**

The Check Bill of Materials window appears.

2. **From the Product Code drop-down list, select the code of the assembly you want to check and click OK.**

The description of the assembly appears in a text box. You can't edit this information.

3. **In the Quantity box, select the number of assemblies you want to make and click the Check icon.**

If you don't have enough of an item of stock, a message appears stating how many assemblies you need to get. Click OK to find out what items you need to order. If you have enough components in stock, a confirmation message appears to tell you.

If you have Sage 50 Accounts Professional, you can create a purchase order automatically by selecting the items you're short of and clicking Create Order.

4. **To print a list of items required, click Print.**

Figure 12-5 shows the parts required for a Jingles Magic Party. Sage states that not all the components and subcomponents are in stock and gives a list of products that Jeanette needs to order.

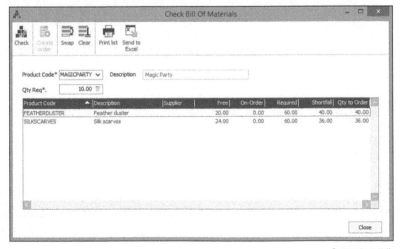

FIGURE 12-5:
Checking parts for a Jingles Magic Party.

Source: Jane Kelly

WARNING

The Check BOM screen shows only product items, not service items. If a BOM includes a service as well as products, you must deal with the service element separately. Alternatively, you can mark the service item as stock in the product record to ensure that it is picked up in the BOM.

Transferring stock for a BOM

You can use the product transfer function to increase the quantity of product assemblies in stock by using components currently in stock. In the Jingles example, to get a Magic Party into stock, Jeanette needs to transfer the Magic Party components and the party itself into stock.

When you use the product transfer facility, Sage automatically calculates the cost of the product assembly by adding together the costs of the component parts.

To complete a product transfer, follow these steps:

1. **From Products and services, click the Stock Transfer icon.**

The Stock Transfer screen appears.

2. **Insert the details for each transfer in the lines provided, using one line per transfer.**

Each transfer must involve a product assembly. In the Jingles example, Jeanette selects a Magic Party and a box of tricks. She enters a quantity of 1 and Sage transfers the necessary component parts into those items of stock, as shown in Figure 12-6.

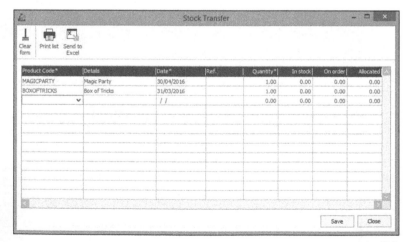

FIGURE 12-6:
Transferring stock to BOMs.

Source: Jane Kelly

3. **If you're happy with the information, click Save – if not, click Discard to cancel.**

   Click Close to exit the Stock Transfer screen.

When you carry out a stock transfer, Sage carries out the following postings:

» Sage increases the in-stock quantity of the finished product by the quantity entered. This transaction is recorded as a *movement in (MI)* on the product activity file.

» Sage reduces the in-stock quantity of each individual component type. The transfer is recorded as a *movement out (MO)*.

» Sage updates the product activity file with each transfer made.

» Sage updates the cost price of the finished product in the product record.

Processing Stock Returns

You may have stock returned for a variety of reasons – maybe the item doesn't fit, doesn't suit the customer's needs, or is the wrong colour or size. When you receive returned stock, you have to adjust your stock levels by issuing a credit note and updating the system (which in turn updates the stock levels) or by making an *adjustment in* to stock.

WARNING

The Stock return option isn't available if you selected the product code as a non-stock or service item. I explain this in more detail in Chapter 3.

If the returned items are damaged or faulty, you use a different method to process the stock return to accommodate the ultimate destination of the defective goods:

» **Damaged goods returned to you (damages in):** If a customer returns a product that is damaged or doesn't work, you can't just add the faulty item back into your stock and sell it again. Instead, you create a record of the stock return that doesn't increase the in-stock quantity, as I show in Figure 12-7.

» **Damaged goods you return to your supplier (damages out):** If you return goods to your supplier for repair or replacement, you don't update the quantity in stock, sales value or sales quantity figures.

» **Write off:** You use this option if you need to *write off* the stock, which means determining that the stock has no value and you can't sell it. Sage makes an adjustment to the stock levels in the same way that an adjustment out does.

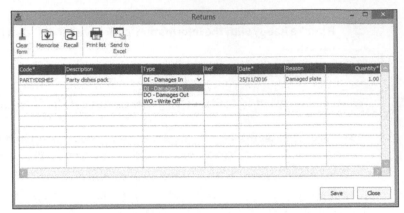

FIGURE 12-7:
Recording a
stock return.

Source: Jane Kelly

TIP

At least once a year, you have to value your stock for accounts purposes. Any written-off stock reduces the value of the stock in the accounts. You can obtain a Product Write Off Details report from the Product reports window, in a subsection of Product damage and write off reports. This report helps you identify the value of stock to be written off in the accounts. I suggest you talk to your accountant about processing this type of adjustment in your accounts.

To record a stock return, follow these steps:

1. **From Products and services, select the product you want to record a return for.**

2. **Click the Returns icon in the Products toolbar.**

   The Returns window appears.

3. **Enter the stock return details.**

   You can complete the following boxes:

   - **Code:** If necessary, change the product code by using the drop-down arrow.

   - **Description:** This field automatically appears when the record is selected.

   - **Type:** Click this box to reveal a drop-down arrow and select Damages In, Damages Out or Write Off.

   - **Reference:** Enter a reference if required.

   - **Date:** Change the date if you don't want to use today's date.

   - **Reason:** Enter a reason for the return.

   - **Quantity:** Note the quantity of stock being returned.

4. **To post the stock return, click Save; otherwise, click Close.**

If you want, click Memorise to temporarily save the stock return details and then post the items at a later date. To access the memorised information, click the Returns icon and then Recall. Open the saved file to bring up your previously memorised items, which you can then save and post.

Allocating Stock

If you run the Plus or Professional version of Sage, you can manually allocate stock for general use or project use and allocate it to a project by way of a purchase order. Both manual and purchase order stock allocations affect the committed costs of a project. *Committed costs* are costs allocated to a project. Committed costs are not formally charged to a project until the stock allocated to a project is issued – see the later section 'Issuing allocated stock' for more on this.

When you record a stock allocation, you can't allot more than the amount of available stock, called *free stock*, unless you set Sage to allow negative stock. After you assign stock, the stock is no longer free and can't be used for other sales orders.

To allocate stock, follow these steps:

1. **From Products and services, click the Allocations icon.**

   A drop-down menu appears, giving you three options. You can allocate stock, amend allocations or issue allocations.

2. **Select Allocate stock.**

   The Allocations window appears.

3. **From the Allocations window, enter the stock allocation details.**

   Using the drop-down arrows, enter the product code, the project reference and the cost code, if required. Figure 12-8 shows allocation information for Jingles – Jeanette decides to allocate 5 balloons to an order, and Sage has calculated that 20 balloons are available.

   Sage automatically shows the amount of free stock, but you need to enter the quantity of stock you want to allocate.

4. **To print a copy of the stock information you've entered, click Print List.**

5. **Click Save to save the allocation, or click Close if you don't want to save it.**

   Click Close to return to the Products window.

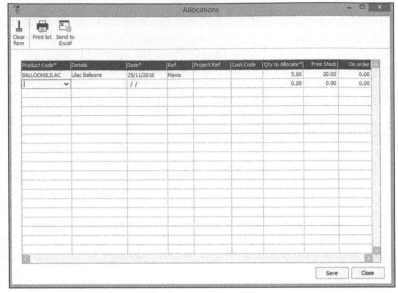

FIGURE 12-8:
Jeanette decides to allocate some lilac balloons to a customer's order.

You can view how much stock is allocated by looking at the bottom left corner of the Product Record, as shown in Figure 12-9. The record shows how much of that item is in stock, how much of the stock is allocated and how much is free stock.

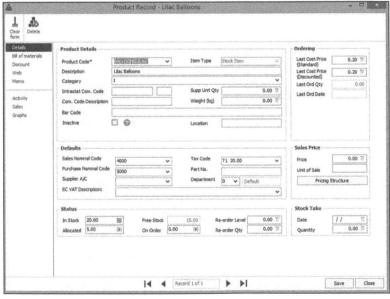

FIGURE 12-9:
The product record after stock is allocated.

Changing stock allocation

You can amend any previous allocations you made to stock by following these steps:

1. **From Products and services, click the arrow under the Allocations icon.**

2. **From the drop-down list, select Amend Allocations.**

The Amend Allocations window appears.

3. **Select the product you want to amend or delete using the drop-down arrow.**

Click OK.

4. **Change the allocated quantity by overtyping.**

You can change only the quantity. Press 0 (zero) to remove a product allocation. By removing a product allocation, you increase the amount of free stock available for that product and reduce the allocated amount.

For example, you may want to do this if you receive a big order from a valued customer and you need to ship it quickly. You can decide to take stock that had been previously allocated to another customer and reallocate it to your priority order.

5. **To generate a copy of the stock allocation information, click Print List.**

6. **Click Save to save the details of the stock allocation. If you want to clear the allocation, click Discard.**

If you allocate any of the stock to projects, the costs are committed to the project. You can view this stock on a committed costs report. You can find this report in the Projects module by clicking the Reports icon and then Committed Costs. Then Run the Committed Costs Per Project report.

Issuing allocated stock

After you have allocated stock, you need to issue the stock. By issuing stock, you update your stock records and stock allocation records. When issuing an allocation associated with a project, the value of the issued stock is applied to the cost of the project. In other words, Sage converts *committed costs* to *actual costs* for the project.

To issue stock, follow these steps:

1. **From Products and services, click the Allocations icon.**

2. **From the drop-down list, select Issue Allocations.**

The Issue Allocations window opens.

REMEMBER

3. **Use the drop-down arrow to select the product you want to issue.**

   The product must be allocated before you can issue it.

4. **Enter the quantity of stock you want to issue and click Save.**

   You can choose to issue less than the whole quantity of stock. Only the stock you choose to issue is allocated and charged to the project – the balance remains as committed stock.

   Alternatively, you can click Issue All, as shown in Figure 12-10.

5. **To print a list of the stock allocation information, click Print List.**

6. **To issue the stock, click Save. To clear the information, click Close.**

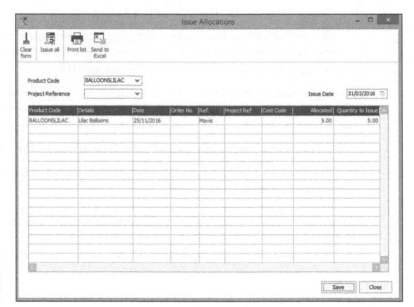

FIGURE 12-10:
Issuing
allocated stock.

Source: Jane Kelly

REMEMBER

Be aware of the following rules when you issue allocated stock:

» When you issue stock to a project, you must ensure the status of the project allows postings.

» You can't change the details of a stock allocation, such as the project reference or cost codes, during a stock issue. You can change only the stock quantity.

» A stock issue can't exceed the allocation amount, regardless of the negative stock setting.

Chapter 13

Managing Projects

S age's Project Costing tool, available to users of Accounts Plus and Accounts Professional, enables large and small businesses to successfully manage a project.

In Chapter 3, I describe how to set up a project using a blank record. You can follow that process or access the Project Record wizard by clicking Projects from the Navigation bar on the left side of the screen and then clicking the New icon. After you set up the project, the information in this chapter comes into play, because here I tell you how to manage projects.

With Sage, you can track costs and ensure you capture every expenditure associated with a project. You can then charge the client a fee that produces a profit for your company. You can evaluate future projects more accurately and target your business toward more profitable ventures.

For illustration purposes, I use a project that has been set up for my fictitious company, Jingles. Jeanette (the business owner) is planning a Fun Day for her business to showcase her party-planning products, and she has decided to use the Project facility to allow her to control the costs associated with this project.

Appointing a Project's Status and Costs

The *project status* helps you track a project's progress. You can set the status to allow or disallow postings. Sage has five status categories for you to use, according to where the project is in its life cycle.

When you first set up a project, the status is automatically shown as Active. This means that the project is currently in progress. This status is the default setting, but you can change this by accessing Settings, Configuration Editor and then Project Costing (I provide more details later in this chapter).

Each status has its own rules as to whether or not you can make postings to it. Postings that assign costs to a project are usually allowed when a project is in full swing, but postings are no longer allowed in a project's later stages. You can also decide at which point in the life cycle to change a status or delete the project record.

Two statuses don't allow postings:

>> The project is complete and you don't expect any more costs to come in.

>> The project has been suspended.

Every project is specific to an individual business, so only you can determine whether you need to change a project's status. For example, when an active project ends, you give it the status *complete* because you don't want additional postings being made in error to a finished project.

WARNING

To be absolutely sure that a completed project doesn't incur further costs, you can delete the project record after you change the status to complete. Personally, I think you should consider deleting a project only if you know for certain that you no longer require any analysis information for the project.

Assigning status

You assign your project one of five default status categories. A project status changes according to the stage of the project. The default status categories are as follows:

>> **Active:** This status indicates that a project is open and ongoing. You can make postings to the project, but you can't delete the record.

>> **Snag:** Although completed, the project remains open so you can still make final postings. You can't delete the record.

An example of a snagged project is a building project that is essentially finished, and you've charged the major costs. You still need to work out the wrinkles to rectify minor defects, however, so you can assign additional costs to the job.

>> **Completed:** The job is closed and you can't post to the project. You can delete the record if you want to.

>> **Suspend:** The project has been suspended. You can't post to the project or delete the record. This status usually indicates a problem with the project.

>> **Initial:** The project is at a pre-acceptance stage. Although you can make postings to the record, you can't delete it. You can use this status for very new projects that are just getting off the ground. You may decide to start recording the costs in case the project gets the official go-ahead. If it doesn't get the go-ahead, no harm is done. But if the project does proceed, you've begun the process of recording costs and can monitor the project effectively.

You can access the Configuration Editor and change the names of the status categories to names that suit your business better, as I explain in the later section 'Changing status and costs'.

Note: I discuss only the default project statuses in this chapter. It is possible to add up to 99 statuses (specific to your business), and you can specify whether you want to allow postings or allow deletions for any of these statuses. You can add or edit your status in the Configuration Editor (Settings, then click the Project Costing tab).

Looking at costs – types and codes

You give each project a project reference and use that reference when recording costs to the project by using cost types and cost codes:

>> **Cost type:** This is a label that describes an activity or resource. Labour and materials are examples of cost types. A cost type on its own is meaningless – it must be associated with a cost code. The default cost type is *other*, which is linked to the default cost codes in the next point. You can have up to 99 cost types.

>> **Cost code:** This is a way to further differentiate cost types. For example, you can further divide the cost type *labour* into plumbers, carpenters, bricklayers and so on. You can create the cost code yourself, according to the needs of

your business. You have just eight characters to name your cost codes, but you don't have to use all eight. The default cost codes are labour (LAB1), materials (MAT1), overheads (OHD1) and mixed (MIX1). Sage allows you to have up to 99 different cost codes.

REMEMBER

A cost type can link to many cost codes, but a cost code can link to only one cost type.

You can set up budgets for a project against each cost code. When you apply costs to a project, the cost code rather than the cost type records the charge. For example, when you enter a purchase invoice, you have a column for the project reference and a column for the cost code. The cost codes are linked to the cost types in the Configuration Editor. You can view cost types and cost codes in the Configuration Editor.

Changing status and costs

If you use the default status set, the only time you need to change the status of the project is when the project reaches a different stage in its life cycle. For example, all projects start at the default status of Active, but when a project is complete, you no longer want to accept costs against that project so you need to change the status, as I outline in the later section 'Completing Your Project'.

You can change the default project status names so they better describe your business needs. You can make the same name changes to the cost types and cost codes.

You amend the project status, cost code and cost type or create further analysis fields by editing the Project custom fields, using the Configuration Editor window:

1. **From the Menu bar, click Settings and then click Configuration.**

   A message appears saying that this option can't be run with any other windows open. Click Yes to close all other open windows. The Configuration Editor appears.

2. **Click the Project Costing tab.**

   Figure 13-1 shows the types of field you can change.

3. **Amend the project status, cost type and cost codes by clicking the relevant Edit button and changing the necessary details.**

   If you want to edit the cost codes, click Edit Code in the cost code section. The Edit Cost Code window appears, and you can change the description or cost type. Then click OK.

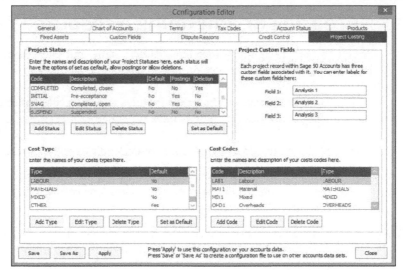

4. **Click Apply to use this configuration on your accounts data.**

5. **Click Close.**

    A message appears asking if you want to save the changes. Click Yes and then click Close again to return to the Welcome screen.

You can edit and apply your own project status names using titles that are more meaningful to your business.

Managing Project Resources

To undertake work on a project, you need personnel and equipment. A plant, machinery, computer equipment and people cost money, and you need to apply these costs to your project.

The term *resource* applies to any cost applied to a project. For example, you apply people costs via a timesheet. You can use the timesheet to apply labour costs to a project. Machinery has some sort of hire charge or other cost associated with it, which you can also apply to the project.

When you record a project charge, you select the type of resource used. You can use the resource information to calculate a total cost for the charge, but you can override this as the charge is recorded.

FIGURE 13-1: Changing your status, cost types and cost codes with the Configuration Editor.

Creating or amending a resource

You can create as many resources as you want, but each resource must have a unique reference. You create or amend a resource as follows:

1. **From the Navigation bar, click Projects and then click the Resources icon.**

The Resources box opens.

2. **Click Add to add a new resource or click Edit to edit an existing resource.**

If you want to add a new resource, enter the details here. You must give each resource a unique reference number, name, unit of measure (such as hour), cost rate and cost code (use the drop-down arrow).

WARNING

When you edit an existing resource, you can change the name, unit of measure, cost rate and cost code – but not the reference number.

3. **Click OK; then close the Resources window.**

When you next click on the Resources icon, your newly created or amended resource will appear.

In Figure 13-2 I have added Jingles's new labour resource, Dave. You can create resources for different people with individual charge rates. For example, you can set up each member of your staff as a resource and charge them to the specific projects they work on.

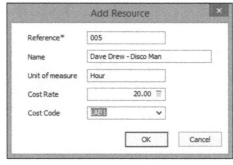

FIGURE 13-2:
Adding a new labour resource.

Source: Jane Kelly

Deleting a resource

You can easily delete a resource if you no longer need it. Follow these steps:

1. **From the Navigation bar, click Projects and then click the Resources icon.**

2. **From the Resources window, highlight the resource you want to delete and click Delete.**

3. **A confirmation message appears.**

   Click Yes to delete or No to return to the Resources window.

4. **Click Close to return to the Projects window.**

Tracking Project Costs

You can record costs or charges against a specific project as soon as you incur them. For example, you can apply timesheets to a specific project as soon as you receive them. The following sections outline the mechanisms for applying project charges, invoices, bank payments and stock issues to the accounts and projects.

REMEMBER

To apply costs to a project, the project must be set up to allow postings. See the earlier section 'Appointing a Project's Status and Costs' section to find out about allowing postings.

Sharing out project charges

A project charge applies a cost to the project but doesn't charge the nominal ledger and therefore doesn't affect the accounts. For example, labour costs go through the accounts by way of wages journals, which directly affect the accounts. But you can't post to Projects directly from a journal – so, at a later stage, you need to allocate the applicable labour costs directly to the project by way of a project charge.

The types of project charge you can make include the following:

>> **Labour charges:** You can take these from the rates and hours entered on timesheets.

>> **Costs:** You can include costs that don't affect your stock, such as costs involving nonstock items or service items. You can't issue nonstock items to a project, so the only way to post a charge to the project for items of this nature is to process a project charge. You can only charge service items to a project this way. (I discuss nonstock and service items in Chapter 3.)

>> **Adjustments or corrections:** You can incorporate amendments to other costs for the project. For example, if you post an invoice to the wrong project, you can do a credit from the project without having to reverse the invoice. You can then put the appropriate charge in the correct project.

Sage shows project charges as transaction type CD (costing debits), but you can also issue a cost credit (CC) if you need to make an adjustment to the project cost.

To record a *project only* cost or credit (the 'only' indicates you're only charging amounts to the project, not affecting your nominal ledger), follow these steps:

1. **From the Navigation bar, click Projects.**

   The Projects window opens. Select the project you want to process a charge for.

2. **Click the Charges icon or the Credits icon if you need to credit the project.**

   The Project Charges or Project Credits window appears.

3. **Enter the details of the charge or credit in the boxes provided, using one line per charge.**

   You must enter a cost code for the cost; otherwise, Sage shows an error message when you try to save the cost.

   If you select a resource for the charge or credit, Sage automatically fills in the rate and cost code as the default rate from when you entered it on the resource list. You can overwrite this rate if you require.

   When you enter the quantity, Sage automatically calculates the total cost and displays it in the Total Cost column.

4. **Click Save to save your entries or click Close to exit without saving.**

5. **Click Close to return to the Projects window.**

Figure 13–3 shows the charge to the Fun Day project for the use of assistant Sarah Daly, who has planned some of the event. Jeanette wants to charge the project for Sarah's time spent on organising the Fun Day. A separate resource has been set up with the reference SARAH and given the cost code LAB1.

Issuing stock to a project

Sometimes you don't use all of the stock on a project. You can use the Products and services module to allocate stock to a project and put returned or unused products back into stock. These stock postings are shown as adjustments in (AI) or adjustments out (AO) on the Product Activity screen. You can find details about allotting stock in Chapter 12. Remember to select a project reference and ensure the project status allows postings.

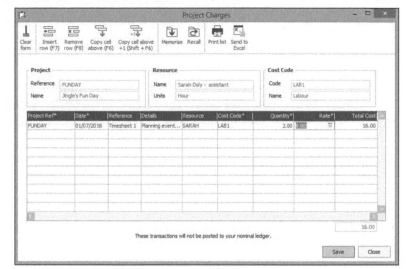

FIGURE 13-3: Applying a project charge to a project for Jingles – Sarah's time has been added as a labour charge to the Fun Day project.

When you allocate stock to a project, that stock is set aside for the use of that project. The cost of the stock becomes a *committed cost* to the project, but it becomes an *actual cost* to the project only when the stock is issued.

You need to use the Products and services module to issue the stock, which then shows up in your project reports. (See the section 'Integrating POP with project costing' later in this chapter for more information.)

Figure 13-4 shows the issue of party poppers stock to Jingles's Fun Day project. The stock shows as an adjustment out of stock and against the project.

If you subsequently view the project record and look at the Analysis page, you will see a field called Committed costs under the Cost Totals section. Here you can click on the little grey arrow, which drills down to the individual items that make up the committed cost total. You can view any stock issues that have been issued to a project.

REMEMBER

Stock issues are a cost to the project. Usually, when stock leaves your hands, you invoice a customer, the customer pays the invoice and money subsequently flows back into your business. When you allocate stock to a project, you don't get paid for it immediately or directly.

You can use the Clear Stock option as part of your month-end or year-end routine. This option involves removing stock transactions from your product activity record, up to and including a specified date. Note that any project active at the point you clear your stock still holds the details of all the transactions showing in its product activity, so you can maintain a complete history for that project.

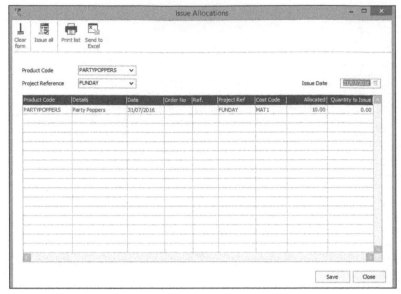

FIGURE 13-4:
Party-popper
stock issued to
Jingles's Fun Day
project.

Source: Jane Kelly

Counting costs from a supplier invoice

You can post purchase invoices (PI), purchase credit notes (PC) and bank payments (BP) to a project. By doing so, you update your accounts with the cost and also link the cost to your project. (To see how to post a supplier invoice, refer to Chapter 7.) Remember to enter the project reference in the Project Reference column and enter a valid cost code in the Cost Code column.

WARNING

When you post an invoice to a project, you post a value but not a quantity to the project. The Batch Entry screen for posting invoices doesn't have a quantity column – it just registers an amount. If you need to post quantities of an item to a project, post the invoice without a project reference and then post a separate project charge to the project.

You can apply costs using bank payments. When you make a bank payment, select a project reference and a cost code. That cost is then applied to the project. (For details on how to process a bank payment, refer to Chapter 8.)

Integrating POP with project costing

As Sage is an integrated system, you can link purchase order processing (POP) and projects. The project is updated at various points of the purchase-order life cycle:

>> **Creating an order:** At the time of creating an order, give the order a project reference and enter a cost code.

>> **On order:** After you place the goods on order, those costs are *committed* to the project, meaning the value of those goods and services is applied to that project.

>> **Goods received:** After you receive the goods, you can automatically allocate them to stock and then allocate the stock to the project. You can see the stock has been allocated to the project by clicking the product record and looking at the Stock Allocated box in the lower left corner of the record.

>> **Stock issued:** After the stock is issued, the amount of allocated stock reduces. *Actual costs* are applied to the project and committed costs are reduced. The transaction is shown as an AO (adjustment out of stock) transaction type and shows the project reference and cost code associated with that transaction.

You can look at the Activity tab of the project record to see the transaction.

>> **Invoice:** For stock items, you apply the actual cost to the project at the point the stock is issued. When stock is issued to a project, the costs convert from *committed costs* to *actual costs*. You can update the invoice at a later point to ensure the accounts and supplier ledger have been updated.

REMEMBER

You must manually issue the stock to the project by going into the Products and services module. The purchase order only allocates stock to your project and labels it a committed cost. When you formally issue the stock to the project, the committed costs change to actual costs.

WARNING

When you update your purchase order, in the Batch Supplier Invoice screen the project reference and cost code are blank. Do not reenter the project reference and cost code, because this posts the actual costs for a second time, thus double-counting. Click Save instead. Sage flashes up a warning message about double-counting. Click Yes to continue and return to the Purchase Order Processing window.

For nonstock items, the actual cost to the project is applied when you generate and update the invoice. When you produce a purchase order for these items, enter the project reference and cost code on the Batch Supplier screen, as this lets you post the actual costs to the project. When you click Save, a warning message appears, stating:

If you have already entered a project reference for these items on the purchase order, they will automatically become a realised cost when the stock is issued. You may be double-counting for these items. Are you sure you want to continue?

Click Yes. You've created a service invoice, not a stock invoice, so you're not issuing any stock and therefore can't be double-counting.

TIP

You can review the value of both committed costs and actual costs by looking at the Analysis tab of the relevant project record.

Analysing Project Costs

Sage has several features that help you track your projects and analyse your costs and revenues. Tracking and analysing give you the ability to respond to customers' enquiries about the projects.

Looking at the project's activity

When you analyse a project, the first thing you may want to do is look at the Project Activity screen. This screen shows you all the transactions with a specific project reference. You can also filter the transactions by type with the Custom Range button, as in the following steps:

1. **From the Navigation bar, click Projects and then click the Activity icon, or select the specific project and click the Activity icon.**

    The transaction information for the project appears.

    If the project you select is a multilevel project, tick the Include Rolled Up Transactions checkbox to show all the transactions for all the projects linked with the one you're viewing.

2. **Filter the transactions by clicking the drop-down arrow next to the Show field to select specific calendar months or by clicking the Custom Range button.**

    Clicking the Custom Range option opens up an Activity Range window, as in Figure 13-5. You can view the project activity by specific transaction types or display all transactions.

REMEMBER

Sage remembers the filter you used, so the next time you view the activity Sage applies the same filter until you change it.

You can look at the transactions that are recorded against a project. These transactions may include the following:

FIGURE 13-5:
Filtering the project activity with the Custom Range button.

Source: Jane Kelly

>> **CD:** Project charge (costing debit)

>> **CC:** Project credit (costing credit)

>> **AO:** Stock adjustment out of stock into the project

>> **AI:** Stock adjustment out of the project back into stock

>> **PI:** Purchase invoice, which you can generate from a purchase order if you have Accounts Professional

>> **PC:** Purchase credit note that may be issued to the project

>> **BP:** Bank payment

>> **VP:** Credit card payment

>> **CP:** Cash payment – for example, something bought using petty cash

>> **CR:** Cash receipt

>> **SI:** Sales invoice issued to charge the customer as part of the project billing process

>> **SC:** Credit note issued to the customer in respect of adjustments to the project billing process

REMEMBER

Stock allocations aren't displayed as part of the project activity.

You can also check the customer record associated with a project. For example, the Fun Day project is being organised for Anytown Parish Council. Jeanette can access the Customer module, open the customer record for Anytown Parish Council and then select the Projects tab. She can then see a list of every project associated with Anytown Parish Council. Figure 13-6 shows the customer record for Anytown Parish Council and the Fun Day project associated with it. The record shows the price quoted for the project and the costs billed to date.

FIGURE 13-6:
A project associated with a customer, viewed from the Projects tab of the customer's record.

Source: Jane Kelly

Note: You must make sure that you have allocated a customer to a project by selecting the project record and then, on the details page, using the drop-down arrow to select the appropriate customer account. This ensures that the project details pull through into the customer record, as shown in Figure 13-6.

Comparing costs and budget

Comparing the actual costs of a project against a budget gives you an indication of how well the project is being managed. Costs at or below budget suggest a well-managed project. Costs starting to exceed the budget indicate the project isn't going as planned and you need to control costs. You may need to investigate each aspect of the project to see why costs are exceeding budget.

To assign a budget to a project, follow these steps:

1. **From the Navigation bar, click Projects, select the project you require and click the Edit icon.**

2. **Click the Budgets tab.**

   The budget information shows all cost codes currently set up in Sage 50 Accounts.

3. **Select the Budget column for each cost type and enter a figure.**

4. **Click Save to save your entries, or click the Clear Form icon if you want to clear the data and start again.**

5. **Click Close to exit the project record and return to the Projects window.**

To see how the project costs compare with the budget, click the Analysis tab on the project record to view a summary of actual costs, budgeted costs and committed costs. You can also enter the project price that has been quoted in the Revenue Totals section of the project record.

You can run many reports to check the progress of your project. You can run reports showing committed costs for each project and cost transactions by cost code, and to check stock issued for a project. You can also run a number of day-book reports to see postings to the project by various transaction types. To print a report, click the Reports icon from the Projects module and select whichever report you require from the array available.

Charging Your Customers for a Project

Ultimately, you need to charge your customers for work carried out on your project. If the project is large, you may want to charge your customers on a continual basis. If the project is a small, one-day affair, as in the Jingles Fun Day example, you probably invoice at the end of the project.

Project costing doesn't automatically bill your customers, but the Analysis tab of the project record helps you calculate how much to charge. You can see how much you've billed a customer already or how much you've quoted a customer and therefore what amount is outstanding. Sage provides a variety of project-costing reports that can help you decide how much to charge your customers.

Figure 13-7 shows that Anytown Parish Council was quoted a price of £2,000 for a Fun Day and currently no bills have been issued, so Jingles needs to raise an invoice for the full £2,000.

After you know how much you need to charge, you can invoice your customer in a number of ways:

>> Issue a service invoice, showing details of work carried out.

>> Issue a product invoice, using special product code S3 if you have Accounts Professional. This product code lets you issue service charges and product charges on the same invoice.

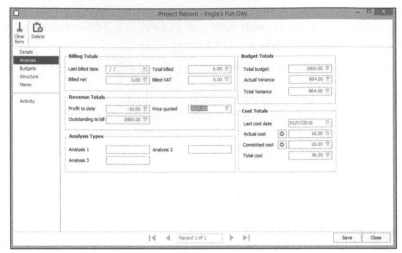

>> Issue a product invoice showing nonstock or service items. You can use this
type of invoice if your business is service-based, but you use product records
to keep track of your services or to produce price lists.

If you overcharge a customer for a project, you can credit your customer by raising
a credit note. (Refer to Chapter 6 for how to raise product and service invoices.)

REMEMBER

When you enter the invoice, you must ensure you include the project reference
and cost code. When the invoice is posted to the ledger, it updates the project
activity information and the Analysis tab.

A number of reports provide you with the information necessary to produce an
invoice based on time and materials used. This process isn't automated, so you
need to produce your bills manually, as I explain in Chapter 6.

Completing Your Project

After the project has come to an end and you no longer have any invoices or transactions to post to it, you mark the project as complete. Changing the status to
complete ensures no further postings can be made to the project. You change the
status of the project with these steps:

1. **From the Projects window, highlight the project you want to complete.**

2. **Click the Edit icon.**

   This takes you to the Details tab.

3. **On the status line, use the drop-down arrow to select the status** *completed*.

4. **Click Save to save your changes, or click the Clear Form icon to exit without saving.**

If you no longer need to view this project record and have no need for any further analysis of the project, you may delete the project. You can delete a project only if the project status is complete. To delete a project, simply highlight the project you want to delete and click Delete.

Chapter 14

Using Foreign Currencies

This chapter is all about getting your head around the foreign currencies element of Sage. I always found the topic of foreign currencies a bit scary, so in this chapter I go through it step by step and make things as easy as possible for you to understand.

In this chapter I show you how to set up foreign currencies and deal with exchange rates in Sage. I introduce you to the Foreign Trader facility and show you how it fits into the day-to-day working of your business. You can find out how to deal with the extra paperwork when it comes to foreign customers, suppliers and banks. And I show you how to use the Revaluation wizard to keep your foreign currency bank accounts in line.

Foreign Trader is available for all variants of Sage Accounts from Sage Instant Accounts, but only as an additional module. This chapter applies mainly to businesses that receive multiple foreign invoices and pay suppliers in foreign currencies. If you have only the occasional foreign invoice, converting the foreign currency to pounds sterling and processing the invoice as usual is probably easier than bothering with the Foreign Trader module. (Head to Chapter 7 for the low-down on how to process invoices.)

Setting Up Foreign Currencies

If you deal with foreign currencies, you need to set up those currencies in Sage. To process an invoice in a foreign currency, you have to convert the foreign currency into your base currency, which you select when you run the Active Setup wizard (which I cover in Chapter 1). For this book, I assume your base currency is pounds sterling.

To do the conversion, Sage needs to have exchange rates in place – but these fluctuate constantly. I suggest you agree on a rate or set a time to check the current rate with your customers and suppliers. For example, you may agree with your supplier to use the exchange rate issued by HM Revenue & Customs (HMRC) on the first day of each week for a month, or you may set a rate to use for the whole of that month.

TIP

The HMRC website at www.hmrc.gov.uk provides useful information on exchange rates. To find the correct exchange rates, enter the words 'exchange rates' in the search box and then click the HMRC exchange rates link that should appear. Select the year you want to find the appropriate rate for, and then choose the month or week. For example, if you have an April 2016 invoice from the United States, you can select April 2016 rates of exchange and find the dollar exchange rate to convert your invoice to pounds sterling.

Entering the exchange rate for a currency

One of the best places to find information on exchange rates is the HMRC website at www.hmrc.gov.uk. You can enter the rates from this website into Sage so that you can use the Sage foreign currencies options. To register the exchange rate, follow these steps:

1. **From the Menu bar, click Settings.**

2. **Select Currencies.**

   The currency you selected when you first set up Sage is displayed as the base currency. (See Chapter 1 for more on setting up Sage.) The Currencies box opens, showing a list of all currencies available in Sage, along with the currency code and symbol (for example, U.S. dollars is USD $). If you want to add a new currency or edit an existing one, do it here.

3. **Select the currency you want to enter an exchange rate for.**

   The currency you select appears at the bottom of the Currencies screen and shows an exchange rate of zero if you haven't already entered an exchange rate.

4. **Enter the exchange rate you want to use.**

   You can enter exchange rates for as many currencies as you require. Figure 14-1 shows how Jeanette of Jingles entered a U.S. dollar exchange rate using April 2016 rates from the HMRC website.

5. **Click Close to exit the Currencies screen and save the exchange rate details.**

Source: Jane Kelly

FIGURE 14-1: Entering a U.S. dollar exchange rate for Jingles.

CONVERTING CURRENCIES WITH F5

The F5 key works as a currency converter if you're in any numeric field. This nifty function comes in handy when you process invoices in pounds sterling and convert the foreign invoice value before you enter invoices into Sage.

Press the F5 key and a currency converter box appears. Type in the amount of foreign currency and specify which currency it is (for example, U.S. dollars), and Sage converts it to your base currency.

You need to set up the exchange rate you want to use to convert the currencies in your Currencies table, as I explain in the nearby section 'Entering the exchange rate for a currency'.

Amending the Countries table

The Countries table consists of a list of countries and their country codes. Sage indicates members of the European Union (EU) with a tick in the EU column. The Countries table is used for Intrastat reporting. *Intrastat* is a system that collects data about the movement of physical goods between member states of the EU. You may have to amend the Countries table when countries join or leave the EU.

Intrastat has been in operation since January 1993 and has replaced the customs declarations. The supply of services is excluded from Intrastat, which is closely linked with the VAT (value-added tax) system. Companies that aren't VAT registered have no obligations under the Intrastat system.

To amend your Countries table:

1. **From the Menu bar, click Settings and then Countries.**

   The Countries table appears. The table has three columns showing the country, the country code and a checkbox indicating with or without a green tick whether the country is a member of the EU.

2. **To add a country, click Add.**

   Type the country name in the Add/Edit Country Details box that opens.

   Alternatively, to edit the details for a country, highlight its name and click Edit.

   Tick the EU Member box if you add a country that's part of the EU. You can change EU status by clicking the EU Member box to add or remove the tick.

FOREIGN CURRENCY CHECKLIST

Use this checklist to get through the maze of working with Sage 50 Accounts and foreign currency:

- Activate the Foreign Trader Setup wizard.

- Enter exchange rates for all currencies you use.

- Set up new customer accounts for customers that use foreign currencies.

- If you have customers who may pay you in more than one currency, use a separate customer account for each currency.

- Set up new foreign currency supplier accounts – with separate accounts for each currency.

- Set up bank accounts for each foreign currency.

3. **Click OK to save the changes, or click Cancel to exit without saving.**

Sage returns to the Countries table.

4. **Click Close to exit the Countries table.**

Tailoring the Foreign Trader Tool

Turning on Foreign Trader is a choice, but if you trade using foreign currencies, you have to activate Foreign Trader.

The Foreign Trader facility is the crux of the foreign currencies part of Sage. When activated, this facility can process customers and suppliers based in a foreign currency; let you use foreign currency bank accounts; and process invoices, credit notes, bank payments and receipts in different currencies.

After you activate the Foreign Trader option, you can't switch it off!

WARNING

You set up the Foreign Trader option using the Foreign Trader Setup wizard as follows:

1. **From the Menu bar, click Tools, Activations and then Enable Foreign Trader.**

A warning message may say you can't run this wizard with other windows open, so click Yes to close all other windows.

2. **The Foreign Trader Setup window opens, as shown in Figure 14-2.**

Work through the following screens of the wizard, clicking Next after you finish each screen:

- **Welcome:** This screen explains that you can process customer, supplier and bank transactions in foreign currencies. Sage offers a link where you can access a complete guide to Foreign Trader.

- **Setup:** This screen explains that you need to use a nominal code to handle exchange rate variances and to choose how you want to update exchange rates. The default nominal code is 7906, and the default update method is 'Always prompt to save exchange rate changes'. You can use the drop-down arrows to change either of these.

- **Finish:** In the Finish screen, Sage recommends you click Settings and then Currencies to check your currency codes and the exchange rates you want to use.

If you need to make any changes, click Back. If you don't want to proceed, click Cancel. Otherwise, click Finish to activate your Foreign Trader option.

Source: Jane Kelly

FIGURE 14-2:
Welcome to the
Foreign Trader
Setup wizard.

REMEMBER

When you run the Foreign Trader option, the Currency Exchange Rate box appears in the Invoice defaults on the General tab. You can use the drop-down arrow to choose a different exchange rate change method from the default setting.

Keeping Trade Status in Mind When Setting Up Accounts

Getting your customer, supplier and bank records ready for foreign trade is as simple as making sure you give them a touch of the exotic when you set them up. In Chapter 3, I explain the basic setup procedures for Sage, so check there for help.

When you set up customer and supplier records for foreign trade, keep the following points in mind for individual records:

>> Click the correct country when you enter the customer or supplier's address.

>> Select the correct currency on the Defaults tab. (If you don't select the currency, the currency rate box won't appear when you issue an invoice for that foreign customer.)

>> Adjust the tax code accordingly. If you supply goods to a VAT-registered customer in another EU member state and the goods are moved from the U.K. to that EU country, your supply may be zero-rated. (See HMRC Notice 725, The Single Market, for more information on this.) Some supplies of services to overseas customers are zero-rated, but many are standard-rated – seek advice from your local tax office.

You need a separate bank account for every currency you deal with. For example, if you trade in pounds sterling, U.S. dollars, euros and Japanese yen, you need four bank accounts. Sage shows you the balance in the original currency and also what it converts to in the base currency. Use these accounts just as you do any other bank account.

After you enter a transaction, you cannot change its currency.

To convert a bank account to foreign currency usage, change the currency by using the drop-down arrow of the Currency box on the Account Details tab within the bank account. Figure 14-3 shows an example of an American bank account setup. Notice the Account Details tab shows a field for both the U.S. dollar balance and the pounds sterling base currency.

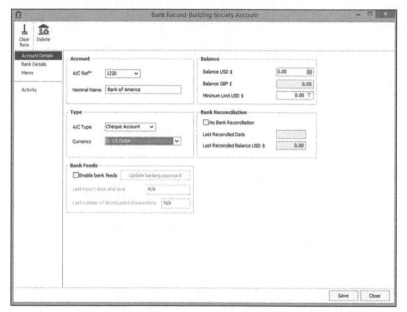

FIGURE 14-3:
Setting up a foreign bank account.

Source: Jane Kelly

Processing the Paperwork

In this section, I show you how to raise sales invoices and purchase invoices using foreign currencies and how to apply receipts and payments using foreign currency bank accounts.

Raising invoices, credit notes and orders

You can raise invoices, credit notes and orders in the usual way. (I explain raising invoices and credit notes in Chapter 6 and raising orders in Chapter 10.) When you open a foreign customer record, a Rate box appears under the Address box on the Details screen of both the Invoice and Sales Order screens, and the currency symbol changes from pounds sterling to the currency you have chosen for that customer.

TIP

You can change the currency rate in the Rate box by overtyping the current rate shown.

REMEMBER

Exchange rates fluctuate all the time, often in the time between processing one foreign invoice and the next. You can apply a new exchange rate as you enter your sales invoice, credit note or order. As soon as you attempt to change the exchange rate (assuming you've accepted the defaults for the exchange-rate method), Sage asks if you want to update your currency record with your new exchange rate. Click Yes or No depending on your requirements.

Choosing VAT codes

You must make sure Sage shows the VAT correctly. For example, exporting goods to a customer outside the EU is normally zero-rated. (Read HMRC Notice 703, Export of Goods from the UK, for more on this.) When you process a sales invoice, credit note or order to a zero-rated country, make sure Sage calculates the VAT using the T0 tax code.

You may need to press F3 and edit the information on your invoice to ensure you've selected the correct VAT code. Click OK to apply these changes. Figure 14-4 shows the VAT code being edited to T0 for goods sold to a business in the United States.

For VAT-registered customers outside the U.K. but within the EU, use the tax code T4 (Sales of goods to VAT registered customers in the EC) and make sure that you include the customer's EC VAT registration number on the customer record.

Other useful VAT codes include the following:

» T7 for zero-rated purchases of goods from suppliers in the EC

» T8 for standard-rated purchases of goods from suppliers in the EC

TECHNICAL STUFF

For EU VAT codes for purchases, Sage allocates a notional rate linked to the U.K. VAT system. For example, T8 is linked to the U.K. standard VAT rate of 20 per cent.

FIGURE 14-4:
Changing the VAT code is easy and often necessary when dealing with foreign trade.

Source: Jane Kelly

Figure 14-5 shows an invoice to American Events for a box of tricks, sold for $50. Sage automatically shows the conversion in the base currency (£35.44 sterling), at the bottom right corner of the invoice.

FIGURE 14-5:
A Jingles sales invoice raised to an American customer.

Source: Jane Kelly

Converting currencies and viewing invoices

REMEMBER

Although you create the invoice in a foreign currency, after saving the invoice, it is displayed on the Invoice list initially in pounds sterling, but then the next column shows the dollar amount.

After you update the invoice to the nominal ledger and the customer ledger, the balance on the Customer screen shows in pounds sterling, just like all the other balances outstanding. If you double-click the customer record and look at the Details screen, the balance in sterling still shows. On the Activity screen, you see the foreign currency, as in Figure 14-6. The right side of the screen shows the customer balance in U.S. dollars and the year-to-date (YTD) turnover is shown in pounds sterling. The invoice details are in U.S. dollars, and the balance outstanding is aged in dollars at the bottom of the screen.

FIGURE 14-6:
Customer activity for an American customer's account.

Source: Jane Kelly

Entering batch invoices and credit notes

You can use the batch-entry method of inputting invoices for customers and suppliers in the currency that appears on their record. For example, if you have a German supplier, you can enter the invoice in euros as it appears on the German invoice.

Figure 14-7 shows an invoice from Tiki Toys in Japanese yen for some robot toys. The Batch Entry has an additional Currency box showing Japanese yen, the exchange rate used for processing the invoice and the T0 tax code used for zero-rated supplies.

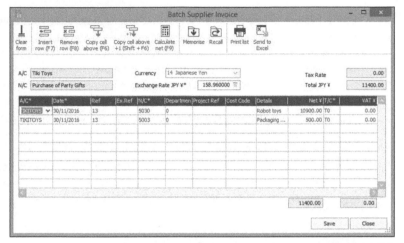

FIGURE 14-7: A batch of invoices from a foreign supplier.

After you enter the batch invoice and are happy with the details, you can save the invoice. You can now view the transaction in the supplier's Activity screen. The transaction is shown in yen and the balance on the account is in yen, but the turnover YTD is in pounds sterling. The balance outstanding is aged into current, 30 days, 60 days, 90 days and older than 90 days.

Banking on Foreign Currencies

Banking tasks with foreign currencies are no different from the same tasks in pounds sterling, although you have additional boxes on some of the screens that highlight the exchange rate, and you see references to the foreign currency.

Coping with customer receipts and supplier payments

When you deal with businesses and customers in foreign countries, you expect to receive and send invoices and payments in different currencies. For example, if you send customer invoices to America, you send the invoice in U.S. dollars and you expect to be paid in U.S. dollars.

REMEMBER

Make sure you process the transaction in the same currency from the customer or supplier account through to the bank account.

Sometimes you may receive money in a foreign currency that doesn't relate to any invoices you issued, or you may need to make foreign currency payments where you have no invoice associated with the payment. To accommodate these invoice-less transactions, follow the procedure I explain in Chapter 8 for bank payments or bank receipts – but note that the Bank Account screen shows the currency and the exchange rate you entered in the Currency table. You can change this rate if required. Depending on the defaults you chose, you may be able to update your currency record here.

The Net and Tax columns show the currency code associated with the bank account. For example, if you have a U.S. dollar account, you see the $ sign at the top of the Net and Tax columns.

Depositing foreign currencies

You process receipts in a foreign currency in the bank account that you set up to deal with that type of money – Japanese yen in the yen bank account, euros in the euros account, and so on. When Jeanette of Jingles receives payment from American Events for the sum of $50, she deposits the money in the U.S. dollar account.

To process a receipt in foreign currency, follows these steps:

1. **From the Navigation bar, click Bank accounts and highlight the foreign bank account you're processing a receipt for.**

   Click Customer Receipt.

2. **Select the customer account.**

   Outstanding invoices appear in the main part of the screen.

3. **Enter the date of the receipt.**

   Sage automatically defaults to the current day's date, so change the date if you need to.

4. **Enter a reference.**

   Putting a paying-in slip or BACS reference is a good idea.

5. **Check you're happy with the exchange rate given (taken from your Currency table) and change it as needed.**

   If you change the currency rate, Sage asks if you would like to update your Currencies List.

   If you used the HMRC website to obtain your previous exchange rate, check to ensure that the rate is still valid; if not, amend the rate.

6. **Enter the amount received against the invoice, or click the Pay in Full icon at the top of the screen.**

7. **Click Save to process the data, or click Close to exit without saving.**

8. **Click Close to exit the Customer Receipt screen.**

   You return to the Bank screen.

Paying a foreign supplier

Businesses generally like to receive payments in the same currency as the invoice. Consider what happens when Jingles pays Tiki Toys for the robot toys. The total amount outstanding on the account is 11,400 yen – you can see the invoice in Figure 14-7. Jeanette processes this transaction through the Japanese bank account in the usual way – check out Chapter 7 for a reminder on how to process supplier payments.

Carrying out a bank transfer

In this section, I describe how to make transfers from your base currency to a foreign currency and from one foreign currency to another.

Use the exchange rate shown in the table at www.hmrc.gov.uk and follow these steps:

1. **From the Navigation bar, click Bank accounts and then click the Bank Transfer icon.**

2. **Use the drop-down arrows to select the account you want to transfer from and the account you want to transfer to.**

   The Reference and Description fields have details entered already, but you can change these to something more meaningful to you.

3. **Use the drop-down arrow to select a department, if required.**

4. **Enter the date of the transaction.**

5. **Enter the amount you want to transfer from the first account.**

    Note that Sage will have already calculated an exchange rate if you are transferring between foreign currencies, but if you want to change this, you can overtype it. Sage also enters the received amount automatically if you are transferring between two different foreign currencies.

6. **Enter the exchange rate you want to use if you're transferring from your base currency to a foreign currency account.**

7. **Click Save or click Close to exit without saving.**

    Alternatively, you can click the Clear Form icon to clear the screen.

    Figure 14-8 shows a 30 November transfer of $200 in U.S. dollars from the Bank of America into Jingles's Japanese bank account. Sage calculates the value to be received in yen for the Bank of Japan and deposits the proper sum – in this case, 22,531.54 yen – in the Japanese bank account. Jingles can use the money in this account to pay its Japanese suppliers and receive payments from Japanese customers.

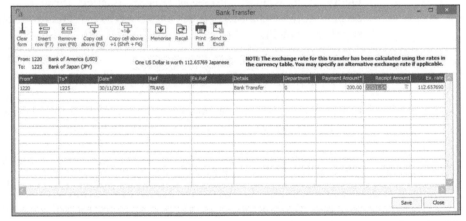

FIGURE 14-8:
A bank transfer between two foreign accounts.

REMEMBER

When you perform bank transfers between foreign accounts and you enter a payment value for a transfer from a particular account, Sage uses the exchange rate information held within the Currency table to calculate the receipt value in the other account. If you decide to change any part of the information in this transaction, Sage may need to recalculate the figures. Sage makes these changes according to the order in which you change the data.

Expecting changing exchange rates

Exchange rates vary from week to week and even from day to day. The exchange rate is likely to change in the time between you receiving and paying an invoice.

When you post invoices and make payments to your ledgers, you do so in the relevant foreign currency. For example, a $100 invoice is likely to prompt a $100 payment in U.S. dollars. That payment clears the balance on the account to zero – but the payment doesn't take into account any exchange rate differences that occurred between posting the invoice and posting the payment.

Sage secretly works in the background to make adjustments for exchange rate fluctuations. To accommodate exchange rate differences, Sage cleverly creates a dummy invoice with the reference Reval (short for Revaluation). Sage works out the differences on the two parts of the invoice and posts the necessary adjustment using the 7906 exchange rate variance nominal code. If the exchange rate works in your favour so you pay less, Sage posts a purchase credit note to account for the fluctuation.

You can view these adjustments by looking at the nominal activity of account 7906. (Chapter 20 covers how to access a Nominal Activity report.) In addition, opening the foreign supplier record and clicking the Activity tab reveals a button at the bottom of the screen that says Pounds. Click this to see the transactions in pounds sterling instead of the foreign currency.

Figure 14-9 shows the Nominal Activity screen for exchange rate variances. You can see the result of a movement in exchange rate for the Tiki Toys transaction. Between the time Jingles ordered robot toys from the supplier and the time Jingles paid the invoice, the exchange rate changed – on 15 December 2016, instead of £71.72, the 11,400 yen were worth £70.24, so the robot toys cost £1.48 less than expected. Sage automatically posted the necessary adjustments into nominal account 7906, which you can see on the Nominal Activity screen in Figure 14-9. The revaluation is shown on two separate lines (£1.41 and £0.07) because there was both the cost of the robot as well as a packaging cost. Both amounts sum to £1.48, which is the adjustment needed to correct the movement in exchange rates.

TIP

Exchange rate revaluations go on all the time as you process your foreign currency transactions. For more information on this subject, type 'exchange rate fluctuations' into Sage Help.

FIGURE 14-9:
Accommodating
exchange rate
fluctuations.

Source: Jane Kelly

Doing Revaluations with the Wizard

The Revaluation wizard is useful for keeping your monthly foreign currency bank accounts straight. Sage does a lot of automatic adjustments in the background, but from a housekeeping point of view, you need to ensure you update and review all your foreign currency bank accounts on a regular basis. Doing so at the end of each month ensures your financial reports are correct.

For example, a bank account with a balance of $1,583.20 at an exchange rate of 1.5832 contains £1,000. But at the month end, if the exchange rate falls to 1.4723, the account contains £1,075.32. You need to take account of these fluctuations by running the Revaluation wizard.

To run the Revaluation wizard, follow these steps:

1. **From the Menu bar, click Modules → Wizards → Foreign Bank Revaluation.**

   Click Yes to the confirmation message that appears. The Revaluation wizard opens with the Welcome screen, as shown in Figure 14-10.

2. **Highlight the account you want to revalue and then click Next.**

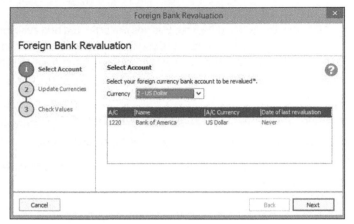

FIGURE 14-10:
Running the
Foreign Bank
Revaluation
wizard.

Source: Jane Kelly

3. **Enter the date you want to revalue.**

The last day of a month is a good choice. Enter the exchange rate for the foreign currency on the date of revaluation. Click Next to continue.

4. **Check the details of the revaluation are correct and then click Post.**

The wizard posts a journal, using your revaluation control account nominal code, to revalue your foreign currency bank accounts.

You can check your journals have been posted by clicking on the Transactions link from the Navigation bar. You can also check revaluations from the Foreign Bank Revaluations icon on the bank record, where you see the date of the revaluation and the exchange rate used. You can make changes to these revaluations.

If you need to correct the exchange rate you used or reverse the revaluation because you made an error, follow these steps:

1. **From the Navigation bar, click Bank accounts, select the bank account you want to make the adjustment for, click the New/Edit icon and select Edit from the drop-down list.**

The bank record opens.

2. **Click the Revaluations tab.**

3. **Click the Show Balances icon.**

The information updates to show the foreign balance and the prior base currency balance. The revalued base balance also shows.

Note that the Edit and Reverse buttons are activated and available to use. The Reverse button comes in handy if you mess up a transaction and want to reverse it. If you click the Reverse button, Sage automatically reverses the revaluation and creates and posts the appropriate journals to the necessary accounts.

4. **Select the revaluation you want to adjust and click Edit.**

5. **Change the exchange rate in the Edit Revaluation box.**

6. **Click OK to complete the adjustment, or click Cancel to take you back to the Bank Record Revaluation tab.**

4

Running Monthly, Quarterly and Annual Routines

IN THIS PART . . .

Discover how to reconcile your bank accounts.

Understand the procedures you need to carry out when you prepare monthly accounts and year-end reports.

If you're a VAT-registered business, ensure you meet the key quarterly deadline of the VAT return.

Chapter 15

Reconciling Your Bank Accounts

I f you like to know to the penny what's in your bank account, you're reading the right chapter. Reconciling your bank accounts normally forms part of your monthly accounting routine. Running through the bank reconciliation process gives you a thorough review of your bank statements and provides a good opportunity to investigate any unusual or incorrect transactions. As a result, you're fully aware of the financial transactions flowing in and out of your bank accounts.

To reconcile your bank accounts, you need to get the bank data into your Sage accounts system. You can enter bank data into Sage in three ways, as you find out in this chapter:

>> Use bank feeds.

>> Enter the bank transactions manually.

>> Import your bank statements (using e-Banking).

Recognising Reasons to Reconcile

Performing a bank reconciliation requires you to check you've matched all the bank transactions in Sage against the entries on your bank statements. Ultimately, you should be able to tick off every item on your bank statement against a corresponding entry in Sage.

Most businesses have at least one current account, a deposit account, a business credit card and a petty cash tin. Each separate account needs statements of one sort or another. Sage assumes you have all of these accounts and provides defaults for each account, which you can rename or add to as required. (Refer to Chapter 3 for the lowdown on amending accounts.) Additionally, Sage includes a building society account and credit card receipts account by default, as Figure 15-1 shows.

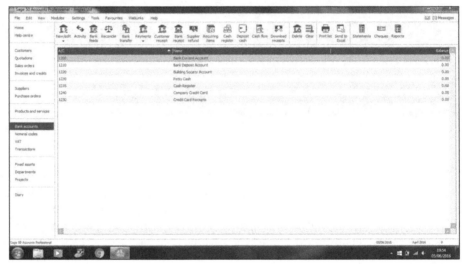

FIGURE 15-1: Sage assumes your business has various bank accounts.

Source: Jane Kelly

After you reconcile your accounts, you can be sure that the data and any reports run from your information are accurate.

You need to reconcile all your bank accounts to ensure the accuracy of your accounting records. Reconciling all your bank accounts is particularly important if you're VAT registered, because reconciling helps you pick up all transactions associated with VAT (value-added tax). Credit card transactions in particular can attract a lot of VAT. If you don't reconcile your credit card statements, you may miss VAT-liable transactions and render your accounts and your VAT return incorrect.

WARNING

When you set up your bank records, Sage lets you determine whether you want each bank account to be a reconciling account. If you don't want to reconcile an account, click the bank record and put a tick in the No Bank Reconciliation box on the account details tab. Use this feature with caution – most bank accounts need to be reconciled to ensure accuracy of information.

REMEMBER

Doing your bank reconciliations on a regular basis guarantees the accuracy of your information and lets you run meaningful reports to help you manage your business and make sensible decisions.

Using Bank Feeds to Post Data into Sage

In recent times, bank feeds have become the most efficient way to manage and reconcile the data that comes in and out of your bank account. Essentially, once set up, your bank account statement data automatically feeds into your Sage bank account (hence the name) and awaits your instructions as to what to do with the data. This speeds up data processing hugely and ultimately eliminates data entry errors.

WARNING

However, before you get too carried away, a word of warning: You must make sure you still check the data to your actual bank statements, because there may be the occasional glitch in the banking download process, and it's possible that a transaction could be missed. So you must always thoroughly check your data and ensure that your statement balance on Sage actually matches the statement balance on your bank statement after you have reconciled a period.

REMEMBER

Bank feeds are available only with the Sage 50 Accounts version 22 subscription and Sage 50 Accounts version 22 with Sage Cover Extra, Essential Cover Plus and Essential Cover Expert.

Setting up bank feeds

Getting up and running with bank feeds is a very simple process, but you do need to have some information to hand before you begin. You need your bank account sort code and account number, as well as your online login bank details that you received when you first set up online banking. These may vary from bank to bank. You also need your Sage ID, which is the username and password that you need to access certain Sage services, such as bank feeds and Sage Drive (find out more on this in Chapter 21).

1. **Click on Bank Accounts, and then click the Bank feeds icon.**

   The Bank feeds setup window opens (see Figure 15-2). This screen tells you a bit more about who is providing the third-party access to your bank details (Yodlee Inc.) and also what information you will need to provide. If you are happy with this information, click the Let's get started button.

FIGURE 15-2:
Bank feeds setup
information.

2. **Sage asks you to enter your Sage ID login.**

   If you don't have these details, you can click 'New User? Create a Sage ID' and follow the on-screen prompts. Once you have your Sage ID, enter these details when prompted.

3. **When requested, enter your Sage account number and the serial number for your software.**

   If you can't remember your serial number, click Help and then About from the Sage menu bar. You can find the serial number displayed under License Information. Then click Register.

4. **You then need to select your bank account information by following the on-screen prompts.**

This enables Sage to locate your correct bank account and begin the process of accessing your bank account details using your secure bank account login credentials. Click OK and then close this screen.

Downloading your bank transactions

Once Sage has set up your bank feed information and successfully enabled the bank feeds, you need to download the data.

WARNING

When you do your first download, make sure that you use the day after your last bank reconciliation. Personally, I would choose the start of a new month and ensure that I had reconciled fully to the end of the previous month.

TIP

It is possible to download bank transactions to Sage once every 15 minutes!

To download the transactions:

1. **From the Bank Accounts module, select the bank account you want to use and click the Bank feeds icon.**

The Bank feeds window opens for that bank account. See Figure 15-3. Note that the window is split into four panes. The top left pane is where your transactions from the bank will ultimately be viewed.

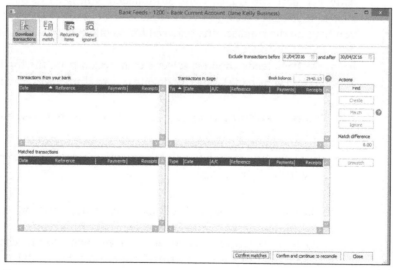

FIGURE 15-3:
Looking at the
Bank feeds
window.

Source: Jane Kelly

2. **Check the dates in the top right-hand corner of the screen.**

   If this is the first download, ensure that the first date is after the date that you last reconciled your bank account. For example, my last bank reconciliation was 31.03.2016, so I make sure that I exclude transactions from before 01.04.2016.

3. **Once you are happy with the dates selected, click the Download transactions icon.**

   Sage warns you that the download time will be affected by the number of transactions being downloaded and the speed of your Internet connection; click OK. Sage now whirs into action, and the screen says that it is retrieving additional information.

WARNING

   Note that you may be asked to provide additional security information. Make sure you have your online PIN details and so forth to hand, as Sage gives you only a couple of minutes to enter your details. Don't be tempted to press any buttons on the keyboard at this stage, even if it doesn't look like anything is happening.

4. **Sage gives you a 'We have successfully updated your account details' message when it has completed downloading your transactions. Click Close when you receive this message.**

   Your downloaded transactions now appear in the top left of the bank feed box.

Reconciling your downloaded transactions

After you have the transactions downloaded, you need to reconcile them. Make sure that you have a copy of your bank statement to hand, just to make sure that you have all the transactions required for reconciling the account.

From the Bank feeds window, select a transaction from the top left pane (Transactions from your bank). You can do one of two things with each transaction:

>> **Create a new transaction** to match with the entry that has been imported from your bank account.

>> **Match the transaction** to a transaction already entered in Sage (which will show in the top right pane).

I describe each of the two processes in the following sections.

TIP

You may have recurring bank entries that you want to process, if you have not already done so. Click the Recurring Items icon followed by the Process icon to process these transactions for the period that you are reconciling. The transactions will appear in the top right pane of the Bank feeds window.

Creating a new transaction in Sage

If no transactions appear in the top right window (Transactions in Sage), it means that you need to create those transactions. Click the Create icon on the right side of the screen (refer to Figure 15-3 to see this button).

Sage recognises whether you have highlighted either a payment or receipt that needs to be created, and a new window opens giving you options as to what type of transaction you want to create. For example, if you select a payment to match, Sage opens the Create Money Out Transaction window (See Figure 15-4), where you can choose a bank payment, supplier payment, customer refund or bank transfer.

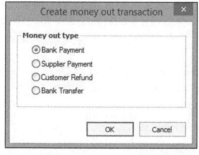

FIGURE 15-4:
Creating a Money
Out transaction.

Source: Jane Kelly

Select the appropriate payment method – for example, bank payment – and click OK. The normal bank payment window opens, and you can process the transaction as normal.

The transaction that you have created is automatically matched with the transaction that you have highlighted from the bank. The transaction then appears in the bottom left pane of the bank feed window, as a Matched transaction, and also appears in the bottom right pane.

Continue to Match or create items (ticking the items off the physical bank statement as you go).

TIP

To speed things up, you can select more than one transaction in the top left pane. It makes sense to select the same type of transactions though. For example, you can select all the bank payment transactions, and they will all then display in the bank payment window, where you can enter them all together rather than enter each individual transaction at a time.

This works better for bank payments and bank receipts where you can batch process. It is better to individually select customer receipts and supplier payments. Then you can make sure you allocate the payment/receipt to the correct account and invoices.

One of the benefits of using bank feeds becomes very apparent when entering customer receipts: When you create a transaction and it takes you through to the normal customer receipt screen, you don't have to reenter all the date and reference information, because it automatically pulls through from the bank statement.

Matching transactions manually

If you have already entered transactions into Sage, they appear in the top right pane of the bank feeds window (you can see this pane in Figure 15-3). Follow these steps to match transactions:

1. **Highlight the transaction in the top left pane (Transactions from your bank) with the matching transaction (no pun intended) in the top right pane (Transactions in Sage).**

2. **Click the Match icon on the right side of the screen.**

   The matched transactions now appear in the bottom two panes of the bank feed screen.

After you have entered and matched your transactions, you have two options. You can either click the Confirm matches icon (which simply saves your matches and exits the bank feed), or you can Confirm and continue to reconcile, which takes you through to the standard bank reconciliation screen (as detailed in the later section 'Doing the Reconciliation').

Matching transactions with the Auto Match option

The benefits of the bank feed option really become apparent here. Once you have entered the dates for the bank reconciliation period and downloaded the transactions from your bank account, Sage automatically shows the items that have been entered into the accounts system for those specified dates (in the top right pane) and the downloaded transactions from the bank account in the top left pane.

To begin with, all transactions will be in the top two panes, as nothing has yet been matched. An icon called Auto Match, when clicked, enables Sage to use certain criteria to be able to match up your downloaded bank transactions with those transactions that you have entered in Sage. It uses transactions types such as payments and receipts with the exact amount and a date range of four days to match up transactions. Once Sage finds a match, it places the matched transactions in the bottom two panes of the reconciliation screen.

However, there may be items from the downloaded bank transactions that cannot be matched with items in Sage, perhaps because you weren't aware of them. For example, bank interest may have been applied to your bank account that you may not be aware of until you see your bank transactions. To deal with these items, you simply highlight the bank transaction and then click Create. Follow the instructions in the earlier section 'Creating a new transaction in Sage'.

You can now either click the Confirm matches icon, which effectively saves your bank reconciliation, or you can continue on to complete the reconciliation process as outlined later in this chapter.

Double-checking everything

After you have matched all the transactions that you are able to, and you are happy that the Match difference box (on the right side of the Bank feeds window) shows a zero total, click the button Confirm and continue to reconcile.

The usual bank reconciliation window appears, and you can reconcile your account as normal – see the later section 'Doing the Reconciliation' for information.

In fact, you will find that because you have already matched your items in the Bank feeds window, you simply need to check that the matched balance and statement balance boxes agree at the bottom of the bank reconciliation page. Don't forget to double-check your statement balance to the actual bank statement balance.

Assuming that everything is in order, click the Reconcile button at the bottom right corner of the screen. That's it; all done!

Manually Entering Your Bank Account Data

If you are not using the bank feeds facility that I describe earlier in this chapter, you will have to manually enter your bank transactions and then perform a manual bank reconciliation.

Before you start a manual reconciliation, make sure you've accomplished the following tasks:

>> **Enter all the payments from your cheque stubs for the period you want to reconcile.** Refer to Chapter 7 for a reminder on how to process supplier payments and Chapter 8 for all other payment types.

>> **Enter the receipts from your paying-in book for the period you want to reconcile.** Refer to Chapter 5 for help with processing customer receipts and Chapter 8 for recording other bank receipts.

TIP

Make sure you enter the cheque numbers and payslip numbers in the Reference field so you can easily identify those items on your statement.

If your bank statements contain any transactions that aren't yet in Sage, input those transactions before the reconciliation. Items in this last-minute batch may include

>> Bank interest (paid and received)

>> Bank charges

>> Direct debits – to pay suppliers, for example

>> Direct credits and BACS from customers

>> Transfers between accounts

TIP

Tick off the items on your bank statement as you enter them in Sage. That way, you can see if you missed anything that needs to be entered.

Using e-Banking to Import Data

You can use the e-Banking option to connect your banking software to your accounts and then process e-Payments and e-Reconcile. I discuss e-Banking in more detail in Chapter 19.

It is a quicker and more accurate way to pay your suppliers. When using e-Payments, Sage creates a file that you can import into your banking software, which means that you can automate payments to your suppliers.

You can also e–Reconcile your bank accounts, which essentially means that you can import a bank statement into Sage 50 accounts and then reconcile the transactions in Sage against your statement.

WARNING

However, you first need to check with your bank that the online banking software that you are using is compatible with Sage. You may find, as I did, that it is not quite as straightforward as it initially seems. For example, to get full access to all the e–Banking functionality, you may need to use a fee-paying bank service, not just a regular online banking service.

To check the compatibility of your banking service, click Help from the main toolbar and then select F1, In product Help. When the search box opens, type in 'e–Banking' and then click Search. Under the title 'Download and Install the required e–Banking component', click the link for www.sage.co.uk. You will then be taken to a list of Sage e–Banking compatible banks. Scroll down the list to find your bank. You will see that the list is split into Payments and Reconciliation/Statement download. There will be a tick against each of these services if your bank is able to provide it. You may find that your bank may not provide both of these services if you are not using a business banking service. For example, Barclays provides only a statement import service for online banking, but if you use its BusinessMaster service (not the Lite option), you have access to both importing statements and electronic payments.

REMEMBER

At the end of the day, you need to choose the service that provides your business with the most benefits for a price that you are happy to pay. If you simply want ease of bank reconciliation and you subscribe to the correct Sage 50 Accounts package, then bank feeds is the way to go. If you don't have the correct version (version 22 upward) for Sage 50, you may want to consider the option of importing your bank statement as described in e–Reconciling in Chapter 19.

Doing the Reconciliation

You need your bank statements in front of you as you work through the reconciliation process. Tick off each item as you enter it into Sage, and then put a line through the tick or use a highlighter pen to indicate you've reconciled that item. Make your mark visible so you can easily spot anything that you haven't reconciled. In Figure 15-5, I show an example of a bank statement with marks for items entered and reconciled. The receipts have been entered into Sage but not yet reconciled – they simply have a tick against them. However, the payments have been entered but have also been reconciled – to show this, I cross through the original tick.

BISI Bank Ltd

Statement Period ended: 30.04.2016

Account No: 51235467   Sort code: 21.45.85

		<u>Payments</u>	<u>Receipts</u>	<u>Balance</u>
01.04.2016	Opening balance			£2000.00
01.04.2016	Transfer to dollar account	£500.00 ✗		£1500.00
10.04.2016	Transfer to petty cash account	£100.00 ✗		£1400.00
12.04.2016	Cash takings		£350.00 ✓	£1750.00
15.04.2016	Cash Sale		£1.50 ✓	£1751.50
24.04.2016	Cash takings		£425.00 ✓	£2176.50
30.04.2016	Closing bank balance			£2176.50

FIGURE 15-5:
A bank statement showing items that are and aren't reconciled.

Source: Jane Kelly

To begin the reconciliation process, follow these steps:

1. **From the Navigation bar, click Bank accounts.**

   Make sure the cursor highlights the bank account you want to reconcile. Sage defaults to account 1200, which is the Bank Current account, so move the cursor if necessary.

2. **Click the Reconcile icon to bring up a Statement Summary, as I show in Figure 15-6.**

FIGURE 15-6:
Statement Summary for bank reconciliation.

Source: Jane Kelly

3. **Enter the Statement Summary information.**

Your statement summary contains the following fields for you to fill in:

- **Statement Reference:** Sage gives you a default reference, with the first four digits being the bank account nominal code and the remaining reference being today's date. You can overwrite this reference with a more meaningful name. Giving your statement a reference lets Sage archive the reconciliation as a PDF document so you can pull up a copy of the bank reconciliation at any time.

TIP

- **Ending Balance:** Enter the final balance shown on the bank statement for the period you're reconciling. Most people reconcile to the end of the month, but I find it easier to reconcile one statement page at a time, as you have fewer transactions to reconcile – which means fewer transactions to check back through in the event of an error. To reconcile by page, use the balance at the bottom of the statement page and reconcile each item on that single page.

- **Statement Date:** Sage automatically defaults to today's date, so change this to the date of the bank statement you want to reconcile.

- **Interest Earned:** If you've earned any interest on the bank statement, enter it here. Alternatively, you can enter any interest as an adjustment in Step 6.

- **Account Charges:** Enter any bank charges on this screen, or enter an adjustment on the Bank Reconciliation screen in Step 6.

4. **Click OK to bring up the Bank Reconciliation screen, as shown in Figure 15-7.**

If you click OK without changing any of the information on the statement summary, you can still change the statement balance and date on the actual Reconciliation screen.

The Bank Reconciliation screen is split into two parts. The top part shows all the transactions currently entered in Sage that need to be matched against the bank statement (up to and including the statement end date, shown at the top of the screen). Items move to the bottom part of the screen after you match them against the bank statement. The bottom part of the screen shows account charges and interest earned, if you entered these on the statement summary, and the last reconciled balance. If you're doing a reconciliation for the first time, the last reconciled balance is zero – otherwise, you see the balance from the previous reconciliation.

REMEMBER

Sage only brings up transactions posted to the system up to the statement end date that you enter on the Statement Summary screen. In Figure 15-7, the end date is 30 April 2016, so only items dated on or before that date appear. If you don't specify a date on the Statement Summary screen, Sage brings up all transactions posted to the system date, which is today's date.

FIGURE 15-7:
The Bank Reconciliation screen.

Source: Jane Kelly

TIP

You can change the statement end balance and the date in the Bank Reconciliation screen by overtyping the date and end balance at the top of the screen.

5. **Match items on Sage against the bank statement.**

   Match each item on your bank statement against the same item in the top part of the Bank Reconciliation screen. To match an item, double-click the item in the top box, or highlight it and click the Match button to the right of the screen. As soon as you match an item, it moves to the bottom part of the screen and the values of the Matched Balance and the Difference boxes at the bottom right of the screen change accordingly.

TIP

As you double-click each item in Sage, make a corresponding mark on the bank statement. If you originally ticked items on the statement, now put a cross through the same tick or highlight the item so you can identify anything not reconciled at the end.

If you move a transaction to the bottom section in error, double-click or highlight the transaction and click Unmatch to move it back to the unmatched items at the top.

The three boxes at the bottom right corner of the screen keep track of the balance between the transactions you match and what your statement says. If you get everything to agree, the Difference box contains a zero.

6. **Click the Adjust button (above Difference at the bottom right of the screen) to make any adjustments.**

You may find you missed inputting an entry that's on the bank statement. Figure 15-8 shows what you can adjust. From version 22 onward, Sage has added another adjustment option that now allows you to adjust for bank transfers, which saves you having to jump in and out of the bank reconciliation if you have missed a bank transfer.

FIGURE 15-8: Adding an adjustment directly to your bank reconciliation.

Source: Jane Kelly

7. **Save the reconciliation.**

Ideally, you work through the bank reconciliation until you've matched all the items from the bank statement. If you need to stop halfway through, however, you can save the work you've done so far by clicking the Save progress button, at the bottom right of the screen, and then clicking OK.

To continue reconciling, click the Reconcile button. A pop-up screen asks whether you want to use or discard the previously saved statement. Click the Use Saved button, and Sage takes you back to the point where you left off.

WARNING

Clicking Discard Saved wipes out your previous work, and you have to start your reconciliation again.

8. Reconcile your bank transactions.

When all your transactions match and the Difference box reads zero, click the Reconcile button at the bottom right of your screen. Sage saves your reconciled statement in a history file (using the reference you gave your reconciliation at the start of the reconciliation process), so you can review it later if you need to.

To access your archived reconciliations, click the Reconcile button and then click OK from the Statement Summary screen. This opens up the Reconciliation screen, where you can click the View History icon at the top left of the screen. A list of PDF files appears, displaying your historical bank reconciliations, as I show in Figure 15-9. Double-click the file you want to view to open the relevant PDF file.

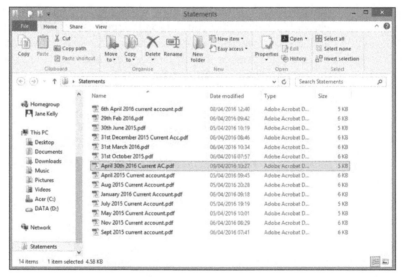

FIGURE 15-9: Viewing the historical bank reconciliations.

Source: Jane Kelly

Troubleshooting When Your Account Doesn't Reconcile

In an ideal world your accounts always reconcile, especially if you follow my recommendations in this chapter. But if your accounts don't reconcile, try the following suggestions:

>> **Check you've ticked off every item on your bank statement.** You may have missed something, which is easy to do when you have lots of transactions on one page or lots of pages in a statement.

>> **Make sure all the items left in the top part of the screen haven't cleared your bank account.** On a bank statement several pages long, you can easily overlook a transaction, especially if you're going through the statement page by page.

>> **Check off each item again to make sure you haven't entered the same entry twice.** If you've entered something twice, double-click the offending item in the matched section of the Bank Reconciliation screen to unmatch it. Then find the transaction number of that item and delete it.

>> **Make sure that the last reconciled figure is the one that you are expecting for the previous month/period.** This just ensures that you have started from the correct point and not missed any transactions.

>> **Double-check the date and whether you have entered the correct bank statement balance.** You may have incorrectly entered the balance, which means that the difference box won't equal zero until you enter the correct statement figure.

When the Difference box reads zero, save or reconcile the account.

TIP

If you reconcile a transaction by mistake, go to File Maintenance, click Corrections and find the transaction. Then Click Edit Item, uncheck the Bank Reconciled box and save your changes. Click Yes to confirm the changes. The next time you open the bank reconciliation, that transaction appears.

Rounding Up Stragglers

You may find that even though the Difference box is zero, you still have some unmatched items in the top part of the screen. This situation is perfectly normal – it just means you've entered cheques or receipts that haven't cleared the bank account and don't show on the current bank statement.

For example, if you're preparing accounts to the end of March, you must enter all cheques up to and including 31 March. However, the 31 March bank statement may not include cheques you wrote on 31 March, 30 March or even 29 March because they haven't cleared your bank yet.

Cheques that show on Sage but aren't yet on your bank statement are known as *unpresented cheques*. You may also have an *outstanding lodgement* or two – a deposit paid in toward the end of the month that doesn't appear on your bank statement because it hasn't cleared the banking system.

At the year end, your accountant usually performs a traditional bank reconciliation and needs to know what your outstanding cheques and lodgements are. In Figure 15-10 I show an example year-end reconciliation using some of Jingles's figures.

Jingles Ltd
Bank Reconciliation as at 30.04.2016

FIGURE 15-10: The accountant's year-end bank reconciliation for Jingles.

	£
Balance per bank statement	2176.50
Less unpresented cheques	387.50
Add back outstanding lodgements	00.00
Balance per the cash book	**1789.00**

Source: Jane Kelly

You can print a list of unpresented cheques and outstanding lodgements at the end of any month. To do this, click the Reports icon within the Bank module; scroll down the report headings on the left of the screen; and at the bottom, click Unreconciled Transactions. Click Bank Report – Unreconciled. If you click the Preview icon, you see this report lists all the unreconciled items for the period selected.

Chapter 16

Running Your Monthly and Yearly Routines

The nominal ledger lists all the nominal codes that your company uses. These nominal codes, when grouped together, form the record of your company's assets, liabilities, income and expenditure. The codes are grouped together in categories identified in your chart of accounts, which I talk about in Chapter 2.

Sage uses the accounting principle of *accrual accounting*. Accrual accounting is all about recording sales and purchases when they occur, not when cash changes hands – you match revenue with expenditure. For example, if you prepare your accounts for the month of June, you need to make sure that you enter all the sales invoices for June, even if your customers haven't paid them yet. You also check that all the purchase invoices relating to June are posted, so you get an accurate reporting position.

In this chapter, I show you how to run wizards and create journals by using the nominal codes to run the monthly and yearly routines. You need these routines to produce timely and accurate reports for management decision making.

TIP

Checklists are vitally important to the smooth running of month-end and year-end processes. You can design your own checklists or use the wizards to guide you through the processes – but either way, you need a routine.

WARNING

If you don't have Accounts Plus or Accounts Professional, you can't perform some of the steps I outline in this chapter. Instead of benefiting from the wizards, you have to manually process your accruals, prepayments and depreciation by using a nominal journal. If you're not happy dealing with journals, I suggest you leave these tasks for your accountant.

Adding Up Accruals

An *accrual* is an amount you know you owe for a product or service you've received but for which you haven't yet received the invoice. An accrual occurs for items that you pay in arrears, such as telephone bills. To maintain an accurate set of accounts, you post an accrual into your nominal ledger by using the appropriate journals. These journals increase the costs to the business and create an accrual for the value of the outstanding invoice. The accrual is treated as a liability within the accounts because the business owes money. As soon as you receive the bill, you can reverse the accrual.

Charging a monthly amount for a service that you normally pay in arrears has a smoothing effect on company profits. For example, if you have a £3,000 telephone bill that you pay quarterly, the bill is accrued in the accounts for the three months before you receive the bill and you put a charge of £1,000 in your accounts each month. If you don't do this, the first two months of the quarter show artificially high profits and the third month shows artificially low profits when the full cost of the telephone bill hits the profit and loss account in one go. The cumulative effect over the three months is the same, but the monthly effect can make the difference between a profit and a loss for your company. Reviewing your accruals and prepayments (which I talk about in the next section) is important for monthly reporting purposes.

TIP

If you don't have Sage 50 Accounts Plus or Professional, then you will need to manually journal your entries. If you're confident with your double-entry bookkeeping, you can post a debit to the cost account and a credit to the accruals account.

Sage likes to make things easy for you and provides a wizard for setting up adjustments for any invoices you're likely to pay in arrears. To access the wizard and set up the accruals, follow these steps:

1. **From the Navigation bar, click Nominal Codes.**

    Click the Accruals icon. The Accruals window opens.

2. **Click the Wizard icon to open the Accruals wizard.**

3. **Select the code you want to set up an accrual for.**

    Enter a transaction description, for example Telephone accrual for April–June 2016. Enter a department (if relevant). Click Next.

4. **Enter the total amount of the accrual, followed by the number of months the accrual should run for.**

    In the three-month telephone bill example, you enter £3,000 in the Total Amount box, followed by 3 in the No. of Months box. Sage automatically calculates the monthly amount.

5. **Click Create to continue.**

    The Accruals window opens, displaying the information for the accrual that you're setting up. If you're happy with the information shown, click Save; if not, close the window. A confirmation message appears saying that the accruals will be posted to the ledgers when you run the month-end option.

If you're happy with the accrual process and don't need step-by-step guidance from your friendly wizard, you can set up a nominal ledger accrual manually as follows:

1. **From the Navigation bar, click the Accruals icon.**

2. **Manually fill in the fields in the Accruals window.**

    Enter the following information:

    -   **Nominal Code:** Using the drop-down arrow, select the nominal code affected by the accrual. In the telephone bill example, Jingles uses 7550 as the nominal code for telephones.

    -   **Details:** Enter details of the accrual. These details show up in the nominal activity reports.

    -   **Department:** Enter the department, if required.

    -   **Accrual Nominal Code:** This field is set to the default accrual nominal code 2109. Don't change this code, because it's a control account. If you're not using the Sage default codes and chose a customised set of nominal codes during Active Setup (which I talk about in Chapter 1), your accrual account may have a different code.

- **Value:** Enter the total value of the accrual. In the telephone bill example, the amount is £3,000.

- **Months:** Put in the number of months to spread the accrual over, between 1 and 12 months.

- **Monthly Amount:** Sage automatically calculates this field after you enter the total amount and the number of months. It shows the monthly amount that's debited when you run the month-end post accruals option.

3. **When you're happy with the information entered for your accruals, click Save.**

    A confirmation message states that these details will be posted to Sage when you run the month-end option. The accrual now appears on the Accruals list.

REMEMBER

If you use the basic Sage Accounts program, you have to complete a nominal journal for your accruals. For the telephone costs example, the double-entry is a debit to the cost code (telephone 7550) and a credit to default accrual code 2109.

Counting Out Prepayments

A *prepayment* is payment in advance for services you haven't completely received. For example, if your business buys a year-long radio advertising campaign for £12,000, which is invoiced in March, you enter the invoice in March for the full value of the advertising campaign – but most of the invoice relates to a future period of time, so you create a prepayment for the 11 months of advertisements to come.

REMEMBER

Registering a prepayment has the effect of decreasing the cost code in the expenses and increasing the prepayments account in the debtors ledger because you've paid in advance for services that haven't been supplied in their entirety (effectively, the supplier owes you).

If you are using Sage 50 Accounts Plus or Professional, you can set up prepayments in much the same way as accruals (which I cover in the preceding section). If you want to use the wizard method, follow these steps:

1. **From the Navigation bar, click the Prepayments icon.**

    The Prepayments window opens.

2. **Click the Wizard icon.**

   The Nominal Ledger Prepayments wizard opens.

3. **Select the nominal code you want to set up the prepayment.**

   In the advertising example, you set up an advertising prepayment for £11,000, using the nominal code 6201.

REMEMBER

   In the nominal record, you can sort the nominal code list into alphabetical or numerical order by clicking the Name or Nominal Code fields. But the system doesn't let you sort differently in the Prepayments screen.

4. **Enter the description of the prepayment and a department if relevant.**

   For example, the advertisement description may read Radio Advertising Prepayment April 2016 – February 2017. (The prepayment is only for 11 months because the initial payment paid the bill for March.)

   Enter a department (if relevant); then click Next to continue.

5. **Enter the total amount, followed by the number of months for the prepayment.**

   Click Create to continue.

6. **Review the summary of the prepayment.**

   Click Save if you're happy with the details, or close to exit without saving.

7. **Click Save.**

   A confirmation message states the payments will be posted only when you run the month-end option. Click OK to return to the Nominal Ledger window.

Alternatively, follow Step 1 in the preceding list and then manually enter the details directly onto the screen (see the example in the section 'Adding Up Accruals' earlier in this chapter). This manual method is quicker than using the wizard, as you don't click through so many screens.

REMEMBER

If you use basic Sage Accounts, your nominal journal double-entry is a debit to prepayments and a credit to the cost code.

If you have to manually journal your prepayments, you will find that when you enter the original invoice, you should code the net amount to prepayments (1103), and then at the end of each month, you need to journal across the appropriate proportion of the bill to the relevant profit and loss nominal code. (In the telephone example in this chapter, it would be £1,000 per month for 12 months to 7550.)

Depreciating Fixed Assets

A *fixed asset* is an item likely to be held in your business for more than 12 months. Fixed assets are usually large and expensive items with a long useful life, such as machinery, land, buildings and cars.

Because fixed assets last so long, you can't charge the profit and loss account with the full asset value. Instead, you *depreciate* the asset, assigning a proportion of the asset to the profit and loss account and offsetting that amount against any profits you make.

Depreciation or *writing down your assets* is an accounting method used to gradually reduce the value of a fixed asset in the accounts. Depreciation applies a charge through the profit and loss account and reduces the value of the asset in the balance sheet.

If you are using Sage 50 Accounts Plus or Professional and you have many different asset types, figuring out individual depreciation amounts can be quite time-consuming. Fortunately, Sage has the useful Fixed Asset Register that lets you enter the details of each asset and the method of depreciation you intend to use. Each time you run your month-end option, Sage calculates the depreciation due for each asset and automatically posts this to the appropriate accounts. Head to Chapter 3 for more on assets.

Writing down your assets

Sage provides two accepted methods of calculating depreciation and a write-off facility. If you use the Fixed Asset Register, Sage calculates the depreciation for you.

If you don't have Accounts Plus or Accounts Professional, you have to depreciate your assets manually by posting a nominal journal each month, as fixed asset records aren't available in the basic Sage Accounts program.

REMEMBER

You can choose your method of depreciation, but after you choose it you must use the same method consistently every year. This method becomes part of your accounting policy and is referred to in the Notes to the Accounts section of your year-end accounts prepared by your accountant.

Your accountant can help you decide which of the methods I explain in the next sections is best for you.

Ruling on the straight line method

In *straight line depreciation*, the value of the asset is depreciated evenly over the period of its useful life. For example, an asset that depreciates over a four-year period has a quarter (25 per cent) of the value depreciated each year. The same amount of depreciation is charged each month. For example, an asset that cost £24,000 and is due to be depreciated over a four-year period is depreciated by £6,000 each year, which equates to £500 per month.

Counting down the reducing balance method

In *reducing balance depreciation*, the value of the asset is depreciated by a fixed percentage but the calculation is based on the net book value (NBV) each year, so the NBV reduces each year. The *net book value* is the cost price of the fixed asset less the accumulated depreciation to date. For example, at the end of year 1, a £12,000 asset with a four-year lifespan depreciates by £3,000 (at 25 per cent), leaving the NBV as £9,000 – as shown in Table 16-1.

TABLE 16-1   ## Depreciation on a £12,000 Asset over Four Years

Year	Depreciation Amount	Net Book Value
1	£3,000	£9,000
2	£2,250	£6,750
3	£1,687.50	£5,062.50
4	£1,265.62	£3,796.88

Using the reducing balance method means the asset never fully depreciates. The amount of depreciation just gets smaller and smaller each year. You're actually likely to write off the asset because it's obsolete before the NBV is anywhere near zero.

Going for the one-time write-off

You may find it necessary to write off the remaining value of an asset in one go. For example, the asset may have been disposed of and you need to remove the value from the books. Alternatively, if the asset is so old that it's no longer worth the value shown in the books, it's a candidate for write-off.

Posting assets and depreciation

You post the actual capital cost of an asset when you make the invoice or bank payment and you've coded the item to fixed assets. You make the depreciation postings when you run month-end routines or if you've chosen to manually post your journals each month end. You can make the postings only once in a calendar month. If you use the month-end option and forget to run the depreciation, you need to set the program date back to the month that you forgot to run and post the depreciation.

If you post your depreciation journals manually, the double-entry way to complete your journals is to debit the depreciation account in the profit and loss account and credit accumulated depreciation in the balance sheet account.

TIP

To ensure you post the correct amount of depreciation, check your fixed asset records are up to date and you correctly set up the asset and the required depreciation.

Entering Journals

If you use the basic Sage Accounts program, pay special attention to this section, as it explains what journals actually do. You need to understand the principles of double-entry bookkeeping to make journal entries competently.

A *journal* is where you transfer values between nominal accounts. You can use journals to correct mistakes if you post incorrectly. You also use journals to do your accruals and prepayments in basic Sage 50 Accounts or if you don't want to use the wizards in Accounts Plus or Accounts Professional.

You use debits and credits to move values between nominal accounts. The journal must balance, so you need your values of debits to equal values of credits before Sage can post the journal.

WARNING

Use journals only if you're confident with double-entry bookkeeping. Otherwise, stick to the wizards because they perform the double-entry for you.

You may need to update several journals on a monthly basis, including depreciation journals if you don't use the Fixed Asset Register, wages journals, and any other journals that you may need to correct *mispostings* – items posted to the wrong account.

Completing journals

To complete a journal, follow these steps:

1. **From the Navigation bar, click Nominal Codes and then click the Journal entry icon at the top of the screen.**

   The Journal Entry screen opens.

2. **Enter the necessary information in the Nominal Ledger Journal sheet.**

   You need to supply the following information:

   - **Reference:** For example, your reference may be April 2016 depreciation if you're manually posting depreciation and not using the Fixed Asset Register.

   - **Posting Date:** The system uses the current day's date, so specify the date on which you want to post the journal.

   - **Nominal Code:** Use the drop-down arrow to select the first nominal code for your journal. For example, if you post a journal for depreciation, you may show a debit entry for depreciation (N/C 8000) for the sum of £200. The detail reads Plant and Machinery Depreciation. The corresponding credit entry uses plant and machinery accumulated depreciation (N/C 0021) for the sum of £200, as shown in Figure 16-1.

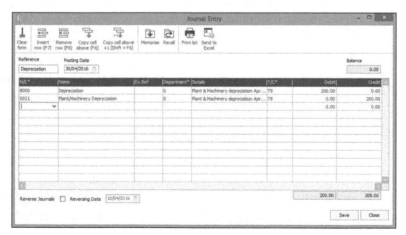

FIGURE 16-1:
An example of posting a journal for depreciation.

Source: Jane Kelly

- **Name:** The nominal code name automatically comes up on the screen.

- **Ex.Ref:** This column lets you provide any extra detail.

- **Department:** Choose a department, if you need one.

- **Details:** Enter details of the journal to appear on the nominal activity report.

- **Tax Code:** The system defaults to T9, but you can change the code using the drop-down arrows.

- **Debit or Credit:** Fill in the appropriate column according to whether it's a debit or a credit.

When you finish, the Balance box shows zero and the totals of the debits and credits are the same.

3. **Click Save if you're happy with the journal.**

The journal is posted to the nominal codes shown.

REMEMBER

Before you save the journal, you can reverse it at a future point in time. This option is particularly useful if you post an accrual or prepayment type of journal. Tick the Reverse Journals box and then enter the date you want the journal to reverse on. These boxes show up on your nominal journal only if you tick the Enable Reversing Journals box on the Parameters tab of Company Preferences, which you access by clicking Settings on the Menu bar.

Rattling skeleton journals

If you use Sage 50 Accounts Plus or Professional and you do the same journals on a regular basis, you can take advantage of the option to create a *skeleton journal*, which you can reuse. After you save a skeleton journal, you can recall the journal and see all the details that you saved.

You can save values in your skeleton journals only if you tick the Copy Skeleton Journal Values box in Settings → Company Preferences → Parameters.

Creating a skeleton journal

To create a skeleton journal, enter the journal details as described earlier but click the Memorise icon instead of saving the journal. The Memorise box opens, and Sage prompts you for a filename and a description of the journals. Type these and then click Save; then close the screen. Sage asks, 'Do you want to save changes?' Click No.

Recalling a journal

When you want to reuse your skeleton journal, from the Navigation bar, click Nominal Codes and then click the Journal entry icon to bring up the Journal Entry window. Click the Recall icon to see a list of the memorised journals. Highlight the journal you want and click Load. The journal comes up on the screen, as if you'd just entered it. If you want to make changes to the journal, you can overtype the details. Click Save to post the journal, or click Close to exit followed by No to discard the journal and return to the Nominal codes window.

Reversing journals

Sometimes you may want to cancel a journal. Making a mistake when you're trying to reverse a journal manually is very easy, especially if you get the double-entry accounting wrong. Sage can help you with the reversing journal option.

The main reason you may want to reverse a journal is because you got the double-entry bookkeeping wrong – maybe you got your debits mixed up with your credits. As long as you can identify both the debit and the credit that need to be corrected and these have individual transaction numbers, you can reverse them. You may not need to reverse the whole thing.

REMEMBER

Before you undertake the nominal journal reversal, take a backup in case things go wrong and you need to restore your data.

To reverse a transaction, follow these steps:

1. **From the Navigation bar, click Nominal Codes and then click the Journal reversal icon.**

   Sage prompts you to take a backup and print a copy of the Nominal Ledger Daybook report.

2. **Click Print Now to obtain a printout or to preview the Nominal Ledger Daybook report.**

   Click Run to produce the reports you need. You can select the date ranges and nominal codes from the usual criteria box.

3. **Click Backup Now.**

   The usual Backup screen appears. Click OK. After the backup is complete, you return to the Journal Reversals screen. Click OK.

4. **Enter the transaction range your journal appears in.**

   You can find this information on the Nominal Ledger Daybook report that you printed or on the Transactions screen.

5. **Enter the date of the original journal and then click OK.**

   The Journal Reversal window opens, showing the journal transactions that you want to reverse.

If the journal you're trying to reverse doesn't come up, check you used the correct transaction number. Make sure the journal you want to reverse actually balances (in other words, the debits equal the credits); otherwise, Sage won't accept the reversal.

6. **Highlight the items for reversal and click Reverse, followed by Save.**

The journal you reversed shows on the audit trail with the reference REVERSE, and the details state Reversal of transaction XX.

After you reverse an offending journal, don't forget to post the correct one.

Carrying Out Your Month-End Routine

Running the month-end process in Sage lets you automatically run the accruals, prepayment and depreciation journals that I describe in other sections in this chapter. When you run the month-end process, you also get the opportunity to clear your customer and supplier month-to-date turnover figures, remove fully paid and reconciled transactions, clear the audit trail and remove stock transactions.

The month-end process gives you the opportunity to review your accounts and prepare for the next accounting period. After you post all your journals and run all monthly routines, you can start running reports (which I cover in Chapter 18).

Ticking off your checklist

Following a checklist is probably the easiest way to run the month end in a controlled manner. Before you run your month-end process, use the following to ensure you remember everything:

>> Change your program date to the month end (Settings → Change Program Date).

>> Enter all transactions for the current period.

>> Process bank recurring entries for the month.

>> Reconcile all bank accounts (including credit cards).

>> Post all journals (including skeleton).

>> Post revaluation journals if you use foreign currency. (Refer to Chapter 14 for more on dealing with foreign currencies.)

>> For Sage Accounts Plus and Professional only, set up prepayments, accruals, fixed assets and depreciation.

>> Post opening and closing stock journals (use Modules → Wizards → Opening Closing Stock Wizard).

>> Take a backup and label it – for example, April 2016 month end.

As you run your month-end processes, be sure to cover the following points:

>> Remove stock transactions, if required.

>> Clear audit trail, if required.

>> Take another backup titled 'After month end' together with the date.

TIP

As you work through the month-end processes, tick off each item in the checklist so you can see which tasks remain.

Running the month-end

The month-end procedure lets you clear down the month-to-date turnover figures on all your customer and supplier records. In clearing the month-to-date turnover figures, Sage zeroes down the sale or purchase values in the Month to Date field, which helps for reporting purposes. If you have Accounts Plus or Accounts Professional, you can process your accruals, prepayments and depreciation as well.

If you have foreign currency set up, you have the option to run the Foreign Bank Revaluation, which ensures exchange rate fluctuations are taken into account at the month end.

You can post transactions beyond the month-end date, and Sage designates them to the appropriate month. Even after you post the month end, you can still post transactions to any previous accounting period: Sage just slots them into the appropriate month. If you don't want this to happen, you can enter a lock date when you run the month end – this means that if you tick the Lock Date box and enter a specific date, you won't be able to post a transaction with a date before the lock date. This helps control the accuracy of the reporting – for example, if you request reports with a prior period date, then the numbers in those reports should remain the same and not be adjusted by late invoices being posted to prior periods.

To run the month end, follow these steps:

1. **Click Tools → Period End → Month End from the Menu bar to bring up the Month End window.**

   A confirmation box appears saying that all other open windows will be closed. Click Yes to continue, and the Month End window then opens as shown in Figure 16-2.

FIGURE 16-2:
Running the month-end procedure.

Source: Jane Kelly

2. **Sage suggests you check your data, take a backup and run your foreign bank revaluation wizard if you have enabled the foreign trader option.**

3. **After you're happy that your data is suitably updated and checked, review the Month End options section and tick the appropriate boxes.**

   You can select the month-end date; run the accruals, prepayments and depreciation journals; and tick the Clear Turnover Figures box to set your month-to-date turnover figures for your customers and suppliers to zero. You can also set a lock date, which ensures you can't post information with a prior date to the date that you tell Sage to lock from.

4. **Click the Run Month End button to begin the month-end process.**

Click Yes to confirm that you want to proceed with the month-end routine. A confirmation message says that the process has been completed. Click OK to close this message.

Clearing stock transactions

Clearing stock transactions is a way to reduce the number of transactions on your product activity ledger. You clear the transactions up to a date you specify. You may decide to do this if your system is slowing down as a result of the vast number of records it has to process. A year end is often a good time to clear stock transactions. Once you have cleared your stock transactions, you can then delete your stock record if you wish.

You don't have to clear the stock transactions, however, and many people prefer not to, as they like to be able to view a complete history of transactions.

If you are using Sage 50 Accounts Plus or Professional, you might want to print off your Product Valuation and Product Activity reports before you clear your stock transactions.

To clear your stock, follow these steps:

1. **Take a backup of your data.**

2. **From the Menu bar, click Tools → Period End → Clear Stock.**

3. **The Data Management box opens and gives you two options:**

- **Clear transactions on all stock records:** This clears all transactions up to the date specified.

- **Clear transactions on selected records:** This lets you select specific product records and clear the transactions for those products only.

4. **After you select one of the options, Sage asks for a date to clear transactions up to.**

Enter the date you want and then click Clear Stock to continue or Close to exit. The Sage backup window appears and suggests you run a backup. Once the backup has completed, the clear stock process begins and a confirmation message tells you the process has been completed. Click OK to close the Clear Stock box, and then click Close to exit the Data Management box to return to the Getting Started screen.

Deleting stock

After you clear stock transactions, you can delete any stock records that you no longer want. Sage scans your product list and checks for any records that meet the following criteria:

» There are no transactions in the stock activity (you can ensure this is the case by clearing stock as I explain in the previous section).

» The stock record is not part of a component for another stock item – for example, a Bill of Materials (BOM) item.

» The product has zero items on order or allocated (which indicates it's part of an active stock item).

If these criteria are met, Sage lets you delete the stock records. To delete stock, work through the following steps:

1. **From the Menu bar, click Tools, Period End, and then Delete Stock.**

2. **If you have other windows open, say Yes to the warning message that asks you to close all other windows before you run the process.**

3. **The Data Management – Delete Stock window opens.**

   Click the Start Scan button for Sage to check for product lists to see if any products meet the criteria listed previously.

4. **The Backup window opens.**

   Sage asks you to back up your data before you select the stock records you want to delete. Click OK.

5. **Sage provides you with a product list highlighting all the products that meet the deletion criteria.**

   Select the records you want to delete. To select all the records in the list, click the Swap button.

6. **After you select the products to delete, click OK.**

   A warning message asks you if you want to permanently delete the selected records. If you aren't sure, click No; otherwise, click Yes. A message confirms the number of records that you've deleted. Click OK.

7. **Close the Data Management window.**

   You can check the Products and services main window to check the products have disappeared from the product list.

Clearing the audit trail

Clearing your audit trail removes transactions that meet specific criteria from the audit trail up to a date that you choose. You're left with fewer transactions on the screen, which makes your life easier and speeds up the process of running reports and backing up your data. The process of clearing your audit trail is usually done at year end. Several criteria must be met before a transaction can be cleared – for example, transactions must be from a prior financial year, transactions must be fully paid and allocated, and all VAT (value-added tax) and bank entries must be reconciled.

WARNING

Taking backups before you run the process of clearing your audit trail is absolutely essential. Clearing your audit trail is irreversible. Make sure you print your audit trail; daybook reports; sales, purchase and nominal activity reports; and any VAT return reports before you run the Clear Audit Trail option.

You can look at the deleted transactions by clicking Transactions from the Navigation bar, followed by the Reports icon. The Transaction Reports window opens. Selecting Cleared Audit Trail Reports shows you a variety of reports on the right side of the screen – if you scroll down the list, you can see that the last report shows Removed Audit Transactions.

During the process of removing transactions, Sage posts journal entries to the nominal codes the transactions were linked to. This posting ensures the balances on the nominal accounts stay the same as before the Clear Audit Trail process was run. The journals are displayed with the detail opening balance and appear at the end of the audit trail when the Clear Audit Trail process is complete.

To run the Clear Audit Trail, follow these steps:

1. **From the Menu bar, click Tools → Period End → Clear Audit Trail.**

   The Data Management – Clear Audit Trail window opens. Enter the date you want to clear transactions up to and including. Then click Clear Audit Trail.

2. **The backup window opens.**

   You may want to amend the name of the backup file to make it clear that it refers to prior Clear Audit Trail data.

   If transactions are removed, you can view the deleted transactions by clicking 'I would like to review details of removed transactions' and then OK. Click OK again and then close the Data Management window.

Managing Cash Flow

You probably wonder sometimes if you have enough money in the bank to pay your suppliers, staff salaries and imminent bills. Keeping an eye on your cash flow is the only way to know how much spare cash you have.

Sage's cash–flow facility helps you plan your payments and work out what monies are due in, so you can calculate whether or not you have the cash to carry out your day–to–day banking transactions.

You need to be in the Bank accounts module to run the cash–flow forecast. Then follow these steps:

1. **From the Navigation bar, click Bank accounts and then click the Cash flow icon.**

   The Cash Flow Forecast screen opens, with two boxes at the top of the screen. The box on the left is a summary of the bank balance and notes any regular receipts or payments (recurring entries). The left-hand box also shows any forecasted receipts and payments and provides a projected bank balance up to the period specified. The box on the right shows bank accounts; the default shows the main bank account only, but you can include more accounts if you want to. The bottom section of the screen shows a list of all outstanding receipts and payments in date order.

2. **In the main body of the screen, remove the tick in the Include? column to remove the corresponding transaction from the cash flow.**

   The forecast bank balance adjusts accordingly. Figure 16-3 shows the Cash Flow screen with the Include? column.

   To make a manual entry to see what effect a transaction may have on the cash flow, place the cursor on the first vacant line on the main body of the cash flow and enter the details of the manual entry. The forecast bank balance adjusts for the new transaction.

3. **Print the cash flow by clicking the Print icon or send the cash flow to Microsoft Excel by clicking Send to Excel.**

   Excel opens and you can view the cash-flow details on a spreadsheet. The spreadsheet allows you a lot more flexibility to play around with the figures.

TIP

The layout of the Sage cash flow exported to the spreadsheet may not suit you. Many people like to see a much more detailed or daily cash–flow analysis. You can design your own spreadsheet layout. Alternatively, most banks can provide you with examples of cash–flow statements – go and have a word with your friendly business banker.

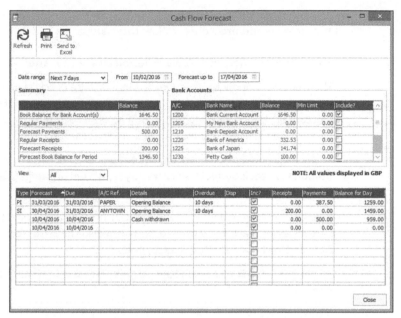

FIGURE 16-3:
Posting a manual entry on to your cash flow.

Source: Jane Kelly

Doing a Year-End Routine

The year-end procedure is principally a financial accounting process. You must run your month end for the last month of your accounting year, which takes care of the usual journal routines.

The year-end procedure clears down the profit and loss accounts to zero and transfers any current-year profit or loss to the retained profit account. You carry forward the balances on the balance sheet to the new year and transfer any future-dated transactions into the relevant months for each nominal record.

You transfer the actual values for the current year to the prior year, so you can make comparisons in the new financial year.

WARNING

You must take a backup before you run this process. Sage actually recommends taking two backups, so you still have a copy if one backup is lost or damaged. You also need to check you've run all the reports that you require for your accounts and you've adjusted your system date to the same as your year-end date by clicking Settings → Change Program Date. Check your chart of accounts doesn't contain any errors, although you should notice these sorts of mistakes when you run your profit and loss and balance sheets for the year.

To run your year-end procedure, follow these steps:

1. From the Menu bar, click Tools → Period End → Year End.

The Year End window appears, which is essentially a checklist of things to do before and during the year-end process. In the Prepare for Year End section, you can check your data and the chart of accounts before you run your backups. You can also archive your data and choose the location of the archive.

2. In the Year End Options section, choose whether to base next year's nominal or stock budgets on current-year actual or budget data by ticking the Budget Options box.

The Budget options window opens. You can increase your budget by a percentage increase if you want to. You must also check the Year End Postings Date and the Lock Date that Sage suggests.

3. In the Run Year End section, Sage summarises the options that you've chosen.

If you're happy with the details, click Run Year End. A message asks you to confirm that you want to run the year-end process. Click Yes if you do, or click No to cancel.

4. If you click Yes, a message says that processing the Year End will apply to any existing layout of accounts.

Click Yes to continue.

5. The Year End Report window asks which method of output you need.

You can choose Printer, Preview or File. I usually choose Printer. Click OK. The Print Year-End Report window opens and you can select your printer and the number of copies. Click OK.

6. A confirmation message says your year end has now completed and gives you the dates of your new financial year.

I suggest you take another backup and label it 'After the year end'.

Chapter 17

Running Your VAT Return

Value-added tax, or VAT, can induce a state of panic when a tax inspection suddenly looms. You can avoid this hysteria by keeping proper accounting records with a system such as Sage and running your VAT returns in a systematic, methodical manner. Running a VAT return takes mere seconds as a result of the integrated nature of the Sage software.

In this chapter, I take you through the various VAT schemes that Sage operates, concentrating in particular on running a standard VAT return, as well as discussing other features such as fuel scale charges, Intrastat reports, EC lists and the VAT audit.

The VAT return involves working through three stages and ticking tasks off as you go along. You can process your whole VAT return from the VAT Return window in Sage, where you can check, reconcile and perform the journal transfers all in one area.

Understanding Some VAT Basics

REMEMBER

You need to worry about VAT only if your business is VAT registered. After you register, you can reclaim VAT on certain purchases, but you also have to charge and pay VAT on your sales.

Your company can voluntarily register for VAT – and doing so is usually worth the extra hassle if you can reclaim VAT on a significant proportion of your purchases. VAT registration is mandatory if you exceed certain VAT thresholds – at the time of writing (2016), you must register for VAT if your VAT taxable turnover reaches £83,000 or more.

A basic knowledge of what you can and can't claim VAT on pays off. You can find many books on this subject, and the VAT office also provides plenty of publications for specific industries. A quick look on the HM Revenue & Customs (HMRC) website at www.hmrc.gov.uk gives you a list of the various publications. You can find the main VAT rules and procedures in HMRC Notice 700/1.

Knowing your outputs from your inputs

VAT inputs and outputs have nothing to do with the Hokey Cokey. I wish they were that enjoyable.

REMEMBER

Output VAT is just a fancy name for the VAT element of your sales. *Input VAT* is the opposite – it represents the VAT element of your purchases.

A VAT return compares the totals of your VAT inputs and outputs, and subtracts one from the other. If the outputs exceed the inputs, you owe HMRC. If the inputs exceed the outputs, HMRC owes you a refund.

Cracking the codes

When you enter invoices, credit notes or orders for your customers and suppliers, you need to know which tax code to use. Sage automatically provides you with the following list of U.K. tax codes, or T codes:

>> **T0:** Zero-rated – VAT is not payable on zero-rated supplies, such as books and children's clothes.

>> **T1:** Standard rate – currently 20 per cent.

>> **T2:** Exempt from VAT – for example, insurance and subscriptions to membership organisations.

>> **T4:** Sales of goods to VAT registered customers in the European Community (EC).

>> **T5:** Lower-rate VAT – usually 5 per cent. This applies to the purchase of energy-saving materials and reclaiming VAT on DIY building work.

>> **T7:** Zero-rated purchases of goods from suppliers in the EC.

>> **T8:** Standard-rated purchases of goods from suppliers in the EC.

>> **T9:** Transactions not involving VAT – for example, wages.

Other Sage standard codes include the following:

>> **T20:** Sales and purchases of reverse charges.

>> **T22:** Sales of services to VAT registered customers in the EC.

>> **T23:** Zero-rated purchases of services from suppliers in the EC.

>> **T24:** Standard-rated purchases of services from suppliers in the EC.

>> **T25:** Flat rate accounting scheme, purchase and sale of individual capital items greater than £2,000.

Sage doesn't use T3 or T6.

Comparing Sage's VAT accounting methods

Sage supports four types of VAT schemes: the standard VAT accounting scheme, VAT cash accounting, Flat rate – invoiced based, and Flat rate – cash based. HMRC provides some helpful information about the VAT schemes available on its website, so go to www.hmrc.gov.uk if you want to find out more.

Set up your accounting method before you enter any transactions onto Sage. The Active Setup wizard I talk about in Chapter 1 includes the VAT accounting method as one of its steps. If you're not sure which method you chose, click Settings → Company Preferences and then click the VAT tab. In the VAT Details box, you'll find the VAT scheme that you selected. Use the drop-down arrow to view the other VAT schemes available for you to use, as shown in Figure 17-1.

Setting the standard scheme

In the standard VAT scheme, Sage calculates the amount of VAT based on when you issue an invoice. As you raise each invoice, you're liable to pay the VAT on it when your next VAT return is due. You can reclaim the VAT on invoices sent to you from your suppliers, regardless of whether or not you've paid them.

Source: Jane Kelly

FIGURE 17-1:
Checking your
VAT scheme.

Considering cash accounting

VAT cash accounting calculates the VAT based on when your customer pays an invoice and when you pay your supplier. You benefit if your customers are slow to pay, as you don't need to pay the VAT until they pay you.

WARNING

VAT cash accounting in the Republic of Ireland is slightly different from VAT cash accounting in the United Kingdom. In the Republic of Ireland, the scheme is also known as the *monies received* scheme – you calculate your VAT on the money you actually receive from customers and on the invoices or credits you receive from your suppliers. Sage 50 Accounts can operate both schemes.

It is useful to note that the Republic of Ireland does have different tax codes, which can be seen if you click F1 for help and then type 'tax codes' into the search box.

Figuring out the flat rate VAT scheme

The flat rate VAT scheme lets you pay VAT as a fixed percentage of your VAT-inclusive turnover. You don't claim VAT back on any purchases, making it a very simple system to operate. The actual percentage you use depends on what type of business you run.

You can join the flat rate scheme only if you estimate your VAT taxable turnover (excluding VAT) in the next year to be £150,000 or less. You can then stay on the scheme until your business income is more than £230,000.

Sage lets you set up both invoice- and cash-based flat VAT rate schemes.

Managing Your VAT

Running a VAT return in Sage is remarkably easy, but you do have to check your VAT return before you send it in.

Also included within the VAT ledger are icons to help you calculate your fuel scale charges, print EC Sales lists and produce a reverse charge Sales list. You can also access a VAT Audit, a Tax Values Audit and a selection of tax analysis reports. The Show Me How icon is like a VAT help centre to help you process your VAT return from start to finish.

Note: For the purposes of demonstration, I explain how to run a standard VAT return using Sage 50 Accounts Professional.

To access the VAT ledger, from the Navigation bar, click VAT and then the VAT Return icon. The VAT Return window opens, where you find three tabs:

>> Prepare the VAT Return

>> Reconcile the VAT Return

>> Complete the VAT Return (which I describe later in this chapter)

When you work out your VAT, appreciating what items carry VAT and what you can reclaim VAT on helps. If you're unsure, contact your accountant or HMRC for help.

Preparing your VAT return

REMEMBER

Before you start figuring out your VAT return, make sure your books are up to date for the period. Enter all your sales invoices, purchase invoices, receipts and payments, and reconcile all your bank accounts and credit card accounts to ensure you've accounted for all elements of VAT. If you use fuel scale charges, make sure you have processed these too. I provide more details on how to process fuel scale charges later in this chapter.

The first step of running your VAT return is to calculate the amount owing or owed by following these steps:

1. **From the Navigation bar, click VAT.**

The VAT window opens.

2. **Click the VAT Return icon.**

The VAT form opens. The screen is split into two parts: The right side of the screen looks like the manual VAT return form that you may have received from HMRC before. The left side of the screen is the data entry part.

3. **Click Backup.**

Sage advises you to run a backup before you run the VAT return.

4. **Under Date Range, enter the period the VAT return relates to.**

In my Jingles example, I use 1 April 2016 to 30 June 2016.

5. **Under VAT Verification, click the Settings button.**

Here you can view the eight checks Sage carries out to ensure your VAT return is as accurate as possible, as I show in Figure 17-2. To return to the main VAT return screen, you can click OK if you have adjusted any of the settings, or Cancel if you haven't made any changes.

FIGURE 17-2: Checking your VAT verification settings.

6. Click Calculate VAT Return.

REMEMBER

If you have any previous period unreconciled items, such as late invoices that you have entered, these will appear in the Earlier unreconciled transactions window. You must check these entries to ensure they are correct before proceeding. Click Include or Ignore.

Sage tells you how many transactions it found for this VAT return, and how many transactions are dated before the specified period but haven't been reconciled. You can choose whether you want to include these, as mentioned earlier. If you choose not to include them, they remain as unreconciled items in the audit trail and appear again when you do your next VAT return.

7. Click OK.

The VAT return fills with figures, and you can see how much Sage thinks you owe HMRC, or vice versa. Sage also jumps to the Reconcile VAT Return tab – note the boxes on the left side of the screen have changed.

Figure 17-3 shows a VAT return for Jingles. Sage calculates that Jingles is owed £756.40.

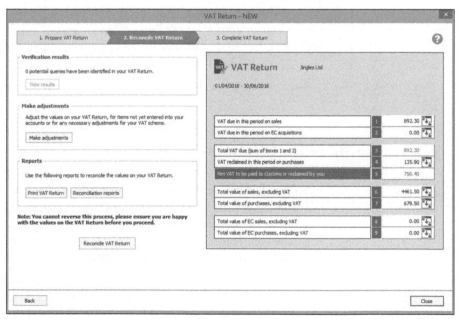

FIGURE 17-3:
A standard VAT return for Jingles.

Source: Jane Kelly

Reconciling your VAT return

After you calculate your VAT, you can reconcile your VAT return. On the Reconcile VAT Return tab, you have the following options:

>> **Check your verification results:** This box shows how many queries have been identified with your VAT return. The Jingles return shows zero queries. Click the View Results button if you have any queries that Sage has targeted. For example, Sage will highlight if you have forgotten to update any invoices or credit notes.

>> **Make adjustments:** Clicking this button opens the VAT Manual Adjustments screen, as shown in Figure 17-4.

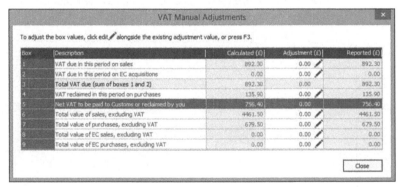

To adjust the box values, click edit 🖉 alongside the existing adjustment value, or press F3.

Box	Description	Calculated (£)	Adjustment (£)	Reported (£)
1	VAT due in this period on sales	892.30	0.00	892.30
2	VAT due in this period on EC acquisitions	0.00	0.00	0.00
3	Total VAT due (sum of boxes 1 and 2)	892.30	0.00	892.30
4	VAT reclaimed in this period on purchases	135.90	0.00	135.90
5	Net VAT to be paid to Customs or reclaimed by you	756.40	0.00	756.40
6	Total value of sales, excluding VAT	4461.50	0.00	4461.50
7	Total value of purchases, excluding VAT	679.50	0.00	679.50
8	Total value of EC sales, excluding VAT	0.00	0.00	0.00
9	Total value of EC purchases, excluding VAT	0.00	0.00	0.00

FIGURE 17-4: Making VAT manual adjustments.

Source: Jane Kelly

>> **Reports:** This section lets you print your VAT return and run reconciliation reports.

● When you click Print VAT Return, the VAT Return Report box opens, as shown in Figure 17-5. The VAT Return box is already ticked, but you can also run the detailed or summary VAT report – I like to always run the detailed VAT report. You can choose to preview, print, email or file – I always print a copy for my VAT return folder.

● After you print your VAT return, you need to check the results by using Sage's reconciliation reports. Click Reconciliation Reports to open the Reconciliation Reports window. Double-click the Reconciliation Reports option on the left side of the screen. Two further options appear: Standard VAT and Transaction Analysis. If you double-click the Standard VAT, a further series of options appears. If you click once on the Bank option, a series of reports appears on the right side of the screen. Here you can print a copy of all the bank reports that contribute toward checking the detail of your VAT report. Work through each of the report options (you see most of them in Figure 17-6) to find all the reports necessary to check your figures.

REMEMBER

Read the next section before you finally reconcile your VAT return.

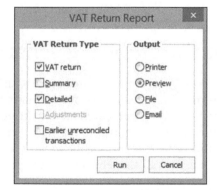

FIGURE 17-5:
Running your
VAT reports.

Source: Jane Kelly

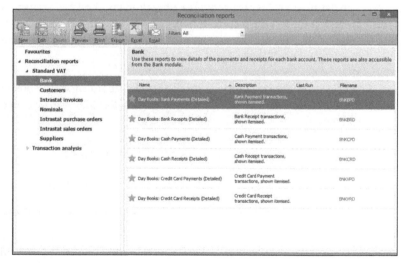

FIGURE 17-6:
VAT reports for
checking your
VAT return.

Source: Jane Kelly

Checking Your VAT Return Using Reconciliation Reports

You have to run some reconciliation reports to check the figures in your VAT return. The information supplied by Sage is only as good as the person who enters it, so you need to check your VAT return against the nominal ledger. The checks are different depending on which VAT scheme you operate. In this section I look at each scheme in turn and examine which reconciliation reports you need to check to ensure the accuracy of your VAT return.

Checking under the standard scheme

Your sales tax and purchase tax control accounts must agree with box 1 and box 4 respectively on the VAT return. To make sure that the accounts agree, print the nominal activity report for the sales tax control account and the purchase tax control account and compare the totals with the relevant boxes on the VAT return. Ensure the dates for the nominal activity report are the same as for the VAT return. The nominal activity report identifies all elements of VAT on sales and purchases. If necessary, you can check each entry line by line and compare it with the information in the VAT return detailed report.

The detailed VAT report provides a breakdown of all the transactions behind each number on the VAT return. If you use the VAT standard accounting scheme, the detailed VAT report shows every sales invoice and credit note and every purchase invoice and credit note.

Sage groups the transactions on the report according to the box they belong in on the VAT return. For example, you see each individual transaction contained within VAT box 1.

Follow these steps to print the nominal activity report:

1. **From within the VAT return process, click Reconciliation Reports.**

   The reconciliation report window opens, initially showing that you have no favourite reports added.

2. **Double-click Reconciliation Reports in the list, and then double-click Standard VAT.**

3. **Choose Nominals with a single click.**

   Some report options appear on the right side of the screen.

4. **Choose the Nominal Activity Report and click on the Preview icon.**

   The Criteria Values box opens, as shown in Figure 17-7. Enter the nominal codes for the sales tax control account and the purchase tax control account – 2200 and 2201, respectively.

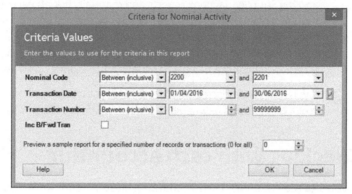

Source: Jane Kelly

FIGURE 17-7:
The Criteria Value box for running the nominal activity for VAT.

5. **Enter the transaction dates.**

   Make sure the dates are for the same period as the VAT return, and then click OK.

6. **View the report and ensure the figures for the sales tax control account and purchase tax control account are the same as the figures on the VAT return in boxes 1 and 4.**

   If the figures are not the same, check through the following reasons:

   - Make sure you select the same dates for the Nominal Activity report and the VAT return. That way, you select data for the same period and it should agree, unless you've said Yes to any unreconciled items from a previous quarter.

   - Check if the VAT control accounts include any totals for tax codes that aren't included in your VAT return. For example, T9 by default isn't included in your VAT return.

   - Check your clear-down journals have been correctly posted from the previous quarter. (The clear-down journals are done automatically by Sage if you select the option when processing your VAT return.)

   - See if any journals were posted to the VAT control ledgers. You don't normally need to post journals to the control accounts.

- Check the audit trail. You can check which items have already been reconciled by looking for R (for reconciled) in the V (VAT) column. Items with an N in the column haven't been reconciled and need checking as part of the current VAT return.

- If you still can't find the discrepancy, print the Customer daybook reports and the Supplier daybook reports and manually tick off each item against the tax control accounts. You can find these reports by clicking the Reconciliation Reports button on the VAT return and then selecting Standard VAT Return followed by either Customers or Suppliers. This last-resort check can be time-consuming, but it does usually work.

- If you still have a discrepancy, print the daybooks for your bank, cash, credit receipts and payments, and check these reports.

Checking with cash accounting

If you operate the VAT cash accounting system and work from a cash-based instead of an invoice-based system, you need to print the following reports:

>> Nominal Ledger daybook reports

>> Customer Receipts and all other daybook reports

>> Supplier Payments and all other daybook reports

You can find all of these reports using the Reconciliation Reports button within the VAT return module. Make sure you select the same dates for your reports and your VAT return. Check the reports against your VAT return for all bank and cash accounts within your business.

Getting ready to reconcile after checking

After you print out your reconciliation reports and are happy with your VAT return, click Reconcile Your VAT Return to continue. Sage asks if you want to Flag Transactions as Reconciled. Click Yes if you're certain you want to complete your VAT return; otherwise, click No.

Sage jumps into action and begins the process of completing all the tasks involving your VAT.

When Sage is finished, the VAT return appears with a big stamp marked RECONCILED on it, as shown in Figure 17-8.

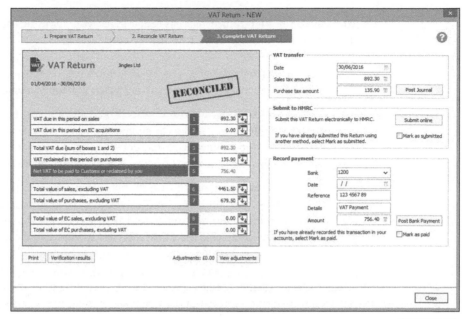

FIGURE 17-8:
Success – you
have reconciled
your VAT return!

Completing Your VAT return

The final screen of the VAT return process is the Complete VAT Return tab, where you can also print a copy of the VAT return. You can click Verification Results to see the verification results summary, as shown in Figure 17-9. This outlines possible duplication entries, missing entries, uncommon tax codes, incorrect EC transactions and other issues. You can also review any adjustments that you made.

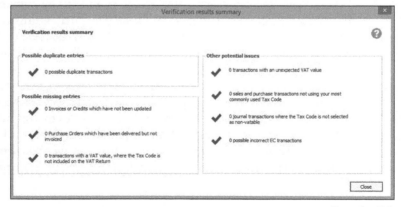

FIGURE 17-9:
Viewing the
verification
results summary.

To finalise the VAT return process, Sage gives you some further options on the right side of the Complete VAT Return screen:

>> **Post the VAT transfer:** If you click Post Journal, Sage automatically does the double-entry bookkeeping for you. A big green tick appears when this is complete.

>> **Submit to HMRC:** You can directly submit your VAT return from this screen if you have your Government Gateway details to hand. You don't have to submit your VAT return straightaway, however, if you're within your deadline period.

>> **Record receipt/payment:** You can submit your payment or receipt, depending on whether you owe VAT or HMRC owes you. You can post the bank payment or receipt directly from this screen, or tick the box to tell Sage if you've already completed the transaction directly through the Bank module.

After you reconcile your VAT return, a copy of the return is archived in Sage. The reconciled and archived VAT return appears on the VAT ledger window and has a return number as a method of identification. The listing shows the period and the amount of the return. The Paid column shows N if the return has not been paid via the VAT window. The status shows as Submitted if the return has been submitted via the VAT window, but it shows as Pending if the VAT return hasn't been submitted to HMRC via the VAT window.

However, just to confuse matters, you can submit the VAT return via the HMRC website and Sage would not be clever enough to know this, so it would still show as Pending. You can, however, tick a box on the VAT return window to mark the return as being submitted and it will change the status to Submitted on the main VAT ledger window. You can also mark the VAT return as having been paid, even if you pay it directly from the Bank module instead of the VAT ledger window.

You can view a saved return by highlighting the return in the VAT ledger and clicking View. You can delete a VAT return from Sage by highlighting the return and clicking Delete, but I suggest you keep your VAT returns on Sage. I recommend you also keep a hard copy of all your VAT returns and put them somewhere safe – you must keep copies for possible VAT inspection for at least six years.

To check if the transactions have definitely been reconciled, try to calculate the VAT return again for the same period. A message appears stating you've selected a date range that's already been reported on. Click Yes to continue. Sage confirms that no transactions were found for that period – evidence that the transactions have been reconciled. You can also check that the individual transactions have been reconciled by viewing the Audit Trail screen and looking for an R in the VAT column.

Posting the VAT transfer

Clearing is transferring the values from your sales tax and purchase tax control accounts to your VAT Liability account. The balance created in your VAT Liability account should agree with the amount due to or from HMRC.

After you make the VAT payment or refund and post it to the VAT Liability account, the balance on the Liability account becomes zero.

Sage has a VAT transfer wizard to help you. You find the wizard on the final page of the VAT Return screen: Click Post Journal in the VAT transfer section and the job is done.

Submitting your VAT return

You can submit your VAT return directly from Sage, as I describe earlier, or you can print off all the reports and submit your VAT return via the HMRC website. I describe both methods in this section, where I assume you've calculated and rec-onciled your VAT return but haven't sent it yet.

Posting your return online via Sage

Nearly all VAT registered businesses have to submit their VAT return online. You also have to pay electronically – this works in your favour as you get an extra week to pay your VAT liability.

REMEMBER

You must have a Government Gateway account to make e-VAT payments. Go to www.hmrc.gov.uk for details on how to obtain an account.

You must ensure that you have completed your eSubmission credentials, includ-ing your User ID and the password given to you when you registered for the Gov-ernment Gateway service. To do so, click Settings → Company Preferences → VAT tab and complete the necessary details.

To send your online VAT return, follow these steps:

1. **From the VAT screen, double-click the VAT return you want to send.**

The VAT Return window opens. The return's status must be pending or partial.

2. **Click the Submit Online button.**

If this is the first time you've sent an online VAT return, Sage asks you to enter your eSubmission credentials. Click Yes to open the eSubmission details window, as shown in Figure 17-10. Follow the on-screen instructions to complete your online submission.

FIGURE 17-10:
Submitting your
credentials.

Submitting your VAT return manually via HMRC

To submit your VAT return manually, you need to print out all the reports and then enter them into the HMRC system. Ensure you have a printed copy of the final VAT return and follow these steps:

1. **Access the HMRC website at www.hmrc.gov.uk and click the HMRC services: sign in or register button.**

   Using the login details you were given when you registered to use the online services, access the VAT Return service.

2. **Submit the figures from the VAT report in Sage into the relevant boxes on the HMRC website.**

   Follow the online instructions to submit your VAT return, and print out a copy of the confirmation that the VAT return has been submitted. File this with your hard copy of the VAT return.

   If the value in box 5 is negative, you have a VAT reclaim and HMRC owes you money. If the figure in box 5 is positive, you owe HMRC.

   You can manually tick a box on the VAT return screen to say that the VAT return has been directly submitted to the HMRC via its website.

Posting your refund or payment in Sage

There are two options available when posting the HMRC bank payment/receipt:

» You can post the payment/receipt directly within the VAT return on the final screen, and once done, Sage will place a big green tick alongside that part of the VAT return.

» Alternatively, you can post the payment/receipt through your bank module in the normal way as described in Chapter 8. To post a VAT refund, post a Bank receipt to the VAT Liability account (2202), coded to T9. To make a VAT payment, post a bank payment via the Bank module, using the nominal code 2202.

As soon as you save the bank payment, the Paid column changes from N (no) to Y (yes) on the VAT ledger list of returns.

Investigating Other Useful Icons in Your VAT Module

As well as the VAT return icon (which is the key to this whole chapter!), additional icons are available to help you complete your VAT return. Some of these may not apply to you (particularly if you don't trade with foreign countries), but others are required to ensure that the accounts data is as accurate as possible before you submit your VAT return.

Posting scale charges

Fuel scale charges occur when you use a company vehicle for private use. According to HMRC, if an employee buys fuel for business use and that vehicle is also used privately, the business must account for output tax on the private use by using scale charges. If the business chooses not to use fuel scale charges, then it must keep detailed mileage records of both business and private mileage incurred each month. The business would then claim VAT back only on the business proportion of mileage.

If you use scale charges, you can claim back all the VAT charged on road fuel without splitting your mileage between private and business use. The calculations are based on the CO_2 emissions of the vehicle and the engine size.

Sage makes claiming back VAT much easier with a wizard that guides you through the process:

1. **From the Menu bar, click Modules, click Wizards and then select Scale Charges, or from within the VAT module, click the Scale Charges icon.**

REMEMBER

Before you continue with the wizard, you need to calculate the scale charge for each vehicle. HMRC publication Notice 700/64 from www.hmrc.gov.uk helps you do this. However, you will need the CO_2 emission data for each car. This can be obtained by using the HMRC's online calculator. You can connect directly with the Driver and Vehicle Licensing Agency (DVLA) and check your CO_2 emissions, which are required in order to calculate the fuel charge. You simply need the car registration number and the Make of the car. Go to www.hmrc.gov.uk, type in 'fuel Scale charge' and follow the link to the fuel charge calculator. Please note, new scales are in effect from 1 May 2016.

2. **The Scale charge window opens.**

Sage confirms the use of nominal code 7350 as the default nominal code for scale charges.

Enter the date you want to post the scale charges for (usually the end of the VAT quarter) and any reference or details that you want to include. Enter the gross scale charge and click Next. Sage calculates the posting.

3. **Review and check the posting, and then click Post.**

The information will be automatically picked up in your VAT return.

Reporting Intrastat

Intrastat is concerned with collecting statistics surrounding the physical movement of goods between countries in the EU. It's closely linked with the VAT system. If you're not VAT registered, you don't have any obligations under the Intrastat system.

The Intrastat data sent is used to produce the European trade statistics, which is an essential part of the United Kingdom's Balance of Payments.

For the majority of businesses, Intrastat compliance involves supplying the information from boxes 8 and 9 from your VAT return. However, if a business exceeds the

Intrastat threshold (currently £250,000 on dispatches and £1.5M on arrivals), then it needs to complete Supplementary Declaration (SD) forms, which Sage can help you prepare. You then transfer the information from Sage on to the official SD forms.

TIP

For information about Intrastat reporting and how Sage can help, press F1 and type 'Intrastat' into the Sage Help function.

Completing the EC Sales list

EC Sales lists are used to collect information on all sales from U.K. VAT-registered traders to VAT-registered traders in other EU member states. The information on the lists is used by the United Kingdom and other member states to ensure the appropriate amount of VAT has been calculated.

Some of the information shown on the sales list comes from details contained within Company Preferences in Sage, but you must enter the appropriate quarter end and click Calculate. Sage extracts all the relevant data and shows it on the EC Sales list. You can see the country code, the customer's VAT registration number, the total value of supplies, an indicator field and a submitted field.

The country codes can be found on Sage via Settings from the main toolbar and then clicking Countries. Any amendments to EU countries can be made here by ticking the appropriate boxes.

TIP

For more information about the EC Sales list, visit www.hmrc.gov.uk and enter 'EC Sales lists' into the search box to reveal lots of information about completing the forms.

Understanding the Reverse Charge Sales list

The Rev Charge icon on the VAT ledger refers to the Reverse Charge Sales list (UK Only), which some businesses have to submit to HMRC. This affects businesses that make wholesale supplies of certain electronic communications services. It is an anti-fraud measure that removes the opportunity for fraudsters to charge VAT and then go missing. For more information on the reverse-charge legislation, visit www.hmrc.gov.uk where there is a policy paper titled 'VAT: reverse charge for electronic communications services'.

Running a VAT audit

Sage has introduced an Audit Assistant, which helps check for problems with VAT values in your accounts. In order to run a VAT audit, follow these steps:

1. **Click VAT from the navigation bar and then click the VAT Audit icon.**

The VAT Audit settings window will open, which contains three tabs. Each of the tabs contains several criteria, which you can tick (all default to unticked to begin with). See Figure 17-11 for an example of the Sales Analysis tab.

Source: Jane Kelly

FIGURE 17-11: VAT audit settings.

- **Sales Analysis:** For example, you can request sales invoices and receipts to be identified if they have a VAT rate of less than 19 per cent (or whatever specified percentage you choose to use).

- **Purchase Analysis:** For example, one of the criteria is that you can specify any purchase transactions where the VAT element is greater than a specified amount, such as £1,500.

- **Financials Analysis:** One of the criteria is that you can check for any journal transactions that have been coded to 2202 (the VAT liability code).

2. **Tick any of the criteria that you want to include in your VAT audit.**

Click OK.

3. **A date range box opens; choose the range of dates that you want to run the audit for.**

Click OK.

4. **The VAT audit window appears, showing details of any transactions that have fallen within the criteria that you have specified for your VAT audit.**

    Note: Once you have set up the audit criteria that you require, you can simply click the Tax Values Audit icon, which skips straight to the VAT audit window and reports any results.

You can now check each of these transactions to ensure that they are correct or, if necessary, amend them before you continue with your VAT return.

REMEMBER

The purpose of the VAT assistant is to allow you to interrogate the information supplied to Sage with a view to finding any potential errors and thus eliminating the errors before they get transferred to a VAT return.

Accessing verification reports

Click the Verification reports icon, which gives you a quick way of accessing the reports you require to verify the information found on your VAT return. Sage opens a Prepare for Audit window, which then allows you to choose between Accounts verification or VAT Audit. There is a multitude of reports that you can print to verify your accounts data. Take some time to familiarize yourself with these reports, as you never know when they might prove to be extremely useful!

5

Using Reports

Chapter 18

Running Monthly Reports

R unning reports is an opportunity to see how well your business is progressing. Reports show you if your business is meeting your targets, if you're bringing in as much revenue as you projected and how actual costs compare with your budgeted or forecasted expenditures. Good reports are easy to understand and use headings that are meaningful to your business.

In this chapter I talk about the reports you can produce at the end of each monthly accounting procedure. I assume you've already run the month-end procedure and processed all the necessary journals, as I explain in Chapter 16.

Making the Most of Standard Reports

Whenever possible, I suggest you use the standard reports provided by Sage, as they're simple to run and provide most of the information you need.

Each section on the Navigation bar (apart from Quotations) contains its own reports. The Report icon is usually the last icon on the right-hand side. For example, if you go to Customer and then Reports, you can bring up a variety of aged debtors and customer-related reports; if you go to Bank and then Reports, you can print copies of unreconciled items and run daybook reports for bank receipts and payments as well as many others. Clicking Nominal codes on the Navigation bar and then selecting the appropriate icon brings up the profit and loss report or the balance sheet report – the key financial reports that tell you how the business is doing.

Whenever you select a report, you have five choices of what to do with the data:

>> **Preview:** This lets you preview the layout of the report on the screen and check that it provides you with the information you require. You can then print, export or email from this screen.

>> **Print:** This lets you print a hard copy of the report without previewing.

>> **Export:** You can save the file in various different formats, such as PDF or CSV.

>> **Export to Excel:** You can send the contents of the report into an Excel document and save and amend as necessary.

>> **Email:** Depending on how your email system is configured, you can send the report as an attachment or you can link to your email software and send the report directly.

Checking the Chart of Accounts

Before you run your financial reports, you must check your chart of accounts (COA) for errors because errors in the COA can affect the accuracy of your reports. (Refer to Chapter 2 for more information on the COA.)

To check the COA for errors, click the Chart of Accounts icon from the Nominal codes module, highlight the COA you want to check, click Edit, and then click the Check box. Sage lets you know if no errors exist. If there are errors, Sage lets you print or preview them.

Figuring Out the Financial Reports

The trial balance, profit and loss, and balance sheet reports give you a view of your business. You generally run each report at the end of your accounting period, which is probably monthly, quarterly or annually. I cover these reports in the following sections.

Trying for an initial trial balance

The trial balance report forms the basis of your profit and loss and balance sheet reports. The trial balance report lists all debit and credit balances in nominal code order for the period you specify. The report shows only nominal codes that have a balance, so any codes with a zero balance don't make the list. As I show in the Jingles example in Figure 18-1, the debits and credits are in separate columns with totals at the bottom of each. Double-entry bookkeeping principles mean the two columns balance.

| Date: | 12/04/2016 | Jingles Ltd | | Page: | 1 |
| Time: | 10:36:26 | Period Trial Balance | | | |

To Period: Month 1, April 2016

N/C	Name	Debit	Credit
0021	Plant/Machinery Depreciation		200.00
1100	Debtors Control Account	2,724.08	
1103	Prepayments	9,000.00	
1200	Bank Current Account	1,789.00	
1220	Bank of America	440.94	
1230	Petty Cash	100.00	
2100	Creditors Control Account		12,030.00
2109	Accruals		1,000.00
2200	Sales Tax Control Account		420.93
2201	Purchase Tax Control Account	5.00	
2301	Directors Loan Accounts (Director 1)		2,000.00
3200	Profit and Loss Account	187.50	
4000	Sales of Greetings Cards		513.75
4020	Sale of Balloons		235.00
4030	Sale of Party Gifts		130.00
4035	Party Organising Fees		0.90
5000	Purchase of cards	25.00	
6201	Advertising	1,000.00	
7550	Telephone and Fax	1,000.00	
7906	Exchange Rate Variance	59.06	
8000	Depreciation	200.00	
	Totals:	16,530.58	16,530.58

FIGURE 18-1: Jingles's trial balance for the period ended April 2016.

Source: Jane Kelly

Jingles is quite a new company – it doesn't have many transactions yet, and it doesn't use many nominal codes. As the Jingles business increases, the number of codes will likely increase, and the trial balance report will get longer.

The trial balance report shows at a glance the extent of your assets and liabilities. You can use the report as an investigative tool. For example, if something seems out of whack, you can run more detailed reports to see where the numbers came from. You can drill down further into each of the numbers in the report: If you want to look at the detail behind any of the figures, clicking on the number takes you to the nominal activity for that nominal code and you can see exactly which transactions make up the number.

To run a trial balance report, follow these steps:

1. **From the Navigation bar, click Nominal codes.**

   The Nominal codes window opens.

   Alternatively, from the Menu bar, click Modules and then Nominal codes.

2. **Click the Trial balance icon.**

3. **In the Print Output box, select Preview and then click Run.**

4. **In the Criteria box, use the drop-down arrow to select the period you want to view.**

   In the example in Figure 18-1, I use April 2016.

5. **Click OK.**

   The trial balance report appears.

6. **Click Print, Email or Export to send the report to the destination of your choice.**

7. **Click Close to exit the report and return to the Financials window.**

Accounting for profit and loss

Owners and directors of businesses really like the profit and loss report because it shows whether they're making any money. The profit and loss report shows the total revenue (sales) your company has made in the specified period and then deducts direct costs and overheads for the same period to arrive at a profit or loss for the period.

The layout of the profit and loss report is a standard format, but you can use the COA function to rename headings and group together your nominal codes so the report appears with terminology suited to your business. (Check out Chapter 2 to see how to edit your COA.)

To run your profit and loss report, follow these steps:

1. **From the Navigation bar, click Nominal codes and then click the Profit and Loss icon.**

2. **Select the print output you want and then click Run.**

   You can print, preview, send to file or email. I suggest you preview first so you can see if you're happy with the report criteria you chose.

3. **In the Criteria box, select the period you want to run the report for by filling in the From and To dates.**

4. **Use the drop-down arrow to select the COA layout you want (which I explain in Chapter 2), and then click OK.**

   The profit and loss report appears. The report has two columns, one showing the current period and the other showing the year to date (YTD).

WARNING

   If you select a full year for your From and To dates, both columns show the same figures. If you choose a single month (for example, April), the Period column differentiates the current period (April) from the YTD figures. The numbers for the first month of the year and the YTD numbers are the same.

5. **Choose to Print, Email or Export the report.**

In Figure 18-2, I selected the period from April 2016 to April 2016. This represents the first month of trading and goes some way to explaining why the business made a loss: low sales and large telephone and advertising costs. You'll also notice that the Period and Year to Date columns contain the same data. As the year progresses, these figures cease to be the same, and you'll see some useful data appearing.

Date: 12/04/2016	Jingles Ltd	Page: 1
Time: 10:34:36	**Profit and Loss**	

| From: | Month 1, April 2016 | | |
| To: | Month 1, April 2016 | | |

Chart of Accounts: Default Layout of Accounts

	Period		Year to Date	
Sales				
Shop Sales	816.25		816.25	
Party Fees	0.90		0.90	
		817.15		817.15
Purchases				
Purchases	25.00		25.00	
		25.00		25.00
Direct Expenses				
Sales Promotion	1,000.00		1,000.00	
		1,000.00		1,000.00
Gross Profit/(Loss):		(207.85)		(207.85)
Overheads				
Telephone and Computer charges	1,000.00		1,000.00	
Bank Charges and Interest	59.06		59.06	
Depreciation	200.00		200.00	
		1,259.06		1,259.06
Net Profit/(Loss):		(1,466.91)		(1,466.91)

FIGURE 18-2:
A profit and loss report for Jingles.

Source: Jane Kelly

Comparing profits and losses

Sometimes you need additional analysis from your reporting. With the comparative profit and loss report, you can compare your current month values against budget and prior year data. You can also include percentage variations. The report shows current period values and YTD values.

Work through the following steps to run the comparative profit and loss report:

1. **From the Navigation bar, click Nominal codes and then click the Comparative Profit and Loss icon.**

2. **Select the print output you want and then click Run.**

3. **In the Criteria box, select the period you want to run the report for by filling in the From and To dates.**

4. **Use the drop-down arrows to select the appropriate COA.**

   Click the drop-down arrow to determine whether you should show, not show, show as a variance or show as a variance with a percentage. You can choose any or all of the variables – but if you choose them all, the report becomes quite difficult to read.

5. **Click OK and the report generates in a preview format.**

   Adjust any variables if necessary, or choose to print, export or email the document.

In Figure 18-3 you can see that Jeanette has printed out Jingles's comparative profit and loss report for April 2016. She has chosen to compare against budget but not prior year periods. Choosing not to show the prior year period figures means the report is much easier to read, as Sage shows fewer columns.

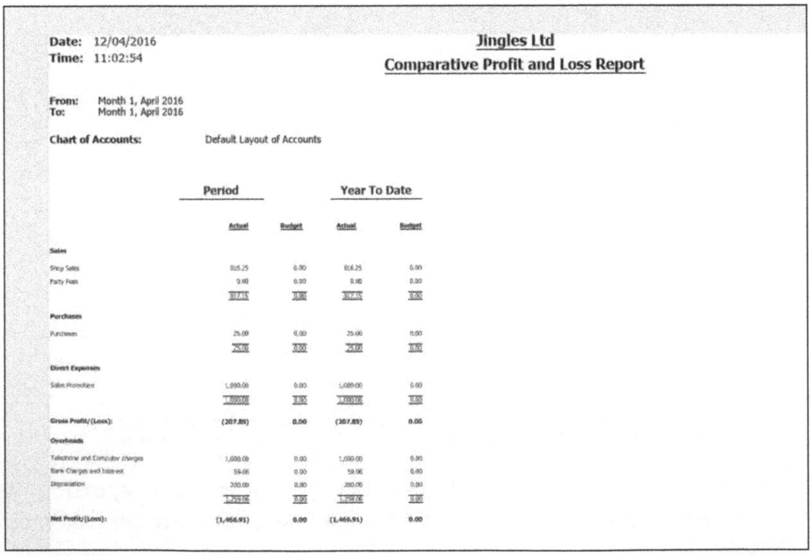

FIGURE 18-3:
The comparative profit and loss report for April 2016 for Jingles.

Weighing the balance sheet

The balance sheet is a really useful tool for establishing your company's financial position. The balance sheet provides a snapshot of the business at a particular point in time. The balance sheet shows your assets, liabilities and sources of funds that helped finance the business. From the balance sheet, you can see how much money people owe to the business and how much money the business owes.

The balance sheet forms part of the management accounts of the business and is traditionally issued at the month end, quarter end and year end. Some people prefer to issue just one set of accounts at the year end, but others prefer to use monthly accounts.

Follow these steps to run a balance sheet for your business:

1. **From the Navigation bar, click Nominal codes and then click the Balance Sheet icon.**

   Alternatively, click Modules and then Nominal codes from the Menu bar.

2. **In the Print Output box, select Preview and then click Run.**

3. **In the Criteria box, use the drop-down arrow to select the period From and To that you want to view.**

   If you have more than one COA layout, select the one you want to preview. Refer to Chapter 2 for details on setting up additional COAs.

   The Jingles example in Figure 18-4 uses the period 1 April 2016 to 31 March 2017 to demonstrate the balance sheet layout. Because the full year has been selected, both columns show the same data.

4. **Click OK to open the Balance Sheet.**

   The balance sheet shows a Period column and a Year to Date column.

REMEMBER

Make sure you understand the component parts of the balance sheet. Try to match the debtors figure in the balance sheet with the aged debtors report, and try to find out what transactions Sage includes in the accruals and prepayments. You can check all your figures by looking at your COA and determining which nominal codes represent each section of the balance sheet. You can review any of the numbers by clicking directly on the number in the balance sheet. Sage provides details of the transactions behind those numbers in the nominal activity report.

Balance Sheet

| From: | Month 1, April 2016 | | | |
| To: | Month 12, March 2017 | | | |

Chart of Accounts: Default Layout of Accounts

	Period		Year to Date	
Fixed Assets				
Plant and Machinery	(200.00)		(200.00)	
		(200.00)		(200.00)
Current Assets				
Debtors	14,652.30		14,927.30	
Deposits and Cash	574.27		574.27	
Bank Account	0.00		1,049.10	
		15,226.57		16,550.67
Current Liabilities				
Creditors : Short Term	13,783.45		14,170.95	
Bank Account	950.90		0.00	
VAT Liability	61.10		73.60	
		14,795.45		14,244.55
Current Assets less Current Liabilities:		431.12		2,306.12
Total Assets less Current Liabilities:		231.12		2,106.12
Long Term Liabilities				
Creditors : Long Term	0.00		2,000.00	
		0.00		2,000.00
Total Assets less Total Liabilities:		231.12		106.12
Capital & Reserves				
Reserves	0.00		(187.50)	
P & L Account	231.12		231.12	
Previous Year Adj			62.50	
		231.12		106.12

FIGURE 18-4:
The Jingles balance sheet for 31 March 2017.

Source: Jane Kelly

Viewing the Audit Trail

Your *audit trail* is a list of all the transactions that have ever occurred in your Sage account, including transactions that you delete. If you make a complete mess of something, you can never quite escape it – Sage displays the mess for all to see, including your accountant and the auditors, who may use it at year end.

Sage lists the transactions in the audit trail chronologically. Each transaction has a unique transaction number. You can use the unique transaction number alongside a search tool to find a particular transaction, which is useful if you need to correct a specific transaction.

You can clear your audit trail periodically to remove the details of the transactions, but Sage keeps the balances and carries them forward so the accounts remain accurate – I explain this properly in Chapter 16. Sage has the capacity to hold 2 billion transactions in your audit trail, so you probably don't ever need to clear it out if you don't want to.

You access the audit trail by clicking the Audit trail report icon in the Transactions module. The Audit reports are available in brief, summary, detailed and deleted transactions. The brief, summary and detailed reports show the transactions in varying levels of detail. The deleted transactions report shows all the transactions you deleted from the system. The report lists one line per transaction, so if you have thousands of transactions, the whole report is extremely long.

To run your audit trail, follow these steps:

1. **From the Navigation bar, click Transactions and then the Audit trail report icon.**

   The Audit Trail Report window opens.

2. **Enter your choice of audit report – brief, summary, detailed or deleted transactions.**

   Choose the method of output and click Run.

3. **In the Criteria box, choose the criteria required for this report.**

   Sage recommends you run the report on a monthly basis, so enter the current month dates.

4. **Click OK to generate the report.**

   If you choose to preview the report, you can now print, export or email it from this screen.

5. **Click Close to exit the report and return to the Financials screen.**

   Printing off your audit trail at the end of each period is a good idea as it provides a hard copy of all your business transactions. Many people print their audit trail at the year end to provide a copy for the auditors, but you can print more regularly if you want. The longer the reporting period, the longer the print-off.

In Figure 18-5 I show an extract from a brief audit trail report for Jingles.

FIGURE 18-5: An extract from Jingles's brief audit trail report.

Date: 12/04/2016   **Jingles Ltd**   Page: 1
Time: 11:31:58   **Audit Trail (Brief)**

| Date From: | 01/01/1980 | | Customer From: | |
| Date To: | 31/12/2019 | | Customer To: | ZZZZZZZZ |

| Transaction From: | 1 | | Supplier From: | |
| Transaction To: | 99,999,99 | | Supplier To: | ZZZZZZZZ |

Exclude Deleted Tran: No

No	Items	Type	A/C	Date	Ref	Details	Net	Tax	Gross
1	1	SI	ANYTOW	31/03/2016	O/Bal	Opening Balance	200.00	0.00	200.00
2	1	PI	PAPER	31/03/2016	O/Bal	Opening Balance	387.50	0.00	387.50
3	1	JC	1100	31/03/2016	O/Bal	Opening Balance	200.00	0.00	200.00
4	1	JC	9998	31/03/2016	O/Bal	Opening Balance	187.50	0.00	187.50
5	1	JD	2100	31/03/2016	O/Bal	Opening Balance	387.50	0.00	387.50
6	1	JD	1100	31/03/2016	O/Bal	From Op Trial	200.00	0.00	200.00
7	1	JC	2100	31/03/2016	O/Bal	From Op Trial	387.50	0.00	387.50
8	1	JD	1200	31/03/2016	O/Bal	From Op Trial	2,000.00	0.00	2,000.00
9	1	JC	2301	31/03/2016	O/Bal	From Op Trial	2,000.00	0.00	2,000.00
10	1	JD	3200	31/03/2016	O/Bal	From Op Trial	187.50	0.00	187.50
11	1	SI	PETE	21/04/2016	1	20 Happy Birthday	40.00	8.00	48.00
12	3	SI	VILLAGE	21/05/2016	2	Snowman cards	49.25	9.85	59.10
15	2	SI	JOHNSON	25/06/2016	3	Wine gift bags	31.00	6.20	37.20
17	2	SI	DAVIS	25/06/2016	4	Party poppers	52.10	10.42	62.52
19	1	SI	BALLOON	13/08/2016	5	Wedding helium	45.00	9.00	54.00
20	1	SC	DAVIS	25/06/2016	1CR	To correct invoice 4	18.00	3.60	21.60
21	1	SC	BALLOON	14/08/2016	2CR	To cancel invoice 5	45.00	9.00	54.00
22	1	SI	BALLOON	15/08/2016	6	Wedding helium	100.00	20.00	120.00
23	1	SR	BALLOON	30/08/2016	BACS	Sales Receipt	120.00	0.00	120.00
24	1	SI	JARVEY	04/08/2016	1	Clown Hire for	250.00	50.00	300.00
25	1	SI	VILLAGE	15/08/2016	2	Happy Birthday	62.50	12.50	75.00
26	1	PI	DERBY	13/05/2016	2	Assorted cards	117.00	23.40	140.40

Source: Jane Kelly

Forgetting the Periods and Going Transactional

Instead of generating reports based on information from a specific period, Sage can produce profit and loss, balance sheet and trial balance reports based on transactions instead of time periods. These transactional reports look very similar to period-based reports, but Sage calculates them in a different way. For example, you have to run period-based reports for a complete month, but with a transactional report you can be more precise in selecting your data.

Transactional reports are handy if you want to look at a specific area or time period in your business. For example, if you ran a promotion over a six-week period and want to view the effects on sales of that promotion, you can run a transactional profit and loss report for that specific six-week period.

You can create transaction-based reports for any date range, taking figures from the audit trail, which I talk about in the preceding section.

To prepare transactional reports, you need to group the transactions obtained from the audit trail into brought-forward figures, current-period figures and YTD figures to help structure the reports. I explain these groupings in more detail in the following sections.

Going by date

You can run transactional reports by selecting a specific date range. The dates you use allow Sage to correctly categorise the transactions into three categories:

>> **Brought Forward figures:** These numbers include the current year's activities and also the balance brought forward from the previous year.

>> **Current Period figures:** These numbers come from the From and To dates you select in the Criteria box for the period you want to report on. (See the later section 'Running the reports' for more on this.)

>> **Year-to-Date figures:** This category encompasses the period from the start of the financial year to the end of the period you select. For example, if you select 1 June 2016 to 15 July 2016, the YTD figures show from 1 January 2016 to 15 July 2016 (assuming you have a December year end). The YTD figures are standard comparative data that Sage uses to compare with the current-period figures.

You need to complete the Criteria box in the report with the specific dates you want to report on. For example, if you choose 1 June to 15 July, that range is your current period – Sage generates the report using those precise dates.

Being number-friendly

You can run transactional reports by selecting a transaction number range rather than a date range. To use transaction numbers, make sure you know what the first transaction number is for the current year. Knowing this number helps Sage determine whether the transaction is prior year or not, which is necessary for balance sheet information. You also need to specify the range of transaction numbers for the specific period you want to report on.

Running the reports

You can run transactional profit and loss, balance sheet and trial balance reports. To run any of these reports, follow these steps:

1. **From the Navigation bar, click Nominal codes and then the Reports icon.**

    The Report Browser screen opens.

2. **Highlight Profit and Loss, Balance Sheet or Trial Balance on the left side of the Report Browser screen.**

    Sage gives you several report options on the right side of the screen.

3. **Scroll down to the bottom of the screen and over the Transactional Report option. Using the floating icons, select Preview, Print, Export, Export to Excel or Email.**

    Clicking an icon once loads the Criteria Values screen, as shown in Figure 18-6. Double-clicking opens the Criteria Values box, where you can preview the report.

4. **When you're happy with the numbers, click OK.**

    Your report is generated.

This method of reporting lets you track your business progress for any accounting period, even for a single day or week. The report gives you much more flexibility over the information that you produce and can aid your business decisions.

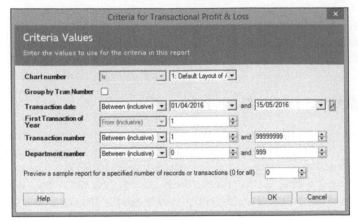

FIGURE 18-6:
Selecting the
criteria for a
six-week period.

Source: Jane Kelly

Designing Reports to Suit Yourself

You may want to personalise one of the many standard reports Sage offers. You can change the existing layouts to suit your needs using Report Designer. Designing reports is a huge topic, and Sage used to produce an entire reference book dealing only with report writing. In this section I scratch the surface by showing you how to take an existing report and tweak it slightly. (Specifically, I look at changing the invoice layout for Jingles Ltd.)

The easiest place to start is to find a report that almost, but not quite, matches your needs. Take this report, save it under a different filename and then reconfigure it with information that suits your business needs.

TIP

Pressing the F1 key in Report Designer opens the very useful Report Designer help module.

To reconfigure a report, follow these steps:

1. **Find the report you want to amend by choosing the Report icon from whichever module you require, and preview the report.**

   If you want to amend an invoice, simply click on Invoices and Credits and highlight any invoice; then click the Print icon. You can now preview the layout of the invoice you require.

2. **In Preview mode, check this is definitely the report you want to adapt, and then click Edit at the top of the preview screen.**

   The Report Designer module opens. Figure 18-7 shows a sales invoice layout as an example – you see the Report Designer layout before any changes have been made.

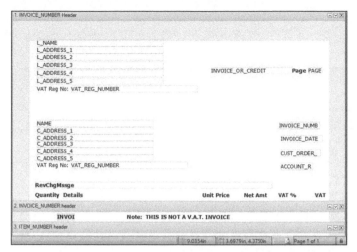

FIGURE 18-7:
Viewing the sales
invoice through
Report Designer.

Source: Jane Kelly

3. **Select the type of change you want to make and follow the on-screen instructions.**

Some of the changes you can make include the following:

- **Insert text:** Click Toolbox → Text Box. Use the mouse to drag and insert a text box in the appropriate part of the screen.

- **Insert new variables:** Click View → Variables to open a list of variables on the left side of the screen. You can then drag and drop suitable variables into the main body of the report.

TIP

If you find you are making a number of changes, it is recommended that you save your file sooner rather than later. See Step 4.

Jeanette decides she wants to insert a new logo on the sales invoice. She clicks on the link in the dynamic help box on the left side of the screen to Add an image or logo. Sage asks you to browse for the image, and then, following on-screen instructions, you can insert and position the image onto your invoice.

4. **After you make the necessary changes, click File on the Menu bar and then click Save As from the drop-down list. Choose an appropriate file format to save the document as.**

The Save As screen opens. On the left are folders containing saved reports. Sage saves the report you're tweaking in the Layouts folder and names it "copy of XX" (XX being the title of the report you have chosen to amend).

TIP

At the top of the Save As screen, Sage shows you where it is saving a copy of the file to. In the case of an invoice, Sage saves the file to Layouts, but for other reports – for example, product reports – Sage saves your file to the My Products and Services reports. For changes to customer reports, your newly saved file will be in My Customer reports.

Having added a new logo, Jeanette saves the updated file as shown in Figure 18-8.

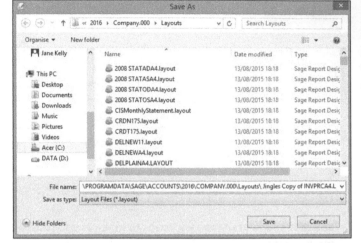

FIGURE 18-8:
Saving the report
with a new
filename in
Report Designer.

Source: Jane Kelly

5. **Click Save, then click File from the Menu bar, and then click Exit to close Report Designer.**

6. **To view the new report, click back into the Layout file (if it is an amended invoice) or the My Reports option (for other report types) and find the newly named file that you have created.**

See Figure 18-9 to see the newly created invoice file for Jingles.

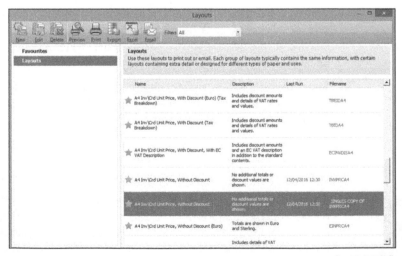

FIGURE 18-9:
Finding your new
report in Sage.

Source: Jane Kelly

It is wise to mark this new report as a favourite so that it appears on your Favourites screen, making it easy to locate for the next time.

7. **You can now preview the file as you would normally to see what your changes look like.**

If you are not happy, simply click the edit button to be taken back into Report Designer to make more tweaks. Figure 18-10 shows the previewed sales invoice for Jingles after some modification.

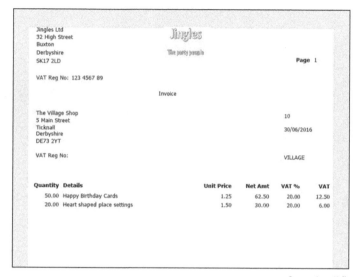

FIGURE 18-10: Jingles's sales invoice after some modification.

Source: Jane Kelly

Play around with the report format until you find something you can work with. If you persist, you may come up with some useful and personalised reports.

Chapter 19

Tackling the Complicated Stuff

When you're confident that you've got to grips with the day-to-day mechanics of the Sage system, you can tackle some of the more advanced options that Sage offers.

The extras I explain in this chapter include the ability to extract data from Sage, make changes within a spreadsheet to that data and then import those changes back into Sage. You can also discover how to relay information to your accountant with minimum disruption to your data and your day-to-day workings.

I also look at the impact of using e-Banking to speed up the processing of banking transactions and how the Document Manager can help you organise your paperwork.

Exporting Data

You can send data from Sage to Microsoft Excel, Word or Outlook. I cover all three in this section.

Sending spreadsheet stuff

You can send all sorts of information from Sage to Microsoft Excel so you can mess about with the data in a spreadsheet without affecting the data in Sage. For example, you may want to edit the data, design specific reports or create what-if scenarios to suit the purposes of your business.

The list of information you can send from Sage to Excel is too long to provide here. To find out whether you can extract what you want from your Sage data, press the F1 key and type 'file export' into the Help field to get a list of the reports you can extract from each module.

TIP

The easiest way to send information to Excel is to use the Send to Excel icon available on the main toolbar for every module: Click the relevant module from the Navigation bar and then click the Send to Excel icon. Sage immediately copies and pastes the contents of the main window into an Excel document, which you can amend as you wish.

Alternatively, click File from the main toolbar, then Microsoft Integration, and then Contents to Microsoft Excel.

You can export to Excel any of the standard reports that you print. Simply choose the Export to Excel floating icon when you want to print the report.

Transferring Outlook contacts

You can send customer and supplier contact information from Sage to Microsoft Outlook. This option is an excellent time-saving device, as it means you don't have to type the information in twice.

The option creates a contact record within Outlook for customers and suppliers who have a name entered on their customer or supplier record.

REMEMBER

If you have two accounts with the same name, Sage creates two contact records in case the two contacts are two different people – for example, you may have two John Smiths.

You can make changes in Sage and then send those changes to Outlook with the amended contact details.

To export account information to Outlook, follow these steps:

1. **From the Sage Menu bar, click File → Microsoft Integration → Microsoft Outlook Import/Export Wizard.**

2. **Select Export Contacts To Outlook.**

   You can choose the other destinations if you prefer.

3. **Follow the wizard's instructions, clicking Next to continue on to each screen.**

TIP

When you've completed the transfer of information, a confirmation message appears, stating that the transfer has been successful. If a different message comes up, follow the advice on the screen. It may be that the folder you're trying to send information to doesn't allow access – Sage then suggests alternatives.

You can copy the following information from your customer and supplier records to Outlook:

>> Contact name and addresses

>> Telephone and fax numbers

>> Websites and email addresses

Exporting to Word

You can send data to Microsoft Word from Sage. You can send information to a new or existing document or as a mail-merge. For example, you can send a list of customer records to Word and mail-merge the contact details with a standard letter from Word.

Exporting to Word can be helpful, for example, if you run a sales promotion and want to contact all your customers to make them aware of the promotion. You can produce a leaflet or letter within Word and send the customer contacts from Sage across to Word so that the names and addresses merge into your Word document. You save time as you don't have to type in the individual names and addresses for all your customers.

To merge customer contact details with a Word document, follow these steps:

1. **From Sage, select the items you want to export data from and click File from the Menu bar.**

   For example, from Customers select a contact to send to Word to complete a mail-merge letter.

2. **Click Microsoft Integration → Contents to Microsoft Word and the option that suits you.**

Your choices are:

- **New Document:** You can create a new Word document to hold the information extracted from Sage.

- **Open Document:** You can open an existing Word document, for example, a promotion letter. You can insert merge boxes so you can personalise the promotion document with the customer details.

- **Run Mail Merge:** You can use the selected data extracted from Sage in a mail-merged document.

For example, here's how Jeanette of Jingles Ltd. sent a promotional letter to a customer:

1. **From the Sage Customer module, select the customer – in this case, The Village Shop – then click File → Microsoft Integration → Contents to Word → Open document.**

   Choose the promotional letter that needs to be sent.

2. **Two documents appear, the first being the mail-merge document that you need to use, and the second being a template on which the document is based.**

   Select the mail-merge document.

3. **Using the first document (referred to in Step 2), place your cursor where you want to insert a merge field, such as the name and address of the recipient of the letter.**

   Click on the Insert Merge Field icon (in Word) and, using the options from the drop-down menu, select the appropriate fields.

   Figure 19-1 shows the document after the mail-merge fields have been selected.

4. **Click the preview results icon (in Word) to see how the information will appear.**

   See Figure 19-2. If you are happy with the results, save the file with a new name.

5. **Click the Finish & Merge icon (in Word), then select Print Documents.**

   The Merge to Printer window opens, and you can select either All records or the record(s) of your choice. Click OK and the print window opens, where you can click OK again to make the document print.

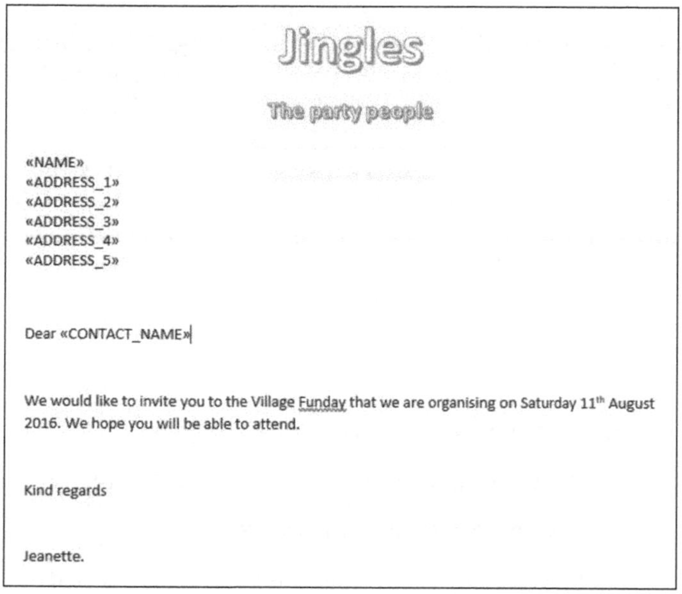

Jingles

The party people

«NAME»
«ADDRESS_1»
«ADDRESS_2»
«ADDRESS_3»
«ADDRESS_4»
«ADDRESS_5»

Dear «CONTACT_NAME»

We would like to invite you to the Village Funday that we are organising on Saturday 11th August 2016. We hope you will be able to attend.

Kind regards

Jeanette.

FIGURE 19-1: Showing the mail-merge document before previewing.

Source: Jane Kelly

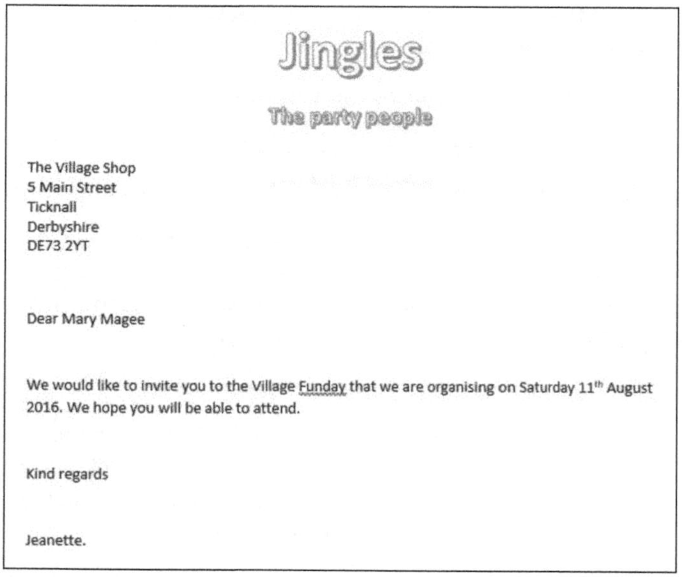

Jingles

The party people

The Village Shop
5 Main Street
Ticknall
Derbyshire
DE73 2YT

Dear Mary Magee

We would like to invite you to the Village Funday that we are organising on Saturday 11th August 2016. We hope you will be able to attend.

Kind regards

Jeanette.

FIGURE 19-2: The promotional letter after mail-merging Sage contact details.

Source: Jane Kelly

Importing Data

The Data Import wizard lets you enhance the existing file import options. You can import from a CSV file or from a Microsoft Excel spreadsheet (.xls or .xlsx file).

To structure your files correctly for importing, take a look at the File Import Templates that are installed with your Sage software. Press F1 to bring up the Help facility if you want to find out more about the templates.

Perhaps an easier method is to access the Data Import wizard, and then once the wizard has started, you can click on the white question mark in a green circle, which will load the help pages related to importing data. You can then click the Import Templates link, which will provide more help and show you where you can access the Import Templates folder.

To use the Data Import wizard, follow these steps:

1. **From the Menu bar, click File and then Import.**

    Follow the screen prompts that open the File Import wizard.

2. **Click Next to work through the wizard.**

    You can access Help at any time while using the wizard and move forward and backward through each screen. Take a backup of your data before proceeding with the Data Import wizard, as the procedure isn't reversible.

3. **From the menu of the Data Type window, select what type of data you want to import.**

4. **Click Next to open the Data Source window.**

    Specify whether the data to import is from a CSV file or an Excel worksheet.

5. **Use the Browse button to choose the file you want to import.**

    If the first line of your CSV file or Excel spreadsheet file contains headings, check the box to say it contains headings. If your Excel spreadsheet contains multiple worksheets, select the one you want to import. Then select the worksheet from the drop-down list provided.

6. **Click Next to open the Field Mappings window**.

    If the field in your imported spreadsheet or CSV files contains the headings appropriate to the supplied template, a mapping template appears, similar to that in Figure 19-3. The imported field name is matched to the corresponding Sage field. In most cases, no remapping is required.

    Where you have no header row in your imported file, no data is shown in the left side of the Field Mappings window, but you still have the Sage headings.

    Where you see an asterisk in the Required? column, you must make a selection in the Imported Field column to match with an entry in the Sage field. For example, if your Account Reference is Column A of your spreadsheet, then use the drop-down list to select A to map with the corresponding Sage field.

    When you've completed your mapping, click Save Map.

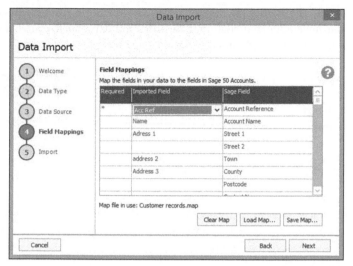

FIGURE 19-3:
Mapping customer record fields before importing.

7. Select a filename and location, and save your Data Import Map file. Click Save.

Your map is saved in your Company.000 Import Maps folder. You can reload maps by using the Load Map function in the Field Mappings window of the Data Import wizard. If you make a mistake while mapping your fields, click Clear Map and start again.

8. Click Next when your field mapping is complete.

The Import window appears. You see a summary of the options you chose in the previous Import wizard windows. If you're happy with the summary, begin importing the data by clicking the Import button. You can modify any of your selections by using the Back button before you click Import.

9. When the data has finished importing, the Import Results Window appears.

The top part of the screen shows the fields you've imported. The bottom part of the screen shows the records that haven't imported. For example, if the file has correctly imported, you should see the names of the records in the top part of the screen, and the bottom part of the screen is blank. However, if you import a file that is not correctly configured, then the file will not successfully import and an error message appears in the bottom part of the screen, indicating where the error lays.

Check your data files after completing the import by clicking File → Maintenance → Check Data options.

If you have imported customer records, you can check your list of customers to check that the records have imported as expected.

WARNING

If you leave a blank line between a heading and the actual information, the data won't import correctly. Delete the line with no information, and the import should then work.

Linking to Your Accountant

If your accountant has access to Sage 50 Client Manager, you can use the Accountant Link to save untold amounts of time for both you and your accountant – and reduce your accountant's bill.

You probably employ an accountant to help you with quarterly VAT (value-added tax) returns, year-end accounts and tax computations. Before the Accountant Link existed, at some point after your year end your accountant took your data files to work on – leaving you unable to use Sage, sometimes for months.

With the Accountant Link, you and your accountant can exchange data in a speedy and accurate fashion. Essentially, you send data to your accountant, who then processes adjustments while you continue to work on your data. Your accountant sends back the adjustments to you to apply to your data. The Accountant Link keeps a log of any changes you make to your data in the intervening period.

The Accountant Link is a wizard that guides you and your accountant through the different stages of the process. To access the wizard, from the Menu bar click Modules → Wizards → Accountant Link. The wizard is split into two parts:

>> One part exports data to your accountant, records material changes and imports your accountant's adjustments.

>> The other part lets your accountant import your data, record adjustments, export the adjustments to a file and send the file back to you, ready for you to apply the changes.

TIP

Ensure your accountant's information is up to date by clicking Settings, Company Preferences and then Accountant from the Menu bar.

WARNING

The Accountant Link is not available if you have activated Sage Drive. To read more about Sage Drive, head to Chapter 21.

Sending accounts to your accountant

If you select the wizard's Export option, Sage guides you through the process of exporting your file in a secure password-protected file to your accountant via email.

From the moment you export the data, Sage begins to record changes you make. You can print a list of material changes to show to your accountant before you import the records back into your system. The changes that Sage considers important are wide-ranging but include deleting customer records, restoring data and creating a nominal account.

When you export your data, Sage generates an export file with an .sae extension. You have two options: Navigate to the filename that Sage has given, or email the file. You select one of the options and then click Exit.

>> If you click Navigate to File, Sage takes you to the folder where you saved the data.

>> If you click Email File, Sage creates an email and attaches a copy of the export file.

Making material changes

After you export your data, Sage begins to record any changes that you make to the dataset. Any amendment to the data is considered a *material change*. You'll know when the system is recording changes, because the word *recording* appears in red at the bottom of the screen.

You can view any of these material changes by clicking on View and then Material Changes from the Menu bar. The Accountant Link – Material Changes window opens. From here, you can view the adjustments that you've made to the data and print the changes if necessary. You can also add comments to the Material Changes file before you click send to email the file to your accountants.

If you think you need to restart the export process, you can stop recording material changes by clicking the Cancel button. Sage flags up a confirmation message asking if you're absolutely sure that you want to cancel the material changes, as any changes made will be lost. Click Yes or No as appropriate. If you click Yes, the material changes recording stops, and the recording message at the bottom of the screen disappears.

Getting back adjustments and narratives

Your accountant makes the adjustments and sends the file back to you for you to apply the adjustments and bring the accounts up to date. The adjustments fall into two categories:

>> **Adjustments:** You can apply these to the accounts automatically from the Comments and Adjustments window. Examples include journals, journal reversals, bank payments and receipts.

>> **Comments:** These are instructions that your accountant sends for changes, which you need to make to your records. You must change the data manually according to your accountant's instructions.

The last section of the wizard helps you import the adjustments your accountant has made to your data.

To import the file from your accountant (which will have an .saa extension), from the Menu bar click Modules → Wizards → Accountant Link → Import. Locate the file and enter your password, and then click Import. You can choose to view the comments and adjustments now or later.

You then click the Adjustments tab, click Begin and then click OK. The adjustments are processed in the order that they appear.

TIP

Allow plenty of uninterrupted time to complete the import process.

You can find further details about the Accountant Link by using the Help system within Sage. Press F1 and type in 'accountant link' to get more information.

Trying e-Banking

Using e-Banking can give you a seamless interface between your bank account and Sage. You can pay your suppliers directly from your bank account, check your online bank statements against your Sage statements and import transactions from your bank so you can reconcile your Sage transactions.

Before you start using this wonderful product, contact your bank and ask for the necessary software. After you set up your banking software, you can then enable the e-Banking options within Sage.

REMEMBER

The e-Banking features available are limited by your bank and your account type. Some banking products let you download statements, which helps with the bank reconciliation, but these products may not have the electronic payments option for your suppliers. You can check whether your bank is compatible by clicking Help from the main toolbar, and then pressing F1. Type 'e-Banking' into the search field; then, underneath the title *Download and Install the required e-Banking component*, click the link www.sage.co.uk. This link takes you to a list of compatible banks, where you can scroll down the list to check what services your bank provides.

The benefits of making electronic payments include the following:

>> **Good control of cash flow:** You know exactly when a payment clears your account – no waiting for cheques to arrive and no delays while cheques are cashed.

>> **Lower costs:** Online banking transactions are usually cheaper than clearing cheques and cash.

>> **Secure:** You don't need to keep cash on the premises if you pay all your debts electronically.

>> **Speed:** You no longer have to write out cheques. Instead, you click and type your way through invoice payments.

Getting your statements online brings benefits too:

>> **Better cash flow:** You can easily see what funds are available at any time.

>> **Efficiency:** You can keep your accounts up to date by seeing current interest payments, direct debits and bank charges.

>> **Environmentally sound:** No paper statements means saving trees and sparing the planet the chemicals used to make paper, ink and stamps.

>> **Saving time:** You don't have to wait for statements to arrive by post and can reconcile straightaway.

Configuring your e-Banking

Before you start, you need to ensure that you have enabled e-Banking in your bank defaults. From the main toolbar, click on Settings followed by Bank defaults. The Bank Defaults window opens as shown in Figure 19-4. You must tick the Enable e-Banking box and then click OK. If you don't do this, the e-Banking fields won't show up on your bank record.

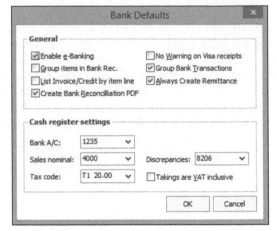

FIGURE 19-4:
Enabling
e-Banking.

Source: Jane Kelly

To make sure Sage can interpret the file format required by your e-Banking system, you need to configure your e-Banking facility. Follow these steps:

1. **From the Navigation bar, click Bank accounts.**

   Choose the account you want to configure.

2. **Click the New/Edit icon and select Edit from the drop-down menu.**

   The bank record opens. Select the Bank Details tab and enter the sort code and account details for your bank account. Figure 19-5 shows the Bank Details tab.

3. **Select the bank type you want to use.**

4. **Click the Configure button.**

   The Sage e-Banking Configuration screen appears for your selected bank type.

5. **Enter the information requested and click OK to save the changes you've made.**

   Click Save in the Bank Details window to close the bank record and save the changes to the record.

You can now access the e-Banking options from the Bank Accounts window.

Opting for e-payments

If your banking software is compatible with Sage 50 Accounts, you can use the e-payments option to pay suppliers directly from your bank account using electronic payments, as shown in Figure 19-6. You need to know the supplier's sort code, account number, BACS reference and account name. You also need to make sure the supplier's record is set to allow online payments – to do this, select a payment method, such as BACS in the Bank tab of your supplier record, which places a tick in the Online Payments box for that supplier record.

FIGURE 19-5:
Configuring
e-Banking
with Sage.

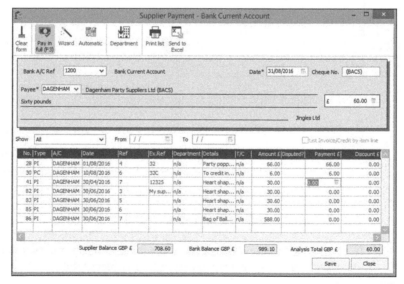

FIGURE 19-6:
Supplier
payments using
e-Banking.

You complete the supplier payment as normal (except the word BACS automatically appears in the Cheque No field) and click Save to process the payment.

After you complete the supplier payment information, you can make the e-payment by following these steps:

1. **From the Navigation bar, click Bank accounts and select the bank account you want to make an e-payment from.**

   Click the Payments icon, and from the drop-down menu select E-Payments at the bottom of the list. The Send Payments window appears, showing details of all the outstanding supplier payments that you've set up to use online banking, as shown in Figure 19-7. You can restrict the number of transactions that appear by selecting a date range.

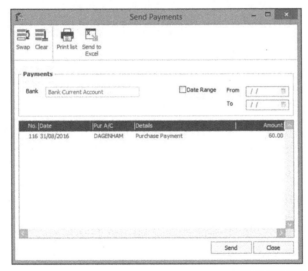

FIGURE 19-7:
Sending an
e-payment.

Source: Jane Kelly

2. **Select the transactions you want to send to your bank and click Send.**

   The transfer of information from Sage to your bank account begins. A confirmation message appears, showing the number and value of payments.

3. **Click OK to continue with the payments.**

   To keep a record of the payment, click Print.

If any problems occur with your e-payment, Sage prompts you to view an error log explaining why the transfer hasn't been successful.

350   PART 5 **Using Reports**

Reconciling electronically

Electronic reconciliation lets you connect to your banking software and see electronic copies of your bank statements so you can reconcile your accounts in Sage.

REMEMBER

Make sure you've configured e-Banking and set up your bank records to allow online reconciliation.

You need to be able to import files from your banking software. Your banking software saves this data into a file on your computer. You use this file to reconcile your electronic bank statement to Sage.

Going automatic

To import your banking transactions, follow these steps:

1. **From the Navigation bar, click Bank accounts, select the bank account you want to reconcile, click the Reconcile icon and then select e-Reconcile.**

   The Amend Bank Statement window appears.

2. **Enter the statement end date and end balance and then click OK.**

   The Reconciliation From screen appears.

3. **Open the File menu and choose Import Bank Transactions, browse to the required file and then click Open.**

   The Open window for your selected bank appears. The left side of the window shows the files on your computer, and the right side shows the bank statement files.

4. **Open the folder where your bank data is saved in the panel on the left.**

   The bank files for the selected bank account are now visible on the right panel.

5. **Select the bank file you want to import from the right panel and click Open.**

   The Reconciliation From window appears, showing your imported transactions. The imported transactions from your bank appear in the top part of the screen, and the Sage account transactions appear in the bottom part of the screen.

6. **Select a method to match transactions.**

   Choose one of the three automatic matching buttons:

   - **Match Full:** Use this button to match items with the same reference and amount.

- **Match Amount:** Click this button to match transactions of the same amount.

- **Match Reference:** Use this option to match transactions that share the same reference as shown on the bank statement, such as 'British Gas DD'.

If no transactions can be matched, a message appears and you can't reconcile your bank transactions with the automatic function. Click OK to go back to the Reconciliation screen.

If Sage finds more than one matching transaction, the Duplicate Transaction window appears. Select the transaction you want to match by clicking the Match button. If you don't want to confirm the matching transactions but want to carry on with the automatic matching process, click Next. To close the window and not match any transactions, click Cancel.

7. **Click Confirm to verify the matched transactions and remove them from the list.**

   You can view your confirmed transactions by clicking View and then Confirmed.

8. **When you're happy with your confirmed transactions, click Reconcile.**

   Sage marks the matched transactions as reconciled, and they no longer appear on the Bank list or the Sage list.

WARNING

If you are using e-reconciliation, you cannot save the matched transactions and return later (as with a standard manual bank reconciliation). Instead, you have to match and then reconcile in one sitting.

Reconciling manually

To do a manual e-reconciliation, follow these steps:

1. **From the Navigation bar, click Bank accounts, click the Reconcile icon and then select e-Reconcile.**

   The Amend Bank Statements window appears.

2. **Enter the statement end date and end balance details, and then click OK.**

   The Reconciliation screen appears.

3. **Match transactions from the bank list or the Sage list by clicking Manual Match.**

   If the Automatically Confirm Manual Matches box is checked, the Manual Match button confirms the transactions. If you haven't ticked this box, the transactions are highlighted in green and you must click Confirm before you reconcile those transactions. You can view the confirmed transactions by clicking View and then Confirmed.

4. **To finish the reconciliation, click Reconcile.**

   If you aren't happy with the reconciliation, you can exit without reconciling by clicking Discard.

5. **Click Yes to the confirmation message that appears, or click No to return to the Reconciliation screen.**

   The matched and reconciled transactions no longer appear on the Sage or Bank transactions.

Working with Document Manager

Sage's Document Manager helps you organise your paperwork. Document Manager lets you match contact information and documents with customers, suppliers and bank records within Sage. You can then link electronic and paper documents to the associated records on Sage.

You can use the Memo tab located on your Sage customer, supplier and bank records to attach electronic files such as Word documents and statements produced in Sage. You can make a filing system reference to note the location of an actual physical document for this record. You can also type free text into the blank section at the bottom of the Memo tab.

Adding attachments and filing system references

A useful feature is the ability to attach a file or even a photograph to a record, using the Memo tab. For example, you could attach a photograph to a project record to provide visual evidence of the project concerned.

To attach a memo to a specific record, use Document Manager and follow these steps:

1. **Open the relevant record and then click the Memo tab.**

2. **Click Add Attachment.**

   Choose the type of attachment to add and click OK.

The Add New Attachment box appears and asks which type of attachment you want to add. Your attachment choices are Electronic (for any electronic file) and Filing System Reference (for a reference to a file location).

3. **Browse your computer to find the electronic file you want to attach.**

If you have selected an electronic attachment, you are requested to browse for that attachment, and the filename of the attachment is shown as the location.

In addition, you are asked if you would like to leave the file in the current location, or move or copy it to a location within Sage 50. Make your choice and then click OK. The file attachment then appears on the memo page of your record.

If you want to add a file system reference, enter the location where your paper document is held, such as the filing cabinet. Type in the name that you want to appear on the Attachment pane for this filing system reference – choose a meaningful name, such as Fun Day Project File Location. Click OK.

Save the record. The memo details have now been saved to that record.

Deleting attachments

If you no longer need an attachment linked to a record, you can delete it. Click the Memo tab of the relevant record and highlight the attachment that you want to delete. Click Delete Attachment and a confirmation message appears. Click Yes to continue. The attachment disappears.

Chapter 20

Running Key Reports

S age produces so many reports that just thinking about them can make your head spin. In this chapter, I pick out the reports I find most useful on a day-to-day basis. I show you how to run each report and use examples to demonstrate how to use them. I provide lots of lovely pictures so you can see what Sage should look like.

REMEMBER

Sage contains lots of other useful reports as well as the ones I talk about in this chapter. I suggest you have a good root through and pick the ones that suit you.

Checking Activity through the Nominal Codes

The nominal activity report identifies transactions posted to specific nominal codes. The report includes transaction types such as purchase invoices, sales invoices, bank payments and receipts, and journals. I use this report on a daily basis. I often just view the activity on-screen, but sometimes I print out the information for further analysis.

This report is useful if you see a figure in the accounts that you want further information on, or if you want to know how much you've spent on an item for a specific time period. For example, Jeanette of Jingles Ltd. notices that the nominal code 4000 – Sales of Greetings Cards shows a balance of £646.25 for the month of April 2016. Jeanette thinks this seems a little high and wants to investigate further. She decides to run a nominal activity report for the nominal code 4000 to give her more details, as shown in Figure 20-1.

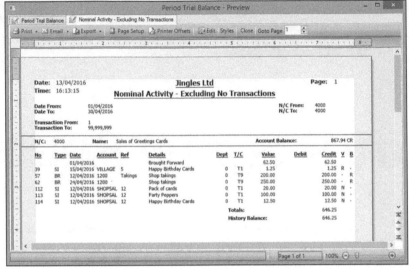

Source: Jane Kelly

FIGURE 20-1:
An example of a nominal activity report, showing Sales of Greetings Cards for Jingles for April 2016.

Jeanette spots a sales invoice for £100 with a description of Party Poppers, which has been posted to the Sales of Greetings Cards nominal code. It looks as though a mistake may have been made when coding this invoice, so she needs to make a correction to the data. It seems as though the mistake was made when journaling the shop takings data. Transaction 113 is the offending item that needs to be corrected.

To investigate your own nominal codes, follow these steps:

1. From the Navigation bar, click Nominal codes and then click the Reports icon.

The Nominal code reports window appears.

2. Click on Nominal activity from the list on the left side of the screen.

A variety of report options appears on the right side of the screen. Highlight the activity report you require and then click the floating preview icon that appears. This brings up the Criteria Values box, as shown in Figure 20-2.

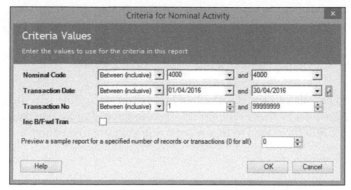

FIGURE 20-2:
Select the
parameters for
your report from
the Criteria
Values box.

3. **Select the nominal code you want to generate a report for and the date range you want to look at.**

If you can't remember the code, use the drop-down arrow to identify the nominal codes. You can run the report by using a range of transaction numbers, if you know them.

WARNING

If you don't put a code in the boxes, Sage uses the default codes 0010–9999. All nominal activities for all nominal codes then print. If you have lots of nominal codes, you'll probably run out of paper before the report finishes printing.

4. **Click OK.**

The report preview appears on screen, unless you've requested to print directly.

5. **Choose to print, email or export the report or just view it on-screen.**

If you select print preview, you can scan the report on-screen to make sure it has presented the information as expected.

If you want to print the report, click the Print icon at the top of the Preview screen. This takes you to the Print Options box, where you can click OK to continue printing or Cancel to return to the report.

TIP

In Chapter 19 you can find out how to export data from Sage into Excel.

6. **Close the report by clicking the white cross in the red box at the top right corner of the screen.**

Alternatively, click Close at the top of the Preview screen.

7. **Click the white cross in the red box to exit the Nominal code reports screen.**

   You return to the Nominal codes window.

You can also access the nominal activity report for the specific nominal code that you require by first highlighting the nominal code and then clicking on the Reports icon. You then need to follow from Step 2 in the preceding list.

Looking into Supplier Activity

How often do you receive supplier statements that don't agree with the figures you think you owe? Performing a quick reconciliation helps you make sure suppliers don't charge you for things you haven't bought.

You can print a supplier's activity screen to show you the transactions you entered in the supplier's account within a specific period and compare that with your supplier's statement. You can then see whether you have any invoices missing.

You can also use a supplier activity report if you want to see how much you spend with a specific supplier or see the volume of transactions for a given period of time.

To run a supplier activity report, follow these steps:

1. **From the Navigation bar, click Suppliers and then click the Reports icon.**

   The Supplier reports window opens.

2. **Click Supplier activity on the left side of the screen and then highlight the report of your choice, shown on the right side of the screen.**

   I recommend looking at the Supplier Activity (Detailed) report. After you highlight the report, click the Preview icon to open the Criteria Values window, as shown in Figure 20-3. Double-clicking on the report you want to view also opens the Criteria Values box.

3. **From the drop-down arrow in the Supplier Reference field, select the supplier and the transaction dates you want to view.**

   In Figure 20-3, Dagenham Party Suppliers is my chosen supplier, and 1 April 2016 to 30 August 2016 are the specified dates.

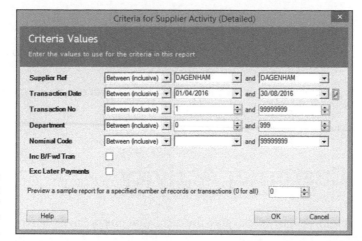

4. Click OK to display the report in preview format.

After you preview the report, you can choose to print, export or email from the toolbar on the report. Figure 20-4 shows the Supplier Activity (Detailed) report for Dagenham Party Suppliers.

FIGURE 20-3:
Choosing the criteria for your supplier activity (detailed) report.

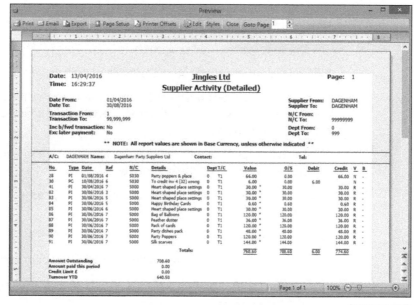

FIGURE 20-4:
A supplier activity report for Jingles's supplier Dagenham Party Suppliers.

5. **Print the report if you want to.**

   To exit, click Close or click the white cross in the red box at the top right of the Preview window.

6. **Click the white cross in the red box to close the Supplier reports screen.**

   You return to the Supplier window.

Tracking Customer Activity

You may be keen to look into the activity of one of your customers for a variety of reasons. You may want to see how much business has tailed off with a particular customer, or you may want to see what goods another customer usually orders you so you can work out what other products to recommend to them. The customer activity report shows you the transactions with a customer for a specified period of time. You can view all transactions, including invoices, credit notes, payments, and payments on account.

To bring up a customer activity report, follow these steps:

1. **From the Navigation bar, click Customers and then click the Reports icon.**

   The Customer reports window opens.

2. **Click on Customer activity on the left side of the screen.**

   Choose a report option from the right side of the screen by highlighting the option and then clicking the Preview icon. I recommend using the Customer Activity (Detailed) report.

   The Criteria Values box opens. You can also double-click on the report you want to view to open the Criteria Values box.

3. **Select the customer and the range of transaction dates you want to look at.**

4. **Click OK to run the report.**

   When the report's done, choose whether to print, email or export.

5. **Click Close or click the white cross in the red box at the top right corner of the Preview screen.**

6. **Close the Customer reports window by clicking on the white cross in the red box in the top right corner.**

   You return to the Customer window.

TIP

You can view customer activity on-screen by selecting the relevant customer and then clicking the Activity icon. The top half of the screen that appears shows all transactions, and the bottom part shows a breakdown of the item highlighted in the top section of the screen.

Checking Numbers with Supplier Daybook Reports

You can find daybook reports in the customer, supplier, nominal and bank ledgers. I use the supplier daybook reports regularly to check the invoice number on the last invoice I posted – I double-check to ensure the last filed invoice is in fact the last invoice posted on the system. Starting off a numbering sequence for your new batch of supplier invoices only to find you've duplicated your numbers is very annoying and time-consuming.

A *daybook* is a list of items entered on the system in the same order you input them. The daybook shows transaction numbers; transaction types; account references; details of the transaction; and the net, VAT (value-added tax) and gross amounts. Detailed reports often show the nominal code and the department the transaction has been allocated to. A daybook is important because it lets your accountant prove the original source documents – such as sales and purchase invoices, cheque stubs, paying-in slips and electronic payments – have been entered onto the system.

You can choose from a number of different daybooks. Using Sage, you can print daybooks for all invoices, paid invoices, credit notes and discounts.

To find the last invoice number, choose the Supplier Invoices (Detailed) report (found within Day books) from the list of reports that Sage provides. This report clearly shows the invoice reference, so if you scroll down to the bottom of the report, you can see the last invoice reference, which is the last invoice posted.

WARNING

Make sure the invoicing sequence runs in order and you have definitely got the last posted invoice number.

To run a supplier daybook report, follow these steps:

1. **From the Navigation bar, click Suppliers and then click the Reports icon.**

   The Supplier reports window opens.

2. **Click on Day books on the left side of the screen. Highlight your chosen report from the right side of the screen and click the Preview icon.**

   I use the Day books: Supplier Invoices (Detailed) report, which shows a list of all purchase invoices entered within your specified date range.

   Specify your criteria in the relevant sections of the Criteria Values box.

3. **Click OK to run the report.**

   If you want the report to list all invoices, don't specify any dates.

TIP

To find the last invoice number, scroll to the bottom of the report and check the Invoice Reference column. Check this number agrees with the last invoice filed. If it does, you can start the next batch of invoices with the subsequent number.

Finding the Customers Who Owe You

If your business is running short of cash because customers aren't paying you promptly, you can produce an aged debtors analysis report to tell you who owes you money, how much and for how long. You can see instantly which customers need a polite kick up the proverbial to help get some cash across to your bank account.

Creating an up-to-date aged debtors analysis report each month helps your business collect debts as efficiently as possible. An aged debtors analysis report builds up a payment profile of your customers, so you can see who pays you within 30 days and who takes more than 90 days to pay. You can use this information to determine who you prefer to continue working with. After all, selling to customers who don't pay you is pointless.

REMEMBER

Make sure you reconcile your bank account on a regular basis so your aged debtors analysis reports are meaningful. You need to be sure that all the money you receive is allocated to the correct customer accounts so you have the most up-to-date information available.

The most sensible time to run an aged debtors analysis report is at the beginning of the month following the month you're trying to chase. For example, you can run the report for the period ended 30 June in the first week of July, when you know that all the sales invoices for June have been posted on the system and you've reconciled the bank account up to the end of June.

TIP

It helps to reconcile your bank account as you proceed through the month; that way, it's not such a big job at the month end, and you can quickly update the bank reconciliation to the month end and produce an accurate aged debtors report in a timely fashion.

To run off an aged debtors analysis report, follow these steps:

1. **From the Navigation bar, click Customers and then click the Reports icon.**

The Customer reports window opens.

2. **Click on Aged debtors on the left side of the screen, and then highlight the report of your choice on the right side of the screen.**

Sage greets you with a raft of options. I suggest you run an Aged Debtors Analysis (Detailed) report (located about a third of the way down the screen), which shows all the individual invoices and credit notes outstanding. Alternatively, you can run the much shorter Aged Debtors Analysis (Summary) report (located about two-thirds of the way down the screen), which shows only the total debt outstanding from each customer. Both reports show the outstanding balance for each customer and also age the debt. You can see the current-month debt, debts that are 30, 60 and 90 days old, and debts that are older than 90 days.

Highlight the report you want and then click the Preview icon to open the Criteria Values box. You can also double-click on the report you want to view to open the Criteria Values box.

3. **Select the customers and dates for which you want to run an aged debtors analysis report.**

You normally select everyone, so leave the Customer Reference box as it is. Selecting the correct dates is important. You need to pick up all transactions outstanding, from day 1 to the end of the period you've decided to run a report for – the end date of the report is the most important one. Choose the end of a period, such as a month or quarter.

TIP

To run a debtors report to tie in with your accounts at the end of a period, run the report to the period end but then select Exclude Later Payments. For example, if you produce accounts to 30 April but continue to process sales receipts into May and then run the aged debtors analysis to 30 April without checking this box, the current amount outstanding is updated by the May sales receipts, and the overall balance of debts outstanding doesn't agree with the balance sheet as at 30 April. By checking Exclude Later Payments, you can run the report to exclude the May receipts, and the report then balances as at 30 April.

4. **Click OK to run the report.**

   You can print or email the report, or export it to Excel. Figure 20-5 shows a detailed aged debtors report for Jingles.

5. **Click Close to exit the report, or click the white cross in the red box to close the Preview window.**

   You return to the Customer reports window. From here, click the white cross in the red box to return to the Customers screen.

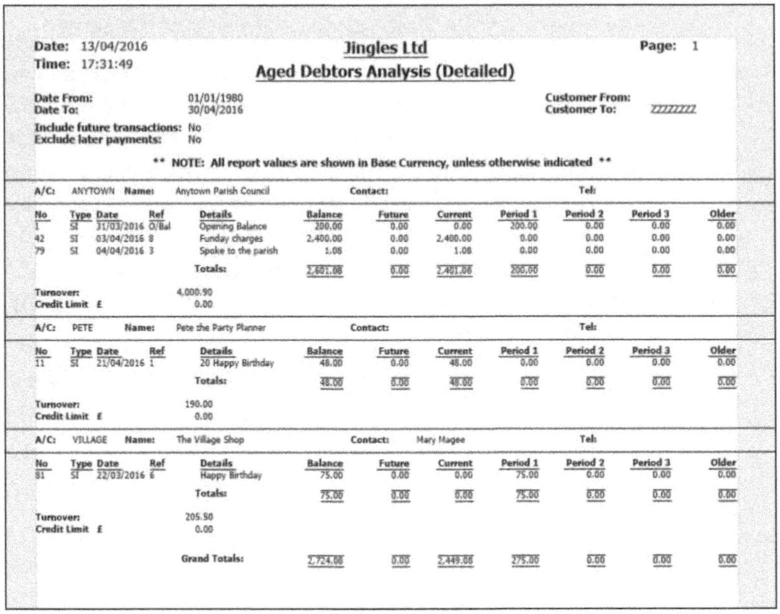

Date: 13/04/2016
Time: 17:31:49

Jingles Ltd

Aged Debtors Analysis (Detailed)

Page: 1

Date From: 01/01/1980
Date To: 30/04/2016
Include future transactions: No
Exclude later payments: No

Customer From:
Customer To: ZZZZZZZZ

** NOTE: All report values are shown in Base Currency, unless otherwise indicated **

A/C: ANYTOWN Name: Anytown Parish Council Contact: Tel:

No	Type	Date	Ref	Details	Balance	Future	Current	Period 1	Period 2	Period 3	Older
1	SI	31/03/2016	O/Bal	Opening Balance	200.00	0.00	0.00	200.00	0.00	0.00	0.00
42	SI	03/04/2016	8	Funday charges	2,400.00	0.00	2,400.00	0.00	0.00	0.00	0.00
79	SI	04/04/2016	3	Spoke to the parish	1.08	0.00	1.08	0.00	0.00	0.00	0.00
				Totals:	2,601.08	0.00	2,401.08	200.00	0.00	0.00	0.00

Turnover: 4,000.90
Credit Limit £ 0.00

A/C: PETE Name: Pete the Party Planner Contact: Tel:

No	Type	Date	Ref	Details	Balance	Future	Current	Period 1	Period 2	Period 3	Older
11	SI	21/04/2016	1	20 Happy Birthday	48.00	0.00	48.00	0.00	0.00	0.00	0.00
				Totals:	48.00	0.00	48.00	0.00	0.00	0.00	0.00

Turnover: 190.00
Credit Limit £ 0.00

A/C: VILLAGE Name: The Village Shop Contact: Mary Magee Tel:

No	Type	Date	Ref	Details	Balance	Future	Current	Period 1	Period 2	Period 3	Older
81	SI	22/03/2016	6	Happy Birthday	75.00	0.00	0.00	75.00	0.00	0.00	0.00
				Totals:	75.00	0.00	0.00	75.00	0.00	0.00	0.00

Turnover: 205.50
Credit Limit £ 0.00

	Balance	Future	Current	Period 1	Period 2	Period 3	Older
Grand Totals:	2,724.08	0.00	2,449.08	275.00	0.00	0.00	0.00

FIGURE 20-5: Reviewing the Aged Debtors Analysis (Detailed) report for Jingles.

Source: Jane Kelly

Paying Attention to Your Creditors

If you find going through your credit card bill terrifying, you probably won't like looking at your aged creditors report, which shows a list of all monies owed to your suppliers.

The aged creditors report looks much like the aged debtors analysis report (which I describe in the preceding section). The report shows how much you owe, to whom and for how long. You can use the aged creditors report to decide which suppliers to pay at the end of the month.

WARNING

Make sure you reconcile all your bank accounts from which you make supplier payments, including credit cards, before you prepare your aged creditors report. If you overlook some payments, your aged creditors analysis report won't be accurate and you may end up paying a supplier twice.

To run an aged creditors analysis report, follow these steps:

1. From the Navigation bar, click Suppliers and then click the Reports icon.

The Supplier reports window opens.

2. Click on Aged creditors on the left side of the screen and highlight the report of your choice from the right side of the screen.

I usually select Aged Creditors Analysis (Detailed) from the raft of options. The Criteria Values box opens. Double-clicking on the report you want to view also opens the Criteria Values box.

TIP

You can save your regular reports as favourites so you don't have to keep scrolling down the list of reports to find the one you want.

3. Use the drop-down arrows to select the supplier you want to run an aged creditors report for.

If you leave the Supplier Reference fields alone, Sage automatically selects all suppliers.

Ensure the Date From and To fields are correct. Tick the Exclude Later Payment box to tell Sage to ignore information beyond the To date.

4. Click OK to run the report.

Choose to print, email or export the report. Figure 20-6 shows a detailed aged creditors report for Jingles.

5. To exit the report, click the white arrow in the red box.

You return to the Supplier reports window. Click the white cross in the red box at the top right corner of the window to return to the Suppliers window.

Date: 13/04/2016 | Jingles Ltd | Page: 1

Time: 17:36:25 | Aged Creditors Analysis (Detailed)

Date From: 01/01/1980 | Supplier From:

Date To: 30/04/2016 | Supplier To: ZZZZZZZZ

Include future transactions: No

Exclude later payments: Yes

** NOTE: All report values are shown in Base Currency, unless otherwise indicated **

A/C: DAGENHAM Name: Dagenham Party Suppliers Ltd Contact: Tel:

No:	Type	Date	Ref	Details	Balance	Future	Current	Period 1	Period 2	Period 3	Older
41	PI	30/04/2016	7	Heart shaped place	30.00	0.00	30.00	0.00	0.00	0.00	0.00
				Totals:	30.00	0.00	30.00	0.00	0.00	0.00	0.00

Turnover: 640.50

Credit Limit £ 0.00

A/C: PAPER Name: Paper Supplies Ltd Contact: Tel:

No:	Type	Date	Ref	Details	Balance	Future	Current	Period 1	Period 2	Period 3	Older
2	PI	31/03/2016	O/Bal	Opening Balance	387.50	0.00	0.00	387.50	0.00	0.00	0.00
32	PA	30/04/2016	1234	Purchase Payment	-387.50	0.00	-387.50	0.00	0.00	0.00	0.00
				Totals:	0.00	0.00	-387.50	387.50	0.00	0.00	0.00

Turnover: 0.00

Credit Limit £ 0.00

A/C: RADIODEN Name: Radio Denby Contact: Tel:

No:	Type	Date	Ref	Details	Balance	Future	Current	Period 1	Period 2	Period 3	Older
107	PI	12/04/2016	9	Radio advertising	12,000.00	0.00	12,000.00	0.00	0.00	0.00	0.00
				Totals:	12,000.00	0.00	12,000.00	0.00	0.00	0.00	0.00

Turnover: 12,000.00

Credit Limit £ 0.00

	Balance	Future	Current	Period 1	Period 2	Period 3	Older
Grand Totals:	12,030.00	0.00	11,642.50	387.50	0.00	0.00	0.00

Source: *Jane Kelly*

FIGURE 20-6: An aged creditors report for Jingles, showing how much Jingles owes.

Handling Unreconciled Bank Transactions

After you reconcile your bank account, you probably have a few transactions that you can't reconcile. They may be unreconciled payments or unreconciled receipts.

You quite often have entries posted in Sage that haven't yet cleared the bank account (see Chapter 15 for more about reconciling). For example, you may post cheques or receipts on Sage before they clear the bank account – these are known as *unpresented cheques* and *outstanding lodgements*.

To print an unpresented cheques report, follow these steps:

1. **From the Navigation bar, click Bank accounts and then click the Reports icon.**

   The Bank reports window opens.

2. **Click Unreconciled transactions.**

   A range of reports appear on the right side of the screen, as shown in Figure 20-7.

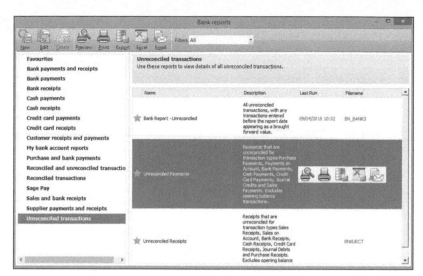

FIGURE 20-7:
The Unreconciled
Payments report.

3. **Highlight the Unreconciled Payments report and then click the Preview icon.**

   The Criteria Values box opens.

4. **Enter the transaction dates you require.**

   You usually put to the end of the month that you've just reconciled.

5. **Click OK to open the report.**

   You can print, email or export the report to your required destination.

6. **Click the white cross in the red box to close the Preview window.**

   This returns you to the Bank reports window. Click the white cross in the red box to close the Bank reports window and return to the Bank accounts window.

Figure 20-8 shows an unreconciled payments report for Jingles from 01 January 1980 to 30 April 2016. The report shows one entry for cheque number 001234, dated 30 April 2016 – this is an unpresented cheque – maybe written on the last day of the month and posted only that day, so it hasn't got as far as the bank yet.

To run an outstanding lodgements report, follow these steps:

1. **From the Navigation bar, click Bank accounts and then click the Reports icon.**

   The Bank reports window opens.

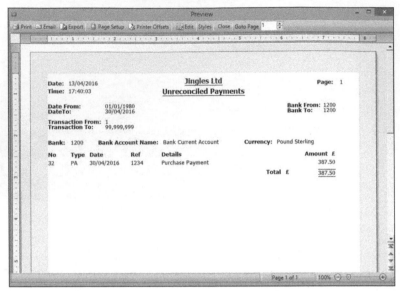

FIGURE 20-8:
Viewing a list of unpresented cheques for Jingles.

Source: Jane Kelly

2. **Click Unreconciled transactions.**

   A range of reports appear on the right side of the screen.

3. **Click Unreconciled Receipts and then click the Preview icon.**

   The Criteria Values box opens.

4. **Enter the transaction dates you require.**

   You generally put to the end of the month you've just reconciled.

5. **Click OK to open the report.**

   You can print, email or export the report to your required destination.

6. **Click the white cross in the red box to exit the Preview window.**

   You return to the Bank reports window. Click the white cross in the red box to close the Bank reports window and return to the Bank accounts window.

TIP

Your accountant probably requires a copy of your unreconciled bank transactions at the year end, so remember to supply your accountant with a copy. Any extra work you do saves on accountancy costs.

Doing a Monthly Breakdown of Profit and Loss

The monthly breakdown report is an incredibly useful report. It shows a month-by-month breakdown of the profit and loss account. You can drill down on any number (except for the totals) to see the breakdown of each number and the nominal code the figures are posted to. Seeing trends developing across the months in income and expenditure is useful.

To run the monthly breakdown report, follow these steps:

1. **From the Navigation bar, click Nominal codes and then click the Reports icon.**

   The Nominal codes reports window opens.

2. **Click Profit and Loss on the left side of the screen.**

   Double-click Profit and Loss (Monthly Breakdown) on the right side of the screen to open the Criteria Values box.

3. **Select the From and To periods and click OK.**

   The report opens, and you can choose to print, export or email it. Figure 20-9 shows a monthly breakdown report for Jingles.

Date: 13/04/2016
Time: 17:45:29

Jingles Ltd
Profit and Loss (Monthly Breakdown)

Page: 1

From: Month 1, April 2016
To: Month 12, March 2017

Chart of Accounts: Default Layout of Accounts

	Apr	May	Jun	Jul	Aug	Sep	Oct	Nov	Dec	Jan	Feb	Mar	Totals
Sales													
Shop Sales	948.75	49.25	157.60	0.00	197.94	0.00	0.00	0.00	0.00	0.00	0.00	0.00	1,353.54
Party Fees	0.90	150.00	2,000.00	0.00	250.00	0.00	0.00	0.00	0.00	0.00	0.00	0.00	2,400.90
	949.65	199.25	2,157.60	0.00	447.94	0.00	0.00	0.00	0.00	0.00	0.00	0.00	3,754.44
Purchases													
Purchases	25.00	89.00	565.50	173.43	50.00	25.00	0.00	71.72	0.00	0.00	0.00	0.00	999.65
	25.00	89.00	565.50	173.43	50.00	25.00	0.00	71.72	0.00	0.00	0.00	0.00	999.65
Direct Expenses													
Sales Promotion	1,000.00	0.00	0.00	0.00	0.00	0.00	0.00	0.00	0.00	0.00	0.00	0.00	1,000.00
	1,000.00	0.00	0.00	0.00	0.00	0.00	0.00	0.00	0.00	0.00	0.00	0.00	1,000.00
Gross	(75.35)	110.25	1,592.10	(173.43)	397.94	(25.00)	0.00	(71.72)	0.00	0.00	0.00	0.00	1,754.79
Overheads													
Gross Wages	0.00	0.00	0.00	250.00	0.00	0.00	0.00	0.00	0.00	0.00	0.00	0.00	250.00
Telephone and Computer charges	1,000.00	0.00	0.00	0.00	0.00	0.00	0.00	0.00	0.00	0.00	0.00	0.00	1,000.00
Bank Charges and	59.06	0.00	0.00	12.50	0.00	2.11	0.00	0.00	0.00	0.00	0.00	0.00	73.67

Source: Jane Kelly

FIGURE 20-9: An extract from the Profit and Loss (Monthly Breakdown) report for Jingles.

4. **To close the Preview report, click the white cross in the red box at the top right corner of the window.**

   You return to the Nominal code reports window.

5. **Click the white cross in the red box at the top right corner of the window.**

   You return to the Nominal codes window.

Ranking Your Top Customers

The top customers report can be a real eye-opener and is a very useful management tool. You may think you know who your best customers are, but this report can reveal some very surprising results.

The report has a simple layout. It shows you the customer's account and name, contact details, when you last invoiced them, their credit limit, and the year-to-date (YTD) or month-to-date (MTD) turnover.

The report lists your customers in order of turnover, so you see which customers are invoiced with the highest value, showing where the bulk of your sales turnover comes from.

You may find your turnover is generated by your top five customers, or you may find you have 20 customers who spend slightly less individually with you. You may consider the second arrangement to be more beneficial as it spreads the risk across a wider customer base. If one customer disappears, you aren't going to feel the effect quite so dramatically.

To run your top customer report, follow these steps:

1. **From the Navigation bar, click Customers and then click the Reports icon.**

   The Customer reports window opens.

2. **Click on Top customers at the bottom left of the screen.**

   Highlight the Top Customer List – Year and click on the Preview icon. The report opens, and you can print, email or export it.

3. **To close the report, click the white cross in the red box.**

   You return to the Customer reports window.

4. **To close the Customer reports window, click the white cross in the red box at the top right corner of the window.**

You return to the Customer window.

TIP

Try exporting your top customers report and play around with the numbers in a spreadsheet. You can then put the information into graphical format to send to your company managers.

WARNING

If you run the Top Customer List – Month, make sure you complete regular month ends and tick the Clear Turnover Figures box in the Month-End window; otherwise, the information is the same as the YTD report. Check out Chapter 16 for more on running your month ends.

Figure 20-10 shows a top customer report for Jingles.

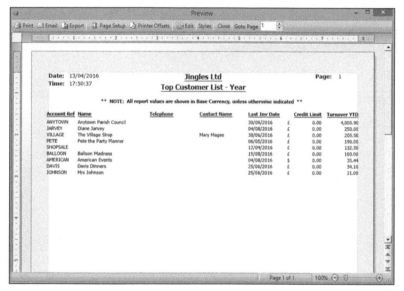

FIGURE 20-10: The top customer report can provide surprising results.

Source: Jane Kelly

Chapter 21

Going Mobile

Sage introduced a service called Sage Drive in the latest-version release of the Sage 50 software; the idea is that you can access your data out of the office. If you're playing a round on your favourite golf course, with Sage apps you can still check whether a customer has paid an invoice, add new customer details or view your price lists. In this chapter I give a brief introduction to the different apps available with Sage 50 Accounts using Sage Drive.

With the addition of any of these apps, you can improve the mobile capability of your accounting software. Never again are you constrained to your desktop. Now you can really do all your work remotely: You can work from home, you can have remote meetings with your accountant, and you can finalise sales orders and produce invoices out on the road.

Setting Up Sage Drive

Sage Drive harnesses cloud technology to let you access your accounts remotely. With Sage Drive you can connect multiple users to your Sage 50 software, access your accounts data using Sage 50 Accounts Tracker via your phone, and use the Sage 50 Accounts Mobile Sales app on your tablet.

Having Sage Drive means you can access your accounts wherever you are, as long as you have an Internet connection. You can then work collaboratively with clients or staff in different locations if they also have Internet access. Sage Drive also means your accountant can access your data remotely without chasing you for backups.

Any changes you make to your data in the cloud are automatically updated to your local data in real time, so everything is always in sync.

In order to set up Sage Drive, you must be logged on as Manager. You need to register for Sage Drive before you can use it. To do this, you need to create a Sage ID by doing the following:

1. **Open Sage 50 Accounts and then click File on the Menu toolbar.**

2. **Click Sage Drive setup.**

   The Sage Drive setup window opens; click Let's get started.

3. **A new window opens, which asks for your Sage ID. Enter your Sage ID and password. Click Sign In.**

   If you do not yet have a Sage ID, then click the Create Sage ID link and follow the on-screen instructions.

4. **You are asked to enter your account number and serial number to register for the Sage Drive service.**

   Your account number can be found on any Sage statement or invoice, and your serial number can be found by clicking on Help from the main toolbar in Sage and then About. Click Register.

5. **Sage requests permission for you to access the Sage 50 data, and you must click Allow if you want to continue.**

6. **You are asked to enter an encryption password, which is not recoverable.**

   Using an encrypted password means that no one can access or read your data, not even Sage. Tick the box to confirm you agree to the terms and conditions and then click the Upload data button.

Sage now whirs into action and begins to upload your data to Sage Drive. You eventually get a congratulations message, saying that you are now connected to the cloud with Sage Drive!

You can continue to the Management Centre to invite other users to access the data, or you can simply close to exit.

To access your data remotely, you need to install Sage 50 Accounts version 22 on the computer that you'd like to use and create a new company. You then need to select Connect to data from Sage Drive and follow the on-screen instructions.

TIP

For more information about setting up Sage Drive, use the F1 function and type 'Sage Drive'. This brings up lots of useful information on Sage Drive, including sharing additional sets of data, managing shared data and adding other users such as your accountant.

Tackling Sage 50 Tracker

Sage 50 Tracker is a free app that lets you manage your accounts on the move. The app uses Sage Drive, which means your Sage data is held securely in the cloud. With this app, you can log into Sage wherever you are and do the following:

>> View a quick account summary on the Home screen

>> View a profit and loss summary, bank balances and bank account details

>> Check account balances for customers and suppliers

>> Keep in touch with your key contacts

>> View maps of where your customers are based

>> Review outstanding debtors and creditors

To use Sage 50 Tracker, you must have Sage 50 version 21 or above with Sage Drive and a Sage ID.

Installing Sage 50 Tracker

In this section, I demonstrate how to access your accounts data via an iPhone. To have the benefit of using this app, you must have either an iPhone 4 or above (and be running iOS7 or above) or an Android smartphone (version 4 or above). You can download the app free of charge from the App Store on your phone. In Figure 21-1 I show the Sage 50 Tracker Info screen.

On your phone, tap the Get button followed by the Install button on the Sage 50 Tracker Info screen to download the app. This process takes a minute or so. Once the app has downloaded, click the Open button.

After the application loads, tap the Sage 50 Tracker icon on your phone to go to the Login screen, which I show in Figure 21-2.

FIGURE 21-1:
Viewing
information
about Sage 50
Tracker in the
iPhone App Store.

Source: Jane Kelly

FIGURE 21-2:
Looking at the
Login screen for
Sage 50 Tracker.

Source: Jane Kelly

Looking at the Sage 50 Tracker dashboard

To login and access your data on Sage 50 Tracker, you need your Sage Passport email address and password. In this section, I use the Demonstration (Demo) Mode to depict the features of Sage 50 Tracker.

Click on the Demo Mode button to go to the Sage 50 Tracker Dashboard screen, which I show in Figure 21-3. The screen shows key data about your business, such as your bank balance details, who owes you money (debtors) and who you owe money to (creditors).

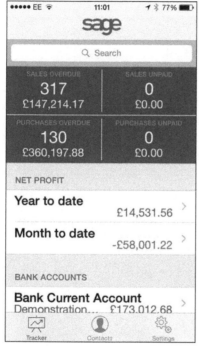

Source: Jane Kelly

FIGURE 21-3: The Sage 50 Tracker Dashboard screen.

Chevrons (>) on the Dashboard screen show you can find further information by drilling down into the data. For example, if you tap the Net Profit year to date figure of £14,531.56, the app shows you a breakdown of how that figure has been achieved, as shown in Figure 21-4.

Clicking on the Sales Overdue line on the dashboard gives you a list of your customers and how much they owe you – I show an example for A1 Design Services in Figure 21-5. You can see the individual invoices outstanding on your phone. You can see the same level of information for your suppliers, so you know who you owe money to.

Source: Jane Kelly

FIGURE 21-4:
Using the
drill-down facility
to investigate
your net profit.

Source: Jane Kelly

FIGURE 21-5:
Taking a look at
the Sales
Overdue
Overview screen.

TIP

A really useful feature of the Tracker app is the ability to drill down to the contact details for customers and suppliers, which I show in Figure 21-6. You can obtain their names, addresses and phone numbers and view their locations via a Google map – great if you're on the road and need to find a client quickly.

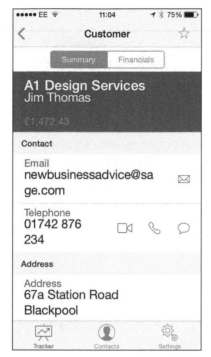

FIGURE 21-6:
Finding a customer's contact details.

Source: Jane Kelly

Sussing Out Sage 50 Mobile Sales

The Mobile Sales app has been designed to provide all the tools necessary to enable your sales force to do an effective job. It is available only in tablet format but allows you to process sales on the road.

The user must have Sage 50 Accounts with Sage Drive and must be using either an iPad mini or iPad 2 or above (running iOS7 or above) or a tablet running Android (version 4 or above). The app can be installed by paying an additional fee to Sage, whereupon an activation email will be sent to the user to allow the app to be set up.

Having this app available to the sales force whilst out with the customer enables the salesperson to check stock availability online and create a quote instantly for the customer. This can be printed at the customer's premises, and an invoice can even be raised before the salesperson has left the client. This is a great tool to gain quick sales and provide salespeople with up-to-date pricing and stock information, allowing them to make informed decisions when negotiating sales with the customer.

Sage 50 Mobile Sales costs £5 plus VAT (value-added tax).

Keeping Connected with Connected Users

Connected Users is part of the added functionality of having Sage Drive. This app gives you and your staff remote access to accounts data, wherever you all are. You automatically have access to one person connecting when you first buy Sage 50, but any additional users cost £5 plus VAT per user per month.

You can add up to 24 connected users, and you can add and delete users whenever you want. You have total control of who can access your secure company data. Users need an Internet connection at all times and a Windows operating system.

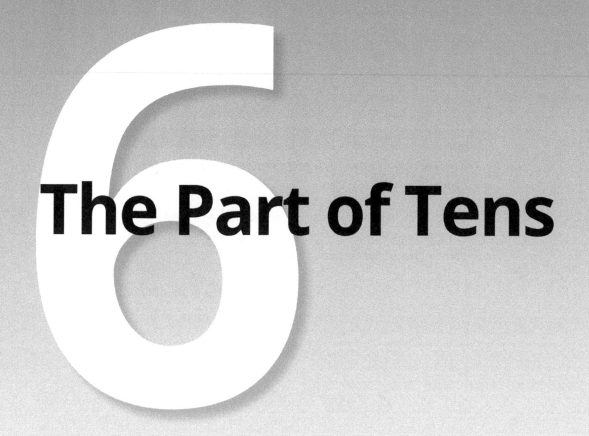

The Part of Tens

Find out how function keys can help to speed up data processing.

Discover the wonderful ways wizards work their magic to help you with the basic setting up of records and some of the trickier aspects of bookkeeping.

Chapter 22

Ten (Okay, Eleven) Funky Functions in Sage

I f you want to wow your friends or your boss with a few neat Sage tricks, look no further than this chapter. Here I show you how to use some of the function keys that give you some great shortcuts – for example, the copy key (F6), which speeds up processing, and F7, which can get you out of a tight spot if you need to insert an extra line somewhere (particularly useful if you miss a line of information from the middle of a journal).

TIP

Since version 22, the function keys 6, 7 and 8 are present on many of the data input screens within Sage. You find icons at the top of many of the module screens for these popular function keys. Instead of actually pressing the function key, you now simply click on the relevant icon. For example, the journal entry screen now has these icons, as well as the batch entry screens for purchase and sales invoices.

Browsing for Help with F1

Pressing F1 launches the Help system. Sage's Help system is intelligent enough to know which part of Sage you're working in and displays the Help screens most suited to your needs. This saves you having to scroll through the Help index list to find the appropriate section. For example, if you're in the Batch Entry screen for suppliers, pressing the F1 key brings up a Help screen related to entering purchase invoices.

Calculating Stuff with F2

Having instant access to a calculator is pretty handy, particularly if you're in the middle of a journal and you need to add up something. Pressing F2 brings up a little calculator on the screen. You can quickly do your sums and then carry on processing information using Sage, without having to dive through your office drawers to find a calculator.

Accessing an Edit Item Line for Invoicing with F3

Pressing F3 displays the Edit Item line when you're entering invoices. You can add additional information and comments to your invoice, whether for a product or service. You need to enter some information first before the Edit box opens.

F3 can also be used to pay in full when creating a payment or receipt. Alternatively, you can use the Pay In Full button, which does the same thing.

Finding Multiple Functions with F4

Pressing F4 does three different things, depending on which screen or field you're in:

>> In a field with a drop-down arrow, press F4 to display the full list.

>> In a Date field, press F4 to show the calendar.

>> In a numeric field, press F4 to make a mini-calculator appear. (F2 opens a calculator in any screen; F4 opens a calculator only if you're in a screen devoted to numbers.)

Calculating Currency or Checking Spelling with F5

Pressing F5 does two different things, depending on which field you're in:

>> In a numeric box, press F5 to show the currency calculator. (You need to ensure your currencies and exchange rates are set up for this to function properly.)

>> In a text box, press F5 to bring up the spellchecker.

Copying with F6

F6 is one of the best Sage inventions ever. Pressing F6 copies entries from the field above, which is particularly useful when you enter batches of invoices. For example, for a batch of invoices with the same date, you can enter the date only once and then press F6 when you get to the Date field as you enter each subsequent invoice. Sage copies the date from the field directly above your line of entry and enters the same date into the invoice on the line of the batch that you're working on.

F6 doesn't work only with dates. You can use the key to copy any field. If you want to enter a mass of invoices from the same customer or supplier, you can use F6 to copy the customer or supplier's details from one invoice into all the other invoices.

F6 has an amazing impact on your data-entry speed, and the key is an absolute godsend when you set up a new system.

TIP

To go up in increments of one, press F6 plus the shift key. This shortcut is very useful when entering dates. For example, when you enter batches of invoices, if you enter the first line with the date 12/05/2016, press F6 plus the shift key when you get to the next line, and the date becomes 13/05/2016.

Inserting a Line with F7

The ability to add a line using F7 may seem pretty mundane, but it's very useful when you enter batches of invoices or journals. If you get halfway through entering a journal and realise you've missed out a line, instead of putting it at the bottom, you can press F7 to insert the line exactly where you want it.

Deleting a Line with F8

F8 is one of my favourite function keys in Sage. Many a time I get to the bottom of a long laborious journal and realise I've started to enter a line of journal that shouldn't be there.

After you enter a nominal code, Sage expects you to continue to post that line of the journal and waits for you to enter a value. When you realise your mistake and try to save the journal with a zero amount on the last line, Sage won't let you post. Instead, it gives you a warning message stating 'No transaction values entered'.

If you click the line you want to delete and press F8, the line miraculously disappears, and Sage lets you save the journal with no further problems.

You can also use the F8 key in other parts of Sage, such as to delete a line from an invoice or order.

Calculating Net Amounts with F9

When you enter an invoice, Sage asks you for the net amount of the invoice, followed by the tax code. After you enter the tax code, Sage calculates the VAT (value-added tax). If you don't know the net amount of the invoice and have only the gross amount, you can type the gross amount in the Net field and press F9. Sage then calculates the net amount for the invoice.

Sage now has a Calculate Net F9 icon that does the same job as pressing F9.

Launching Windows with F11

Pressing F11 launches the Windows control panel. The control panel is useful if you accidentally send a report to the printer and want to cancel the job. Press F11 to open the control panel and select the Printer icon. Double-click the printer where the job is waiting to print, and delete the report from the queue. Click the black cross in the right corner to exit the control panel.

You can also configure F11 to launch another program. Use the Help menu for instructions on how to do this.

Opening Report Designer with F12

F12 launches Report Designer, a Sage feature that lets you create your own or modify existing reports. If you can't find a standard report that produces your information in the way that you want, Report Designer lets you design a report with exactly the details you need for your business. (I explain how to use Report Designer properly in Chapter 18.)

You can also configure F12 to launch another program. Use the Help menu for instructions on how to do this.

Chapter 23

Ten (Plus One) Wizards to Conjure Up in Sage

Sage comes with a number of *wizards*. No, I don't mean little characters with pointy hats and wands – I mean step-by-step instructions on how to carry out specific procedures. Some Sage wizards are a bit laborious to use, but many of them provide much-needed expertise. For example, some of the wizards in Sage help you complete complicated journal entries – and even the most dedicated bookkeepers use these sometimes. In this chapter I talk about the most helpful wizards Sage offers.

Creating a New Customer Account

Using the Navigation bar on the left side of your screen, click Customers and then the Wizard icon. The New Customer wizard starts, taking you step by step through the seven-window process of setting up your customers.

This wizard can take a long time, so I don't use it very often. Instead, I use the quicker method of clicking Customer and then the New icon, which immediately opens a customer record so you can start entering your data.

To have a look at the questions Sage asks as you work through the wizard, press the F1 function key. The Sage Help facility describes in detail the information you need to enter in each of the seven windows.

The final stage of the New Customer wizard lets you enter your opening balances, so you don't need to do this again when you work through other wizards. I talk about opening balances in detail in Chapter 4.

Setting Up a New Supplier

On the Navigation bar, click Suppliers and then the Wizard icon. The New Supplier wizard walks you through the process of setting up your supplier records. The windows that you complete help you set up suppliers' names, addresses, contact details, credit details, bank details and settlement discounts.

If you want to preview the information Sage needs from you to complete the wizard, press the F1 function key to bring up Sage Help.

You don't have to complete every field in the wizard to set up a supplier, but you do need to click through all seven windows to get to the end and save the information you've entered. You can add information to a supplier's record at a later date if you feel you've missed something – simply open the relevant record, make your changes and click Save.

The final stage of the New Supplier wizard lets you enter your opening balances, so you don't need to do this again when you work through other wizards. I talk about opening balances in detail in Chapter 4.

Initiating a New Nominal Account

You use the Nominal Record wizard to create new nominal accounts for your chart of accounts. You need to work through only two screens with this wizard. From the Navigation bar, click Nominal codes and then the Wizard icon.

The wizard asks you to enter the name of your new nominal account and confirm what type of account it is – sales, purchase, direct expenses, overheads, assets, liabilities and so on.

The wizard then asks you to enter your nominal category from within the chart of accounts – for example, product sales – and to type in your nominal code.

WARNING

Decide on your nominal code before you start the wizard. At this point in the wizard, you don't have the option to search your nominal code list to check whether your code is suitable.

After you click Next, the wizard asks if you want to post an opening balance. Click the appropriate answer and then click Create. Some new boxes appear asking you whether it's a debit or a credit balance and the date and amount. Click Create and the new account is prepared.

REMEMBER

Always check your chart of accounts for any errors after you enter new nominal accounts. You can find details on how to do this in Chapter 2.

Creating a New Bank Account

To access the New Bank Account wizard, click the Bank accounts link from the Navigation bar and then the New/Edit icon. Select Wizard from the drop-down menu that appears. The first four windows ask the usual bank details, such as bank name, sort code, account number and so on.

TIP

The last window lets you enter your opening balances so you don't need to do this again when you work through other wizards. See Chapter 4 for the lowdown on opening balances.

Launching a New Product

You use the New Product wizard to create a new product record. To access the wizard, click Products and services on the Navigation bar and then click the Wizard icon.

The wizard asks you to enter a description of the product, selling price, cost price, nominal codes and supplier details. The wizard also lets you enter your opening balances.

Starting Up a New Project

You use the New Project wizard to create a new project record. In Chapter 13 I talk in more depth about creating projects to keep track of a job's progress. To access the New Project wizard, click Projects on the Navigation bar and then click the Wizard icon.

The wizard asks you to enter details, such as the project name, and a unique reference, such as a shortened name or number to identify the project. You can also enter information such as the project start and end dates, choose one of five predefined statuses for the project and link the project to a certain customer. The next couple of windows are optional and contain questions such as the site address and site contact details. The last window asks you to enter the price you quoted for the project.

Helping Out at Month End: Opening/Closing Stock

The Opening/Closing Stock wizard forms part of the month-end routine and is a welcome method of recording your closing stock. The wizard records the amount of closing stock you have at the end of a period and then transfers it to the start of the next period. To access the wizard, click Modules on the Menu bar and then click Wizards.

By recording your opening and closing stock figures, the wizard can accurately calculate the cost of sales figures for your profit and loss report. If you don't post opening and closing stock figures, the cost of sales reflects only the purchase cost and doesn't reflect any stock you have left to sell.

The wizard asks you to confirm the closing stock nominal accounts in your balance sheet and your profit and loss report. Sage asks you to enter the value of this month's closing stock and the previous closing stock. Sage then calculates the double-entry bookkeeping when you click the Calculate button and then posts those entries when you click the Post Transactions button.

Fuelling Up: Scale Charges

If your organisation uses company cars, the Scale Charges wizard is really handy. The wizard lets you calculate the fuel scale charges levied against any fuel used when an employee drives a company car for personal rather than business purposes. Once you have entered the required details, Sage creates the journals necessary to post to the nominal ledger.

You can access the wizard from the toolbar by clicking Modules, then Wizards and then Scale Charges. A new window opens, and you need to complete the screen instructions that ask you for a date, details, reference and amount. You should ensure that the date is set to the quarter end for your VAT (value-added tax) period and not just the current date. When you click Next, Sage confirms the journal post, which takes place to post the fuel scale charges to your accounts. Just click Post if you're happy with the details.

WARNING

Before you proceed with this wizard, you need to calculate the scale charge for each company vehicle, using the details held on the HM Revenue & Customs (HMRC) website (www.gov.uk/fuel-scale-charge). You need to know the CO_2 emissions of your car in order to find the correct fuel scale charge. Both the fuel scale charge and the CO_2 emission data can be obtained from the HMRC website.

Saving Time: Global Changes

The Global Changes wizard helps you make global changes to information in customer, supplier or product accounts without changing each account individually. For example, you can raise the selling price of all your products by 10 per cent, as the sample business in Figure 23-1 did. (I don't recommend such an abrupt and significant change, however, lest you lose 10 per cent of your customers!)

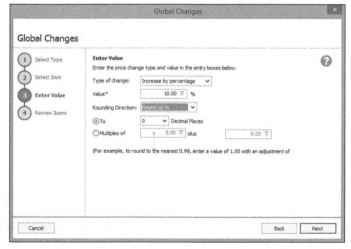

FIGURE 23-1:
The results of applying a 10 per cent increase in selling prices, using the Global Changes wizard.

Source: Jane Kelly

You can access the wizard by clicking Modules from the main toolbar and then Wizards, followed by Global Changes. Work through each of the windows of the wizard, selecting the appropriate boxes for your global change. When you're happy with the details and can see the results shown on-screen, click Finish. Sage then activates the changes.

Handling Currencies: Foreign Bank Revaluation

The Foreign Bank Revaluation wizard takes into account currency rate fluctuations and lets you update currency rates at specific dates so you can report your accounts accurately.

WARNING

After you activate the Foreign Trader option, you can't switch it off.

You have to complete the Foreign Trader Setup wizard to activate the foreign currency functionality in Sage Accounts Professional. Follow these steps to set it up:

1. **From the main toolbar, select Modules → Wizards → Foreign bank revaluation.**

2. **Select your currency followed by the appropriate foreign bank account.**

   Click Next.

3. **Enter the date you want to revalue – for example, the month end.**

4. **Enter an exchange rate you want to use for that date.**

   Click Next.

5. **Sage calculates the revaluation figures and shows you what it will post.**

   If you're happy with the calculation, click Post. Otherwise, click Back to amend your details.

Keeping Others in the Loop: Accountant Link

The Accountant Link is a very useful facility that lets you send a copy of your data to your accountant via email or post. In the past, if you sent data to your accountant, you had to stop work and wait for any adjustments to your accounts.

The Accountant Link lets you send the data and carry on working on the data yourself, minimising disruption within your business.

After you export the data to your accountant, Sage begins to record any material changes you make to the data. You can print a list of these changes to send to your accountant. The accountant can send the data, with adjustments, back to you via a secure file, which you can then import. The Accountant Link helps you apply your accountant's adjustments to your data to bring it up to date. At this point, Sage stops recording material changes.

You can access the Accountant Link wizard by clicking Modules from the main toolbar, then Wizards, followed by Accountant Link. You then need to choose whether you want to import data from your accountant or export data to your accountant. Whichever option you choose, you will be taken step by step through the process via on-screen instructions. I go through this process in more detail in Chapter 19.

WARNING

You don't need the Accountant Link if you already have Sage Drive (see Chapter 21), because Sage Drive lets your accountant dip into your live data at any time – with your permission.

Index

About the Author

Jane Kelly trained as a chartered management accountant while working in industry. Her roles ranged from company accountant in a small advertising business to financial controller for a national house builder. For the last few years, Jane has specialised in using Sage accounting software and has taught a wide variety of small businesses and employees the benefits of using Sage. More recently, Jane has been involved in writing *For Dummies* books, including *Bookkeeping For Dummies*, 4th Edition, and *Bookkeeping & Accounting All-in-One For Dummies*.

Dedication

I would like to dedicate this book to my daughter, Megan, and my husband, Malcolm. Without their support, none of my books would ever have been created.

Author's Acknowledgements

I hope that this book will help many of the small-business owners who currently struggle keeping up-to-date with their finances. I want people to understand that if a system is set up properly, it's very easy to use and the business gains a huge benefit from it.

I want to thank all the people at Wiley, who have been very kind and supportive, particularly Michelle Hacker and the rest of the development team, who have turned my words and pictures into the *For Dummies* book that you see before you.

Finally, I would like to thank my husband, Malcolm, and my daughter, Megan, who have put up with me disappearing into the office to work on the book for what must have seemed like a never-ending time.

Publisher's Acknowledgements

Executive Commissioning Editor: Annie Knight

Project Manager: Michelle Hacker

Development Editor: Georgette Beatty

Copy Editor: Christine Pingleton

Technical Editor: Donna Curling, FMAAT, MICB CB.Dip PM.Dip

Production Editor: Kumar Chellappan

Cover Image: © CWIS/Shutterstock

Take Dummies with you everywhere you go!

Whether you're excited about e-books, want more from the web, must have your mobile apps, or swept up in social media, Dummies makes everything easier.

FOR DUMMIES

A Wiley Brand

BUSINESS

978-1-118-73077-5

978-1-118-44349-1

978-1-119-97527-4

MUSIC

978-1-119-94276-4

978-0-470-97799-6

978-0-470-49644-2

DIGITAL PHOTOGRAPHY

978-1-118-09203-3

978-0-470-76878-5

978-1-118-00472-2

Algebra I For Dummies
978-0-470-55964-2

Anatomy & Physiology For Dummies, 2nd Edition
978-0-470-92326-9

Asperger's Syndrome For Dummies
978-0-470-66087-4

Basic Maths For Dummies
978-1-119-97452-9

Body Language For Dummies, 2nd Edition
978-1-119-95351-7

Bookkeeping For Dummies, 3rd Edition
978-1-118-34689-1

British Sign Language For Dummies
978-0-470-69477-0

Cricket for Dummies, 2nd Edition
978-1-118-48032-8

Currency Trading For Dummies, 2nd Edition
978-1-118-01851-4

Cycling For Dummies
978-1-118-36435-2

Diabetes For Dummies, 3rd Edition
978-0-470-97711-8

eBay For Dummies, 3rd Edition
978-1-119-94122-4

Electronics For Dummies All-in-One For Dummies
978-1-118-58973-1

English Grammar For Dummies
978-0-470-05752-0

French For Dummies, 2nd Edition
978-1-118-00464-7

Guitar For Dummies, 3rd Edition
978-1-118-11554-1

IBS For Dummies
978-0-470-51737-6

Keeping Chickens For Dummies
978-1-119-99417-6

Knitting For Dummies, 3rd Edition
978-1-118-66151-2